Rick Steves®

IRELAND

Rick Steves & Pat O'Connor

2019

CONTENTS

Welcome to Rick Steves' Europe

Travel is intensified living—maximum thrills per minute and one of the last great sources of legal adventure. Travel is freedom. It's recess, and we need it.

I discovered a passion for European travel as a teen and have been sharing it ever since—through tours, my public television and radio shows, and travel guidebooks. Over the years, I've taught thousands of travelers how to best enjoy Europe's blockbuster sights—and experience "Back Door" discoveries that most tourists miss.

Written with my talented co-author, Pat O'Connor, this book covers the highlights of the entire island of Ireland, offering a balanced mix of exciting cities and great-to-be-alive-in small towns. And it's selective—there are plenty of manor-house gardens, but we recommend only the best ones. Our self-guided museum tours and city walks give insight into the country's vibrant history and today's living, breathing culture.

We advocate traveling simply and smartly. Take advantage of our money- and time-saving tips on sightseeing, transportation, and more. Try local, characteristic alternatives to expensive hotels and restaurants. In many ways, spending more money only builds a thicker wall between you and what you traveled so far to see.

We visit Ireland to experience it—to become temporary locals. Thoughtful travel engages us with the world, as we learn to appreciate other cultures and new ways to measure quality of life.

Judging from positive feedback from readers, this book will help you enjoy a fun, affordable, and rewarding vacation—whether it's your first trip or your tenth.

Have a grand holiday! Happy travels!

Rick Steves

IRELAND

Flung onto the foggy fringe of the Atlantic pond like a mossy millstone, Ireland drips with mystery, drawing you in for a closer look. You may not find the proverbial pot of gold, but you'll treasure your encounters with the engaging, feisty Irish people. The Irish culture—with its intricate art and mesmerizing music—is as intoxicating as the famous Irish brew, Guinness.

The Irish revere their past and love their proverbs, such as "When God made time, he made a lot of it." Ireland is dusted with prehistoric stone circles, burial mounds, and standing stones...some older than the pyramids, and all speckled with moss. While much of Europe has buried older cultures under new, Ireland still reveals its cultural bedrock. It's a place to connect with your Neolithic roots, even if you're not Irish.

The 300-mile-long island (about the size of Maine) is ringed with some of Europe's most scenic coastal cliffs. It's only 150 miles across at its widest point. No matter where you go in Ireland, you're never more than 75 miles from the sea. Despite being as far north as Newfoundland, Ireland has a mild maritime climate, thanks to the Gulf Stream. Rainfall ranges from more than 100 inches a year in soggy, boggy Connemara to about 30 inches a year in Dublin. Any time of year, bring rain gear. As Ireland's own Oscar Wilde once quipped, "There is no bad weather...only inappropriate clothing."

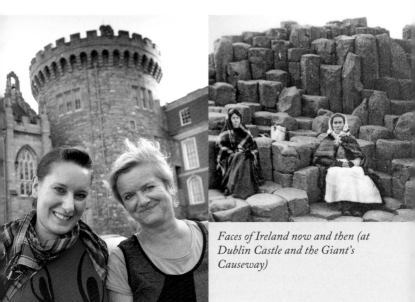

Faces of Ireland now and then (at Dublin Castle and the Giant's Causeway)

Though a small island, Ireland has had a large impact on the rest of the world. Geographically isolated in the damp attic of Dark Age Europe, Christian Irish monks tended the flickering flame of literacy, then bravely reintroduced it to the barbaric Continent. Ireland later turned out some of modern literature's greatest authors, including W. B. Yeats, George Bernard Shaw, Samuel Beckett, and Oscar Wilde. In the 1800s, great waves of Irish emigrants fled famine and colonial oppression, seeking new opportunities abroad and making their mark in the US and beyond. (Every Irish family seems to have a relative in America; about 50 million people claim Irish descent in North America alone.) And although peace now prevails in Northern Ireland, the religious and political conflict there long held the world's attention.

Northern Ireland (with 1.8 million people) is a province of the United Kingdom (like Scotland and Wales), while the Republic (with 4.8 million people and 80 percent of the land) is an independent nation. No visit to Ireland is complete without a look at both.

The Republic of Ireland boasts more sights, from the famous Book of Kells manuscript, prehistoric ruins, Celtic artifacts, and evocative monastic settlements to Iron Age

Traditional Irish Music

A *ceilidh* (KAY-lee) is an evening of music and dance...an Irish hoedown—and can be one of the great Irish experiences. You'll find traditional Irish music in pubs all over Ireland. "Sessions" (musical evenings) may be advertised events or impromptu (and quality can be hit or miss), but either way things get going at about 21:30—though Irish punctuality is unpredictable. Last call for drinks is just before midnight.

Pub music ranges from traditional instrumentals (merry jigs and reels) to ballads (songs of tragic love lost or heroic deeds done) to sing-along strummers. Sessions generally feature a fiddle, a flute or tin whistle, a guitar, and a *bodhrán* (BO-run, goatskin drum), sometimes joined by an accordion or mandolin. The music often comes in sets of three songs. The wind and string instruments embellish melody lines with lots of tight ornamentation.

Percussion generally stays in the background. The *bodhrán* is played with a small, two-headed club; the performer stretches its skin by hand to change tone and pitch. More rarely, you'll hear the crisp sound of a set of bones: two cow ribs (boiled and dried) that are rattled in one hand like spoons or castanets, substituting for the sound of dancing shoes in olden days.

Watch the piper closely. The Irish version of Scottish Highland bagpipes, the *uilleann* (ILL-in) pipes are played by inflating the airbag (under the left elbow) with a bellows (under the right elbow) rather than with a mouthpiece. *Uilleann* is Irish Gaelic for "elbow," and its sound is more melodic, with a wider range than Highland pipes. The piper ▶▶▶

Irish dancing at a pub, accompanied by a bodhrán *player*

Rick Steves Ireland

▶▶▶ fingers the chanter to create individual notes, and taps the chanter on his thigh to close the end and raise the note one octave. He uses the heel of his right hand to play chords on one of three regulator pipes. It takes amazing coordination to play this instrument well, and the sound can be haunting.

During your night out, it's worth staying until the wee hours for the magical moment when a rare *sean nós* (Irish for "old style") lament is sung to a hushed and attentive pub crowd. This slightly nasal vocal style may be a remnant of the ancient storytelling tradition of the bards whose influence died out when Gaelic culture waned 400 years ago. Stories—often of love lost, emigration to a faraway land, or a heroic rebel death struggling against English rule—are always heartfelt.

Sometimes a session hits all the right notes and the atmosphere is spellbinding. The drummer dodges the fiddler's playful bow. Sipping their pints, the musicians skillfully maintain a faint but steady buzz. The floor on their platform is stomped paint-free, and barmaids scurry artfully through the commotion, gathering towers of empty, cream-crusted glasses. Make yourself right at home, "playing the boot" (tapping your foot) under the table in time with the music. ▣

A uilleann *player, entertaining a pub crowd, fueled by beer*

ring forts. The country is bordered by green hilly peninsulas, craggy islands, and sheer cliffs rising up from the crashing waves of the Atlantic.

The people of the Republic of Ireland are best known for the legendary "gift of gab," which has its roots in the ancient Celtic culture. With no written language (until the arrival of Christianity), the ancient Celts passed their history, laws, and folklore verbally from generation to generation. Even today, most transactions come with an ample side-helping of friendly banter. As an Irishman once joked, "How can I know what I think until I hear what I say?"

Listening to the thick Irish brogue, you'll get the fun sensation you're understanding a foreign language. But if you can't understand a thing, you're probably hearing Irish Gaelic, spoken in a Gaeltacht. These government-subsidized cultural preserves are found mostly in far western coastal regions (where English works, too).

The shamrock—used by St. Patrick to explain the concept of the Holy Trinity—is the most recognizable symbol of the Republic of Ireland. Another national symbol you'll see during your visit is the harp (on the back of Irish euro coins and reversed on every pint of Guinness). The Irish seem born with a love of music. Live music is a weekly (if not nightly) draw at any town pub worth its salt.

Northern Ireland is an underrated and often overlooked region that surprises visitors with its striking scenery and friendly people. Its coast boasts the alligator-skin volcanic

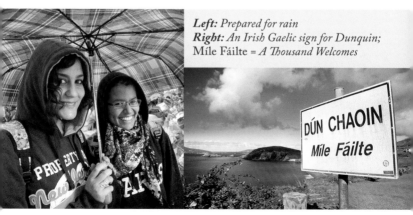

Left: *Prepared for rain*
Right: *An Irish Gaelic sign for Dunquin;*
Míle Fáilte = *A Thousand Welcomes*

DÚN CHAOIN
Míle Fáilte

Left: The serene, green Antrim Coast
Right: Raise a glass in Belfast's historic Crown Liquor Saloon

geology of the Giant's Causeway and the lush Glens of Antrim, while its interior is dominated by rolling hills of pastoral serenity and Lough Neagh, the UK's biggest lake.

An interesting hybrid of Irish and Scottish cultures, Northern Ireland is only 17 miles from Scotland at its closest point. The accents you'll hear in the North are distinctly different from their counterparts south of the border. With a population just a bit larger than that of Phoenix, it's small enough to have one phone book for the entire province, yet is twice as densely populated as the Republic to the south.

The people of the North generally fall into two categories: those who feel they're British (Unionists) and those who feel they're Irish (Nationalists). Those born in the North can choose which of the two passports they want. The turmoil of the Troubles—the decades-long conflict between Unionists and Nationalists, starting in the 1960s—has essentially ended, and Northern Ireland is now statistically one of the safer places in the Western world.

Today's Ireland is vibrant and cosmopolitan, yet warm and down to earth. Want to really get to know Ireland? Belly up to the bar in a neighborhood pub and engage a local in conversation. The Irish people have a worldwide reputation as witty, musical, moody romantics with a quick laugh and a ready smile. Come join them.

Ireland's Top Destinations

There's so much to see in Ireland and so little time. This overview breaks the country's top destinations into must-see sights (to help first-time travelers plan their trip) and worth-it sights (for those with extra time or special interests). I've also suggested a minimum number of days to allow per destination.

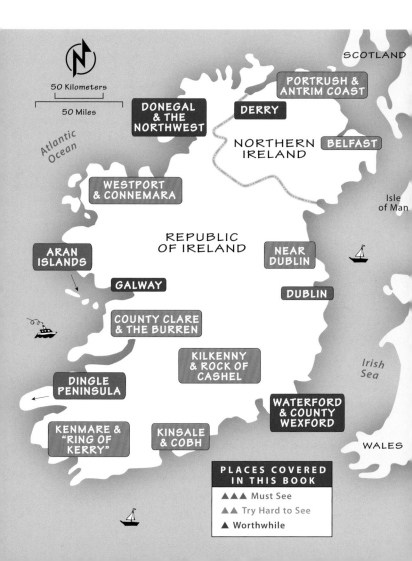

SCOTLAND

50 Kilometers

50 Miles

Atlantic
Ocean

DONEGAL & THE NORTHWEST

PORTRUSH & ANTRIM COAST

DERRY

NORTHERN IRELAND

BELFAST

Isle of Man

WESTPORT & CONNEMARA

REPUBLIC OF IRELAND

ARAN ISLANDS

NEAR DUBLIN

GALWAY

DUBLIN

COUNTY CLARE & THE BURREN

KILKENNY & ROCK OF CASHEL

Irish Sea

DINGLE PENINSULA

WATERFORD & COUNTY WEXFORD

KENMARE & "RING OF KERRY"

KINSALE & COBH

WALES

PLACES COVERED IN THIS BOOK

▲▲▲ Must See
▲▲ Try Hard to See
▲ Worthwhile

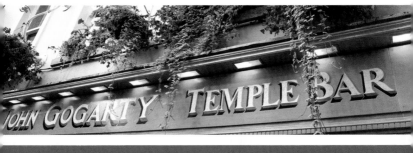

MUST-SEE DESTINATIONS

The island's top three destinations are Dublin, the capital city of the Republic of Ireland, on the east coast; the lush Dingle Peninsula on the west coast; and the rocky Aran Islands to the north, just off the coast of Galway. Each stop has a distinctly different flavor: from big-city Dublin and small-town Dingle to the remote and ancient Aran Islands. If you build your trip around these destinations, you'll get an unforgettable introduction to the best of Ireland.

▲▲▲ Dublin (allow 2 days)

The bustling Irish capital offers fascinating tours (historical, musical, and literary), passionate rebel history (Kilmainham Gaol), treasured Dark Age gospels (starring the monk-illustrated Book of Kells), and intricate Celtic artifacts (National Museum: Archaeology). For evening fun, pub-hop through the rambunctious Temple Bar district, cocking your ear to seek out traditional music.

▲▲▲ Dingle Peninsula (1-2 days)

My favorite fishing village, Dingle town, is a traditional Irish-music pub paradise. It's also a launchpad for a gorgeous loop drive (or bike ride) around the tip of the Dingle peninsula, awash with striking scenery and a wealth of Celtic and early Christian sites.

▲▲▲ Aran Islands (1 day)

Three windswept, treeless islands in the Atlantic are ringed by cliffs, crowned by striking ruins, and home to sparse villages of hardy fisherfolk. The island of Inishmore hosts the star attraction, the 2,000-year-old Dun Aengus fort, perching precariously at the edge of a sheer cliff.

Stone church on Dingle Peninsula, a Dingle pub, celebrating Bloomsday in Dublin, Dun Aengus perch

WORTH-IT DESTINATIONS

You can weave any of these destinations—rated ▲ or ▲▲—into your itinerary. It's easy to add some destinations based on proximity, but some out-of-the-way places can merit the journey, depending on your time and interests.

▲▲ Near Dublin (1 day)

Of the varied sights near Dublin, the best is the Boyne Valley's ancient pre-Celtic burial mounds of Brú na Bóinne, with the majestic Norman castle in Trim nearby. Other choices are the green horse-racing pastures of the Irish National Stud, the graceful Gardens of Powerscourt, and the evocative monastic ruins of Glendalough.

▲▲ Kilkenny and the Rock of Cashel (1 day)

These are the best two destinations in Ireland's interior: the medieval town of Kilkenny, with its narrow lanes, colorful facades, and stocky castle; and the Rock of Cashel, with its dramatic hilltop of church ruins, overlooking the Plain of Tipperary.

▲ Waterford and County Wexford (1-2 days)

This gritty, historic port sparkles with the Waterford Crystal Visitor Centre. There's also a 12th-century lighthouse, the *Dunbrody* Famine Ship replica, the Irish National Irish Heritage park, and the Kennedy ancestral homestead.

▲▲ Kinsale and Cobh (1-2 days)

County Cork has two quaint harbor towns: Kinsale, beloved by foodies, fun for strolling, and guarded by the squat Charles Fort; and the emigration hub of Cobh—the *Titanic's* last stop.

Rock of Cashel ruins, shepherds, color-ful Kinsale, bikers at Muckross House (Ring of Kerry)

▲▲ Kenmare and the Ring of Kerry (1 day)
The tidy town of Kenmare is the ideal home base for side-stepping the throngs flocking to drive Ireland's most-famous peninsula. The scenic loop route connects fairy forts and villages, with options for a boat excursion to the hermitage island of Skellig Michael.

▲▲ County Clare and the Burren (1-2 days)
Ireland's western fringe has the breathtaking Cliffs of Moher, the stony prehistoric landscape of the Burren, the trad music crossroads of cozy Doolin, and the friendly town of Ennis.

▲ Galway (1 day)
This energetic university city has a thriving pedestrian street scene and great people-watching pubs. For tourists, it's the west coast's best home base for reaching the Burren, Aran Islands, and Connemara region.

▲▲ Westport and Connemara (1 day)
This region is a lushly green, hilly Irish outback of cottages, lakes, and holy peaks, dotted with photogenic settlements such as Cong, Kylemore Abbey, and the leafy riverside town of Westport.

▲ Donegal and the Northwest (half-day to 1 day)
Drivers will enjoy this far-flung section of the Republic and its ruggedly beautiful landscape. The region's main town, Donegal, has a striking castle.

▲ Derry (half-day to 1 day)

This Northern Ireland town, which became a 17th-century British settlement encircled by stout town walls, is infamous as the powder keg that ignited Ireland's tragic "Troubles." Its insightful city history museum tells the tale.

▲▲ Portrush and the Antrim Coast (1 day)

Portrush, an unpretentious beach resort, is the pleasant gateway to the geologic wonderland of the Giant's Causeway, the Old Bushmills Distillery, the cliff-edge ruins of Dunluce Castle, and the exhilarating Carrick-a-Rede Rope Bridge.

▲▲ Belfast (1 day)

The no-nonsense capital of Northern Ireland has stirring sectarian political murals, the *Titanic* museum, a grandly domed City Hall, and the charming Victorian seaside retreat of Bangor nearby.

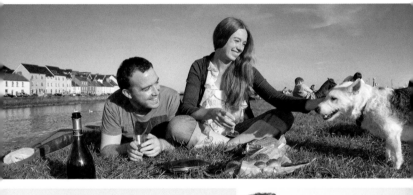

Opposite: Ashford Castle in Cong
This page: Galway picnic, Belfast's City Hall, crossing Carrick-a-Rede Rope Bridge

Planning Your Trip

To plan your trip, you'll need to design your itinerary—choosing where and when to go, how you'll travel, and how many days to spend at each destination. For my best advice on sightseeing, accommodations, restaurants, and transportation, see the Practicalities chapter.

DESIGNING AN ITINERARY

As you read this book and learn your options...

Choose your top destinations.

My recommended itinerary (on page 20) gives you an idea of how much you can reasonably see in 21 days, but you can adapt it to fit your own interests and time frame. If you like what big cities have to offer—museums and nightlife—linger longer in Dublin. If trad music strikes a chord with you, your top stops are—in this order—Dingle, Doolin, Galway, Westport, and Dublin. Food lovers savor Kinsale.

If you're partial to prehistory, you can go back in time in the Burren, Brú na Bóinne burial tombs, and Aran Islands. Modern historians appreciate Belfast. If you're researching Irish roots, Cobh's a great place to start.

Drivers like to joyride around the Dingle and Kerry peninsulas and explore sights scattered throughout County Clare, Connemara, and the Antrim Coast. Nature lovers find inspiration at the Cliffs of Moher and the surprising rock formations of the Giant's Causeway. Photographers want to go everywhere.

Decide when to go.

Peak season (June through Aug) is my favorite time to visit because of the longer days (with daylight from 4:30 until 22:30—Dublin is as far north as Edmonton, Canada). Note though that summer crowds have grown over the years due partly to the cruise-ship industry, which affects mostly Dublin, the Cobh/Cork region, and Belfast.

Travel during "shoulder season" (mid-April through May, plus Sept through early Oct) offers fewer crowds, less competition, and all the tourist fun.

Winter travelers experience no crowds, soft room prices, colder rain, and shorter sightseeing hours (such as 10:00-16:00 instead of the usual 9:00-18:00, or sights open only on weekends, or even closed entirely Nov-Feb). Winter weather can be chilly, dreary, and blustery, dampening the island's rural charm, though city sightseeing is fine.

No matter when you go, expect rain. Just keep on traveling and take full advantage of "bright spells." For weather specifics, see the climate chart in the appendix.

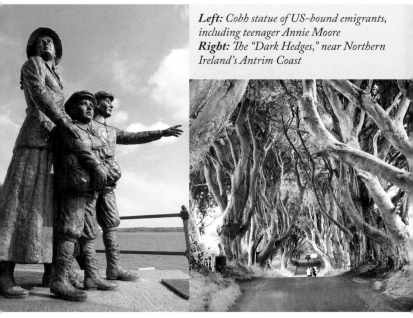

Left: Cobh statue of US-bound emigrants, including teenager Annie Moore
Right: The "Dark Hedges," near Northern Ireland's Antrim Coast

Ireland's Best Three-Week Trip by Car

Day	Plan	Sleep in
1	Fly into Dublin	Dublin
2	Dublin	Dublin
3	Dublin	Dublin
4	Rent car at Dublin Airport, then drive through Glendalough	Kilkenny
5	Rock of Cashel	Waterford
6	Waterford	Waterford
7	Explore County Wexford and Cobh	Kinsale
8	Kinsale	Kinsale
9	Drive to Kenmare	Kenmare
10	Ring of Kerry	Dingle
11	Dingle Peninsula Loop	Dingle
12	Blasket Island, Dingle town	Dingle
13	Cliffs of Moher, the Burren, Dunguaire Castle banquet	Galway
14	Aran Islands	Galway
15	Explore Connemara	Westport
16	Drive to Northern Ireland	Derry
17	Derry	Portrush
18	Explore Antrim Coast	Portrush
19	Drive to Belfast	Belfast
20	Drive to Boyne Valley sights	Trim
21	Return car and fly home from Dublin	

Notes: Spend your first three nights in Dublin, using buses and taxis, then pick up a car for the rest of this itinerary. For three weeks without a car, cut back on the recommended sights with the most frustrating public transportation (County Wexford, the Ring

Connect the dots.

Link your destinations into a logical route. Determine which cities you'll fly into and out of. Begin your search for transatlantic flights at Kayak.com.

Decide if you'll travel by car or public transportation. For the efficiency and freedom, I recommend driving. You won't need a car in big cities (park it), but a car is ideal for exploring regions, stopping wherever you like.

If relying on public transportation, you'll likely use a mix of Kerry, the Burren, Connemara, and the Boyne Valley). You can book day tours by bus for some of these areas at local TIs. For at least two people traveling together, taxis—though expensive—can work in a pinch if bus schedules don't fit your plans (e.g., Cork to Kinsale). If you have time for only one idyllic peninsula on your trip, I'd suggest the Dingle Peninsula over the Ring of Kerry. If you're picking up a car at Dublin Airport, consider starting your trip in small-town Trim, and let Dublin be your finale, when you're rested and ready to tackle the big city.

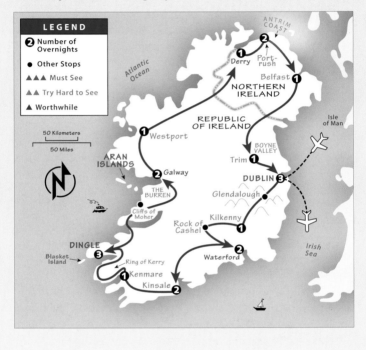

of trains and buses, and fill in transit gaps by taking minibus tours to outlying sights.

To determine approximate transportation times between your destinations, study the driving chart in the Practicalities chapter, or train and bus schedules (see www.discoverireland.ie and select "Getting Around").

If your trip will include other European countries, check Skyscanner.com for intra-European budget flights.

Happy travels!

Write out a day-by-day itinerary.

Figure out how many destinations you can comfortably fit in your timeframe. Don't overdo it—few travelers wish they'd hurried more. Allow enough days per stop (see estimates in "Ireland's Top Destinations," earlier). Minimize one-night stands, especially consecutive ones. It can be worth taking a late-afternoon drive or train ride to get settled into a town for two nights. Include sufficient time for transportation; whether you travel by car, train, or bus, it'll take you a half-day to get between most destinations.

Staying in a home base (like Dublin or Galway) and making day trips can be more time-efficient than changing locations and hotels.

Take sight closures into account. Avoid visiting a city on the one day a week its must-see sights are closed. Check if any holidays or festivals fall during your trip—these attract crowds and can close sights (for the latest, visit Ireland's tourist website, www.discoverireland.ie).

Give yourself some slack. Every trip—and every traveler—needs downtime for doing laundry, picnic shopping, people-watching, and so on. Pace yourself. Assume you will return.

Trip Costs Per Person

Run a reality check on your dream trip. You'll have major transportation costs in addition to daily expenses.

Flight: A round-trip flight from the US to Dublin costs about $1,000-2,000, depending on where you fly from and when.

Car Rental: Allow at least $300 per week, not including tolls, gas, parking, and insurance.

Public Transportation: For a three-week trip, allow $350 per person. Because Ireland's train system has gaps, a rail pass probably won't save you money, but buying train tickets online in advance can save as much as 50 percent.

AVERAGE DAILY EXPENSES PER PERSON

$185
applies to cities, figure on less for towns

Lodging
Based on two people splitting the cost of a $150 double room (includes breakfast).
$75

Meals
$20 for lunch, $30 for dinner, $10 for snacks or Guinness
$60

City Transit
Buses or taxi
$10

Sights and Entertainment
This daily average works for most people.
$40

Budget Tips

You can cut my suggested average daily expenses by taking advantage of the deals you'll find throughout Ireland and mentioned in this book.

Transit passes (for all-day or multiple-day usage) in bigger cities decrease your cost per ride. In Dublin and Belfast, using a hop-on, hop-off bus to get around isn't cheap, but it provides a live guide, a city introduction, and an efficient way to reach far-flung sights (cheaper than taxis and less time-consuming than city buses).

Avid sightseers consider two different sightseeing passes—the Heritage Card and the Heritage Island Visitor Attraction Map—that cover dozens of sights across ▶▶▶

Rick Steves Ireland

▶▶▶ Ireland (see "Sightseeing Passes," in the Practicalities chapter). On a smaller scale, some cities offer combo-tickets or passes that cover multiple museums. If a town doesn't offer deals, visit only the sights you most want to see, and seek out free sights and experiences (people-watching counts).

Some businesses—especially hotels and walking-tour companies—offer discounts to my readers (look for the RS% symbol in the hotel listings in this book).

Book your rooms directly with the hotel. Some hotels give you a discount if you pay in cash and/or stay three or more nights (check online or ask). Rooms cost less outside of peak season (mid-June-Aug). And even seniors can sleep cheap in hostels (some have double rooms) for about $30 per person. Or check Airbnb-type sites for deals.

It's no hardship to eat cheap in Ireland. You can get hearty, affordable meals at pubs and early-bird dinner deals at nicer restaurants. Cultivate the art of picnicking in atmospheric settings.

When you splurge, choose an experience you'll always remember, such as the Dunguaire Castle medieval banquet or a flight to the Aran Islands. Minimize souvenir shopping—how will you get it all home? Focus instead on collecting wonderful memories. ▪

A teachable moment, a soaring sculpture (Rock of Cashel), a Dingle drive

BEFORE YOU GO

You'll have a smoother trip if you tackle a few things ahead of time. For more info on these topics, see the Practicalities chapter (and www.ricksteves.com, which has helpful tips and travel talks).

Make sure your passport is valid. If it's due to expire within six months of your ticketed date of return, you need to renew it. Allow up to six weeks to renew or get a passport (www.travel.state.gov).

Arrange your transportation. Book your international flights. Figure out your main form of transportation within Ireland: You can rent a car, or buy train and bus tickets (either as you go, or you can book train tickets in advance online at a discount).

Book rooms well in advance, especially if your trip falls during peak season or any major holidays or festivals.

Reserve or buy tickets ahead for major sights, ensuring entry and saving you from long ticket-buying lines. It's smart to book online for Dublin's Book of Kells and Kilmainham Gaol, and for Brú na Bóinne (near Dublin) and Titanic Belfast. Garden tours at Glenveagh Castle and National Park in Donegal are only available with an advance reservation. Boat trips to Skellig Michael can sell out weeks in advance—reserve ahead.

Consider travel insurance. Compare the cost of the insurance to the cost of your potential loss. Check whether your existing insurance (health, homeowners, or renters) covers you and your possessions overseas.

Call your bank. Alert your bank that you'll be using your debit and credit cards in Europe. Ask about transaction fees, and get the PIN number for your credit card. You don't need to bring euros or pounds for your trip; you can withdraw local currency from cash machines in Europe.

Use your smartphone smartly. Sign up for an international service plan to reduce your costs, or rely on Wi-Fi in Europe instead. Download any apps you'll want on the road, such as maps, translation, transit schedules, and Rick Steves Audio Europe.

Rip up this book! Turn chapters into mini-guidebooks: Break the book's spine and use a utility knife to slice apart chapters, keeping gummy edges intact. Reinforce the chapter spines with clear wide tape; use a heavy-duty stapler; or make or buy a cheap cover (see Travel Store at www.ricksteves.com), swapping out chapters as you travel.

Pack light. You'll walk with your luggage more than you think. Bring a single carry-on bag and a daypack. Use the packing checklist in the appendix as a guide.

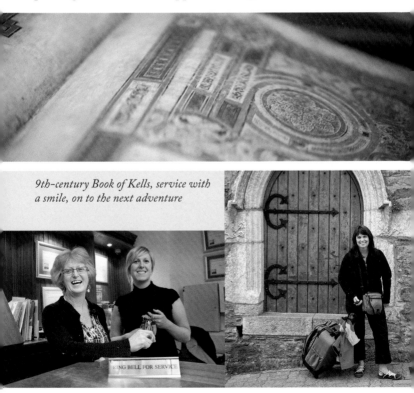

9th-century Book of Kells, service with a smile, on to the next adventure

Travel Smart

If you have a positive attitude, equip yourself with good information (this book), and expect to travel smart, you will.

Read—and reread—this book. To have an "A" trip, be an "A" student. Note opening hours of sights, closed days, crowd-beating tips, and whether reservations are required or advisable. Check the latest at www.ricksteves.com/update.

Be your own tour guide. As you travel, get up-to-date info on sights, reserve tickets and tours, reconfirm hotels and travel arrangements, and check transit connections. Visit local tourist information offices (TIs). Upon arrival in a new town, lay the groundwork for a smooth departure; confirm the road, train, or bus you'll take when you leave.

Outsmart thieves. Although pickpockets aren't prevalent in Ireland, it's wise to be cautious in crowded places where tourists congregate. Keep your cash, credit cards, and passport secure in a money belt tucked under your clothes; carry only a day's spending money in your front pocket. Don't set valuable items down on counters or café tabletops, where they can be quickly stolen or easily forgotten.

Minimize potential loss. Keep expensive gear to a minimum. Bring photocopies or take photos of important documents (passport and cards) to aid in replacement if they're lost or stolen.

Guard your time and energy. Taking a taxi can be a good value if it saves you a long wait for a cheap bus or an exhausting walk across town. To avoid long lines, follow my crowd-beating tips, such as making advance reservations, or sightseeing early or late.

Be flexible. Even if you have a well-planned itinerary, expect changes, closures, sore feet, bad weather, and so on. Your Plan B could turn out to be even better.

Connect with the culture. Interacting with locals carbonates your experience. Enjoy the friendliness of the Irish people. Ask questions; most locals are happy to point you in their idea of the right direction. Set up your own quest for the best pub, traditional music, ruined castle, or ring fort. When an opportunity pops up, make it a habit to say "yes."

Ireland...here you come!

REPUBLIC
OF
IRELAND

REPUBLIC OF IRELAND

The resilient Irish character was born of dark humor, historical reverence, and a scrappy, "we'll get 'em next time" rebel spirit. The Irish people maintain an unsinkable and optimistic belief in the future.

The modern Irish state has existed since 1922, but its inhabitants proudly claim their nation to be the only contemporary independent state to sprout from purely Celtic roots (sprinkled with a few Vikings and ship-wrecked Spanish Armada sailors to spice up the gene pool). The Romans never bothered to come over and organize the wild Irish. Through the persuasive and culturally enlightened approach of early missionaries such as St. Patrick, Ireland is one of the very few countries to have initially converted to Christianity without much bloodshed. The religious carnage came a thousand years later, with the Reformation. Irish culture absorbed the influences of Viking raiders and Norman soldiers of fortune, eventually enduring the 750-year shadow of English domination (1169-1922).

For most of the 20th century, Ireland was an isolated, agricultural economic backwater that had largely missed out on the Industrial Revolution. Things began to turn around when Ireland joined the European Community (precursor to the EU) in 1973, and really took off during the "Celtic Tiger" boom years (1995-2007), when American corporations saw big tax and labor advantages in locating here. Ireland's "Silicon Bog" became the European base for such big names as IBM, Intel, Microsoft, Apple, Facebook, and Google.

Today, the Republic of Ireland attracts both expatriates returning to their homeland and new foreign investment. As the

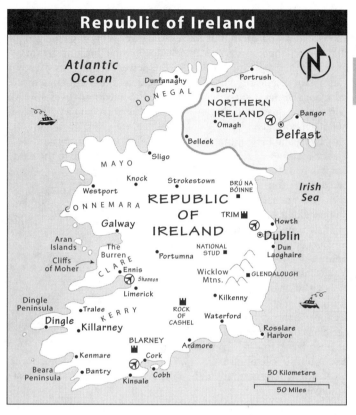

Republic of Ireland

Atlantic Ocean

Dunfanaghy
Portrush
• Derry
DONEGAL
NORTHERN IRELAND
•Omagh
Bangor
Belfast

Belleek

MAYO
• Sligo

Knock
Strokestown
BRÚ NA BÓINNE

Westport
REPUBLIC OF IRELAND
TRIM
Irish Sea

CONNEMARA
Galway
Howth
Dublin

Aran Islands
The Burren
Portumna
NATIONAL STUD
Dun Laoghaire

Cliffs of Moher
CLARE
Ennis
Shannon
Wicklow Mtns.
GLENDALOUGH

Limerick
Kilkenny

Dingle Peninsula
• Tralee
KERRY
ROCK OF CASHEL
Waterford

Dingle
Killarney
BLARNEY
Ardmore
Rosslare Harbor

• Kenmare
Cork

Beara Peninsula
• Bantry
Cobh
Kinsale

50 Kilometers

50 Miles

only officially English-speaking country to have adopted the euro currency, Ireland makes an efficient base from which to access the European marketplace. About 35 percent of the Irish population is under 25 years old, leading many high-tech and pharmaceutical firms to locate here, taking advantage of this young, well-educated labor force. More Viagra is made in Ireland than in any other country...though proudly virile Irish males claim it's all for export.

Other famous exports from the Republic of Ireland include rock and contemporary music (U2, Thin Lizzy, Hozier, Imelda May, the Corrs, Sinéad O'Connor, Enya), traditional Irish music (the Chieftains, Dubliners, the Clancy Brothers), opera (the Irish Tenors and John McCormack), dance (Riverdance), trivia (Guinness World Records), crystal (Waterford), beer (Guinness), iconic authors (Jonathan Swift, W. B. Yeats, James Joyce, George Bernard Shaw, Samuel Beckett, and Oscar Wilde), and a slew of memorable actors (Pierce Brosnan, Colin Farrell, Richard Harris, Michael Gambon, Colm Meaney, Saoirse Ronan, Michael Fassbender, and Maureen O'Hara).

Until recently, Ireland was one of the most ethnically homogenous nations on earth, but the Celtic Tiger economy changed all that, when the country became a destination for immigrants—mostly from the Third World and the newer EU nations. Eastern Europeans (especially Poles) came in search of higher pay...a reversal from the days when many Irish fled to start new lives abroad. A recent census found that over 15 percent of Ireland's population had been born elsewhere.

Everyone here speaks English, though you'll encounter Irish Gaelic (commonly referred to as "Irish") if you venture to the western fringe of the country. The Irish love of conversation shines through wherever you go. All that conversation is helped along by the nebulous concept of Irish time, which never seems to be in short supply. Small shops post their hours as "9:00ish 'til 5:00ish." The local bus usually makes a stop at "10:30ish." A healthy disdain for being a slave to the clock seems to be part of being Irish. And the warm welcome you'll receive has its roots in ancient Celtic laws of hospitality toward stranded strang-

ers. You'll see the phrase *"Céad míle fáilte"* in tourism brochures and postcards throughout Ireland—it translates as "a hundred thousand welcomes."

Founded in the late 1800s to preserve and promote Gaelic culture, the Gaelic Athletic Association (GAA) operates popular Irish hurling and football (not to be confused with soccer) leagues. Other sports in the Republic of Ireland include horse racing and dog racing. And it's hard to go 25 miles in Ireland without running into a golf course (there are more than 300 on the island).

Long a predominant cultural force, the influence of the Catholic Church is less apparent these days. Thirty percent of Irish weddings are now civil ceremonies, and weekly church attendance in Ireland is below the US average, having decreased dramatically over the years. (It would be even lower if not for the influx of devout Catholic Poles.) But the Church still plays a part in Irish life. Most Irish claim to be Catholic, and shrines to the Virgin Mary still grace rural roadsides. The average Irish family spends almost €500 on lavish celebrations for the First Holy Communion of each child. And the national radio and TV station, RTE, pauses for 30 seconds at noon and at 18:00 to broadcast the chimes of the Angelus bells—signaling the start of Catholic devotional prayers. The Irish say that if you're phoning heaven, it's a long-distance call from the rest of the world, but a local call from Ireland.

Republic of Ireland Almanac

Official Name: The Republic of Ireland (a.k.a. "Ireland" or, in Irish, Éire).

Size: 27,000 square miles—half the size of New York State—it occupies the southern 80 percent of the island of Ireland. The country is small enough that radio broadcasts cover traffic snarls nationwide. Population 4.8 million people (same as Louisiana).

Geography: The isle is mostly flat, ringed by a hilly coastline. The climate is moderate, with cloudy skies about every other day.

Latitude and Longitude: 53°N and 8°W. The latitude is equivalent to Alberta, Canada.

Biggest Cities: The capital of Dublin (550,000 people) is the only big city; more than one in four Irish live in the greater Dublin area (1.9 million). Cork has about 125,000 people, Limerick 94,000, Galway 79,000, and Waterford 53,000.

Economy: The Gross Domestic Product is $294 billion, and the GDP per capita is $62,562—one of Europe's highest and 30 percent more than Britain's. Major moneymakers include tourism and exports (especially to the US and UK) of machines, medicine, Guinness, glassware, crystal ware, and software. Traditional agriculture (potatoes and other root vegetables) is fading fast, but dairy still does well.

Government: The elected president, Michael Higgins, appoints the Taoiseach (TEE-shock) or prime minister (youthful Leo Varadkar), who is nominated by Parliament. The Parliament consists of the 60-seat Senate, chosen by an electoral college, and the House of Representatives, with 166 seats apportioned after the people vote for a party. Major parties include Fianna Fáil, Fine Gael, and Sinn Fein—the political arm of the (fading) Irish Republican Army. Ireland is divided into 28 administrative counties (including Kerry, Clare, Cork, Limerick, and so on).

Flag: The Republic of Ireland's flag has three vertical bands of green, white, and orange.

The Average Irish: A typical Irish person is 5'7", 37 years old, has 1-2 kids, and will live to be 80. An Irish citizen consumes nearly 5 pounds of tea per year and spends $5 on alcohol each day. He or she speaks English, though Irish Gaelic is spoken in pockets along the country's west coast (less than 5 percent of Irish people are fluent in the Irish language). Nearly eight in 10 are nominally Catholic (a sharp decline in the last few years), though only one in three attends church.

RTE: The Voice of Ireland

Many a long drive or rainy evening has been saved by the engaging programs I've happened upon on RTE: Raidió Teilifís Éireann. What the BBC is to Britain, RTE is to Ireland: This government-owned company and national public broadcaster produces and broadcasts a wide range of programs on television, radio, and online. Look for it as you travel (via RTE's smartphone apps, on the radio in your car, or on TV at your B&B).

First hitting the airwaves on New Year's Eve 1961, today's RTE TV broadcasts are all digital and in the English language on RTE channels 1 and 2. But don't shy away from channel 4 (TG4), with Irish language TV shows subtitled in English—it's a great way to get a feel for the sound of the language. You couldn't find a richer or more accessible introduction to Irish culture.

Got a serious appetite for all things Irish? Online at www.rte.ie/archives, you'll find a treasure trove of fascinating archived RTE programs—everything from coverage of JFK's 1963 visit, to elderly recollections of the 1916 Rising, to the poetry of Seamus Heaney, to Gaelic sports.

Modern sensibilities continue to make inroads in once-traditional Ireland. A 2003 law required shops to charge customers for plastic sacks for carrying goods, with revenue going to an environmental fund—one of the world's first plastic-bag taxes. In 2004, smoking was banned in all Irish workplaces (including pubs). The Irish were the first nation in the world to enact such a comprehensive law (some pubkeepers initially grumbled about lost business, but the air has cleared). In the past decade, the Irish Department of Health has reported a 30 percent reduction in strokes and a 25 percent reduction in heart disease. Tourism is up as well.

Keeping up this progressive trend, in 2015 Ireland became the first country to legalize marriage equality by popular vote. And the republic in 2017 selected as its new prime minister (known as the "Taoiseach," meaning "Chieftain") the 38-year-old Leo Varadkar, a first-generation son of an Indian emigrant. A medical doctor, the openly gay Varadkar now leads a nation that, only a generation earlier, officially considered homosexuality unlawful as well as immoral.

As time has passed, relations between Ireland and her former colonial master Britain have improved. In May 2011, Queen Elizabeth II became the first British monarch to visit the Republic of Ireland since Ireland's 1921 split from the United Kingdom, which occurred during her grandfather's reign. Her four-night visit (to Dublin, Cashel, and Cork) unexpectedly charmed the Irish people and did much to repair old wounds between the two countries, establishing them, in the words of the Queen, as "firm friends and equal partners."

The big question now is how Brexit (Britain's impending exit from the EU) might complicate Ireland's easy trading relationship with their UK neighbors. Although the UK as a whole voted to leave the EU, the citizens of Northern Ireland voted to remain (recognizing the advantage of their soft border with the Republic). A possible "hardening" of this border is generally seen as a step backward that both countries want to avoid.

At first glance, Ireland's landscape seems unspectacular, with few mountains higher than 3,000 feet and an interior consisting of grazing pastures and peat bogs. But its seductive beauty slowly grows on you. The gentle rainfall, called "soft weather" by the locals, really does create 40 shades of green— and quite a few rainbows as well. Ancient, moss-covered ring forts crouch in lush valleys, while stone-strewn monastic ruins and lone castle turrets brave the wind on nearby hilltops. Charming fishing villages dot the coast near rugged, wave-battered cliffs.

You can't drive too far without running into road construction, as the recently affluent Irish improve their infrastructure with new motorways aimed at making travel between bigger cities faster. But the country is still laced with plenty of humble country lanes—perfect for getting lost in the wonders of Ireland. Slow down to contemplate the checkerboard patterns created by the rock walls outlining the many fields. Examine the colorful small-town shop fronts that proudly state the name of the proprietor. Embrace the laid-back tempo of Irish life.

DUBLIN

With reminders of its stirring history and rich culture on every corner, Ireland's capital and largest city is a sightseer's delight. Dublin punches above its weight class in arts, entertainment, food, and fun. The vibe is infectious and by the time you depart, Dublin's fair city will have you humming, "Cockles and mussels, alive, alive-O."

Founded as a Viking trading settlement in the ninth century, Dublin grew to be a center of wealth and commerce, second only to London in the British Empire. As the seat of English rule in Ireland for 750 years, Dublin was the heart of a "civilized" Anglo-Irish area (eastern Ireland) known as "the Pale." Anything "beyond the Pale" was considered uncultured and almost barbaric...purely Irish.

The Golden Age of English Dublin was the 18th century. The British Empire was on a roll, and the city was right there with it. Largely rebuilt during this Georgian era, Dublin became an elegant and cultured capital.

Those glory days left a lasting imprint on the city. Squares and boulevards built in the Georgian style, such as Merrion Square, give the city an air of grandeur ("Georgian" is British for Neoclassical...named for the period when four consecutive King Georges occupied the British throne from 1714 to 1830). The National Museum, the National Gallery, and many government buildings are in the Georgian section of town.

Throughout the 19th century, as Ireland endured the Great Potato Famine and saw the beginnings of the modern struggle for independence, Dublin was treated—and felt—more like a British colony than a partner. The tension culminated in the Easter Rising of 1916, followed by a successful guerilla war of independence against Britain and Ireland's tragic civil war. With many of its grand streets in ruins, war-torn Dublin emerged as the capital of the British Empire's only former colony in Europe.

While bullet-pocked buildings and dramatic statues keep memories of Ireland's struggle for independence alive, the city is looking ahead to a brighter future. In the last decade, the tentative "green shoots" of a hoped-for financial recovery from the devastating 2008 crash have sprouted into a forest of cranes sweeping over booming construction blocks and expanding light rail infrastructure. Dubliners are energetic and helpful, and visitors enjoy a big-town cultural scene wrapped in a small-town smile.

PLANNING YOUR TIME

This bustling city is a must for travelers interested in Celtic/Viking artifacts, Irish literature, or rebel history. For most people, Dublin deserves three nights and two days.

Be aware that some important sights close on Mondays. Reserve Kilmainham Gaol in advance or risk it being sold out. Consider this ambitious sightseeing plan:

Day 1

9:00 Visit the Book of Kells and Old Trinity Library ahead of mid-morning crowds (book ahead).

11:00 Take the guided Historical Walking Tour.

12:30 Browse Grafton Street, have lunch there, or picnic on St. Stephen's Green.

14:00 Head to the National Museum: Archaeology branch (closed Mon).

16:00 Visit Epic: The Irish Emigration Museum.

17:30 Return to hotel, rest, have dinner.

19:30 Go for an evening guided pub tour (musical or literary).

22:00 If you still have the energy, find a pub with live Irish music.

Day 2

9:00 Tour Kilmainham Gaol (reserve ahead).

11:00 Take the Dublin Castle tour.

13:00 Grab lunch.

14:30 Follow the self-guided "O'Connell Street Stroll" in this chapter, taking in the GPO Witness History exhibit en route (in the General Post Office).

Evening Options: Catch a concert, a play, the storytelling dinner at The Brazen Head (or one of the other recommended dinner shows), another guided pub tour (musical or literary), or more live folk music in a pub.

Orientation to Dublin

Greater Dublin sprawls with well over a million people—more than a quarter of the country's population. But the center of tourist interest is a tight triangle between O'Connell Bridge, St. Stephen's Green, and Christ Church Cathedral. Within or near this triangle, you'll find Trinity College (Book of Kells), a cluster of major museums (including the National Museum: Archaeology), touristy and pedestrianized Grafton Street, Temple Bar (touristy nightlife center), Dublin Castle, and the hub of most city tours and buses. The

major sights outside this easy-to-walk triangle are the General Post Office ("GPO" to locals; north of the center), and Kilmainham Gaol and the Guinness Storehouse (west of the center).

The River Liffey cuts the town in two, and most of your sightseeing will take place on its south bank. Many long Dublin streets change names every few blocks, including the wide main axis that cuts north/south through the tourist center. North from the O'Connell Bridge, it's called O'Connell Street; south of the bridge, it becomes Westmoreland, passes Trinity College, and becomes the pedestrian-only Grafton Street to St. Stephen's Green.

Two suburbs, Dun Laoghaire to the south and Howth to the north, offer quiet home-base alternatives to Dublin (with easy 25-minute transit connections into town). By staying outside the city, you'll save about 25 percent on your hotel costs.

TOURIST INFORMATION

Dublin's busy main TI has lots of info and brochures on Dublin and all of Ireland (Mon-Sat 9:00-17:30, Sun 10:30-15:00, a block off Grafton Street at 25 Suffolk Street, tel. 01/884-7700, www.visitdublin.com). A smaller but equally helpful TI is just past the Spire, on the east side of O'Connell Street (Mon-Sat 9:00-17:00, closed Sun). Watch out for other shops that claim to be TIs, especially on O'Connell Street. They're aiming to sell you tours and collect commissions.

Dublin Pass: This sightseeing pass covers 30 sights and landmarks (but not the Book of Kells), hop-on, hop-off buses, and the Aircoach airport bus—one-way from the airport to the city only (pass-€59/1 day, multiday options available, purchase online and collect at TIs, www.dublinpass.ie). If you already have the Heritage Card (see page 532), skip this one, as the card already covers two big Dublin sights (Kilmainham Gaol and Dublin Castle).

Maps: At any TI, you can pick up the free *Dublin Pocket Guide*, but the best free city map is the one created by the Kilkenny Shop (6 Nassau Street, bordering the south side of the Trinity College campus)—available at tourist outlets throughout the city.

ARRIVAL IN DUBLIN

For details on Dublin's airport, as well as ferry connections between the UK and Dublin, see "Dublin Connections," at the end of this chapter.

By Train: Dublin has two train stations. Heuston Station, on the west end of town, serves west and southwest Ireland (45-minute walk from O'Connell Bridge; take the LUAS light rail or bus #90—see below). Connolly Station, which serves the north, northwest, and Rosslare, is closer to the center (15-minute walk from O'Connell Bridge). Each station has ATMs but no lockers.

The train stations are connected by the red line of the LUAS light-rail system (see "Getting Around Dublin" on page 42) and by bus #90, which runs along the river (€2, 4/hour). From the city center, to reach Heuston Station, catch bus #90 on the south side of the river; to get to Connolly Station and Busáras Central Bus Station, catch #90 on the north side of the river.

By Bus: Bus Éireann, Ireland's national bus company, uses the Busáras Central Bus Station (pronounced bu-SAUR-us). Located next to Connolly Station, it's a 10-minute walk or a short ride on bus #90 to the city center.

By Car: Don't drive in downtown Dublin—traffic's terrible, parking is expensive, and there are plenty of smarter options. If you have to park in central Dublin, a good option is Q-Park Christ Church, on Werburgh Street behind Jurys Inn Christ Church (€3.50/hour, €16/day, tel. 01/454-9001). For more on driving around Dublin, including its toll road, see page 109.

HELPFUL HINTS

Pickpockets: Irish destinations, especially Dublin, are not immune to this scourge. Be on guard—use a money belt or carefully zip things up (see page 527).

Festivals: Book ahead during festivals and for any weekend. **St. Patrick's Day** is a four-day March extravaganza in Dublin (www.stpatricksday.ie). June 16 is **Bloomsday,** dedicated to the Irish author James Joyce and featuring the Messenger Bike Rally (www.jamesjoyce.ie). Hotels raise their prices and are packed on rugby weekends (about four per year), during

DUBLIN

the all-Ireland Gaelic football and hurling finals (Sundays in September), and during summer rock concerts.

Meet a Dubliner: The **City of a Thousand Welcomes** offers a free service that brings together volunteers and first-time visitors. Sign up online in advance and pick an available time slot. In Dublin you'll meet your "ambassador," head for a nearby tea-room or pub, and enjoy a drink (paid for by the city) and a friendly, informal conversation (of up to an hour). It's a great way to get oriented to the city (meet at Little Museum of Dub-

Orientation to Dublin 41

DUBLIN

lin, 15 St. Stephens Green—see map on page 58, tel. 01/661-1000, www.cityofathousandwelcomes.com).

Mass in Latin: The Roman Catholic Mass is said in Latin daily at St. Kevin's Church (Mon-Fri at 8:00, Sat at 9:00, Sun at 10:30, corner of Harrington and Synge, about six blocks south of St. Patrick's Cathedral, www.latinmassdublin.ie).

Bookstores: The giant granddaddy of them all is **Eason's,** five minutes north of the O'Connell Bridge (Mon-Sat 8:00-19:00,

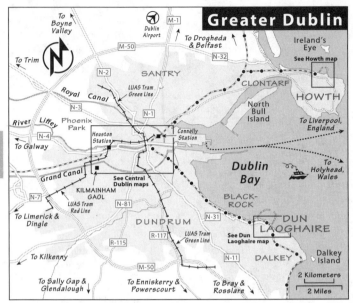

Greater Dublin

Sun 12:00-18:00, 40 O'Connell Street Lower, tel. 01/858-3800, www.easons.com).

Laundry: Krystal Launderette, a block southwest of Jurys Inn Christ Church on Patrick Street, offers same-day full service (Mon-Sat 8:00-20:00, Sun 12:00-17:00, tel. 01/454-6864). The **All-American Launderette** offers self- and full-service options (Mon-Sat 8:30-19:00, Sun 10:00-18:00, 40 South Great George's Street, tel. 01/677-2779). For locations, see the map on page 96.

Bike Rental: River Cycles is right along the south side of the River Liffey on Usher's Island quay, about four blocks west of The Brazen Head pub. From here, consider a low-stress ride into the huge, bike-friendly Phoenix Park (€4/2 hours, €5/4 hours, €10/day, daily 10:00-19:00 "weather depending," 10 Usher's Island, mobile 086-265-6258, www.rivercyclesphoenixparkbikehire.com).

GETTING AROUND DUBLIN

You'll do most of Dublin on foot, though when you need public transportation, you'll find it readily available and easy to use. With a little planning, sightseers can make excellent use of a two-day hop-on, hop-off bus ticket to link the best sights (see page 46). Also, keep in mind that (for cross-city travel) the expanding LUAS light-rail system does not get bogged down in traffic like buses and taxis do.

By Public Transportation

You can buy individual tickets for the bus, DART, and LUAS, or get a transit card that can be used on all three (described below).

Bus: Public buses are cheap and cover the city thoroughly. Most lines start at the four quays (riverfront streets) that are nearest O'Connell Bridge. If you're away from the center, nearly any bus takes you back downtown. Some bus stops are "request only" stops: Be alert to the bus numbers (above the windshield) of approaching buses, and when you see your bus coming, flag it down. Tell the driver where you're going, and he'll ask for €2-3.30 depending on the number of stops. Bring coins, as drivers don't make change.

The Dublin Bus office has free route maps and sells the transit cards described below (Mon-Fri 9:00-17:30, Sat-Sun 9:30-14:00, 59 Upper O'Connell Street, tel. 01/873-4222, www.dublinbus.ie).

DART Train: Speedy commuter trains run along the coast, connecting Dublin with suburban Dun Laoghaire (south) and Howth (north). Think of the DART line as a giant "C" that serves coastal suburbs from Bray in the south up to Howth (€3.25, €6.15 round-trips valid same day only, buy at machine, 4/hour, tel. 01/703-3504, www.irishrail.ie/home).

LUAS Light Rail: The city's light-rail system has two main lines, red and green. The most useful for tourists is the red line, with an east-west section connecting the Heuston and Connolly train stations (15-minute ride apart) at opposite edges of the Central Zone. In between, the Busáras, Smithfield, and Museum stops can be handy. Useful north-south green line stops are at St. Stephen's Green, Trinity College, and both ends of O'Connell Street (€2.10, buy at machine, 6/hour, runs until 24:45, tel. 1-800-300-604, www.luas.ie). Monitors at each boarding platform display the time and end destination of the next LUAS train; check to make sure you're on the right platform for the direction you want to go.

Transit Cards: The Leap Card is good for travel on Dublin's bus, DART, and LUAS routes, and fares are lower than buying individual tickets. Leap Cards are sold at TIs, newsstands, and markets citywide—look for the leaping-frog logo—and can be topped up (€5 refundable deposit, www.leapcard.ie).

For those staying in Dun Laoghaire or Howth—or on a long-term stay in Dublin—the **Leap Visitor Card** may be a better option. It enables unlimited travel on Dublin's buses (including Airlink Express to and from the airport), DART, and LUAS trams (€10/1 day, €19.50/3 days, €40/7 days, each "day" equals 24 hours from first use, http://about.leapcard.ie/leap-visitor-card). It's possible to buy the card online in advance, but it's just as easy to pick one up at the airport (transportation desk in Terminal 1 or at the Spar in Terminal 2) or from several Dublin city center locations (main TI, Dublin Bus office, or Discover Ireland Centre at 14 Upper O'Connell Street).

The **Do Dublin** transit and discount card covers the Airlink Express, public buses in Dublin, and the Do Dublin hop-on, hop-off bus, while offering some sight discounts. Purchase in advance online, at the Do Dublin airport desk (Terminal 1), or the Dublin Bus office (€35/72 hours, tel. 01/844-4265, www.dodublin.ie).

DUBLIN

By Taxi or Uber

Taxis are everywhere and easy to hail. Cabbies are generally honest, friendly, and good sources of information (drop charge—€3.60 daytime, €4 nighttime, €1/each additional adult, figure about €12-15 for most crosstown rides, €40/hour for guided joyride).

Your Uber app will get you two choices in Dublin: "Uber" is actually a taxi (with the standard metered rate, but no tipping and billed to your account); "Uber Black" is an expensive chauffeur-driven car.

Tours in Dublin

While Dublin's physical treasures are lackluster by European standards, the gritty city has a fine story to tell and people with a natural knack for telling it. It's a good town for walking tours, and competition is fierce. Pamphlets touting creative walks are posted all over town. Choices include medieval walks, literary walks, Georgian Dublin walks, and traditional music or literary pub crawls. Taking an evening walk is a great way to meet other travelers. The Dublin TI also offers a variety of free, good-quality, downloadable "Dublin Discovery Trails" audio tours.

For help finding the departure points of the following recommended tours, see the map on page 58.

ON FOOT
▲▲Historical Walking Tour

This is your best introductory walk. A group of hardworking history graduates enliven Dublin's basic historic strip (Trinity College, Old Parliament House, Dublin Castle, and Christ Church Cathedral). You'll get the story of their city, from its Viking origins to the present. Guides speak at length about the roots of Ireland's struggle with Britain. As you listen to your guide, you'll stand in front of buildings that aren't much to look at, but are lots to talk about (April-Oct daily at 11:00, May-Sept also at 15:00; Nov-March Fri-Sun at 11:00). All walks last 90 minutes and cost €12 (ask for discount with this book, free for kids under 14, departs from front gate of Trinity College, private tours available, mobile 087-688-9412 or 087-830-3523, www.historicalinsights.ie).

▲▲Traditional Irish Musical Pub Crawl

This entertaining tour visits the upstairs rooms of three pubs; there, you'll listen to two musicians talk about, play, and sing traditional

Irish music. While having only two musicians makes the music a bit thin (Irish music aficionados will say you're better off just finding a good session), the evening—though touristy—provides a real education in traditional Irish music. The musicians clearly enjoy introducing rookies to their art and are very good at it. And they are really funny. In the summer, this popular 2.5-hour tour frequently sells out, but it's easy to reserve ahead online (€14, ask for discount with this book—use code RSIRISH online, beer extra, at 19:30 April-Oct daily, Jan-March Thu-Sat only, no shows Dec, maximum 65 people, meet upstairs at Gogarty's Pub at the corner of Fleet and Anglesea in the Temple Bar area, tel. 01/475-3313, www.musicalpubcrawl.com). They also offer a dinner-show version; for details and location, see page 107.

Dublin Literary Pub Crawl

Two actors take 40 or so tourists on a walk, stopping at four pubs, and with clever banter introduce the high *craic* of James Joyce, Seán O'Casey, and W. B. Yeats. The two-hour tour is punctuated with 20-minute pub breaks (free time). This is an easygoing excuse to drink beer in busy pubs, meet other travelers, and get a dose of Irish witty lit (€13, at 19:30 April-Oct daily, Nov-March Thu-Sun only; just show up, but reserve ahead in July-Aug when it can fill up; meet upstairs in the Duke Pub—off Grafton on Duke Street, tel. 01/670-5602, mobile 087-263-0270, www.dublinpubcrawl.com). Connoisseurs of Irish pubs enjoy the excellent *Dublin Literary Pub Crawl* guidebook by pub-crawl founder Colm Quilligan.

1916 Rebellion Walking Tour

This two-hour walk breathes gritty life into the most turbulent year in modern Irish history, when idealistic Irish rebels launched the Easter Rising—eventually leading to independence from Britain. Guide Lorcan Collins has written a guidebook called *The Easter Rising*—worth seeking out—and is passionate about his walks (€13, ask for discount with this book; March-Oct Mon-Sat at 11:30, Sun at 13:00; Nov-Feb Fri-Sun at 11:30; departs from International Bar at 23 Wicklow Street, mobile 086-858-3847, www.1916rising.com).

Pat Liddy's Walking Tours

Pat Liddy, one of Dublin's top historians, and his guides take groups on enthusiastic and informal two-hour walks of hidden Dublin districts. Unlike most Dublin walks, this one does a good job of covering the often overlooked but historic north side of town. His "Highlights and Hidden Corners" tour starts near the General Post Office building, winds down across the river to City Hall, through Temple Bar, and ends at Trinity College (€12, April-Oct daily at 11:00, no tours Sun, Tue, or Thu in off-season, meet in front of Dublin Bus office at 59 Upper O'Connell Street, tel. 01/832-9406, mobile 087-905-2480, www.walkingtours.ie).

Local Guides

Two proud Dubliners will show you around town when they're not on the road leading Rick Steves tours: **Joe Darcy** is a friendly guy with a passion for Irish literature, who enjoys unpeeling the urban layers of his hometown for visitors (€120 for up to 4 people for 2.5-hour walking tour, mobile 086-218-0357, josdarcy@gmail.com). Witty **Dara McCarthy** offers similar services for the same rates (mobile 087-291-6798, dara@daramccarthy.com).

BY BIKE
Dublin City Bike Tours

You'll "get your *craic* on a saddle" with Dublin City Bike Tours as you pedal across this flat city on a fun, innovative tour that covers five miles and visits 20 points of interest north and south of the River Liffey. Designed for riders of average fitness, they set a casual pace, and rarely let a little rain stop them (€27 includes bike, helmet, snack, and water; ask for discount with this book; cash only, reserve in advance, 2.5 hours; March-Nov daily at 10:00, additional tours Fri and Sat at 14:00; departs Isaac's Hostel a half-block west of Busáras bus station at 2 Frenchman's Lane—see map on page 80, mobile 087-134-1866, www.dublincitybiketours.com).

Lazy Bike Tour Company

For a less strenuous option, you can grab a bright orange electric bike and matching vest, and buzz along on a guided tour that covers sights from Dublin Castle to Kilmainham Gaol. Tours start in Temple Bar and last two hours (€30, daily at 10:00, 12:30, and 15:00; book in advance in summer; meet at 4 Scarlet Row on Essex Street West in Temple Bar near Christ Church Cathedral, 01/443-3671, www.lazybiketours.com).

BY BUS (ON LAND AND WATER)
▲Hop-on, Hop-off Bus Tours

Taking a hop-on, hop-off bus tour is an excellent way to orient yourself on arrival in Dublin. Several companies running roofless double-deckers do similar 1.5-hour circuits of the city (up to 30 stops, buses circle every 10-15 minutes daily 9:00-17:00, usually until 19:00 in summer). This type of tour, with running commen-

taries (either live or recorded), is made-to-order
for Dublin, and buses run
so frequently that they
make your sightseeing su-
per-efficient. Stops include
the far-flung Guinness
Storehouse and Kilmain-
ham Gaol. Each company

offers various discounts to museums and sights in town, and two
kids ride free with each adult.

Do Dublin (green buses) has drivers who provide fun and
quirky narration, and your ticket includes free entry into the Little
Museum of Dublin and a free walking tour from Pat Liddy's Walking Tours (€19/24 hours, €23/48 hours, tel. 01/703-3028, www.
dublinsightseeing.ie).

Dublin CityScape (yellow buses) offers three routes (€15/24
hours, €18/72 hours, tel. 01/465-9972, http://cityscapetours.ie).

City Sightseeing Dublin (red buses) has a handy "blue
route" that takes you as far as Glasnevin Cemetery and Croke
Park (€19/24 hours, €25/48 hours, tel. 01/898-0700, https://
citysightseeingdublin.ie). They also offer a 90-minute musical **evening tour** (without stops) with a live guide who narrates but also
sings and plays guitar (€10, June-Sept nightly at 20:00 and 21:30,
buy ticket from driver, leaves from the Gresham Hotel at 14 Upper
O'Connell Street—see map on page 80).

▲Viking Splash Tours

If you'd like to ride in a WWII-amphibious vehicle—driven by a
Viking-costumed guide who spouts jokes and historic factoids as
you ramble through town—this is it. The tour starts with a group
roar from the Viking within us all. At first, the guide talks as if he
were a Viking ("When we came here in 841…"), but soon the patriot emerges as he tags Irish history onto the sights you pass. Near
the end of the 75-minute tour (punctuated by occasional group
roars at passersby), you take a slow spin up and down a boring canal
(€22, Feb-Nov daily 10:00-17:00, no tours Dec-Jan, departs about
hourly from the north side of St. Stephen's Green opposite Dawson Street, buy ticket from driver, dress warmly, tel. 01/707-6000,
www.vikingsplash.com).

TOUR PACKAGES FOR STUDENTS

Andy Steves (Rick's son) runs Weekend Student Adventures
(WSA Europe), offering 3-day and 10-day budget travel packages
across Europe including accommodations, skip-the-line sightseeing, and unique local experiences. Locally guided and DIY options

DUBLIN

Dublin at a Glance

▲▲▲**National Museum: Archaeology** Interesting collection of Irish treasures from the Stone Age to today. **Hours:** Tue-Sat 10:00-17:00, Sun from 14:00, closed Mon. See page 60.

▲▲▲**Kilmainham Gaol** Historic jail used by the British as a political prison—today a museum that tells a moving story of the suffering of the Irish people. **Hours:** Guided tours daily June-Aug 9:00-19:00, April-May and Sept until 18:00, Oct-March 9:30-17:30. See page 86.

▲▲▲**Book of Kells in the Trinity Old Library** An exquisite illuminated manuscript, Ireland's most important piece of art from the Dark Ages. **Hours:** Mon-Sat 8:30-17:00, Sun from 9:30; Oct-April Mon-Sat 9:30-17:00, Sun 12:00-16:30. See page 56.

▲▲**Historical Walking Tour** Your best introduction to Dublin. **Hours:** April-Oct daily at 11:00, May-Sept also at 15:00; Nov-March Fri-Sun at 11:00. See page 44.

▲▲**Traditional Irish Musical Pub Crawl** A fascinating, practical, and enjoyable primer on traditional Irish music. **Hours:** April-Oct daily at 19:30, Nov and Jan-March Thu-Sat only. See page 45.

▲▲**Chester Beatty Library** American expatriate's sumptuous collection of literary and religious treasures from Islam, Asia, and medieval Europe. **Hours:** Mon-Fri 10:00-17:00, Sat from 11:00, Sun from 13:00; closed Mon Nov-Feb. See page 71.

▲▲**GPO Witness History Exhibit** Immersive presentation on the 1916 Easter Rising and its impact on Irish history, situated in the building that served as the rebel headquarters. **Hours:** Mon-Sat 10:00-17:30, Sun from 12:00. See page 83.

▲▲**Temple Bar** Dublin's rowdiest neighborhood, with shops, cafés, theaters, galleries, pubs, and restaurants—a great spot for live (but touristy) traditional music. See page 76.

▲▲**Trinity College Tour** Ireland's most famous school, best visited with a 30-minute tour led by one of its students. **Hours:** Departs every 30 minutes daily 9:15-16:00, Oct-April Sat-Sun only, no tours Dec-Jan. See page 56.

▲▲**O'Connell Street** Dublin's grandest promenade and main drag, packed with history and ideal for a stroll. See page 50.

▲▲**Epic: The Irish Emigration Museum** Creative displays about the Irish diaspora that highlight the emigrants' influences on their new homelands. **Hours:** Daily 10:00-18:45. See page 77.

▲**Dublin Castle** The city's historic 700-year-old castle, featuring or-nate English state apartments (interior tourable only with a guide). **Hours:** Mon-Sat 10:00-16:45, Sun from 12:00. See page 70.

▲**Guinness Storehouse** The home of Ireland's national beer, with a museum of beer-making, a gallery of clever ads, and Gravity Bar with panoramic city views. **Hours:** Daily 9:30-19:00, July-Aug 9:00-20:00. See page 87.

▲**National Gallery of Ireland** Fine collection of top Irish paint-ers and European masters. **Hours:** Mon-Sat 9:30-17:30, Thu until 20:30, Sun 11:00-17:30. See page 65.

▲**Jeanie Johnston Tall Ship and Famine Museum** Floating exhib-it on the River Liffey explaining the Famine period that prompt-ed desperate transatlantic crossings (by tour only). **Hours:** Daily 10:00-16:00, Oct-March 11:00-15:00. See page 78.

▲**Grafton Street** The city's liveliest pedestrian shopping street. See page 69.

▲**St. Stephen's Green** Relaxing park surrounded by fine Geor-gian buildings. See page 69.

▲**Dublinia** A fun, kid-friendly look at Dublin's Viking and medi-eval past with a side order of archaeology and a cool town model. **Hours:** Daily 10:00-18:30, Oct-Feb until 17:30. See page 74.

▲**Merrion Square** Enjoyable and inviting park with a fun statue of Oscar Wilde. See page 68.

▲**Hugh Lane Gallery** Modern and contemporary art, starring Monet, Bacon, and Irish artists. **Hours:** Tue-Thu 10:00-18:00, Fri-Sat until 17:00, Sun 11:00-17:00, closed Mon. See page 82.

▲**Dublin Writers Museum** Collection of authorial bric-a-brac. **Hours:** Mon-Sat 9:45-17:00, Sun from 11:00. See page 78.

▲**National Museum: Decorative Arts and History** Shows off Irish dress, furniture, silver, and weaponry with a special focus on the 1916 rebellion, fight for independence, and civil war. **Hours:** Tue-Sat 10:00-17:00, Sun from 14:00, closed Mon. See page 89.

▲**Gaelic Athletic Association Museum** High-tech museum of tra-ditional Gaelic sports (hurling and Irish football). **Hours:** Mon-Sat 9:30-17:00, June-Aug until 18:00, Sun 10:30-17:00 year-round. On game Sundays, it's open to ticket holders only. See page 90.

DUBLIN

are available for student and budget travelers in 13 of Europe's most popular cities, including Dublin (guided trips from €199, see www. wsaeurope.com for details). Check out Andy's tips, resources, and podcast at www.andysteves.com.

O'Connell Street Stroll

This self-guided walk, worth ▲▲, follows Dublin's grandest street from the O'Connell Bridge through the heart of north Dublin. Since the 1740s, the street has been a 45-yard-wide promenade, and ever since the first O'Connell Bridge connected it to the Trinity side of town in 1794, it's been Dublin's main drag. (It was named O'Connell only after independence in 1922.) These days, the city has made the street more pedestrian-friendly, and a LUAS line runs along the median. Though lined with touristy fast-food joints and souvenir shops, O'Connell Street echoes with history.

• *Start your walk on the...*

❶ **O'Connell Bridge:** This bridge—actually wider than it is long—spans the River Liffey, which historically has divided the wealthy, cultivated south side of town from the working-class north side. While there's plenty of culture on the north bank, even today the suburbs (a couple of miles north of the Liffey) are considered rougher and less safe. Dubliners joke that "north-siders" are known as "the accused," while "south siders" are addressed as "your honor."

From the bridge, look as far upstream (west) as you can. On the left in the distance, the concrete building before the green dome marks the birthplace of the city. It squats on the still-buried site of the first Viking settlement, established in Dublin in the ninth century. On the right side of the river, a pleasant boardwalk leads upriver to the elegant iron Ha' Penny Bridge. That bridge leads into the Temple Bar nightlife district (on the left).

Turn 180 degrees and look downstream (east) to see the tall Liberty Hall union headquarters (16 stories tall, some say in honor of the 1916 Easter Rising). Modern Dublin is developing downstream. During the Celtic Tiger boom in the mid-1990s, the Irish subsidized and revitalized this formerly dreary quarter. While "the Tiger" died with the great recession of 2008-2009, Dublin's economy is booming again—as illustrated by the forest of cranes marking building sites in the east end of town.

A short walk downstream along the north bank leads to a powerful series of gaunt statues memorializing the Great Potato Famine of 1845-1849. Beyond, you'll see the masts of the *Jeanie Johnston*, a replica transport ship (see page 78).

• *Now start north up O'Connell Street, walking on the wide, tree-lined median strip toward the spike in the sky.*

Statues and Monuments: Ireland's history is celebrated all

O'Connell Street Stroll

To Airport &
M-1 to Belfast

DUBLIN
WRITERS
MUSEUM

HUGH
LANE
GALLERY

JAMES JOYCE
CENTRE

To Croke Park
Stadium & GAA
Museum

WALK
ENDS

Pool

Garden of
Remembrance

GATE
THEATRE

Parnell

N. GREAT GEORGE'S ST.

W. RUTLAND

PARNELL SQ. E.

SUMMERHILL

CATHAL BRUGHA ST.

DUBLIN

O'Connell
Upper

UPPER O'CONNELL ST.

ST. MARY'S
PRO-CATHEDRAL

PARNELL SQ. W.

LOWER
DOMINICK ST.

Dominick

PARNELL ST.

MOORE LANE

MOORE STREET

STREET
MARKET

150 Meters
150 Yards

SAMPSONS
LANE

HENRY
PL.

GPO WITNESS
HISTORY EXHIBIT

HENRY ST.

MARY ST.

PRINCE'S ST.
NORTH

O'Connell
GPO

LUAS Tram
Red Line

ABBEY ST. MIDDLE

LIFFEY ST. UPPER

ABBEY ST. UPPER

Jervis

NORTH LOTTS ST.

BACH. WAY

GREAT STRAND ST.

MILLENNIUM WALK

BACHELORS WALK

To
Temple Bar

HA' PENNY
BRIDGE

River Liffey

ASTON QUAY

West-
moreland

To Trinity
College

O'CONNELL
BRIDGE

LOWER O'CONNELL ST.

EARL ST.

SACKVILLE
PLACE

ABBEY ST. LOWER

Abbey
Street

ABBEY
THEATRE

MARLBOROUGH ST.

TALBOT ST.

Marlborough

Eden Quay

ROSIE
HACKETT
BRIDGE

BURGH
QUAY

HAWKINS ST.

D'OLIER ST.

WALK
BEGINS

Liffey

GARDINER ST.

- ❶ O'Connell Bridge
- ❷ Daniel O'Connell Statue
- ❸ William Smith O'Brien Statue
- ❹ Abbey Theatre
- ❺ Sir John Gray Statue
- ❻ James Larkin Statue
- ❼ General Post Office & Witness History Exhibit
- ❽ The Spire
- ❾ Moore Street Market
- ❿ St. Mary's Pro-Cathedral
- ⓫ Father Matthew Statue
- ⓬ Gresham Hotel
- ⓭ Charles Stewart Parnell Monument
- ⓮ Gate Theatre
- ⓯ Garden of Remembrance
- ⓰ Dublin Writers Museum
- ⓱ Hugh Lane Gallery
- ⓲ James Joyce Centre

along O'Connell Street. The median is dotted with statues remembering great figures from Ireland's past—particularly the century (c.1830-1930) when Ireland rediscovered its roots and won its independence. At the base of the street stands the man for whom Dublin's main street is named—❷ **Daniel O'Connell** (1775-1847). He was known as the "Liberator" for founding the Catholic Association and demanding Irish Catholic rights in the British Parliament. He organized thousands of nonviolent protestors into "monster meetings," whose sheer size intimidated the British authorities.

Farther along is ❸ **William Smith O'Brien**, O'Connell's contemporary and leader of the Young Ireland Movement, who was more willing to use force to reach his goals. After a failed uprising in Tipperary, he was imprisoned, sentenced to death in 1848, but then exiled to Australia.

At Abbey Street, a one-block detour to the east (right) leads to the famous ❹ **Abbey Theatre,** where turn-of-the-century nationalists (including the poet-playwright W. B. Yeats) staged Irish-themed plays. The original building suffered a fire and was rebuilt

into a nondescript, modern building, but it's still the much-loved home of the Irish National Theatre.

• *Continue up O'Connell Street.*

Look for the statue of ❺ **Sir John Gray,** who, as a newspaperman and politician, was able to help O'Connell's cause. The statue of ❻ **James Larkin,** arms outstretched, honors the founder of the Irish Transport Workers Union.

• *On your left is the...*

❼ **General Post Office (GPO):** This is not just any P.O. It was from here that Patrick Pearse read the Proclamation of Irish Independence in 1916, kicking off the Easter Rising. The building itself—a kind of Irish Alamo—was the rebel headquarters and scene of a bloody five-day siege that followed the proclamation. The post office was particularly strategic because it housed the telegraph nerve center for the entire country. Its pillars are still pockmarked with bullet holes. The engaging GPO Witness History exhibit, on your right as you go inside, brings the dramatic history of this important building to life (see page 83).

• *Arch way back (at the intersection of O'Connell and Henry streets) and marvel up at...*

❽ **The Spire:** There used to be a monument here that didn't wave an Irish flag—a tall column crowned by a statue of the British hero of Trafalgar, Admiral Horatio Nelson. It was blown up in 1966—the IRA's contribution to the local celebration of the Easter Rising's 50th anniversary. The spot is now occupied by the Spire: 398 feet of stainless steel. While it trumpets rejuvenation on its side of the river, it's a memorial to nothing and has no real meaning. Dubliners call it the tallest waste of €5 million in all of Europe. Its nickname? Take your pick: the Stiletto in the Ghetto, the Stiffy on the Liffey, the Pole in the Hole, or the Poker near the Croker (after nearby Croke Park). The "erection at the intersection" was built for the millennium, but Dublin was only able to get it up by 2004. Before leaving, have fun standing close and looking way up.

• Detour a block west (left) down people-filled Henry Street (Dubliners' favorite shopping lane), then wander to the right into the nearby...

❾ Moore Street Market: Many merchants here have staffed the same stalls for decades (Mon-Sat 8:00-18:00, closed Sun). Start a conversation. It's a great workaday scene. You'll see lots of mums with strollers—a reminder that Ireland is one of Europe's youngest countries, with about 35 percent of the population under the age of 25. At the end of the 1916 Easter Rising, the rebel leaders retreated from the burning post office to #16 on this street, where they finally surrendered to British troops (see plaque high up).

• Return to O'Connell Street. A block east (right) of O'Connell, down Cathedral Street, detour to...

❿ St. Mary's Pro-Cathedral: Although this is Dublin's leading Catholic church, it isn't a cathedral but a "pro-cathedral" (as in "provisional")—essentially a parish church serving temporarily as a cathedral. The pope declared Christ Church to be a cathedral in the 12th century—and later, gave St. Patrick's the same designation (and they remain "cathedrals" even though they haven't been Catholic for centuries).

St. Mary's sits on the site of the 12th-century Abbey of St. Mary. With the Reformation leading to Henry VIII's dissolution of the monasteries in 1539, the abbey's "popish trappings" were tossed out and the land confiscated.

In the 18th century, with Catholic worship legal but better done with a low profile, a modest Catholic "Mass house" opened on Liffey Street. Church fathers, however, envisioned a bold new St. Mary's on the main street (where the GPO is today), but they eventually backed away from that high-profile location, and instead built this Neoclassical church here (completed 1825). It's set back from the action, with no big steeple or fancy facade—looking more like a bomb shelter than a dignified church. An unhappy alteration to increase the church's capacity caused it to grow with an odd floor plan. Don't miss the fine Victorian windows (behind the altar) dating from the 1880s. For two centuries, St. Mary's has been part of the stage upon which Irish history has played out:

Daniel O'Connell gave a rousing speech here in 1825 at its dedication, and later lay in state here in 1847. It hosted the funeral Mass of Michael Collins in 1922, and Éamon de Valera (a leader of the Easter Rising) also lay in state here in 1975.

· *Back on O'Connell Street, head up the street (north) until you find the statue of...*

❶ **Father Matthew:** A leader of the temperance movement of the 1830s, Father Matthew was responsible, some historians claim, for enough Irish peasants staying sober to enable Daniel O'Connell to organize them into a political force.

Nearby, the fancy ❷ **Gresham Hotel** is a good place for an elegant tea or beer. In an earlier era, the beautiful people alighted here during visits to Dublin.

· *Standing boldly at the top of O'Connell Street is a monument to...*

❸ **Charles Stewart Parnell:** Ringing the monument are the names of the four ancient provinces of Ireland and all 32 Irish counties (north and south, since this was erected before Irish partition). It's meant to honor Charles Stewart Parnell (1846-1891), the member of Parliament who nearly won Home Rule for Ireland in the late 1800s (and who served time at Kilmainham Gaol). A Cambridge-educated Protestant of landed-gentry stock, Parnell envisioned a modern, free Irish nation of Catholics—but not as a religious state. The Irish people, who remembered their grandparents' harsh evictions during the Famine, came to love Parnell (despite his privileged birth) for his tireless work to secure fair rents and land tenure. Momentum seemed to be on his side. With the British prime minister of the time, William Gladstone, favoring a similar form of Home Rule, it looked as if Ireland was on its way toward independence as a Commonwealth nation, similar to Canada or Australia.

Then a sex scandal broke around Parnell and his mistress, the wife of another Parliament member. The press, egged on by the powerful Catholic bishops (who didn't want a secular, free Irish state), battered away at the scandal until finally Parnell was driven from office. Wracked with exhaustion and only in his mid-40s, Parnell died brokenhearted.

After that, Ireland became mired in the conflicts of the 20th century: an awkward independence (1921) featuring a divided island, a bloody civil war, and sectarian violence for decades afterward.

· *Continue uphill, straight up Parnell Square East. At the* ❹ *Gate Theatre (on the left), actors Orson Welles, Geraldine Fitzgerald, and James*

Mason had their professional stage debuts. One block up, on the left, is the...

⓯ Garden of Remembrance: Honoring the victims of the 1916 Rising, this spot was where the rebel leaders were held before being transferred to Kilmainham Gaol. The park was dedicated in 1966 on the 50th anniversary of the revolt that ultimately led to Irish independence. The bottom of the cross-shaped pool is a mosaic of Celtic weapons, symbolic of how the early Irish proclaimed peace by breaking their weapons and throwing them into a lake or river. The Irish flag flies above the park: green for Catholics, orange for Protestants, and white for the hope that they can live together in peace (park open daily 8:30-18:00).

One of modern Ireland's most stirring moments occurred here in May 2011, when Queen Elizabeth II made this the first stop on her historic visit to Ireland. She laid a wreath at the *Children of Lir* sculpture under this flag and bowed her head in silence out of respect for the Irish rebels who had fought and died trying to gain freedom from her United Kingdom. This was a hugely cathartic moment for both nations. Until this visit, no British monarch had set foot in the Irish state since its founding 90 years earlier.

• *Your walk is over. Two excellent museums are nearby, standing side-by-side: the* ⓰ *Dublin Writers Museum (in a splendidly restored Georgian mansion, see page 78) and the art-filled* ⓱ *Hugh Lane Gallery (page 82). Here at the north end of town, it's also convenient to visit the* ⓲ *James Joyce Centre (a short walk away, see page 80), or the Gaelic Athletic Association Museum at Croke Park Stadium (described on page 90, a 20-minute walk or short taxi ride away). Otherwise, hop on your skateboard and zip back to the river.*

Sights in Dublin

SOUTH OF THE RIVER LIFFEY
Trinity College

Founded in 1592 by Queen Elizabeth I to establish a Protestant way of thinking about God, Trinity has long been Ireland's most prestigious college. Originally, the student body was limited to rich Protestant men. Women were admitted in 1903, and Catholics—though allowed entrance by the school much earlier—were given formal permission by the Catholic Church to study at Trinity in the 1970s (before that they risked excommunication). Today, half of Trinity's 12,500 students are women, and 70 percent are culturally Catholic (although only about 20 percent of Irish youth are church-going).

Tickets for Trinity College Sights: There are two worthwhile experiences here—the Book of Kells exhibit in the library and a half-hour tour of the campus led by students.

It's highly recommended that you buy timed-entry tickets in advance online for the **Book of Kells** (€14, €11 off-peak ticket is good before 10:00 or after 15:00); otherwise you'll likely wait in a long line (worst midday, roughly 10:00-15:00). The **campus tour** ticket is only available on-site (€6), but if you already have a Book of Kells ticket, you can add the tour for €4 (buy at college gate, cash preferred).

A €14 **combo-ticket** covers both, but you can only buy this on-site—and you may still need to wait in line for the Book of Kells (confirm locally).

▲▲Trinity College Tour

Trinity students lead 30-minute tours of their campus (look just inside the gate for posted departure times and a ticket seller on a stool—see map on page 58). You'll get a rundown of the mostly Georgian architecture; a peek at student life past and present; and the enjoyable company of your guide, a witty Irish college kid.

Cost and Hours: Buy on-site—see ticket options above; tours run daily 9:15-16:00, Oct-April Sat-Sun only, no tours Dec-Jan; tours depart roughly every 30 minutes, weather permitting, www.tcd.ie/visitors/tours.

▲▲▲Book of Kells in the Trinity Old Library

The Book of Kells—a 1,200-year-old version of the four gospels—was elaborately inked and meticulously illustrated by faithful monks. Combining Christian symbols and pagan styles, it's a snapshot of medieval Ireland in transition. Arguably the finest piece of art from what is generally called the Dark Ages, the Book of Kells shows that monastic life in this far fringe of Europe was far from dark.

Cost and Hours: Buy timed-entry tickets online in advance—see ticket options above; Mon-Sat 8:30-17:00, Sun from 9:30; Oct-April Mon-Sat 9:30-17:00, Sun 12:00-16:30; audioguide-€5, tel. 01/896-2320, www.tcd.ie/visitors/book-of-kells.

Background: The Book of Kells was a labor of love created by dedicated Irish monks cloistered on the remote Scottish island of Iona. They slaughtered 185 calves, soaked the skins in lime, scraped off the hair, and dried the skins into a cream-colored writing surface called vellum. Only then could the tonsured monks pick up their swan-quill pens and get to work.

The project may have been underway in 806 when Vikings savagely pillaged and burned Iona, killing 68 monks. The survivors fled to the Abbey of Kells (near Dublin). Scholars debate exactly where the book was produced: It could have been made entirely at Iona or at Kells, or started in Iona and finished at Kells.

For eight centuries, the glorious gospel sat regally atop the high altar of the monastery church at Kells, where the priest would read from it during special Masses. In 1654, as Cromwell's puritanical rule settled in, the book was smuggled to Dublin for safety. Here at Trinity College, it was first displayed to the public in the mid-1800s. In 1953, the book got its current covers and was bound into four separate volumes.

DUBLIN

Visiting the Book of Kells: Your visit has three stages: 1) an exhibit on the making of the Book of Kells, including poster-sized reproductions of its pages (your best look at the book's detail); 2) the Treasury, the darkened room containing the Book of Kells itself and other, less ornate contemporaneous volumes; and, upstairs, 3) the Old Library (called the Long Room), containing historical objects.

The Exhibit: The first-class "Turning Darkness into Light" exhibit, with a one-way route, puts the illuminated manuscript in its historical and cultural context, preparing you to see the original book and other precious manuscripts in the treasury. Make a point to spend time in the exhibit (before reaching the actual Book of Kells). Especially interesting are the short, continuously running video clips that show the ancient art of bookbinding and the exacting care that went into transcribing the monk-uscripts. They vividly depict the skill and patience needed for the monks' work.

The Book: The Book of Kells contains the four gospels of the Bible (typically only two of the gospels are on display at any given time). Altogether, it's 680 pages long (or 340 "folios," the equivalent of one sheet, front and back). The Latin calligraphy—all in capital letters—follows ruled lines, forming neat horizontal bars across the page. Sentences end with a "period" of three dots. The black-brown ink was made from the galls of oak trees.

The text is elaborately decorated—of the hundreds of pages, only two are without illustration. Each gospel begins with a full-page depiction of the Evangelists and their symbols: Matthew (angel), Mark (lion), Luke (ox), and John

South Dublin

HENRY ST.
LIFFEY ST. UPPER
ST. MARY'S
GREEN ST.
CAPEL ST.
JERVIS ST.
ABBEY ST. UPPER
ABBEY
LIFFEY ST. LOWER
LOTTS

OLD JAMESON DISTILLERY
MARY'S LANE
SMITHFIELD
Smithfield
ST. MICHAN'S STREET MARKET
ABBEY
Jervis
GREEK ST.
CHURCH ST.
CHANCERY ST.
HAMMOND LN.
The Four Courts
MICHAN'S
Ormond Sq.
GREAT STRAND
ORMOND QUAY LOWER
HA' PENNY BRIDGE

To Collins Barracks & Phoenix Park
FOUR COURTS
INNS QUAY
ORMOND QUAY UPPER
ORMOND QUAY UPPER
MILLENNIUM BRIDGE
QUAY

ARRAN QUAY
FATHER MATTHEW BRIDGE
WELLINGTON
TEMPLE BAR
Temple Bar Sq.

USHERS QUAY
MERCHANTS QUAY
WOOD QUAY
River
SMOCK ALLEY THEATRE
ESSEX ST. EAST
TEMPLE

To Heuston Station
POST
ST. FRANCIS'
ESSEX W.
Mtg. House Sq.
EUSTACE ST.
COPE ST.

COOK ST.
DUBLINIA
IRISHAMBLE
ESSEX W.
6
DAME ST.
DAME LN.
CROW ST.

HIGH ST.
BACK LANE
CHRIST CHURCH CATHEDRAL
LORD EDWARD ST.
CASTLE ST.
CITY HALL
DAME

AUGUSTINE ST.
FRANCIS ST.
LAMB ALLEY
DUBLIN CASTLE
EXCHEQUER ST.
GREAT GEORGE'S ARCADE

THOMAS
To Guinness Storehouse & Kilmainham Gaol
GREAT SHIP ST.
CHESTER BEATTY LIBRARY
LWR. STEPHEN ST.
SOUTH GREAT GEORGE'S ST.
DRURY ST.
WILLIAM ST.

NICHOLAS ST.
BRIDE ST.
GOLDEN LN.
KING ST.

Tour Departure Points

1 Historical Walking Tour
2 Traditional Irish Musical Pub Crawl
3 Literary Pub Crawl
4 1916 Rebellion Walking Tour
5 Pat Liddy's Walking Tours
6 Lazy Bike Tour Co.
7 Viking Splash Tours
8 Trinity College Tour
9 Little Museum of Dublin & City of a Thousand Welcomes

PATRICK ST.
ST. PATRICK'S CATHEDRAL
PETER ST.
PETER ROW
AUNGIER ST.
LWR. MERCER ST.
GLOVERS ALLEY
YORK ST.

KEVIN ST. UPPER
BISHOP ST.
UPR. MERCER ST.
KEVIN ST. LOWER
CUFFE ST.

N

150 Meters
150 Yards

(eagle). The apostles pose stiffly, like Byzantine-style icons, with almond-shaped eyes and symmetrically creased robes. The true beauty lies in the intricate designs that surround the figures.

The colorful book employs blue, purple, red, pink, green, and yellow pigments (all imported)—but no gold leaf. Letters and borders are braided together. On most pages, the initial letters are big and flowery, like in a children's fairytale book.

Notice how the playful monks might cross a "t" with a fish, form an "h" from a spindly-legged man, or make an "e" out of a coiled snake. Animals crouch between sentences. It's a jungle of intricate designs, inhabited by tiny creatures both real and fanciful.

Scholars think three main artists created the book: the "goldsmith" (who did the filigree-style designs), the "illustrator" (who specialized in animals and grotesques), and the "portrait painter" (who did the Evangelists and Mary). Some of the detail work is unbelievably minute.

The Old Library: The Long Room, the 200-foot-long main chamber of the Old Library (from 1732), is stacked to its towering ceiling with 200,000 books. Among the displays here, you'll find one of a dozen surviving original copies of the Proclamation of the Irish Republic. Patrick Pearse read out its words at Dublin's General Post Office on April 24, 1916, starting the Easter Rising that led to Irish independence. Notice the inclusive opening phrase ("Irishmen and Irishwomen") and the seven signatories (each of whom was later executed).

Another national icon is nearby: the oldest surviving Irish harp, from the 15th century (sometimes called the Brian Boru harp, although it was crafted 400 years after the death of this Irish king). The brass pins on its oak and willow frame once held 29 strings. In Celtic days, poets—highly influential with kings and druid priests—wandered the land, uniting the people with songs and stories. The harp's inspirational effect on Gaelic culture was so strong that Queen Elizabeth I (1558-1603) ordered Irish harpists to be hung and their instruments smashed. Even today, the love of music is so intense that Ireland is the only country with a musical instrument as its national symbol. You'll see this harp's likeness on the back of Irish euro coins, on government documents, and (respectfully reversed) on every pint of Guinness.

▲▲▲National Museum: Archaeology

Showing off the treasures of Ireland from the Stone Age to modern times, this branch of the National Museum is itself a national trea-

sure. The soggy marshes and peat bogs of Ireland have proven perfect for preserving old objects. You'll see 4,000-year-old gold jewelry, 2,000-year-old bog mummies, 1,000-year-old Viking swords, and the collection's superstar—the exquisitely wrought Tara Brooch. Visit here to get an introduction to the rest of Ireland's historic attractions: You'll find a reconstructed passage tomb like Newgrange, Celtic art like the Book of Kells, Viking objects from Dublin, a model of the Hill of Tara, and a sacred cross from the Cong Abbey. Hit the highlights of my tour, then browse the exhibits at will, all well-described throughout. For background information on Irish art, see page 505.

Cost and Hours: Free, Tue-Sat 10:00-17:00, Sun from 14:00, closed Mon, €3 audioguide (or free audio download) covers only Treasury room, good café, between Trinity College and St. Stephen's Green on Kildare Street, tel. 01/677-7444, www.museum.ie.

◐ Self-Guided Tour

• *On the ground floor, enter the main hall and get oriented (with the help of this book's map): In the center (down four steps) are displays of prehistoric gold jewelry. To the left are the bog bodies, to the right is the Treasury, and upstairs is the Viking world. We'll start at Ireland's beginning.*

❶ Stone Age Tools: Glass cases hold flint and stone ax-heads and arrowheads (7,000 B.C.). Ireland's first inhabitants—hunters and fishers who came from Scotland—used these tools. These early people also left behind standing stones (dolmens) and passage tombs.

❷ Reconstructed Passage Tomb: At the corner of the room,

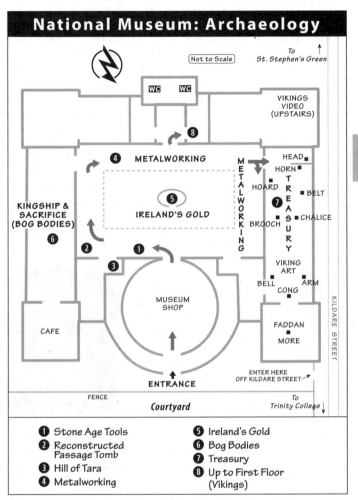

National Museum: Archaeology

Not to Scale

To St. Stephen's Green

VIKINGS VIDEO (UPSTAIRS)

❹ METALWORKING

METALWORKING

HEAD

HORN

HOARD

T R E A S U R Y

BELT

❺ IRELAND'S GOLD

❼

CHALICE

KINGSHIP & SACRIFICE (BOG BODIES)

❻

BROOCH

VIKING ART

BELL

CONG

ARM

❷

❸

❶

MUSEUM SHOP

CAFE

FADDAN

MORE

KILDARE STREET

ENTER HERE OFF KILDARE STREET →

ENTRANCE

FENCE

To Trinity College ↓

Courtyard

❶ Stone Age Tools
❷ Reconstructed Passage Tomb
❸ Hill of Tara
❹ Metalworking
❺ Ireland's Gold
❻ Bog Bodies
❼ Treasury
❽ Up to First Floor (Vikings)

DUBLIN

you'll see a typical tomb circa 3,000 B.C.—a mound-shaped, heavy stone structure, covered with smaller rocks, with a passage leading into a central burial chamber where the deceased's ashes were interred. This is a modest tomb; the vast passage tombs at Newgrange and Knowth (see page 124) are similar but many times bigger.

❸ **The Hill of Tara:** The famous passage-tomb burial site at Tara, known as the Mound of the Hostages, was used for more than 1,500 years as a place to inter human remains. The cases in this side gallery display some of the many exceptional Neolithic and Bronze Age finds uncovered at the site.

Over the millennia, the Mound became the very symbol of Irish heritage. This is where Ireland's kings claimed their power, where St. Patrick preached his deal-clinching sermon, and where, in 1843, Daniel O'Connell rallied Irish patriots to demand their independence from Britain (see illustration in poster on the left wall).

❹ The Evolution of Metalworking: Around 2500 B.C., Ireland discovered how to make metal—mining ore, smelting it in furnaces, and casting or hammering it into shapes. The rest is prehistory. You'll travel through the Bronze Age (ax-heads from 2000 B.C.) and Iron Age (500 B.C.) as you examine assorted spears, shields, swords, and war horns. The cauldrons made for everyday cooking were also used ceremonially to prepare elaborate ritual feasts for friends and symbolic offerings for the gods. The most impressive metal objects are four steps down in the center of the hall.

❺ Ireland's Gold: Ireland had only modest gold deposits, mainly gathered by prehistoric people panning for small nuggets and dust in the rivers. But the jewelry they left, some of it more than 4,000 years old, is exquisite. The earliest fashion choice was a broad necklace hammered flat (a *lunula,* so called for its crescent-moon shape). This might be worn with accompanying earrings and sun-disc brooches. The Gleninsheen Collar (c. 700 B.C.) was found by a farmer in a crevice of the exposed bedrock of the Burren. It's thought that this valuable status symbol was hidden there during a time of conflict, then forgotten (or its owner killed)—if it had been meant as an offering to a pagan god it more likely would have been left in a body of water (the portal to the underworld). Later Bronze Age jewelry was cast from clay molds into bracelets and unique "dress fasteners" that you'd slip into buttonholes to secure a cloak. Some of these gold objects may have been gifts to fertility gods, offered by burying them in marshy bogs.

❻ Bog Bodies: When the Celts arrived in Ireland (c. 500 B.C.-A.D. 500), they brought with them a mysterious practice: They brutally murdered sacrificial slaves or prisoners and buried them in bogs. Four bodies (each in its own tiny theater with a description outside)—shriveled and leathery, but remarkably preserved—have been dug up from around the Celtic world.

Clonycavan Man is from Ireland. One summer day around 200 B.C., this twenty-something man was hacked to death with an ax and disemboweled. In his time, he stood 5'9" tall and had a Mohawk-style haircut, poofed up with pine-resin hair product imported from France. Today you can still see traces of his hair. Only his upper body survived; the lower part may have been lost in the threshing machine that unearthed him in 2003.

Why were these people killed? It appears to have been a form of ritual human sacrifice of high-status people. Some may have been enemy chiefs or political rivals. The sacrifices could have been offerings to the gods to ensure rich harvests and good luck. Other items (now on display) were buried along with them—gold bracelets, royal cloaks, and finely wrought cauldrons.

❼ **Treasury:** Irish metalworking is legendary, and this room holds 1,500 years of exquisite objects. Working from one end of the long room to the other, you'll journey from the world of the pagan Celts to the coming of Christianity, explore the stylistic impact of the Viking invasions (9th-12th century), and consider the resurgence of ecclesiastical metalworking (11th-12th century).

Pagan Era Art: The carved stone head of a mysterious pagan god greets you (#19, circa A.D. 100). The god's three faces express the different aspects of his stony personality. This abstract style—typical of Celtic art—would be at home in a modern art museum. A bronze horn (#17, first century B.C.) is the kind of curved war trumpet that Celts blasted to freak out the Roman legions on the Continent (the Romans never invaded Ireland). The fine objects of the Broighter Hoard (#15, first century B.C.) include a king's golden collar decorated in textbook Celtic style, with interlaced vines inhabited by stylized faces. The tiny boat was an offering to the sea god. The coconut-shell-shaped bowl symbolized a cauldron. By custom, the cauldron held food as a constant offering to Danu, the Celtic mother goddess, whose mythical palace was at Brú na Bóinne.

Early Christian Objects: Christianity officially entered Ireland in the fifth century (when St. Patrick converted the pagan king), but Celtic legends and art continued well into the Christian era. You'll see various crosses, shrines (portable reliquaries containing holy relics), and chalices decorated with Celtic motifs. The Belt Shrine (#32)—a circular metal casing that held a saint's leather belt—was thought to have magical properties. When placed around someone's waist, it could heal the wearer or force him or her to tell the truth.

The Ardagh Chalice (#30) and the nearby Silver Paten (#31) were used during Communion to hold blessed wine and bread. Get close to admire the elaborate workmanship. The main bowl of the chalice is gilded bronze, with a contrasting band of intricately patterned gold filigree. It's studded with colorful glass, amber, and enamels. Mirrors below the display case show that even the underside of the chalice was decorated. When the priest grabbed the chalice by its two handles and tipped it to his lips, the base could be admired by God.

Tara Brooch: A rich eighth-century Celtic man fastened his cloak at the shoulder with this elaborate ring-shaped brooch (#29), its seven-inch stickpin tilted rakishly upward. Made of cast and gilded silver, it's ornamented with fine, exquisitely filigreed gold panels and studded with amber, enamel, and colored glass. The motifs include Celtic spirals, snakes, and stylized faces, but the symbolism is neither overtly pagan nor Christian—it's art for art's sake. Despite its name, the brooch probably has no connection to the Hill of Tara. In display cases nearby, you'll see other similar (but less impressive) brooches from the same period—some iron, some bronze, and one in pure gold.

Viking Art Styles: When Vikings invaded Dublin around A.D. 800, they raped and pillaged. But they also opened Ireland to a vast and cosmopolitan trading empire, from which they imported hoards of silver (see the display case of ingots). Viking influence shows up in the decorative style of reliquaries like the Lismore Crozier (#43, in the shape of a bishop's ceremonial shepherd's crook) and the Shrine of St. Lochter's Arm (raised in an Irish-power salute). The impressive Bell of St. Patrick (#24) was supposedly owned by Ireland's patron saint. After his death, it was encased within a beautifully worked shrine (displayed above) and kept safe by a single family, who passed it down from generation to generation for 800 years.

Cross of Cong: "By this cross is covered the cross on which the Creator of the world suffered." Running along the sides of the cross (#44), this Latin inscription tells us that it once held a sacred relic, a tiny splinter of the True Cross on which Jesus was crucified. That piece of wood (now lost) had been given in 1123 to the Irish high king, who commissioned this reliquary to preserve the splinter (it would have been placed right in the center, visible through the large piece of rock crystal). Every Christmas and Easter, the cross was fitted onto a staff and paraded through the abbey at Cong (see page 364), then placed on the altar for High Mass. The extraordinarily detailed decoration features gold filigree interspersed with colored glass, enamel, and (now missing) precious

stones. Though fully Christian, the cross has Celtic-style filigree patterning and Viking-style animal heads (notice how they grip the cross in their jaws).

Before leaving the Treasury, enter the room behind the Cross of Cong and check out the Faddan More Psalter—a (pretty beat-up) manuscript of the Book of Psalms from the same era as the Book of Kells.

• *Now head up to the first floor to the Viking world. Start in the long hall directly above the Treasury, with the informative 25-minute video on the Viking influence on Irish culture.*

❽ Viking Ireland (c. 800-1150): Dublin was born as a Viking town. Sometime after 795, Scandinavian warriors rowed their long ships up the River Liffey and made camp on the south bank, around the location of today's Dublin Castle and Christ Church. Over the next two centuries, they built "Dubh linn" ("black pool" in Irish) into an important trading post, slave market, metalworking center, and the first true city in Ireland. (See a model of Dublin showing a recently excavated area near Kilmainham Gaol.)

The state-of-the-art Viking boats worked equally well in the open ocean and shallow rivers, and were perfect for stealth invasions and far-ranging trading. Soon, provincial Dublin was connected with the wider world—Scotland, England, northern Europe, even Asia. The museum's displays of swords and spears make it clear that, yes, the Vikings were fierce warriors. But you'll also see that they were respected merchants (standardized weights and coins), herders and craftsmen (leather shoes and bags), fashion-conscious (bone combs and jewelry), fun-loving (board games), and literate (runic alphabet). What you won't see are horned helmets, which, despite the stereotype, were not Viking. By 1050, the pagan Vikings had intermarried with the locals, become Christian, and were melting into Irish society.

• *With time and interest, you could explore the...*

Rest of the Museum: Part of the ground floor is dedicated to medieval Ireland—daily life (ploughs, cauldrons), trade (coins, pottery), and religion (crucifixes and saints). Up one more flight, the Egyptian room has coffins, *shabtis*, and canopic jars—but no mummies.

Other National Museums South of Trinity College

Adjacent to the archaeology branch are these other major museums. Also nearby is Leinster House. Once the Duke of Leinster's home, it now hosts the Irish Dáil (parliament) and Seanad (senate), which meet here 90 days each year.

▲National Gallery of Ireland

While not as extensive as national galleries in London or Paris, the collections here are well worth your time. The beautifully renovated museum boasts an impressive range of works by European masters and displays the works of top Irish painters, including Jack B. Yeats (brother of the famous poet).

Cost and Hours: Free, Mon-Sat 9:30-17:30, Thu until 20:30,

Modern Ireland's Turbulent Birth: A Timeline

Imagine if our American patriot ancestors had fought both our Revolutionary War and our Civil War over a span of seven chaotic years...and then appreciate the remarkable resilience of the Irish people. Here's a summary of what happened when.

Easter Rising, 1916: A nationalist militia called the Volunteers (led by **Patrick Pearse**) and the socialist Irish Citizen Army (led by **James Connolly**) join forces in the Easter Rising, but they fail to end 750 years of British rule. The uprising is unpopular with most Irish, who are unhappy with the destruction in Dublin and preoccupied with the "Great War" on the Continent. But when 16 rebel leaders (including Pearse and Connolly) are executed, Irish public opinion reverses as sympathy grows for the martyrs and the cause of Irish Independence.

Two important rebel leaders escape execution. Brooklyn-born **Éamon de Valera** is spared because of his American passport (the British don't want to anger their potential ally in World War I). **Michael Collins,** a low-ranking rebel officer who fought in the Rising at the General Post Office, refines urban guerrilla-warfare strategies in prison, and then blossoms after his release as the rebels' military and intelligence leader in the power vacuum that followed the executions.

General Election, 1918: World War I ends and a general election is held in Ireland (the first in which women can vote). Outside of Ulster, the nationalist **Sinn Fein** party wins 73 out of 79 seats in Parliament. Only four out of 32 counties vote to maintain the Union with Britain (all four lie in today's Northern Ireland). Rather than take their seats in London, Sinn Fein representatives abstain from participating in a government they see as foreign occupiers.

War of Independence, 1919: On January 19, the abstaining Sinn Fein members set up a rebel government in Dublin called Dáil

Sun 11:00-17:30, Merrion Square West, tel. 01/661-5133, www.nationalgallery.ie.

Tours: Take advantage of the free audioguide (donations accepted) as well as free 45-minute guided tours (Sat at 12:30; Sun at 12:30 and 13:30).

Visiting the Museum: Be sure to walk through the series of rooms on the ground floor devoted to Irish painting and get to know artists you may not have heard of before. Visit the National

Éireann. On the same day, the first shots of the Irish War of Independence are fired as rebels begin ambushing police barracks, which are seen as an extension of British rule. De Valera is elected by the Dáil to lead the rebels, with Collins as his deputy. Collins' web of spies infiltrates British intelligence at Dublin Castle. The Volunteers rename themselves the **Irish Republican Army**; meanwhile the British beef up their military presence in Ireland by sending in tough WWI vets, the Black and Tans. A bloody and very personal war ensues.

Anglo-Irish Treaty, 1921: Having lived through the slaughter of World War I, the British tire of the extended bloodshed in Ireland and begin negotiations with the rebels. De Valera leads rebel negotiations, but then entrusts them to Collins (a clever politician, De Valera sees that whoever signs a treaty will be blamed for its compromises). Understanding the tricky position he's been placed in, Collins signs the Anglo-Irish Treaty in December, lamenting that in doing so he has signed his "own death warrant."

The Dáil narrowly ratifies the treaty (64 to 57), but Collins' followers are unable to convince De Valera's supporters that the compromises are a stepping-stone to later full independence. De Valera and his antitreaty disciples resign in protest. **Arthur Griffith,** founder of Sinn Fein, assumes the presidential post.

Irish Civil War, 1921: In June, the antitreaty forces, holed up in the Four Courts building in Dublin, are fired upon by Collins and his protreaty forces—thus igniting the Irish Civil War. The British want the treaty to stand and even supply Collins with cannons, meanwhile threatening to reenter Ireland if the antitreaty forces aren't put down.

Aftermath, 1922/23: In August 1922, Griffith dies of stress-induced illness, and Collins is assassinated 10 days later. Nevertheless, the protreaty forces prevail, as they are backed by popular opinion and better (British-supplied) military equipment.

By April 1923, the remaining IRA forces dump (or stash) their arms, ending the civil war...but many bitter IRA vets vow to carry on the fight. De Valera distances himself from the IRA and becomes the dominant Irish political leader for the next 40 years.

Portrait Gallery on the mezzanine level for an insight into the great personalities of Ireland. You'll find European masterworks on the top floor, including a rare Vermeer (one of only 30-some known works by the Dutch artist), a classic Caravaggio (master of chiaroscuro and dramatic lighting), a Monet riverscape, and an early Cubist Picasso still life.

Perhaps the most iconic of all the Irish art in this museum is the melodramatic (and huge) c. 1854 depiction of the *Marriage*

DUBLIN

of Strongbow and Aiofe by Daniel Maclise. It captures the chaotic union of Norman and Irish interests that signaled the start of English domination of Ireland 850 years ago. Notice how the defeated Irish writhe and lament in the bright light of the foreground, while the scheming Norman warlords skulk in the dimly lit middle ground. The ruins of conquered Waterford smolder at the back.

National Museum: Natural History

Called "the dead zoo" by Dubliners, this cramped collection of stuffed exotic animals comes across like the locker room on Noah's Ark. But if you're into beaks, bones, bugs, and boars, this Victorian relic is for you. Standing tall above a sea of taxidermy is the regal skeleton of a giant Irish elk from the last Ice Age; it dwarfs a modern moose.

Cost and Hours: Free, Tue-Sat 10:00-17:00, Sun from 14:00, closed Mon, Merrion Square West, tel. 01/677-7444, www.museum.ie.

National Library of Ireland

Literature holds a lofty place in the Irish psyche. To feel the fire-and-ice pulse of Ireland's most influential poet, visit the W. B. Yeats exhibit in the library basement. The artifacts flesh out the very human passions of this poet and playwright, with samples of his handwritten manuscripts and surprisingly interesting mini documentaries of the times he lived in. Upstairs, you can get help making use of library records to trace your genealogy. Take a moment to view the gorgeous baby-blue upstairs reading room under the expansive dome.

Cost and Hours: Free, Mon-Wed 9:30-19:30, Thu-Fri until 16:30, Sat until 12:30, Sun 13:00-16:30, café, tel. 01/603-0200, 2 Kildare Street, www.nli.ie.

Merrion Square and Nearby
▲Merrion Square

Laid out in 1762, this square is ringed by elegant Georgian houses decorated with fine doors—a Dublin trademark. (If you're inspired by the ornate knobs and knockers, there's a shop by that name on nearby Nassau Street.) The park, once the exclusive domain of the residents (among them, Daniel O'Connell at #58 and W. B. Yeats at #82), is now a delightful public escape and ideal for a picnic. To learn what "snogging" is, walk through the park on a sunny day, when it's full of smooching lovers. Oscar Wilde, lounging wittily on a boulder on the corner nearest the town center and surrounded by his clever quotes, provides a fun photo op (see photo on page 82).

▲Number Twenty-Nine Georgian House

The carefully restored house at Number 29 Lower Fitzwilliam Street gives an intimate glimpse of middle-class Georgian life—but is closed for renovation until 2020 (tel. 01/702-6163, www.esb.ie/no29).

Grafton Street and St. Stephen's Green Area

▲Grafton Street

DUBLIN

Once filled with noisy traffic, today's Grafton Street is Dublin's liveliest pedestrian shopping drag and people-watching paradise. A 10-minute stroll past street musicians takes you from Trinity College to St. Stephen's Green. You'll pass two venerable department stores: the Irish Brown Thomas and the English Marks & Spencer. Johnson's Court alley leads to the Powerscourt Townhouse Shopping Centre, which tastefully fills a converted Georgian mansion. The huge, glass-covered St. Stephen's Green Shopping Centre and the peaceful green itself mark the top of Grafton Street.

▲St. Stephen's Green

This city park was originally a medieval commons, complete with gory public executions. The park got its start in 1664, when the city leased some of the land as building lots—and each tenant was obligated to plant six trees. Gradually the green was surrounded with fine Georgian buildings. Today (like New York's Central Park) it provides a grassy refuge for Dubliners. At the northwest corner (near the end of Grafton Street) you'll be confronted by a looming marble arch erected to honor British officers killed during the Boer War. Locals nicknamed it "Traitor's Arch," as most Irish sympathized with the underdog Boers.

During the 1916 Easter Rising, a group of passionate rebels—a mishmash of romantic poets, teachers, aristocratic ladies, and slum dwellers—dug trenches in the park to hunker down, believing they were creating fortified positions. They hadn't figured on veteran British troops easily trumping their move by placing snipers atop the Shelbourne Hotel (with a bird's-eye view into the trenches).

On a sunny afternoon, this open space is a wonderful world apart from the big city. When marveling at the elegance of Georgian Dublin, remember that it was the second-most important city in the British Empire in that era.

Little Museum of Dublin

This boisterous little museum facing St. Stephen's Green, just five rooms in a Georgian mansion from 1776, is a creative labor of love. Volunteers have covered its walls with historic bits and pieces of

Dublin history—all donated by locals. This museum also sponsors the City of a Thousand Welcomes Meet a Dubliner program (see page 40).

Cost and Hours: €8 includes required 30-minute tour, daily 9:30-17:00, Thu until 20:00, tours depart on the hour 10:00-16:00, 15 St. Stephen's Green, tel. 01/661-1000, www.littlemuseum.ie.

Visiting the Museum: Your visit starts with an entertaining 30-minute talk mixing modern Dublin history and pop culture as illustrated in two rooms. Then you're free to wander the remaining rooms (including one on Irish rock 'n' roll for U2 fans and another on local pub culture). Memorabilia range from historic letters written by Irish nationalists Éamon de Valera and Michael Collins to mementos of JFK's 1963 Dublin visit and Muhammad Ali's 1972 fight here.

Dublin Castle and Nearby

If you are in the castle area at lunchtime, consider the recommended Silk Road Café in the Chester Beatty Library (located in the castle gardens; see listing under "Eating in Dublin").

▲Dublin Castle

Built on the spot of the first Viking fortress, this castle was the seat of English rule in Ireland for 700 years. Located where the Poddle and Liffey rivers came together, making a black pool (*dubh linn* in Irish), Dublin Castle was the official residence of the viceroy who implemented the will of the British royalty. In this stirring setting, the Brits handed power over to Michael Collins and the Irish in 1922. Today, it's used for fancy state and charity functions (which may sporadically close it to the public).

Cost and Hours: Visiting the courtyard is free, €10 for one-hour guided tour, €7 to visit on your own (state apartments only); Mon-Sat 10:00-16:45, Sun from 12:00, tours depart every 30 minutes; tickets sold in courtyard under portico opposite clock tower, tel. 01/645-8813, www.dublincastle.ie.

Visiting the Castle: Standing in the courtyard, you can imagine the ugliness of the British-Irish situation. Notice the statue of justice above the gate—pointedly without her blindfold and admiring her sword. As Dubliners say, "There she stands, above her station, with her face to the palace and her arse to the nation."

The fancy interior is viewable on a guided tour, which offers a fairly boring room-by-room walk through the lavish state apartments of this most English of Irish palaces. The tour also includes a look at the foundations of the Norman tower as well as original Viking defenses, and the best remaining chunk of the 13th-century town wall.

▲▲Chester Beatty Library

This library—located in the gardens of Dublin Castle (follow the signs)—is an exquisite, delightfully displayed collection of rare ancient manuscripts and beautifully illustrated books from around the world, plus a few odd curios. These treasures were bequeathed by Alfred Chester Beatty (1875-1968), a rich American mining magnate who traveled widely, collected 66,000 objects assiduously, and retired to Ireland.

DUBLIN

Cost and Hours: Free; Mon-Fri 10:00-17:00, Sat from 11:00, Sun from 13:00, closed Mon Nov-Feb; library's Silk Road Café is fine for a light lunch—see listing under "Eating in Dublin"; tel. 01/407-0750, www.cbl.ie.

◐ Self-Guided Tour: Start on the ground floor, with a 10-minute film about Beatty. Then head upstairs to the second floor to see the treasures he left to his adopted country. Note that exhibits often rotate, so they may not be on display in the order outlined here.

Sacred Traditions Gallery: This space is dedicated to sacred texts, illuminated manuscripts, and miniature paintings from around the world. The doors swing open, and you're greeted by a video highlighting a diverse array of religious rites—a Christian wedding, Muslims kneeling for prayer, whirling dervishes, and so on.

• *Tour the floor clockwise, starting with Christian texts on the left side of the room. There you'll find several glass cases containing...*

Ancient Bible Fragments: In the 1930s, Beatty acquired these 1,800-year-old manuscripts, which had recently been unearthed in Egypt. The Indiana Jones-like discovery instantly bumped scholars' knowledge of the early Bible up a notch. There were Old Testament books, New Testament books, and—rarest of all—the Letters of Paul. Written in Greek on papyrus more than a century before previously known documents, these are some of the oldest versions of these texts in existence. Unlike most early Christian texts, the manuscripts were not rolled up in a scroll but bound in a book form called a "codex." On display you may see pages from a third-century Gospel of Luke or the Gospel of John (c. A.D. 150-200). Jesus died around A.D. 33, and his words weren't recorded until decades later. Most early manuscripts date from the fourth century, so these pages are about as close to the source as you can get.

Letters (Epistles) of Paul: The Beatty has 112 pages of Saint Paul's collected letters (A.D. 180-200). Paul, a Roman citizen (c.

A.D. 5-67; see Albrecht Dürer's engraving of the saint), was the apostle most responsible for spreading Christianity beyond Palestine. Originally, Paul reviled Christians. But after a mystical experience, he went on to travel the known world, preaching the Good News in sophisticated Athens and the greatest city in the world, Rome, where he died a martyr to the cause. Along the way, he kept in touch with Christian congregations in cities like Corinth, Ephesus, and Rome with these letters.

Continuing up the left side of the room, you'll find gloriously illustrated medieval Bibles and prayer books, including an intricate, colorful, gold-speckled Book of Hours (1408).

• *Turn the corner into the center of the room, to find the sacred texts of...*

Islam: Muslims believe that the angel Gabriel visited Muhammad (c. 570-632), instructing him to write down his heavenly visions in a book—the Quran. You'll see Qurans with elaborate calligraphy, such as one made in Baghdad in 1001. Nearby are other sacred Islamic texts, some beautifully illustrated, where you may find the rare illuminated manuscript of the "Life of the Prophet" (c. 1595), produced in Istanbul for an Ottoman sultan.

• *On the right side of the room, you enter the world of...*

East Asian Religions: Statues of Gautama Buddha (c. 563-483 B.C.) and Chinese Buddhist scrolls attest to the pervasive influence of this wise man. Buddha was born in India, but his philosophy spread to China, Japan, and Tibet (see the mandalas). Continuing clockwise, you'll reach the writings from India, the land of a million gods—and the cradle of Buddhism, Hinduism, Sikhism, and Jainism.

• *Your visit continues downstairs on the first floor, in the gallery devoted to the...*

Arts of the Book: The focus here is on the many forms a "book" can take—from the earliest clay tablets and papyrus scrolls, to parchment scrolls and bound codexes, to medieval monks' wondrous illustrations, to the advent of printing and bookbinding, to the dawn of the 21st century and the digital age.

• *Tour the floor clockwise. Immediately to the left, find a glass case containing...*

Egyptian and Other Ancient Writings: A hieroglyph-covered papyrus scroll from the Book of the Dead (c. 300 B.C.) depicts a pharaoh on his throne (left) presiding over a soul's judgment in the afterlife. The jackal-headed god Anubis (center-right) holds a scale, weighing the heart of a dead woman to see if it's light enough for her to level up to the next phase of eternity. Nearby (in a free-standing glass case, near the bottom) are a few small cuneiform tablets and cylinder seals from as far back as 2,700 B.C. These objects from ancient Sumeria (modern-day Iraq) are older than the pyramids and represent the very birth of writing.

• *Continue up the left side of the room, perusing displays on...*

Printing, Illustrating, and Bookbinding: The printing press with movable type was perfected by Johannes Gutenberg in Germany around 1450. The printed sheets were folded, sewn together, and wrapped in a cover. With the engraving process, beautiful illustrations could also be reproduced on a mass scale. Until the 20th century, it was common for a book buyer to acquire the printed sheets and then select a lavish custom-made cover.

• *Turn the corner to the center of the room.*

Islamic World: These are secular books—science textbooks and poetry—many from the rich Persian culture (modern-day Iran). Some are richly illustrated with elaborate calligraphy. While Islam avoids representations of living things, as you can see, that restriction doesn't apply to nonreligious texts.

• *Continue to the right side of the room.*

Far East: Besides albums and scrolls, you might see eye-catching Japanese woodblock prints, ornate Chinese snuff bottles, rhino-horn cups, and the silk dragon robes of Chinese emperors of the Qing dynasty (1644-1911). The Qianlong Emperor (r. 1736-1795)—a poet and arts patron—welcomed European Jesuits to his court and commissioned a huge collection of books, including some carved from jade.

Dublin City Hall

The first Georgian building in this very Georgian city stands proudly overlooking Dame Street, in front of the gate to Dublin Castle. Built in 1779 as the Royal Exchange (where one changed money), it introduced Ireland to the Georgian style then very popular in Britain. In 1852, the building became the City Hall.

Cost and Hours: Free, Mon-Sat 10:00-17:15, closed Sun, coffee shop, tel. 01/222-2204.

Visiting City Hall: Step inside to feel the prosperity and confidence of Dublin in her 18th-century glory days. Under the grand rotunda, a cycle of heroic paintings tells the city's history in a rare example of Arts and Crafts artwork from 1919. The mosaics on the floor convey such homilies as "Obedience makes the happiest citizenry."

Pay your respects to the 18-foot-tall statue of Daniel O'Connell, the great orator and liberator who, in 1829, won emancipation for Catholics in Ireland from the much-despised Protestants over in London. The body of modern Irish rebel leader Michael Collins lay in state here after his assassination in 1922 (the greeter is happy to give you more information).

Downstairs, don't miss the free **"Story of the Capital" exhibit**. It is the best history of Dublin exhibit I have found, traced through

DUBLIN

artifacts and models as well as excellent video clips, including *The City in Turmoil.*

Dublin's Cathedrals Area

Because of Dublin's English past (particularly Henry VIII's Reformation, and the dissolution of the Catholic monasteries in both Ireland and England in 1539), the city's top two churches are no longer Catholic. Christ Church Cathedral and nearby St. Patrick's Cathedral are both Church of Ireland (Anglican). In the late 19th century, the cathedrals underwent extensive restoration. The rich Guinness brewery family forked out the dough to try to make St. Patrick's Cathedral outshine Christ Church—whose patrons were the equally rich, rival Jameson family of distillery fame.

Christ Church Cathedral

Occupying the same site as the first wooden church built on this spot by King Sitric in late Viking times (c. 1030), the present structure is a mix of periods: Norman and Gothic, but mostly Victorian Neo-Gothic from the late 19th century.

Cost and Hours: €6.50 includes downstairs crypt exhibition, €14.50 combo-ticket includes Dublinia (described next); Mon-Sat 9:30-17:00, Sun 12:00-14:30; €4 guided tours Mon-Fri at 11:00, 12:00, 14:00, and 15:00; tel. 01/677-8099, www.christchurchdublin.ie.

Church Services and Evensong: There's a full Anglican service Sun at 11:00, and the public is welcome to a 45-minute evensong service, sung by the esteemed Christ Church choir (Wed-Thu at 18:00, Sun at 15:30).

Visiting the Cathedral: The interior is Victorian, from the 1870s. Highlights are the finely carved wooden quire (with the grand bishop's seat) and the tomb of Strongbow, the Norman warlord who helped conquer Ireland, leading to centuries of British domination. (While he was buried here in 1176, this stone is a 14th-century replacement.) From the south transept, stairs lead down into the crypt—considered the oldest structure in town (open to the public). Running the entire length of the church (with a forest of stout supporting columns), it's filled with historic odds and ends (and a WC).

▲Dublinia

This exhibit, which highlights Dublin's Viking and medieval past, is a hit with youngsters (but meaty enough for adults as well).

Cost and Hours: €9.50, €14.50 combo-ticket includes Christ Church Cathedral; daily 10:00-18:30, Oct-Feb until 17:30, last entry one hour before closing; top-floor coffee shop, across from Christ Church Cathedral, tel. 01/679-4611, www.dublinia.ie.

Visiting the Exhibits: The displays are laid out on three floors.

The ground floor focuses on Viking Dublin, explaining life aboard a Viking ship and inside a Viking house. Viking traders introduced urban life and commerce to Ireland—but kids will be most interested in gawking at their gory weaponry.

The next floor up reveals Dublin's day-to-day life in medieval times, from chivalrous knights and damsels in town fairs to the brutal ravages of the plague. Like so much of Europe at that time (1347-1349), Ireland lost one-third of its population to the Black Death. The huge scale model of medieval Dublin is especially well done. The top floor's "History Hunters" section is devoted to how the puzzles of modern archaeology and science shed light on Dublin's history. From this floor, you can climb a couple of flights of stairs into the tower for so-so views of Dublin, or exit across an enclosed stone bridge to adjacent Christ Church Cathedral.

DUBLIN

St. Patrick's Cathedral

This Anglican cathedral is a thoughtful learning experience as well as a living church. The first church here was Catholic, supposedly built on the site where St. Patrick baptized local pagan converts. While the core of the Gothic structure you see today was built in the 13th century, most of today's stonework is 19th century. After the Reformation, it passed into the hands of the Anglican Church. A century later, Oliver Cromwell's puritanical Calvinist troops—who considered the Anglicans to be little more than Catholics without a pope—stabled their horses here as a sign of disrespect.

Cost and Hours: €6.50 donation to church; Mon-Fri 9:30-17:00, Sat-Sun 9:00-18:00—but on Sun it's closed 10:30-12:30 and 14:30-16:30, last entry one hour before closing; at the intersection of Patrick Street and Upper Kevin Street, www.stpatrickscathedral.ie.

Tours: Free guided tours are given several times a day in summer; check website for schedule but typically at 10:30, 11:30, 14:30, 15:00, and 15:30.

Evensong: You'll get chills listening to the local "choir of angels" Mon-Fri at 17:30 and Sun at 15:15.

Visiting the Cathedral: The inside feels like an Irish Westminster Abbey, with venerable tombs and memorials to great Irish figures everywhere. The fine Victorian glass is from a Guinness-funded restoration in the 1870s. The regimental flags of the British army hang from the ceiling, colors slowly fading, in remembrance of soldiers lost. The north transept is dedicated to music (they claim Handel's *Messiah* was first performed here in 1742). The south transept is "The Discovery Space," a delightful learning center with thousand-year-old gravestones and free brass rubbing.

Jonathan Swift (author of *Gulliver's Travels*) was dean of the cathedral from 1713 to 1745. His grave and death mask are located near the front door (on the right side of the nave), where his cutting, self-penned epitaph reads: "He lies where furious indignation can no longer rend his heart."

▲▲Temple Bar

This much-promoted area—with shops, cafés, theaters, galleries, pubs with live music, and restaurants—feels like the heart of the old city. It's Dublin's touristy "Left Bank," on the south shore of the river, filling the cobbled streets between Dame Street and the River Liffey.

Three hundred years ago, this was the city waterfront, where tall sailing ships offloaded their goods (a "bar" was a loading dock along the river, and the Temples were a dominant merchant family). Eventually, the city grew eastward, filling in tidal mudflats, to create the docklands of modern Dublin. Once a thriving Georgian center of craftsmen and merchants, this neighborhood fell on hard times in the 20th century. Ensuing low rents attracted students and artists, giving the area a bohemian flair. With government tax incentives and lots of development money, the Temple Bar district has now become a thriving entertainment (and beer-drinking) hot spot.

Sights and Activities in Temple Bar: Temple Bar Square, just off Temple Bar Street (near Ha' Penny Bridge), is the epicenter of activity. It hosts free street theater and a **Saturday book market**. On busy weekends, people-watching here is a contact sport (and pickpocketing is not).

Irish music fans find great CDs at humble **Claddagh Records** (Cecilia Street, just around the corner from Luigi Malone's, Mon-Sat 11:00-17:30, closed Sun, tel. 01/677-0262). Unlike big, glitzy chain stores, this is a little hole-in-the-wall shop staffed by informed folks who love turning visitors on to Irish tunes. Grab a couple of CDs for your drive through the Irish countryside.

Farther west and somewhat hidden is Meeting House Square, with a lively **organic-produce market** (Sat 10:00-18:00). Bordering the square is the **Irish Film Institute** (main entry on Eustace Street), which shows a variety of art-house flicks. A bohemian crowd relaxes in its bar/café, awaiting the next film (6 Eustace Street, box office daily 13:30-21:00, tel. 01/679-5744, www.irishfilm.ie).

Less commercial plays can be seen nearby at **Smock Alley Theatre,** with seating surrounding a tiny stage, in a space on the site of the city's first custom-built theater from 1662 (for details, see page 93).

Eating in and near Temple Bar: I've listed my recommendations later in this chapter (see "Eating in Dublin," later). But if you want to wander on your own without following particular rec-

ommendations, venture down a few side lanes off the main drag to see what looks good. If the rowdy Temple Bar scene gets to be too much, cross over to the north bank of the River Liffey on the Millennium Pedestrian Bridge (next bridge west of the Ha' Penny Bridge), where you'll find a mellower, more cosmopolitan choice of restaurants with outdoor seating in the Millennium Walk district (see page 92).

Nighttime Rowdiness: Temple Bar can be an absolute spectacle in the evening, when it bursts with revelers. The noise, pushy crowds and inflated prices have driven most Dubliners away. But even if you're just gawking, don't miss the opportunity to wander through this human circus. It's craziest on summer weekend nights, holidays, and nights after big sporting events let out. Women in funky hats, part of loud "hen" (bachelorette) parties, promenade down the main drag as drunken dudes shout from pub doorways to get their attention. You're bound to meet some characters and might even have to step around some "sidewalk pizza."

NORTH OF THE RIVER LIFFEY

O'Connell Street and the historic core north of the river is covered by the self-guided walk on page 50. After you're oriented with the walk, consider the following sights.

▲▲Epic: The Irish Emigration Museum

Telling the story of the Irish diaspora, this museum celebrates how this little island has had an oversized impact on the world. While the museum has no actual artifacts, this is an entertaining and educational experience.

Cost and Hours: €14, daily 10:00-18:45, last entry at 17:00, one-hour tours at 11:00 and 14:00, in the CHQ building on Custom House Quay (at the modern pedestrian bridge a few steps from the famine statues along the riverfront), tel. 01/906-0861, www. epicchq.com.

Visiting the Museum: The museum fills the wine vaults in the basement of an iron-framed warehouse from the 1820s (where the customs house stood on the River Liffey). Its 20 themed galleries take an interactive, high-tech approach to explain the forces that propelled so many Irish around the globe. Featured illustrious emigrants include labor agitator Mother Jones, Caribbean pirate Anne

Bonny, Australian bush bandit Ned Kelly, and musical Chicago police chief Francis O'Neill. Historic photos of filthy tenements and early films of bustling urban scenes document the plight of the common Irish emigrant. And all along you celebrate Irish heritage in music, literature, sports, and more.

Genealogy Help: Upstairs from the museum, the **Irish Family History Centre** can help you research your Celtic roots (€10 to access research stations, €40 for 30-minute consultation, daily 10:00-17:00, tel. 01/905-9216, www.irishfamilyhistorycentre.com).

Nearby: Today the modern **food court** in the CHQ building serves the glassy office towers that now energize what, 30 years ago, was an urban wasteland. A modern **pedestrian bridge**—shaped like an old Irish harp and designed by Santiago Calatrava—leads to Dublin's strikingly contemporary convention center.

Before leaving the riverside area, cross Customs House Quay (the main road) and wander 50 yards up the River Liffey toward the city to contemplate the skeletal sculptures of the city's evocative **Famine Memorial.** A few steps in the opposite direction, downriver, you'll spot the masts of the Jeanie Johnston Tall Ship and Famine Museum (see next). A visit here ties in well with the area's emigration theme.

▲Jeanie Johnston Tall Ship and Famine Museum

Docked on the River Liffey, this seagoing sailing ship is a replica of a legendary Irish "famine ship." The original *Jeanie Johnston* embarked on 16 eight-week transatlantic crossings, carrying more than 2,500 Irish emigrants (about 200 per voyage) to their new lives in America and Canada in the decade after the Great Potato Famine of the 1840s. While many barely seaworthy hulks were known as "coffin ships," the people who boarded the *Jeanie Johnston* were lucky: The ship was Irish owned and crewed, with a humanitarian captain and even a doctor on board, and not one life was lost. Your tour guide will introduce you to the ship's main characters and help illuminate day-to-day life aboard a cramped tall ship 160 years ago.

Note that, because this ship makes goodwill voyages to Atlantic ports, it may be away during your visit—check ahead.

Cost and Hours: €10, visits by 50-minute tour only, easy to book slot in advance online; daily 10:00-16:00, Oct-March 11:00-15:00, tours depart on the hour (but no tours at 13:00); on the north bank of the Liffey just east of Sean O'Casey Bridge, tel. 01/473-0111, www.jeaniejohnston.ie.

▲Dublin Writers Museum

No other country so small has produced such a wealth of literature. As interesting to those who are fans of Irish literature as it is boring to those who aren't, this three-room museum features the lives and works of Dublin's great writers. It's a low-tech museum, where you read informative plaques while perusing display cases with minor memorabilia—a document signed by Jonathan Swift, a photo of Oscar Wilde reclining thoughtfully, an early edition of Bram Stoker's *Dracula,* a George Bernard Shaw playbill, a not-so-famous author's tuxedo, or a newspaper from Easter 1916 announcing "Two More Executions Today." If unassuming attractions like that stir your blood—or if you simply want a manageable introduction to Irish lit—it's worth a visit.

DUBLIN

Cost and Hours: €7.50, includes helpful 45-minute audioguide; Mon-Sat 9:45-17:00, Sun from 11:00; 18 Parnell Square North, tel. 01/872-2077, www.writersmuseum.com.

Visiting the Museum: The collection is chronological. While you'll follow the audioguide, here are some highlights:

Room 1 starts with Irish literature's deep roots in the roving, harp-playing bards of medieval times. By telling stories in the native language, they helped unify the island's culture. But "literature" came only with the arrival of the English language. **Jonathan Swift** (1667-1745)—Ireland's first great writer—was born in Dublin and served as dean of St. Patrick's Cathedral, though he spent much of his life in London. His stinging satire of societal hypocrisy set the tone of rebellion found in much Irish literature. The theater has been another longstanding Irish specialty, starting with the 18th-century playwright Oliver Goldsmith. In the 1890s, sophisticated Dublin (and Trinity College) was a cradle for great writers who ultimately found their fortunes in England: the playwright/poet/wit Oscar Wilde, Bram Stoker (who married Wilde's girlfriend), and the big-idea playwright George Bernard Shaw. Poet **W. B. Yeats** stayed home, cultivating Irish folklore at soirees (hosted by the literary patron Lady Augusta Gregory).

Room 2 continues into the 20th century with Yeats' **Abbey Theatre**, the scene of premieres by great Irish playwrights (including Yeats, Shaw, and Wilde), and an important force in the developing sense of Irish national identity in the early part of the century. Dublin was also a breeding ground for bold new ideas, producing Modernist writers Samuel *(Waiting for Godot)* Beckett and James Joyce (a center devoted to him is described next). As the 20th century progressed, writers like Sean O'Casey, Brendan Behan, Seamus Heaney, John B. Keane, and Brian Friel kept Dublin at the forefront of modern theater.

Finish your visit by going **upstairs** to see an elegant Georgian library with portraits, busts, and temporary exhibits on Irish literature.

DUBLIN

North Dublin

Accommodations

1 The Castle Hotel

2 Jurys Inn Parnell Street

3 Belvedere Hotel

4 Charles Stewart Guesthouse

James Joyce Centre

Only aficionados of James Joyce's work will want to visit this micromuseum.

Cost and Hours: €5, Mon-Sat 10:00-17:00, Sun from 12:00, closed Mon Oct-March, two blocks east of the Dublin Writers Museum at 35 North Great George's Street, tel. 01/878-8547, www.jamesjoyce.ie. The center offers walking tours of Joyce sights several times a week.

Background: Born and raised in Dublin, James Joyce (1882-1941) wrote in great detail about his hometown, and mined the local dialect for his pitch-perfect dialogue. His best-known work, *Ulysses,* chronicles one day (June 16, 1904) in the life of the fictional Leopold Bloom as he wanders through the underside of Dublin. Joyce himself left Dublin (on June 17, 1904) for Paris and lived away from the city for most of his life. He never took up the cause of Irish nationalism and rarely delved into Irish mythology. He instead wrote with a new Modernist focus on linguistic invention and social frankness.

Visiting the Center: Your visit begins (top floor) with videos on Joyce's life and his enormous influence on subsequent writers. Next, a touchscreen display traces Bloom's Dublin Odyssey. Photos of Joyce and quotes from his books decorate the walls. A recreation of a messy, cramped study evokes Joyce's struggles through poverty and criticism as he forged his own path. Down one flight, see portraits of Joyce and his wife and muse, Nora Barnacle. (The first time they, um, went on a date was June 16, 1904. Joyce later set the events depicted in his masterpiece, *Ulysses,* on that date, which is commemorated annually as Bloomsday in honor of Leopold Bloom.) On the ground floor, a film version of one of Joyce's short stories, *The Dead,* plays eternally. In a tiny back courtyard, you can see the original door from 7 Eccles Street, the address of Leopold Bloom.

DUBLIN

Dublin's Literary Life

Dublin in the 1700s, grown rich from a lucrative cloth trade, was one of Europe's most cultured and sophisticated cities.

The buildings were decorated in the Georgian style still visible today, and the city's Protestant elite shuttled between here and London, bridging the Anglo-Irish cultural gap. Jonathan Swift (1667-1745) was the era's greatest Anglo-Irish writer—a brilliant satirist and author of *Gulliver's Travels*. He was also dean of St. Patrick's Cathedral (1713-1745) and one of the city's eminent citizens.

Around the turn of the 20th century, Dublin produced some of the world's great modern writers. Bram Stoker (1847-1912) was creator of *Dracula*. Oscar Wilde (1854-1900) penned *The Picture of Dorian Gray* and a clutch of fine plays. George Bernard Shaw (1856-1950) wrote *Pygmalion*, *Major Barbara*, *Man and Superman*, and a host of other dramas. William Butler Yeats (1865-1939) was a prolific poet and playwright on Irish themes. And James Joyce (1882-1941) whipped up a masterpiece called *Ulysses*. For more on Irish literature (and to see which of these writers won the Nobel Prize), see page 509.

To dip your toe into the occasionally unfathomable depths of classic Irish lit, drop by the tiny **Sweny's Pharmacy** for one of its daily readings from *Ulysses*. This shrine for devotees of Joyce is a time capsule, looking just as the writer described it in his novel more than a hundred years ago. The text is passed around for all to read a section aloud, and even if you don't understand its obscure local references, appreciate the rhythm of its stream-of-consciousness verbal flow...and buy a bar of lemon soap on your way out (daily, usually at 13:00, check schedule at www.sweny.ie, sometimes read in other languages...might make it easier to figure out, 1 Lincoln Place between Trinity College and Merrion Square).

▲Hugh Lane Gallery

This stimulating and well-described exhibit of art from the 1870s onward includes a sampling of Impressionist masterpieces from the gallery's founding collection, once owned by Sir Hugh Lane, an Irish art dealer. Genteel and bite-sized, the museum is particularly worth a visit for a well-known Monet painting, an exhibit on modern artist Francis Bacon, and a few select paintings by Irish artists.

Cost and Hours: Free, Tue-Thu 10:00-18:00, Fri-Sat until 17:00, Sun 11:00-17:00, closed Mon, in the Dublin City Gallery on Parnell Square North, tel. 01/222-5550, www.hughlane.ie.

Visiting the Gallery: Head to Room 1, where you'll find **Monet's *Waterloo Bridge*** (1900). On a visit to London, the once-bohemian, now-famous Impressionist Claude Monet checked into Room 618 of the Savoy Hotel and set to work painting Waterloo Bridge at different times of day and in various weather conditions. This painting is just one of 41 versions of the scene. Monet—the master of capturing hazy, filtered light—loved London for its fog. With the Thames in the foreground, the bridge in the middle, and belching smokestacks in the distance, Monet had three different layers of atmospheric depth to explore.

In 1905, Sir Hugh bought Monet's *Waterloo Bridge* as part of his mission to bring modern art to the British Isles and provincial Dublin. Unfortunately, Sir Hugh went down on the *Lusitania* in 1915 and didn't see this gallery open. To see a depiction of dapper Sir Hugh—by the American society portraitist John Singer Sargent—find the room to the right of Room 3.

Francis Bacon Studio: Although he spent most of his life in London, Francis Bacon (1909-1992) was born in Dublin and raised nearby. After his death, his entire London studio was reconstructed here, just as the artist had left it.

After a wandering youth of odd jobs and petty crime, Bacon took up painting in his late thirties. He jumped onto the art stage in 1945 with his bleak canvases of twisted, deformed, screaming-mouthed men caged in barren landscapes—which hauntingly captured the mood of post-WWII Europe. He would become Britain's premier painter, but he continued to live simply. He stayed in his small, cramped flat with an even smaller studio (this one) for his entire life. Here he painted his famous series of "Heads"—portraits of his friends, especially of his life partner, George Dyer.

The place is a mess—empty paint cans, slashed canvases, books, photos, and newspapers everywhere—leaving only enough space for Bacon to set up his canvas in the middle of it all and paint. As trashed as the studio is, it reflects Bacon's belief that "chaos breeds energy."

Spend 10 minutes with the 1985 filmed interview of Bacon, which was conducted in the studio. He speaks about his work and reminisces about his down-and-out days. In nearby rooms are photos of Bacon, a few unfinished works, and personal items, such as his coffee-table book on Velázquez, the Old Master who inspired Bacon's famous portrait of a screaming pope.

▲▲GPO Witness History Exhibit

During the 1916 Easter Rising, Irish nationalists took over buildings in Dublin, including the General Post Office (GPO), which became the rebel headquarters. Initial euphoria led to chaotic street battles and ended with the grim realization among the insurgents that surrender was the best option—trusting that their martyrdom would inspire the country to rise more effectively. This engaging exhibit—in the working GPO—explores that pivotal Easter Week.

Cost and Hours: €14, cheaper online, Mon-Sat 10:00-17:30, Sun from 12:00, last entry one hour before closing, audioguide-€1, tel. 01/872-1916, www.gpowitnesshistory.ie.

Background: A sideshow for European nations preoccupied with World War I, the Easter Rising was critical to Irish nationalists. Almost every Irish generation for the preceding 125 years had launched doomed insurrections. But this one had a lasting effect, although it may not have seemed so in its immediate wake—a couple of weeks later, the patriot leaders who held their ground at the GPO were executed in Kilmainham Gaol (see page 86). Public sympathies shifted seismically. After seven centuries of dominance, the British were on a slippery slope leading to the eventual granting of independence to its nearest and oldest colony.

Visiting the Exhibit: You'll find the exhibit, with many interesting artifacts, on the right as you enter the building. It features a fairly balanced view of the rebellion, including the less popular realities (like the lack of widespread support at the beginning of the movement and the civilians who died in the crossfire). Don't miss the excellent 15-minute wide-screen depiction of events (called "The Rising") in the tiny theater. An interactive map of Dublin zooms in and out of various neighborhoods, tracking the week's confrontations, with actors dramatizing the events and conversations that shaped the conflict. In video presentations, historians give their take on how the rebellion affected Irish history.

14 Henrietta Street

This Georgian house morphed from affluent 18th-century mansion to cramped, impoverished, multifamily 19th-century hovel. Now a new museum (should be open by the time you visit), it brings high-density urban poverty into focus and explains tenement life in Dublin.

Cost and Hours: €9, check website for hours, 14 Henrietta Street, tel. 01/524-0383, www.14henriettastreet.ie.

National Leprechaun Museum

This corny, low-tech attraction is fine for kids and lighthearted adults. On this 45-minute guided meander through Irish mythology, you'll visit a wishing well, a giant's living room, and a fairy fort, listening to tales that will enchant your wee ones.

Cost and Hours: €14, daily 10:00-18:30, last entry one hour before closing, a block north of the River Liffey on Abbey Street across from Jervis LUAS stop, tel. 01/873-3899, www.leprechaunmuseum.ie.

Evening Visits: For adults only, a one-hour, interactive "This Dark Land" storytelling performance explores the macabre side of Irish folklore (€16, May-Sept Fri-Sat at 19:30 and 20:30).

From Famine to Revolution

After the Great Potato Famine (1845-1849), destitute rural Irish moved to the city in droves, seeking work and causing a housing shortage. Unscrupulous landlords came up with a solution: Subdivide the city's once-grand mansions, vacated when gentry moved to London after the 1801 Act of Union. The mansions' tiny rooms could then be crammed with poor renters. Dublin became one of the most densely populated cities in Europe—one of every three Dubliners lived in a slum. On Henrietta Street, once a wealthy Dublin address, these new tenements bulged with humanity. According to the 1911 census, one district counted 835 people living in 15 houses (many with a single outhouse in back or a communal chamber pot in the room). In cramped, putrid quarters like this, tuberculosis was rampant, and infant mortality skyrocketed.

Those who could get work tenaciously clung to their precious jobs. The terrible working conditions prompted many to join trade unions. A 1913 strike and employer lockout, known as the "Dublin Lockout," lasted for seven months. The picket lines were brutally put down by police in the pocket of rich businessmen, led by newspaper owner and hotel magnate William Murphy. In response, James Larkin and James Connolly formed the Irish Citizen Army, a socialist militia to protect the poor trade unionists.

Murphy eventually broke the unions. Larkin headed for the US to organize workers there. During World War I, he praised the rise of the Soviet Union and later was persecuted during the postwar "Red Scare" (even doing time in Sing Sing prison for advocating "unlawful means" to overthrow the US government). Meanwhile, Connolly stayed in Ireland and brought the Irish Citizen Army into the 1916 Easter Rising as an integral part of the rebel forces. During the uprising, he slyly had a rebel flag flown over Murphy's prized hotel on O'Connell Street. The uninformed British artillery battalions took the bait and pulverized it.

Connolly was the last of the rebel leaders executed in Dublin in 1916. Unable to stand in front of the firing squad in Kilmainham Gaol (his gangrenous ankle had been shattered by a bullet while he was defending the General Post Office), Connolly was tied to a chair and shot sitting down. Of the 16 rebel executions, Connolly's was most credited with turning Irish public opinion in favor of the rebel martyrs (due to his devoted following among poor tenement dwellers).

Today you'll find heroic Dublin statues to honor both men. James Larkin, arms outstretched, is in front of the post office on O'Connell Street. James Connolly is on Beresford Place, behind the Customs House.

DUBLIN

DUBLIN

Old Jameson Distillery

Whiskey fans enjoy visiting the old distillery. You get a 40-minute tour and a free shot in the pub. Unfortunately, the "distillery" feels corporate, overpriced, and put together for tourists. The Bushmills tour in Northern Ireland (in a working factory, see page 440) and the Midleton tour near Cork (in the huge original factory, page 213) are better experiences. If you do take this tour, volunteer energetically when offered the chance: This will get you a coveted seat at the whiskey taste-test table at the tour's end.

Cost and Hours: €20, Mon-Sat 9:30-18:00, Sun from 10:00, last tour at 17:15, late tours possible in summer; Bow Street, tel. 01/807-2355, www.jamesonwhiskey.com.

Nearby: The neighborhood called **Smithfield** was on the fast track to gentrification prior to the 2008-2009 economic crash. Today, it's getting back on its feet and is home to both the Old Jameson Distillery and Dublin's most authentic traditional-music pub (see page 94). Both are on the long Smithfield Square, two blocks northwest of the Four Courts—the Supreme Court building. The **Fresh Market,** near the top of the square, is a handy grocery stop for urban picnic fixings (daily until 22:00).

OUTER DUBLIN

The Kilmainham Gaol (GAY-ol) and the Guinness Storehouse are located west of the old center and can be linked by a 20-minute walk, a five-minute taxi ride, or public bus #40 or #13. (To ride the bus from the jail to the Guinness Storehouse, leave the prison and take three rights—crossing no streets—to reach the bus stop.) Another option is to take a hop-on, hop-off bus, which stops at both sights (see page 46).

▲▲▲Kilmainham Gaol

Opened in 1796 as Dublin's county jail and a debtors' prison, Kilmainham was considered a model in its day. In reality, this jail was frequently used by the British as a political prison. Many of those who fought for Irish independence were held or executed here, including leaders of the rebellions of 1798, 1803, 1848, 1867, and 1916. National heroes Robert Emmett and Charles Stewart Parnell each did time here. The last prisoner to be held in the jail was Éamon de Valera, who later became president of Ireland. He was released on July 16, 1924, the day Kilmainham was finally shut down. The buildings, virtually in ruins, were restored in the 1960s. Today, it's a shrine to the Nathan Hales of Ireland.

Cost and Hours: Buy in advance online—€8, includes guided one-hour jail tour and unguided museum visit; daily June-Aug 9:00-19:00, last tour at 17:45; April-May and Sept until 18:00, last tour at 16:45; Oct-March 9:30-17:30, last tour at 16:45; tours run 2/hour, tel. 01/453-5984, www.kilmainhamgaolmuseum.ie.

Advance Tickets Recommended: Book online at least a few days in advance to guarantee a spot on a tour. While you can try to buy a €9 ticket in person, you'll likely wait in a long line, and walk-up spots go quickly. If you need to wait for your tour departure, visit the museum first.

Getting There: Hop-on, hop-off buses stop here, or take bus #69 or #79 from Aston Quay or #13 or #40 from O'Connell Street or College Green—confirm with driver.

Visiting the Jail: Start your visit with a one-hour guided tour (includes 15-minute prison-history slide show in the prison chapel). It's touching to tour the cells and places of execution—hearing tales of oppressive colonialism and heroic patriotism—alongside Irish schoolkids who know these names well. The museum has an excellent exhibit on Victorian prison life and Ireland's fight for independence.

Don't miss the dimly lit "Last Words 1916" hall upstairs, which displays the stirring final letters that patriots sent to loved ones hours before facing the firing squad. Regrettably, transcriptions of the letters are not posted, denying visitors a better understanding of the passion and patriotism of Ireland's greatest in their own last words—a lost opportunity for Americans not realizing that there are other Nathan Hales in this world who wish they had more than one life to give for their country. (Fortunately, the little bookshop for budding patriots carries the inspirational *Last Words* book.)

Nearby: The free Irish Museum of Modern Art is a 15-minute walk from here.

▲Guinness Storehouse

A visit to the Guinness Storehouse is, for many, a pilgrimage. Arthur Guinness began brewing the renowned stout here in 1759, and by 1868 it was the biggest brewery in the world. Today, the sprawling complex fills several city blocks (64 acres busy brewing 1.5 million pints a day).

Visitors (1.5 million annually) are welcomed to the towering storehouse, where the vibe is glitzy entertainment. Don't look for conveyor belts of beer bottles being stamped with bottle caps, or displays of historic artifacts. Rather than a brewery

The Famous Record-Breaking Records Book

Look up "beer" in the *Guinness World Records*, and you'll discover that the record for removing beer bottle caps with one's teeth is 68 in one minute. But aside from listing records for amazing—or amazingly stupid—feats, this famous record book has a more subtle connection with beer.

In 1951, while hunting in Ireland's County Wexford, Sir Hugh Beaver, then the managing director at Guinness Breweries, got into a debate with his companions over which was the fastest game bird in Europe: the golden plover or the red grouse. That night at his estate, after scouring countless reference books, they were disappointed not to find a definitive answer.

Beaver realized that similar questions were likely being debated nightly across pubs in Ireland and Britain. So he hired a fact-finding team in London to compile a book of answers to various questions. In 1955, the *Guinness Book of Records* (later renamed *Guinness World Records*) was published. By Christmas, it topped the British bestseller list.

In the beginning, entries mostly focused on natural phenomena and animal oddities, but grew to include a wide variety of extreme human achievements.

The iconic books are now available in more than 100 countries and 26 languages, with more than 3.5 million copies sold annually. As the bestselling copyrighted book of all time, it even earns a record-breaking entry within its own pages.

tour, this is a Disneyland for beer lovers—huge crowds, high decibel music, and dreamy TV beer ads on big screens.

Cost and Hours: Buy in advance online—€23, includes a €5 pint; daily 9:30-19:00, July-Aug 9:00-20:00, last entry two hours before closing, last beer served 45 minutes before closing; tel. 01/408-4800, www.guinness-storehouse.com.

Advance Tickets Recommended: The only smart way to visit is by booking a timed-entry ticket online. You'll save 10 percent on admission and avoid waiting in long lines outside the brewery. Visit by 10:30 for 20 percent off admission.

Getting There: Ride the hop-on, hop-off bus (your HOHO ticket gives you a €1 discount here), or take bus #13, #40, or #123 from Dame Street and O'Connell Street. Enter the brewery on Bellevue Street.

Visiting the Brewery: The exhibit fills the old fermentation plant, used from 1902 through 1988, which reopened in 2000 as a huge shrine to the Guinness tradition. Step into the middle of the ground floor and look up. A tall, beer-glass-shaped glass atrium—14 million pints big (that's about 10 days' production)—soars upward past four floors of exhibitions and cafés to the skylight. Then look down at Arthur's original 9,000-year lease, enshrined under Plexiglas in the floor. At £45 per year, it was quite a bargain.

As you escalate ever higher, you'll notice that each floor has a theme. The first floor is dedicated to cooperage—the making of wooden barrels (with 1954 film clips showing master kegmakers working at their now virtually extinct trade); the second floor has the tasting rooms (described below); the third floor features advertising and a theater with classic TV ads; the fourth floor is where you can pull your own beer (at the Academy); and the fifth floor has Arthur's Bar. The top floor is the Gravity Bar, providing visitors with a commanding 360-degree view of Dublin—with vistas all the way to the sea—and an included pint of the beloved stout.

The tasting rooms (on level 2) provide a fun detour. In the "white room" you're introduced to using your five senses to appreciate the perfect porter. Then, in the "velvet chamber," you're taught how to taste it from a leprechaun-sized beer glass.

Claiming Your Beer: Your admission includes a ticket for a beer, which you can claim on one of three levels. On level 4, you can pull your own pint (and then drink it). On level 5, at Arthur's Bar, you can choose among extra stout (4.2%, carbonated), Dublin Porter (3.8%, 1796 recipe), West Indies Porter (6%, toffee flavor, 1801 recipe), Hop House 13 (4.1%, a hoppy lager), and Black Velvet (half and half sparkling wine and Guinness). On the top floor (where there's the most energy and fun), drinks are limited to the basic stout or soft drinks.

▲National Museum: Decorative Arts and History

This branch of the National Museum, which occupies the huge, 18th-century stone Collins Barracks in west Dublin, displays Irish dress, furniture, weapons, silver, and other domestic baubles from the past 700 years. History buffs will linger longest in the "Soldiers & Chiefs" exhibit, which covers the Irish at war both at home and abroad since 1500 (including the American Civil War). The sober finale is the "Proclaiming the Republic" room, offering Ireland's best coverage of the painful birth of this nation. Guns, flags, and personal letters help illustrate the 1916 Easter Rising, the War of Independence against Britain, and Ireland's civil war. Croppies Acre, the large park between the museum and the river, was the site of Dublin's largest soup kitchen during the Great Potato Famine in 1845-1849.

Cost and Hours: Free, Tue-Sat 10:00-17:00, Sun from 14:00, closed Mon, good café; on north side of the River Liffey in Collins Barracks on Benburb Street, roughly across the river from Guinness Storehouse, LUAS red line: Museum stop; tel. 01/677-7444, www.museum.ie.

DUBLIN

▲Gaelic Athletic Association Museum

The GAA was founded in 1884 as an expression of an Irish cultural awakening (see sidebar on page 91). It was created to foster the development of Gaelic sports, specifically Gaelic football and hurling, and to exclude English sports such as cricket and rugby. The GAA played an important part in the fight for independence. This museum, at 82,000-seat Croke Park Stadium in northeast Dublin, offers a high-tech, interactive introduction to Ireland's favorite games. Relive the greatest moments in hurling and Irish-football history. Then get involved: Pick up a stick and try hurling, kick a football, and test your speed and balance. A 15-minute film (played on request) gives you a "Sunday at the stadium" experience.

Cost and Hours: €7, Mon-Sat 9:30-17:00, June-Aug until 18:00, Sun 10:30-17:00 year-round—except on game Sundays, when the museum is open to ticket holders only; café, located under the stands at Croke Park Stadium, enter from St. Joseph's Avenue off Clonliffe Road, tel. 01/819-2323, www.crokepark.ie/gaa-museum.

Tours: The €14, one-hour museum-plus-stadium-tour option (daily at 11:00, 13:00, and 15:00) is worth it only for rabid fans who want a glimpse of the huge stadium and locker rooms. The €20 rooftop tour offers views 17 stories above the field from lofty catwalks (Mon-Fri at 11:30 and 14:30, Sat-Sun hourly from 10:30 to 14:30; fewer tours Oct-April).

Hurling or Gaelic Football at Croke Park Stadium

Actually seeing a match here, surrounded by incredibly spirited Irish fans, is a fun experience. Hurling is fast and rough: like air-

borne hockey with no injury time-outs. Gaelic football resembles a rugged form of soccer; you can carry the ball, but must bounce or kick it every three steps. Matches are held most Saturday or Sunday afternoons in summer (May-Aug), culminating in the hugely popular all-Ireland finals on Sunday afternoons in September. Tickets are available at the stadium except during the finals. Choose a county to support, buy their colors to wear or wave, scream yourself hoarse, and you'll be a temporary local.

Cost and Hours: €20-55, box office open Mon-Fri 9:30-13:00 & 14:15-17:30, www.gaa.ie.

Getting There: Croke Park is located on the north bank of the Royal Canal, about 10 blocks north of the Connolly train station. It can be reached by bus #40 or #41, or by taxi.

Ireland's Gaelic Athletic Association

The GAA has long been a powerhouse in Ireland. Ireland's national pastimes of Gaelic football and hurling pack stadiums all over the country. When you consider that 82,000 people—paying about €25 each—stuff Dublin's Croke Park Stadium and that all the athletes are strictly amateur, you might wonder, "Where does all the money go?"

Ireland has a long tradition of using the revenue generated by these huge events to promote Gaelic athletics and Gaelic cultural events throughout the country in a grassroots and neighborhood way. So, while the players (many of whom are schoolteachers whose jobs allow for evenings and summers free) participate only for the glory of their various counties, the money generated is funding children's leagues, school coaches, small-town athletic facilities, and traditional arts, music, and dance—as well as the building and maintenance of giant stadiums such as Croke Park.

In Ireland, sports have a deep emotional connection as a heartfelt expression of Irish identity. There was a time when membership in the GAA was denied to anyone who also attended "foreign games," defined as rugby, soccer, or cricket. If the Brits played it, it was viewed as cultural poison. So intractable was this rule that in 1938, Douglas Hyde (then president of Ireland) was kicked out of the GAA for attending an international soccer match. (The rule was abolished in 1971 with the advent of TV sports.)

In 1921, during the War of Independence, IRA leader Michael Collins orchestrated the simultaneous assassination of a dozen British intelligence agents around Dublin in a single morning. The same day, the Black and Tans retaliated. These grizzled British WWI veterans, clad in black police coats and tan surplus army pants, had been sent to Ireland to stamp out the rebels. Knowing Croke Park would be full of Irish Nationalists, they entered the packed stadium during a Gaelic football match and fired into the stands, killing 13 spectators as well as a Tipperary player.

Today Croke Park's "Hill 16" grandstands are built on rubble dumped here after the 1916 Rising; it's literally sacred ground. And the Hogan stands are named after the murdered player from Tipperary. Queen Elizabeth II visited the stadium during her historic visit in 2011. Her warm interest in the stadium and in the institution of the GAA did much to heal old wounds.

Glasnevin Cemetery Museum

This is the final resting place for Ireland's most passionate patriots, writers, politicians, and assorted personalities. What Père Lachaise is to Paris, Glasnevin is to Dublin. Here you'll find the graves of Michael Collins, Charles Stewart Parnell, and teenage rebel/martyr Kevin Barry (of patriot song fame), surrounding a replica round tower atop the crypt of Daniel O'Connell. The cemetery's 120 leafy acres are surrounded by a tall wall and a half-dozen watchtowers used to deter grave robbers. Guided tours of the cemetery are fascinating to those who love Irish culture and history. A wall of memorials commemorate all who were lost during the struggle for Irish independence a hundred years ago, including civilians and British soldiers. The adjacent museum offers more detail—you'll dig the graveyard superstitions.

Cost and Hours: Cemetery-free, museum-€6.50, €13 includes tour; daily 10:00-18:00, 1.5-hour tours hourly from 10:30 to 15:30, more in summer; tel. 01/882-6550, www.glasnevinmuseum.ie.

Getting There: It's two miles north of the city center (get here on the hop-on, hop-off bus, or take buses #40 or #140 from O'Connell Street).

Shopping in Dublin

Shops are open roughly Monday-Saturday 9:00-18:00 and until 20:00 on Thursday. Hours are shorter on Sunday (if shops are open at all). Good shopping areas include:

• **Grafton Street,** with its neighboring streets and arcades (such as the fun Great George's Arcade between Great George's and Drury Streets), and nearby shopping centers (Powerscourt Townhouse and St. Stephen's Green). Francis Street creaks with antiques.

• **Henry Street,** home to Dublin's top department stores (pedestrian-only, off O'Connell Street).

• **Nassau Street,** lining Trinity College, with the popular Kilkenny Shop (Irish design) and lots of touristy stores.

• **Temple Bar,** worth a browse for art, jewelry, New Age paraphernalia, books, music (try Claddagh Records), and gift shops. On Saturdays, a couple of markets—one for food and another for books—set up shop. For details on this area, see page 76.

• **Millennium Walk,** a trendy lane stretching two blocks north from the River Liffey to Abbey Street. It's filled with hip restaurants, shops, and coffee bars. It's easy to miss—look for the south entry at the pedestrian Millennium Bridge, or the north entry at Jervis Street LUAS stop.

• **Street markets,** such as Moore Street (produce, noise, and lots of local color, Mon-Sat 8:00-18:00, closed Sun, near General Post Office), and St. Michan Street (food, Tue-Sat 7:00-15:00, closed Sun-Mon, behind Four Courts building).

Entertainment in Dublin

Ireland has produced some of the finest writers in the English and Irish languages, and Dublin houses some of Europe's best theaters. Though the city was the site of the first performance of Handel's *Messiah* (1742), these days Dublin is famous for the rock bands that have started here: U2, Thin Lizzy, Sinéad O'Connor, and Live Aid founder Bob Geldof's band the Boomtown Rats.

Theater

Abbey Theatre is Ireland's national theater, founded by W. B. Yeats in 1904 to preserve Irish culture during British rule (performances generally nightly at 20:00, Sat matinees at 14:30, 26 Lower Abbey Street, tel. 01/878-7222, www.abbeytheatre.ie). **Gate Theatre** does foreign plays as well as Irish classics (Cavendish Row, tel. 01/874-4045, www.gatetheatre.ie). The **Gaiety Theatre** offers a wide range of quality productions (King Street South, toll tel. 0818-719-388, www.gaietytheatre.ie). The **Bord Gáis Energy Theatre** is the newest and spiffiest venue (Grand Canal Square, tel. 01/677-7999, www.bordgaisenergytheatre.ie). Intimate little **Smock Alley Theatre** hides at the western fringe of Temple Bar, offering less mainstream performances on the site of Dublin's first theater (6 Lower Exchange Street, tel. 01/677-0014, www.smockalley.com). Street theater takes the stage in Temple Bar on summer evenings. Browse the listings and fliers at the TI.

Concerts

The **3 Arena**, sited on what was once a dock railway terminus (easy LUAS access), is now sponsored by a hip phone company. Residents call it by its geographic nickname: The Point. It's considered one of the country's top live-music venues (East Link Bridge, toll tel. 01/819-8888, http://3arena.ie).

At the **National Concert Hall**, the National Symphony Orchestra performs most Friday evenings (off St. Stephen's Green at Earlsfort Terrace, tel. 01/417-0077, www.nch.ie).

Pubs and Live Traditional Music

For guided pub crawls (focusing on either Irish literature or music), see page 45.

Temple Bar and Nearby

The Temple Bar area in particular thrives with music—traditional, jazz, and pop. Although it's pricier than the rest of Dublin and extremely touristy, it really is the best place in town to mix beer and music. For locations, see the "Dublin Restaurants" map on page 102.

Gogarty's Pub has foot-tapping sessions downstairs daily at 13:00 and upstairs nightly from 21:00 (at corner of Fleet and Anglesea, tel. 01/671-1822). Use this pub as a kickoff for your Temple Bar evening. It's also where the Traditional Irish Musical Pub Crawl starts (see page 45).

The **Palace Bar** is a well-preserved gin joint, with almost 135 years of history. It attracted Dublin's literary greats from the start, and contrasts sharply (and refreshingly) with the prefab offerings down the street in the Temple Bar mayhem (east end of Temple Bar, where Fleet Street hits Westmoreland Street at 21 Fleet Street, tel. 01/671-7388, www.thepalacebardublin.com).

Porterhouse has an inviting and varied menu, Dublin's best selection of microbrews, and live music. You won't find Guinness here, just tasty homebrews. Try one of their sampler trays (corner of Essex Street East and Parliament Street, tel. 01/671-5715, check music schedule at www.theporterhouse.ie).

Near Temple Bar: A 10-minute hike up the river west of Temple Bar takes you to two pubs with a local and less touristy ambience. **The Brazen Head,** which claims to be the oldest pub in Dublin, is a hit for an early dinner and late live music (nightly from 21:30), with atmospheric rooms and a courtyard perfect for balmy evenings. They also host great "Food, Folklore, and Fairies" storytelling dinner evenings (see page 107). **O'Shea's Merchant Pub,** just across the street, is encrusted in memories of County Kerry football heroes. It's filled with locals taking a break from the grind. There's live traditional music nightly at 21:30 (the front half is a restaurant, the magic is in the back—enter on Bridge Street, tel. 01/679-3797, www.themerchanttemplebar.com).

More Pub Action

In Smithfield: Hiding in a nondescript building at the top of Smithfield Square north of the River Liffey, the **Cobblestone Pub** offers Dublin's least glitzy and most rewarding traditional-music venue. The candlelit walls, covered with photos of honored trad musicians, set the tone. Music is revered here, as reflected in the understated sign: "Listening area, please respect musicians" (trad-music sessions Mon-Tue at 21:00, Wed-Sat at 19:00, Sun at 14:00; 100 yards from Old Jameson Distillery's brick chimney tower at 77 King Street North, tel. 01/872-1799, www.cobblestonepub.ie).

Southeast of St. Stephen's Green: Down the axis of Merrion Row and Lower Baggot Street, you'll find three venerable pubs filled with businessmen and staff from nearby governmental buildings blowing off steam. **O'Donoghue's** was famously the home pub of the Dubliners, for decades one of Ireland's premier traditional Irish music groups. The pub still offers nightly trad sessions (15 Merrion Row, tel. 01/660-7194). **Doheny & Nesbitt** is a photogenic choice, with wonderful woodwork and cozy conversational alcoves as well as great pub grub (5 Lower Baggot Street, tel. 01/676-2945). **Toner's** is another well-varnished choice—it's already celebrated its 200th anniversary. It has the added attraction of a large beer garden out back to enjoy on fine days (139 Lower Baggot Street, tel. 01/676-3090).

Near Trinity College: The **Dingle Whiskey Bar** boasts its namesake libation but also features 170 whiskeys from Ireland, Scotland, and North America. Tasting flights are available for novice to connoisseur palates (Mon-Thu 15:00-23:00, Fri-Sun 13:00-late, 45 Naussau Street, tel. 01/644-4180).

Sleeping in Dublin

Choosing the right neighborhood in Dublin is as important as choosing the right hotel. All of my recommended accommodations are in safe areas convenient to sightseeing.

Central Dublin is popular, loud, and expensive. You'll find big, practical, central places south of the river, near Christ Church Cathedral (on the edge of Temple Bar), Trinity College, and St. Stephen's Green. For classy, older Dublin accommodations in a quieter neighborhood, stay a bit farther out, southeast of St. Stephen's Green. North of the river are a few reliable options in an urban area well-served by LUAS streetcars. If you're on a tight budget, get a room in outlying Dun Laoghaire (page 114) or Howth (page 119), where rooms are cheaper—and quieter (both an easy 25-minute DART train ride into the city).

I rank accommodations from **$** budget to **$$$$** splurge. My recommendations include everything from €25 bunks to deluxe €270 doubles, though most of the hotels listed here cluster around €170. Prices are often discounted on weeknights (Mon-Thu) and from November through February. For some travelers, short-term, Airbnb-type rentals can be a good alternative; search for places in my recommended hotel neighborhoods.

Rooms can be tight. Book any accommodations well in advance, especially if you'll be traveling during peak season (June-

Dublin Accommodations

1 Jurys Inn Christ Church
2 Kinlay House
3 Four Courts Hostel
4 Trinity Lodge
5 Trinity College Accomm. Office
6 Brooks Hotel
7 Buswells Hotel
8 Albany House
9 Fitzwilliam Townhouse
10 Avalon House Hostel
11 Launderettes (2)
12 To Bike Rental

August), weekends any time of year (particularly during rugby weekends), or if your trip coincides with a major holiday or festival (see the appendix). On Sundays in September, fans converge on Dublin from all over the country for the all-Ireland finals in Gaelic football and hurling.

To get the best deal, contact my family-run hotels directly by phone or email. By going direct, the owner avoids a roughly 20 percent commission and may be able to offer you a discount. For more information and tips on hotel rates and deals, making reservations, and finding a short-term rental, see page 534.

SOUTH OF THE RIVER LIFFEY
Near Christ Church Cathedral

These lodging options cluster near Christ Church Cathedral, a 5-minute walk from the rowdy and noisy evening scene (at Temple

Bar), and 10 minutes from the sightseeing center (Trinity College and Grafton Street). The cheap hostels in this neighborhood have some double rooms. If your hotel charges extra for a full Irish breakfast, you can eat for less at the many small cafés nearby; try the Queen of Tarts or Chorus Café (see listings under "Eating in Dublin," later).

$$$$ Jurys Inn Christ Church is central and offers business-class comfort in 182 identical rooms. This no-nonsense, American-style hotel chain has a winning keep-it-simple-and-affordable formula. If "ye olde" is getting old—and you don't mind big tour groups—this is a good option. Request a room far from the noisy elevator (breakfast extra, book long in advance for weekends, pay parking, Christ Church Place, tel. 01/454-0000, US tel. 800-423-6953, www.jurysinns.com, jurysinnchristchurch@jurysinns.com).

¢ Kinlay House is the backpackers' choice—definitely the place to go for cheap beds, a central location, and an all-ages-welcome atmosphere. This huge, red-brick, 19th-century Victorian building has 200 metal, prison-style beds in spartan rooms. It fills up most days—reserve well in advance, especially for summer weekends (private and family rooms available, includes continental breakfast, travel desk, kitchen, lots of stairs, Christ Church, 2 Lord Edward Street, tel. 01/679-6644, www.kinlaydublin.ie, info@kinlaydublin.ie).

¢ **Four Courts Hostel** is a 234-bed hostel well-located immediately across the river from the Four Courts. It's within a five-minute walk of Christ Church Cathedral and Temple Bar. Bare and institutional, it's also spacious and well-run, with a focus on security and efficiency (private rooms available, elevator, game room, some pay parking, 15 Merchant's Quay, from Connolly Station or Busáras Bus Station take LUAS to Four Courts stop and cross river via Father Matthew Bridge, tel. 01/672-5839, www.fourcourtshostel.com, info@fourcourtshostel.com).

Trinity College Area

You can't get more central than Trinity College; these listings offer a good value for the money.

$$$$ Trinity Lodge offers fine, quiet lodging in 26 rooms split between two Georgian townhouses on either side of South Frederick Street, just south of Trinity College (12 South Frederick Street, tel. 01/617-0900, www.trinitylodge.com, trinitylodge@eircom.net).

$$ Trinity College turns its 800 student-housing dorm rooms on campus into no-frills, affordable accommodations in the city center each summer. Look for the Accommodations Office (open Mon-Fri 8:00-18:00) through the door on the right before you come into the courtyard (rooms available late-May-mid-Sept, some en suite rooms but most with shared bath, breakfast extra, tel. 01/896-1177, www.tcd.ie/accommodation/visitors, reservations@tcd.ie).

Near St. Stephen's Green

$$$$ Brooks Hotel is a fine choice for great service, tending 98 plush rooms in an ideal central location. This splurge rarely disappoints (Drury Street, tel. 01/670-4000, www.brookshotel.ie, reservations@brookshotel.ie).

$$$$ Buswells Hotel, one of the city's oldest, is a pleasant Georgian-style haven with 67 rooms in the heart of the city (breakfast extra, between Trinity College and St. Stephen's Green at 23 Molesworth Street, tel. 01/614-6500, www.buswells.ie, info@buswells.ie).

$$$ Albany House's 50 good-value rooms come with high

Southeast Dublin

Accommodations
1. Number 31
2. The Schoolhouse Hotel
3. Mespil Hotel
4. Roxford Lodge Hotel
5. Waterloo House

Eateries & Pubs
6. Bloom Brasserie & Wine Bar;
   Zakura Izakaya
7. Searsons Pub & Langkawi
8. La Peniche Dinner Barge
9. O'Donoghue's; Doheny & Nesbitt;
   Toner's

DUBLIN

ceilings, Georgian ambience, and some stairs. Ask for a quieter room in back, away from streetcar noise (just one block south of St. Stephen's Green at 84 Harcourt Street, tel. 01/475-1092, www.albanyhousedublin.com, info@albanyhousedublin.com).

$$$ Fitzwilliam Townhouse rents 14 basic rooms in a Georgian townhouse near St. Stephen's Green (family rooms, breakfast extra, 41 Upper Fitzwilliam Street, tel. 01/662-5155, www.fitzwilliamtownhouse.com, info@fitzwilliamtownhouse.com).

¢ Avalon House Hostel, near Grafton Street, rents simple, clean backpacker beds (private rooms available, includes continental breakfast, elevator, a few minutes off Grafton Street at 55 Aungier Street, tel. 01/475-0001, www.avalon-house.ie, info@avalon-house.ie).

Away from the Center, Southeast of St. Stephen's Green

The Grand Canal, Dublin's urban waterway, sports a lovely narrow greenbelt of trees and lily pads that's ideal for a pleasant stroll or jog. This neighborhood—stretching roughly east-west from Leeson Street to Grand Canal Street—is a perfect compromise between busy central lodging options and more sedate choices that are farther out. These listings are unique places (except for the business-class Mespil Hotel), and they charge accordingly. If you're going to break the bank, do it here.

$$$$ Number 31 is a hidden gem reached via gritty little Leeson Close (a lane off Lower Leeson Street). Ask Noel about the VIPs who attended dinner parties here 50 years ago. Its understated elegance is top-notch, with six rooms in a former coach house and 15 rooms in an adjacent Georgian house; the two buildings are connected by a quiet little garden. Guests appreciate the special touches (such as a sunken living room with occasional peat fires) and tasty breakfasts served in a classy glass atrium (family rooms, free parking, 31 Leeson Close, tel. 01/676-5011, www.number31. ie, info@number31.ie).

$$$$ The **Schoolhouse Hotel** taught as many as 300 students in its heyday (1861-1969) and was in the middle of the street fight that was the 1916 Easter Rising. Now it's a serene hideout with 31 pristine rooms and a fine restaurant (breakfast extra, book early, 2 Northumberland Road, tel. 01/667-5014, www.schoolhousehotel. com, reservations@schoolhousehotel.com).

$$$ Mespil Hotel is a huge, modern, business-class hotel renting 254 identical three-star rooms at a good price with all the comforts. This place is a cut above Jurys Inn (breakfast extra, elevator; small first-come, first-served free parking; 10-minute walk southeast of St. Stephen's Green or take bus #37, #38, #39, or #46A; 50 Mespil Road, tel. 01/488-4600, www.mespilhotel.com, mespil@leehotels.com).

$$$ Roxford Lodge Hotel is well managed and a great value. In a quiet residential neighborhood a 20-minute walk from Trinity College, it has 24 tastefully decorated rooms awash with Jacuzzis and saunas. The executive suite is honeymoon-worthy (family rooms, breakfast extra, elevator, parking, 46 Northumberland Road, tel. 01/668-8572, www.roxfordlodge.ie, reservations@ roxfordlodge.ie).

$$$ Waterloo House sits proudly Georgian on a quiet residential street with 19 comfortable and relaxing rooms and a pleasant back garden (family rooms, parking, 8 Waterloo Road, tel. 01/660-1888, www.waterloohouse.ie, info@waterloohouse.ie).

NORTH OF THE RIVER LIFFEY
Near Parnell Square
A swanky neighborhood 250 years ago, this is now workaday Dublin with a steady urban hum, made accessible by LUAS streetcars. To locate these hotels, see the map on page 80.

$$$$ The **Castle Hotel** is a formerly grand but still comfortable Georgian establishment embedded in the urban canyons of

North Dublin. A half-block east of the Garden of Remembrance, it's a good value with pleasant rooms and the friendly Castle Vaults pub with live music in its basement (Great Denmark Street, tel. 01/874-6949, www.castle-hotel.ie, info@castle-hotel.ie).

$$$$ Jurys Inn Parnell Street has 253 predictably soulless but modern rooms. It's a block from the north end of O'Connell Street and the cluster of museums on Parnell Square (breakfast extra, tel. 01/878-4900, www.jurysinns.com, jurysinnparnellst@jurysinns.com).

$$$$ Belvedere Hotel has 92 plain-vanilla rooms that are short on character but long on dependable, modern comforts (Great Denmark Street, tel. 01/873-7700, www.belvederehotel.ie, reservations@belvederehotel.ie).

$$$ Charles Stewart Guesthouse, big and basic, offers 60 acceptable rooms in a good location for a fair price (family rooms, breakfast extra, ask for a quieter room in the back, just beyond top end of O'Connell Street at 5 Parnell Square East, tel. 01/878-0350, www.charlesstewart.ie, info@charlesstewart.ie).

Eating in Dublin

It's easy to find fine, creative eateries all over town. While you can get decent pub grub for under €20 on just about any corner, consider saving that for the countryside. There's just no pressing reason to eat Irish in cosmopolitan Dublin. In fact, going local these days is the same as going ethnic. The city's good restaurants are packed from 19:00 on, especially on weekends. Eating early (17:30-19:00) saves time and money, as many better places offer an early-bird special. Most restaurants serve free jugs of ice water with a smile.

I rank restaurants from **$** budget to **$$$$** splurge. For general advice on eating in Ireland, including typical dishes, breakfasts, picnicking, tipping, pub grub, and beer, see the "Eating" section of the Practicalities chapter.

FAST, EASY, AND CHEAP IN THE CENTER
Near Grafton Street
$$ Cornucopia is a small, earth-mama-with-class, proudly vegetarian, self-serve place two blocks off Grafton. It's friendly and youthful, with hearty lunches and dinner specials (daily generally until 21:00, 19 Wicklow Street, tel. 01/677-7583).

$$$ The Farm is a hardworking and practical place with a passion for fresh, organic, free-range fare that's affordable and tasty. Lunch and early-bird specials are a smart value (good vegetarian options, Wed-Sat 12:00-23:00, Sun-Tue until 22:00, half-block south of Trinity College at 3 Dawson Street, tel. 01/671-8654).

$$ The Hairy Lemon has a weird name, but its friendly staff,

Dublin Restaurants

1. Cornucopia
2. The Farm
3. The Hairy Lemon Pub
4. O'Neill's Pub
5. Avoca Café & Sandwich Counter
6. The Duke Pub
7. Davy Byrnes Pub
8. Wagamama & Dunnes Grocery
9. Yamamori
10. Silk Road Café
11. Queen of Tarts
12. Chorus Café
13. Leo Burdock
14. Spar Market
15. Fallon & Byrne Food Hall; Boulevard Café
16. Dunnes Grocery
17. Marks & Spencer

central location, and fun and creative menu keep me coming back. Hearty eaters will love their famous stew-like Dublin Coddle. Dine in the pub zone or in the brighter annex. Part of the movie *The Commitments* (1991) was filmed here (daily 11:30-22:00, 41 Lower Stephen Street, tel. 01/671-8949).

$$ O'Neill's Pub is a venerable, multilevel, dark, and tangled retreat offering good grub, including inexpensive breakfasts and

⑱ Trocadero	㉗ Gogarty's Pub
⑲ Eden Bar & Grill	㉘ Palace Bar
⑳ The Bank	㉙ Porterhouse
㉑ Gallagher's Boxty House	㉚ O'Shea's Merchant Pub
㉒ Luigi Malone's	㉛ Dingle Whiskey Bar
㉓ The Shack	㉜ Arlington Hotel (Celtic Show)
㉔ Bad Ass Café	㉝ The Shelbourne Hotel
㉕ To Grand Canal Eateries	(Afternoon Tea)
㉖ The Brazen Head Pub	

dependable carvery lunches (daily 12:00-22:30, Suffolk Street, tel. 01/679-3656).

$$ Avoca Café, on the second floor above the Avoca department store, is a cheap and cheery eatery with healthy foodie plates, great salads, and an enthusiastic local following (Mon-Sat 9:30-17:30, Sun from 11:00, 11 Suffolk Street, tel. 01/672-6019). In the store basement, the **$ Avoca Sandwich Counter** has simple seating and a cheap buffet counter that sells food priced by weight. They also offer deli sandwiches and enticing baked goodies (great for takeaway, daily generally 10:00-18:00).

$$ The Duke and **Davy Byrnes,** neighbors on Duke Street, serve reliable pub lunches. Davy Byrnes (at #21, tel. 01/677-5217) feels like pub-meets-diner, and The Duke (at #9, tel. 01/679-9553) has a buffet counter in the back from 12:00 to 16:00. Both are favorites for Irish lit fans whose heroes frequented them (James Joyce, Brendan Behan, and Patrick Kavanagh). Davy Byrnes is where Leopold Bloom ate his gorgonzola cheese sandwich in *Ulysses*.

$$ Wagamama is a pan-Asian slurp-a-thon with great and healthy noodle and rice dishes served at long communal tables by energetic waiters (daily 12:00-22:00, South King Street underneath St. Stephen's Green Shopping Centre, tel. 01/417-1878).

$$ Yamamori is a plain, mellow, and modern Japanese place serving seas of sushi and noodles (daily 12:00-22:30, 71 South Great George's Street, tel. 01/475-5001).

Near Christ Church Cathedral

$ The Silk Road Café at the Chester Beatty Library serves a delightful selection of Middle Eastern and Mediterranean cuisine (in keeping with the theme of the library's collections). The dishes are always fresh, with a good variety of soups, *panini*, falafel, and vegetarian options (Mon-Fri 10:00-16:45, Sat from 11:00, Sun from 12:00, on the grounds of Dublin Castle, tel. 01/407-0770). While you're there, be sure to pop into the amazing (free) library (see listing in "Sights in Dublin").

$ Queen of Tarts, with nice outdoor seating, does yummy breakfasts, light lunches, sandwiches, and wonderful pastries (Mon-Fri 8:00-19:00, Sat-Sun from 9:00, just off Dame Street, go 100 yards up from City Hall and left on Cow's Lane, tel. 01/670-7499).

$ Chorus Café is a friendly and plain little hole-in-the-wall diner serving salads, *panini*, and pastas (daily 8:30-17:00, 7 Fishamble Street, next door to the site of the first performance of Handel's *Messiah*, tel. 01/616-7088, Cyrus).

$ Leo Burdock has been serving authentic fish-and-chips, in large splittable portions, for more than a hundred years. You'll find it around the corner from Jurys Inn—just follow the line of Dubliners waiting for their haddock (daily 12:00-23:30, no seating—takeaway only, 2 Werburgh Street, tel. 01/454-0306).

Delis and Groceries

Grocery Delis with Seating: If you want to eat fast, cheap, and healthy in the tourist center, two high-end groceries offer fresh sandwiches and a salad bar, and a place to sit while you eat. The **Spar** market (corner of Dame Street and South Great George's

Street; more branches throughout the city) is open 24/7 and has huge windows overlooking the Dame Street action. The very proper **Fallon & Byrne Food Hall** is like eating at an upscale Trader Joe's (Mon-Sat 8:00-21:00, Sun until 19:00, 11 Exchequer Street).

Supermarkets: Many of Dublin's grocery stores sell cheap salads, microwaved meat pies, and made-to-order sandwiches. **Dunnes,** at 11 South Great George's Street, is your one-stop shop for assembling a picnic meal (Mon-Sat 8:30-19:00, Sun from 11:00). They have another outlet in the basement of St. Stephen's Green Shopping Centre. **Marks & Spencer** department store has a fancy grocery store in the basement, with fine takeaway sandwiches and salads (daily 8:00-20:00, 20 Grafton Street). **Centra** markets, some open 24 hours, are spread all over Dublin.

HIP AND FUN IN NORTH DUBLIN

The Church is a trendy café/bar/restaurant/nightclub/beer garden housed in the former St. Mary's Church. In its former life as a church, it hosted the baptism of Irish rebel Wolfe Tone and the marriage of brewing legend Arthur Guinness. The **$$$ choir balcony** has a huge pipe organ and a refined menu (daily 17:00-22:30). The ground floor **$$ nave** is dominated by a long bar and pub grub (daily 12:00-21:00). A disco thumps away in the bunker-like basement. On warm summer nights, the outdoor terrace is packed. Eating here is as much about the scene as the cuisine (reservations smart Fri and Sat nights, corner of St. Mary's and Jervis Streets, tel. 01/828-0102, www.thechurch.ie).

$$$ Mr Fox is an elegant and serene little basement operation serving locally sourced dishes created by chef Anthony Smith (Tue-Fri 12:00-14:00 & 17:00-21:30, Sat 17:30-22:00, closed Sun-Mon; behind the Garden of Remembrance at 38 Parnell Square West, see map on page 80, tel. 01/874-7778, www.mrfox.ie).

$$ Brannigan's is an inviting and family-run traditional pub—it's been a "beer emporium since 1909." They offer a non-touristy lunch buffet (Mon-Fri 12:00-15:00), and it's convenient for theatergoers—located roughly halfway between the Gate and Abbey theaters (daily 10:30-23:30, 9 Cathedral Street, just off O'Connell Street 50 yards from the Spire—see map on page 80, tel. 01/874-0137).

CLASSY DINING SOUTH OF TEMPLE BAR

These stylish restaurants serve well-presented food at fair prices. They're located within a block of each other, just south of Temple Bar and Dame Street, near the main TI.

$$$$ Trocadero serves beefy European cuisine to Dubliners interested in a slow, romantic meal. The dressy, red-velvet interior is draped with photos of local actors. Come early or make a reservation—it's a favorite with theatergoers (Mon-Sat 17:00-23:30, closed Sun, 4 St. Andrew Street, tel. 01/677-5545, www.trocadero. ie). The three-course pretheater special is a fine value at €27 (17:00-19:00, leave by 19:45, Robert).

$$$ Eden Bar & Grill lurks on funky William Street with a varied menu from monkfish to pizza, highlighted by especially creative lamb dishes (daily 12:00-16:00 & 17:30-22:00, 7 South William Street, tel. 01/670-6887).

$$$ Boulevard Café is mod, trendy, and likeable, dishing up Mediterranean cuisine that's heavy on the Italian. It's smart to reserve for dinner (Mon-Sat 12:00-22:00, Sun 12:30-20:00, 27 Exchequer Street, tel. 01/679-2131, www.boulevardcafe.ie).

$$$ The Bank wows visitors with its grand Victorian bank-lobby ambience, lit by an arched Tiffany skylight. You'll find great food—the mussel and oyster starters are a hit—in a central location (daily 11:00-23:30, 20 College Green, tel. 01/677-0677).

IN TEMPLE BAR

$$ Gallagher's Boxty House is touristy and traditional—a good, basic value with creaky floorboards and old Dublin ambience. They serve stews and corned beef, but the specialty is boxty, the generally bland-tasting Irish potato pancake filled and rolled with various meats, veggies, and sauces (Mon-Fri 12:00-22:00, Sat-Sun from 11:00, reservations wise, 20 Temple Bar, tel. 01/677-2762, www. boxtyhouse.ie).

$$ Luigi Malone's, with its fun atmosphere and varied menu of pizza, ribs, pasta, sandwiches, and fajitas, is just the place to take your high-school date (Mon-Sat 12:00-22:00, Sun 13:00-21:30, corner of Cecilia and Fownes streets, tel. 01/679-2723).

$$$ The Shack, while touristy, has a reputation for good quality. It serves traditional Irish, chicken, seafood, and steak dishes (daily 12:00-22:00, in the center of Temple Bar, 24 East Essex Street, tel. 01/679-0043).

$$ The **Bad Ass Café** serves pizza, pasta, burgers, and salads that are cheap by Temple Bar standards. There's even a fun kids' menu. Their big patio fronts the Temple Bar action, and there's live music nightly in the dark, sprawling, pubby interior (daily 12:00-22:00, 9 Crown Alley, tel. 01/675-3005).

NEAR THE GRAND CANAL

These places are within a long block of one other in the emerging Grand Canal neighborhood—an area southeast of St. Stephen's Green that's (as yet) undiscovered by the tourist crowds. You'll find them just over the Grand Canal about a 20-minute walk from the center (near the intersection of Baggot Street and Mespil Road).

$$$ Bloom Brasserie & Wine Bar has a woody, candlelit ambience with beautifully presented dishes based on locally sourced meats (beef, lamb, duck) and seafood (Irish salmon). The modern menu changes with the seasons (Mon-Sat 12:00-14:30 & 17:00-22:30, closed Sun, 11 Upper Baggot Street, tel. 01/668-7170).

$$ Searsons Pub, a sprawling neighborhood favorite, is a gastropub with an open kitchen, a classy-for-a-sports-bar energy, and friendly service. If there's a horse race or rugby match on, it'll be on the screens here (it's located near the rugby stadium and a betting office). You can escape the clamor out back on the patio (daily 12:00-23:30, 42 Upper Baggot Street, tel. 01/660-0330).

$$ Zakura Izakaya is a classy-if-noisy Japanese place—small and tight, like a sushi wine-bar (daily 12:00-22:00, 7 Upper Baggot Street, tel. 01/563-8000).

$$ Langkawi is a cozy, traditional family operation serving Malaysian fusion food, with spicy Indian influences and rice-based Chinese favorites (daily 12:30-14:00 & 18:00-23:30, 46 Upper Baggot Street, tel. 01/668-2760).

$$$$ La Peniche is a floating barge sailing relaxed diners slowly up the leafy Grand Canal on twice-evening departures. Their French-inspired dishes, served in a novel nautical setting, are unique among Dublin dining experiences. While the seating is tight, it's a romantic meal. The boat moves very slowly—just a couple of hundred yards—and if it's dark, there's no real view (daily at 18:00 and 21:00, reservations smart, Grand Canal Jetty, mobile 087-790-0077, www.lapeniche.ie).

DINNER WITH ENTERTAINMENT

$$$$ The Brazen Head hosts "Food, Folklore and Fairies" evenings, which are more culturally highbrow than the title might suggest, while still remaining fun. Even at €48, the evening is a great value. You get a hearty, three-course meal that's punctuated by soulful Irish history and fascinating Irish mythology, delivered by an engaging local folklorist, with occasional live trad tunes in-between (daily 19:00-22:00, Jan-Feb Thu and Sat only; reservations smart; by south end of Father Matthew Bridge, 2 blocks west of Christ Church Cathedral at 20 Bridge Street; pub tel. 01/677-9549, show tel. 01/218-8555, www.irishfolktours.com).

$$$$ The **Musical Pub Crawl Dinner Show** is a handy intro to Irish traditional music and dancing. Two accomplished musicians take time between tunes to humorously point out what makes this music uniquely Irish—it's a great primer. Then you'll move on to dinner with Irish dancing as part of the entertainment (€43, May-Sept daily at 18:00, meet at Oliver St. John's Gogarty's on Fleet Street in Temple Bar, tel. 01/475-8345, www.musicalpubcrawl.com).

$$$ Celtic Nights combines traditional music and dancing into a big-stage, high-energy, family-friendly, Irish variety show. This touristy dinner act hits all the clichés, from *Riverdance*-style choreography to fun fiddling and comedic *craic*. It comes with a traditional three-course dinner and lots of audience participation (€35, €15 for children under 12, nightly show at 20:30, downtown by the O'Connell Bridge at the Arlington Hotel, 23 Bachelors Walk, tel. 01/687-5200, www.celticnights.com).

AFTERNOON TEA

$$$$ **The Shelbourne Hotel** has been a Dublin landmark since 1824, built to attract genteel patrons and Dublin's upper-crust socialites (not to mention British Army snipers during the 1916 Easter Rising). But schlubs like us can dip our toes in the aristocratic fantasy by enjoying the tradition of afternoon tea (no shorts, tank tops, or T-shirts). The menu is a swirl of finger sandwiches, buttermilk scones, clotted cream, strawberry jam, ginger loaf, and fine coffee...as well as 22 varieties of tea. You'll find it in the ground floor Lord Mayor's Lounge (seatings Mon-Thu at 13:00, 15:15, and 17:30; Fri-Sun at 11:45, 14:00, 16:15, and 18:30; reservations smart, especially on weekends; 27 St. Stephen's Green, tel. 01/663-4500).

Dublin Connections

BY PLANE

Dublin Airport has two terminals located an easily walkable 150 yards apart (airport code: DUB, tel. 01/814-1111, www.dublinairport.ie). Both have ATMs, cafés, Wi-Fi, and luggage storage (www.leftluggage.ie). There is no TI at the airport.

Getting Downtown by Bus: You have two main choices—Airlink (double-decker turquoise bus) or Aircoach (single-deck blue bus). Both pick up on the street directly in front of arrivals, at ground level at both terminals.

Airlink Express: Airlink bus #747 generally runs an east-west route that parallels the River Liffey, and includes stops at the Busáras Central Bus Station, Connolly Station, O'Connell Street, Temple Bar, Christ Church, and Heuston Station. Airlink bus #757 links the airport to the center along a generally north-south axis, including Trinity College, St. Stephen's Green (eastern end), and the National Concert Hall. Ask the driver which stop is closest to your hotel (€7, pay driver, 3-5/hour, about 40 minutes; runs Mon-Sat 5:00-late, Sun from 7:25; tel. 01/873-4222, www.dublinbus.ie). This bus is covered by the Leap Visitor and the Do Dublin transit cards; both cards can be purchased at the airport (see page 43).

Aircoach: This bus generally runs a north-south route that follows the O'Connell and Grafton streets axis. To reach recommended hotels south of the city center, the Aircoach bus #700 works well (€8 if paying driver, discount if booked online, covered by Dublin Pass, 4/hour, fewer late-night, runs 24 hours, tel. 01/844-7118, www.aircoach.ie).

By Taxi: Taxis from the airport into Dublin cost about €30 (see page 44).

Sleeping at the Airport: A safe bet is the **$$$ Radisson Blu Dublin Airport** (tel. 01/844-6000, www.radissonblu.ie).

BY TRAIN OR BUS

The frequencies listed below are for Monday-Saturday. Trains and buses generally run less frequently on Sundays.

By Train from Dublin's Heuston Station to: Tralee (every two hours, most change in Mallow but one direct evening train, 4 hours), **Ennis** (11/day, 3-4 hours, change in Limerick, Limerick Junction, or Athenry), **Galway** (8/day, 3 hours), **Westport** (5/day, 3 hours). Irish Rail train info: Toll tel. 1850-366-222, www.irishrail. ie.

By Train from Dublin's Connolly Station to: Rosslare (3-4/ day, 3 hours), **Portrush** (7/day, 5 hours, transfer in Belfast or Coleraine). The **Dublin-Belfast train** connects the capitals in two hours at 90 mph (8/day Mon-Sat, 5/day Sun). Northern Ireland train info: Tel. 048/9089-9400, www.translink.co.uk.

By Bus to: Belfast (hourly, most via Dublin Airport, 3 hours), **Trim** (almost hourly, 1 hour), **Ennis** (almost hourly, 5 hours), **Galway** (hourly, 3.5 hours; faster on CityLink—hourly, 2.5 hours, tel. 091/564-164, www.citylink.ie), **Westport** (6/day, 5 hours), **Limerick** (7/day, 3.5 hours), **Tralee** (7/day, 6 hours), **Dingle** (4/day, 8.5 hours, transfer at Limerick and Tralee). Bus info: Toll tel. 1850-836-611, www.buseireann.ie.

BY CAR

It's best to avoid driving in hectic Dublin. If you plan to drive in Ireland, save your car rental for the countryside. Consider renting a car at the airport, where you'll find all the standard car-rental agencies with longer hours and easier access to the M-50.

M-50 Toll Road: Drivers renting a car at Dublin Airport and heading for the countryside can bypass the worst of the big-city traffic by taking the M-50 ring road south or west. The M-50 uses an automatic tolling system called eFlow. Your rental should come with an eFlow tag installed; confirm this when you pick up your car. The €3.10 toll per trip is automatically debited from the credit card with which you rented the car (for pass details, see www. eflow.ie).

Other Toll Roads: Your rental car's eFlow tag will work only for the M-50 ring road around Dublin. On any other Irish toll roads, you'll have to pay with cash (about €2/toll). These roads mostly run outward from Dublin toward Waterford, Cork, Limerick, and Galway (roads farther west are free).

CONNECTING IRELAND AND BRITAIN

It's worth spending a few minutes researching your transportation options across the Irish Sea. Most airline and ferry companies routinely offer online discounts. Before sorting out rail/ferry prices with individual companies, try www.arrivatrainswales.co.uk/sailrail, which deals with several companies and has fares low enough to compete with cheap airlines. Ferries work for rural Wales or Scotland; for everywhere else, fly.

Flights: If you're going directly to London, flying is your best bet. Ryanair and Aer Lingus are the predominant discount carriers, but note that their London-bound flights often land at Luton or Stansted—airports some distance from the city center. If you need to get to Heathrow, try British Airways; some Aer Lingus flights land there, too.

Ferries: Irish Ferries and Stena Line combine to make eight daily crossings between Dublin Port (two miles east of O'Connell Bridge) and Holyhead, Wales. Most trips take 3.5 hours (€39), but Irish Ferries offers a twice-daily fast boat that makes the trip in 2 hours (€44). You must board at least 30 minutes before the scheduled sailing time. Since these boats can fill up on summer weekends, book at least a week ahead during the peak period.

Irish Ferries depart at 2:40, 11:50, 14:10, and 17:15 (Dublin tel. 0818-300-400, UK tel. 08717-300-400, www.irishferries.com); Stena Line sails at 2:15, 8:20, 15:10, and 20:40 (Dublin tel. 01/907-5555, UK tel. 08447-707-070, www.stenaline.ie).

Dublin Bay

Dangling from opposite ends of Dublin Bay's crescent-shaped shoreline, Dun Laoghaire (dun LEERY) and Howth (rhymes with "growth") are two peas in a pod. They offer quiet, cheaper lodging alternatives to Dublin and have easy light-rail access to the city center, just a 25-minute ride away. Dun Laoghaire is bigger and has more going on, while Howth has a sleepier vibe and a fishing fleet.

Dun Laoghaire

Dun Laoghaire is seven miles south of Dublin. This snoozy suburb, with easy connections to downtown Dublin, is a convenient small-town base for exploring the big city.

The Dun Laoghaire harbor was strategic enough to merit a line of martello towers, built in 1804 to defend against an expected Napoleonic invasion (one tower now houses the James Joyce Museum). By the mid-19th century, massive breakwaters were completed to protect the huge harbor. Ships sailed regularly from here to Wales (75 miles away), and the first train line in Ireland connected the terminal with Dublin. Since the ferries left, Dun Laoghaire has gotten quieter, and it no longer has a TI.

GETTING TO DUN LAOGHAIRE

The DART commuter train connects to Dublin in 25 minutes (4/hour, runs daily until about 23:30, €3.25 one-way, €6.15 round-trips are good same day only, www.irishrail.ie). If you're coming from Dublin, catch a DART train marked *Bray* or *Greystones* and get off at the Sandycove/Glasthule or Dun Laoghaire stop, depending on your B&B's location. If you're leaving Dun Laoghaire, catch a train marked *Howth* to get to Dublin. Get off at the central Tara Street Station to sightsee in Dublin, or, for train connections north, ride one stop farther to Connolly Station.

Aircoach bus #703 makes it easy to connect Dun Laoghaire and Dublin Airport. To return to the airport from Dun Laoghaire, catch the bus by the Pavilion Theatre on Marine Road or at the front steps of the Royal Marine Hotel (€10, runs hourly, 50 minutes, tel. 01/844-7118, www.aircoach.ie).

With the DART and Aircoach options, taking a taxi is like throwing money away. But if you really need one, try ABC Taxi service (about €30 to Dublin, €40 to the airport, tel. 01/285-5444).

Dun Laoghaire is ideal for those who want to leave their cars and sightsee Dublin by DART, as parking is cheap and sometimes free (pay-and-display parking enforced Mon-Sat 8:00-19:00, €1.50/hour, 3-hour maximum, free on Sun).

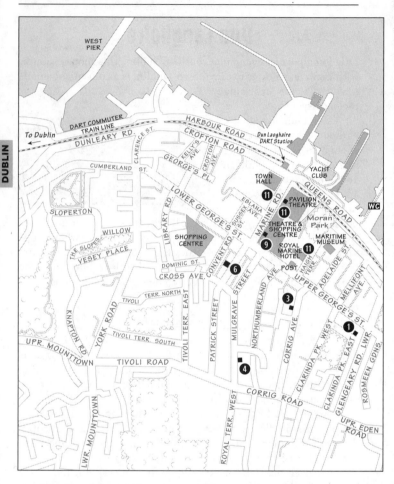

Orientation to Dun Laoghaire

Once a busy transportation hub, Dun Laoghaire has a coastline defined by its nearly mile-long breakwaters—reaching like two muscular arms into the Irish Sea. The breakwaters are popular for strollers, bikers, bird-watchers, and fishermen.

Helpful Hints: For **laundry,** try Q-Clean, located in the village of Glasthule, a five-minute downhill walk from Sandycove/Glasthule DART station (full-service only, Mon-Sat 9:00-18:00, closed Sun, 34 Glasthule Road, tel. 01/230-1120). For the **best views,** hike out to the lighthouse (at the end of the East Pier) or climb the tight stairs to the top of the James Joyce Tower and Museum.

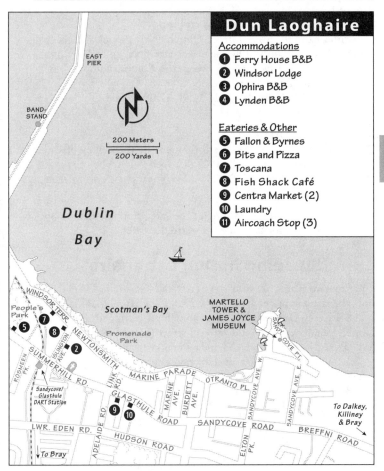

DUBLIN

Sights in Dun Laoghaire

James Joyce Tower and Museum

This squat martello tower at Sandycove was originally built to repel a possible Napoleonic invasion, but it became famous chiefly because of its association with James Joyce. The great author lived here briefly and made it the setting for the opening of his novel *Ulysses*. The museum's round exhibition space is filled with literary memorabilia, including photographs and rare first editions. For a fine view, climb the claustrophobic, two-story spiral stairwell sealed inside the thick wall to reach the rooftop gun mount.

Cost and Hours: Free, daily 10:00-18:00, Nov-Feb until 16:00; the museum is run by volunteers—call ahead to be sure it's open, tel. 01/280-9265, www.joycetower.ie.

National Maritime Museum of Ireland

Maritime exhibits fill a former church with model steamships, brass fittings, accounts of heroic rescue attempts, and a huge lighthouse optic (lamp lens, installed where the altar once stood). Landlubbers may find it underwhelming.

Cost and Hours: €6, daily 11:00-17:00, Haigh Terrace, tel. 01/214-3964, www.mariner.ie.

Plays and Concerts

The Pavilion Theatre offers performances in the center of town (box office open Mon-Sat 12:00-17:00, open 2 hours before performances, Marine Road, tel. 01/231-2929, www.paviliontheatre.ie).

Swimming

Kids of all ages enjoy swimming at the safe, sandy little cove bordered by rounded rocks beside the martello tower.

Sleeping in Dun Laoghaire

The first two places are near the Sandycove/Glasthule DART Station; the last two places are near the Dun Laoghaire DART Station.

$$ Ferry House B&B, with four high-ceilinged rooms, is a family-friendly place on a dead-end street (family room, 15 Clarinda Park North just off Clarinda Park West, tel. 01/280-8301, mobile 087-267-0511, www.ferryhousedublin.ie, ferry_house@hotmail.com, Eamon and Pauline Teehan).

$ Windsor Lodge rents four fresh, inviting rooms on a quiet street a block off the harbor and a block from the DART station (cash only, 3 Islington Avenue, tel. 01/284-6952, mobile 086-844-6646, www.windsorlodge.ie, windsorlodgedublin@gmail.com, Mary O'Farrell).

$ Ophira B&B is a historic house with four comfortably creaky rooms run by active diver-hiker-biker John O'Connor and his wife, Cathy (family room, parking, 10 Corrig Avenue, tel. 01/280-0997, www.ophira.ie, johnandcathy@ophira.ie).

$ Lynden B&B, with a classy 180-year-old interior hiding behind a somber front, rents four big rooms (cash only, cheaper rooms with shared bath, go past Mulgrave Street to 2 Mulgrave Terrace, tel. 01/280-6404, www.lyndenbandb.com, mariatgavin@gmail.com, Maria Gavin).

Eating in Dun Laoghaire

George's Street—Dun Laoghaire's main drag, three blocks inland—has plenty of reasonably priced eateries and pubs, many with live music.

DUBLIN

$$ Fallon & Byrnes is your best bet for fine wine and good food in a lovely glassed-in space beside the pleasant People's Park (daily 12:00-21:00, Summerhill Road, tel. 01/230-3300).

$$ Bits and Pizza is kid-friendly and a good bet for families (daily 12:00-22:00, off George's Street at 15 Patrick Street, tel. 01/284-2411).

$$ Toscana, on the seafront, is a popular little cubbyhole, serving hearty Italian dishes and pizza. Its location makes it easy to incorporate into your evening stroll. Reserve for dinner (early-bird specials before 18:30, daily 12:00-22:00, 5 Windsor Terrace, tel. 01/230-0890, http://toscana.ie).

$$ Fish Shack Café, on the stroll-worthy waterfront, serves fresh fish dishes to beachcombers (daily 12:00-22:00, takeout available, 1 Martello Terrace, tel. 01/284-4555).

Groceries: For picnic shopping, try **Centra Market,** right on Marine Road (daily until 22:00).

In Glasthule: Called simply "the village" locally, Glasthule is just down the street from the Sandycove/Glasthule DART station and has an array of fun, hardworking little restaurants plus a Centra Market.

Howth

Eight miles north of Dublin, Howth rests on a teardrop-shaped peninsula that pokes the Irish Sea. Its active harbor chugs with

fishing boats earnestly bringing in the daily catch, and seals trolling for scraps. Weary Dubliners come here for refreshing coastal cliff walks near the city. Located at the north terminus of the DART light-rail line, Howth makes a good place for travelers to settle in, with easy connections to Dublin for sightseeing. But there are only a couple centrally located and worthwhile lodging options.

Howth was once an important gateway to Dublin. Near the neck of the peninsula is the suburb of Clontarf, where Irish High King Brian Boru defeated the last concerted Viking attack in 1014. Eight hundred years later, a squat martello tower was built on a bluff above Howth's harbor to defend it from a Napoleonic invasion that never came. The harbor then grew as a port for shipping from Liverpool and Wales. It was eventually eclipsed by Dun Laoghaire, which was first to gain rail access. Irish rebels smuggled German-supplied guns into Ireland via Howth in 1914, making the 1916 Easter Rising possible. Soon after, Howth became a favorite safe-

DUBLIN

Howth

1. King Sitric's Accommodation, Fish Rest. & East Café Bar
2. Glenn-na-Smol B&B
3. The Oar House Rest.
4. The House Rest.
5. Abbey Tavern
6. Bloody Stream Pub
7. Country Market
8. Centra Market

LIGHTHOUSE

KING'S FOOTSTEPS

Howth Harbor

Irish Sea

To Dublin

HOWTH DART STATION

YACHT CLUB

WC

To National Transport Museum, Howth Castle (closed) & Dublin

HARBOUR RD.

CHURCH ST.

ABBEY ST.

MARTELLO TOWER & MUSEUM OF VINTAGE RADIO

To Cliff Walk & Lighthouse

EVORA PK.

ST. LAWRENCE RD.

GRACE O'MALLEY RD.

Deer Park Golf Course

GRACE O'MALLEY DR.

LIBRARY

MAIN ST.

ASGARD PK.

BALSCADDEN

KILROCK RD.

NASHVILLE RD.

TUCKETT'S LN.

ST. PETER'S TERR.

BALGLASS RD.

ASGARD RD.

THORMANBY

BALKILL PK.

200 Meters
200 Yards

house refuge for rebel mastermind Michael Collins. These days, this is a pleasant, coastal hamlet.

GETTING TO HOWTH

The DART light-rail system zaps travelers between Howth and the city (4/hour, 25 minutes, daily until about 23:30, €3.25 one-way, €6.15 round-trips good same day only, www.irishrail.ie). If you're coming from Dublin, catch a DART train marked *Howth* (not *Howth Junction, Malahide,* or *Drogheda*) and ride it to the end of the line—passing through Howth Junction en route. All trains departing Howth head straight to Dublin's Connolly Station, and then continue on to Tara and Pearse stations (get off at Tara for most sightseeing). Grab a morning train to minimize the jam on sunny summer weekends.

A taxi from the airport takes about 20 minutes and costs about €25. Try Executive Cabs (tel. 01/839-6020).

Orientation to Howth

Howth perches on the north shore of the peninsula and generally divides along the east-west harborfront and the north-south street that winds uphill to the village.

The quarter-mile harborfront promenade stretches from the DART station (in the west) to the martello tower on the bluff (in the east). Dominating the view are two stony piers that clutch like crab claws at the Irish Sea. The West Pier has the fishing action, while the East Pier extends to a stubby 200-year-old lighthouse and views of a rugged nearby island, Ireland's Eye. The village is reached via Abbey Street (becoming Main Street), extending uphill from the harbor near the base of the martello tower bluff. Along the street, you'll find a church, most of the shops and pubs, and a grocery store.

There are two **ATMs** in town: the tiny Ulster Bank kiosk across the street from the DART station (to the left of the Gem Market) and inside the Centra Market. The helpful **TI** is located on the harborfront, in a tiny wooden hut on Harbour Road, across from Howth's old courthouse (daily 9:30-17:00, shorter hours off-season, tel. 085/858-1695, www.howthismagic.com).

Sights in Howth

Other than coastal walks, sightseeing here pales in comparison to Dublin. Privately owned Howth Castle cannot be toured.

Museum of Vintage Radio

The three-story martello tower on the bluff overlooking the East Pier is the only sight in Howth worth a glance. Curator Pat Herbert has spent decades acquiring his collection of lovingly preserved radios, phonographs, and even a hurdy-gurdy (a crank-action musical oddity)—all of which still work. Check out the radio disguised as a picture frame, which was used by the resistance in occupied France during World War II.

Before leaving the compact bluff, catch the views of the harbor and the nearby island of Ireland's Eye. Spot the distant martello tower on the island's west end and the white guano coating its eastern side, courtesy of a colony of gannets.

Cost and Hours: €5, daily 11:00-16:00, Sat-Sun only Nov-April, entry up driveway off Abbey Street, mobile 086-815-4189.

National Transport Museum

Housed in a large shed on the castle grounds, this is a dusty waste of time unless you find rapture in old trams and buses (€3, Sat-Sun only 14:00-17:00, tel. 01/848-0831, www.nationaltransportmuseum. org).

St. Mary's Abbey

Looming above Abbey Street, the abbey ruins date from the early 1400s. Before that, a church built by Norse King Sitric in 1042 stood at this site. The entrance to the ruins is on Church Street, above the abbey grounds.

East and West Piers

The piers make for mellow strolls after a meal. Poke your head into the various fishmonger shops along the West Pier to see the day's

catch. At the end of the pier (on the leeward side), you'll find the footprints of King George IV carved into the stone after his 1821 visit. The East Pier is a quiet jetty barbed with a squat lighthouse and the closest views of Ireland's Eye. If you want to get even closer to the island, book a boat excursion (€15 round-trip, daily in summer on demand 10:30-18:00, call for off-season trips, mobile 086-845-9154, www.islandferries.net).

Hiking Trails

Trails above the eastern cliffs of the peninsula offer enjoyable, breezy exercise. For a scenic three-hour round-trip, walk past the East Pier and martello tower, following Balscadden Road uphill. You'll soon pass Balscadden House, where writer W. B. Yeats spent part of his youth (watch for plaque on left). A 10-minute stroll beyond that, the road dead-ends, where you'll find the well-marked trailhead and easy-to-follow trail; soon you'll be walking south around the craggy coastline to grand views of the Bailey Lighthouse on the southeast rim of the peninsula. The gate to the lighthouse grounds is always locked, so enjoy the view from afar before retracing your steps back to Howth.

Sleeping in Howth

$$$$ King Sitric's Accommodation is Howth's best lodging option and has a fine harborfront seafood restaurant. It fills the old harbormaster's house with eight well-kept rooms and a friendly staff (discounts for 2-night stay with dinner, East Pier below martello tower, tel. 01/832-5235, www.kingsitric.ie, info@kingsitric.ie, Aidan and Joan MacManus).

$ Glenn-na-Smol B&B is a homey house with six unpretentious rooms in a quiet setting, a 15-minute walk uphill along the coast behind the martello tower (family room, cash only, parking, corner of Nashville Road & Kilrock Road, tel. 01/832-2936, mobile 085-758-1083, rickards@indigo.ie, Sean and Margaret Rickard).

Eating in Howth

$$$$ King Sitric's Fish Restaurant, one of the area's most famous seafood experiences, serves Irish versions of French classics in a dining room (upstairs) with harbor views. Chef Aidan MacManus rises early each morning to select the best of the day's catch on the pier to be enjoyed that evening (Wed-Sat 18:00-21:30, Sun 13:00-17:00, closed Mon-Tue, reservations a good idea, tel. 01/832-5235, www.kingsitric.ie). They also operate the more economical **$$ East Café Bar** on the ground floor with extra seating out front. Their soups, salads, steak sandwiches, and fish dishes are a good value (daily 10:00-22:00).

$$$ The Oar House sits halfway down the West Pier, serving a variety of fresh fish dishes in a bustling atmosphere (daily 12:00-"the cows come home," 8 West Pier, tel. 01/839-4568).

$$$ The House is the best value up the hill in the village. Here you'll find a comfortable local vibe, a contemporary creative menu, and a rumor that Captain Bligh once lodged here (Tue-Sun 12:00-21:00, Mon open for lunch only, 4 Main Street, tel. 01/839-6388).

For standard pub grub, try the **$$ Abbey Tavern** up the hill on Abbey Street (occasional trad music and dance, call for schedule, tel. 01/839-0307). Another good choice is the **$$ Bloody Stream Pub** in front of the DART station (tel. 01/839-5076). The **Country Market** sells picnic supplies, and its cheap and friendly upstairs tearoom offers lunch (daily 9:00-18:00, Main Street). The **Centra Market** is a block closer to the waterfront (daily until 22:00, Main Street).

NEAR DUBLIN

*Boyne Valley • Trim • Glendalough • Wicklow Mountains •
Irish National Stud*

Not far from urban Dublin, the stony skeletons of evocative ruins sprout from the lush Irish countryside. The story of Irish history is told by ancient burial mounds, early Christian monastic settlements, huge Norman castles, and pampered estate gardens. In gentler inland terrain, the Irish love of equestrian sport is nurtured in grassy pastures ruled by spirited thoroughbreds. These sights are separated into three regions: north of Dublin (the Boyne Valley, including Brú na Bóinne and the town of Trim), south of Dublin (Powerscourt Estate Gardens, Glendalough, and the Wicklow Mountains), and west of Dublin (the Irish National Stud).

Boyne Valley

The peaceful, green Boyne Valley, just 30 miles north of Dublin, has an impressive concentration of historical and spiritual sights: The enigmatic burial mounds at Brú na Bóinne are older than the Egyptian pyramids. At the Hill of Tara (seat of the high kings of Celtic Ireland), St. Patrick preached his most persuasive sermon. The valley also contains the first monastery in Ireland and several of the country's finest high crosses. You'll see Trim's 13th-century castle—Ireland's biggest—built by Norman invaders, and you can wander the site of the historic Battle of the Boyne (1690), which cemented Protestant British domination over Catholic Ireland until the 20th century.

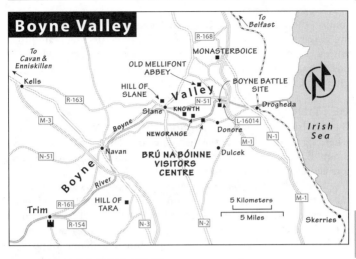

PLANNING YOUR TIME

Of these sights, only Brú na Bóinne is worth ▲▲▲ (and deserves a good three or four hours). The others, while relatively meager physically, are powerfully evocative to anyone interested in Irish history and culture. If you have a car, get an early start, and eat your Weetabix, you could see the entire region in a day.

As you plan your Ireland itinerary, if you're flying into or out of Dublin but want to avoid the intensity and expense of that big city, consider using Trim as an overnight base (45-minute drive from airport; accommodations listed on page 134) and tour these sights from there.

GETTING AROUND BOYNE VALLEY

The region is a joy by car, because all of the described sights are within a 30-minute drive of one another. Though the sights are on tiny roads, they're well-marked with brown, tourist-friendly road signs. You'll navigate best using an Ordnance Survey atlas.

It's also possible to get to the Boyne Valley from Dublin with a tour. **Newgrange Tours** visits Brú na Bóinne (including inside the Newgrange tomb), the Hill of Tara, and the Hill of Slane in a seven-hour trip (€40, daily pickup from several Dublin hotels, book direct via website, mobile 086-355-1355, www.newgrangetours. com, newgrangetours@gmail.com).

Brú na Bóinne

The famous archaeological site of Brú na Bóinne—"dwelling place of the Boyne"—is also commonly called "Newgrange," after its star attraction. Here you can visit two ▲▲▲ 5,000-year-old passage tombs—**Newgrange** and **Knowth** (rhymes with "south"). These are massive grass-covered burial mounds built atop separate hills, with a chamber inside reached by a narrow stone passage. Mysterious, thought-provoking, and mind-bogglingly old, these tombs can give you chills.

GETTING THERE

By **car,** drive 45 minutes north from Dublin on N-1 to Drogheda, where signs direct you to the visitors center. If you're using a GPS, input "Brú na Bóinne" rather than "Newgrange" to get to the visitors center, where you must check in.

Without a car, you can combine **train and taxi** service. First take a train departing Dublin Connolly station at 8:00, which puts you in the town of Drogheda around 9:00 (€12 round-trip; confirm train times at www.irishrail.ie). From here it's a short taxi ride to the Brú na Bóinne visitors center (approximately €8 one-way).

PLANNING YOUR VISIT

Access to Newgrange and Knowth is by guided tour only (book ahead). You'll start your visit at the state-of-the-art visitors center with its excellent museum, then catch a shuttle bus to the tomb sites, where a guide gives a 30-minute tour.

Each tomb site takes about 1.5 hours to visit (30-minute round-trip bus ride plus 30-minute guided tour plus 30 minutes of free time). The museum at the visitors center is well worth an additional 30-60 minutes. If you add in waiting time for the next available shuttle bus, you're looking at a minimum of 2.5 hours to visit one of the tombs (along with the museum), or 4 hours to visit both tombs (and museum).

Which tomb is best? If you can't see both, I'd pick Newgrange because it's more famous and allows you inside. (On the other hand, wait times for the Newgrange shuttle bus can be longer.) Knowth is bigger and flanked by small mounds, but you can't access its narrow passages. Each site is different enough and worthwhile, but for many, seeing just one is adequate. You might pick your tomb according to whichever shuttle bus is leaving next.

ORIENTATION TO BRÚ NA BÓINNE

Cost: Newgrange-€7, Knowth-€6, both-€13; museum is included in tomb prices.

Hours: Daily 9:00-19:00, slightly shorter hours mid-Sept-May, last bus to the tombs leaves 1.75 hours before closing, last entry to visitors center 45 minutes before closing, Newgrange is open year-round, while Knowth is open May-Oct only.

Information: Tel. 041/988-0300, www.heritageireland.ie.

Advance Tickets Recommended: It's smart to reserve timed-entry tickets online at https://brunaboinne.admit-one.eu. Otherwise, on busy summer days, tickets can sell out. Without a tour reservation, arrive early—ideally before 9:30.

VISITING BRÚ NA BÓINNE

At the visitors center, check in and spend your waiting time in the excellent museum, grabbing lunch in the cheery downstairs cafeteria, and using the WCs (there are none at the tomb sites).

Brú na Bóinne Visitors Center Museum

The museum introduces you to the Boyne River Valley and its tombs. No one knows exactly who built the 40 burial mounds found in the surrounding hills. Exhibits re-create what these pre-Celtic people might have been like—simple farmers and hunters living in huts, fishing in the Boyne, equipped with crude tools of stone, bone, or wood.

Then around 3200 B.C., someone had a bold idea. They constructed a chamber of large stones, with a long stone-lined passage leading up to it. They covered it with a huge mound of dirt and rocks in successive layers. Sailing down the Boyne to the sea, they beached at Clogherhead (12.5 miles from here), where they found hundreds of five-ton stones, weathered smooth by the tides. Somehow they transported them back up the Boyne, possibly by tying a raft to the top of the stone so it was lifted free by a high tide. They then hauled these stones up the hill by rolling them atop logs and up dirt ramps, and laid them around the perimeter of the burial mound to hold everything in place. It would have taken anywhere from five years to a generation to construct a single large tomb.

Why build these vast structures? Partially, it was to bury VIPs. A dead king might be carried up the hill to be cremated on a pyre. Then they'd bring his ashes into the tomb, parading by torchlight down the passage to the central chamber. The remains were placed in a ceremonial basin, mingled with those of his illustrious ancestors.

To help bring the history to life, the museum displays replicas of tools and objects found at the sites, including the ceremonial basin stone and a head made from flint, which may have been carried atop a pole during the funeral procession. Marvel at the craftsmanship of the perfectly spherical stones (and the phallic one), and wonder at their purpose.

The tombs also served an astronomical function; they're precisely aligned to the movements of the sun, as displays and a video illustrate. You can request a short tour and winter solstice light-

NEAR DUBLIN

show demo at a full-size replica of the Newgrange passage and interior chamber.

Since the tombs are aligned with the heavens, it begs the question: Were these structures sacred places where primal Homo sapiens gathered to ponder the deepest mysteries of existence?

▲▲▲Newgrange

This grassy mound atop a hill is 250 feet across and 40 feet high. Dating from 3200 B.C., it's 500 years older than the pyramids at Giza. The base of the mound is ringed by dozens of curbstones, each about nine feet long and weighing five tons.

The entrance facade is a mosaic of white quartz and dark granite. This is a reconstruction done in the 1970s, and not every archaeologist agrees it originally looked like this. Above the doorway is a square window called the roofbox, which played a key role (as we'll see). In front of the doorway lies the most famous of the curbstones, the 10- by 4-foot entrance stone. Its left half is carved with three mysterious spirals, which have become a kind of poster child for prehistoric art.

Most of Newgrange's curbstones have designs carved into them. This was done with super-hard flint tools; the Neolithic ("New Stone Age") people had not mastered metal. The stones feature common Neolithic motifs: not people or animals, but geometric shapes—spirals, crosshatches, bull's-eyes, and chevrons. (For more information on prehistoric art, see page 505.)

Entering the tomb, you walk down a narrow 60-foot passage lined with big boulders. Occasionally you have to duck or turn sideways to squeeze through. The passage opens up into a central room—a cross-shaped central chamber with three alcoves, topped by a 20-foot-high igloo-type stone dome. Bones and ashes were placed here in a ceremonial stone basin, under 200,000 tons of stone and dirt.

While we know nothing of Newgrange's builders, it most certainly was a sacred spot—for a cult of the dead, a cult of the sun, or both. The tomb is aligned precisely east-west. As the sun rises around the shortest day of the year (winter solstice—usually on Dec 21—and two days before and after), a ray of light enters through the roofbox and creeps slowly down the passageway. For 17 minutes, it lights the center of the sacred chamber (your guide will demonstrate this). Perhaps this was the moment when the souls of the dead were transported to the afterlife, via that ray of life-giving and life-taking light. Then the light passes on, and, for the next 361 days, the tomb sits again in total darkness.

▲▲▲Knowth

This site is an impressive necropolis, with one grand hill-topping mound surrounded by several smaller satellite tombs. The central mound is 220 feet wide, 40 feet high, and covers 1.5 acres.

You'll see plenty of mysteriously carved curbstones and new-feeling grassy mounds that you can look down on from atop the grand tomb.

Knowth's big tomb has two passages: one entering from the east, and one from the west. Like Newgrange, it's likely aligned so the rising and setting sun shone down the passageways to light the two interior chambers, but these are aligned to the equinox rather than the solstice. Neither passage is open to the public, but you can visit a room carved into the mound by archaeologists, where a cutaway lets you see the layers of dirt and rock used to build the mound. You also get a glimpse down one of the passages.

The Knowth site thrived from 3000 to 2000 B.C. The central tomb dates from about 2000 B.C. It was likely used for burial rituals and sun-tracking ceremonies to please the gods and ensure the regular progression of seasons for crops. The site then evolved into the domain of fairies and myths for the next 2,000 years, and became an Iron Age fortress in the early centuries after Christ. Around A.D. 1000, it was an all-Ireland political center, and later, a Norman fortress was built atop the mound. Now, 4,000 years after prehistoric people built these strange tombs, you can stand atop the hill at Knowth, look out over the surrounding countryside, and contemplate.

More Boyne Valley Sights

▲▲Battle of the Boyne Site

One of Europe's lesser-known battlegrounds (but huge in Irish and British history), this is the pastoral riverside site of the pivotal battle in which the Protestant British decisively broke Catholic resistance, establishing Protestant rule over all of Ireland and Britain.

Cost and Hours: €5, daily 9:00-17:00, Oct-April until 16:00, last entry one hour before closing, tearoom/cafeteria, tel. 041/980-9950, www.battleoftheboyne.ie.

Getting There: The visitors center is on the south bank of the Boyne River, about two miles north of the village of Donore. It's well signposted for drivers from M-1, N-51, or N-2. Once you pass through the main gates, you'll find the visitors center in the mansion a quarter-mile up the driveway.

"Living History" demonstrations: The Sunday afternoon "Living History" demonstrations (March-Sept) are a treat for history buffs and photographers, with guides clad in 17th-century garb. You'll get a bang out of the musket loading and firing demo. Or catch the cavalry combat in full gallop and learn that to be an Irish watermelon is to fear the sword. Check the event program online for schedules and additional offerings such as battlefield walks.

Background: It was here in 1690 that Protestant King William III, with his English/Irish/Dutch/Danish/French Huguenot army, defeated his father-in-law—who was also his uncle—Catholic King James II and his Irish/French army. At stake was who would sit on the British throne, who would hold religious power in Ireland, and whether or not French dominance of Europe would continue.

King William's forces, on the north side of the Boyne, managed to fight their way across the river, and by the end of the day, King James was fleeing south in full retreat. He soon left Ireland, but his forces fought on until their final defeat a year later. James II (called "James da Turd" by those who scorn his lack of courage and leadership) never returned, and he died a bitter ex-monarch in France. His "Jacobite" claim to the English throne lived on among Catholics for decades, and was finally extinguished in 1745, when his grandson, Bonnie Prince Charlie, was defeated at the Battle of Culloden in Scotland.

King William of Orange's victory, on the other hand, is still celebrated in Northern Ireland every July 12, with controversial marches by Unionist "Orangemen." The battle actually took place on July 1, but was officially shifted 11 days later when the Gregorian calendar was adopted in 1752. (Even the calendar has been affected by religious strife: Protestant nations were reluctant to use a calendar developed by a Catholic—Pope Gregory in 1582. So England delayed adoption of Gregory's calendar for 170 years.)

The 60,000 soldiers who fought here made this one of the largest battles ever to take place in the British Isles. Yet it was only a side skirmish in an even larger continental confrontation pitting France's King Louis XIV against the "Grand Alliance" of nations threatened by France's mighty military and frequent incursions into neighboring lands.

Louis ruled by divine right, answerable only to God—and James modeled himself after Louis. Even the pope (who could control neither Louis nor James and was equally disturbed by Catholic France's aggressions) backed Protestant King William against

Catholic King James—just one example of the pretzel logic that was the European mindset at the time.

The site of the Battle of the Boyne was bought in 1997 by the Irish Office of Public Works, part of the Republic's governmental efforts to respect a place sacred to Unionists in Northern Ireland—despite the fact that the battle's outcome ensured Catholic subordination to the Protestant minority for the next 230 years.

Visiting the Site: The **visitors center** is housed in a mansion built on the battlefield 50 years after the conflict. The exhibits do a good job of illustrating the international nature of the battle and its place in the wider context of European political power struggles. The highlight is a huge battleground model with laser lights that move troops around the terrain, showing the battle's ebb and flow on that bloody day. A separate 15-minute film (shown in the former stable house) runs continuously and does a fine job of fleshing out the battle.

As you exit the site to the north (on the L-16014 access road that connects to the main N-51 road), you'll cross the River Boyne on a **metal bridge,** locally referred to as "Old Bridge." This spot is where the most frantic action took place on that bloody day.

Pull over and gaze down at the river. Picture crack Dutch troops (from King William's homeland) marching south in formation. They were the first to cross the river here, while their comrades behind on the north bank covered their exposed position with constant protective fire. Low tides (the sea is only 7 miles downstream) allowed these soldiers to cross the river in water up to their waists. Between the gun smoke, weapon fire, and shouts filling the air, it was tough to tell friend from foe in the close, chaotic combat. Neither force had standard uniforms, so King William's troops wore sprigs of green while the troops of King James pinned white paper to their coats. Both sides bled red.

▲Hill of Tara

This site was the most important center of political and religious power in pre-Christian Ireland. While aerial views show plenty of mystifying circles and lines, wandering with the sheep among the well-worn ditches and hills leaves you with more to feel than to see. Visits are made meaningful by an excellent 20-minute video presentation and the insightful 20-minute guided walk that usually follows (walk times unpredictable due to frequent big bus tours; worth calling ahead to confirm availability). Wear good walking shoes—the ground is uneven and often wet.

Cost and Hours: €5, includes video and guided walk (if available when you visit), buy tickets from old church in the trees above parking lot; daily 10:00-18:00, last tour at 17:00, from mid-Sept-mid-May access is free but visitors center is closed; WCs in café next to parking lot, tel. 046/902-5903, http://hilloftara.org.

Visiting the Site: You'll see the Mound of Hostages (a Bronze Age passage grave, c. 2500 B.C.), a couple of ancient sacred stones, a war memorial, and vast views over the Emerald Isle. While ancient Ireland was a pig pile of minor chieftain-kings scrambling for power, the high king of Tara was king of the mountain. It was at this ancient stockade that St. Patrick directly challenged the king's authority. When confronted by the high king, Patrick convincingly explained the Holy Trinity using a shamrock: three petals with one stem. He won the right to preach Christianity throughout Ireland, and the country had a new national symbol.

This now-desolate hill was also the scene of great modern events. In 1798, passionate young Irish rebels chose Tara for its defensible position, but were routed by better organized (and more sober) British troops. (The cunning British commander had sent three cartloads of whiskey along the nearby road earlier in the day, knowing the rebels would intercept it.) In 1843, the great orator and champion of Irish liberty Daniel O'Connell gathered 500,000 Irish peasants on this hill for his greatest "monster meeting"—a peaceful show of force demanding the repeal of the Act of Union with Britain (kind of the Woodstock of its day). In a bizarre final twist, a small group of British Israelites—who believed they were one of the lost tribes of Israel, who had ended up in Britain—spent 1899 to 1901 recklessly digging up parts of the hill in a misguided search for the Ark of the Covenant.

Stand on the Hill of Tara. Think of the history it's seen, and survey Ireland. It's understandable why this "meeting place of heroes" continues to hold a powerful place in the Irish psyche.

Old Mellifont Abbey

This Cistercian abbey (the first in Ireland) was established by French monks who came to the country in 1142 to bring the Irish monks more in line with Rome. (Even the abbey's architecture was unusual, marking the first time in Ireland that a formal, European-style monastic layout was used.) Cistercians lived isolated rural lives; lay monks worked the land, allowing the more educated monks to devote all their energy to prayer. After Henry VIII dissolved the abbey in 1539, centuries of locals used it as a handy quarry. Consequently, little survives beyond the octagonal lavabo, where the monks would ceremonially wash their hands before entering the refectory to eat. The lavabo gives a sense of the abbey's former grandeur.

The excellent 45-minute tours, available upon request and included in your admission (late May-Aug only), give meaning to what you're seeing. To get a better idea of the extent of the site, check out the model of the monastery in its heyday, located at the back of the small museum next to the ticket desk.

Cost and Hours: €5; daily 10:00-18:00, last tour at 17:30, last entry 45 minutes before closing; from Sept-late May site is free but there are no tours; tel. 041/988-0300, www.heritageireland.ie.

Monasterboice

This ruined monastery is visit-worthy for its round tower and its ornately carved high crosses—two of the best such crosses in Ireland. In the Dark Ages, these crosses, illustrated from top to bottom with Bible stories, gave monks a teaching tool as they preached to the illiterate masses. Imagine the crosses in their prime, when they were brightly painted (before years of wind and rain weathered the paint away). Today, Monasterboice is basically an old graveyard.

Cost and Hours: Free and always open.

Visiting the Site: The 18-foot-tall **Cross of Murdock** (Muiredach's Cross, c. 923, named after an abbot) is considered the best high cross in Ireland. The circle—which characterizes the Irish high cross—could represent the perfection of God. Or, to help ease pagans into Christianity, it may represent the sun, which was worshipped in pre-Christian Celtic society. Whatever its symbolic purpose, its practical function was to support the weight of the crossbeam.

Face the cross (with the round tower in the background) and study the carved sandstone. The center panel shows the Last

Judgment, with Christ under a dove, symbolizing the Holy Spirit. Those going to heaven are on Christ's right, and the damned are being ushered away by a pitchfork-wielding devil on his left. Working down, you'll see the Archangel Michael weighing souls, as the Devil tugs demonically at the scales; the adoration of the three—or four—Magi; Moses striking the rock to bring forth water; scenes from the life of David; and, finally, Adam, Eve, and the apple next to Cain slaying Abel. Imagine these carvings with their original, colorful paint jobs. Check out the plaque at the base of the nearby tree, which further explains the carvings on the cross.

Find the even taller cross nearest the tower. It seems the top section was broken off and buried for a period, which protected it from weathering. The bottom part remained standing, enduring the erosive effect of Irish weather, which smeared the once-crisp features.

The door to the round tower was originally 15-20 feet above the ground (accessible by ladder). After centuries of burials, the ground level has risen.

Trim

The sleepy, workaday town of Trim, straddling the River Boyne, is marked by the towering ruins of Trim Castle. Trim feels littered with mighty ruins that seem to say, "This little town was big-time...800 years ago." The tall Yellow Steeple (over the river from the castle) is all that remains of the 14th-century Augustinian Abbey of St. Mary. Not far away, the Sheep's Gate is a humble remnant of the once-grand medieval town walls. Near the town center, the modest, 30-foot-tall Wellington Column honors native son Arthur Wellesley, the First Duke of Wellington (1769-1852), who spent his childhood in Trim, defeated Napoleon at Waterloo, and twice became prime minister.

Trim makes a great landing pad into—or launching pad out of—Ireland. If you're flying into or out of Dublin Airport and don't want to deal with big-city Dublin, this is a perfect alternative—an easy 45-minute, 30-mile drive away. You can rent a car at the airport and make Trim your first overnight base (getting used to driving on the other side of the road in easier country traffic). Or spend your last night here before returning your car at the airport. Weather permitting, my evening stroll makes for a fine first or last night in the Emerald Isle.

Orientation to Trim

Trim's main square is a traffic roundabout, and everything's within a block or two. Most of the shops and eateries are on or near Market Street, along with banks and a supermarket.

TOURIST INFORMATION

The TI is right next to the castle entrance and includes a handy coffee shop. Drop in to pick up a free map (Mon-Fri 9:30-17:30, Sat-Sun 12:00-17:00, shorter hours Sept-May, Castle Street, tel. 046/943-7227). Outside, 100 feet to the right of the TI door, you'll find a plaque with photos showing the castle dolled up for the filming of *Braveheart*.

HELPFUL HINTS

Laundry: The launderette is located close to Market Street (Mon-Sat 9:00-13:00 & 13:30-17:30, closed Sun, Watergate Street, tel. 046/943-7176).

Parking: To park on the street or in a public lot, use the pay-and-display parking system (€1/hour, 2-hour maximum, Mon-Sat 9:00-18:00, free Sun).

Taxi: Donie Quinn can give you a lift to nearby Boyne sites (tel. 046/943-6009).

Adventure Tours: Boyne Valley Activities offers kayaking, rafting, high-rope walks, and archery excursions...luckily not simultaneously (€25 for archery; €40 for rafting, kayaking, and high-rope walks; call ahead to reserve, mobile 086-734-2585, www.boynevalleyactivities.ie).

Marc O'Regan leads backcountry trout and pike fishing tours, making a splash with anglers who want to experience Ireland's bountiful lakes and rivers (tel. 046/943-1635, www.crannmor.com). O'Regan and his wife also run the recommended Crannmór Guest House.

Sights in Trim

▲▲Trim Castle

This is the biggest Norman castle in Ireland. Set in a grassy riverside park at the edge of this sleepy town, its mighty keep tow-

ers above a very ruined outer wall. It replaced a wooden fortification that was destroyed in 1173 by Irish High King Rory O'Connor, who led a raid against the invading Normans. The current castle was completed in the 1220s and served as a powerful Norman statement to the restless Irish natives. It remained a sharp barb at the fringe of "the Pale" (English-controlled territory), when English rule shrank to just the area around Dublin in the 1400s. By that time, any lands farther west were "beyond the Pale."

Cost and Hours: €5 for entrance to keep and required tour, €2 for gardens only; daily 10:00-17:00, Nov-mid-March open Sat-Sun only 9:30-16:00, last entry one hour before closing, 45-minute tours run 2/hour but spots are limited and can fill up—so arrive early in peak season, tel. 046/943-8619, www.heritageireland.ie.

Visiting the Castle: Today the castle remains an impressive sight—so impressive that it was used in the 1994 filming of *Braveheart* (which was actually about Scotland's—not Ireland's—fight

NEAR DUBLIN

Trim

To Athboy & Kells
ATHBOY RD.
To ❸
L-4023
KILDALKEY RD.
KELLS RD.
RING RD.
❶❷ Groceries
❶❷
ST. PATRICK'S CHURCH OF IRELAND
ST. LOMAN'S ST.
CHURCH LN.
HAGGARD ST.
HIGH ST.
To Navan & Brú na Bóinne
R-161
LACKANASH RD.
❷
P
NAVAN GATE ST.
SARSFIELD AVE.
❾
YELLOW STEEPLE
ABBEY LN.
SHELL GAS STATION
❶❶
WATERGATE ST.
MARKET ST.
BRIDGE ST.
ST. MARY'S ABBEY
SHEEP'S GATE
River Boyne
N
200 Meters
200 Yards
POST &
❶❷
❺
P
❼
P
❻
CASTLE ST.
❶
B
TRIM CASTLE
EMMET ST.
FINNEGAN'S WAY
NEW DUBLIN RD.
B
River Walk
ST. PATRICK'S CATHOLIC CHURCH
NEW HAGGARD RD.
P
PATRICK ST.
❶
R-154
WELLINGTON COLUMN
SUMMERHILL RD.
❽
To ❿ Sts. Peter & Paul Cathedral, Airport & Dublin
RING RD.
APPLEGREEN MINIMART
R-160
R-158
To ❹ & Longwood
To Enfield

❶ Highfield House B&B
❷ White Lodge B&B
❸ To Crannmór Guest House
❹ To Tigh Catháin B&B
❺ Franzini's Restaurant
❻ The Stockhouse
❼ Rachel's Café
❽ Castle Arch Hotel Rest.
❾ James Griffin Pub
❿ To Marcie Regan's Pub
⓫ Launderette
⓬ Groceries (2)

for freedom from the English). The best-preserved walls ring the castle's southern perimeter and sport a barbican gate that contained two drawbridges.

At the base of the castle walls, notice the cleverly angled "batter" wall—used by defenders who hurled down stones that banked off at great velocity into the attacking army. Notice also that the castle is built directly on bedrock, visible along the base of the walls. During sieges, while defenders of other castles feared that attackers would tunnel underground to weaken the defensive walls, that was not an issue here.

The massive 70-foot-high central keep, which is mostly a hollow shell, has 20 sides. This experimental design was not implemented elsewhere because it increased the number of defenders needed to cover all the angles. You can go inside the keep only with the included tour, where you'll start by checking out the cool ground-floor models showing the evolution of the castle. Then you'll climb a series of tightly winding original staircases and modern, high catwalks, learn about life in the castle, and end at the top with great views of the walls and the countryside.

Make time to take a 15-minute walk outside, circling the castle walls and stopping at the informative plaques that show the castle from each viewpoint during its gory glory days. Night strollers are treated to views of the castle hauntingly lit in blue-green hues.

NEAR DUBLIN

Trim Evening Stroll

Given good weather, here's my blueprint for a fine night in Trim. Start the evening by taking the pleasant **River Walk** stroll along the River Boyne from Trim Castle. Cross the wooden footbridge over the river behind the castle and turn right (east). The paved, level trail eventually leads under a modern bridge/overpass and extends a mile along fields that serfs farmed 750 years ago. During the filming of *Braveheart*, Mel Gibson's character met the French princess in her tent in these fields, with the castle looming in the background.

The trail ends in the medieval ruins of **Newtown.** This was indeed once the "new town" (mid-1200s) that sprouted as a religious satellite community to support the political power housed in the castle. Wander the sprawling, ragtag ruins of **Saints Peter and Paul Cathedral** (1206), once the largest Gothic church in Ireland. Seek out the tomb with a carved lid depicting a medieval lord and lady; this is known locally as the tomb of the "jealous man and woman" (because they do not touch each other). Upon close inspection, you'll notice hundreds of tiny pins in the creases of the carving, left behind by superstitious visitors. Why? If you rub a pin on your stubborn wart and then leave it here...presto: wart-be-gone.

Just beyond the ruins, cross the old Norman bridge to the 13th-century scraps of the **Hospital of St. John the Baptist.** Medieval medicine couldn't have been fun, but this hospital was the best you could hope for back when life was nasty, brutish, and short. Many a knight was spent here.

Cross back over the bridge and stop for a pint at tiny, atmospheric **Marcie Regan's,** one of the oldest pubs in Ireland (an exterior sign calls it "Regan's," but most locals call it "Marcie's"). Explore its dimly lit back rooms. The pub sits beside one of the oldest bridges in Ireland (the one you just crossed).

Then walk back along the river the way you came and have dinner at the recommended **Franzini's** restaurant beside the castle. After dinner, assist your digestion by walking a lap around the castle (beautifully lit at night). End the evening a few blocks away with a pint at the recommended **James Griffin** pub. A fine night 'tis...or 'twas.

Sleeping in Trim

Because Trim is a popular spot for weddings, book as early as possible if you are visiting on a summer weekend.

$$ Highfield House B&B, across the street from the castle and a five-minute walk from town, is a stately 210-year-old former maternity hospital, with hardwood floors and 10 spacious, high-ceilinged rooms (family rooms; above the roundabout where Dublin Road hits Trim, just before castle at Castle Street; tel. 046/943-6386, mobile 086-857-7115, www.highfieldguesthouse.com, info@highfieldguesthouse.com, Geraldine and Edward Duignan).

$ White Lodge B&B, a 10-minute walk northeast of the castle, has six comfortably unpretentious rooms with an oak-and-granite lounge (open May-Oct, family room, parking, New Road, tel. 046/943-6549, www.whitelodge.ie, info@whitelodge.ie, Todd O'Loughlin). They also offer a family-friendly self-catering house next door. A handy 300-yard trail leads from across the street to the castle.

Countryside B&Bs: These two B&Bs are in the quiet countryside about a mile outside Trim (phone ahead for driving directions).

$ At ivy-draped Crannmór Guest House, Anne O'Regan decorates five rooms with cheery color schemes (family room; north of the Ring Road on Dunderry Road L-4023, then veer right at the first fork; tel. 046/943-1635, mobile 087-288-7390, www.crannmor.com, cranmor@eircom.net). Anne's professional-guide husband Marc knows all the best fishing holes (listed earlier, under "Helpful Hints").

$ Marie Keane's Tigh Catháin B&B, southwest of town, has four large, bright, lacy rooms with a comfy, rural feel and organically grown produce at breakfast (cash only, on R-160/Longwood Road, 200 yards past the Applegreen minimart, tel. 046/943-1996, mobile 086-257-7313, www.tighcathain-bnb.com, tighcathain.bnb@gmail.com).

Eating in Trim

A country market town, Trim offers basic meat-and-potatoes lunch and dinner options. My first two listings are really the only full restaurants in town. Otherwise, the spots along Market Street are friendly, wholesome, and unassuming.

$$$ Franzini's has a fun dinner menu and an excellent location next to the castle. They serve pasta, steak, fish, and great salads in a modern, plush space (Mon-Sat 17:00-21:00, Sun 14:00-20:00, on French's Lane across from the castle parking lot, tel. 046/943-1002).

$$$ The Stockhouse serves hearty steaks and poultry, plus creative desserts. Sit upstairs and take in the history of Trim from the walls while you wait (Mon-Thu 17:00-21:00, Fri-Sat until 22:00, Sun 13:00-20:30, Finnegan's Way, tel. 046/943-7388).

$$ Rachel's Café is a good bet along Market Street for salads, sandwiches, and meat pies (Mon-Sat 8:30-17:30, Sun until 17:00, tel. 046/943-1636).

$$ The **Castle Arch Hotel,** popular with locals, serves hearty pub grub at reasonable prices in its bistro on Summerhill Road (daily 12:30-21:00, tel. 046/943-1516).

Pubs: For a fun pub experience, check out Trim's two best watering holes. The **James Griffin** (on High Street) is full of local characters with traditional Irish music sessions on Monday, Wednesday, and Thursday nights. Locals fill the tiny, low-ceilinged **Marcie Regan's,** a creaky, unpretentious pub at the north end of the old Norman bridge over the River Boyne—it's a half-mile stroll outside town, next to the ruins of Newtown.

Supermarkets: Several stores offer picnic supplies. These include **Spar Market** (Mon-Sat 7:30-20:00, Sun 8:30-19:00, Emmett Street) and the larger **Super Valu** (daily 8:00-22:00, on Haggard Street, a bit farther from the town center).

Trim Connections

Trim has no train station; the nearest is in Drogheda, 25 miles away on the coast. Buses from Trim to **Dublin** (almost hourly, 1 hour) pick you up at the bus shelter next to the TI and castle entrance on Castle Street. For details, see www.buseireann.ie.

Glendalough and the Wicklow Mountains

The Wicklow Mountains, while only 15 miles south of Dublin, feel remote—enough so to have provided a handy refuge for opponents to English rule. Rebels who took part in the 1798 Irish uprising hid out here for years. The area only became more accessible in 1800, when the frustrated British built a military road to help flush out the rebels. Today, this same road—now R-115—takes you through the Wicklow area to Glendalough at its south end. While the valley is the darling of Dublin day-trip tour organizers, for the most part it doesn't live up to the hype. But two blockbuster sights—Glendalough and the Powerscourt Estate Gardens—make a visit worth considering.

GETTING AROUND THE WICKLOW AREA

By car or tour, it's easy. If you lack wheels, take a tour. It's not worth the trouble on public transport.

By Car

It's a delight. Take N-11 south from Dublin toward Bray, then R-117 to Enniskerry, the gateway to the Wicklow Mountains. Signs direct you to the gardens and on to Glendalough. From Glendalough, if you're heading west, you can leave the valley (and pick up the highway to the west) over the famous but dull mountain pass called the Wicklow Gap.

By Tour from Dublin

Bus Tours: Several companies offer tours around the region. **Wild Wicklow Tours** gives you an entertaining guide who packs every minute of an all-day excursion with information and *craic* (interesting, fun conversation). With a gang of 40 packed into tight but comfortable, mountain-gripping buses, the guide kicks into gear from the first pickup in Dublin. Tours cover the windy military road over scenic Sally Gap and the Glendalough monasteries (€28, ask for discount with this book, runs daily year-round, stop for lunch at a pub—cost not included, several Dublin hotel pickup points, return to Dublin by 18:00, advance booking required, tel. 01/280-1899, www.wildwicklow.ie).

Do Dublin Tours offers a shorter trip focusing on Wicklow's two main sights, Glendalough and Powerscourt Gardens, aboard bright-green, double-decker buses (€22, daily departure at 10:30,

South of Dublin

To Sligo

To Airport & Belfast

To Galway

M-4 Liffey

CASTLETOWN HOUSE

River

Dublin

Howth

To Liverpool, England

Dublin Bay

Dun Laoghaire

To Holyhead, Wales

N-11

N-7

To Galway

M-50

N-31

Dalkey

Naas

M-7

R-114

R-117

Killiney

To National Stud, Limerick, Killarney & Cork

N-81

R-759

GARDENS OF POWERSCOURT

M-11

Bray

Irish Sea

R-117

RUSSBOROUGH HOUSE

R-115

OLD MILITARY ROAD

Enniskerry

River Liffey

R-760

Poulaphouca Reservoir

Sally Gap

Great Sugar Loaf

Greystones

Hollywood

R-756

N-81

Wicklow Mountains

R-115

Lough Tay

R-759

R-755

R-761

Lough Dan

Roundwood

N-11

Wicklow Gap

R-756

Annamoe

R-764

To Kilkennny

Laragh

R-763

GLENDALOUGH
See detail map

R-752

Wicklow

R-755

Rathdrum

R-752

R-750

■AVONDALE

R-747

N-11

Avoca

R-747

5 Kilometers

5 Miles

R-747

To Rosslare

Arklow

NEAR DUBLIN

return by 17:00, tours depart from Dublin Bus head office, 59 Upper O'Connell Street, tel. 01/844-4265, www.dodublin.ie).

Local Guide: Friendly and knowledgeable **Lisa Tully** knows the region and can show you the worthwhile stops on your drives around County Wicklow (when she's not on the road leading Rick Steves tours). If you're without a car, she also offers scenic walking tours—meet her by train from Dublin or she'll arrange a driver to get you to and from the countryside (€40/hour, available March-Nov, tel. 086/898-6457, www.wicklowguidedtours.ie, lisa@wicklowguidedtours.ie).

Sights in the Wicklow Area

▲▲Powerscourt Estate Gardens

A mile above the village of Enniskerry, the Powerscourt Estate Gardens cover 47 acres within a 700-acre estate. The dreamy driveway alone is a mile long. The mansion's interior is only partially restored after a 1974 fire (and only available for special events). But its meticulously kept aristocratic gardens are Ireland's best. The house was commissioned in the 1730s by Richard Wingfield, first viscount of Powerscourt. The gardens you see today were created during the Victorian era (1858-1875).

Upon entry, you'll get a flier laying out 40-minute and one-hour walks. The "one-hour" walk takes 30 minutes at a relaxed amble. With the impressive summit of the Great Sugar Loaf Mountain as a backdrop, and a fine Japanese garden, Italian garden, and goofy pet cemetery along the way, this attraction provides the scenic greenery I hoped to find in the rest of the Wicklow area. Parts of the lush movies *Barry Lyndon* and *The Count of Monte Cristo* were filmed in this well-watered aristocratic fantasy.

Spend 10 minutes checking out the easy-to-miss film room, which provides a history of the estate and a model of Powerscourt House before the fire.

Cost and Hours: €10, daily 9:30-17:30, Nov-Feb until dusk, great cafeteria, tel. 01/204-6000, www.powerscourt.com.

Other Sights: Kids may enjoy a peek at the antique dollhouses of the upstairs **Tara's Palace Museum of Childhood** (€5, proceeds go to children's charities, Mon-Sat 10:00-17:00, Sun from 12:00). Skip the Powerscourt Waterfall (4 miles away).

▲Old Military Road over Sally Gap

This trip is only for those with a car. From the Powerscourt Gardens and Enniskerry, go to Glencree, where you drive the tiny old military road (R-115) over Sally Gap and through the best scenery of the Wicklow Mountains (on Sundays, watch for dozens of bicycle racers). Look for the German military cemetery, built for U-boat sailors who washed ashore in World War II. Near Sally Gap, notice the peat bogs and the freshly cut peat bricks drying in the wind. Many locals are nostalgic for the "good old days," when homes were always peat-fire heated. At the Sally Gap junction, turn left, where a road winds through the vast Guinness estate. Look down on the glacial lake (Lough Tay) nicknamed "Guinness Lake," as the water looks like Ireland's favorite dark-brown stout, and the sand of the beach actually looks like the head of a Guinness beer. The History Channel series *Vikings* was primarily filmed on a temporary set built on the shores of the lake. From here, the road meanders scenically down into the village of Roundwood and on to Glendalough.

▲▲Glendalough

The steep wooded slopes of Glendalough (GLEN-da-lock, "Valley of the Two Lakes"), at the south end of Wicklow's old military road, hide Ireland's most impressive monastic settlement. Founded by St. Kevin in the sixth century, the monastery flourished (despite repeated Viking raids) throughout the Age of Saints and Scholars until the English destroyed it in 1398. A few hardy holy men continued to live here until it was finally abandoned during the Dissolution of the Monasteries in 1539. But pilgrims kept coming, especially on St. Kevin's Day, June 3. (This might have something to do with the fact that a pope said seven visits to Glendalough had the same indulgence—or forgiveness from sins—value as one visit to Rome.) While much restoration was done in the 1870s, most of the buildings date from the 10th to 12th century.

In an Ireland without cities, these monastic communities were mainstays of civilization. At such remote outposts, ascetics (with a taste for scenic settings, but abstaining from worldly pleasures) gathered to commune with God. In the 12th century, with the arrival of grander monastic orders such as the Cistercians, Benedictines, Augustinians, Franciscans, and Dominicans, and with the growth of cities, these monastic communities were eclipsed. Today, Ireland is dotted with the reminders of this age: illuminated manuscripts, simple churches, carved crosses, and about 100 round towers.

The valley sights are split between the two lakes. The smaller, lower lake is just beyond the visitors center and nearer the best remaining ruins. The upper lake has scant ruins and feels like a state park, with a grassy lakeside picnic area and school groups. Walkers and hikers will enjoy a choice of nine different trails of varying lengths through the lush Wicklow countryside (longest loop takes four hours, hiking-trail maps available at visitors center).

Planning Your Time: Summer tour-bus crowds are terrible all day on weekends and 11:00-14:00 on weekdays. If you're there at midday, your best bet is to take the once-daily, 45-minute tour of the site (June-Aug only at 13:30, departs from visitors center). Otherwise, ask if you can tag along with a prebooked tour group's tour. If you're on your own, find the markers that give short descriptions of the ruined buildings.

Here's a good day-plan: Park for free at the visitors center. Visit the center; take the guided tour if possible; wander the ruins surrounding the round tower on your own (free); or walk the traffic-free Green Road a half-mile to the upper lake, and then walk back to the visitors center and your car along the trail that parallels the public road (an easy, roughly one-mile loop). Or you can drive to the upper lake. If you're rushed, skip the upper lake.

Cost and Hours: Free to enter site, €5 for visitors center, €4 to park at upper lake; open daily 9:30-18:00, mid-Oct-mid-March until 17:00; last entry 45 minutes before closing, tel. 0404/45352.

Visiting Glendalough: Start out at the **Glendalough Visitors Centre,** where a 15-minute video provides a good thumbnail background on monastic society in medieval Ireland. While the video is more general than specific to Glendalough, the adjacent museum room does feature this particular monastic settlement. The model in the center of the room re-creates the fortified village of the year 1050. Interactive exhibits show the contributions these monks made to intellectual life in Dark Age Europe (such as illuminated manuscripts and Irish minuscule, a more compact alphabet developed in the seventh century).

When you're ready to visit the site, head out behind the visitors center, cross the bridge over the brook, and follow the lane 100 yards to the original stone **gateway.** From here you enter the sacred inner-monastic grounds that provided sanctuary for anyone under threat. Look for the cross carved into the sanctuary stone in the gateway (at knee level). A refugee had 90 days to live safely within the walls. But on the 91st day, he would be tossed out to the waiting authorities...unless he became a monk (in which case he could live there indefinitely, no matter what his crime).

The graceful **round tower** rises from an evocative tangle of tombstones. Easily the best ruins of Glendalough gather within 100 yards of this famous 110-foot-tall tower. Towers like this (usually 60-110 feet tall with windows facing the four cardinal compass points) were standard features in such monastic settlements. They functioned as bell towers, storage lofts, beacons for pilgrims, and last-resort refuges during Viking raids. (But given enough warning, monks were safer hiding in the surrounding forest.) The towers had a high door with a pull-up ladder—both for safety and because a door at ground level would have weak-ened the tower's foundation. Several ruined churches (10th-12th century) lurk nearby...seek them out.

The **cathedral** is the largest and most central of all the ruins. It evolved over time with various expansions and through the reuse of stones from previous structures. The larger nave came first, and the chancel (up the couple of stairs where the altar later stood) was an addition. The east window faces toward Jerusalem and the rising sun, symbolic of Christ rising from the dead. Under the southern window is a small wall cupboard with a built-in basin. The holy vessels used during Mass were rinsed here so that the holy sacra-mental water would drain directly into the ground, avoiding any contamination (look for the tiny drain in the center).

Nearby is **St. Kevin's Cross.** At 10 feet tall and carved from a single block of granite, this cross was a statement of utter devo-tion. (Most other famous Irish high crosses were carved of softer sandstone, allowing their carvers to create more ornate depictions of biblical stories than you'll see here.) According to legend, if you hug this cross and can reach your hands around to touch your fin-gers on the other side, you'll have your wish granted (and your jeal-ous friends labeling you a knuckle dragger). St. Kevin: the patron saint of dislocated shoulders.

Heading downhill, you'll pass the tiny **priests' house,** which was completely reconstructed (using the original stones) from a 1779 sketch. It might have originally acted as a kind of treasury, housing the relics of St. Kevin.

Farther down, you'll come to perhaps the prettiest structure surviving on the site: **St. Kevin's "kitchen"** (actually a church).

Its short round tower appeared to earlier visitors to be a chimney, but its function was always as a belfry. The steeply stacked stone roof conceals a croft (upper story) perhaps used as a scriptorium for copying holy manuscripts. Nearby is the less impressive stone footprint of **St. Kieran's Church,** possibly dedicated to the saint and contemporary of St. Kevin who founded Clonmacnoise Monastery (another scenic sanctuary, on the banks of the River Shannon south of the town of Athlone).

From here, pass through the kissing gate and cross the bridge over the brook. On the other side, if you're short of time, turn left to go back to the visitors center and parking lot. With more time, turn right and explore the lovely tree-shrouded **Green Road,** which leads past the **lower lake** for a half-mile to the **upper lake** as part of a pleasant one-mile loop.

The oldest ruins—scant and hard to find—lie near the upper lake. **St. Kevin's bed** is a cave where the holy hermit-founder of the monastery took shelter. It lies above the left (southern) shore and is visible and reachable only by boat. The story goes that St. Kevin's devotion was so strong that he would strip off his clothes and jump into thorn bushes rather than submit to the pleasures of the flesh. Another tale has him standing in pious stillness with arms outstretched while a bird builds its nest in his hand. If you want a scenic Wicklow walk, begin here.

NEAR DUBLIN

Avondale House

Located in south County Wicklow (known as the Garden County), this mansion is the birthplace and lifelong home of Charles Stewart Parnell, the Nationalist politician and dynamo often called the "uncrowned King of Ireland" (see page 54).

Cost and Hours: €7, Thu-Sun 11:00-17:00, closed Mon-Wed and all of Nov-Easter, café, tel. 0404/46111, www.heritageisland. com.

Getting There: It's best to visit by car, as Avondale House is too far for the Dublin day-tour buses (45 miles south of Dublin). In good weather, avoid the €5 parking fee by leaving your car along the road (R-752) just outside the estate gate and walking 200 yards to the house. You can also take a train from Dublin's Connolly station to Rathdrum (4/day, 1.5 hours). From there, Avondale is a short taxi ride away (1.5 miles south of town; try Aughrim Cabs— mobile 086-852-5553).

Visiting the House: Upon entering the opulent Georgian "big house" (built in 1777), you'll first view an informative 20-minute video on Parnell's life. Then you're set free to roam with a handout outlining each room's highlights. A fine portrait of Parnell graces the grand, high-ceilinged entry hall, and a painting of his American grandfather, who manned the USS *Constitution* in the War of

1812, hangs in one room. The dining room is all class, with fine plasterwork and hardwood floors. Original furniture, such as Parnell's sturdy canopied bed, graces the remaining rooms, many of which come with cozy fireplaces and views. The lush surrounding estate of over 500 acres, laced with pleasant walking trails, was used by the Irish Forestry Service (Coillte) to try out forestry methods.

Irish National Stud

Ireland's famed County Kildare—just west of Dublin—has long been known to offer the perfect conditions for breeding horses. Its reputation dates all the way back to the 1300s, when Norman war horses were bred here. Kildare's grasslands lie on a bedrock table of limestone, infusing the soil with just the right mix of nutrients for grazing horses. And the nearby River Tully sparkles with high levels of calcium carbonate, essential for building strong bones in the expensive thoroughbreds (some owned by Arab sheikhs) raised and raced here.

In 1900, Colonel William Hall-Walker (Scottish heir to the Johnny Walker distilling fortune) bought a farm on the River Tully and began breeding a line of champion thoroughbreds. His amazing successes and bizarre methods were the talk of the sport. In 1916, the colonel donated his land and horse farm to the British government, which continued breeding horses here. The farm was eventually handed over to the Irish government, which in 1945 created the Irish National Stud Company to promote the thoroughbred industry.

Today, a guided tour of the grounds at the Irish National Stud gives you a fuller appreciation for the amazing horses that call this place home. Animal lovers and horse-racing fans driving between Dublin and Galway can enjoy a couple of hours here, combining the tour with a stroll through the gardens.

GETTING THERE

From M-7, **drivers** take exit #13 and follow the signs five minutes south (don't take exit #12 for the Curragh Racecourse). **Trains** departing Dublin's Heuston station stop at Kildare town (1-3/hour, 45 minutes). A shuttle bus runs from Kildare's train station to the National Stud (2/hour), or you can take a taxi (about €12-15). One **bus** departs Dublin's Busáras station Monday through Saturday at 9:30 and returns from the National Stud at 15:45. On Sunday, two buses run, departing Busáras at 10:00 and 12:00, with returns at 15:00 and 17:30. Confirm this schedule at the Dublin bus station.

NEAR DUBLIN

When Irish Horses Are Running

Every Irish town seems to have a betting shop for passionate locals who love to closely follow (and wager on) their favorite horses. A quick glance at the weekend sports sections of any Irish newspaper gives you an idea of this sport's high profile. Towns from Galway to Dingle host annual horse races that draw rabid fans from all over. Interestingly, Irish horse races run the track clockwise (the opposite direction from races in the US).

The five most prestigious Irish races take place at the **Curragh Racecourse,** just south of Kildare town (March-Oct, 1 hour west of Dublin, 10 minutes from the National Stud, www.curragh.ie). Horses have been raced here since 1741. The broad, open fields nearby are where the battle scenes in *Braveheart* were filmed (the neighboring Irish army base provided the blue-face-painted extras).

ORIENTATION TO IRISH NATIONAL STUD

Cost: €12.50 includes guided tour, plus entry to Japanese Gardens, St. Fiachra's Garden, and Horse Museum.

Hours: Daily 9:00-18:00, closed Nov-Jan, last entry one hour before closing, 30-minute tours depart at 10:30, 12:00, 14:00, and 16:00, tel. 045/521-617, www.irishnationalstud.ie.

Eating: There's a decent cafeteria, or bring your own food and eat at a picnic table by the parking lot.

VISITING IRISH NATIONAL STUD

The guided tour begins in the **Sun Chariot Yard** (named for the winner of the 1942 Fillies Triple Crown), surrounded by stables housing pregnant mares. A 15-minute film of a foal's birth runs continuously in a stall in the corner of the yard.

The adjacent **Foaling Unit** is where births take place, usually from February through May. The gestation period for horses is 11 months, with 90 percent of foals born at night. (In the wild, a mare and her foal born during the day would have been vulnerable to predators as the herd moved on. Instead, horses have adapted so that foals are born at night—and are able to keep up with the herd within a few hours.) Eccentric Colonel Hall-Walker noted the position of the moon and stars at the time of each foal's birth, and sold those born under inauspicious astrological signs (regardless of their parents' stellar racing records).

From here, you'll pass a working saddle-making shop and a forge where horseshoes are still hammered out on an anvil.

At the **Stallion Boxes,** you'll learn how stargazing Colonel Hall-Walker installed skylights in the stables—allowing the heavens maximum influence over the destiny of his prized animals. A brass plaque on the door of each stall proudly states the horse's name and its racing credentials. One stall bears the simple word, "Teaser." The unlucky occupant's job is to identify mares in heat... but rarely is the frustrated stallion given the opportunity to breed. Bummer.

After the tour, meander down the pleasant tree-lined **Tully Walk,** with paddocks on each side. You'll see mares and foals running free, with the occasional cow thrown in for good measure (cattle have a calming effect on rowdy horses). To ensure you come home with all your fingers, take full note of the *Horses Bite and Kick* signs. These superstar animals are bred for high spirits—and are far too feisty to pet.

Other Sights: Visitors with extra time can explore three more attractions (all included in your entry ticket). The tranquil and photogenic **Japanese Gardens** were created by the colonel to depict the trials of life (beware the Tunnel of Ignorance). A wander through the more extensive and natural **St. Fiachra's Garden** (the patron saint of gardening) demands more time. Equestrian buffs may want to linger among the memorabilia in the small **Horse Museum,** where you can get a grip on how many hands it takes to measure a horse.

NEAR DUBLIN

KILKENNY & THE ROCK OF CASHEL

Driving from Dublin (on Ireland's east coast) to Dingle (on Ireland's west coast), the best two stops to break the long journey across the Irish interior are Kilkenny, Ireland's finest medieval town; and the Rock of Cashel, a thought-provoking early Christian site crowning the Plain of Tipperary.

Counties Kilkenny and Tipperary ("Tipp" to locals) are friendly neighbors geographically, yet blood sporting rivals on the hurling field, with the lion's share of the GAA national championships split between them. (Kilkenny locals are quick to point out that their 34 championships top all Irish counties.) Watch for kids heading home from school, carrying hurlies (ash-wood sticks with broad, flat ends) and dressed in their local colors (black and yellow, like bumblebees, for Kilkenny; blue and gold for Tipperary).

These two counties also boast some of the finest agricultural land on this rocky and boggy island. That's why Norman invaders fought to wrestle it away and make it one of their first Irish breadbaskets 750 years ago, soon after they secured their County Wexford beachhead. These days, farm tractors rumble the back roads where it's not a long way to Tipperary.

PLANNING YOUR TIME

With one day, drivers connecting Dublin with Kinsale can get an early start, stop in Kilkenny for lunch, and then tour the Rock of Cashel before ending up in Kinsale to spend the night. For a longer visit, Kilkenny makes a good overnight for drivers from Dublin who want to visit Powerscourt Gardens and Glendalough (see previous chapter).

I've listed accommodations for both Kilkenny and at the Rock of Cashel: A night in Kilkenny comes with plenty of traditional folk music in its pubs, and more to do (additional sights nearby include Jerpoint Abbey and Kells Priory). If you're driving between Dublin and Dingle (or Kenmare), the Rock of Cashel is a more direct overnight.

With a few extra days, consider worthwhile destinations along the southeast coast, such as Waterford and County Wexford (see next chapter). Folks with more time can continue on the scenic southern coastal route west via Cobh, Kinsale, Kenmare, and the Ring of Kerry (all covered in later chapters).

Kilkenny

The country's loveliest inland city—past winner of Ireland's "Tidy Town" award—Kilkenny gives you a feel for salt-of-the-earth Ireland. The town earned its nickname, the "Marble City," because of the stone from the local quarry (actually black limestone, not marble). You can see white seashells fossilized within the black stone steps around town. While an average size town today (around 25,000 residents), Kilkenny has a big history. It was even the capital of Ireland for a short spell in the turbulent 1640s. Actor George Clooney traces his roots to Kilkenny.

Kilkenny's castle and cathedral stand like historic bookends on a higgledy-piggledy High Street of colorful shops and medieval facades. This stretch of town has been rebranded as "The Medieval Mile." Other Irish towns can't quite claim such a colorful and concentrated window into those feudal times.

Orientation to Kilkenny

TOURIST INFORMATION
The TI is a block off the bridge in the 16th-century Shee (a wealthy medieval donor family) Alms poorhouse (Mon-Sat 9:00-17:30, Sun 11:00-17:00, shorter hours and closed Sun off-season; Rose Inn Street, tel. 056/775-1500). The Kilkenny Medieval Mile Pass sold by the TI isn't worth the trouble for most travelers.

ARRIVAL IN KILKENNY

The train/bus station is four blocks from John's Bridge, which marks the center of town.

If you're arriving by car, the Market Yard Car Park behind Kyteler's Inn is handy for a few hours (€1.50/hour, daily 8:00-18:00, entry off Bateman's Quay). The multistory parking garage on Ormonde Street is the best long-term bet (€1.50/hour, or get the 3-day pass for €10 if staying overnight—it allows you to come and go; open 7:00-23:00, Fri-Sat until 24:00). If parking overnight, wait until you depart to pay as some hotels will validate parking. Otherwise, you can use the pay-and-display meters on the street (€1.50/hour, enforced Mon-Sat 8:00-19:00).

HELPFUL HINTS

Market: The square in front of Kilkenny Castle hosts a friendly produce, cheese, and crafts market on Thursday (8:00-14:30).

Laundry: At the south end of town, the **Laundry Basket** trumpets its existence in vivid red at 21 Patrick Street (Mon-Fri 9:00-18:00, Sat 10:00-15:00, closed Sun, tel. 056/777-0355).

Bookstore: With a cheap and cheery café upstairs, **The Book Centre** is a great place to hang out on a rainy day (Mon-Sat 9:00-18:00, Sun 13:00-17:00, 10 High Street, tel. 056/776-2177).

Bike Rentals: Kilkenny Cycling rents bikes for €20 a day (€50 refundable deposit). They provide safety gear, and have route maps for exploring the pastoral charms of County Kilkenny (office behind The Wine Center shop at 15 John Street, mobile 086-895-4961, www.kilkennycyclingtours.com).

KILKENNY & CASHEL

Tours in Kilkenny

Walking Tour

Pat Tynan and his staff offer the only regularly scheduled walking tours in town. They last one hour and depart from the TI (€10, daily at 11:00 and 14:00, Nov-mid-March by prior arrangement only, mobile 087-265-1745, www.kilkennywalkingtours.ie).

Local Guides

For more than 40 years, **Frank Kavanagh** helped visitors appreciate Kilkenny Castle. These days, he's available for custom walks of the town and castle. He also offers handy full- or half-day driving tours to destinations as far away as Cashel and Waterford (available Feb-Nov, book ahead, €75/half-day, €150/full day, gas and lunch cost extra, mobile 086-839-2468, http://visitkilkenny.ie/franks_medieval_tours, fkav1948@gmail.com).

Amanda Pitcairn runs scholarly tours focusing on the history of medieval Kilkenny and the daily life of its inhabitants—witchcraft and skullduggery included. Ask about her connection to mutineers from the *HMS Bounty* (€8, book ahead, mobile 087-277-6107, www.touchthepastireland.com, pitcaira@tcd.ie).

Bike Tours

At **Kilkenny Cycling,** Jason Morrissey is the man with the plan for a two-hour "easy-paced" guided tour (€20), which takes in a half-dozen of the town's best sights, including Kilkenny Castle, Rothe House and Garden, and St. Canice's Cathedral (usually departs at 10:00 and 14:00, also at 19:00 May-Sept). Ask about his four-hour unguided "bike-and-hike" recommended route, which includes a six-mile ride to Bennettsbridge (he'll explain where to leave the bikes). Your route home is a pretty hike back along the river. He also offers a €20 medieval mile cycling treasure hunt for history buffs (ask for discount with this book, cash only, see "Bike Rentals," earlier, for contact info).

Sights in Kilkenny

▲▲Kilkenny Castle

Dominating the town, this castle is a stony reminder that the Anglo-Norman Butler family controlled Kilkenny for 500 years. The castle once had four sides, but Oliver Cromwell's army knocked down one wall when it took the castle, leaving it as the roughly "U" shape we see today.

Cost and Hours: €8, daily June-Aug 9:00-17:30, slightly shorter hours off-season, tel. 056/770-4100, www.kilkennycastle.ie.

Visiting the Castle: Enter the castle gate, turn right in the courtyard, and head into the base of the turret. Here you'll find the continuously running 12-minute video explaining how the wooden fort, built here by Strongbow in 1172, evolved into a 17th-century château. Then go into the main castle entrance, diagonally across the courtyard from the turret, to buy your entry ticket. You'll be free to walk through the castle. A pamphlet explains the exhibits, and you can also talk to stewards in the important rooms.

Now restored to its Victorian splendor, the castle's highlight is the beautiful family-portrait gallery, which puts you face-to-face with the wealthy Butler family ghosts.

Nearby: The **Kilkenny Design Centre,** across the street from the castle in some grand old stables, is full of local crafts and offers handy cafeteria-style lunches in its food hall (shops open Mon-Sat 10:00-19:00, Sun until 18:00; food hall open daily 8:30-18:30; tel. 056/772-2118, www.kilkennydesign.com).

▲Rothe House and Garden

This is the crown jewel of Kilkenny's medieval architecture: a well-preserved merchant's house that expanded around interior courtyards as the prosperous Rothe family grew in the early 1600s.

Cost and Hours: €5.50; Mon-Sat 10:30-17:00, Sun 12:00-17:00; Nov-March closes at 16:30 and all day Sun; Parliament Street, tel. 056/772-2893, http://rothehouse.com.

Visiting the House and Garden: Check out the graceful top-floor timberwork supporting the roof, which uses wooden dowels (pegs) instead of nails. The museum, which also serves as the County Kilkenny genealogy center, gives a glimpse of life here in late Elizabethan and early Stuart times. The walled gardens at the far back were a real luxury in their time.

The Rothe family eventually lost the house when Oliver Cromwell banished all Catholic landowners, sending them to live on less desirable land west of the River Shannon. In the late 1800s, the building housed the Gaelic League, devoted to the rejuvenation of Irish culture through preservation of the Irish language and promotion of native Irish sports (such as hurling). One of the future leaders of the 1916 rebellion—Thomas McDonagh, who was executed at Dublin's Kilmainham Gaol—taught here.

▲Medieval Mile Museum

This fine museum, opened in 2017, covers Kilkenny's brutal yet pious Dark Age past and rounds out the story that the Rothe House (listed above) starts.

Cost and Hours: €7, €12 with 45-minute tour; open daily 10:00-18:00, Nov-March 11:00-16:30; tours leave daily at 10:30,

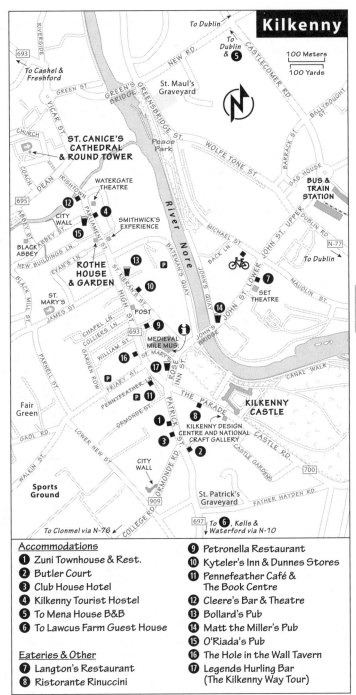

KILKENNY & CASHEL

Accommodations
1. Zuni Townhouse & Rest.
2. Butler Court
3. Club House Hotel
4. Kilkenny Tourist Hostel
5. To Mena House B&B
6. To Lawcus Farm Guest House

Eateries & Other
7. Langton's Restaurant
8. Ristorante Rinuccini
9. Petronella Restaurant
10. Kyteler's Inn & Dunnes Stores
11. Pennefeather Café & The Book Centre
12. Cleere's Bar & Theatre
13. Bollard's Pub
14. Matt the Miller's Pub
15. O'Riada's Pub
16. The Hole in the Wall Tavern
17. Legends Hurling Bar (The Kilkenny Way Tour)

12:30, 14:30, and 16:30; 2 Mary's Lane, tel. 056/781-7022, www.medievalmilemuseum.ie.

Visiting the Museum: Housed in the 13th-century St. Mary's Church (much of which was rebuilt in the 1700s), the museum displays medieval artifacts, including ornately carved tomb lids, ceremonial swords and scepters, and neatly penned 800-year-old civic records (with exhibits enhanced by modern touchscreen displays). You'll also find peekaboo glimpses of hidden burial vaults through Plexiglas flooring and visit the private chapel of the Rothes (the wealthy merchant family). Guided tours put flesh on the bones of this museum's stony skeleton.

The site itself also has an interesting history. This is where the famous witch trial of Alice Kyteler and her son took place in 1324. The two beat the rap with money: She paid to engineer a secret escape while her son funded the reroofing of the church. That left her destitute maid to take the heat...literally. Then, as now, the poor are at a disadvantage in court. The evocative graveyard out back whispers the righteous claims to heaven of the rich donors who built this medieval town.

▲Hurling Museum and Stadium Experience

The sport of hurling is historically and culturally important to the Irish. And Kilkenny is a hurling mecca (check out the cool statue of three players in leaping action, at the southwest end of John's Bridge). Run by PJ Lanigan, "The Kilkenny Way" is a walking tour that includes visits to a hurling pub/museum and the stadium where the Kilkenny Cats play. You'll learn about the long history and rules of this lightning-fast field game, and also get a chance to play as you figure out how to balance your *sliotar*—and how to pronounce it.

Cost and Hours: €25 for two-hour tour, includes pub meal; daily at 13:45, reserve ahead in summer; leaves from Legends Hurling Bar, 28 Rose Inn Street, tel. 056/772-1718, www.thekilkennyway.com.

St. Canice's Cathedral

This 13th-century cathedral is early-English Gothic, rich with stained glass, medieval carvings, and floors paved in history. Check out the model of the old walled town in its 1641 heyday, as well as a couple of modest audiovisuals. The 100-foot-tall **round tower,** built as part of a long-gone pre-Norman church, recalls the need for a watchtower, treasury, and refuge. The fun ladder-climb to the top affords a grand view of the countryside.

Cost and Hours: Cathedral-€4, tower-€3, combo-ticket-€6; Mon-Sat 9:00-18:00, Sun 13:00-18:00; Sept-May slightly shorter hours and closed for lunch; tel. 056/776-4971, www.stcanicescathedral.com.

Smithwick's Experience Kilkenny

Smithwick's (pronounced SMITH-icks) reddish ale was born in Kilkenny...and has been my favorite Irish beer since my first visit to Ireland. Older than Guinness (but now owned by the same parent company), Smithwick's marked its tercentennial (300th anniversary) in 2010. After a corporate shake-up in 2013, the brewery consolidated its operations in Dublin and opened an "Experience" visitors center here on the former brewery grounds.

Tours focus on the historic origins of the tasty ale, first brewed by the monks of St. Francis Abbey (the 14th-century ruins of the abbey lie adjacent to the site). In the days of the monks, beer was a safer and healthier alternative to local water sources that were often contaminated. I'll drink to that.

Note that—like the Guinness Storehouse in Dublin—this is not a tour of a working brewery. It's a corporate-sponsored homage to the history of the brewery that once operated here.

Cost and Hours: €13, discount if booked online, entry includes a pint at the tour's end; daily 10:00-18:00, Nov-Feb 11:00-16:00, one-hour tours run hourly, last tour departs one hour before closing; 44 Parliament Street, tel. 056/778-6377, www.smithwicksexperience.com.

Nightlife in Kilkenny

Pubs and Traditional Music Sessions

Kilkenny has its fair share of atmospheric pubs. Visitors seeking fun trad music sessions can try the first four places listed here. Those seeking friendly conversation in utterly unvarnished Irish surroundings should seek out the memorable duo at the end of these listings. A fun pub crawl could link all of these places with 20 minutes of walking (30 minutes crawling). Check on nightly pub trad session schedules as you explore town during the day (they may change unpredictably).

Starting at the north end of town and working south, **Cleere's Bar & Theatre** is a friendly throwback with surprisingly good pub grub served until 20:00 (music Mon and Wed at 21:30, 28 Parliament Street). **Bollard's Pub,** an unpretentious landmark at the north end of St. Kieran's Street, is a good bet for lively traditional music sessions (Tue and Thu-Fri at 21:00). Or sit out front under the awning and enjoy a pint as Kilkenny's humanity flows past you. Just down the same street is **Kyteler's Inn,** with a stony facade and medieval witch-haunted cellar (music nightly in summer at 18:00, 27 St. Kieran's Street). You can saunter over John's Bridge to check out the tunes at **Matt the Miller's Pub,** with its multilevel, dark-wood interior (around 21:00 most nights, next to bridge on John Street across the river from the castle).

Lacking music but high on character, **O'Riada's** is an endangered species—a wonderful, old-fashioned place that your Irish grandfather would recognize and linger in. This is an ideal place to chat with engaging locals (across from the Watergate Theatre at 25 Parliament Street).

At the other end of the conversational spectrum, **The Hole in the Wall** is a tiny, restored Elizabethan tavern (c. 1582) hidden down an alley (capacity 15-20, mostly standing). Charmingly eccentric owner Michael Conway—cardiologist by day and historian/playwright/actor/barman by night—presides over the speakeasy-like space as a labor of love. His sporadic music sessions (which mostly take place in the slightly larger, but equally creaky, timber-beamed upstairs hall) can't be pigeon-holed. But when they're on, they are usually an uninhibited, go-for-broke thump-a-thon (he plays bass drum). Spontaneous, but always entertaining, Conway conducts sing-alongs of Irish classics that include helpful lyrics and explanations of Irish idioms (unpredictable hours but typically Fri-Sat from 20:00 and sometimes weeknights, confirm ahead, look for the alley beside Bourkes shop at 17 High Street, tel. 087/807-5650, www.holeinthewall.ie).

Theater

The **Watergate Theatre** houses live plays and other performances in its 300-seat space (€12-25, Parliament Street, tel. 056/776-1674, www.watergatetheatre.com).

The **Set Theatre,** adjacent to sprawling Langton's Restaurant, is a fine, modern, 250-seat music venue attracting top-notch Irish acts in an intimate setting (€10-25, John Street, tel. 056/772-1728, www.set.ie).

Sleeping in Kilkenny

My first three listings are more central, clustered within a block of each other along Patrick Street; in general, options for smaller places in town are shrinking as they struggle to compete with bigger hotels.

Note: Kilkenny is a popular weekend destination for loud and rowdy stag and hen (bachelor and bachelorette) parties, thanks to its easy train access from Dublin (no risk of drunk driving). For quiet at night, avoid hotels with bars downstairs or nearby, and stick with smaller B&Bs, guesthouses, or rural lodging (especially Fri-Sat nights). Except for the Zuni and Club House, my recommendations should be free of these disturbances.

IN THE CENTER

$$$ Zuni Townhouse, above a fashionable restaurant, has 13 boutique-chic rooms sporting colorfully angular furnishings. Ask about two-night weekend breaks and midweek specials that include a four-course dinner (parking in back, 26 Patrick Street, tel. 056/772-3999, www.zuni.ie, info@zuni.ie).

$$ Butler Court is Kilkenny's best lodging value. Ever-helpful Yvonne and John offer 10 modern, spacious rooms behind the beige, flag-draped archway. Bo the dog quietly patrols the courtyard (wheelchair-accessible, continental breakfast in room, will validate parking in nearby multistory garage on Ormonde Street for length of your stay, 14 Patrick Street, tel. 056/776-1178, www.butlercourt.com, info@butlercourt.com).

$$ Club House Hotel, originally a gentlemen's sporting club, comes with fading Georgian elegance; a musty, creaking ambience; a palatial, well-antlered breakfast room; and 35 comfy bedrooms (secure parking, 19 Patrick Street, tel. 056/772-1994, www.clubhousehotel.com, info@clubhousehotel.com).

¢ Kilkenny Tourist Hostel fills a fine Georgian townhouse with ramshackle fellowship at the north end of the town center, right in the action. It offers 70 cheap beds, a friendly family room, a well-equipped members' kitchen, and a wealth of local information (private rooms available, cash only, pay self-serve laundry, 2 blocks from cathedral at 35 Parliament Street, tel. 056/776-3541, www.kilkennyhostel.ie, info@kilkennyhostel.ie).

FARTHER OUT

$ Mena House B&B is a traditional, good-value option quietly nestled a mile north of town, about a 15-minute walk from the center and easy for drivers (parking, just south of the Kilkenny Golf Club on Castlecomer Road, tel. 056/776-5362, www.menahousebandb.com, menahouse@eircom.net).

$$ Lawcus Farm Guest House is a quirky, seductive confection of rural comfort 10 miles south of Kilkenny between Kells Priory and the village of Stoneyford. Hosts Mark and Ann Marie have a passion for recycled materials and an environmental sensitivity. Mark, an inventive craftsman, renovated the original house and built the rest. A menagerie of friendly pets and farm animals shares the tasteful 20-acre property straddling the Kings River. Ask about the tiny secluded tree house (family rooms, cash only, parking, mobile 086-603-1667 or 087-291-1056, www.lawcusfarmguesthouse.com, lawcusfarm@hotmail.com). To reach the farm, go south out of Kilkenny on N-10, which becomes R-713 after crossing over the M-9 motorway. Just as you enter the village of Stoneyford, turn right onto L-1023. Go 500 yards down that lane and watch for a

KILKENNY & CASHEL

brown sign directing you to turn right into a 100-yard-long gravel driveway.

Eating in Kilkenny

$$$ **Langton's** is every local's first choice, serving high-quality Irish dishes under a labyrinthine, multichambered, Tiffany-skylight expanse (daily 12:00-22:00, 69 John Street, tel. 056/776-5133, www.langtons.ie).

$$$$ **Ristorante Rinuccini** serves classy, romantic, candlelit Italian meals (daily 12:00-14:30 & 17:00-22:00, reservations smart, 1 The Parade, tel. 056/776-1575, www.rinuccini.com).

$$ **Petronella Restaurant** warms its medieval surroundings with dependable traditional dishes and a welcoming vibe (Mon-Sat 12:00-15:00 & 17:00-21:00, closed Sun, Butterslip Lane off High Street, tel. 056/776-1899, www.petronella.ie).

$$$$ **Zuni,** in one of my recommended accommodations, is a stylish splurge offering international cuisine (daily 12:30-17:00 & 18:00-20:45, weekend reservations a good idea, 26 Patrick Street, tel. 056/772-3999, www.zuni.ie).

$$$ **Kyteler's Inn** serves decent pub grub in a timber-and-stone atmosphere with a heated and covered beer garden out back. Visit their fun 14th-century cellar and ask about their witch. Watch your head or risk leaving some of your DNA embedded in the low stone arches (Mon-Sat 12:00-21:00, Sun until 20:00, 27 St. Kieran's Street, tel. 056/772-1064).

$ **Pennefeather Café,** above the Kilkenny Book Centre, is good for a quick, cheap, light lunch (Mon-Sat 9:00-17:30, closed Sun, 10 High Street, tel. 056/776-4063).

Grocery Store: You'll find an ample selection of supplies for a grassy picnic at **Dunnes Stores** (a few doors down from Kyteler's Inn on St. Kieran's Street, Mon-Sat 8:00-22:00, Sun 10:00-20:00).

Kilkenny Connections

From Kilkenny by Train to: Dublin (6/day, 1.5 hours), **Waterford** (6/day, 45 minutes). For details, see www.irishrail.ie.

By Bus to: Dublin (8/day, 2.5 hours), **Waterford** (2/day, 1 hour), **Tralee** (3/day, 5.5 hours, change in Cork), **Galway** (3/day, 5 hours). For details, see www.buseireann.ie.

Between Kilkenny and Waterford

The fast M-9 motorway links Kilkenny and Waterford on a 45-minute drive. But drivers in no rush can savor the journey by spending a couple of enjoyable backroad hours taking in two pastoral sights: Jerpoint Abbey and Kells Priory. (You can also stitch these places into a more leisurely itinerary for an easy, triangular day trip beginning and ending in Kilkenny—about 28 miles/45 km total.) The rural roads come with old stone bridges spanning placid rivers that weave among tiny villages and abandoned mills. Bring an Ordnance Survey atlas (available at most bookstores) to navigate. It's easier to visit Jerpoint Abbey first. There are no guided tours at Kells Priory; ask at the abbey for directions and pointers.

▲▲Jerpoint Abbey

Evocative abbey ruins dot the Irish landscape, but few are as well-presented as Jerpoint (founded in 1180). Its claim to fame is fine stone carvings on the sides of tombs and on the columns of the cloister arcade. If you visit only one abbey in Ireland, make sure it's this one.

Without the excellent guided tours, the site is a cold, rigid ruin. But once in the hands of the unusually well-versed hosts, the place truly comes alive with insights into the monastic culture that imprinted Ireland 850 years ago.

Cost and Hours: €5; daily 9:00-17:30; shorter hours Oct-Nov; Dec-March by appointment only; tel. 056/772-4623.

Getting There: It's located about 11 miles (17 km) south of Kilkenny or 2 miles (3 km) south of Thomastown, beside R-700.

Visiting the Abbey: The Cistercian monks, who came to Ireland from France in the 12th century, were devoted reformers bent on following the strict rules of St. Benedict. Their holy mission was to bring the wild Irish Christian church (which had evolved, unsupervised, for centuries on the European fringe) back in line with Rome. With an uncompromising my-way-or-the-hell-way attitude, they steamrolled their belief system across the island and stamped the landscape with a network of identical, sprawling monasteries. The preexisting form of Celtic Christianity that had thrived in the Dark Ages was no match for the organization and determination of the Cistercians.

For the next 350 years, these new monasteries held the moral high ground and were the dominant local religious authority. Monks got closer to God by immersing themselves in the hardships of manual field work, building water mills, tending kilns, and advancing the craft of metallurgy. The wealth created by this turbo-charged industriousness caused communities to form around these magnetic monastic cores.

What eventually did them in? King Henry VIII's marriage problems, his subsequent creation of the (Protestant) Church of England, and his eventual dissolution of the (Catholic) monasteries. Walls were knocked down and roofs were torn off monasteries such as Jerpoint to make them uninhabitable. Their lands were forfeited to the king, who sold them off and enriched his treasury. It's good to be king.

▲▲Kells Priory

This place is a wonderful lonely gem. Locals claim that the massive religious complex of Kells Priory (more than 3 acres) is the largest monastic site in Europe. It's an isolated, deserted ruin that begs a curious wander, a nimble shutter finger on your camera, and alert side-stepping of sheep droppings.

Don't confuse this Kells with the identically named town farther north in County Meath (that's the Kells that produced the famous Book of Kells, now housed in Trinity College Library in Dublin).

Cost and Hours: Free, no set hours.

Getting There: You'll find Kells Priory about 9 miles (15 km) south of Kilkenny or 6 miles (10 km) west of Jerpoint Abbey, just off the R-697 road. From Jerpoint Abbey, turn left, then take your first right through the village of Stoneyford. At the end of the village, turn left (at the sign for Kells Priory), then continue straight.

The main parking lot lies on a slope above the south side of the ruins (a good place for a quick overview photo stop). But I prefer to park beside the Kings River on the north side of the ruins. To get there, cross the pretty stone bridge over the river, and turn right onto the L-5067 road. Drive about 100 yards past the first mill (with a craft shop in an adjacent building); when you come to the second mill (completely shuttered and abandoned), park in the gravel lot in front.

Visiting Kells Priory: From the parking lot by the abandoned mill (described above), stroll past the mill's rusty waterwheel and enjoy the wander downstream for the remaining 100 yards along the riverside path. It's a photogenic approach to the priory ruins. Once inside the complex, watch where you walk and explore at your leisure. Consider bringing a picnic to enjoy. But please respect the site and leave no trash.

Founded in 1193 by Norman soldiers of fortune with Augustinian monks in tow, this priory grew into the intimidating structure that locals call "the seven castles" today. These "castles," however, were actually Norman tower houses connected by a wall that enclosed the religious functions within. Inside the walls, the site is divided into two main areas: One is a huge interior courtyard (larger than a football field) dominated by the encircling tower houses;

the other is a tangled medieval maze of rock walls (remnants of a cloister, a church, cellars, a medieval dormitory, and a graveyard).

The most dramatic 75-year period of the site's history took place between 1252 and 1327, when it was attacked and burned three times (once by Edward the Bruce's army of Scots). The contrast between those violent times and today's pastoral decay is striking.

Rock of Cashel

Rising high above the fertile Plain of Tipperary, the Rock of Cashel is one of Ireland's most historic and evocative sights. Seat of

the ancient kings of Munster (c. A.D. 300-1100), this is where St. Patrick baptized King Aengus in about A.D. 450. Strategically located and perfect for fortification, the Rock was fought over by local clans for hundreds of years. Finally, in 1101, clever Murtagh O'Brien gave the Rock to the Church. His seemingly benevolent donation increased his influence with the Church, while preventing his rivals, the powerful McCarthy clan, from regaining possession of the Rock. As Cashel evolved into an ecclesiastical center, Iron Age ring forts and thatch dwellings gave way to the majestic stone church buildings enjoyed by visitors today. Queen Elizabeth II's history-making, four-day visit to Ireland in 2011 included a visit to the Rock.

ORIENTATION TO THE ROCK OF CASHEL

Cost and Hours: €8, families-€20, ticket includes guided tour—see below; open daily 9:00-19:00, mid-March-early June and mid-Sept-mid-Oct until 17:30, winter until 16:30, last entry 45 minutes before closing; tel. 062/61437, www.heritageireland. ie.

Crowd-Beating Tips: Summer crowds flock to the Rock (worst June-Aug 11:00-15:00). Try to plan your visit for early or late in the day.

Dress Warmly: Bring a coat—while the parking lot can be sheltered, the Rock is exposed and often cold and windy.

Tours: Guided walks are included with your entrance (2/hour, about 45 minutes). Otherwise, set your own pace with my self-guided tour.

Parking: Pay the €4.50 fee at the machine (under the Plexiglas shelter to the left of the exit) before returning to your car.

KILKENNY & CASHEL

Rock of Cashel

VIEW TO
HORE ABBEY

O'SCULLY
CRYPT

6 ROUND
TOWER

WELL

7

CASTLE
8

CATHEDRAL

MAGRATH'S
TOMB

"BIG WIND
CHUNK"

5

FRESCOES
(14TH
CENT.)

CORMAC'S
CHAPEL

4

TOUR
ENDS

TOMB
CARVINGS
OF SAINTS

FRESCOES
(15TH CENT.)

3

ST. PATRICK'S
CROSS
(COPY)

2

Cliffs

TICKETS

DORMITORY
(VIDEO)

1

HALL OF
VICARS CHORAL
(MUSEUM
DOWNSTAIRS)

50 Meters

50 Yards

TOUR
BEGINS

GATE

STONE
WALL

To Hore Abbey

To **P**, Sounds of
History Museum
& Cashel Town

1 Hall of the Vicars Choral
2 St. Patrick's Cross
3 Cormac's Chapel (Exterior)
4 Chapel Interior & Sarcophagus

5 Forgotten Void
6 Graveyard & Round Tower
7 Cathedral
8 Castle (or Tower)

KILKENNY & CASHEL

WCs: Use the basic ones at the base of the Rock next to the parking lot (there are none up on the Rock).

OVERVIEW

From the parking lot, it's a steep 100-yard walk up to the Rock itself. On this 200-foot-high outcrop of limestone, the first building you'll enter is the 15th-century Hall of the Vicars Choral, housing the ticket desk, a tiny museum (with a stunted original 12th-century high cross dedicated to St. Patrick and a few replica artifacts), and a 20-minute video (2/hour, shown in the hall's former dormitory). From there you'll explore the following: a round tower, an early Christian cross, a delightful Romanesque chapel, and a ruined Gothic cathedral, all surrounded by my favorite Celtic-cross graveyard with views for miles.

◉ SELF-GUIDED TOUR

Nowhere else in Ireland can you better see the evolution of Irish devotion expressed in stone. This large lump of rock is a pedestal supporting a compact tangle of three dramatic architectural styles: early Christian (round tower and St. Patrick's high cross), Romanesque (Cormac's Chapel), and Gothic (the main cathedral).

• *Follow this tour counterclockwise around the Rock. Start by descending the indoor stairs opposite the ticket desk into the one-room, vaulted cellar museum.*

❶ Hall of the Vicars Choral

You are in the cellar of the youngest building on the Rock (early 1400s). This would have been the storage room for the vicars (minor clerics) appointed to sing during cathedral services. Today it contains a sparse collection of artifacts (some copies) associated with the religious site. Two glass cases display brooches and primitive axes, while the walls are hung with stone slab carvings. The impressively ornate shrine bell of St. Patrick is a reproduction (the bell would not have been used by him, but rather, dedicated to him, centuries later). But the star of the vault is the **original Cross of St. Patrick** at the far end. The massive stone base is hollow (see the mirror underneath it). Was it a hiding place for valuable religious objects during raids? Or just too heavy to move otherwise? The cross stood outside for centuries, but hundreds of years of wind and rain slowly buffeted away important detail, scouring it into the stubby shape that remains. On my first visit here, almost 40 years ago, the original cross still stood outside; today, a copy occupies the original location (for history on the cross, see next page).

• *Climb back up to the ticket desk level and continue up the indoor stairs into the living space of the vicars.*

Walk to the **great hall** with the big brown tapestry. Vicars were granted nearby lands by the archbishop and lived comfortably here, with a large fireplace and white, lime-washed walls (to reflect light and act as a natural disinfectant that discouraged bugs). Window seats gave the blessedly literate vicars the best light to read by. The furniture is original, but the colorfully ornamented oak timber roof is a reconstruction, built to medieval specifications using wooden dowels instead of nails. The large wall tapestry shows King Solomon with the Queen of Sheba.

The vicars, who formed a sort of corporate body to assist the bishop with local administration, used a special seal to authorize documents such as land leases. You can see an enlarged wooden copy of the seal (hanging above the fireplace), depicting eight vicars surrounding a seated organist. It was a good system—until some of the greedier vicars duplicated the seal for their own less holy purposes, forcing the archbishop to curtail its use.

• *Go outside the hall into the grassy space, veer left about 30 feet, and find...*

❷ St. Patrick's Cross

St. Patrick baptized King Aengus on the Rock of Cashel in about A.D. 450. This 12th-century cross, a stub of its former glory, was carved to celebrate the handing over of the Rock to the Church 650 years after St. Patrick's visit (the cross that stands here is a copy; the original is in the museum in the Hall of the Vicars Choral, described earlier). Typical Irish high crosses use a ring around the cross' head to support its arms and to symbolize the sun (making Christianity more appealing to the sun-worshipping Celts). But instead, this cross uses the Latin design: The weight of the arms is supported by two vertical beams on each side of the main shaft, representing the two criminals who were crucified beside Christ (today only one of these supports remains).

• *Walk about 100 feet slightly uphill along the gravel path beside the cathedral. Roughly opposite the far end of the Hall of the Vicars Choral is the entry (a glass door) to the chapel.*

❸ Cormac's Chapel (Exterior)

As the wild Celtic Christian church was reined in and reorganized by Rome 850 years ago, new architectural influences from

continental Europe began to emerge on the remote Irish landscape. This small chapel—Ireland's first and finest Romanesque church, constructed in 1134 by King Cormac MacCarthy—reflects this evolution. Imagine being here in the 12th century, when this chapel and the tall round tower were the only stone structures sprouting from the Rock (among a few long-gone, humble wooden structures).

The "new" Romanesque style reflected the ancient Roman basilica floor plan. Its columns and rounded arches created an overall effect of massiveness and strength. Romanesque churches were like dark fortresses, with thick walls, squat towers, and few windows. Irish stone churches of this period (like the one at Glendalough in the Wicklow Mountains) were simple rectangular buildings emphasizing function.

The two square towers resemble those in Regensburg, Germany, further suggesting that well-traveled medieval Irish monks brought back new ideas from the Continent.

Before stepping inside, notice the weathered tympanum above the door. The carved "hippo" is actually an ox, representing Gospel author St. Luke.

• *The modern, dark-glass chapel door is a recent addition to keep out nesting birds. Enter the chapel and let your eyes adjust to the low light.*

❹ Chapel Interior

Just inside, on your left, is an empty stone **sarcophagus.** Nobody knows for sure whose body once lay here (possibly the brother of King Cormac MacCarthy). The damaged front relief is carved in a Viking style. Vikings had been raiding Ireland for more than 200 years by the time this was carved; they had already intermarried with the Irish, and were seeping into Irish society. Some scholars interpret the relief design (a tangle of snakes and beasts) as a figure-eight lying on its side, looping back and forth forever, symbolizing the eternity of the afterlife.

You're standing in the **nave,** dimly lit by three small windows. Overhead is a round vaulted ceiling with support ribs. The strong round arches support not only the heavy stone roof, but also the unseen second-story scriptorium chamber, where monks once carefully copied manuscripts by candlelight (their work was amazingly skillful and ornate, considering the poor light).

The big main arch overhead, studded with fist-size heads, framed the altar (now gone). Walk into the chancel and look up at the ceiling, examining the faint **frescoes,** a labor of love from 850 years ago. Frescoes are rare in Ireland because of the perpetually moist climate. (Mixing pigments into wet plaster worked better in dry climates like Italy's.) Once vividly colorful, then fading over time, these frescoes were further damaged during and after the Reformation, when Protestants piously whitewashed them. These surviving frescoes were discovered under multiple layers of whitewash during painstaking modern restoration. Take a moment to imagine the majesty of this chapel before its fine ornamentation was destroyed by those Reformation iconoclasts.

• *Walk through the other modern, dark-glass doorway, opposite the door you used to enter the chapel. You'll find yourself in a...*

❺ Forgotten Void

This enclosed little space was created when the newer cathedral was wedged between the older chapel and the round tower. Once the main entrance into the chapel, this forgotten doorway is crowned by a finely carved tympanum that decorates the arch above it. It's perfectly preserved because the huge cathedral shielded it from the wind and rain. The large lion (symbol of St. Mark's gospel) is being hunted by a centaur (half-man, half-horse) archer wearing a Norman helmet.

• *Exit the chapel, turning left, and tiptoe through the tombstones around the east end of the cathedral to the base of the round tower.*

❻ Graveyard and Round Tower

This graveyard is full. The 20-foot-tall stone shaft at the edge of the graveyard, marking the O'Scully family crypt, was once crowned by an elaborately carved Irish high cross—destroyed during a lightning storm in 1976. The fortified wall dates from the 15th century, when the riches of this outpost merited a little extra protection.

Look out over the **Plain of Tipperary.** Called the "Golden Vale," its rich soil makes it Ireland's most fertile farmland. In St. Patrick's time, it was covered with oak forests. From the corner of the church, beyond the fortified wall on the left, you can see the ruined 13th-century **Hore Abbey** dominating the fields below (free, always open and peaceful).

Gaze up at the **round tower,** the first stone structure built on the Rock after the Church took over in 1101. The shape of these towers is unique to Ireland. Though you might think towers like this were chiefly intended as a place to hide in case of invasion, they were instead used primarily as bell towers and lookout posts. The tower stands 92 feet tall, with walls more than three feet thick. The doorway, which once had a rope ladder, was built high up not only for security, but also because having it at ground level would have weakened the foundation of the top-heavy structure. The interior once contained wooden floors connected by ladders, and served as safe storage for the monks' precious sacramental treasures. The tower's stability is impressive when you consider its age, the winds it has endured, and the shallowness of its foundation (only five feet below present ground level).

Continue walking around the cathedral's north transept, noticing the square "put-log" holes in the exterior walls. During construction, wooden scaffolding was anchored into these holes. After the structure was completed, the builders simply sawed off the scaffolding, leaving small blocks of wood embedded in the walls. With time, the blocks rotted away, and the holes became favorite spots for birds to build their nests.

On your way to the cathedral entrance find the small **well** (in the corner on the left, built into the wall). Its stone lip is groovy from ropes after centuries of use. Without this essential water source, the Rock could never have withstood a siege and would not have been as valuable to clans and clergy. In 1848, a chalice was dredged from the well, likely thrown there by fleeing medieval monks intending to survive a raid. They didn't make it. (If they had, they would have retrieved the chalice.)

• *Now enter the...*

❼ Cathedral

Traditionally, churches face east toward Jerusalem and the rising sun. Because this cathedral was squeezed between the preexisting chapel, round tower, and drinking well, to make it face east the builders were forced to improvise by giving it a cramped nave and an extra-long choir (where the clergy gathered to celebrate Mass).

Built between 1230 and 1290, the church's pointed arches and high, narrow windows proclaim the Gothic style of the period (and let in more light than earlier Romanesque churches). Walk under the central bell tower and look up at the rib-vaulted **ceiling.** The hole in the middle was for a rope used to ring the church bells. The wooden roof is long gone. When the Protestant Lord Inchiquin (who became one of Oliver Cromwell's generals) attacked the Catholic town of Cashel in 1647, hundreds of townsfolk fled to the sanctuary of this cathedral. Inchiquin packed turf around the exterior and burned the cathedral down, massacring those inside.

Ascend the terraces at the choir end of the cathedral, where the main altar once stood. Stand on the gravestones (of the 16th-century rich and famous) with your back to the east wall (where the narrow windows have crumbled away) and look back down toward the nave. The right wall of the choir is filled with graceful Gothic windows, while the solid left wall hides Cormac's Chapel (which would have blocked most sunlight). The line of stone supports on the left wall once held the long, wooden balcony where the vicars sang. Closer to the altar, high on the same wall (directly above the pointed doorway), is a small, rectangular window called the "lep-

er's squint"—which allowed unsightly lepers to view the altar during Mass without offending the congregation.

The grand **wall tomb** on the left contains the remains of archbishop Miler Magrath, the "scoundrel of Cashel," who lived to be 100. From 1570 to 1622, Magrath was the Protestant archbishop of Cashel who simultaneously profited from his previous position as Catholic bishop of Down. He married twice, had lots of kids, confiscated the ornate tomb lid here from another bishop's grave, and converted back to Catholicism on his deathbed.

KILKENNY & CASHEL

• *Walk back down the nave and turn left into the south transept.*

Peek into the modern-roofed wooden structure against the wall on your left. It's protecting 15th-century **frescoes** of the Crucifixion of Christ that were rediscovered during renovations in 2005. They're as patchy and hard to make out (and just as rare, for Ireland) as the century-older frescoes in the ceiling of Cormac's Chapel.

On the opposite side of this transept, in alcoves built into the wall, enjoy the wonderful **carvings** of early Christian saints lining the outside walls of tombs (look down at shin level).

• *Exit the cathedral opposite where you entered.*

❽ Castle (or Tower)

Back outside, stand beside the huge chunk of wall debris. (This is not "the rock" of Cashel.) Try to picture where it might have perched in the ragged puzzle of ruins above. This end of the cathedral was converted into an archbishop's castle in the 1400s (shortening the nave even more). Looking high into the castle's damaged top floors, you can see the bishop's residence chamber and the secret passageways that were once hidden inside the thick walls. Lord Inchiquin's cannons weakened the structure during the 1647 massacre, and in 1848, a massive storm (known as "Night of the Big Wind" in Irish lore) flung the huge chunk next to you from the ruins above.

In the mid-1700s, the Anglican Church transferred cathedral status to St. John's in town, and the archbishop abandoned the drafty Rock for a more comfortable residence, leaving the ruins that you see today.

NEAR THE ROCK
Sounds of History Museum

In the Brú Ború Cultural Centre (below the Rock of Cashel parking lot, below the statue of the three blissed-out dancers) is a small museum dedicated to the story of Ireland's ancient and traditional music. The exhibit starts with a video display tracing the physical evolution of Cashel from ancient ring fort to grand religious complex. Then come displays about ancient wind instruments. To wrap it up, there's a small theater where you'll enjoy a 15-minute film introduction to Ireland's beloved traditional music scene.

Cost and Hours: €5, Mon-Sat 9:00-17:00, closed Sun, tel. 062/61122, www.bruboru.ie.

Performances: If sleeping in Cashel in the summer, consider taking in a performance of the Brú Ború musical dance troupe in the center's theater (€20, €50 with dinner, Tue-Sat in late-June-mid-Aug, dinner at 19:00, 75-minute performance at 21:00, informal music session in the café/bar after).

Town of Cashel

The huggable town at the base of the Rock affords a good break on the long drive from Dublin to Dingle (**TI** open daily 9:30-17:30 in season, tel. 062/61333). The Heritage Centre, next door to the TI, presents a modest six-minute audio explanation of Cashel's history around a walled town model. Parking requires a pay-and-display ticket (€1, enforced Mon-Sat 9:00-18:00, free Sun).

Sleeping in Cashel: If you spend the night, you'll be treated to beautifully illuminated views of the ruins. The first listing is a classy hotel in the center of town (15-minute walk from the Rock). The rest are cozy, old-fashioned, and closer to the Rock.

$$ Bailey's Hotel is Cashel's best boutique hotel, housed in a fine Georgian townhouse (1709). Its 19 refurbished rooms are large, inviting, and well-appointed, perched above a great cellar-pub restaurant (parking, 42 Main Street, tel. 062/61937, www.baileyshotelcashel.com, info@baileyshotelcashel.com).

$$ Joy's Rockside House B&B is closest to the Rock, resting on its lower slopes. With four large, fresh rooms (three with views of the Rock), it's the best value in Cashel (family room, cash only, parking, Rock Villas Street, tel. 062/63813, mobile 087-222-1676, www.joyrockside.com, joyrocksidehouse@eircom.net, Joan and Rem Joy).

$$ Cashel Lodge is a well-kept rural oasis housed in an old stone grain warehouse, a 10-minute walk from the Rock near the Hore Abbey ruins. Its seven comfortable rooms combine unpretentious practicality with Irish country charm. Guests have a ringside seat for beautiful views of the Rock lit up at night (camping spots, parking, Dundrum Road R-505, tel. 062/61003, www.cashel-lodge.com, info@cashel-lodge.com, Tom and Brid O'Brien).

$ Rockville House, 100 yards from the Rock, is a traditional place run by gentleman owner Patrick Hayes. The house itself has six fine rooms, and its old stablehouse, lovingly converted by Patrick, has five more (family room, cash only, 10 Dominic Street, tel. 062/61760, rockvillehse@eircom.net).

$ Wattie's B&B has three rooms that feel lived-in and comfy (cash only, parking, 14 Dominic Street, tel. 062/61923, www.wattiesbandb.ie, wattiesbandbcashel@gmail.com, Maria Dunne).

Eating in Cashel: The following places are good lunch options near the Rock. **$ Granny's Kitchen** is a tiny, violet-colored place with basic soup-and-sandwich lunches (daily 11:00-16:00, just past parking lot at the base of the Rock). **$$ Café Hans** has the best lunch selection and biggest crowds (Tue-Sat 12:00-17:30, closed Sun-Mon, 75 yards down the road from the parking lot).

$$$$ Chez Hans, filling an old stone church, is good for a splurge dinner (Tue-Sat 18:00-21:30, closed Sun-Mon, a block below the Rock, tel. 062/61177, www.chezhans.net).

KILKENNY & CASHEL

In town, you'll find several options. Next door to the TI, **$ Feehan's Bar** is a convenient stop for a pub grub lunch (daily 12:00-16:00, tel. 062/61929). A couple of blocks farther into town, the **$$ Cellar Pub** hides beneath Bailey's Hotel and serves satisfying dishes (daily 12:00-21:30, tel. 062/61937). **Super Valu** is the town's supermarket (Mon-Sat 7:00-22:00, Sun 8:00-21:00, 30 Main Street).

Cashel Connections: Cashel has no train station; the closest one is 13 miles away in the town of Thurles. Buses run from Cashel to **Dublin** (4/day, 3 hours), **Kilkenny** (3/day, 2.5 hours), and **Waterford** (6/day, 2 hours). Bus info: www.buseireann.ie.

KILKENNY & CASHEL

WATERFORD &
COUNTY WEXFORD

If you need an overnight stop in southeast Ireland, the historic Viking port and Norman beachhead town of Waterford is your best choice. From here, you can explore the varied sights of County Wexford (including a 12th-century lighthouse, the Kennedy homestead—now a museum—the re-creation of a famine ship, and more). But humble Waterford town is of most interest to crystal devotees and Irish history enthusiasts. If that's not you, give it a miss. Or consider staying in more appealing Kilkenny (see the previous chapter) and sample this area via day trips.

This region has a pastoral serenity and a strong history of trading from its sheltered ports facing England. The Vikings built the ports and developed the trade routes. Their cousins, the Normans, came along 200 years later and carefully fortified the ports. In 1170, King Henry II visited his new Irish realm with a huge fleet, calling Waterford the "Gateway to Ireland." With more efficient farming techniques and advanced military technology, the Normans cranked up their dominant culture and shoved the locals aside.

But the Irish made them fight to hang on to it. Like medieval Fort Apaches, Norman-fortified tower-house castles dot the landscape. And throughout your travels here, you'll see evidence of the region's Norman (French) roots in its high concentration of family names with old Norman prefixes: De Berg, De Lacy, Devereux, Fitzgilbert, Fitzsimmons, Fitzgerald, and so on.

And how about this: Zorro was from Wexford. Or so say some historians, who claim that the inspiration for the colorful fictitious character was none other than locally born, multilingual, 17th-century Catholic adventurer William Lamport. Lamport ran afoul of the English, fled to Spain, became a pirate, then joined a Spanish regiment fighting Swedes in the Thirty Years War. He was sent to Mexico as a spy (El Zorro means "the fox") but was executed for sympathizing with native slaves against the Mexican Inquisition.

Waterford

The oldest city in Ireland, Waterford was once more important than Dublin, and its three fine museums reflect this history. But today, while tourists associate the town's name with its famous crystal, locals are quick to remind you that the crystal is named after the town, not vice versa (come for the crystal, stay for the history). That said, Waterford is a plain, gray, workaday town of 45,000. Pubs outnumber cafés, and freighters offload cargo at the dock. Wandering the back streets, you'll get a dose of gritty Ireland, with fewer leprechauns per capita than other Irish destinations (though you'll also see some recent sprucing-up efforts as the town tries to shake its mediocre image).

PLANNING YOUR TIME

A day is enough time for Waterford's compact historic core. Visit the Waterford Crystal Visitor Centre early or late to avoid the midday big bus-tour crowds. Beyond that, your best activity is the historic walking tour (listed under "Helpful Hints," later), followed by a visit to the branch of the Waterford Museum of Treasures housed in Reginald's Tower. History buffs may want to dig deeper with visits to the other two branches of this three-museum complex: Chorister's Hall (medieval life) and Bishop's Palace (Georgian to modern age). To feel the pulse of contemporary Waterford, hang out on Barronstrand Street—the town's pedestrian artery.

Orientation to Waterford

Waterford's main drag runs along its homely harbor; all of my recommended accommodations and sights are within a 15-minute walk from here. The sights and TI cluster within a four-block area nicknamed the "Viking Triangle." The TI and Reginald's Tower are opposite a modern, white, tent-like structure covering a raised stage called the Millennium Plaza, at the far eastern end of the harborfront from Rice Bridge. The other museums, the Waterford

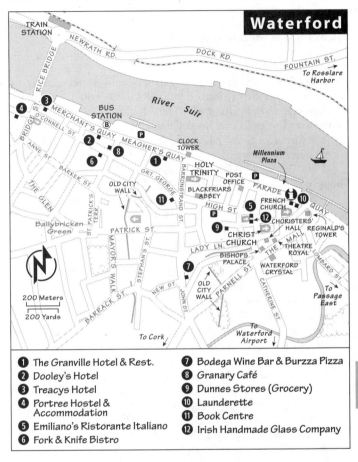

Waterford

① The Granville Hotel & Rest.
② Dooley's Hotel
③ Treacys Hotel
④ Portree Hostel & Accommodation
⑤ Emiliano's Ristorante Italiano
⑥ Fork & Knife Bistro
⑦ Bodega Wine Bar & Burzza Pizza
⑧ Granary Café
⑨ Dunnes Stores (Grocery)
⑩ Launderette
⑪ Book Centre
⑫ Irish Handmade Glass Company

WATERFORD & COUNTY WEXFORD

Crystal Visitor Centre, and the Theatre Royal are inland from Reginald's Tower, facing a street called The Mall.

A stubby three-story Victorian clock tower marks the middle of the harbor. It's also the start of the pedestrian Barronstrand Street, which runs two blocks inland to the town square. Also along the harbor are the bus station and easy parking lots (€1.80/hour). The best overnight lot—enter next to the bus station—costs €5 for a stay from 17:00 to 11:00. Some harborfront lots, including the overnight lot, have machines where you pay before exiting (check the payment/exit procedures as you walk out of the lot; you may need exact change in coins).

TOURIST INFORMATION

The TI sits on the harborfront, where Greyfriars Street meets Parade Quay, facing Millennium Plaza (Mon-Sat 9:00-17:00, usually closed Sun, shorter hours Nov-March; 120 Parade Quay, tel. 051/875-823, www.discoverireland.ie/waterford).

HELPFUL HINTS

Laundry: A-Class Cleaners does full-service loads the same day if you drop off early (Mon-Fri 9:00-18:00, Sat 9:30-17:30, closed Sun, 129 Parade Quay, tel. 051/844-100).

Bookstore: The multilevel **Book Centre,** right off the main square, is a fun browse and has a cozy soup and sandwich café on an upstairs balcony (Mon-Sat 9:00-18:00, Fri until 21:00, Sun 13:00-17:00, 25 John Roberts Square, tel. 051/873-823).

Shopping: The **Irish Handmade Glass Company** features artisans trained at the old Waterford Crystal factory, who work right in front of you fashioning unique crystal creations (Mon-Fri 9:00-17:00, Sat from 10:00, closed Sun, behind the Kite Design Studio storefront, 11 Henrietta Street, tel. 051/858-914, www.theirishhandmadeglasscompany.com).

Taxis: Try **Premiere Taxi Service** (tel. 051/373-373) or **Rapid Cabs** (tel. 051/858-585). **Rapid Express** offers coaches to Dublin's airport (tel. 051/872-149).

Historic Walking Tour: Jack Burtchaell and his partners lead entertaining, informative, hour-long, historical town walks (worth ▲▲) that go from the TI to the Waterford Crystal Visitor Centre, giving you a good handle on the story of Waterford. They meet at the TI every day at 11:45 and 13:45—or you can join the tour as it swings by the Granville Hotel at 12:00 and 14:00 (just show up, pay €8 at the end, mid-March-mid-Oct only, tel. 051/873-711, www.jackswalkingtours.com).

Theater: Waterford's small but lively **Theatre Royal** claims a 225-year tradition. Given the dearth of other nighttime options in Waterford beyond pubs, it's worth checking out their schedule of plays, concerts, and light opera (€15-30 tickets, located on The Mall across from the Waterford Crystal Visitor Centre, tel. 051/874-402, www.theatreroyal.ie).

Sights in Waterford

▲▲WATERFORD CRYSTAL VISITOR CENTRE

With a tradition dating back to 1783 (absent about 100 years, from the late 1840s Famine until the post-WWII boom), Waterford was once the largest—and still is the most respected—glassworks in the world. The economic downturn of 2008 shattered the market for luxury items like crystal, forcing the huge Waterford Crystal factory outside town to close. The company was bought by American investors who opened a new, scaled-down factory in the town center (and later sold it to a Finnish company for a handsome profit).

Waterford's History

Arriving in 819, Vikings first established Waterford as their base for piracy. Waterford was a perfect spot for launching their ships, since it's located at the gateway to one of the most extensive river networks in Ireland. From here, raiders could sail and row 50 miles into Ireland, an island with no towns, just scattered monastic settlements and small gatherings of clans—perfect for the Vikings' plan of rape, pillage, and plunder.

Later, the Vikings decided to "go legit." They turned to profiteering, setting up shop in an established trading base

they named Vandrafjord, or "safe harbor." Ireland's first permanent town eventually became known as Waterford. It was from this base that the Norsemen invaded northern England.

In the 12th century, a deposed Irish king named Diarmuid Mac-Murrough opened the Irish version of Pandora's box by inviting the Normans over from England, hoping to use their advanced military technology to regain his land from a rival clan. The great warrior knight Strongbow came... and never left, beginning Ireland's long and troublesome relationship with the English. In 1170, Strongbow married the Irish princess Aoife in here in Waterford (in a Gothic church where Waterford's Christ Church Cathedral stands today). One of Ireland's most famous and melodramatic paintings (hanging in the National Gallery in Dublin) depicts this event, and a copy of it covers a wall in Chorister's Hall Medieval Museum. With this marriage, Strongbow was next in line for the title of King of Leinster, which he was named after the death of his father-in-law, MacMurrough, a year later.

Strongbow's success was so rapid that King Henry II got worried about a rival kingdom blossoming on his flank. He quickly gathered his navy and sailed over from England to make sure Strongbow knew who was boss—and to intimidate Irish clan leaders into swearing loyalty to the Crown. England's first roots in Ireland had been planted.

For the English, Waterford has often proved to be a tough nut to crack. During Oliver Cromwell's brutal scorched-earth campaign of 1649-1650, he destroyed any town still loyal to King Charles I (see "The Curse of Cromwell" sidebar, later). Waterford was the only Irish city to withstand Cromwell's siege.

While 70 percent of Waterford Crystal is now manufactured by cheaper labor in Poland, Slovenia, and the Czech Republic, the finest glass craftsmen still reside here, where they create "prestige pieces" for special-order customers. The one-hour tour of this hardworking little factory is a joy. It's more intimate than the old, larger factory, and you're encouraged to interact with the craftsmen. Large tour groups descend midday, so try to visit before 10:00 or after 15:30.

Cost and Hours: Tours cost €14 and depart every 30 minutes (cheaper online); Mon-Sat 9:00-18:00 (last tour at 16:15), Sun from 9:30, shorter hours Nov-March, call to confirm, shop open longer hours; on The Mall, one block south of Reginald's Tower; tel. 051/317-000, www.waterfordvisitorcentre.com.

Visiting the Factory: The tour begins with a bit of history and a look at an impressive six-foot-tall crystal grandfather clock. It then loses momentum as you're ushered into a glitzy and pointless five-minute fireworks film montage set to a techno beat. But things pick up again as your guide takes you into the factory to meet the craftsmen in their element. Glassblowers magically spin glowing blobs of molten crystal into exquisite and recognizable shapes in minutes. If you get dizzy blowing up balloons for a kid's party, consider the lung stamina that these craftsmen display. Watch closely as the glassblower puts his thumb over the opening between breaths to keep the heat and pressure inside the blob constant.

Heavy molten crystal has an intentionally high lead content (it's what distinguishes fine crystal from common glassware). A cooling-off stage allows the crystal to set. Then glasscutters deftly cradle the fragile creations against diamond-edged cutting wheels, applying exactly enough pressure to ensure that the grooves are replicated with surgical skill. The glasscutters will be glad to demonstrate if you ask.

Watch the skilled cutters muscle rough unfinished pieces—weighing as much as bowling balls—and cut intricate patterns. The crystal vases and bowls may look light and delicate, but hold an unfinished piece (with its lead-enhanced heft) and you'll gain a new appreciation for the strength, touch, and hand-eye coordination of the glasscutters.

Afterward, visit the glittering salesroom, surrounded by hard-to-pack but easy-to-ship temptations. Take a look at the copies of famous sports trophies (they make backups of their most important commissions, just in case). If you make a significant purchase, be sure to ask about getting a VAT refund (see page 529).

MUSEUM OF TREASURES COMPLEX

Waterford presents its impressive history in a three-museum complex called the Museum of Treasures, with locations just a damsel's handkerchief-drop from each other. The museums line up along the southern flank of the "Viking Triangle," the footprint of the original Viking-fort section of town, about a two-minute walk apart (the museum's tagline is "Vikings to Victorians: 1,000 years of history in 1,000 paces").

To see the branches in historical sequence, first visit Reginald's Tower on the harborfront to understand the Viking roots of the city. Then stroll up The Mall to find Chorister's Hall Medieval Museum, a modern structure tucked behind the Theatre Royal. This branch shows Norman and Tudor artifacts above an original 13th-century vaulted wine cellar. Finally, right next door, you can visit the imposing Bishop's Palace, a fine mansion full of everything Waterford from 1700 to the present. Few Irish towns can claim a meatier bite of Irish history than Waterford.

Note: Entry to Reginald's Tower is covered by the Heritage Card (see "Sightseeing Passes," page 532). The Chorister's Hall and Bishop's Palace are not, but they do offer a combo-ticket for entry into both.

▲Reginald's Tower

This oldest part of the oldest town in Ireland is named after Regnall, the first (Norwegian) Viking leader of Waterford, who built

a fortified oaken tower here in A.D. 914 and later invaded Jorvik (York, England). Dating from the late 1100s, the stone Norman tower you see today replaced the wooden one and was once the most important corner of the town wall. The tower is Ireland's oldest intact building and the first made with mortar. Today, its four floors creak with Viking artifacts.

Cost and Hours: €5; includes guided tour upon request—ask for the one-hour version, which adds a historical walk around the block to French Church; daily 9:30-17:30, Jan-Feb until 17:00, tel. 051/304-220, www.waterfordtreasures.com.

Visiting the Museum: Before you enter, look for the **cannonball** embedded high above the entrance, courtesy of Cromwell's siege cannons.

Once inside, you'll find an interesting Viking town **model** opposite the ticket counter. Upstairs, a display of early coins explains how the Vikings introduced the concept of coinage to the Irish after they eventually settled down and set up trade posts. Look for the tiny **Kite Brooch** that delicately blends both Scandinavian and Irish styles. In their day, brooches were considered badges of

WATERFORD & COUNTY WEXFORD

Thomas Francis Meagher (1823-1867)

Waterford's favorite son had a short but amazing life. The son of the town's mayor, Meagher joined Daniel O'Connell's non-violent movement to repeal the Act of Union with Britain. Impatient with the slow-moving political process of constant compromise, Meagher joined the radical Young Irelander movement that advocated separation from Britain by force of arms. He became an inspiring and fiery speaker nicknamed "Meagher of the Sword." He went to France in 1848 and returned with the first Irish tricolor flag—a gift from the French that represented the Catholics (green), the Protestants (orange), and peaceful coexistence between the two (white).

Involved in a failed uprising, Meagher was sentenced to hang, but his sentence was commuted to life in prison in Tasmania. In 1852, Meagher escaped Tasmania via an American whaling ship and sailed to New York, where he eventually became a lawyer and started an Irish newspaper. After a trip to Nicaragua (to study the feasibility of building a canal or railway across the isthmus), he returned to New York to fight in the American Civil War. Meagher was made a Union general, raised a regiment of Irish immigrants, and famously led them into battle at Antietam and Fredericksburg. After the war, he became the first governor of the Montana territory. At age 44, Thomas Francis Meagher fell off a riverboat one night and drowned in the Missouri River. Sheer accident, foul play, or careless drunkenness? Nobody knows for sure—but his body was never found.

To learn more about this little-known, but fascinating Irish leader, read Timothy Egan's *The Immortal Irishman* (2016), which offers a vivid account of the contrasting events and locales in Meagher's life.

status, and this one's owner must have been at the top of the heap. As you climb the narrow stone stairways, watch your head (people were shorter 800 years ago). And be sure to go all the way to the top floor, where an informative 10-minute animated **video** traces the evolution of the town from muddy fort to modern city.

The **statue** outside (in the middle of the street) is of Thomas Francis Meagher (see sidebar), whose short, hell-bent-for-leather life took him on precarious adventures from Waterford to Tasmania to Nicaragua to Montana and, finally, to an unknown watery grave.

Chorister's Hall Medieval Museum

This middle branch of the museum triumvirate uses its three floors to focus on life in Waterford from the Norman invasion of the late 1100s to the Williamite English triumph of the late 1600s. Your visit is enhanced by an excellent free audio/videoguide that plays automatically as you move from room to room (pay attention to the changing images it displays—they'll help you navigate among artifacts).

Cost and Hours: €7, €10 combo-ticket with Bishop's Palace; June-Aug Mon-Sat 9:15-18:00, Sun 11:00-18:00; Sept-May Mon-Sat 10:00-17:00, Sun 11:00-17:00; last entry one hour before closing, tel. 051/304-500, www.waterfordtreasures.com.

Visiting the Museum: Begin by descending under the modern building and into an original wine-vault cellar from the 1200s (long on atmosphere but otherwise empty).

Ride the elevator to the top floor to see a grand collection of well-described Anglo-Norman artifacts. The Great Charter Roll of 1372 was compiled to reinforce Waterford's claim to a monopoly of the lucrative wine-import trade. Check out the wall-size copy of the famous painting depicting the pivotal marriage of Norman leader Strongbow to Irish princess Aoife, then bring it to life on your audioguide. Detailed town models and an informative 10-minute audiovisual presentation complete the history here.

Down one floor, you'll learn how religion played out on Waterford's historic stage. Watch this floor's audiovisual presentation first to understand the broader context of this town's role in Irish history. Then feast your eyes on "Heaven's Embroidered Cloths," a collection of priestly vestments produced in Medici Florence, decorated in affluent Bruges, and shipped to conflicted Waterford. Hidden under a flagstone in the floor of Christ Church Cathedral during a siege, they were rediscovered 123 years later during renovation.

▲Bishop's Palace

Housed in the former mansion (built 1743) of the local Protestant bishop (with his Christ Church Cathedral looming right behind it), this museum presents a grand sweep through the history of Waterford since 1700, and contains the world's largest collection of old Waterford glass.

Cost and Hours: €7, €10-combo ticket with Chorister's Hall, same hours and contact info as Chorister's Hall. Entertaining 45-minute free tours are led by actors in period dress, who inhabit the palace as servants of the bishop (hourly June-Aug 9:30-18:00, Sept-May 10:00-16:00).

Visiting the Palace: The refined interior hints of the privileged lifestyle of the holy resident. Back then, a visit with the bishop would depend on social class. The bishop would meet upper-class visitors at the top of the grand stairway, greet middle-class merchants at his office doorway, and not budge from his desk chair for anyone from the lower class. Under no circumstances would he come downstairs to greet anyone.

These days, you'll work your way through three floors spiced with characters like Waterford-born action hero Thomas Francis Meagher (see sidebar). You'll learn why the province of Newfoundland in Canada owes over 50 percent of its population to immigrants from Waterford. And if you've ever wondered what bull baiting was, you'll be filled in on this equally cruel (and long outlawed) Irish version of a bullfight.

Particularly poignant is the top-floor coverage of local WWI loyalists (Waterford was more loyal to the British crown than most Irish towns) contrasted with the 1916 Rising and flowering of Irish Republicanism.

OTHER SIGHTS IN WATERFORD
Cathedral of the Holy Trinity

The year is 1793. With Catholic France (30 million) threatening Protestant Britain (8 million) on one side, and Catholic Ireland (6 million) stirring things up on the other, English King George III was stuck between a rock and a hard place. To lessen Irish resentment, the king granted Ireland the Irish Relief Act, which, among other things, allowed the Irish to build Catholic churches and worship publicly for the first time since the penal laws forbade them a hundred years earlier. Allowed new freedom, the Irish built this interesting cathedral in 1796. It's Ireland's first Catholic post-Reformation church and its only Baroque church. The building was funded by wealthy Irish wine merchants who were flourishing in Cádiz, Spain. Among its treasures are 10 Waterford Crystal chandeliers.

Cost and Hours: Free, daily 8:00-19:00.

Nearby: The cathedral faces **Barronstrand Street,** which leads from the clock tower on the harborfront through the pedestrian-friendly **town square** to Patrick Street. The street separates the medieval town (on your left with the river behind you) from the 18th-century city (on your right). A river once flowed here—part of the town's natural defenses just outside the old wall. The huge **shopping center** that dominates the old town was built right on top of the Viking town. In fact, the center is built over a church dating from 1150, whose stone foundation you can see at the bottom of the escalator (behind the glass, next to the kiddie rides).

Christ Church Cathedral

This Protestant cathedral, with 18th-century Georgian architecture, is the third church to stand here. Look for the exposed Gothic column six feet below today's floor level, a remnant from an earlier church where the Norman conqueror Strongbow was married (see sidebar on page 173).

Wander over to the macabre tomb of 15th-century mayor James Rice, which bears a famous epitaph: "I am what you will be, I was what you are, pray for me." To emphasize the point, he requested that his body be dug up one year after his death (1482) and his partially decomposed remains be used to model his likeness, now seen on the tomb's lid...complete with worms and frogs.

Cost and Hours: Free, €2 donation requested, Mon-Fri 10:00-17:00, Sat until 16:00, closed Sun except for services, tours available on request.

Sleeping in Waterford

Waterford is a working-class city. Cheap accommodations are fairly rough; fancy accommodations are venerable old places that face the water. I recommend one historic option, two modern places, and a budget choice. Many find sleepy Ardmore, an hour southwest down the coast, a smaller and more scenic home base (see page 212).

$$$ The Granville Hotel is Waterford's best and most historic hotel, grandly overlooking the center of the harborfront. The place is plush, from its Old World lounges to its 98 well-tended rooms (super breakfasts, Meagher's Quay, tel. 051/305-555, www. granville-hotel.ie, stay@granville-hotel.ie).

$$$ Dooley's Hotel, a more modern, family-run place on the harbor with 113 big rooms, can be less expensive than the Granville but is still high quality (Merchant's Quay, tel. 051/873-531, www.dooleys-hotel.ie, hotel@dooleys-hotel.ie).

$$$ Treacys Hotel—family-run and modern—is on the waterfront, close to the Rice Bridge with 163 pleasant, earth-toned rooms (1 Merchants Quay, tel. 051/877-222, www. treacyshotelwaterford.com, res@thwaterford.com).

$ Portree Hostel & Accommodation is the central budget option. It's just across the bridge from the train station and combines 24 basic rooms upstairs with 15 dorm beds in its basement hostel (breakfast €7 extra, guest kitchen in hostel section, parking, 10 Mary Street, tel. 051/874-574, www.portreehostel.ie, portreeguesthouse@gmail.com).

Eating in Waterford

For something livelier than tired pub grub, consider these good restaurants found on less-frequented back streets. They're small and popular with locals.

$$$ Emiliano's Ristorante Italiano is the most romantic place in town, hidden on a tiny lane behind Reginald's Tower. They serve a great selection of tasty pasta dishes and fine wines (Tue-Sat 17:00-22:00, also open Sat-Sun for lunch 12:30-14:30, closed Mon all day, 21 High Street, tel. 051/820-333).

$$ Fork & Knife Bistro is a friendly Polish place with a B.Y.O.B. liquor policy. It serves hearty Eastern European fare, including potato pancakes stuffed with pork goulash and topped with sour cream (Tue-Sun 10:00-21:00, closed Mon, 11a O'Connell Street, tel. 087/171-8688).

$$ Bodega is my favorite wine bar, run by laid-back Cormac in a warm-glow Mediterranean atmosphere. Their lamb sliders get raves (Mon-Sat 12:00-22:00, closed Sun, 54 John Street, tel. 051/844-177).

$ Burzza Pizza, right next door and under the same ownership, serves not only pizza but also "proper" hamburgers (Mon-Sat 12:00-22:00, closed Sun, 53 John Street, tel. 051/844-969).

$ Granary Café occupies the bottom floor of an old stone warehouse facing the waterfront (café on back side, away from traffic). It's a soup/salad/sandwich cafeteria that tries harder than most (Mon-Sat 8:00-17:00, Sun from 10:00, Hanover Street, tel. 051/854-428).

On the Harborfront: With a central waterfront location, the **$ Granville Hotel**'s carvery is the traditional budget lunch option (daily 12:30-14:30, otherwise good bar food daily 10:30-21:30, Meagher's Quay).

Pub Grub and Music: Waterford's staple food seems to be pub grub. Several typical pubs serve dinner in the city center. But for your musical entertainment, you'll need to hum a medley of your favorite show tunes. For some reason, not much live music exists in town. Ask at your hotel, or just wander around, read the notices, and follow your ears. Anything with a pulse will be found on George Street, Barronstrand Street, and Broad Street.

Supermarket: The best grocery option is **Dunnes** in the shopping center (daily).

Waterford Connections

From Waterford by Train to: Dublin (8/day, 2.5-3 hours), **Kilkenny** (6/day, 45 minutes). For details, see www.irishrail.ie.

By Bus to: Cork (almost hourly, 2 hours), **Kilkenny** (2/day,

1 hour), **Rosslare** (4/day, 3 hours), **Wexford** (5/day, 1 hour). Waterford bus station info: Tel. 051/879-000. For details, see www.buseireann.ie.

County Wexford

The southeast corner of Ireland, peppered with pretty views and historic sites, is easily accessible to drivers as a day trip from Kilkenny or Waterford. Five sights worth considering are within an hour's drive of Waterford and can also be done as a day loop from Kilkenny (if you get an early start).

The dramatic Hook Head Lighthouse—capping an intriguing and remote peninsula—comes with lots of history and a good tour. The Kennedy Homestead is a pilgrimage site for Kennedy fans. These two stops involve more back-roads navigation, but they feel more intimate (study your map south of the town of New Ross).

The *Dunbrody* Famine Ship in New Ross gives a sense of what 50 days on a "coffin ship" with dreams of "Americay" must have been like. The Irish National Heritage Park near Wexford is like a Knott's Berry Farm...circa the Stone Age. And the National 1798 Centre in Enniscorthy explains the roots of the Irish struggle for liberty. These three stops, which are no strangers to tour buses, form an easy driving triangle whose legs are N-25, N-11, and N-30.

If you're driving from Waterford to Kilkenny, consider a visit to the ruins at Jerpoint Abbey and Kells Priory on the way (see the "Between Kilkenny and Waterford" section in the previous chapter.)

PLANNING YOUR TIME

New Ross, Enniscorthy, and Wexford, which form a three-town triangle, are about 30 minutes apart and connected by fast roads. The Kennedy Homestead is a 15-minute drive south of New Ross, and the lighthouse is a one-hour trip from Waterford to the end of the Hook Peninsula. All are well-signposted and easy to find... except for Hook Head Lighthouse (see details later).

Connecting Dublin with Waterford, you could visit several of these sights in a best-of-County Wexford day en route. On a quick trip, the sights are not worth the trouble by public transit. If you'll be spending the night, blue-collar Enniscorthy (with decent hotels and B&Bs) provides a good glimpse of workaday Ireland.

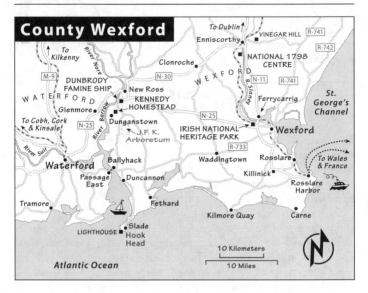

Sights in County Wexford

▲Hook Head Lighthouse

This claims to be the oldest operating lighthouse in Europe. According to legend, St. Dubhan arrived in the fifth century and discovered the bodies of shipwrecked sailors. Dismayed, he and his followers began tending a fire on the headland to warn future mariners. What you see today is essentially a structure from the 12th century, built by the Normans, who first landed five miles up the east coast (at Baginbun Head, in 1169). They established Waterford Harbor—a commercial beachhead for the rich Irish countryside they intended to conquer. This beacon assured them safe access.

Today's lighthouse is 110 feet tall and looks modern on the outside. (It was automated in 1996, and its light can be seen for 23 miles out to sea.) But, except for its modern light, it's actually 800 years old, built following a plan inspired by the lighthouse of Alexandria in Egypt—one of the seven wonders of the ancient world. Since it's a working lighthouse, it can be toured only with a guide.

Cost and Hours: Fine 45-minute tours cost €9 and depart every half-hour July-Aug, every hour off-season, last tour usually at 16:00; daily July-Aug 9:30-18:00, May and Sept until 17:30, Oct-April until 17:00; tel. 051/397-055, www.hookheritage.ie.

Getting There: The lighthouse can be a bit tricky to find. But if you follow the brown *Hook Scenic Route* signs south of Ballyhack and remind yourself that you're on a narrow peninsula with the lighthouse at the southern tip, you'll be funneled straight there (more or less).

If connecting Waterford to Hook Head, use the car-ferry shortcut from Passage East to Ballyhack. Buy a round-trip and carefully save the tiny receipt for the return journey...the scrap of paper seems determined to ride the next breeze out to sea (€12 round-trip, €8 one-way, 5-minute crossing; runs continuously Mon-Sat 7:00-22:00, Sun 9:30-22:00; Oct-March daily until 20:00, www.passageferry.ie). To reach the ferry from Waterford, take Lombard Street (near Reginald's Tower) south, and follow it all the way to Passage East (it becomes R-683).

Visiting the Lighthouse: As you view the black-stained, ribbed, vaulted ceilings and stout, 10-foot-thick walls, you can

almost feel the presence of the Cistercian monks who tended this coal-burning beacon for the Normans. Climbing 115 steps through four levels rewards you with a breezy, salt-air view from the top.

Oliver Cromwell passed through here to secure the English claim to this area (see "The Curse of Cromwell" sidebar, later). He considered his two options and declared he'd take strategic Waterford "by Hook or by Crooke." Hook is the long peninsula with the lighthouse. Crooke is a little village on the other side, just south of Passage East.

There's a decent cafeteria and a shop with fliers explaining other sights on the peninsula. Kids-at-heart can't resist climbing out on the rugged rocky tip of the windy Hook Head.

▲Kennedy Homestead

Patrick Joseph Kennedy, President John F. Kennedy's great-grandfather, left Ireland in 1858. Distant relatives have turned the family homestead into a little museum/shrine

for Kennedy pilgrims. Physically, it's not much: A barn and a wing of the modern house survive from 1858. JFK and his entourage visited here in June 1963, a few months before he was assassinated. While it's now just a private home, anyone interested in the Kennedys will find it worth driving the long narrow lane to see.

Cost and Hours: €7.50, daily 9:30-17:30, tel. 051/388-264, www.kennedyhomestead.ie.

JFK in Ireland

JFK arrived in Ireland for a three-day visit in late June 1963, straight from the Berlin Wall and his inspiring "Ich bin ein Berliner" speech. The Irish gave him a deliriously warm welcome in those Cold War days. Bursting with pride in his presidency (he was the first Catholic to hold the office), the Irish saw what was possible at a time when the state of the Irish economy was dire and emigration was high. Kennedy's every move was televised. Only 10 percent of Irish households had a TV at that time, so people crowded into pubs with TVs to watch. Kennedy's whirlwind itinerary included stops in Dublin, Galway, Limerick, Cork, and County Wexford, where he visited the farm of his Irish ancestors near Dunganstown.

As the third-born son, JFK's great-grandfather Patrick Joseph Kennedy had little hope of inheriting the family farm. He had learned the trade of coopering (barrel making) at a brewery in nearby New Ross and decided to emigrate to Boston in 1848 near the end of the Great Potato Famine. There he clawed out a new start from desperate poverty and started a family. But he succumbed to cholera in 1858...105 years to the day (November 22) before his great-grandson would be assassinated.

JFK's death came only five months after his triumphant Irish visit, at perhaps the peak of his popularity. After the assassination, Kennedy staffer and later New York senator Daniel Patrick Moynihan was quoted as saying, "To be Irish is to know that in the end the world will break your heart."

An old Irish superstition holds that it's bad luck to take a stone away from a "fairy fort" (the Iron Age ring forts that dot the landscape). Some say that the reason the Kennedy clan has suffered so many tragedies over the years is that an ancestor may have taken a stone from a fort, way back when.

Getting There: It's four miles (6 km) south of New Ross near Dunganstown (from R-733 follow brown signs with JFK's face in profile, down a long one-lane road; park behind the modern visitors center). Don't confuse the Kennedy Homestead with the nearby JFK Arboretum—a huge park with 4,500 species of trees. It's nice if you like trees and plants, but there's no Kennedy history there.

Visiting the Homestead: Inside is a fascinating exhibition on Kennedy's Irish heritage, his brief visit here, and the aftermath of his tragic death. A little barnyard houses one long shed with knick-knacks and photos of his visit. Look for the old bench-style car seat (with furniture legs added by Kennedy's second cousin). This was the nicest seat in the homestead's modest home, where the eminent visitor sat to take tea. There are a couple of short videos: JFK chatting with his distant relatives, and then being whisked away by helicopter to continue his triumphant tour of the country. JFK's assassin denied him the opportunity of a promised return visit. But his widow, Jackie, made sure that his Irish relatives here got some of his precious memorabilia.

▲▲*Dunbrody* Famine Ship

Permanently moored on a river in the tiny port of New Ross, this ship was built as a re-creation of similar vessels that sailed to America full of countless hungry Irish emigrants. The *Dunbrody* is a full-scale reconstruction of a 19th-century three-masted bark built in Quebec in 1845. It's typical of the trading vessels that originally sailed, empty, to America to pick up goods; during the Famine, shipowners found that they could make a little money on the westward voyage. On board, extended families camped out for 50 days on bunk beds no bigger than a king-size mattress. Commonly, boats like this would arrive in America with

only 80 percent of their original human cargo (in the worst cases, only 50 percent). Those who succumbed to "famine fever" (often typhus or cholera) were dumped overboard, and the ships gained their morbid moniker: "coffin ships."

Cost and Hours: €10, daily 9:00-18:00, Oct-March 10:00-17:00, 45-minute tours go 2/hour, last tour starts one hour before closing, upstairs café handy for lunch with nice views of the ship, tel. 051/425-239, www.dunbrody.com.

Getting There: The *Dunbrody* is in New Ross, near the Kennedy Homestead. During work hours, you'll need to feed the parking meters in the lot (€1/hour, free on Sun).

Visiting the Ship: Your visit starts with an audiovisual presentation on the life Irish emigrants were leaving behind, followed by coverage about the building of the vessel. Then you'll follow an excellent guide on board the ship, encountering a couple of passengers (one traveling first class, the other second) who tell vivid tales about life onboard. At the end, you'll get a glimpse of the new life Irish immigrants would encounter in New York. Most arrived filthy (try skipping a shower for six weeks), illiterate, penniless, and speaking only Irish.

Roots seekers are welcome to peruse the computerized file of the names of the million immigrants who sailed on these ships from 1846 through 1865. Before you leave, check out the Irish America Hall of Fame, commemorating the contributions Irish men and women have made to US history (with short videos on Henry Ford and JFK, whose roots lie in this part of Ireland).

The Curse of Cromwell

The scariest bogeyman in all of Irish history was Oliver Cromwell. In 1649, he led Parliamentary forces to victory in the English Civil War and had King Charles I beheaded. As-suming the title of Lord Protector, he created a commonwealth (instead of a kingdom) and initiated one of the longest periods in the past 1,000 years during which England func-tioned without a monarch. Cromwell then turned his attention to Ireland, determined to root out the last royalists loyal to the English monarchy and to punish the Irish for the 1641 massacre of Protestant settlers.

Driven by his Puritan Calvinist beliefs, Cromwell claimed a divine right to carry out God's work as he saw it. He thought buttons to be a sign of vanity and so he fastened his clothes with hidden hooks. To him, all Catholics were complicit in the Protestant deaths by virtue of their misguided faith. He saw priests as little more than witch doctors. Even Protestant An-glicans (the faith founded by Henry VIII a century before) were looked on with suspicion as "Catholics without a pope." Crom-well's self-righteous army of 12,000 soldiers had God on their side and Ireland in their musket-sights.

Cromwell and his tough New Model Army landed in Dublin on August 15, 1649, and marched north to the town of Drogheda. In a bloody siege lasting three days, his soldiers massacred al-most all of the town's 3,000 inhabitants. A handful of lucky survi-

Ros Tapestry

Before you leave New Ross, consider a short visit to see the Ros Tapestry. Outlining the colorful Norman history of the region, it's a bit like a recently woven version of the ancient Bayeux Tapestry in Normandy. Consisting of 15 large embroidered panels, not all of which are complete yet, this is a labor of love that local women have been working on for more than 20 years. Visitors are invited upstairs to take part in its creation by doing one stitch themselves.

Cost and Hours: €8, includes audioguide, Mon-Sat 10:00-17:00, Sun 11:00-15:00, tel. 051/445-396, www.rostapestry.ie. It's housed on the ground floor of an old six-story stone warehouse about 100 yards north of the *Dunbrody* Famine Ship, across the street; leave your car in the *Dunbrody* parking lot.

▲Irish National Heritage Park

This 35-acre wooded park, which contains an 1857 tower com-memorating local boys killed in the Crimean War, features replicas of buildings from each era of Irish history. Since Ireland's countvors silently slipped into the River Boyne and played dead, floating downstream out of harm's way. Cromwell then turned south to Wexford, where his army again massacred 3,000-some civilians and Irish troops. Few garrison towns resisted after that. Cromwell's merciless efficiency brought almost the entire island under English control in less than a year.

Catholic landowners were forced to give up their land or face execution...a deal with the devil known as "to hell or to Connaught." About 11 million acres of productive land was taken from Catholic landowners and handed over to Cromwell's soldiers as payment for service. In "exchange," these Catholics got unfertile ground west of the River Shannon. This forced mass migration essentially destroyed Ireland's Catholic landowning class. (In 1641, Catholics owned 59 percent of Ireland—by 1714 they owned 7 percent.) Some Catholics were allowed to stay on as tenants, providing labor for their new English masters.

Upon Cromwell's death in 1658, his less-dynamic son took over, and the English began to miss their monarchy. In 1660, Charles I's son, Charles II, was invited back from exile in France and the monarchy was restored. Soon after, Cromwell's body was dug up, hung, and beheaded—his head was stuck on a pike and displayed in front of London's Parliament for 20 years (curiously, a heroic statue of him stands there today). But most of Ireland's Catholics never regained their land, and for the next 250 years Ireland continued its slow downward cultural spiral at the hands of the English government.

WATERFORD & COUNTY WEXFORD

less ancient sights are generally unrecognizable ruins—hard to re-create in your mind—this park is intended to help out. You'll find buildings and settlements illustrating life in Ireland from the Stone Age through the 12th-century Norman Age. As a bonus, you'll see animal-skin-clad characters doing their prehistoric thing—gnawing on meat, weaving, making arrowheads, and so on.

Cost and Hours: €9.50, daily 9:30-18:30, winter until 17:30, last entry 1.5 hours before closing, audioguide-€2, free guided tours leave throughout the day until about 16:00—reserve in advance, tel. 053/912-0733, www.inhp.com, info@inhp.com.

Getting There: It's clearly signposted on the west end of Wexford—you'll hit it before entering town on the N-11 Enniscorthy road.

Visiting the Park: Your visit begins with a 15-minute video. From there, follow the audioguide, or better, do the hour-long guided tour. There are 16 stops, each covering a different stage of Irish civilization. The highlight is a monastic settlement from the age when Europe was dark, and Ireland was "the island of saints and scholars." While you can wander around on your own, there's hardly anything actually old here, and the visit is most worthwhile if you take the included tour.

National 1798 Centre

Located in Enniscorthy, this museum creatively tells the story of the rise of revolutionary thinking in Ireland, which led to the ill-fated rebellion of 1798 (Ireland's deadliest). Enniscorthy was the crucial Irish battleground of a populist revolution (inspired by the American and French revolutions). The town witnessed the bloodiest days of the doomed uprising. The material is compelling for anyone intrigued by the struggles for liberty, but there's little more here than video clips of reenactments and storyboards on the walls.

Cost and Hours: €7; Mon-Fri 9:30-17:00, Sat 12:00-17:00, closed Sun; shorter hours Oct-March; last entry one hour before closing, tel. 053/923-7596, www.1798centre.ie.

Getting There: Enniscorthy is 12 miles (19 km) north of Wexford town. The National 1798 Centre is the town's major sight and is well-signposted (follow the brown *Aras 98 Centre* signs).

Nearby: Leaving the center, look east across the River Slaney, which divides Enniscorthy, and you'll see a hill with a stumpy tower on it. This is **Vinegar Hill.** The tower is the old windmill that once flew the green rebel flag. Drive to the top for the views that the rebels had of the surrounding British forces. The doomed rebels tried desperately to hold the high ground, with no shelter from the merciless British artillery fire.

KINSALE & COBH

County Cork, on Ireland's south coast, is fringed with historic port towns and scenic peninsulas. The typical tour-bus route here includes Blarney Castle and Killarney—places where most tourists wear nametags. But rather than kissing the spit-slathered Blarney Stone, spend your time in County Cork enjoying the bustling, historic maritime towns of Kinsale and Cobh. Although Cobh is a growing cruise ship port, most cruise travelers are booked on day excursions that clog iconic stops like Blarney Castle, and blessedly spare Kinsale and Cobh all but the briefest of drive-by glimpses.

Cobh can be reached from Dublin by train (via Cork city). Meanwhile, more remote—but more charming—Kinsale lies 15 miles south of Cork's train station and makes a great home base for a visit to the coast of County Cork.

Most drivers approach the region from the northeast and visit Cobh en route to Kinsale. Drivers coming from Waterford can easily visit Ardmore and the Old Midleton Whiskey Distillery along the way. Blarney Castle and Macroom make convenient stops when connecting to the Ring of Kerry or Dingle.

Avoid the mistake many travelers make—allowing destinations into their itineraries simply because they're famous from a song or as part of a relative's big-bus-tour memory. If you have the misfortune to spend the night in Killarney town (next door in County Kerry), you'll understand what I mean.

The town is a sprawling line of chain hotels and outlet malls littered with pushy shoppers looking for plastic shamrocks.

Kinsale

While Cork is the biggest town in southern Ireland, nearby Kinsale is actually more historic and certainly cuter. Pint-sized and friendly, it's delightful to visit. Thanks to the naturally sheltered bay barbed by a massive 17th-century star fort, you can submerge yourself in maritime history, from the Spanish Armada to the sailor who inspired Daniel Defoe's *Robinson Crusoe* to the *Lusitania* (torpedoed by the Germans just off the point in 1915). Apart from all the history, Kinsale has a laid-back feel with a touch of wine-sipping class.

PLANNING YOUR TIME
Kinsale is worth two nights and a day. Spend the morning checking out one or two of the town's sights, and make sure to take Don and Barry's excellent Kinsale walking tour (9:15 or 11:15 most days). After lunch, head out to Charles Fort for great bay views and insights into British military life in colonial Ireland. (You can drive, or take a taxi out and walk back.) On the way back, stop for a pint at the Bulman Bar. Finish the day with a good dinner and live music in a pub. Those blitzing Ireland can give Kinsale four hours—see the fort, wander the town, and enjoy a nice lunch—before driving on.

Orientation to Kinsale

Kinsale has a great natural harbor and is older than Cobh (the city of Cork's harbor town). While the town is prettier than the actual harbor, the harbor was its reason for being. Today, Kinsale is a vibrant bustle of about 5,000 residents. Its population swells to 9,000 with the many "blow-ins" who live here each summer. The town's long and skinny old center is part modern marina (attracting wealthy yachters) and part pedestrian-friendly medieval town (attracting scalawags like us). It's an easy 20-minute stroll from end to end.

TOURIST INFORMATION
The TI is centrally located, at the head of the harbor (Mon-Sat 9:00-17:00, closed Sun, shorter hours Dec-Feb; tel. 021/477-2234, www.kinsale.ie).

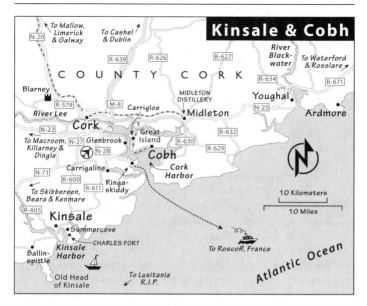

ARRIVAL IN KINSALE

Kinsale doesn't have a train station. The **bus** stop is on Pier Road, 100 yards behind the TI, just before the gray swooping modern sculptures at the south end of town.

Drivers should park and walk. While Kinsale's windy medieval lanes are narrow and congested, parking lots ease the hassle. The most central lot is at the head of the harbor behind the TI (€1.50/hour, 2-hour maximum, use pay-and-display machine, exact coins required, enforced Mon-Sat 10:30-18:00, free on Sun). There's a big, safe, free parking lot across the street from St. Multose Church at the top of town, a five-minute walk from most recommended hotels and restaurants. An even larger free lot is farther away, a 10-minute walk east of town by the fire station. Parking on the street is pay-and-display. Outlying streets, a 10-minute stroll from the action, have wide-open parking.

HELPFUL HINTS

Crowds: The Kinsale Rugby Sevens Tournament draws dozens of teams and hundreds of loud-and-proud, rowdy rugby fans on the first weekend in May (with its associated Bank Holiday Monday). If you're not up for the scrum, then scram.

Market: Check out the lively open-air market on Wednesdays (June-Sept, 9:00-14:00) in the town square on Market Quay.

Money: The two banks in town have ATMs (on Pearse Street and on Emmett Street).

Bookshop: The **Kinsale Bookshop** is on Main Street (Mon-Sat

KINSALE & COBH

10:00-18:00, Sun from 12:00, 8 Main Street, tel. 021/477-4244).

Laundry: Elite Laundry does an average-sized load for about €12 (Mon-Fri 9:00-17:30, Sat 10:00-17:00, closed Sun, The Glen, tel. 021/477-7345).

Bike Rental and a Good Ride: Mylie Murphy's, run by helpful Julian, rents bikes from a handy spot near the Centra Market (€15/day, includes lock and helmet; Mon-Sat 9:30-18:00, Sun 11:00-17:00 May-Aug only, shorter hours in winter; arrangements can be made for pickup or drop-off, tel. 021/477-2703). They can recommend paths good for biking or walking that stretch around the harbor.

For a good short-and-scenic route, bike south on the Pier Road, past the marina a couple miles, and turn left across the first bridge. Turn left again at the far end of the bridge to reach the dead end of the road marked by the Dock pub. Jump off your bike and explore the great views from the grassy ruins of James Fort, uphill behind the pub (2 miles each way). Or head out to Kinsale's only beach, a couple of hundred yards south of James Fort on the east side of its peninsula (over the hill, behind the Dock pub).

Taxi: Tom Canty can drive you where you need to go, including Cork Airport for €25 or Cork city for €30 (mobile 087-237-1022).

Tours in Kinsale

▲▲Don & Barry's Kinsale Historic Stroll

To understand the important role Kinsale played in Irish, English, and Spanish history, join gentlemen Don Herlihy or Barry Moloney on a fascinating 1.5-hour walking tour (€8, daily mid-March–mid-Oct at 11:15, also Mon-Sat at 9:15 in May-Sept, no reservation necessary, by appointment only off-season, meet outside the TI, private tours possible, tel. 021/477-2873 or 087/250-0731, www.historicstrollkinsale.com). Both guides are a joy, creatively bringing to life Kinsale's

past, placing its story in the wider sweep of history, and making the stony sights more than just buildings. They collect payment at the end, giving anyone disappointed in the talk an easy escape midway through. Don't get hijacked by imitation tours that pretend to be recommended by me on my forum—ask for Don or Barry. This walk is Kinsale's single best attraction.

Ghost Walk Tour

This is not just any ghost tour; it's more Monty Python-style slapstick comedy than horror. Two high-energy actors (Brian and David) weave funny stunts and stories into a loose history of the town, offering 75 minutes of entertainment on Kinsale's after-dark streets (€10, April-Oct Sun-Fri at 21:00, no tours Sat, leaves from The Tap Tavern, call ahead to confirm, mobile 087-948-0910). You'll spend the first 15 minutes in the back of The Tap Tavern— time to finish your drink and get to know some of the group. This tour doesn't overlap with the more serious historic town walk described earlier.

Kinsale Harbour Cruise

Enjoy a 45-minute voyage around the historic harbor aboard the nimble little 50-passenger *Spirit of Kinsale*. The voyage offers sea-level views of both Charles and James forts, as well as seal and seafowl sightings with informative commentary from captain/historian/naturalist Jerome (€13, June-Sept daily at 14:00 and 15:00, July-Aug also at 11:00 and 12:00, one sailing per day April-May and Oct, check schedule online; departs from Pier Road in front of Acton's Hotel roughly 200 yards south of the TI; not necessary to book ahead; mobile 086-250-5456, www.kinsaleharbourcruises. com).

Sights in Kinsale

Kinsale's top sight is the town walking tour with Don and Barry (listed earlier, under "Tours in Kinsale"). But with extra time, there's much more to explore.

▲▲Kinsale Town Wander

Here's a very simple town stroll to get your historic bearings.

• Start on the harbor (just below the TI and across from Dinos Fish & Chips). To trace the route, see the map on the next page.

Harborfront: The medieval walled town's economy was fueled by its harbor, where ships came to be stocked. The old walls defined the original town and created a fortified zone that facilitated the taxation of goods. In the 17th and 18th centuries, this small and easily defended harbor was busy with rich and hungry tall ships. Kinsale was the last stop for ships making the two-month trip to America. Ships gathered here for provisions and to assemble into convoys that made the crossing safer.

Look for the **memorial** shaped like the mast of a tall ship, farther out toward the marina. It's a reminder that this was also

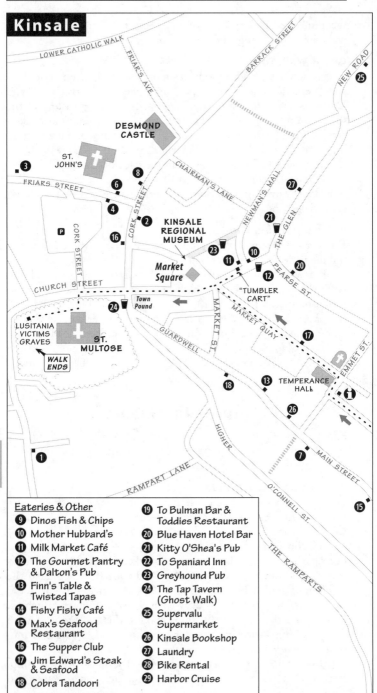

Kinsale

KINSALE & COBH

Eateries & Other

9 Dinos Fish & Chips
10 Mother Hubbard's
11 Milk Market Café
12 The Gourmet Pantry & Dalton's Pub
13 Finn's Table & Twisted Tapas
14 Fishy Fishy Café
15 Max's Seafood Restaurant
16 The Supper Club
17 Jim Edward's Steak & Seafood
18 Cobra Tandoori
19 To Bulman Bar & Toddies Restaurant
20 Blue Haven Hotel Bar
21 Kitty O'Shea's Pub
22 To Spaniard Inn
23 Greyhound Pub
24 The Tap Tavern (Ghost Walk)
25 Supervalu Supermarket
26 Kinsale Bookshop
27 Laundry
28 Bike Rental
29 Harbor Cruise

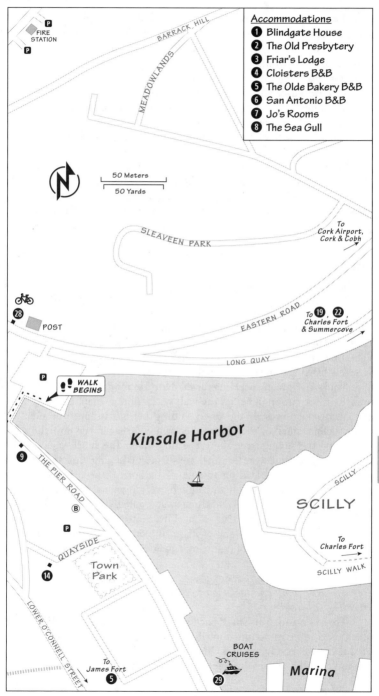

Accommodations

1. Blindgate House
2. The Old Presbytery
3. Friar's Lodge
4. Cloisters B&B
5. The Olde Bakery B&B
6. San Antonio B&B
7. Jo's Rooms
8. The Sea Gull

50 Meters
50 Yards

BARRACK HILL

MEADOWLANDS

FIRE STATION

SLEAVEEN PARK

To Cork Airport, Cork & Cobh

POST

EASTERN ROAD

To 19, 22, Charles Fort & Summercove

LONG QUAY

WALK BEGINS

Kinsale Harbor

9

THE PIER ROAD

SCILLY

SCILLY

To Charles Fort

SCILLY WALK

QUAYSIDE

Town Park

14

LOWER O'CONNELL STREET

To James Fort

5

BOAT CRUISES

29

Marina

KINSALE & COBH

a port of military consequence. Dozens of ships from the Spanish Armada could moor here, threatening England. Since Spain and Ireland had a common religion and common enemy (Catholicism and England), Kinsale had a more prominent place in history than its size might suggest.

You're standing on reclaimed land. What seems like part of the old center was actually built later on land reclaimed from the harbor. The town sits on the floor of a natural quarry, with easy-to-cut shale hills ideal for a ready supply of fill. Notice the mudflats in the harbor at low tide.

Clear-cutting of the once-plentiful oak forest upriver (for shipbuilding and barrel-making) hastened erosion and silted up the harbor. By the early 1800s—when British ships needed lots of restocking for the Napoleonic Wars—ships were bigger, Kinsale's port was slowly dying, and nearby Cobh's deep-water port took over the lion's share of shipping. Kinsale settled into a quieter existence as a fishing port.

• *From the TI, walk inland (between the Temperance Hall and the old Methodist church) up Market Quay. Take your first right on Market Street and find an old vehicle on big wheels at the Milk Market Café, across from Dalton's Pub.*

Town Center: Parked like a big flowerbox here is a 19th-century **"tumbler cart."** This rolled through town like a garbage service collecting sewage from the townsfolk, then spread the human waste as fertilizer on the fields outside of town.

Study the green metal medieval **Kinsale model** (circa 1381) and the information panel on the wall with another map. It shows the narrow confines of the town, hiding behind its once-proud walls, before much of the bay was reclaimed. You can see how the wall lined the main street along the tidal flats. The subtle curves of Main Street trace the original coastline. (Walking this street, you'll see tiny lanes leading to today's harbor. These originated as piers—just wide enough to roll a barrel down to an awaiting ship.) Notice the town wall had three "water gates." One was called "World's End," which felt true in the 14th century.

Find **Dalton's Pub**—one of 25 pubs in this small-but-never-thirsty town. This is one of many inviting local pubs famous for live folk and trad music.

• *Backtrack to cross Market Square, pass the old courthouse (now the Regional Museum), and take Church Street to a vacant little lot across from The Tap Tavern.*

Town Pound: This small enclosure was where goods and livestock used to be impounded until the owner could pay the associated tax. After the James and Charles forts were built in the 1600s, the town wall became obsolete—and also boxed in the town, preventing further expansion. So the townspeople disassembled the wall and used its ready-cut stones for building projects like this.

• *Walk uphill past The Tap Tavern to the church.*

St. Multose Church: This Anglican church (open after noon) comes with a fortress-like tower. While rebuilt in recent centuries, it goes back to the Middle Ages. In its very proper Anglican interior, you'll see a list of vicars going back to 1377. The humble base of the baptismal font dates from the 6th century.

• *Leaving the church, walk 20 paces, veering left and uphill to two gray, concrete, gravelly graves (near the gate to the street).*

***Lusitania* Victims Graves:** This remembers "Victims of the *Lusitania* Outrage 1915." Nine months into World War I, just off the coast of Kinsale, the Germans torpedoed the *Lusitania* with many Americans on board. It sank within 20 minutes, and more than half of the 2,000 passengers drowned. This tragedy led to the United States going "over there" and joining what was called "The Great War."

▲▲Charles Fort

Strategically set to be the gatekeeper for this critical harbor, Kinsale's star-shaped Charles Fort is a testimony to the importance of this little town in the 17th century.

Cost and Hours: €5, daily 10:00-18:00, Nov-mid-March until 17:00, last entry one hour before closing, a half-mile south of town, tel. 021/477-2263. Free guided walks are included (45 minutes, generally on the hour). A little coffee-and-pastry café stands inside the walls. To visit the castle you'll need to drive, catch a taxi, or walk (see the "Scilly Walk," later).

Visiting the Fort: When built, Charles Fort was Britain's biggest star-shaped fort—a state-of-the-art defense when artillery made the traditional castle obsolete (low, thick walls were tougher for cannons to breach than the tall, thinner walls of older castles). The star design made defending any attack on its walls safer and more effective. Notice how the strongest walls face the sea and how the oldest buildings are crouched down below the potential cannon fire of attacking ships.

Red buoys mark the navigable lane for shipping in this shallow harbor—making any ship entering or leaving well within cannon range.

The British occupied this fort until Irish independence in 1922. Its interior buildings were torched in 1923 by antitreaty IRA forces to keep it from being used by Free State troops during the Irish Civil War.

Guided tours (free with admission) engross you in the harsh daily life of 18th-century British soldiers and the few "lucky" wives allowed to live in the fort and earn their keep doing laundry for an army.

While most of the fort is just ruined buildings with nice views, there is an important exhibit filling two floors of the Barracks Stores building (the tall intact building, just below and to the right of the entry).

Climb the ramparts to enjoy the view, marvel at the cleverness of a "star-designed fort," and gaze out to Kinsale Head where, in 1915, the *Lusitania* was torpedoed by Germans and sank.

After Your Visit: For a beer or meal nearby, try the recommended **Bulman Bar** in Summercove, where the road runs low near the water on the way back to town (with small parking lot). And to see how easily the forts could bottle up this key harbor, pull over at the grand harbor viewpoint at the high point on the road back into town (between Summercove and The Spaniard pub).

Scilly Walk (Kinsale to Charles Fort)

The 45-minute walk between Kinsale and Charles Fort offers a delightful chance to connect the town with its leading attraction. (There's no convenient alternative other than a car or taxi.) Along the way you'll pass great harbor views, quaint cottages, dry stone walls, and the recommended Bulman Bar. While the couple of hundred yards at the beginning and end are along roads (without sidewalks), the middle 80 percent of the walk is along a peaceful, pedestrian-only trail through lush vegetation. Look for *Scilly Walk* signs on the left when walking towards town (near top of hill, 100 yards beyond Bulman Bar).

James Fort

Older, overgrown with yellow gorse, and filling a forgotten peninsula, James Fort is Kinsale's other star fort, guarding the bay opposite Charles Fort. Built in the years just after the famous 1601 battle of Kinsale (when a Spanish force disembarked here—see the "Kinsale's History" sidebar), this fort is more ruined, less interesting, and less visited than Charles Fort. Its military usefulness ended with a bang in 1690 when the magazine containing the fort's ammunition was hit by a direct and fatal shell fired by King William's besieging army. Check out the satellite blockhouse (down a straight, 75-yard trail from the main walls), which sits below the fort at the water's edge opposite Summercove. It controlled a strong chain boom that could be raised to block ships from reaching Kinsale's docks (free, always open).

Getting There: Easily accessible by car or bike, it's two miles

(3 km) south of town along Pier Road on the west shore of the bay (cross the bridge and turn left; you'll dead-end at Castle Park Marina, where you can park or leave your bike). It's up the hill behind the Dock pub. When facing the pub, the trailhead to the fort is at the far left end of the buildings, where the parking lot ends.

▲Desmond Castle

This 15th-century fortified customs house has had a long and varied history. It was the Spanish armory during Spain's 1601 occupation of Kinsale. Nicknamed "Frenchman's Prison," it served as a British prison and once housed 600 cramped prisoners of the Napoleonic Wars (not to mention earlier American Revolutionary War prisoners captured at sea—who were treated as rebels, not prisoners, and chained to the outside of the building as a warning to any rebellion-minded Irish). In the late 1840s, it was a famine-relief center.

Today, the evocative little tower comes with a scant display of its colorful history, as well as the modest two-room Museum of Wine, highlighting Ireland's little-known connection to the international wine trade. In the late Middle Ages, Kinsale was renowned for its top-quality wooden casks. Developing strong trade links with Bordeaux and Jerez, local merchants traded their dependable empty casks for casks full of wine. Later, Kinsale became a "designated wine port" for tax-collection purposes.

Cost and Hours: €5; daily 10:00-18:00, closed Oct-Easter, last entry at 17:15; tours generally at 10:15, 12:00, 14:15, and 16:00; Cork Street, tel. 021/477-4855.

▲Kinsale Regional Museum

In the center of the old town, traffic circles the market, which later became a courthouse and is now the Regional Museum. Its Dutch architecture reflects the influence of Dutch-born King William of Orange at the end of the 1600s. Drop by at least to read the fun 1788 tax code for all Kinsale commercial transactions (outside at the front door).

Cost and Hours: Free, Tue-Sat 10:30-13:30, closed Sun-Mon, staffed by volunteers—hours can be erratic, Market Square, tel. 021/477-7930.

Visiting the Museum: The modest museum is worth a quick visit for its fun mishmash of domestic and maritime bygones. It also gives a good perspective on the controversial *Lusitania* tragedy. Kinsale had maritime jurisdiction over the waters 12 miles offshore, where the luxury liner was torpedoed in 1915. Hearings were held upstairs here in the courthouse shortly afterward to investigate the causes of the disaster—which helped propel America into World War I—and to paint the German Hun as a bloodthirsty villain. Claims by Germany that the *Lusitania* was illegally carrying munitions (and using innocent passengers as human shields)

KINSALE & COBH

Kinsale's History

Kinsale's remarkable harbor has made this an important port since prehistoric times. The bay's 10-foot tide provided a natural

shuttle service for Stone Age hunter-gatherers: They could ride it, at two miles per hour twice a day, for the eight miles up and down the River Bandon. In the Bronze Age, when people discovered that it takes tin and copper to make bronze, tin came from Cornwall (in southwest England) and copper came from this part of Ireland. From 500 B.C. to A.D. 500, Kinsale was a rich trading center. The result: Lots of Stonehenge-type monuments are nearby. The best is Drombeg Stone Circle (a one-hour drive west, just off R-597/Glandore Road).

Kinsale's importance peaked during the 16th, 17th, and 18th centuries, when sailing ships ruled the waves, turning maritime countries into global powers. Kinsale was Ireland's most perfect natural harbor and the gateway to both Spain and France—potentially providing a base for either of these two powers in cutting off English shipping. Because of this, two pivotal battles were fought here in the 17th century: in 1601 against the Spanish, and in 1690 against the French. Two great forts were built to combat these threats from the Continent. England couldn't rule the waves without ruling Kinsale.

To understand the small town of Kinsale, you need to understand the big picture: In about 1500, the pope divided newly discovered lands outside Europe between Spain and Portugal. With the Reformation breaking Rome's lock on Europe, maritime powers such as England were ignoring the pope's grant. This was important because trade with the New World and Asia brought huge wealth in spices (necessary for curing meat), gold, and silver.

England threatened Spain's New World piñata, and Ireland was Catholic. Spain had an economic and a religious reason to defend the pope and Catholicism. The showdown between Spain and England for mastery of the seas (and control of all that trade) was in Ireland. The excuse: to rescue the dear Catholics of Ireland from the terrible treachery of Protestant England.

So the Irish disaster unfolded. The powerful Ulster chieftains Hugh O'Neill and Red Hugh O'Donnell and their clans had been on a roll in their guerilla battles against the English on their home turf up in Ulster. With Spanish aid, they figured they could actually drive the English out of Ireland. In 1601, a Spanish fleet dropped off 3,000 soldiers, who established a beachhead in Kinsale. After the ships left, the Spaniards were pinned down in Kinsale by the English commander (who, breaking with martial etiquette, actually fought in the winter). In harsh winter conditions, virtually the entire Irish-clan fighting force left the north and marched to the south coast, thinking they could liberate their Spanish allies and win freedom from England.

The numbers seemed reasonable (8,000 Englishmen versus 3,000 Spaniards with 7,000 Irish clansmen approaching). The Irish attacked on Christmas Eve in 1601. But, holding the high ground around fortified and Spanish-occupied Kinsale, a relatively small English force kept the Spaniards hemmed in, leaving the bulk of the English troops to rout the fighting Irish, who were adept at ambushes but not at open-field warfare. (Today's visitors will be reminded of this crucial battle as they wander past pubs with names like "The 1601" and "The Spaniard"—see pub sign on opposite page.)

The Irish resistance was broken, and its leaders fled to Europe (the "flight of the Earls"). England made peace with Spain and began the "plantation" of mostly Scottish Protestants in Ireland (the seeds of today's Troubles in Ulster). England ruled the waves, and it ruled Ireland.

The lesson: Kinsale is key. England eventually built two huge, star-shaped fortresses to ensure control of the narrow waterway, a strategy it would further develop in later fortifications built at Gibraltar and Singapore.

Kinsale's maritime history continued. Daniel Defoe used the real-life experience of Scottish privateer Alexander Selkirk, who departed from Kinsale in 1703 and was later marooned alone on a desert island, as the basis for his book *Robinson Crusoe*. (Selkirk was lucky to have been marooned when he was—his ship and all aboard later perished in a hurricane off Costa Rica.)

It was just 10 miles offshore from Old Kinsale Head that the passenger liner *Lusitania* was torpedoed by a German submarine in 1915. At the time, the liner was the fastest vessel on the seas (with a top speed of 25 knots). The primitive U-boats of the day were much slower (8 knots), giving Lusitania's crew a false sense of security. Because World War I was the first conflict to employ submarine warfare, evasion tactics were largely untested. As the *Lusitania* sank, nearly 1,200 people were killed, sparking America's eventual entry into the war.

KINSALE & COBH

may have been inspired by the huge explosion and rapid sinking of the vessel. As the wreck slowly succumbs to a century of gravity and rust, it's collapsing on itself and the truth of its cargo may forever be lost in the ocean floor muck.

The museum displays are sparse, but include *Lusitania* flotsam such as a wicker deck chair and a US mail bag. A flickering black-and-white film shows the last happy glory days of the vessel in port. Apart from the *Lusitania* footage, you'll find a gritty little model of medieval Kinsale surrounded by its once-proud walls. Perhaps even more memorable, in the side room is the boot of the 8-foot-3-inch Kinsale giant, who lived here in the late 1700s.

Nightlife in Kinsale

Live Folk and Trad Music
In the Town Center: Kinsale's town pubs are packed with atmosphere and live music (more likely folk, but plenty of traditional Irish too). Rather than target a certain place, simply walk the area between Guardwell, Pearse Street, and the Market Square. Music starts up after 21:00—you'll hear it as you wander. Pop into each pub that has live music and then settle in to your favorite. **Dalton's Pub** hosts informal amateur sessions with locals after 21:00 (grab a seat by 20:30). The **Blue Haven Hotel Bar** and **Kitty O'Shea's** are also good bets.

Outside of Town: Irish music purists will be rewarded if they take the five-minute taxi ride (€10 one-way) out to the **Bulman Bar** near the base of Charles Fort. This is one of Kinsale's two best pubs for traditional Irish music sessions (Thu-Sat at 21:30, Sun at 17:00, get there early to ensure a seat, tel. 021/477-2131). Otherwise, get your trad fix at the charmingly claustrophobic **Spaniard Inn,** a 10-minute walk out to the Scilly peninsula across the harbor from town. It fills the center of a hairpin turn on the crest of the peninsula. The darkly atmospheric interior is about the size of a rail car, with the long bar taking up half the space, so only about 10 seats get an actual view of the musicians (most nights at 21:30, you'll stand all night unless you arrive before 20:30, tel. 021/477-2436).

Pubs for *Craic* Rather than Music
For conversation or an introspective pint, I like the **Greyhound** (off Newman's Mall, behind the Milk Market Café)—no live music, just a scruffy, multichambered throwback with no pretenses. Another joint filled with characters who haven't changed in decades is **The Tap Tavern** (corner of Church Street and Guardwell). It's presided over by Mary O'Neill, the unofficial godmother of Kinsale, and her slyly humorous son Brian, who runs the town's recom-

mended ghost tours. Check out the ancient holy well that came to light when they built their appealing back patio.

Sleeping in Kinsale

Kinsale is a popular place in summer for yachters and golfers (who don't flinch at paying $300 for 18 holes out on the exotic Old Head of Kinsale Golf Course). It's wise to book your room in advance. These places are all within a 15-minute walk of the town center.

$$$ Blindgate House, high up on the fringe of town behind St. Multose Church, offers 11 pristine rooms in fine modern comfort (tel. 021/477-7858, mobile 087-237-6676, www.blindgatehouse.com, info@blindgatehouse.com, Maeve Coakley).

$$$ The Old Presbytery is a fine, quiet house a block outside the commercial district, with a meandering floor plan, plush lounge, and nine pleasant rooms. Listed in most guidebooks, it has lots of American guests. The breakfasts are a delight, the rooms are stocking-feet cozy, and Noreen McEvoy runs the place with a passion for excellence. Join the other guests for a complimentary wine-and-cheese happy hour every afternoon (RS%, 10 percent discount with cash, family rooms, private parking, 43 Cork Street, tel. 021/477-2027, www.oldpres.com, info@oldpres.com).

$$ Friar's Lodge is a slate-shingled hotel, perched up the hill past St. John's Catholic Church. What its 17 spacious rooms lack in Old World character, they make up for in dependable quality (family rooms, private parking, 5 Friar Street, tel. 021/477-7384, www.friars-lodge.com, mtierney@indigo.ie).

$$ Cloisters B&B has four snug but bright and inviting rooms with a friendly atmosphere fostered by Orla Kenneally and Aileen Healy (2 Friars Street, tel. 021/470-0680, www.cloisterskinsale.com, info@cloisterskinsale.com).

$ The Olde Bakery B&B makes you feel at home, with six quilt-bedded rooms, Lilly the loveable mute mutt, and charmingly chatty hostess Chrissie Quigley (cash only, 56 Lower O'Connell Street, tel. 021/477-3012, www.theoldebakerykinsale.com, oldebakery@gmail.com).

$ San Antonio B&B is a 200-year-old house with five rooms and a funky budget feel, lovingly looked after by gentleman Jimmie Conron (cash only, 1 Friar Street, tel. 021/477-2341, mobile 086-878-9800, jimmiesan@yahoo.ie).

$ Jo's Rooms is a good value, offering five fresh, practical rooms in the center of town (breakfast extra, cash only, small rooms with smaller double beds, 55 Main Street, mobile 087-948-1026, www.joskinsale.com, joskinsale@gmail.com).

$ The Sea Gull, perched up the hill right next to Desmond Castle, offers six retro-homey rooms. It's run by Mary O'Neill, who also runs The Tap Tavern down the hill (RS%, cash only, Cork Street, tel. 021/477-2240, mobile 087-241-6592, marytap@iol.ie).

Eating in Kinsale

Back in the 1990s, when Ireland was just getting its cuisine act together, Kinsale was the island's self-proclaimed gourmet capital.

While good restaurants are commonplace in Irish towns today, Kinsale still has an edge at mealtime. Local competition is fierce, and restaurants offer creative and tempting menus. Seafood is king. With so many options in the ever-changing scene, it's worth a short stroll to assess your options. Reservations are smart, especially if eating late or on a weekend. Restaurant connoisseurs can check the menu details of Kinsale's top restaurants at www.kinsalerestaurants.com.

CHEAP AND CHEERY

$ Dinos Fish & Chips, with big windows overlooking the harbor, is a fun and family-friendly chain for budget fish-and-chips. It's modern and spacious, with a nautical theme. Try the large €14 plate, designed for two (daily 9:00-21:30, across from the TI facing the harbor, tel. 021/477-4561).

$ Mother Hubbard's, tiny with six tables and packed with happy locals near Market Square, serves all-day breakfast, toasties, sandwiches, and salads (daily 8:30-14:00, 1 Market Street, tel. 021/477-2440).

$ Milk Market Café—right next door—is a hit with kids, offering burgers, pizza, and fish-and-chips (daily 10:00-18:00, 3 Market Street).

$ The Gourmet Pantry is an above-average takeout option (Mon-Sat 9:00-17:30, Sun from 10:00, 4 Market Street, tel. 021/470-9215).

Groceries: You can gather picnic supplies at the **SuperValu** supermarket (daily 8:00-21:00, New Road, tel. 021/477-2843).

GOOD DINNERS IN THE OLD CENTER

$$$$ Finn's Table is dressy, refined, and romantic, with white tablecloths, candles, and elegant service. John Finn cooks and Julie Finn serves enticing dinner plates ranging from lamb to lobster. Meat is their passion—John comes from a long line of butchers and still gets the best cuts from his dad's butcher shop. Their three-course early-bird menu, served until 18:30, makes this pricey place more affordable (Thu-Tue 18:00-22:00, closed Wed; Nov-April Thu-Sat only, if open at all; 6 Main Street, tel. 021/470-9636, www.finnstable.com).

$$$ Fishy Fishy Café, a high-energy destination seafood restaurant with spacious seating (indoor, balcony, and terrace) and a wonderful menu, is run by Martin and Maria Shanahan. When I asked, "What's your secret?" they pointed to the portraits of fishermen on the wall and said, "Local, local, local." It's a good lunch or early dinner option for those on a tighter budget. Martin's culinary prowess has led him to host a weekly cooking show on Irish TV (daily 12:00-21:00, reservations recommended, Pier Road, tel. 021/470-0415, www.fishyfishy.ie).

$$$ Max's Seafood Restaurant is a spacious and stylish—but not overly romantic—place. There's no pretense—the focus is simply on great seafood. Chef Olivier Queva from France offers a fresh and classic selection and a French flair (nice wine by the glass), while wife Anne Marie serves. While this place gets pricey, there's a good early-bird special until 19:15 (daily 18:00-21:30, 48 Main Street, tel. 021/477-2443).

$$$ The Supper Club is a linen-and-leather upmarket joint with a meat smoker, strong cocktails, and creative desserts (Tue-Sat 18:30-22:00, closed Sun-Mon, 3 Cork Street, tel. 021/477-2847).

$$$ Jim Edward's Steak & Seafood Restaurant and Bar is an energetic place that's clearly a local favorite for its steaks, seafood, and vegetables. Choose between the restaurant's maritime setting or the more intimate, pub-like bar (same menu, bar open daily 12:00-22:00, restaurant from 18:00, Market Quay, tel. 021/477-2541).

$$ Twisted Tapas is hip and youthful, serving Spanish tapas and lighter fare "with a twist" (Wed-Sun 18:00-21:00, closed Mon-Tue, 5 Main Street, tel. 021/477-4218).

$$ Cobra Tandoori is good for tasty Punjabi/Indian cuisine (daily 16:00-23:00, 69 Main Street, tel. 021/477-7911).

NEAR CHARLES FORT

$$$ Bulman Bar and Toddies Restaurant serves seafood with seasonal produce. The mussels are especially tasty; on a balmy day or evening, diners take a bucket and a beer out to the seawall. This is the only way to eat on the water in Kinsale. The **$$ pub**, strewn with fun decor and sporting a big fireplace, is also good for a coffee or beer after your visit to the fort (pub open daily 12:30-21:00, restaurant open Tue-Sat from 18:30, 200 yards toward Kinsale from Charles Fort in hamlet of Summercove, tel. 021/477-2131).

Kinsale Connections

BY PUBLIC TRANSPORTATION

The closest train station is in Cork, 15 miles north. But buses run frequently between Kinsale (stop is on Pier Road, 100 yards behind TI, at south end of town) and Cork's bus station (14/day Mon-Sat, fewer on Sun, 50 minutes, www.buseireann.ie).

In **Cork,** the bus station and train station are a 10-minute walk apart. The bus station (corner of Merchant's Quay and Parnell Place) is on the south bank of the River Lee, just over the nearest bridge from the train station (north of the river on Lower Glanmire Road).

From Cork by Train to: Dublin (hourly, 3 hours, www.irishrail.ie).

From Cork by Bus to: Dublin (every 2 hours, 3.5 hours), **Galway** (hourly, 4.5 hours), **Tralee** (hourly, 2.5 hours), **Kilkenny** (4/day, 2 direct, 3.5 hours). Bus info: Tel. 021/450-8188 or www.buseireann.ie.

BY PLANE

Cork Airport is handy for travelers starting or ending their trip in southern Ireland. Located four miles south of Cork city (on N-27/R-600 to Kinsale, a 30-minute drive away), it offers connecting flights from London Heathrow and Edinburgh on Aer Lingus, as well as from London's Stansted and Gatwick on Ryanair. You can also fly from here directly to many European cities (tel. 021/431-3131, airport code: ORK, www.corkairport.com).

Citylink airport buses run to Kinsale (hourly Mon-Sat, fewer on Sunday) and less frequently to other destinations, including Galway (6/day, 4 hours).

To sleep near Cork Airport, consider **$$$ Cork Airport Hotel** (book directly on their website for best prices, tel. 021/494-7500, www.corkairporthotel.com, reservations@corkairporthotel.com).

Cobh

If your ancestry is Irish, there's a good chance that this was the last Irish soil your ancestors had under their feet. Cobh (pronounced "cove") was the major port of Irish emigration in the 19th century. Of the six million Irish who have emigrated to America, Canada, and Australia since 1815, nearly half left from Cobh.

The first steam-powered ship to make a transatlantic crossing departed from Cobh in 1838—cutting the journey time from 50 days to 18. When Queen Victoria came to Ireland for the first time in 1849, Cobh was the first Irish ground she set foot on. Giddy, the town renamed itself "Queenstown" in her honor. It was still going by that name in 1912, when the *Titanic* made its final fateful stop here before heading out on its maiden (and only) voyage...just over 100 years ago. To celebrate their new independence from British royalty in 1922, locals changed the town's name back to its original Irish moniker. Today the town's deep harbor attracts dozens of cruise ships per year (with their large packs of eager visitors).

Orientation to Cobh

Cobh sits on a large island in Cork Harbor, connected to the mainland via a short bridge (on the north shore) and a drive-on ferry (on the west shore). The town's inviting waterfront is colorful yet salty, with a playful promenade. The butcher's advertisement reads, "Always pleased to meet you and always with meat to please you." Stroll past the shops along the water. Ponder the large and dramatic *Lusitania* memorial on Casement Square and the modest *Titanic* memorial nearby on Pearse Square.

A hike up the hill to the towering Neo-Gothic St. Colman's Cathedral rewards you with a fine view of the port. To get to the cathedral, walk behind the *Lusitania* memorial, go under the stone arch, and strut up steep Westview Street, passing the photogenic row of colorful houses on your right (nicknamed the "deck of cards" by locals). After panting your way to the top, turn right—you can't miss the cathedral steeple.

Tourist Information: The TI is in the old library right at the base of Westview Street (Mon-Fri 9:00-17:30, Sat-Sun 10:30-16:30, tel. 021/481-3301, www.cobhharbourchamber.ie).

Helpful Hints: If you're driving into Cobh, follow the *Heritage Centre* signs to The Queenstown Story, where you'll find easy **parking** at the museum. There's a two-hour parking maximum anywhere in town (first hour free, second hour is €1, pay at machines on street).

Michael Martin and his staff lead one-hour **Titanic Trail walking tours** that give you unexpected insights into the tragic *Titanic* and *Lusitania* voyages, Spike Island, and Cobh's maritime history (€9.50, ask for Rick Steves discount and show this book when you pay, daily at 11:00, also 14:00 in summer with required

KINSALE & COBH

Cobh

To Cork
To Cuskinny → East Ferry

BISHOP STREET
PARK RD.
LAUNDRY HILL
JOHN O'CONNELL ST.
WEST VIEW
LAKE ROAD
OLD STREET
CASEMENT
WOLFE TONE ST.
ROCHE'S TERR.
ST. COLMAN'S CATHEDRAL
CATHEDRAL PL.
CHURCH ST.
HARBOUR HILL
RAHILLY ST.
LUSITANIA MEMORIAL
Pearse Square
TITANIC MEM.
Casement Square
WEST BEACH
EAST BEACH
LYNCH'S QUAY
TITANIC EXPERIENCE
SPY HILL
BURMA STEPS
To Carrigloe & Cork
SPY HILL
WESTBOURNE PLACE
BUS TERMINUS
KENNEDY PIER
100 Meters
100 Yards

QUEENSTOWN STORY MUSEUM & HERITAGE CENTRE
TRAIN STATION
Cork Harbor

1 Commodore Hotel
2 Waters Edge Hotel & Jacob's Ladder Restaurant
3 Ard na Laoi B&B
4 Trade Winds Rest.
5 Titanic Bar & Grill
6 Centra Market & Post Office

prebooking, call ahead to confirm tour times in winter, private tours available, meet in lobby of Commodore Hotel, tel. 021/481-5211, mobile 087-276-7218, www.titanic.ie, info@titanic.ie). Seriously interested travelers should look for his book, *RMS Lusitania: It Wasn't and It Didn't.*

Sights in Cobh

▲The Titanic Experience

It's stirring to think that this modest little port town was the ship's final anchorage—and the last chance to get off. Occupying the former White Star Line building where the *Titanic*'s final passengers boarded, this compact museum packs a decent punch as it recounts the story of the ship and its final moments.

Cost and Hours: €9.50, daily 9:00-18:00, Oct-April until 17:30, last entry 45 minutes before closing, Casement Square, tel. 021/481-4412, www.titanicexperiencecobh.ie.

Visiting the Museum: As you look off the back balcony into the harbor, note the decayed pilings in front of you. These once supported the old pier and represent the passengers' last chance to turn back. One lucky surviving crewman with a premonition did.

Inside the museum, you travel room to room with your host, the ship's fourth mate, in audiovisual form. He meets you at the boarding dock, full of pride in the new vessel. He joins you in replicas of a posh first-class cabin and a no-frills third-class cabin before his commentary is interrupted by the sound of ice tearing at the hull. You then enter an exhibition room featuring an animation that silently depicts the ship sinking in its steel-twisting, slow-motion ballet to the bottom (settling as two crunched hulls 600 yards apart and 12,000 feet deep).

The last stop is a room highlighting the luxurious ship's innovative firsts. It was one of the first equipped with a wireless "Marconi room" to send messages from sea to shore—or to other ships. *Titanic* was the first ever to issue an SOS message by Morse code. Another wall explains in grim detail the effects of hypothermia on the human body.

Before you leave, check out the list of 123 passengers who boarded the *Titanic* in Cobh. Your entry ticket has one of these passenger's names on it. See if you survived (you've got a 30 percent chance). A passenger with the same name as one of this book's coauthors is listed among the third-class passengers lost.

▲The Queenstown Story

Filling a harborside Victorian train station, this museum is an earnest attempt to make the city's history come to life. The topics—the Famine, Irish emigration, Australia-bound prison ships, the sinking of the *Lusitania,* and the ill-fated voyage of the *Titanic*—are interesting enough to make it a worthwhile stop.

Cost and Hours: €9.50; Mon-Sat 9:30-18:00, Sun 11:00-18:00; Nov-April until 17:00; last entry one hour before closing, Cobh Heritage Centre, handy café, tel. 021/481-3591, www.cobhheritage.com, info@cobhheritage.com.

Visiting the Museum: Coverage of the *Titanic* and the *Lusitania* was beefed up for the centennials of these famous ships' sinking (2012 and 2015, respectively). You'll learn about one priest who got off the *Titanic* at Cobh. His photos of the early legs of the voyage are a priceless historical reference. But in general, the museum itself, while kid-friendly and engaging, is weak on actual historical artifacts. It reminds me of a big, interesting history picture book with the pages expanded and tacked on the wall.

Before departing, walk over to the Annie Moore statue next to the water, 25 yards from the front door. She emigrated from Cobh and was the first person to be processed through Ellis Island when it opened on January 1, 1892.

Nearby: Those with Irish roots to trace can use the Heritage Centre's **genealogy search service,** located right across from the Queenstown Story ticket booth. Since Cobh was the primary Irish emigration port, this can be a great place to start your search (€50/hour consultation and research assistance by appointment only,

Irish Genealogy

Lots of travelers come to the Emerald Isle intent on tracing their Irish ancestry. But too few give it enough thought before they set foot on the old sod, and instead head straight to what they think might be the right town or region to start "asking around." While this approach may bear fruit (or at least give you an opportunity to meet nice Irish people), a bit of preparation can save time and increase your chances of making a real connection to your Celtic bloodlines.

First, a common false assumption: Many novice root-searchers think their Irish ancestors were from County Cork, because Cobh is listed as their emigration departure port. But Cobh was the primary departure port for the vast majority of Irish emigrants—regardless of where they had resided in Ireland. An even earlier wave of Irish emigrants (mostly Scots-Irish from Ulster) sailed from the port of Derry (the second busiest emigration port).

If you have an idea of what town your ancestors hailed from, search for its location (www.google.com/maps is a good starting point). Correct spelling is essential: Ballyalloly is up north in County Down while Ballyally is down south in County Cork (close enough only counts in horseshoes and hand grenades). Just as there's a Springfield in almost every state in the Union, the same goes for some common Irish town names: There's a town named Kells in four different Irish counties.

Fáilte Ireland, the official government-sponsored Irish tourist board, is a safe bet for reputable genealogy sources (www.discoverireland.ie). Some fertile websites to consider browsing are www.irishgenealogy.ie or www.ancestry.com. The recently enabled online access to both the 1901 and 1911 Irish censuses has been a boon (www.census.nationalarchives.ie). However, it's not

email ahead to book—genealogy@cobhheritage.com). See the sidebar for more tips on researching your Irish heritage.

Sleeping in Cobh

These hotels are all centrally located near the harbor, less than a five-minute walk from the Queenstown Story.

$$$ Commodore Hotel is a grand 170-year-old historic landmark with 40 rooms. This place was once owned by the Humbert family, wealthy Germans who opened it up to *Lusitania* refugees after the 1915 sinking. Its high-ceilinged rooms creak with Victorian character (Westbourne Place, tel. 021/481-1277, www.commodorehotel.ie, commodorehotel@eircom.net).

$$$ Waters Edge Hotel, located 50 yards from the Queenstown Story, has 19 bright, modern rooms and a pleasant hara perfect science: Many precious birth records (some dating back to the 1200s) went up in smoke when offices in the Four Courts building in Dublin burned in 1922 during the Irish Civil War.

Before you get to Ireland, make contact with the Genealogy Advisory Service at the National Library in Dublin (tel. 01/603-0213, www.nli.ie, genealogy@nli.ie). Others to contact in advance of your trip include the helpful genealogy search service in Cobh (tel. 021/481-3591, www.cobhheritage.com/genealogy, genealogy@cobhheritage.com).

If you think your heritage might be Scots-Irish, check the Discover Ulster-Scots Centre in Belfast (tel. 028/9043-6710, http://discoverulsterscots.com, discoverulsterscots@gmail.com). Also consider the Mellon Centre for Migration Studies, near Omagh in Northern Ireland (tel. 028/8225-6315, www.qub.ac.uk/cms, mcms@librariesni.org.uk).

Another option is to hire a qualified expert to assist you in drilling deeper and navigating obstacles; Fáilte Ireland may be able to give you a recommendation. This kind of help doesn't come cheap, but if you're willing to invest in an experienced researcher, you may get better results. One worth considering is Sean Quinn of My Ireland Heritage (tel. 01/689-0213, www.myirelandheritage.com, sean@myirelandheritage.com, based near Dublin in Trim, County Meath, but able to work across Ireland). Top-end services like Sean's can then drive you to the locations where your ancestors lived.

With a few emails, phone calls, and Internet searches, you may just end up having a pint with some Irish guy who looks a lot like you. (For tips on dialing Irish phone numbers from North America, see page 556.)

bor-view restaurant (Yacht Club Quay, tel. 021/481-5566, www.watersedgehotel.ie, info@watersedgehotel.ie).

$ Ard na Laoi B&B is a friendly place with five fresh rooms in a great central location (cash only, 15 Westbourne Place, tel. 021/481-2742, www.ardnalaoi.ie, info@ardnalaoi.ie, Michael O'Shea).

Eating in Cobh

The nicest place in town is **Trade Winds,** with both a **$$$ pub** (downstairs) and **$$$$ restaurant** (upstairs). It's near the Commodore Hotel, facing the waterfront at 16 Casement Square. **$$$ Titanic Bar & Grill** is sunken under the Titanic Experience, with fun outdoor seating on fine days. I also like **$$$ Jacob's Ladder** restaurant in the Waters Edge Hotel. For picnic fixings, there's the **Centra Market**, facing the water on West Beach Street.

Cobh Connections

BY TRAIN
Cork's **Kent Station** has frequent short-hop service to both Cobh and Midleton, which are on separate lines (€5 one-way, €8.50 round-trip, 25 minutes, usually depart on the hour, return on the half-hour, www.irishrail.ie).

ROUTE TIPS FOR DRIVERS
Between Cobh and Cork or Waterford: If you're driving to Cobh from either Cork or Waterford, exit N-25 about 8 miles (13 km) east of Cork, following little R-624 over a bridge, onto the Great Island, and directly into Cobh.

Between Cobh and Kinsale: The 30-mile (50 km) drive takes 45 minutes and involves navigating Cork city traffic on well-marked roads. Driving from Cobh to Kinsale, you'll head north out of Cobh on R-624 and get on N-25 heading west, then follow the airport signs (with a little jet airplane icon) the whole way. You'll pass Cork Airport, which is conveniently located on R-600 leading south straight into Kinsale.

Between Waterford and Kinsale

If you're driving from Waterford (see previous chapter) to Cobh and Kinsale, you can easily visit these sights just off N-25 (listed roughly from east to west).

Ardmore
This funky little beach resort, with a famous ruined church and round tower, is a handy stop (just east of Youghal, 3 miles/5 km south of N-25 between Waterford and Cobh). A couple of buses run daily from Ardmore to Cork and to Waterford.

This humble little port town is just a line of pastel houses that appear frightened by the sea. Its beach claims (very modestly) to be "the most swimmable in Ireland."

The town's historic claim to fame: Christianity came to Ireland here first (thanks to St. Declan, who arrived in A.D. 416—15 years before St. Patrick...but with a weaker public-relations team). As if to proclaim that feat with an 800-year-old exclamation mark, one of Ireland's finest examples of a round tower stands perfectly intact, 97 feet above an evocative graveyard and a ruined church (noted for the faint remains of some early Christian carvings on its west facade). You can't get into the tower—the entrance is 14 feet off the ground.

An easy, scenic coastal loop hike (3 miles, 1 hour) leads from the parking lot of the ritzy Cliff House Hotel along the coast, eventually cutting inland and back into town (simple to follow, ask for free rudimentary map in newsstand at end of Main Street).

Sleeping in Ardmore: $$$$ Cliff House Hotel is a died-and-gone-to-heaven splurge with 39 impeccably modern and decadently expensive rooms, all with ocean views (tel. 024/87800, www.thecliffhousehotel.com, info@thecliffhousehotel.com).

$$ Duncrone B&B, run by Jeanette Dunne, has four vividly colorful rooms (half-mile outside town, up past the round tower, tel. 024/94860, www.duncronebandb.com, info@duncronebandb.com).

Eating in Ardmore: The local favorite is **$$ White Horses Restaurant** (Tue-Sun 11:00-22:00, closed Mon, Main Street, tel. 024/94040). For a fine lunch or dinner with cliff-perch views, check out the restaurant in the luxurious **$$$$ Cliff House Hotel** (turn right at the coastal end of Main Street and drive up narrow lane to dead end, tel. 024/87800). **An Tobar,** the only pub in town, is down near the water (but does not serve food).

▲Old Midleton Distillery

Sometime during your Ireland trip, even if you're a teetotaler, you'll want to tour a whiskey distillery. Of the three major distillery tours (this one, Jameson in Dublin, and Bushmills in Northern Ireland), the Midleton experience is the most interesting. After a 10-minute video, you'll walk with a guide through a great old 18th-century plant on a 45-minute tour; see waterwheel-powered

crankshafts and a 31,000-gallon copper still—the largest of its kind in the world; and learn the story of whiskey. Predictably, you finish in a tasting room and enjoy a free, not-so-wee glass. The finale is a Scotch vs. Irish whiskey taste test. Your guide will take two volunteers for this. Don't be shy, and enjoy an opportunity to taste the different brands.

Cost and Hours: €18, daily 10:00-18:00, tours run regularly 10:00-16:30 in summer—4/day in winter, cafeteria, tel. 021/461-3594, www.jamesonwhiskey.com.

Getting There: It's 12 miles (19 km) east of Cork in Midleton, about a mile off N-25, the main Cork-Waterford road. There's easy parking at the distillery lot.

Between Kinsale and Killarney

If you're driving between Kinsale and the Ring of Kerry (see next chapter), you can easily visit these sights (listed from east to west).

Blarney Stone and Castle

The town of Blarney is of no importance, and the 15th-century Blarney Castle is an empty hulk (with little effort put forth to make it meaningful or interesting). It's only famous as the place of tourist pilgrimage, where bus-loads line up to kiss a stone on its top rampart and get "the gift of gab." The stone's origin is shrouded in myth (perhaps brought back from the Holy Land by crusaders).

The best thing about this lame sight is the opportunity to watch a cranky man lower lemming tourists over the edge, belly up and head back, to kiss the stone while an automated camera snaps a photo—which will be available for purchase back by the parking lot. After a day of tour groups mindlessly climbing up here to perform this ritual, the stone can be literally slathered with spit and lipstick.

The tradition goes back to the late 16th century, when Queen Elizabeth I was trying to plant loyal English settlers in Ireland to tighten her grip on the rebellious island. She demanded that the Irish clan chiefs recognize the Crown, rather than the clan chiefs, as the legitimate titleholder of all lands.

One of those chiefs was Cormac MacCarthy, Lord of Blarney Castle (who was supposedly loyal to the queen). He was smart enough never to disagree with the queen—instead, he would cleverly avoid acquiescing to her demands by sending a never-ending stream of lengthy and deceptive excuses, disguised with liberal doses of flattery (while subtly maintaining his native Gaelic loyalties). In her frustration, the queen declared his endless words nothing but "blarney."

While the castle is a shell, the surrounding grounds are beautiful and well kept. There are even some

KINSALE & COBH

hints of Ireland's pre-Christian past on the grounds; you can see dolmens beside the trail in the forested Rock Close.

Cost and Hours: €15, Mon-Sat 9:00-18:30, Sun until 18:00, later in peak season, shorter hours in winter, free parking lot, helpful TI, tel. 021/438-5252, www.blarneycastle.ie.

Getting There: It's 5 miles (8 km) northwest of Cork, the major city in south Ireland. Looking for shopping galore? Adjacent Blarney Woolen Mills has it all (right next to the castle parking lot).

Beal na Blath: Michael Collins Ambush Site

Irish history fans may want to make a brief detour en route from Kinsale to Macroom to visit nearby Beal na Blath (BALE-nuh-

BLAH), where dynamic Irish rebel leader Michael Collins was assassinated on August 22, 1922, during the Irish Civil War. The site is not much more than a bend in a country road, with an Irish high cross on a raised platform to mark the spot. But it's Ireland's equivalent of Dallas' infamous "grassy knoll." (For an engrossing view of this and Collins' life, see the 1996 movie *Michael Collins*.)

Take a moment to step out of the car and climb the steps onto the fenced platform. Next to the high cross, a plaque with a photo shows the road as it appeared in 1922, with arrows approximating the position of the Collins convoy and the spots from which the ambushers fired.

Dusk was falling as the convoy carrying Collins to Cork came under attack. Collins could have ordered his driver to speed off, but chose instead to stand and fight. The identity of the antitreaty IRA guerilla who fired the fatal shot (thought to have been an errant ricochet) remains in dispute. Following his death, Collins' body lay in state for three days at Dublin City Hall, drawing massive crowds. Although his pro-treaty Free State army later won the civil war, it's likely that modern Irish history would have been much different had Collins lived. While Éamon de Valera directed his country down the "comely maiden at the crossroads" vision, had Collins survived and taken power, Ireland would have been more secular and more integrated into the European economy—richer and more mainstream European.

Getting There: Beal na Blath is just off N-22, the road that runs west from Cork to Macroom, and is easiest to find if you have a detailed Ordnance Survey atlas (it covers all tiny rural lanes). About halfway between Cork and Macroom, take R-585 south off N-22 through the tiny village of Crookstown. From Crookstown,

KINSALE & COBH

follow *Beal na Blath* signs south for about a mile to the ambush site (well-marked, but be alert in case foliage on leafy rural lanes obscures a sign at a crossroads).

Macroom

This busy, one-street market town makes a convenient coffee or lunch stop for those driving between Cork or Kinsale and Killarney. The romanticized gateway where its ruined castle once stood was owned by the father of William Penn (who founded Pennsylvania). It overlooks an entertaining main square, where you'll find limited parking. The weekly market fills the square with "casual trading" each Tuesday. The 2006 Irish Civil War saga *The Wind That Shakes the Barley* was filmed in this area.

Lynch's Coffee Shop and Bakery (the bright-yellow storefront at the far end of the square) is a welcoming place, with cheap and cheery food and drink, a WC in the back, and historic town photos on the walls. The Lynch family has run the bakery since 1869 (say "hi" to Humphrey and his wife Pat). The **Next Door Café**, in the Castle Hotel (a block from the square on the main street), serves good, fast lunches and made-to-order sandwiches.

If Macroom parking is challenging, continue driving west on N-22 another 10 miles to the little hamlet of **Ballyvourney,** where you'll find a friendly lunch at the Mills Inn (on right with easy parking behind).

KENMARE &
THE RING OF KERRY

It's no wonder that, since Victorian times, visitors have been attracted to this dramatic chunk of Ireland. Mysterious ancient ring forts stand sentinel on mossy hillsides. Beloved Irish statesman Daniel O' Connell maintained his ancestral estate here, far from 19th-century politics. And early Christian hermit-monks left a lonely imprint of their devotion, in the form of simple stone dwellings atop an isolated rock crag far from shore...a holy retreat on the edge of the then-known world.

Today, it seems like every tour bus in Ireland makes the ritual loop around the scenic Ring of Kerry, using the bustling and famous tourist town of Killarney as a springboard. Killarney National Park is gorgeous and well worth driving through. But I prefer to skip Killarney town (useful only for its transportation connections). Instead, make the tidy town of Kenmare your home base, and use my suggestions to cleverly circle the much-loved peninsula—entirely missing the convoy of tour buses.

PLANNING YOUR TIME

All you need in compact Kenmare is one night and an early start the next day to drive the Ring of Kerry. The Ring is best driven clockwise, leaving Kenmare by 8:30; for route specifics, see page 233. Without a car, you can take a minibus tour from Kenmare, though it's not as enjoyable as driving the loop yourself.

Here's a good strategy for your visit: Whether you're coming to Kenmare from Kinsale or elsewhere, you'll likely drive through the town of Killarney. After Killarney, you can see any of these sights on your way to Kenmare: Muckross House, Killarney National Park, and the Kissane Sheep Farm. Ideally, arrive in Kenmare by late afternoon and see the town's sights, then get an early start on the Ring of Kerry in the morning. After driving the Ring, head to Dingle for the night.

Hardy hikers might consider adding another day here to visit the rugged island of Skellig Michael, which requires an overnight in Portmagee or St. Finian's Bay. Be aware that island access is unpredictable—boats can book up weeks in advance and are only able to make the crossing about five days out of seven due to rough seas, even in summer.

Kenmare

Cradled in a lush valley, this charming little town (known as Neidín, or "little nest," in Irish) hooks you right away with its rows of vividly colored shop fronts and go-for-a-stroll atmosphere. The nearby finger of the gentle sea feels more like a large lake (called the Kenmare River, just to confuse things). Far from the assembly-line tourism of Killarney town, Kenmare (rhymes with "been there") also makes a great launchpad for enjoying the sights along the road around the Iveragh (eev-er-AH) Peninsula—known to shamrock lovers everywhere as the Ring of Kerry.

Check out the Heritage Centre in the back rooms of the TI to get an overview of the region's history. Visit the Kenmare Lace and Design Centre above the TI to get a close look at the town's famously delicate lace. A five-minute walk from the TI gives you hands-on access to a pre-historic stone circle at the edge of town. Finish up by taking a peek inside Holy Cross Church to see the fine ceiling woodwork.

Orientation to Kenmare

Carefully planned Kenmare is shaped like an "X," forming two triangles. The upper (northern) triangle contains the town square—where fairs and markets have been held for centuries (colorful market Wed in summer), the adjacent TI and Heritage Centre, and a cozy park. The lower (southern) triangle contains three one-way streets busy with shops, lodgings, and restaurants. Use the tall Holy Cross Church spire to get your bearings (next

to the northeast parking lot, handy public WC across the street).

Accommodations

1 Lansdowne Arms Hotel/Bar
2 Sallyport House
3 Hawthorn House
4 Willow Lodge
5 Whispering Pines B&B
6 Virginia's Guesthouse
7 Limestone Lodge
8 Watersedge B&B
9 Rockcrest House
10 Kenmare Fáilte Hostel
11 To Parknasilla Hotel & Ring of Kerry Golf

Eateries & Other

12 Jam Deli
13 Café Mocha
14 Bookshop Vegetarian Café
15 The Lime Tree Rest.
16 Packies Restaurant
17 Mulcahy's Restaurant
18 Horse Shoe Pub & Rest.
19 P. F. McCarthy's Pub & Rest.
20 Crowley's Pub
21 Foley's Pub
22 Supermarket
23 Launderette
24 Bike Rental
25 Kenmare Bookshop
26 To River Valley Riding Stables
27 To Star Sailing (Boat Rental)

Tourist Information: The helpful TI is on the town square (Mon-Sat 9:30-17:30; closed Thu in spring and fall, Sun year-round, and all of Nov-March; tel. 064/664-1233 or 086/240-0484). The short "The Trail" self-guided tour can help shape a town stroll. The TI also sporadically offers a 1.5-hour, €10 guided town walk (get details and book at the TI).

HELPFUL HINTS

Money: You'll find two banks with ATMs—one facing the town square, the other on the corner of Henry and Main streets.

Laundry: O'Shea's Cleaners and Launderette is across from the Lansdowne Arms Hotel, hidden in the back recesses of O'Shea's photography shop (Mon-Sat 9:00-20:00, Sun 12:00-18:00, tel. 064/664-0808).

Bookstore: Kenmare Bookshop is a cozy one-room cottage run by friendly John O'Connor (Mon-Sat 10:00-13:00 & 14:00-17:30, Sun 12:00-17:30, July-Aug until 21:00, on Shelbourne Street at roundabout across from Lansdowne Arms Hotel, tel. 064/664-1578).

Cultural Events: Carnegie Arts Center is a small-town venue offering a mixed bag of concerts in its 140-seat theater (€5-20), art exhibitions, and films. In summer (June-Aug), Thursday is movie night at 20:00 for €7 (across Shelbourne Street from Lansdowne Arms Hotel, tel. 064/664-8701, www.carnegieartskenmare.ie).

Bike Rental: Finnegan's Corner rents bikes and has route maps and advice on maximizing scenery and minimizing traffic (standard bike-€15/day, €20/24 hours, beefed-up road bike-€30/day; Mon-Sat 9:30-18:30, July-Aug until 19:00; Sun 12:00-18:00; leave ID for deposit, office in gift shop at 37 Henry Street, tel. 064/664-1083, www.finneganscycles.com).

Parking: Two large public parking lots (behind the TI and across from the church, free overnight) cling to the two main roads departing town to the north. Street parking is free (2 hours).

Taxi: Try **Murnane Cabs** (mobile 087-236-4353) or **Kenmare Coach and Cab** (mobile 087-248-0800).

Tours: Finnegan's Tours runs day tours with guides who give a casual, anecdotal narration. The tour—little more than a scenic joyride—generally makes three rest stops and one sightseeing stop (route depends on day: Ring of Kerry on Mon, Wed, and Fri; Ring of Beara on Tue; Glengarriff and Garnish Island on Thu). In July and August tours leave from the TI at 10:00 and return by 17:00 (€30 for any tour, reserve a day in advance by phone or three days in advance by email; for Sept-June, call to arrange tours; private tours for small groups possible with ad-

Kenmare's History:
Axes, Xs, Nuns, and Lace

Bronze Age people (2000 B.C.), attracted to this valley for its abundant game and fish, stashed their prized ax heads and daggers in hidden hoards. Almost 4,000 years later (in 1930), a local farmer from the O'Sullivan clan pried a bothersome boulder from one of his fields and discovered it to be a lid for a collection of rare artifacts that are now on display in the National Museum in Dublin (the "Killaha hoard"). The O'Sullivans (Irish for "descendants of the one-eyed") were for generations the dominant local clan, and you'll still see their name on many Kenmare shop fronts.

Oliver Cromwell's bloody Irish campaign (1649), which subdued most of Ireland, never reached Kenmare. However, Cromwell's chief surveyor, William Petty, knew good land when he saw it and took a quarter of what is now County Kerry as payment for his valuable services, marking the "lands down" on maps. His heirs, the Lansdownes, created Kenmare as a model 18th-century estate town and developed its distinctive "X" street plan. William Petty-Fitzmaurice, the first Marquis of Lansdowne and landlord of Kenmare, became the British prime minister who negotiated the peace that ended the American War of Independence in 1783.

Sister Margaret Cusack, a.k.a. Sister Mary Francis Clare, lived in the town from 1862 to 1881, becoming the famous Nun of Kenmare. Her controversial religious life began when she decided to become an Anglican nun after her fiancé's sudden death. Failing to be accepted as one of Florence Nightingale's nurses during the Crimean War, she converted to Catholicism, joined the Poor Clare order as Sister Mary Francis Clare, and moved with the order to Kenmare.

Sister Clare became an outspoken writer who favored women's rights and lambasted the tyranny of the landlords during the Great Potato Famine (1845-1849). She eventually took church funds and attempted to set herself up as abbess of a convent in Knock. Her renegade behavior led to her leaving the Catholic faith, converting back to Protestantism, writing an autobiography, and lecturing about the "sinister influence of the Roman Church."

After the devastation of the Famine, an industrial school was founded in Kenmare to teach trades to destitute youngsters. The school, run by the Poor Clare sisters, excelled in teaching young girls the art of lacemaking. Inspired by lace created earlier in Italy, Kenmare lace caught the eye of Queen Victoria and became much coveted by Victorian society. Examples of it are now on display in the Victoria and Albert Museum (London), the Irish National Museum (Dublin), and the US National Gallery (Washington, DC).

vance notice; tel. 064/664-1491, mobile 087-248-0800, www.kenmarecoachandcab.com, info@kenmarecoachandcab.com).

Kerry Experience Tours offers a customized approach rather than a set route. Offerings include Ring of Kerry tours, Beara Peninsula tours, and taxi service (generally €250/day for 2 passengers, tel. 086/255-4098, www.kerryexperiencetours.ie, info@kerryexperiencetours.ie).

Sights in Kenmare

Heritage Centre

This humble museum, in the back rooms of the TI, consists of a series of storyboards and a model of the planned town. A 20-minute visit here explains the nearby ancient stone circle, the history of Kenmare's lacemaking fame, and the story of a feisty, troublemaking nun (see the sidebar on Kenmare's history).

Cost and Hours: Free, same hours as TI.

Kenmare Lace and Design Centre

A single large room above the TI displays the delicate lacework that put Kenmare on the modern map. From the 1860s until World

War I, the Poor Clare convent at Kenmare was the center of excellence for Irish lacemaking. Inspired by antique Venetian lace, but creating their own unique designs, nuns taught needlepoint lacemaking as a trade to girls in a region struggling to get back on its feet in the wake of the catastrophic famine. Queen Victoria commissioned five pieces of lace in 1885, and by the end of the century tourists began visiting Kenmare on their way to Killarney just for a peek at the lace. Nora Finnegan, who runs the center, usually has a work in progress to demonstrate the complexity of fine lacemaking to visitors.

Cost and Hours: Free, Mon-Sat 10:15-17:30, closed mid-Oct-Easter and Sun year-round, tel. 064/664-2978, www.kenmarelace.ie.

Ancient Stone Circle

Of the approximately 100 stone circles that dot southwest Ireland (Counties Cork and Kerry), Kenmare's is one of the most accessible. More than 3,000 years old, it may have been used both as a primitive calendar and as a focal point for rituals. The circle has a diameter of 50 feet and consists of 15 stones ringing a large center boulder (possibly a burial monument). Experts think this stone circle (like most) functioned as a celestial calendar—it tracked the position of the setting sun to determine the two solstices (in June and December), which mark the longest and shortest days of the year.

Cost and Hours: €2, drop coins into honor box in hut by entry when attendant is away, always open.

Getting There: It's a five-minute walk from the TI. From the city center, face the TI, turn left, and walk 200 yards down Market Street, passing a row of cute 18th-century houses on your right. Beyond the row of houses, veer right through an unmarked modern gate mounted in stone columns, and continue 50 yards down the paved road. You'll pass the entry hut on your right. The stone circle is behind the adjacent hedge.

Holy Cross Church

Finished in 1864, this is Kenmare's grand Catholic church. It's worth a quick visit to see the ornate wooden ceiling supported by 10 larger-than-life angels (carved in Bavaria), the fine 1914 altar carved of Italian marble, and the Victorian stained-glass windows.

Experiences near Kenmare

Horseback Riding: River Valley Riding Stables offers day treks for all levels of experience through beautiful hill scenery in the Roughty River Valley (adults-€20/hour, kids-€15/hour, group discounts, long hours, based at Sheen Falls Lodge 1.5 miles southeast of Kenmare—cross Our Lady's Bridge and turn left on N-71, mobile 087-958-5895, rivervalleystables@hotmail.com).

Boating and Hiking: Star Sailing rents boats, gives sailing lessons, and organizes hill walks. Hop on a small two-person sailboat (€45 for 1 hour, €35/additional hour) or a six-person boat (€65 for 1 hour, €55/additional hour). Or kick around in a kayak (single-€20/hour, double-€36/hour). Phone ahead to reserve boats (daily 10:00-17:00, located 5 miles southwest of Kenmare on R-571 on Beara Peninsula, courtesy shuttle can pick you up in Kenmare, tel. 064/664-1222, www.staroutdoors.ie; adjacent Con's Restaurant is open daily 12:00-20:00).

Golfing: Another way to experience Ireland's 40 shades of green is to splurge on a scenic day on the links. The Kenmare Golf Club is right on the edge of town (€40 greens fee June-Aug, €35 Sept-May, €30 Oct-April, on R-569 toward Cork, tel. 064/664-1291, www.kenmaregolfclub.com). Or try the Ring of Kerry Golf and Country Club (weekdays-€60 greens fee, weekends-€75, 4 miles west of town on N-70, prebook on weekends, tel. 064/664-2000, www.ringofkerrygolf.com).

Beara: The Other Peninsula

This sleepy yet scenic wedge of land (just south of Kenmare) deserves honorable mention as a distant third choice after the Dingle and Ring of Kerry peninsulas. But locals rave about it like we would our home sports team. If you have the luxury of two nights in Kenmare, Beara is worth considering. If you don't have a full day to spare to drive the length of it, you can spend a memorable half-day enjoying Garnish Island and Healy Pass, skipping the western half of the peninsula.

Garnish Island is a rocky island refuge, cloaked by a lush garden, plopped down in the corner of Bantry Bay. Crowned by a martello tower (a stout bunker built to repel feared Napoleonic invasions, free to climb for views), the gardens were the creation of a rich landlord, who turned the barren 37 acres into a lushly vegetated fantasy in the early 1900s. You'll meander past Italian reflecting pools, a Grecian temple framing views of a placid bay, and a walled garden nursery clad in roses. Pine-forested trails, punctuated with rhododendrons, connect it all. Boats depart from the well-marked pier in Glengarriff, about 18 miles (30 km) south of Kenmare, for the scenic 15-minute cruise past seals sunning on rocks to the island (boat-€12 round-trip, 2/hour; gardens-€5, June-Aug Mon-Sat 9:30-18:00, Sun from 11:00, shorter hours off-season and closed Nov-March; tearoom, snacks, and WCs at island's pier; tel. 027/63116, www.harbourqueenferry.com).

A narrow, eight-mile mountain road (R-574) feels like a toboggan run as it squiggles over the peninsula's lumpy spine at **Healy Pass.** The road linked the north coast (County Kerry) to the south coast (County Cork) to facilitate food-relief deliveries 170

Nightlife in Kenmare

Wander the compact Kenmare town triangle and stick your head in wherever you hear something you like. Music usually starts at 21:30 (although some pubs have early 18:30 sessions—ask at the TI) and ranges from Irish traditional sessions to sing-along strummers. **Crowley's** is an atmospheric little shoebox of a pub with an unpretentious clientele. **Foley's** whiskey tube collection adorns its window, inviting you in for a folksy songfest. The recommended Lansdowne Arms Hotel sponsors live traditional sessions in their **Bold Thady Quill Bar.**

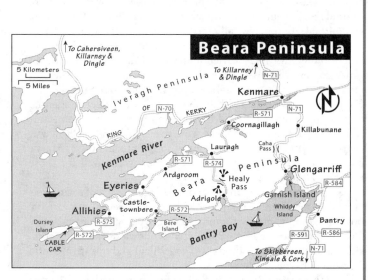

years ago. The views from the 1,000-foot summit make you marvel at the road-building skills of the famine-era workmen. The barren, rocky landscape makes it easy to spot approaching cars (remember to look up on hairpin turns). Be cooperative by pulling over at wide spots to allow safe passage, and honk to alert other cars as you approach blind, rocky curves.

The rest of the peninsula is pastoral in the middle and edged with scenic cliffs near the tip. Ireland's only cable car connects the headland with mellow Dursey Island. Cattle can be transported on it (one at a time). The floor is slatted so water can be sloshed over the boards to wash out the dung. Castletownbere (on the south coast) is a fishing port with plenty of pubs for lunch. Allihies and Eyeries (on the north coast) are two of the most colorfully painted towns in Ireland, splattered with pastels and vivid hues.

Sleeping in Kenmare

$$$ Lansdowne Arms Hotel is the town's venerable grand hotel, with generous public spaces. This centrally located, 200-year-old historic landmark rents 25 large, crisp rooms (music in pub until late on Fri-Sat, parking, corner of Main and Shelbourne Streets, tel. 064/664-1368, www.lansdownearms.com, info@lansdownearms. com).

$$$ Sallyport House, an elegant, quiet house with five rooms filled with antique furniture, has been in Helen Arthur's family for generations. Ask her to point out the foot-worn doorstep that was salvaged from the local workhouse and built into her stone chimney (cash only, no kids, parking, closed Nov-mid-March, 5-minute walk south of town before crossing Our Lady's Bridge, tel. 064/664-2066, www.sallyporthouse.com, port@iol.ie).

$$ Hawthorn House is a fine, modern, freestanding house with a lounge, warm and friendly hostess Mary O'Brien, and 10 comfy rooms. Mary's front parlor is a homage to her son Stephen's hard-won success as a player for the dominant County Kerry Irish football team. The house is set in a quiet residential location just a block from all the pub and restaurant action (family rooms, parking, Shelbourne Street, tel. 064/664-1035, www.hawthornhousekenmare.com, hawthorn@eircom.net). Mary's modern, self-catering apartment next door works well for those wanting to linger (weekly rentals).

$$ Willow Lodge, on the main road at the edge of town, feels American-suburban, with friendly hosts and seven comfortable rooms (cash only, family rooms, parking, 100 yards beyond Holy Cross Church, tel. 064/664-2301, www.willowlodgekenmare.com, willowlodgekenmare@yahoo.com, jovial Paul and talkative Gretta Gleeson-O'Byrne).

$ Whispering Pines B&B offers five rooms with sincere, traditional Irish hospitality in a spacious house warmed by the presence of hostesses Mary Fitzgerald and daughter Kathleen (cash only, closed Oct-March, at the edge of town on Bell Height, tel. 064/664-1194, www.whisperingpineskenmare.com, wpines@eircom.net).

$ Virginia's Guesthouse, ideally located near the best restaurants, is well kept by Neil and Noreen. Its nine rooms are fresh, roomy, and appealing (breakfast extra in downstairs café, 36 Henry Street, mobile 086-306-5291, www.virginias-guesthousekenmare.com, virginias.guesthouse@gmail.com).

$ Limestone Lodge stands rock-solid beside a holy well, with five comfy rooms in a quiet location. Friendly hosts Sinead and Siobhan Thomas are experts on Kenmare's famous lace, and Casey, their wiggly Jack Russell terrier, is an expert at being cute (cash only, family rooms, parking, tel. 064/664-2231, mobile 087-757-4411, www.limestonelodgekenmare.com, info@limestonelodgekenmare.com).

$ Watersedge B&B is a mile south of town, serenely isolated on a forested hillside and overlooking the estuary. The modern house has four clean, colorful rooms and a kid-pleasing backyard (cash only, parking, tel. 064/664-1707, mobile 087-413-4235, www.watersedgekenmare.com, watersedgekenmare@gmail.com, Noreen and Vincent O'Shea). To get here, drive south over Our Lady's Bridge, bear left, immediately look for the B&B sign, and take the first right onto the road heading uphill. Go 100 yards up the paved road, then—at the end of the white cinder-block wall (on left)—turn right onto the private lane and drive 100 yards to the dead-end. It's worth it.

$ Rockcrest House is secluded down a quiet, leafy lane, with six large rooms and a fine front-porch view (cash only; as you pass the TI heading north out of town, take the first left after crossing the bridge; tel. 064/664-1248, mobile 087-904-3788, www. visit-kenmare.com, info@visit-kenmare.com, Marian and David O'Dwyer). Ask about their two self-catering cottage rentals.

¢ Kenmare Fáilte Hostel (fawl-chuh) maintains 34 budget beds in a well-kept, centrally located building with more charm than most hostels (private rooms available, closed mid-Oct-April, Shelbourne Street, tel. 064/664-2333, mobile 087-711-6092, run by Finnegan's Corner bike rental folks directly across street, www. kenmarehostel.com, info@kenmarehostel.com).

SLEEPING IN LUXURY ON THE RING OF KERRY

$$$$ Parknasilla Hotel is a 19th-century luxury hotel (82 rooms) lost in 500 plush acres of a subtropical park overlooking the wild Atlantic Ocean. The tranquility, combined with old-fashioned service and Victorian elegance, makes this a good stop for anyone interested in luxuriating on the Ring of Kerry. Originally an old railroad hotel for Romantic Age tourists, in recent decades it has been a ritual splurge for Irish families and wedding groups (highest rates July-Aug, 19th-century diversions, park walks, tel. 064/667-5600, www.parknasillahotel.ie, reservationsinfo@parknasillahotel.ie).

Eating in Kenmare

This friendly little town offers plenty of quality options. If dining, make a reservation or get a table early, as many finer places book up later in the evening during the summer. Pub dinners are a good value and easier on the budget, but pub kitchens close earlier than restaurants.

LUNCH

Soup-and-sandwich lunch options abound. **$ Jam** is an inviting place with delightful seating inside and out, and soups, salads, and sandwiches on the menu. They make sandwiches or wraps to go for picnics (daily 8:00-17:00, Henry Street, tel. 064/664-1591). **$ Café Mocha** is a basic sandwich shop (daily 9:00-17:30, on the town square, tel. 064/664-2133). **Murphy's Daybreak** supermarket is a good place to stock up for a Ring of Kerry picnic (Mon-Sat 8:00-22:00, Sun 9:00-21:00, Main Street). **$ The Bookshop Vegetarian Café** is delightful for a healthy, peaceful lunch or some coffee, cakes, and pastries (daily, on Bridge Street just around the corner from the TI, tel. 064/667-9911).

DINNER

$$$ The Lime Tree Restaurant occupies the former Lansdowne Estate office, which gave more than 4,000 people free passage to America in the 1840s. These days, it serves delicious, locally caught seafood dishes in a modern yet cozy dining hall (daily 18:30-21:30, closed Nov-March, reservations smart, Shelbourne Street, tel. 064/664-1225, www.limetreerestaurant.com).

$$$$ Packies is a popular bistro that has a leafy, low-light interior and cottage ambience, and serves traditional cuisine with French influence. Their seafood gets rave reviews (Mon-Sat 18:00-22:00, closed Sun, reservations wise, Henry Street, tel. 064/664-1508).

$$$$ Mulcahy's Restaurant has a jazz-mellowed, elegant ambience and creatively presented gourmet dishes. Given the Indian, Japanese, and American influences, there's always a good vegetarian entrée (Thu-Tue 17:00-22:00, closed Wed, reservations smart, Main Street, tel. 064/664-2383).

$$$ Horse Shoe Pub and Restaurant, specializing in steak and spareribs, somehow turns rustic farm-tool decor into a romantic candlelit sanctuary (daily 17:00-22:00, Main Street, tel. 064/664-1553).

$$ P. F. McCarthy's Pub and Restaurant feels like a sloppy saloon, serving reasonable salad or sandwich lunches and filling dinner fare (daily 12:00-21:00, 14 Main Street, tel. 064/664-1516).

Kenmare Connections

Kenmare has no train station (the nearest is in Killarney, 20 miles away) and only a few bus connections (www.buseireann.ie). Most buses transfer in Killarney.

From Kenmare by Bus to: Killarney (3/day, 45 minutes), **Tralee** (3/day, 2 hours), **Dingle** (3/day, 3-4 hours, change in Killarney), **Kinsale** (3/day, 4 hours, 2 changes), **Dublin** (4/day, 7.5 hours, change in Killarney and Limerick).

Near Kenmare

These attractions are near Kenmare, at the eastern (inland) end of the Ring of Kerry. If you're approaching the region from Kinsale and Cobh, drive through Killarney and hop on the Ring to visit Muckross House and Muckross Traditional Farms (near the lakes), Killarney National Park, and Kissane Sheep Farm (in the mountains) en route to Kenmare. By taking a bite out of the Ring the day before you sleep in Kenmare, you'll be better situated to drive most of the remainder of the Ring of Kerry loop the next day. Get an early start from Kenmare and you should be able to avoid the worst of the bus traffic on the Ring.

KILLARNEY

Killarney is a household word among American tourists, and it seems to be on every big-bus tour itinerary. Springing from the bus and train station of this thriving regional center are a few colorful streets lined with tourist-friendly shops and restaurants. Killarney's suburbs sprawl with vast hotels that, except for the weather, feel more like Nebraska than Ireland. Killarney's elegant Neo-Gothic church stands tall, as if to say the town existed and mattered long before tourism. But then you realize it dates from 1880...just about when Romantic Age tourism here peaked. For nonshoppers, Killarney's value is its location at the doorstep of the lush Killarney National Park. And for most tour organizers, it's the logical jumping-off point for excursions around the famous Ring of Kerry peninsula.

If you're traveling in the region without a car, you'll have to stop here. The Killarney bus and train stations flank the big, modern Killarney Outlet Centre mall. (In some touristy parts of Ireland, like this one, every other shopping center is called an "outlet"—implying factory-direct values.) If you have a layover between connections, walk five minutes straight out from the front of the mall, and check out Killarney's shop-lined High Street and New Street. The **TI** is a 15-minute walk from the train station, on Beech Street.

Killarney Connections

From Killarney Around the Ring of Kerry: Bus Éireann drives the loop around the Ring of Kerry from Killarney—suitable for a quick peek. While it generally stops only long enough to pick up and drop off travelers en route, there is a 50-minute stop in Sneem (€25, daily July-mid-Sept, departs the Killarney bus station at 12:45 and returns to Killarney at 17:45, no reservation needed, www.buseireann.ie). You can catch this same bus from Tralee at 11:50, returning to Tralee by 18:45 (€28).

By Bus to: Kenmare (3/day, 45 minutes), **Tralee** (hourly, 40 minutes), **Dingle** (2/day direct, 1.5 hours, 2/day with change in Tralee, 2.5 hours), **Shannon Airport** (6/day, 3.5 hours), **Dublin** (every 2 hours, 6 hours, change in Limerick). The bus station has a left-luggage desk. For bus schedules: Toll tel. 1850-836-611, www.buseireann.ie.

By Train to: Tralee (8/day, 35 minutes), **Cork** (every 2 hours, 2 hours, most with change in Mallow), **Waterford** (5/day, 4-6 hours), **Dublin** (every 2 hours, fewer on Sun, 3.5 hours, 1 direct in morning, rest with change in Mallow). For train schedules, call 01/836-6222 or visit www.irishrail.ie.

To Muckross House: There's no bus service. You can hike 30 minutes (get directions from TI), rent a bike, hire a horse buggy, or catch a cab (€12).

SIGHTS NEAR KILLARNEY
▲Muckross House and Farms
Perhaps the best stately Victorian home you'll see in the Republic of Ireland, Muckross House (built in 1843) is magnificently set at

the edge of Killarney National Park. It's adjacent to Muckross Farms, a fascinating open-air farm museum that shows rural life in the 1930s (worth ▲). Besides the mansion and farms, this regular stop on the tour-bus circuit also includes a fine garden idyllically set on a lake and an information center for the national park. The poignant juxtaposition of the magnificent mansion and the humble farmhouses illustrates in a thought-provoking way the vast gap that once separated rich and poor in Ireland.

Cost and Hours: House–€9, farms–€9, €15 combo-ticket includes both (Heritage Cards not accepted for farms). House open daily 9:00-17:30, July-Aug until 19:00, last entry one hour before closing. Farms open daily June-Aug 10:00-18:00, May and Sept daily 13:00-18:00, March-April and Oct Sat-Sun only 13:00-18:00, closed Nov-Feb, tel. 064/667-0144, www.muckross-house.ie, info@muckross-house.ie.

Tours: The only way to see the interior of the house is with the 45-minute guided tour, which gives meaning to your visit (included with admission, offered frequently throughout the day). Book your tour as soon as you arrive (they can fill up). Then enjoy a walk in the gardens or lunch in their better-than-average cafeteria until your tour begins.

Getting There: Muckross House is conveniently located for a break on the long ride from Kinsale or Cashel to Dingle or Kenmare. From Killarney, follow signs to Kenmare, where you'll find Muckross House three miles (5 km) south of town. As you approach from Killarney, you'll see a small parking lot two miles before the actual parking lot. This is used by horse-and-buggy bandits to hoodwink tourists into thinking they have to pay to clip-clop to the house. Giddy-up on by to find a big, safe, and free parking lot right at the mansion.

Visiting the House and Farms: A visit to **Muckross House**

takes you back to the Victorian period—the 19th-century boom time when the sun never set on the British Empire and the Industrial Revolution (born in England) was chugging the world into the modern age. Of course, Ireland was a colony back then, with big-shot English landlords. During the Great Potato Famine of 1845-1849, most English gentry lived very well—profiting off the export of their handsome crops to lands with greater buying power—while a third of Ireland's population starved.

Muckross House feels lived-in (and it was, until 1933). Its fine Victorian furniture is arranged around the fireplace under Waterford crystal chandeliers and lots of antlers. You'll see Queen Victoria's bedroom (ground floor, since she was afraid of house fires). The owners of the house spent a couple of years preparing for the royal visit in 1861, eager to gain coveted titles and nearly bankrupting themselves in the process. The queen stayed only three nights and her beloved Prince Albert died soon after the visit. The depressed queen never granted the titles that the grand house's owners had so hoped for.

The house exit takes you through an **information center** for Killarney National Park, with a relaxing 15-minute video on "Ireland's premier national park," featuring lots of geology, flora, and fauna (free, shown on request).

The **garden** is a hit for those with a green thumb, and a €1.50 booklet makes the nature trails interesting. A bright, modern cafeteria (with indoor/outdoor seating) faces the garden. The adjacent crafts shop shows weaving and pottery-making in action.

The **Muckross Traditional Farms** consists of six different vintage farmhouses. The farms are strung along a mile-long road, with an old bus shuttling those who don't want to hike (free, 4/hour).

For those interested in Irish farm life from the 1920s until electricity arrived in 1955, this is a great experience—but only if you engage the attendants in conversation. Each farm is staffed by a Kerry local who enjoys telling tales of life on the farm in the old days. When they first got electricity in 1955, they'd pull on their rubber Wellington boots for safety and nervously "switch it on." Poor farmers could afford electricity only with the help of money from relatives in America. They'd have one bulb hanging from the ceiling and, later, one plug for a hot pot. Every table had a Sacred Heart of Jesus shrine above it. The plug went directly below it. No one dreamed of actually heating the house with electricity. Children slept six to a bed, "three up and three down...

feet in your face." You'll learn what happened when you had the only radio in the area, and how one flagstone on the mud floor was enough for the fiddler and dancer to set the beat. Probe with your questions...get personal.

▲Killarney National Park

As you drive from Killarney to Kenmare, heading south on N-71, you'll sweep through scenic Killarney National Park (just south of Killarney town) on the most mountainous stretch of the Ring of Kerry. This 25,000-acre park (Ireland's oldest) was established when Muckross Estate was donated to the nation in 1932. Glacially sculpted rock ridges cradle three large lakes teeming with trout and salmon, which lure sport fishermen.

Hikers enjoy an easy 10-minute stroll along a mossy trail from the roadside up to **Torc Waterfall** (look for small parking lot beside N-71, 2 miles—3 km—south of Muckross House), then lace up their boots to take on more strenuous trails beyond. If you go early or late in the day, keep an eye out for Ireland's only native herd of red deer. The park's old-growth oak, yew, and alder groves are the best preserved in Ireland, and rhododendrons explode beside the road in late May and June.

Take a quiet moment to contemplate your lush surroundings. This is what the majority of Ireland looked like 8,000 years ago, before Neolithic man settled and began rudimentary slash-and-burn farming. Later English colonial harvesting of timber exacerbated the deforestation process. Today, Ireland has the smallest proportion of forested land—10.5 percent—of any EU nation.

Enjoy expansive lake views from **Ladies View,** right beside the N-71 road, half a mile (1 km) from the park's southern exit. Just south of the park exit, you'll pass long, thin Looscaunagh Lough (beside the road on the left). A few hundred yards farther, the Black Valley opens up beneath you on the right. This remote valley was the last chunk of Ireland to get electricity—in 1978. The highest bump on the distant ridge across the Black Valley to the west is Carrauntoohil, Ireland's tallest mountain at 3,400 feet.

▲▲Kissane Sheep Farm

Call ahead to arrange an hour's visit to this hardworking 2,500-acre Irish farm, perched on a scenic slope above the Black Valley. John Kissane, whose family has raised sheep here for five generations, gives hands-on demonstrations of sheep shearing. John (or his brother Noel) explains the process and invites you to touch the pile of fresh wool afterward. You can feel the lanolin, which acts as natural waterproofing for the sheep and is extracted from the wool to sell to pharmaceutical firms (synthetic manufacturing has driven the price of wool so low, it's not worth selling otherwise). But the highlight of any visit is the demonstration of sheepherding by the highly alert family dogs (border collies trained here since puppy-hood). John commands the dogs from afar using an array of verbal calls and hand signals. Little Sean is at his dad's side, learning the trade, though these days the farm makes more money from visiting tourists than it does in the traditional sheep-and-wool trade.

Cost and Hours: €7, by appointment only most afternoons April-Sept (minimum 15 people)—call ahead and coordinate your visit with a visiting big bus tour as they don't do private demonstrations; closed Oct-March, on N-71 between Ladies View and Moll's Gap, tel. 064/663-4791, mobile 087-260-0410, www.kissanesheepfarm.com, noel@kissanesheepfarm.com.

From Kissane Sheep Farm to Kenmare: Continue driving south on N-71. Going over Moll's Gap (WCs and Avoca Café beside parking lot), you'll descend into Kenmare. The rugged, bare rock on either side of the road was rounded and smoothed by the grinding action of glaciers over thousands of years. In the distance to the north (on your right) you can see the Gap of Dunloe, a perfect example of a U-shaped glacial valley notch.

Ring of Kerry

The Ring of Kerry (the Iveragh Peninsula) has been the perennial breadwinner of Irish tourism for decades now. Lassoed by a winding coastal road (the Ring), this mountainous, lake-splattered region comes with breathtaking scenery and the highest peak in Ireland. While a veritable fleet of big, tourist-laden buses circles it each day, they generally stay together and seem to stop at the same handful of attractions. Therefore, if you avoid those places at rush hour, the Ring feels remarkably unspoiled and dramatically isolated. Armed with a good map and a reliable alarm clock, you can avoid the crowds and enjoy one of the most rewarding days in Ireland.

PLANNING YOUR TIME
More than twice the size of the Dingle Peninsula (see the next chapter) and backed by a muscular tourism budget that promotes every sight as a "must-see," the Iveragh Peninsula can seem overwhelming. Be selective, and don't let them pull the turf over your eyes.

KENMARE & RING OF KERRY

By Car: You can explore the Ring (primarily on N-70) in one satisfying day. Travelers linking overnights in Kinsale and Dingle can insert a night between them in Kenmare (a good base for enjoying the best of the Ring of Kerry). If visiting Muckross House and Kissane Sheep Farm (on the mountainous section of the Ring), do so in the morning on your way to Kenmare to avoid afternoon buses and save the following day for the rest of the Ring.

Tackling the Kinsale-to-Dingle drive plus the Ring of Kerry all in the same day is doable with an early start (no later than 8:30)—but you add about two hours of driving just to reach the actual Ring, meaning you have little time to stop and enjoy what you came here to see. You also run the risk of meeting the big-bus convoy head on (see "Driving the Ring of Kerry," below).

To include a boat trip out to the remote, evocative island of Skellig Michael, add another day and plan an overnight in the Portmagee area.

By Public Transportation: You have three options for seeing the Ring of Kerry without a car, none of which is as enjoyable as driving the loop yourself: minibus tour from Kenmare (see page 220); big-bus tour from Killarney (TI tel. 064/663-1633); or public bus from Killarney (see page 229).

DRIVING THE RING OF KERRY (MADE LESS SCARY)

The entire Ring of Kerry loop is 135 miles and takes 4.5 hours to drive without making any stops. Drive clockwise around the Ring to entirely miss the chain of tour buses. Be sure to factor in time to stop for lunch and to see the sights. Tank up before leaving, as gas in Kenmare is cheaper than out on the Ring. You'll pass a handy Topaz gas station on your right a half-mile north of Kenmare, just before you turn left onto the N-70 main Ring of Kerry road.

On a one-day visit to the Ring, I'd leave Kenmare by 8:30 and head clockwise (against the prevailing tour-bus traffic). Allow time for stops at Staigue Ring Fort (45 minutes) and Derrynane House (1 hour), and get to Waterville before noon. Shortly after Waterville, leave the main Ring for the Skellig Ring (a road that's too narrow for big buses). Plan to have lunch out on the Skellig Ring, either as a picnic on the lovely beach at St. Finian's Bay, or in Portmagee. By the time you rejoin the main route, the big buses have slunk by. On the last half of the route, there are two more hour-long stops: the Skellig Experience Centre (near Portmagee) and two additional big ring forts (near Cahersiveen).

For me, the two most photogenic coastal stretches are out near the tip of the peninsula: between Caherdaniel and Waterville (on the Ring of Kerry) and from Ballinskelligs to Portmagee (on the Skellig Ring). For a stop-by-stop description of this route, follow my "Ring of Kerry Driving Tour."

The only downside of going against all the bus traffic is that, on the narrow parts of the Ring road, buses always have the right-of-way. If there's a bottleneck, it's up to you to back up to the nearest wide spot in the road to let a less-nimble bus get through a tight curve. But every year I notice that the road has been improved and bottlenecks widened. Very few remain. There are also lots of scenic-view pullouts. With an early start, you can avoid these hassles: On my last circuit, I got to Waterville by 11:30, from where I slipped happily into the bus-free Skellig Ring...and didn't encounter a single bus the rest of the day.

Smart drivers equip themselves with a good map before driving the Ring of Kerry loop. If you don't have one already, pick up the *Complete Road Atlas of Ireland* by Ordnance Survey (€10-13, sold in most TIs and bookstores in Ireland). The *Fir Tree Aerial* series provides a useful map that covers both the Iveragh (Ring of Kerry) and Dingle peninsulas, giving you a bird's-eye feel for the terrain (€9, sold in most bookstores in County Kerry).

The flat, inland, northeastern section of the Ring—from Killorglin to Killarney on N-72—is skippable.

Ring of Kerry Driving Tour

Here's a self-guided sightseeing tip sheet for my preferred clockwise route, kilometer by kilometer. If you do any exploring, you'll likely get hopelessly off pace, but the kilometer references still help—just do the arithmetic to figure out how far various stops are from each other. Several of these stops are explained in far greater detail later in this chapter, in the same order in which they're listed here. To understand your options, read the rest of this chapter before you start on your tour.

0 km: Leave Kenmare.

17.6 km: On the right is Glacier Lake, with a long, smooth limestone "banister" carved by a glacier 10,000 years ago.

22.8 km: The recommended Parknasilla Hotel—a posh 19th-century hotel—is a great stop for tea and scones.

26 km: Visit the town of Sneem.

40.4 km: Turn off for the Staigue Ring Fort.

41.5 km: On the left, enjoy great views across the bay of the Beara Peninsula beyond a ruined hospital with IRA ties. It was

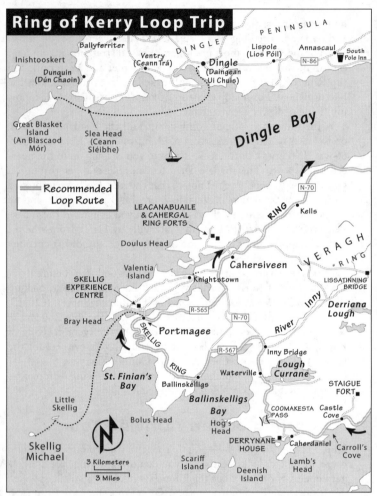

Ring of Kerry Loop Trip

funded about 1910 by a local Englishwoman sympathetic to the Irish Republican cause. No one wants to touch these ruins today, out of fear of "kicking up a beehive."

43.5 km: Carroll's Cove has a fine beach with some of the warmest water in Ireland, grand views of Kenmare Bay, a local trailer park, and "Ireland's only beachside bar."

46.4 km: Take the turnoff for Derrynane House (home of Daniel O'Connell).

50.4 km: Enjoy brilliant views for the next two kilometers to Coomakesta Pass.

52.4 km: The Coomakesta Pass lookout point (700-foot altitude) offers grand vistas in both directions.

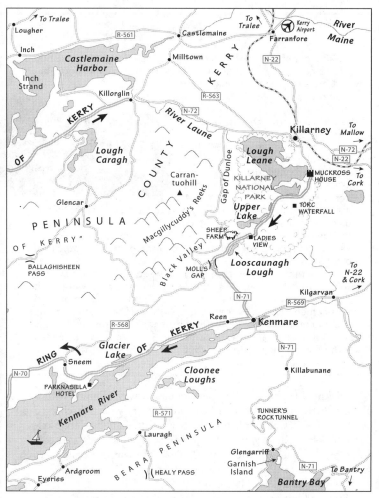

54.5 km: On a clear day, watch for fine views of the distant Skellig Islands with their pointy summits.

59.6 km: In the town of Waterville, you'll see a sculpture of Charlie Chaplin standing on the waterfront on the left. Waterville is also home to the Butler Arms Hotel—a fine stop for tea and scones in its Charlie Chaplin room (with lots of photos of the silent-film icon and his young wife frolicking as they lived well in Ireland).

65 km: After rejoining the main road, cross the small bridge that's locally famous for salmon fly-fishing. Take the first left (R-567) for the Skellig Ring loop (follow brown *Skellig Ring* signs through Ballinskelligs, and then scenically to Portmagee). At this point, you've left the big-bus route.

The Ring Forts of Kerry

The Ring of Kerry comes with three awe-inspiring prehistoric ring forts—among the largest and best preserved in all of Ireland. Staigue Fort (near the beginning of my recommended clockwise Ring route) is most impressive but in a desolate setting. The two others— Cahergal and Leacanabuaile, 200 yards apart just north of Cahersiveen (closer to the end of the Ring, after Valentia Island)—are easier to visit and plenty evocative. Each ring fort is about a 2.5-mile (4-km) side-trip off the main drag. If you're trying to beat the tour-bus convoy, Staigue Fort is problematic because it eats up morning time before the buses have passed you. The Cahersiveen ring forts are your last stop in the Ring of Kerry, once bus traffic is of no concern.

All of these ring forts are roughly the same age and have the similar basic features. The circular drystone walls were built sometime between 500 B.C. and A.D. 300 without the aid of mortar or cement. About 80 feet across, with walls 12 feet thick at the base and up to 25 feet high, these brutish structures would have taken 100 men six months to complete. Expert opinion is divided on the reason they were built, but most believe that the people

75 km: St. Finian's Bay lies about halfway around, with a pleasant little picnic-friendly beach that's recently been discovered by surfers (no WCs). Just before the bay is the small, modern Skelligs Chocolate Factory, with free, tasty samples as well as a café for coffee and muffins (Mon-Fri 10:00-17:00—but longer hours in summer, Sat-Sun 12:00-17:00, especially fun for kids, tel. 066/947-9119, www.skelligschocolate.com).

80 km: Photographers and walkers will want to turn left into the driveway that advertises "Best View in County Kerry." Park and pay the €4 fee at the hut. Then walk 10 minutes straight up the gravel road, where you'll be confronted by a dramatic coastal cliff that opens up onto dramatic coastal views. The beehive huts nearby are replicas but true to the originals.

83 km: You reach Portmagee, a small port town and jumping-off point for boats to the Skellig Islands.

83.2 km: Cross the bridge to the Skellig Experience Centre. You're now on Valentia Island, its name hinting at medieval trading connections with nearby Spain—which lies due south. Dinosaur who built them would have retreated here at times of clan conflict. Civilization was morphing from nomadic hunter-gatherers to settled farmers, so herders used these forts to gather their valuable cattle inside and protect them from ancient rustlers. Other

experts see the round design as a kind of amphitheater, where local clan chieftains would have gathered for important meetings or rituals. However, the ditch surrounding the outer walls of Staigue Fort suggests a defensive, rather than ceremonial, function. Without written records, we can only imagine the part these magnificent piles of finely stacked stones played in ancient dramas.

Because this region had copper mines, southwest Ireland has a wealth of prehistoric sights. The Bronze Age wouldn't have been the Bronze Age without copper, which was melted together with tin to make bronze for better weapons and tools (2000 to 500 B.C.). The many ring forts and stone circles reflect the affluence that the abundance of copper brought to the region.

hunters may want to detour and follow the signs to the modest but ancient tetrapod tracks, frozen in stone, on the north side of the island (ask for directions at the visitors center).

91.2 km: At the church in Knightstown, turn left for the Knightstown Heritage Museum.

93 km: Return to the main road and go through Knightstown to the tiny ferry (€7/car, runs constantly 8:00-21:00, 1-km trip).

95 km: Leaving the ferry, rejoin N-70 (the main Ring of Kerry route), turning left for the town of Cahersiveen. From here, you can detour a few kilometers to two impressive stone ring forts, Cahergal and Leacanabuaile.

100 km: Return to N-70 at Cahersiveen and follow signs for *Glenbeigh* and *Killorglin*. Enjoy views of the Dingle Peninsula across Dingle Bay to your left. Eagle eyes can spot stumpy Eask Tower and Inch Beach.

The rest of the loop is less scenic. At Killorglin, you've seen the best of it. From here, go either to Dingle (left) or to Kenmare/Killarney/Kinsale (right).

Sights on the Ring of Kerry

FROM KENMARE TO PORTMAGEE

Sneem

Although it's inundated by tour buses daily from 14:00 to 16:00, the town of Sneem is peaceful and laid-back the rest of the day. This humble town has two entertaining squares. The Irish joke, "Since we're in Kerry, the square on the east side is called South Square and the one on the west is called North Square." On the first (South) square, you'll see a statue of Steve "Crusher" Casey, the local boy who reigned as world champion heavyweight wrestler (1938-1947). A sweet little peat-toned rapid gurgles under the one-lane bridge connecting the two Sneem squares. The North Square features a memorial to former French president Charles de Gaulle's visit (Irish on his mother's side, de Gaulle came here for two weeks of R&R after his final retirement from office in 1969). Locals call it "da gallstone."

▲Staigue Fort

This impressive ring fort is worth a stop on your way around the Ring (always open, drop €1 in the little gray donation box beside the gate). While viewing the imposing pile of stone, read "The Ring Forts of Kerry" sidebar, earlier.

Getting There: The fort is 2.5 miles (4 km) off the main N-70 road up a narrow rural access lane (look for signs just after the hamlet of Castle Cove). Honk on blind corners to warn oncoming traffic as you drive up the hedge-lined lane.

▲Derrynane House

This is the home of Daniel O'Connell, Ireland's most influential 19th-century politician, whose tireless nonviolent agitation gained equality for Catholics 185 years ago. The coastal lands of the O'Connell estate that surround Derrynane (rhymes with Mary-Ann) House are now a national historic park. A visit here is a window into the life of a man who not only liberated Ireland from the last oppressive anti-Catholic penal laws, but also first developed the idea of a grassroots movement—organizing on a massive scale to achieve political ends without bloodshed (see sidebar).

Cost and Hours: €5; May-Sept daily 10:30-18:00; mid-March-April and Oct Wed-Sun 10:30-17:00, closed Mon-Tue; open weekends only in Nov, closed Dec-mid-March; last entry 45 minutes before closing, tel. 066/947-5113.

Getting There: Just outside the town of Derrynane, pick up a handy free map of the area from the little private TI inside the brown Wave Crest market (TI open daily May-Sept 9:00-18:00, closed Oct-April, tel. 066/947-5188; market is a great place to buy

The Ring of Kerry vs. the Dingle Peninsula

If I had to choose one spot to enjoy the small-town charm of traditional Ireland, it would be Dingle and its history-laden scenic peninsula. But the Ring of Kerry—a much bigger, more famous, and more touristed peninsula just to its south—is also great to visit. If you go to Ireland and don't see the famous Ring of Kerry, your uncle Pat will never forgive you. Here's a comparison to help with your itinerary planning.

Both peninsulas come with a scenic loop drive. Dingle's is 30 miles. The Ring of Kerry is 120 miles. Both loops come with

lots of megalithic wonder. Dingle's prehistory is more intimate, with numerous little evocative stony structures. The Ring of Kerry's prehistory shows itself in three massive ring forts—far bigger than anything on Dingle.

Dingle town is the perfect little Irish burg—alive with traditional music pubs, an active fishing harbor, and the sturdy cultural atmosphere of an Irish-speaking Gaeltacht region. You can easily spend three fun nights here. In comparison, Kenmare (the best base for the Ring of Kerry loop) is pleasant but forgettable. Those spending a night on the west end of the Ring of Kerry find a rustic atmosphere in Portmagee (the base for a cruise to magical Skellig Michael).

Near Dingle, the heather-and-moss-covered Great Blasket Island and the excellent Great Blasket Centre offer insights into the storytelling traditions and simple lives of hardy fisherfolk who—until 60 years ago—lived just off the tip of the Dingle Peninsula. Skellig Michael is a brutally rugged and remote chunk of rock in the Atlantic off the tip of the Ring of Kerry, with evocative medieval stone ruins of its long-gone hermit-monks. It's a world-class sight, but the Skellig Experience Centre near Portmagee on the mainland is less impressive than Dingle's Great Blasket Centre.

Muckross House, with its fascinating open-air farmhouse museum and beautiful lake views of Killarney National Park, is on the eastern side of the Ring of Kerry. It's also an efficient and natural stop for those driving between Kinsale and Dingle—so you can see it regardless of which scenic peninsula drive you take.

Both regions are beyond the reach of the Irish train system and require a car or spotty bus service to access. Both offer memorable scenery, great restaurants, warm B&B hospitality, and similar prices. The bottom line: With limited time, choose Dingle. If you have a day or two to spare, the Ring of Kerry is also a delight.

picnic food). One mile after the market, take a left and follow the signs into Derrynane National Historic Park.

Visiting the House: The house has a quirky floor plan. Ask about the next scheduled 20-minute audiovisual show, which fleshes out the highlights of O'Connell's turbulent life and makes the contents of the house more interesting. Self-guided info sheets are available in the main rooms (in both English and Irish).

Downstairs in the study, look for the glass case containing the pistols used in O'Connell's famous duel. Beside them are his black gloves, one of which he always wore on his right hand when he went to Mass (out of remorse for the part it played in taking a man's life). The dining room is lined with family portraits. Upstairs in the drawing room, you'll find his ornately carved chair with tiny harp strings and wolfhound collars made of gold. In a drawer in an upstairs bedroom is a copy of O'Connell's celebrated speech imploring the Irish not to riot when he was arrested. And in another upstairs room is his deathbed, brought back from Genoa.

The coach house (out back) shows off the enormous grand chariot that carried O'Connell through throngs of joyous Dubliners after his release from prison in 1844. He added the small chapel wing to the house in gratitude to God for his prison release. O'Connell's summer retreat, a small tower down the path behind the coach house, should be open by the time you visit.

Portmagee

Just a short row of snoozy buildings lining the bay, Portmagee is the best harbor for boat excursions out to the Skellig Islands (see "Getting There" on page 247). It's a quiet village with a handful of B&Bs, two pubs, a bakery, a market, and no ATMs—the closest ATM is 6 miles (10 km) east in Cahersiveen. On the rough harborfront, a slate memorial to sailors lost at sea from here reads, "In the nets of God may we be gathered."

A 100-yard-long bridge connects Portmagee to gentle Valentia Island, where you'll find the Skellig Experience Centre (on the left at the Valentia end of the bridge). A public parking lot is at the Portmagee end of the bridge, with award-winning WCs (no kidding: look for the proudly displayed "Irish Toilet of the Year 2002 runner-up" plaque). The first permanent transatlantic cable (for telegraph communication) was laid from Valentia Island in 1866.

Sleeping in Portmagee: The first two listings are in town. The last listing is south of Portmagee, on St. Finian's Bay.

$$$ Moorings Guesthouse feels like a small hotel, with 17 rooms, a pub and a fine restaurant downstairs, and the most convenient location in town, 50 yards from the end of the pier (family rooms, tel. 066/947-7108, www.moorings.ie, moorings@iol.ie, Gerard and Patricia Kennedy).

KENMARE & RING OF KERRY

Daniel O'Connell (1775-1847)

Born in Cahersiveen and elected from Ennis as the first Catholic member of the British Parliament, O'Connell was the hero of Catholic emancipation in Ireland. Educated in France at a time when punitive anti-Catholic laws limited schooling for Irish Catholics at home, he witnessed the carnage of the French Revolution. Upon his return to Ireland, he saw more bloodshed during the futile Rebellion of 1798. He chose law as his profession and reluctantly killed a man who challenged him to a duel.

Abhorring all this violence, O'Connell dedicated himself to peacefully gaining equal rights for Catholics in an Ireland dominated by a wealthy Protestant minority. He formed the Catholic Association with a one-penny-per-month membership fee and quickly gained a huge following (especially among the poor) with his persuasive speaking skills. Although Catholics weren't allowed to hold office, he ran for election to Parliament anyway and won a seat in 1828. His unwillingness to take the anti-Catholic Oath of Supremacy initially kept him out of Westminster, but the moral force of his victory caused the government to give in and concede Catholic emancipation the following year.

Known as "the Liberator," O'Connell was working toward his next goal—repealing the Act of Union with Britain—when he was imprisoned in 1844 for what the British considered seditious conspiracy. His massive "monster meeting" rallies attracted thousands of peaceful poor, and his popularity spooked the British authorities, who threw him in jail on trumped-up charges. When the Great Potato Famine hit in 1845, some in the Irish ranks advocated for more violent action against the British, something O'Connell had long opposed. He died two years later in Genoa on his way to Rome, but his ideals lived on: His Catholic Association was the model of grassroots organization for the Irish, who later emigrated and rose within American big-city political "green machines."

$$$ Portmagee Heights B&B is a modern, solid slate home up above town, renting eight fine rooms (cash only, family rooms, on the road into town, tel. 066/947-7251, www.portmageeheights. com, portmageeheights@gmail.com, hostess Monica Hussey can arrange Skellig boat trips).

$$ Beach Cove B&B offers three comfortable, fresh, and lovingly decorated rooms in splendid isolation four miles south of Portmagee, over lofty Coomanaspic ridge, beside the pretty beach at St. Finian's Bay (100 yards from the Skelligs Chocolate Factory). Charming Bridie O'Connor will arrange a boat trip out to the Skelligs for you. Her adjacent cottage out back has two double rooms, making it ideal for families (two-story family cottage out back sleeps four but no breakfast, tel. 066/947-9301, mobile 087-139-0224, www.stayatbeachcove.com, beachcove@eircom.net). Bridie's husband, Jack, was the head coach of the Kerry football team until he retired in 2012...making him a very important person in this part of Ireland (Kerry has won more football titles than any other Irish county, three of them with Jack at the helm).

Eating in Portmagee: These options all line the waterfront (between the pier and the bridge to Valentia Island). **$$$ The Moorings** is a nice restaurant with great seafood caught literally just outside its front door (March-Oct Tue-Sun 18:00-22:00, closed Mon and in winter, reservations a good idea, tel. 066/947-7108, www.moorings.ie). The **$$ Bridge Bar,** next door, does traditional pub grub. Call ahead to check on their traditional music and dance schedule (daily 12:00-22:00, live music Fri and Sun nights, tel. 066/947-7108). The **$$ Fisherman's Bar** is less flashy, with more locals and cheaper prices (daily 10:00-21:00, tel. 066/947-7103).

For picnic supplies, **O'Connell's Market** is the only grocery (Mon-Sat 9:00-19:00, Sun 9:30-12:30). **Skellig Mist Bakery** can make basic lunch sandwiches to take on Skellig boat excursions (daily 9:00-17:30, tel. 066/947-7250).

VALENTIA ISLAND

These two sights are on Valentia Island, across the bridge from Portmagee.

Skellig Experience Centre

Whether or not you're actually sailing to Skellig Michael (described later), this little center (with basic exhibits and a fine 15-minute film) explains it well—both the story of the monks and the natural environment.

Cost and Hours: €5, daily July-Aug 10:00-19:00, May-June and Sept until 18:00, March-April and Oct-Nov until 17:00, closed Dec-Feb, last entry one hour before closing, call ahead outside of peak season as hours may vary, on Valentia Island beside bridge linking it to Portmagee, tel. 066/947-6306, www.skelligexperience.com.

Boat Trips: The Skellig Experience Centre arranges two-hour boat trips, circling both Skellig Michael and Little Skellig (without actually bringing people ashore)—ideal for those who want a close look without the stair climb and vertigo that go with a visit to the island (€30, sailing daily about 14:45 and returning by 17:00, weather permitting, depart from Valentia Island pier 50 yards below the Skellig Experience Centre).

Evolution in Ireland: Tetrapods to Marconi

Evolution, literacy, communication—Ireland has played a starring role in all three.

Many Irish paleontologists believe that the fossilized tetrapod tracks preserved on Valentia Island are the oldest in Europe. It was here that some of the first fish slithered out of the water on four stubby legs 385 million years ago, onto what would become the Isle of Saints and Scholars. Over time, those tetrapods evolved into the ancestors of today's amphibians, reptiles, birds, mammals...and humans, with the desire to record their thoughts and history, and communicate with others across the miles.

Irish scribes—living in remote outposts like the Skellig Islands, just off this coast—kept literate life alive in Europe through the darkest depths of the so-called Dark Ages. In fact, in about the year 800, Charlemagne imported monks from this part of Ireland to be his scribes.

Just more than a thousand years later, in the mid-19th century, Paul Julius Reuter—who provided a financial news service in Europe—knew his pigeons couldn't fly across the Atlantic. So he relied on ships coming from America to drop a news capsule overboard as they rounded this southwest corner of Ireland. His boys would wait in their little boats with nets to "get the scoop." They say Europe learned of Lincoln's assassination (1865) from a capsule tossed out of a boat here.

The first permanent telegraph cables were laid across the Atlantic from here to Newfoundland, giving the two hemispheres instantaneous electronic communication. Queen Victoria was the first to send a message—greeting American president James Buchanan in 1858. The cable broke more than once, but it was finally permanently secured in 1866. Radio inventor Guglielmo Marconi, who was half-Irish, achieved the first wireless transatlantic communication from this corner of Ireland to America in 1901.

Today, driving under the 21st-century mobile-phone and satellite tower that crowns a hilltop above Valentia Island, while gazing out at the Skellig Islands, a traveler has to marvel at humanity's progress—and the part this remote corner of Ireland played in it.

Valentia Heritage Museum

The humble Knightstown schoolhouse, built in 1861, houses an equally humble but interesting little museum highlighting the quirky things of historic interest on Valentia Island. Coming from Portmagee, take a hairpin left as you enter the village (at the lighthouse sign) and find it on your right past the church. You'll see a 19th-century schoolroom and learn about tetrapods (those first fish to climb onto land—which locals claim happened here). You'll also follow the long story of the expensive, frustrating, and heroic battle to lay telegraph cable across the Atlantic, which—after some false starts—finally succeeded in 1866, when the largest ship in the world connected this tiny island of Valentia with Newfoundland. This project was the initiative of the Atlantic Telegraph Company, which later became Western Union. These stories and more are told with intimate black-and-white photos and typewritten pages.

Cost and Hours: €3.50, daily 10:30-17:00, closed Oct-March, tel. 066/947-6985, www.valentiaisland.ie.

Nearby: If you're interested in those tetrapods, the actual "first footprints" are a 15-minute drive from the museum, on a rugged bit of rocky shoreline, a 10-minute hike below a parking lot (free, always viewable, get details locally).

CAHERGAL AND LEACANABUAILE RING FORTS

Crowning bluffs in farm country, 2.5 miles (4 km) off the main road at Cahersiveen, these two windy and desolate forts are each different and worth a look. Just beyond the Cahersiveen town church at the tourist office, turn left, cross the narrow bridge, turn left again, and follow signs to the ancient forts—you'll see the huge stone structures in the distance. You'll hike 10 minutes from the tiny parking lot (free, always open, no museum). Both forts are roughly 100 yards off the road (uphill on the right) and are 200 yards from each other. For details, see "The Ring Forts of Kerry" sidebar, earlier.

Skellig Michael

A trip to this jagged, isolated pyramid—the Holy Grail of Irish monastic island settlements—rates as a truly memorable ▲▲▲ experience. After visiting Skellig Michael a hundred years ago, Nobel Prize-winning Irish playwright George Bernard Shaw called it "the most fantastic and impossible rock in the world."

Rising seven miles offshore, the Skelligs (Irish for "splinter") are two gigantic slate-and-sandstone rocks crouched aggressively on the ocean horizon. The larger of the two, Skellig Michael, is more than 700 feet tall and a mile around, with a tiny cluster of abandoned beehive huts clinging near its summit like stubborn barnacles. The smaller island, Little Skellig, is home to a huge colony of gannet birds (like large, graceful seagulls with six-foot wingspans), protected by law from visitors setting foot onshore.

Skellig Michael (dedicated to the archangel) was first inhabited by sixth-century Christian monks. Inspired by earlier hermit-monks in the Egyptian desert, they sought the purity of isolation to get closer to God. Neither Viking raids nor winter storms could dislodge them, as they patiently built a half-dozen small, stone, igloo-like dwellings and a couple of tiny oratories. Their remote cliff-terrace perch is still connected to the sea 600 feet below by an amazing series of rock stairs. Viking Olav Trygvasson, who later became king of Norway and introduced Christianity to his country, was baptized here in 993.

Chiseling the most rudimentary life from solid rock, the monks lived a harsh, lonely, disciplined existence here, their colony surviving for more than 500 years. They collected rainwater in cisterns and lived off fish and birds. To supplement their meager existence, they traded bird eggs and feathers with passing boats for cereals, candles, and animal hides (used for clothing and for copying scripture). They finally moved their holy community ashore to Ballinskelligs in the early 1100s. But Christian pilgrims continued to visit Skellig Michael for centuries as penance...edging out onto a ledge to kiss a stone cross that has since toppled into the ocean.

In 2014, the ruggedly exotic Skellig Michael was used as a filming location for the final scenes of *Star Wars: The Force Awakens*. To keep the filming top-secret, the Irish Navy was called in to enforce a two-mile exclusionary zone around the island. But controversy soon arose: Environmental groups voiced concerns about the impact on the island's fragile ecosystem, especially native seabirds who are sensitive to disturbances in the Force and might be spooked into seeking other nesting grounds. Disney scrapped plans for filming the next installment, *Star Wars VIII,* on the island. Instead it built its own version of the location at Sybil Head on the Dingle Peninsula. Expect a steady stream of *Star Wars* tourists at both filming locations. *Go mbeidh an Fórsa leat!* (May the Force be with you!)

GETTING THERE

Boat trips cost €60 and officially run to Skellig Michael daily from mid-May to September, but the schedule is heavily dependent on

KENMARE & RING OF KERRY

weather conditions. If the seas are too choppy, the boats cannot safely drop people at the concrete island pier (it's a bit like jumping off a trampoline onto an ice rink). Experienced boat captains say they are able to bring visitors ashore roughly five days out of seven in an average summer week.

Boat trips normally depart Portmagee at 10:00 (depending on tides), sail for an hour, leave you on the island from roughly 11:00 until 13:30, and get you back into Portmagee by 14:30 (with plenty of time to drive on to Dingle). Fifteen small boats (from Portmagee, Ballinskelligs, Waterville, and Valentia Island) have permits to land on Skellig Michael. Each boat can carry a dozen passengers. This limits the number of daily visitors and minimizes the impact on the sensitive island ecosystem.

To book a trip, call as soon as you know your dates—these trips can fill up weeks in advance. Contact **Patrick Murphy** (tel. 087-676-2983 or 087-234-2168, www.skelligcruises.com, murphysseacruises@gmail.com), **Joe Roddy** (mobile 087-284-4460), or **Brendan Casey** (tel. 066/947-2437, mobile 087-228-7519). For a list of everyone that runs trips to the island, see www.skelligexperience.com/other-sea-tours.

Bring your camera, a sandwich lunch (easy to buy at the recommended Skellig Mist Bakery in Portmagee), water, sunscreen, rain gear, hiking shoes, and your sense of wonder.

Planning Tips: Your best bet is to reserve a room near Portmagee or St. Finian's Bay—whichever best fits your itinerary. (It's possible to sleep in Kenmare and get up early to drive two hours straight to Portmagee—but you'll be frustrated by not having time to enjoy the Ring's attractions along the way.) Keep your fingers crossed for good weather, then contact the boat operator on the morning of departure to get the final word. If the seas are too rough, he can tell from Portmagee and will make a decision that morning whether to go (rather than taking passengers halfway out, then aborting).

VISITING SKELLIG MICHAEL

Since you'll have only 2.5 hours to explore the island, begin by climbing the seemingly unending series of stone stairs to the monastic ruins (600 vertical feet of uneven steps with no handrails). Save most of your photographing for the way down. Photo-bugs who linger too long below risk missing the enlightening 20-minute free talk among the beehive huts, given by guides who camp on the island from April through October. Afterward, poke your head into some of the huts and try to imagine the dark, damp, and devoted life of a monk here more than 1,000 years ago. After rambling through the ruins, you can give in to the puffin-spotting photo frenzy as you wander back down the stairs.

The two lighthouses on the far side of the island are now automated, and access to them has been blocked off. There are no WCs or modern shelters of any kind on Skellig Michael.

If you visit between May and early August, you'll be surrounded by fearless rainbow-beaked puffins, which nest here in underground burrows. Their bizarre swallowed cooing sounds like a distant chainsaw. These portly little birds live off fish, and divers have reported seeing them 20 feet underwater in pursuit of their prey.

Your return boat journey usually includes a pass near Little Skellig, which looms like an iceberg with a white coat of guano—courtesy of the 20,000 gannets that circle overhead like feathered confetti. These large birds suddenly morph into sleek darts when pursuing a fish, piercing the water from more than 100 feet above. You're also likely to get a glimpse of gray seals lazing on rocks near the water's edge.

DINGLE PENINSULA

Dingle Town • Dingle Peninsula Loop Trip • Blasket Islands • Tralee

The Dingle Peninsula, the westernmost tip of Ireland (and Europe, for that matter), offers just the right mix of far-and-away beauty, isolated walks and bike rides, and ancient archaeological wonders—all within convenient reach of its main town. Dingle town is just large enough to have all the necessary tourist services and the steady nocturnal beat of Ireland's best traditional music scene.

For more than 35 years, my Irish dreams have been set here on this sparse but lush peninsula, where locals are fond of saying, "The next parish over is Boston." There's a feeling of closeness to the land in Dingle. When I asked a local if he was born here, he thought for a second and said, "No, it was about six miles down the road." I asked his friend if he'd lived here all his life. He said, "Not yet."

Dingle feels so traditionally Irish because it's part of the Gaeltacht, a region where the government subsidizes the survival of the Irish language and culture. While English is always there, the signs, chitchat, and songs come in Irish Gaelic. Children carry Gaelic footballs to class, and the local preschool brags "ALL Gaelic." And although Dingle is crowded in summer, it still feels like the fish and the farm really matter. A half-dozen fishing boats sail from here, tractors leave tracks down the main drag, and a faint whiff of peat fills the nighttime streets.

But Dingle is a destination in transition—it's discovered by more travelers each year, and big-bus crowds crush in during midday after touring the peninsula. Small cruise ships eye the harbor from a distance with the hope of docking here a few years down the road (if infrastructure and dredging plans go through). And weekend stag and hen (bachelor and bachelorette)

parties are starting to appear, attracted by Dingle's growing reputation as "a drinking town with a fishing problem." The filming of the most recent *Star Wars* movie at the tip of the peninsula has once again put this Irish paradise on the big screen (it was previously featured in *Ryan's Daughter* and *Far and Away*).

Despite growing more touristy, Dingle's charms are resilient. As the older generation slows down and fades away, a new generation of entrepreneurs—either local kids or "blow ins" from out of town—is giving Dingle fresh vitality. While residents hold a "goodbye to Dingle" party with the start of each tourist season in the spring and a "no more tourists" party at the end of the season, their welcome is warm and genuine.

PLANNING YOUR TIME

For the shortest visit, give **Dingle** two nights and a day. By car, it takes five hours to get here from Dublin, four hours from Galway, and three hours from Cork. By spending two nights, you'll feel more like a local on your second evening in the pubs. You'll need the better part of a day to explore the 30-mile loop around the peninsula by bike or car (following my **"Dingle Peninsula Loop Trip"** on page 283). To do any serious walking or relaxing, you'll need three nights and two days. It's not uncommon to find Americans slowing way, way down in Dingle.

In good weather, **Great Blasket Island** (off the western tip of the Dingle Peninsula, with the best ferry options from Dingle town) is a rewarding and easy to navigate hiking option (see page 293).

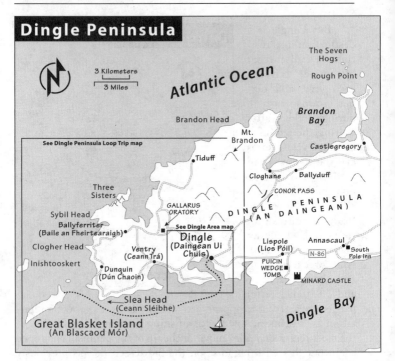

Dingle Peninsula

The Seven Hogs

Rough Point

Atlantic Ocean

Brandon Bay

Brandon Head

Mt. Brandon

Castlegregory

See Dingle Peninsula Loop Trip map

Tiduff

Cloghane   Ballyduff

CONOR PASS

Three Sisters

GALLARUS ORATORY

DINGLE   PENINSULA
(AN DAINGEAN)

Sybil Head
Ballyferriter
(Baile an Fheirtearaigh)

See Dingle Area map

Dingle
(Daingean Ui Chuis)

Lispole
(Lios Póil)

Annascaul

N-86

South Pole Inn

Clogher Head

Ventry
(Ceann Trá)

PUICIN WEDGE TOMB

Inishtooskert

Dunquin
(Dún Chaoin)

MINARD CASTLE

Slea Head
(Ceann Sléibhe)

Dingle Bay

Great Blasket Island
(An Blascaod Mór)

3 Kilometers

3 Miles

Dingle's activity level ramps up in late April, peaks through July and August, and slows by late September. It's smart to book your lodging as soon as you know what dates you'll be in town. I've generally listed hours for the tourist season (April-Sept). Hours may be longer in July and August, and many places cut back or shut down entirely from October to March.

Dingle Town

Of the peninsula's 10,000 residents, about 2,000 live in Dingle town (Daingean Ui Chuis). Its few streets, lined with ramshackle but gaily painted shops and pubs, run up from a rain-stung harbor always sheltering fishing boats and leisure sailboats. Traditionally, the buildings were drab gray or whitewashed, but Ireland's "Tidy Town" competition a few decades back prompted everyone to paint their buildings in playful pastels.

The courthouse (1832) is open one day per month. The judge does his best to wrap up business within a few hours. During the day, you'll see teenagers—already working on ruddy, beer-glow cheeks—roll kegs up the streets and into the pubs in preparation

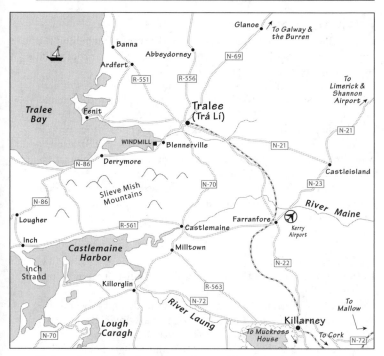

for another night of music and *craic* (fun conversation and atmosphere). It's a friendly town.

Orientation to Dingle

Dingle—extremely comfortable on foot—hangs on a medieval grid of streets between the harbor (where the bus to Tralee, with the nearest train station, stops) and Main Street (three blocks inland). Nothing in town is more than a 10-minute walk away. Street numbers are rarely used. Everyone knows each other, and people on the street are fine sources of information. Locals love their soda bread, and they understand that tourism provides the butter.

TOURIST INFORMATION

The TI has a great town map (free) and a staff who know the town, but less about the rest of the peninsula (Mon-Sat 9:00-13:00 & 13:30-17:00, generally closed Sun, shorter hours off-season, on Strand Street by the water, tel. 066/915-1188). For additional advice on outdoor activities, drop by the Mountain Man shop on Strand Street (see "Helpful Hints," later), or talk to your B&B host.

ARRIVAL IN DINGLE

By Bus: Dingle has only one bus stop, on the waterfront behind the SuperValu supermarket (look for the bus shelter with the roof made from an overturned black-tarred boat).

By Car: Drivers choose two roads into town: the easy southern route on N-86 or the much more dramatic, scenic, and treacherous Conor Pass on R-569 (see "Route Tips for Drivers" at the end of this chapter). It's 30 miles (48 km) from Tralee either way. If you're not staying overnight (i.e., parking at your B&B), use the waterfront parking lot extending west from the TI (€1/hour, pay-and-display, daily 8:00-18:00).

By Plane: Kerry Airport, halfway between Tralee and Killarney, is a one-hour drive from Dingle. Short puddle-jumper flights connect the region to Dublin. For more on Kerry Airport, see the end of this chapter.

HELPFUL HINTS

Before You Go: Check the local website for a list of festivals and events (www.dingle-peninsula.ie).

Crowds: Crowds trample Dingle's charm throughout July and August. The craziest times are during the Dingle Races (early Aug), Dingle Regatta (early to mid-Aug), Blessing of the Boats (end of Aug or beginning of Sept), and Dingle Food Festival (first weekend in October). Easter week brings Irish families. The first Mondays in May, June, and August are Bank Holidays—three-day weekends when Dingle fills up. The town's metabolism (prices, schedules, activities) rises and falls with the tourist crowds, so late October through March is sleepy.

Farmers Market: From mid-April to mid-October on Fridays from 9:00 to 15:00, farmers sell fresh produce, homemade marmalade, and homespun crafts in a small parking lot across the street from SuperValu grocery store.

Money: Two banks with ATMs are staggered across from each other on Main Street. Expect to use cash (rather than credit cards) to pay for most peninsula activities.

Bookstore: An Café Liteartha is a perfect rainy-day hideout, with stacks of books and a backroom café. It lurks across the lane from Paddy's Bike Hire (daily 10:00-18:00, closed Sun Oct-May, Dykegate Street, tel. 066/915-2204).

Laundry: Dingle Cleaners is convenient (Mon-Sat 9:00-18:00, closed Sun, beside Moran's Market and gas station, tel. 066/915-0680, run by Ciarán—pronounced key-a-RAWN). There's no self-service laundry in Dingle.

Biking: To rent a bike, try **Paddy's Bike Hire,** with reliably maintained 21-speed hybrids (€15/day, includes helmet and lock, daily 9:00-19:00, must leave driver's license, directly across

Dykegate from An Café Liteartha, tel. 066/915-2311). **Dingle Electric Bike Experience** rents less-tiring electric bikes as well as 24-speed hybrid bikes, and can deliver them to your hotel and pick them up later (electric-€40/day, hybrid-€20/day, tel. 086/084-8378, www.dinglebikes.com, info@dinglebikes.com).

To bike the peninsula, get a bike with skinny street tires, not slow and fat mountain-bike tires. Be aware that Dingle and the Dingle Peninsula have no bike lanes and increasing traffic volume.

Taxi: Try **Diarmuid Begley** (mobile 087-250-4767), Sean with **S.O.L. Cabs** in Dingle (mobile 087-660-2323), or **Tom Kearney** in Dunquin (mobile 087-933-2264).

Travel Agency: Maurice O'Connor at **Galvin's Travel Agency** can book plane tickets, as well as ferry rides to Britain (Mon-Fri 9:30-18:00, Sat 10:00-14:00, closed Sun, John Street, tel. 066/915-1409).

Activities: The **Mountain Man,** a hiking shop run by local guide Adrian Curran, is a clearinghouse for information on hiking, horseback riding, sea kayaking, climbing, and peninsula tours. Call a few days ahead to see which guided, scenic, mountain day-hikes are scheduled (daily 9:00-18:00, June-mid-Sept until 21:00, just off harbor at Strand Street, tel. 066/915-2400, www.themountainmanshop.com).

The **Dingle Hillwalking Club** is an informal, visitor-friendly hiking group and a great way to connect with fun, active locals. But you must have serious footwear for the rugged terrain (free, every other Sun at 10:00, meets in front of SuperValu, www.dinglehillwalkingclub.com).

At the **Dingle Falconry Experience,** master falconer Eric leads encounters with hawks, falcons, owls, and eagles (€15, reserve in advance, most days at 17:00 at Milltown House, just over the bridge west of town, www.dinglefalconry.com).

Tours in Dingle

Minibus Tours
Sciúird Archaeology Tours, worth ▲▲▲, are offered by a father-son team with a passion for sharing the long history of the Dingle Peninsula. Tim Collins (the retired Dingle police chief) and son Michael give informative 2.5-hour minibus tours with running commentary that

Dingle at a Glance

▲▲▲**Dingle Peninsula Loop Trip** Scenic 30-mile loop (easy by car, demanding four hours by bike) featuring the Gallarus Oratory (impressive early-Christian church), Iron Age stone huts and "fairy forts," Norman ruins, and spectacular coastal views. See page 283.

▲▲▲**Sciúird Archaeology Tours** Fascinating 2.5-hour minibus tours helmed by a father-son team who offer an up-close look into the peninsula's ancient history. **Hours:** Tours generally depart at 10:30 and 14:00 in peak season. See page 255.

▲▲▲**Dingle Town Walk** This short stroll introduces you to the town, its finest craft shops, and its characteristic pubs.

▲▲▲**Traditional Music** Best enjoyed at one of Dingle's many pubs; early birds can take in early-evening folk concerts at St. James' Church or the Siopa Ceoil music shop. See page 271.

▲▲**Harry Clark Windows** Imaginative stained-glass Bible scenes inside a lovely Neo-Gothic chapel in the middle of Dingle town. **Hours:** Mon-Fri 9:00-17:00, Sat 10:00-15:00, closed Sun, shorter hours off-season. See page 265.

▲▲**Great Blasket Island** Until quite recently home to one of Ireland's most traditional communities; best appreciated after visit to the excellent Great Blasket Centre in Dunquin on the mainland. **Hours:** Great Blasket Centre open Mon-Sat 10:00-18:00, Sun 11:00-18:00, closed Nov-Easter. See page 293.

▲**Fungie** Dingle Harbor's resident dolphin (and town mascot), who makes regular appearances in the bay (hop a boat tour for a chance at a personal encounter). **Hours:** Boats depart 11:00-17:00; frequency depends on demand. See page 266.

▲**Oceanworld** Aquarium with penguin exhibit, petting pools, and no shortage of Fungie lore. **Hours:** Daily 10:00-17:00, shorter hours off-season. See page 266.

▲**Short Hikes** Bike-ride-plus-hike to nearby Eask Tower for great town and peninsula views, or mellow waterside stroll out to the town's lighthouse. See page 267.

basically follows the self-guided route in this book (Tim helped me write it). Dress for the weather and wear durable shoes. (In a gale storm with slashing winds Tim kept telling me, "You'll survive it.") Stops include beehive huts, the Reasc Monastery, the Gallarus Oratory, and Kilmalkedar Church—but not the Great Blasket Centre (€30, departs daily at 10:30 and 14:00 from the Fungie statue at the

TI or at your B&B by request, book by email as soon as you know your dates, tel. 066/915-1606, www.collinskirrary.com/#sciuird, collinskirrary@eircom.net). Off-season, you may have to call back to see if a minimum of six people have signed up.

Dingle Slea Head Tours is a small company (just Rory, Eibhlis, and Colm) that does single-and multiday private driving tours of the region from their Dingle home base (tel. 087-218-9430, www.dinglesleaheadtours.com, info@dinglesleaheadtours.com). They also run Slea Head tours daily at 10:00 and 14:00 (3 hours, €30, minimum 4 people).

Rural Walking Tours

Claire Galvin & Kevin O'Shea take fit hikers (with proper footwear) into the scenic back country of the Dingle Peninsula, ranging from climbing Mount Brandon to hiking the Great Blasket Island. Routes can be tailored to your interests (tel. 087/624-7230 or 087/790-3950, www.celticnature.com).

Boat Tours

When hard times fell on the local fishing industry, hardworking captains converted to sightseeing operators. From April to September, a guerilla flotilla of former fishing boats load up with tourists and crisscross Dingle harbor. Most churn around the sheltered bay to spot Fungie the friendly dolphin. Others offer half-day "eco-voyages" beyond the mouth of the harbor to spy seabirds and seals, or dependable transport to Great Blasket Island off the tip of the peninsula.

Amid the confusing smattering of options, it mostly boils down to these major operators:

Dingle Dolphin Boat Tours, with a fleet of six boats, offers the widest variety of options, including a one-hour bay cruise with a guarantee to see Fungie or get your money back (€16, at least 4/day in summer), a 2.5-hour "Sea Safari" focusing on coastal wildlife (€45, daily at 12:30), and a day trip to Great Blasket Island (6-hour round-trip voyage puts you on the island for about 3.5 hours). In good weather, it departs at 11:00, arrives on the island by 12:30, and returns to Dingle by 17:30 (€55, must book ahead, schedules vary with weather and tides, office in back corner of TI beside Fungie sculpture, tel. 066/915-6422, www.dingledolphin.com).

Dingle Bay Charters covers a similar lineup at competitive prices. Their office is at the base of the large Dingle Marina jetty—not to be confused with the shorter commercial fishing pier (tel. 066/915-1344, mobile 087/672-6100, https://dingleboattours.com, info@dinglebaycharters.com).

Blasket Island Ferry shuttles visitors from Dunquin Pier at the far west end of the peninsula to Great Blasket Island (€30, kids-€15, hourly starting at 10:00, weather permitting, advanced booking recommended, tel. 066/915-6422, mobile 085/775-1045, www.blasketisland.com, blasketislandferries@hotmail.com).

Dingle Town Walk

This quick, self-guided circle through town gives you a once-over-lightly historical overview and good orientation.

• *Start just beyond the "old roundabout" and beside the playground at the...*

❶ **Tiny Bridge:** This pedestrian bridge, with its black-and-gold wrought-iron railing, was part of the original train line coming into Dingle (the westernmost train station in all of Europe from 1891 to 1953). The train once picked up fish in Dingle; its operators boasted that the cargo would be in London markets within 24 hours. The narrow-gauge tracks ran right along the harborfront.

All the land beyond the old buildings you see today has been reclaimed from the sea. Look inland and find the building on the left with the slate siding (the back wall of O'Flaherty's pub), facing the worst storms coming in from the sea. This was the typical design for 19th-century weatherproofing. The radio tower marks the sky-blue police station.

• *From here, cross the roundabout and walk up the big street called...*

❷ **The Mall:** After about 20 yards, two stubby red-brick pillars mark the entry to the police station. These pillars are all that remain of the 19th-century British Constabulary, which afforded a kind of Green Zone for British troops when they tried to subdue the local insurgents here. It was burned down in 1922, during the Civil War; the present building dates from 1938. Today, in a small, peaceful town like Dingle, the police department is virtually unarmed.

The big white **crucifix** across the street and 50 yards up The Mall is a memorial to heroes who died in the 1916 Rising. Note that it says in the people's language, "For honor and glory of Ireland, 1916 to 19__." The date is unfinished until Ireland is united and free. The names listed are of local patriots who died fighting the British, and one (Thomas Ashe) who died while on a hunger strike.

• *Just past the Russels B&B sign, take 15 paces up the B&B's driveway to see an old stone etched with a cross sitting atop the wall (on the right).*

This marks the site of a former **Celtic holy well,** a sacred spot for people here 2,000 years ago. Now, cross over the street, and continue walking uphill along the delightful gurgling stream.

Fifty yards farther up is another much-honored spot: the distribution center for **Guinness.** From this warehouse with its rusty, red, corrugated second-floor, pubs throughout the peninsula are

Dingle Town Walk

To Gallarus Oratory, Ballyferriter & Slea Head

MAIN ST.

TEMPERANCE HALL

SMALL GALLERY

CURRAN'S PUB

CHAPEL WITH HARRY CLARK WINDOWS

GREEN ST.

ST. JAMES'

FOXY JOHN'S PUB

BANK

To Tralee via Conor Pass

200 Meters
200 Yards

ST. MARY'S

CAROL CRONIN GALLERY

POST OFFICE

MAIN ST.

DICK MACK'S

BENNER'S HOTEL

FIADH SHOP

SPA RD.

LISBETH MULCAHY WEAVER

DINGLE CRYSTAL

GATE

JOHN ST.

JOHN WELDON JEWELER

LITTLE CHEESE SHOP

Park

GUINNESS DIST. CTR.

LIBRARY

GREY'S

DYKE

COURT-HOUSE

HOLYGROUND

CINEMA

THE MALL

COURT-HOUSE PUB

STRAND

BRIDGE

CELTIC HOLY WELL MARKER

THE WOOD

SUPER VALU

LN.

CRUCIFIX

WC

MURPHY'S

THE TRACKS

FUNGIE STATUE

B

TINY BRIDGE

MORAN'S MARKET

Fishing Boat Harbor

PLAYGROUND

WALK BEGINS

SPORTS GROUND

FISHING PIER

WALK ENDS

MAIL RD.

Dingle Harbor

HOSPITAL

FUNGIE

N-86

To Tralee & Killarney

Trail to Lighthouse

1 Tiny Bridge
2 The Mall
3 Main Street
4 Green Street
5 Harbor & Fungie Statue

stocked with beer. The wooden kegs have been replaced by what locals fondly call "iron lungs."

Across the street is the blocky, riot-resistant 19th-century **courthouse**, made of gray stone. Once a symbol of British oppression, today it's a laid-back place where the roving County Kerry judge drops by to adjudicate cases on the last Friday of each month (mostly domestic disputes and drunken disorderliness). Next door, with the blue walls, is the popular (and recommended for trad music) **Court House Pub.**

• *Continue to the big intersection and pause at the small bridge over a little stream. Notice the colors. A century ago, all these buildings were just shades of black and white. Their exteriors were originally exposed stonework (like the houses upstream). Then in the 1920s came the plaster (notice the bumps on the yellow Small Bridge Pub), and in the 1970s— cheery pastels (along with modern tourism). Now head left into the commercial heart of the town on...*

❸ **Main Street:** First, find the little **Fiadh Handwoven Design Shop**, on the left just past the first little corner, across from Ashes Bar. Fiadh (pronounced Fia) Durham creates locally inspired contemporary designs with local wool at her loom and welcomes curious visitors (check out her fine scarves).

A few steps farther up on the left is **Benner's Hotel**. This was Dingle's first hotel, where the old Tralee stagecoach route ended. Note the surviving Georgian facade and door.

Across the street, up a short gravel alley, is **St. James' Church**. Since the 13th century, a church has stood here (just inside the medieval wall, closed to public during the day). Today, it's Anglican on Sundays and filled with great traditional music several nights a week. In 2003, a midwinter concert series sprang up at the church, featuring internationally known artists seeking an intimate venue. It became known as the "Other Voices" series and grew to become an annual event. (Amy Winehouse filmed her "One Shining Moment" TV concert here in 2006.)

• *Farther uphill on the same side is a co-op gallery.*

The Small Gallery (An Gailearai Beagg) is the cute little showroom of the West Kerry Craft Guild, a collective of 14 local artists and artisans who each man the shop two days a month to show off their work. Drop in and see who's working today and learn about their work.

Facing each other just uphill are two of Dingle's most unapologetically **traditional drinking holes,** Curran's and Foxy John's. You're welcome to pop in and look around, though you'll feel a little more welcome if you order a drink (a small beer is "a glass" or half-pint). The publicans are happy to reminisce about old Dingle. These pubs are throwbacks to the humble day when a single hole-in-the-wall address would do double duty: commercial shop by day, pub by night.

James Curran runs **Curran's Pub** out of what was once his grandma's general store. On the last Saturday of every month— when farm families were in town for the market—the wives would pick up their basics here, ordering butter, tea, sugar, jams, and salted meat through the little window. (Just about everything else they consumed was homegrown.) The same shelves grandma

Dingle, An Daingean, or Daingean Ui Chuis?

Linguistic politics have stirred up a controversy over the name of this town and peninsula. As a Gaeltacht, the entire region gets subsidies from the government (which supports the survival of the traditional Irish culture and language). A precondition of this financial support is that towns use their Irish Gaelic name. In 2005, well-meaning government officials in Dublin dictated that Dingle convert its name to the Irish Gaelic "An Daingean" ("on DANG-un"). But as it turns out, four separate Irish towns are named Daingean ("fortress"), so in 2012 Dingle's name was changed again—to Daingean Ui Chuis ("Fortress of the Husseys," a Norman founding family back in the late Middle Ages).

The town has resisted these dictates from Dublin. Dingle has become so wealthy from the tourist trade that it sees its famous name as a trademark, and doesn't want to become "the cute tourist town with the unpronounceable name, formerly known as Dingle." Until recently, official road signs identified the town only as *Daingean Ui Chuis;* however, so many were modified by stubborn locals, who stenciled in a crude *DINGLE,* the government eventually gave up and changed the signs back to *Dingle.* In town, most businesses, all tourist information, and nearly all people—locals and tourists alike—refer to it as Dingle.

For the sake of clarity, in this book I follow the predominant convention: Dingle instead of An Daingean or Daingean Ui Chuis, Great Blasket Island instead of An Blascaod Mór, and so on. But for ease of navigation, I've also generally included the place's Irish name in parentheses. For a list of these bilingual place names, see the sidebar on page 282.

used for jams and socks today stock beer and whiskey. Notice the "snug" in front. Until the 1950s, women weren't really welcome to drink in Irish pubs, but they could discreetly nurse a sherry in the "snug" while their men enjoyed the main room. The great photos all around give you a sense for the old days. This was one of American actor Robert Mitchum's favorite pubs while here to film *Ryan's Daughter* in 1969. Buy a beer and chat with Mr. Curran.

Foxy John's Pub, across the street, is still a working hardware store. Any time of day, you can order a bag of nails with your pint. Notice the back room; while pubs historically have had a legal "last call" at 11:30, the action would often migrate to the back room after the front door was locked.

• *Walk uphill to the Green Street intersection.*

On your right, notice the big **Temperance Hall,** which dates back to a 19th century church-promoted movement that attempted to cut down the consumption of alcohol. To this day Ireland has a serious alcohol problem behind the happy veneer of all this pub fun. You'll see pickled old timers who spend every morning of their last years on the same barstool. Today the Temperance Hall is a meeting place for AA groups, youth clubs, scouts, and other various social and support groups.

Directly across the street, you'll find a small **plaque** on the wall. This marked a safe house prepared during the French Revolution for the French Queen, Marie Antoinette. But the queen refused to leave France and was beheaded in 1789.

• *Now head downhill opposite the Temperance Hall to discover...*

❹ **Green Street:** Green Street is a reminder that 16th-century Dingle traded with Spain and was a port of embarkation for pilgrims on their way to Santiago de Compostela. A few steps down Green Street on the left, look above Kanon's Korner Fish shop to find a stone carved with the year "1586"—perhaps a remnant of that Spanish influence.

Farther along on the left, look for the **Carol Cronin Gallery**, an art gallery that clearly loves the sea. Popping in, you're likely to meet Carol at work. Many find her seascape paintings absolutely mesmerizing.

Down the street on the right, pop into the beautiful, modern **St. Mary's Church.** The former convent behind it shows off its delightful **Harry Clark stained-glass windows**—the single most important cultural sight in Dingle. Don't miss them (described later, under "Sights in Dingle"). Then, wander in the backyard to check out the tranquil nuns' cemetery, with its white-painted iron crosses huddling peacefully together under a big copper beech tree.

Across from St. Mary's (hence the nickname "the last pew") is **Dick Mack's Pub,** another traditional pub well worth a peek, even for nondrinkers. This was once a tiny leather shop that expanded into a pub at night. The pub was established in 1899 by great-grandpa Mack (master of the westernmost train station in Europe), whose mission was to provide "liquid replenishment" to travelers. Today, Dick Mack retains its old leather-shop ambience. In fact it's popular for handcrafted belts. (Their motto: "Step up and get waisted.") The latest Mack, Finn, has changed the focus to whiskey—very trendy in Ireland—and is also starting up a microbrewing operation in the back lot. Finn has no menu—guests just ask him for their options. Exploring the pub, you'll see a classic snug by the window, wonderful photos of generations past, and

Dingle's History

The wet sod of Dingle is soaked with medieval history. In the dimmest depths of the Dark Ages, peace-loving, bookish monks fled the chaos of the Continent and its barbarian raids. They sailed to the drizzly fringe of the known world—to places like Dingle. These monks kept literacy alive in Europe, and later provided scribes to Charlemagne, who ruled much of central Europe in the year 800.

It was from this peninsula that the semi-mythical explorer-monk St. Brendan is said to have set sail in the sixth century in search of a legendary western paradise. Some think he beat Columbus to North America by almost a thousand years (see sidebar on page 305).

Dingle was a busy seaport in the late Middle Ages. Dingle and Tralee (covered later in this chapter) were the only walled towns in Kerry. Castles stood at the low and high ends of Dingle's Main Street, protecting the Normans from the angry and dispossessed Irish outside. Dingle was a gateway to northern Spain—a three-day sail due south. Many 14th- and 15th-century pilgrims left from Dingle for the revered Spanish church in Santiago de Compostela, thought to house the bones of St. James.

In Dingle's medieval heyday, locals traded cowhides for wine. When Dingle's position as a trading center waned, the town faded in importance. In the 19th century, it was a linen-weaving center. Through most of the 20th century, fishing dominated, and the only visitors were scholars and students of old Irish ways. Then, in 1970, the movie *Ryan's Daughter* introduced the world to Dingle. The trickle of Dingle fans has grown to a flood as word of its musical, historical, gastronomical, and scenic charms—not to mention its friendly dolphin—has spread.

Hollywood-style stars on the sidewalk outside that recall famous visitors.

Green Street continues downhill past inviting boutiques, cafés, and estate agents (showing the current price of houses here). Many fine Dingle shops show off work by local artisans.

Dingle Crystal features Sean Daly and his Waterford-trained crystal-cutting skills. Sean prides himself on the deep, sharp cuts in his designs—see the video of him at work. The shop is run by his daughter Bella.

A few steps farther on is the shop of **Lisbeth Mulcahy Weaver,** filled with traditional but stylish woven woolen wear. It's also the Dingle sales outlet of her husband, a well-known potter from Slea Head. Across the street is **John Weldon Jewellers**—ideal for those interested in handcrafted gold and silver with Celtic designs.

• *At the corner, take a left on Grey's Lane and follow your nose to...*

The **little cheese shop** is a foodie shrine playfully governed by Maja Binder, a German who trained in Switzerland. Poke your head inside, even if only for a whiff of her various traditional handmade cheeses.

Back on Green Street you'll see **Dingle's library,** a gift from the Carnegie Foundation, with a small exhibit about local patriot Thomas Ashe and the Blasket Island writers. The best historic photos you'll find in town decorate the library's walls with images of 19th-century Dingle.

• At the bottom of Green Street, take a right and head (past the best ice cream in town—at the recommended Murphy's) to...

❺ **The Harbor and the Fungie Statue:** The harbor was built in 1992 on reclaimed land. The string of old stone shops facing the harbor was the loading station for the railway that hauled the fish from Dingle until 1953. Dingle's fishing industry survives, but it's an international endeavor. Most fishing boats that now ply these waters are Spanish, French, and Basque. Rather than going home with their catch, they offload their fish (mackerel, tuna, cod, herring, and prawns) onto trucks that lumber directly to their homelands. (European Union member countries can fish in other countries' waters, which can leave a little country like Ireland at the mercy of other nations that have many times the people, appetite, and purchasing power.)

In the old days, sailors would hang out at the Marina Inn Pub. But today they barely get off their boats. The trucks that haul their catch home return to Ireland loaded with provisions for their fishermen, a situation that does very little to bolster Dingle's economy. But don't be too sad for Dingle. The parking lot to the right is often filled with tour buses, as Dingle is on the big-bus route from Killarney to Slea Head (in season, thousands stop here daily for a few hours).

Enjoy the kid-friendly scene around the **bronze statue** of Dingle's beloved dolphin, Fungie (described later). From the Fungie statue, look straight out. Dead ahead on the distant hill is the Eask Tower. While it serves the useful purpose of marking this hidden harbor for those far out at sea, it was built primarily as a Famine-era make-work project. A bit to the right, the big, yellow 18th-century manor house across the harbor was owned by Lord Ventry, the dominant English landlord of the time, and is now a school. The pyramid in the distance is Mount Eagle, marking Slea Head at the end of Dingle Peninsula. The building to the left with two big basement doors is a boathouse. At high tide, boats would float in, and be dry-docked at low tide for repairs. Beyond the boathouse and the harbor wall is the mouth of Dingle Harbor, playful Fungie, and the open sea. The booking office for harbor and Fungie boat tours (which leave from here; see page 257) faces the statue.

• *Your walk is over. For a little extra charm, stroll straight ahead to the end of the dock for pier for a salty view, a look at the fishing boats, and a chat with fisherman or two.*

Sights in Dingle

▲▲Harry Clark Windows

Just behind Dingle's St. Mary's Church stands the former Presentation Sisters' convent, now home to the Díseart (dee-SHIRT, rhymes with "T-shirt") Institute of Education and Celtic Culture. The sisters of this order, who came to Dingle in 1829 to educate local girls, worked heroically during the Famine. The convent contains the beautiful Neo-Gothic Chapel of the Sacred Heart, built in 1884. During Mass in the chapel, the Mother Superior would sit in the covered stall in the rear, while the sisters—filling the carved stalls—chanted in response.

The chapel was graced in 1922 with 12 windows—the work of Ireland's top stained-glass man, Harry Clark. Long appreciated only by the sisters, these special windows—showing scenes from the life of Christ—are now open to the public. The convent has become a center for sharing Christian Celtic culture and spirituality.

Cost and Hours: €3, Mon-Fri 9:00-17:00, Sat and Sun 10:00-15:00, tel. 066/915-2476, www.diseart.ie.

Visiting the Chapel: Stop at the reception room to pay and pick up a loaner description with a self-guided walk. While Harry Clark's windows are the big draw, it's also worth noting the recently painted, charming art of Coloradan Eleanor Yates, especially her *Last Supper* that pictures Dingle Harbor out the window. Upstairs is the chapel with the beloved stained glass of Harry Clark. While the windows behind the altar are Victorian, Clark's early-20th-century windows ring the chapel with six easy-to-read scenes. Clockwise from the back entrance, they are the visit of the Magi, the Baptism of Jesus, "Let the little children come to me," the Sermon on the Mount, the Agony in the Garden, and Jesus appearing to Mary Magdalene. Each face is lively and animated in the imaginative, devout, neo-medieval, and fun-loving style of Harry Clark.

DINGLE PENINSULA

▲Fungie

In 1983, a bottlenose dolphin moved into Dingle Harbor and became a local celebrity. Fungie (FOON-ghee) is now the darling of the town's tourist trade and one reason you'll find so many tour buses parked along the harbor. A recent study theorizes that he may be one of a half-dozen dolphins released from "Dolphinariums" (under pressure from animal rights activists) on the southern coast of Britain. This would account for Fungie's loner ways and comfort around humans.

Hardy little tour boats thrive by baiting passengers with the chance of an up-close Fungie encounter, then motoring out to the mouth of the harbor, where they troll around looking for him (see page 257). You don't pay unless you see the dolphin. Fungie is slowing down a bit as he ages and locals are gearing up for a day when tour boats will have to settle for puffins. Still, if there's a group of boats at the mouth of the harbor, Fungie always comes out to play.

▲Oceanworld

This aquarium offers a little peninsula history, 300 different species of fish in thoughtfully described tanks, and the easiest way to see Fungie the dolphin: on video. Walk through the tunnel while fish swim overhead. You'll see local fish as well as a colorful Amazon collection. The penguin exhibit has a dozen of the little tuxedo torpedoes darting underwater and splashing up onto their fake Arctic ice block. Newer additions include young otters and tiny crocodiles. The aquarium's mission is to teach, and you're welcome to ask questions. The petting pool is fun. Splashing attracts the rays, which are unplugged.

Cost and Hours: €14, €38-44 for families with children (4-6 people, daily 10:00-18:00, shorter hours off-season, cafeteria, just past harbor on west edge of town, tel. 066/915-2111, www.dingle-oceanworld.ie).

Dingle Distillery Tour

Whiskey is as trendy as Dingle, and the hometown distillery would love to give you a sample. The one-hour tour includes earnest explanations and two hard drinks—a whiskey and a gin or vodka. The distillery is a 20-minute walk from town, just over the bridge on Slea Head Drive (€15, tours run daily in season at 12:00, 14:00, and 16:00—more with demand, see map on page 277 for location, tel. 086/777-5551, www.dingledistillery.ie).

Music Shops
Danlann Gallery sells violins made by the owner, tin whistles, woodcrafts, and traditional toys, with a tiny vegetarian café upstairs (Mon-Fri 10:00-18:00 in summer, "flexible hours" on weekends and off-season, Dykegate Street).

Siopa Ceoil (literally "The Music Shop") is an inviting little music shop worth seeking out. It's enthusiastically run by Michael Herlihy, who plays a mean accordion and offers free quick-and-dirty *bodhrán* (traditional drum) lessons. Michael, his son Dara, and omni-pleasant Caitriona are virtual encyclopedias of Irish music knowledge (Mon-Sat 9:30-20:00, Sun 14:00-19:00, shorter hours off-season, near the waterfront on a short dead-end lane called The Colony, tel. 066/915-2618, mobile 087-914-5826). The shop hosts "unplugged" traditional music concerts several nights a week, and sells advance discounted tickets for concerts at St. James' Church (see "Folk Concerts," later).

WALKS, RIDES, AND GOLF
▲Short Harbor Walk from Dingle
This easy stroll along the harbor out of town gives you a chance to see Fungie and takes about 1.5 hours round-trip. Head east from the old roundabout (just past O'Flaherty's pub) and walk uphill past the Esso station. Just after Bambury's B&B, take a right, then immediately bear left (toward the cell-phone tower). The road curls downhill and dead-ends at a tiny Irish Coast Guard station beside the bay. Turn left at the station, climbing the steps over the low wall and following the seashore path to the mouth of Dingle Harbor (passing Hussey's folly, an empty two-story shell of a tower built by a 19th-century fat cat). Ten minutes beyond that is a two-story (white with red trim) lighthouse. This is Fungie's neighborhood. If you see tourist boats out, you're likely to see the dolphin. The trail continues another half-mile to dramatic cliff views and an intimate little beach.

▲Bike and Hike to Eask Tower
The bike-and-hike trek to Eask Tower, totaling about 10 miles round-trip, is a good compromise for those wanting more exercise than the mellow harbor walk to the lighthouse, but less sweat than biking the entire 30-mile Dingle Peninsula Loop (described on page 283). The lazy option: Skip the bike, drive to the trailhead, and walk up from there.

Rent a bike in town and pedal west past the aquarium, going left at the roundabout that takes you over the bridge onto R-559 toward Slea Head. After almost two miles, turn left at the brown sign to *Holden's Leather Workshop*. A narrow leafy lane leads another two miles or so to a hut on the right marked *Eask Tower* (the tower looms on the bare hill above). Pay the €2 trail fee at the hut (if unattended, feed the honor box) and hike about a mile straight up the hill. It's a steep trail. You'll zigzag around sheep and tiptoe over their droppings. You'll also need to navigate through (possibly climb) a couple of waist-high, metal-rung gates. After 45 minutes,

you'll reach the stone signal tower on the crown of the hill. Enjoy fantastic views of Dingle town (to the north) and Dingle Bay with the Iveragh Peninsula (home of the Ring of Kerry to the south). Spot the two jagged Skellig Islands off the distant tip of the Iveragh Peninsula.

Horseback Riding

Dingle Horse Riding takes out beginners for a 1.5-hour (€60) trail ride. More experienced riders can choose between two-hour

(€75), half-day (€180), and full-day (€300) excursions (call ahead to book, follow Main Street out of Dingle, turn right at sign, tel. 066/915-2199, www. dinglehorseriding.com). **Long's Horseriding Centre** is farther out on the peninsula just past Ventry (sign on right)—an easy stop for drivers doing the Slea Head Loop (one-hour beach ride-€35, two-hour beach and mountain trail ride-€70, half-day ride-€140, full-day ride-€200, call to book, tel. 066/915-9034, mobile 087-225-0286, www.longsriding.com). In either case, mountain rides are only for advanced riders, and all horses come with English-style saddles (no horns to hang on to).

Dingle Pitch & Putt

This course's scenic 18 holes (ranging from 30 to 95 yards in length) offer a relaxing diversion for average duffers on a green headland overlooking the harbor. They also have a "crazy course" (miniature golf).

Cost and Hours: €7, includes gear, daily 10:00-19:00, closed Nov-March; located behind Milltown House about a 25-minute walk out of town—after crossing over the bridge, take the first left and then the first right; tel. 066/915-2020.

Golf

Located out west, near the wildly scenic tip of the Dingle Peninsula and the town of Ballyferriter, Ceann Sibéal/Dingle Links offers a round of golf in a hard-to-beat setting.

Cost and Hours: €70-85 July-Aug, €60-70 April-June and Sept, €30-55 Oct-March, open daily till dusk, Baile an Fheirtearaigh, 9 miles west of Dingle town, tel. 066/915-6255, www.dinglelinks.com.

EAST OF DINGLE TOWN

▲Minard Castle

Three miles southwest of the town of Annascaul (Abhainn an Scáil), off the Lispole (Lios Póil) Road, is the largest fortress on the peninsula. Built by the Knights of Kerry in 1551, Minard Castle was destroyed by Cromwell's troops in about 1650. With its corners undermined by Cromwellian explosives, it looks ready to split—it's no longer safe to enter this teetering ruin.

From the outside, look for the faint scallop in the doorway, the symbol of St. James. Medieval pilgrims would stop here before making a seafaring pilgrimage from Dingle to St. James' tomb at Santiago de Compostela in northern Spain. Imagine the floor plan of the castle: ground floor for animals and storage, main-floor living room with fireplace, then a floor with sleeping quarters, and, on top, the defensive level.

The setting is dramatic, with the Ring of Kerry across the way and Storm Beach below. The beach is notable for its sandstone boulders that fell from the nearby cliffs. Grinding against each other in the wave and tidal action, the boulders eroded into cigar-shaped rocks. Pre-Christian Celts would carry them off and carve them into ogham stones to mark clan boundaries.

Next to the fortress, look for the "fairy fort," an Iron Age fort from about 500 B.C. Locals thought it unlucky to pluck stones from these ring forts, so they remain undisturbed, overgrown with greenery, all across Ireland.

Puicin Wedge Tomb

While pretty obscure, this is worth the trouble for its evocative setting. Above the hamlet of Lispole (Lios Póil) in Doonties, park your car and hike 10 minutes up the ridge. At the summit is a pile of rocks made into a little room with one of the finest views on the peninsula. Beyond the Ring of Kerry you may just make out the

DINGLE PENINSULA

Tom Crean, Unsung Antarctic Explorer

Kerrymen are known as a hardy lot, and probably none more so than Antarctic explorer and Annascaul native Thomas Crean. As a 15-year-old lad looking for steady employment and a chance to see the world, Crean left these shores in 1893 to join the British Royal Navy, and in 1901 volunteered to join the crew of the RSS *Discovery*. Onboard were Captain Robert Falcon Scott and other soon-to-be famous explorers, including Ernest Shackleton. Their mission: to be the first men to reach the South Pole.

It was the world's first serious attempt to reach the pole, an effort that required pulling sleds laden with tons of supplies across miles and miles of ice in extreme conditions. One of the team's most able man-haulers, Crean quickly gained his mates' trust and respect for his hard work, calm presence, and cheerful (if tuneless) singing. The *Discovery* Expedition pushed the boundaries of Antarctic exploration, but didn't reach the pole (Britain's second attempt, in 1909 under Shackleton, got much closer before also turning back).

Determined to try again, Scott chose Crean among the first of his handpicked crew for the *Terra Nova* Expedition (1910-1913). Early on, Crean saved some expedition members stranded on a drifting ice floe—encircled by orcas (who can tip ice to make vulnerable seals slide off)—by leaping between floating chunks of ice, then scaling an ice wall to get help. Later, Crean and two others were the last support team ordered to turn back as Scott made the final push to the pole (having come so close, the unshakable Crean wept at the news). Near the end of the 730-mile

jagged Skellig Michael, noted for its sixth-century monastic settlement (see previous chapter).

South Pole Inn

This pub, once owned by modest-yet-heroic Antarctic explorer Tom Crean, is still open for business. You'll see it as you pass through Annascaul on N-86 (at the bottom of a hill, on the left if you're heading east). Consider dropping in to have a pint and peruse the walls of lovingly maintained photos devoted to Crean's incredible adventures (see sidebar).

Inch Strand

This four-mile sandy beach was made famous by the movie *Ryan's Daughter*. It's rated a "Blue Flag" beach for its clean water and safe swimming (usually has a lifeguard in summer).

DINGLE PENINSULA

return trip, Crean's two mates, sick and freezing, could go no farther. Exhausted and provisioned with only three cookies and two sticks of chocolate, Crean made a nonstop, solo, 35-mile march through a blizzard to reach help, saving his mates' lives. (Though Scott's party did reach the pole, a Norwegian team led by Roald Amundsen beat them to it—by a month; Scott and his men didn't survive the trip back.)

Crean's most famous act of heroism took place on his third and final polar expedition (1914-1917), led by Shackleton. Their ship, the *Endurance*, was crushed by ice, marooning the crew on Elephant Island. Hoping to find help at a whaling station, Shackleton, Crean, and four others sailed a modified open lifeboat 800 miles in 17 days to South Georgia Island. There they were forced to hike across the rugged, unexplored interior to reach the station on the other side. A ship was sent to rescue the exhausted and malnourished crew, all of whom had miraculously survived the 18-month ordeal.

Crean never did reach the South Pole himself, turning down Shackleton's request to join him on his next (and last) trek. But Crean distinguished himself as a hero among explorers—who named both a mountain and a glacier after him in Antarctica—and was honored by King George V. In 1920, he retired from the navy, returned to County Kerry, and stashed his medals away, never again speaking of his experiences—partly out of modesty, and partly because his service in the (British) navy could have made him a target for Irish nationalists. An uneducated farmer's son, Crean left few records of his exploits and didn't achieve the fame of his lauded (and more well-to-do) contemporaries. Crean married, bought a pub (South Pole Inn—see "East of Dingle Town"), and raised three daughters. After bravely escaping many near-deaths in the Antarctic, he finally died in 1938 of a burst appendix.

Nightlife in Dingle

▲▲▲Music in Dingle Pubs

Traditional pub music is Dingle town's best experience. Even if you're not into pubs, take an afternoon nap and then give these an evening whirl. Dingle is renowned among traditional musicians as an ideal place to perform. The town has piles of pubs that feature music most nights, and there's never a cover charge—just buy a beer. The scene is a decent mix of locals, Americans, Brits, and Germans. Music normally starts at 21:30-ish, and the last call for drinks is at "half eleven" (23:30), sometimes later on weekends. For a seat near the music, arrive early. If the place is chockablock with people, power in and find breathing room in the back. By midnight, the door is usually closed and the chairs are stacked.

DINGLE PENINSULA

Make a point to wander the town and follow your ear. Smaller pubs may feel a bit foreboding to a tourist, but rest assured that

people—locals as well as travelers—are out for the *craic*. Irish culture is very accessible in the pubs; they're like highly interactive museums waiting to be explored. If you sit at a table, you'll be left alone. But stand or sit at the bar and you'll be engulfed in conversation with new friends. Have a glass
in an empty, no-name pub and chat up the publican. Pubs are no longer smoky, but can be stuffy and hot, so leave your coat at home. I know it's going to be a great trad music session when my eyeglasses steam up as I enter.

For some background, see "Traditional Irish Music" on page 7. For locations of the following pubs, see the map on page 280.

Dingle Pub Crawl

The best place to start a pub crawl is at **O'Flaherty's,** the first music pub in Dingle, located on Holyground street. Quietly intense owner Fergus O'Flaherty, a fixture since my first visit to Dingle, can belt out a song as he joins a varying lineup of loyal local musicians. Talented Fergus sings and plays a half-dozen different instruments during almost nightly traditional-music sessions. His domain has a high ceiling and is dripping in old-time photos and town memorabilia—it's unpretentious, cluttered fun.

Moving up Strand Street, find **John Benny's.** Its dependably good traditional-music sessions come with John himself joining in on accordion when he's not pouring pints. **Paddy Bawn Brosnan's Pub** (also on the Strand) brags no music and no food—just beer and sports. If any game's on TV—especially Gaelic football or hurling—you can watch it here with the locals.

Then head up Green Street. **Dick Mack's,** across from the church, is nicknamed "the last pew." Once a leather shop, today the pub sells only drinks, with several rooms, a fine snug, ample beer choices, and a fascinating ambience. The latest Mack, Finn, focuses on whiskey and craft beers.

Green Street climbs to Main Street, where two more Dick Mack-type places are filled with locals deep in conversation (but no music): **Foxy John's** (a hardware shop by day) and **Curran's** (across the street, a small clothing shop by day). For more on each of these (and Dick Mack), see the town walk, earlier.

Wander down Main Street. The **Dingle Pub** seems designed for John Denver and Irish Rovers fans. It's well established as *the* place for folk-ballad singing rather than the churning traditional beat of an Irish folk session. Just downhill, **Neligan's** is another lively traditional music session option with fun dance lessons for beginners on summer Thursday nights. At the bottom of Main Street, **Small Bridge Bar** offers live music nightly. These days, its dimly lit confines are popular with a younger, late-night crowd.

I'd finish my night at the **Court House Pub** (on The Mall, next to the old gray courthouse). This is a steamy little hideaway with low ceilings and high-caliber musicians who perform nightly at 21:00, and my favorite men's room in Ireland—with kegs for urinals. Owner Tommy O'Sullivan is a guitar-strumming fixture on the trad music scene. His wife, Saundra, is from Houston and also sings.

Off-Season: From October through April, the music hibernates for the most part. But on weekends, your best bets are the Small Bridge Bar, O'Flaherty's, the Court House Pub, and John Benny's. Check for winter performances of the "Other Voices" series at St. James Church (see "Folk Concerts," next).

▲▲Folk Concerts

If you're not a night owl, these are your best opportunities to hear Irish traditional music in a more controlled, early evening environment. (In these settings, many of the musicians find flash photography to be an irritating distraction.)

St. James' Church: Top local musicians offer a quality evening of live, acoustic, traditional Irish music in the fine little St. James' Church (100 seats), just off Main Street. If you prefer not to be packed into a pub with the distractions of conversation, these concerts are a good option. They are organized by local piper Eoin Duignan, whose command of the melodic *uileann* bagpipes is a highlight most nights. Surprisingly, this humble church is the home venue of the acclaimed "Other Voices" winter concert TV series that has drawn the likes of Amy Winehouse, Sinéad O'Connor, and Donovan, among others (€13 in advance, €15 at the door; Mon, Wed, and Fri at 19:30, May-Oct only; mobile 087-284-9656; see sign on church gate or, for more details or to book a ticket, drop by Paul Geaneys Pub, Leac a Ré craft shop, or Siopa Ceoil music shop).

The Siopa Ceoil Trad Concert: The Siopa Ceoil music shop hosts intimate traditional Irish music sessions in its cozily cramped, 45-seat space. The show is casual and run by the family, with a running commentary to explain the local music culture. It generally features two musicians playing two 45-minute sets with a 20-minute break (€20, includes a tasty Irish decaf between sets; May-Sept Tue, Thu, Sat at 19:00, plus Sun July-Sept; 2 The Colony, mobile 086-080-8448, www.siopaceoil.ie).

Cinema

Dingle's little theater is The Phoenix on Dykegate. Its film club (50-60 locals) meets here Tuesdays year-round at 20:45 for coffee and cookies, followed by a film at 21:00 (€8 for film, anyone is welcome). The leader runs it almost like a religion, with a sermon on the film before he rolls it. The regular film schedule for the week is posted on the door.

Sleeping in Dingle

Prices vary with the season, with winter cheap, and July and August tops.

IN OR NEAR THE TOWN CENTER

$$$ **Greenmount House** sits among chilly palm trees at the top of town. A five-minute hike up from the town center, this guesthouse commands a fine view of the bay and mountains. Gary Curran runs one of Ireland's best B&Bs, with two fine rooms, three superb rooms, and nine sprawling suites in a modern building with lavish public areas and wonderful breakfasts (parking, top of John Street, tel. 066/915-1414, www.greenmounthouse.ie, info@greenmounthouse.ie). Seek out the hot tub in their back-garden cabin.

$$ **Bambury's Guesthouse,** hosted by cheerful Bernie Bambury, is big and modern with views of grazing sheep and the harbor. The 12 rooms are airy and comfy (coming in from Tralee it's on your left on Mail Road, 2 blocks before Esso station; tel. 066/915-1244, www.bamburysguesthouse.com, info@bamburysguesthouse.com).

$$$$ **Benners Hotel** was the only hotel in town a hundred years ago. It stands bewildered by the modern world on Main Street, with sprawling public spaces and 52 abundant, overpriced rooms (tel. 066/915-1638, www.dinglebenners.com, info@dinglebenners.com).

$$ **Alpine Guesthouse** looks like a Monopoly hotel, and is fittingly comfortable and efficient. Its 14 bright and fresh rooms come with pastoral views, a cozy lounge, and friendly owner Paul O'Shea (RS%, family rooms, easy parking, Mail Road, tel. 066/915-1250, www.alpineguesthouse.com, alpinedingle@gmail.com). Driving into town from Tralee, this will be the first lodging on your right, next to the sports field and a block uphill from the Dingle Esso station.

$ **Eileen Collins Kirrary B&B,** which takes up a quiet corner in the town center, is run by the same Collins family that does archaeological tours of the peninsula (see page 255). They offer five pleasant rooms, great prices, a large garden, and a homey friendliness (cash only, tel. 066/915-1606 or mobile 087-150-0017,

Kirrary House, just off The Mall on Avondale at Dykegate and Grey's Lane, www.collinskirrary.com, collinskirrary@eircom.net, Eileen Collins). They also rent a cozy, family-friendly, self-catering cottage a couple hundred yards up behind town with good views (sleeps 5, 3-night minimum, contact their son Hugh to reserve, hughocoileanin@gmail.com).

$$ Sraíd Eoin House offers five pleasant, top-floor rooms above Galvin's Travel Agency (RS%, cash only, family rooms, John Street, tel. 066/915-1409, www.sraideoinbnb.com, sraideoinhouse@hotmail.com, friendly Kathleen and Maurice O'Connor).

$$ Barr Na Sráide Inn, central and hotel-like, has 29 basic rooms (family deals, self-service laundry, bar, parking, past McCarthy's pub on Upper Main Street, tel. 066/915-1331, www.barrnasraide.com, barrnasraide@eircom.net).

$ O'Neill's B&B is homey and friendly, with six decent rooms on a quiet street at the top of town (cash only, parking, John Street, tel. 066/915-1639, www.oneillsbedandbreakfast.com, info@oneillsbedandbreakfast.com, Mary and Stephen O'Neill).

BEYOND THE PIER

These accommodations are a 10-15-minute walk from Dingle's town center. They tend to be quieter, since they are farther from the late-night pub scene.

$$$ Heaton's Guesthouse, big, peaceful, and comfortable, is on the water just west of town at the end of Dingle Bay—a five-minute walk past Oceanworld on The Wood. The 16 thoughtfully appointed rooms come with all the amenities (creative breakfasts, parking, The Wood, tel. 066/915-2288, www.heatonsdingle.com, info@heatonsdingle.com, David Heaton).

$$$ Castlewood House is a palatial refuge with 12 tasteful rooms, classy furnishings, and delicious breakfasts. The breakfast room and patio have a wonderful view of Dingle Harbor (parking, The Wood, tel. 066/915-2788, www.castlewooddingle.com, info@castlewooddingle.com, Brian and Helen Heaton).

$ Harbour Nights B&B weaves together a line of old row houses to create a 14-room guesthouse facing the harbor (just past the aquarium on The Wood, parking, tel. 066/915-2499, mobile 087-686-8190, www.dinglebandb.com, info@dinglebandb.com, Seán and Kathleen Lynch).

ABOVE TOWN

Arcing inland above the town's western slope are four good lodging choices on a road that changes names three times in a half mile. Starting from the corner of Green Street and Main Street

Accommodations
1 Greenmount House
2 Bambury's Guesthouse
3 Benners Hotel
4 Alpine Guesthouse
5 Eileen Collins Kirrary B&B & Sciúird Arch. Tours
6 Sraíd Eoin House & Galvin's Travel Agency
7 Barr Na Sráide Inn
8 O'Neill's B&B
9 Heaton's Guesthouse
10 Castlewood House
11 Harbour Nights B&B
12 Tower View B&B
13 The Lighthouse B&B
14 Bolands B&B

(headed uphill) you'll be on Goat Street, then Ashmount Terrace, then High Road.

$$ Tower View B&B is a big, modern home just outside of town on a lovely quiet lot. This kid-friendly mini farm rents eight fine rooms (family rooms, High Road, tel. 066/915-2990, www. towerviewdingle.com, info@towerviewdingle.com, Aiden & Helen Murphy).

$$ The Lighthouse B&B is a cozy place, with six prim rooms, wonderful views near the crest of the hill, and Lucky the fluffball mutt (family rooms, High Road, tel. 066/915-1829, www.lighthousedingle. com, info@lighthousedingle.com, Denis & Mary Murphy).

$$ Bolands B&B is family-run with a traditional, welcoming atmosphere and six comfortable rooms (family rooms, Goat Street, tel. 066/915-1426, http://bolandsdingle.ie, bolanddingle@eircom. net, Breda & Michael Boland).

Dingle Accommodations & Services

15 Devane's B&B
16 Dingle Harbour Lodge
17 Hideout Hostel

Services
18 SuperValu Grocery/Dep't Store
19 Cinema

20 Library
21 Laundry
22 Bike Rental
23 Mountain Man Shop
24 Danlann Gallery
25 Siopa Ceoil Shop
26 Boat Tours

$ Devane's B&B caters to the active bike-and-hike crowd, with six clean and practical rooms that are a good value given their close proximity to town (cash only, Goat Street, tel. 066/915-1193, www.devanesdingle.com, devanesdingle@eircom.net, Kevin & Geraldine Devane).

HOSTELS AND DORMS

$$ Dingle Harbour Lodge is a former hostel, pleasantly refurbished and morphing into a hotel hybrid with 29 rooms on the edge of town. You have the feeling of being a guest in a comfy hotel without the fancy prices (family rooms, up a long driveway off The Wood past the aquarium, tel. 066/915-1577, www.dingleharbourlodge.com, info@dingleharbourlodge.com).

¢ Hideout Hostel is friendly and central, just across the lane from the movie theater. Michael (ME-hall) grew up on this street and manages a relaxed, fun atmosphere (private rooms available, Dykegate Street, tel. 066/915-0559, www.thehideouthostel.com, info@thehideouthostel.com).

On Great Blasket Island

You can really get away from it all on Great Blasket Island, a couple of miles off the tip of the peninsula (and described later in this chapter). No phone, no lights, no cars. Not a single luxury. Like Robinson Crusoe (or Gilligan), it's primitive as can be. Book your boat crossing in advance (see page 257).

$ Blasket Hostel is the only lodging or modern amenity on the otherwise uninhabited island. This very basic seasonal crash pad, in the fishing village ghost town on the east end of the island, consists of four houses (two toilets per house), with dorm rooms and a few doubles in an unforgettable setting (private rooms available, no electricity or Wi-Fi, self-serve kitchen—bring your own food, closed off-season, mobile 086-057-2626, www.greatblasketisland. net, info@greatblasketisland.net, Billy O'Connor).

Eating in Dingle

THE ONLY CHEAP MEAL IN DINGLE: PICNIC

The **SuperValu** supermarket/department store, at the base of town, has everything and stays open late (Mon-Sat 8:00-21:00, Sun until 19:00, daily until 22:00 July-Aug). Smaller groceries, such as **Centra** on Main Street (daily 8:00-21:00), are scattered throughout the town. Consider a grand-view picnic out on the end of the newer pier (as you face the harbor, it's the pleasure-boat pier on your right). You'll find picnic tables on the harbor side of the roundabout and benches along the busy harborfront.

DINING IN DINGLE

All of these restaurants are good, but I've listed them in order of my personal preference. The top-end places generally offer good-value, multicourse, early-bird specials from about 17:30 to 19:00. Remember that while seafood is a treat here, so is the lamb.

$$$$ Out of the Blue Seafood-Only Restaurant is the locals' choice for just plain great fresh fish. The interior is bright and elegantly simple. The chalkboard menu is dictated by what the fishermen caught that morning. If they're closed, there's been a storm and the fishermen couldn't go out. Dinners are artfully presented, with a touch of nouvelle cuisine and certainly no chips (Mon-Sat 17:00-21:30, Sun 12:30-15:00, reservations smart, some outdoor picnic-table seating, just past the TI, facing the harbor on The Waterside, tel. 066/915-0811, www.outoftheblue.ie).

$$$ James G. Ashe Pub and Restaurant, an old-fashioned joint, is popular with locals for its nicely presented, top-quality, traditional Irish food and seafood at good prices. Check out the photos of Gregory Peck, who was related to the Ashe family and visited the pub often. I like their beef-and-Guinness stew (daily 12:00-15:00 & 17:30-21:30, Main Street, tel. 066/915-0989).

$$$$ Global Village Restaurant is where Nuala Cassidy and Martin Bealin concoct their favorite dishes. Martin has a passion for making things from scratch and giving dishes a creative twist with inspiration gleaned from his world travels. No chips, no deep-fat-fried anything. It's an eclectic, healthy, fresh seafood-eaters' place (daily 17:30-22:00, Nov-Feb open Fri-Sun only, good salads, top of Main Street, tel. 066/915-2325, mobile 087-917-5920).

$$$$ Chart House Restaurant serves contemporary cuisine in a sleek, well-varnished dining room. Settle back into the ship-shape, lantern-lit space. The menu is shaped by what's fresh and seasonal, and the chef is committed to always offering a good vegetarian entrée (daily 18:00-22:00 except closed Mon Oct-May, reservations wise, at roundabout at base of town, tel. 066/915-2255, www.thecharthousedingle.com, Jim McCarthy).

$$$$ Lord Baker's is the venerable elder among fine Dingle dining options. John Moriarty and his family concoct quality dishes served in a friendly yet refined atmosphere. The seafood soup is a memorable specialty (Fri-Wed 18:00-21:30, closed Thu, reservations smart, Main Street, tel. 066/915-1277 or 066/915-1141, www.lordbakers.ie).

$$$$ Fenton's is good for seafood meals with a memorable apple-and-berry-crumble dessert (Tue-Sun 18:00-21:30, closed Mon, reservations smart, on Green Street down the hill below the church, tel. 066/915-2172, mobile 087-248-2487, www.fentonsrestaurantdingle.com).

LESS EXPENSIVE DINGLE MEALS

While the top-end restaurants charge on average €25-35, you can eat well for €15-20 in Dingle's pubs and ethnic eateries. Many cheap and cheery lunch places close at 18:00. Most pubs stop serving food at about 21:00 (to make room for their beer drinkers and musicians). Anyone will serve tap water for free. Here are some ideas:

$$ John Benny's Pub is a waterfront pub dishing up traditional Irish fare. John, the proprietor, hopes people will come here for dinner, and stay for a drink and to enjoy his nightly live music (food daily 12:30-21:30, music after 21:30, The Pier).

$$ Danno's Restaurant and Bar is a sprawling and fun-loving eatery popular with tourists and locals for inexpensive burgers, fish-and-chips, and pub grub. Danno's interior is a mix of railroad

Dingle Center Restaurants & Pubs

1. Out of the Blue Restaurant
2. James G. Ashe Pub/Rest.
3. Global Village Restaurant
4. Chart House Restaurant
5. Lord Baker's Restaurant
6. Fenton's Restaurant
7. John Benny's Pub
8. Danno's Restaurant & Bar
9. The Blue Zone Wine Bar
10. Anchor Down Restaurant
11. Reel Dingle Fish & Chips
12. The Wren's Nest
13. An Café Liteartha
14. Bean in Dingle
15. Small Bridge Bar & Neligan's Pub
16. O'Flaherty's Pub
17. Paddy Bawn Brosnan's Pub
18. Dick Mack Pub
19. Foxy John's Pub
20. Curran's Pub
21. Dingle Pub
22. Court House Pub
23. SuperValu Grocery/Dep't Store

and rugby memorabilia. He offers some of the best outdoor seating in town with a heated and leafy patio out back (closed Mon, Strand Street, tel. 086/236-4404).

$$ The Blue Zone is a hip jazz wine bar offering pizza, salad, and an international cosmopolitan vibe. Tight, busy, and family-friendly, it's a tasty alternative to Dingle's pub grub and fish-dominated fare. Or just kick back and enjoy a late-night conversation over a glass of wine set to eclectic background music (Thu-Tue 17:30-11:30, closed Wed, Green Street across from St. Mary's Church, tel. 066/915-0303).

$$ Anchor Down is a fresh fish option that's easy on the wallet. The Sheehy family, who are local fishermen, supply their simple little cottage with a variety of fresh fish—and chips if you want them (daily 11:30-21:30, closed Dec-Feb, up a lane off Strand Street, behind Out of the Blue restaurant, 3 The Colony, tel. 066/915-1545).

$ Reel Dingle Fish & Chips is the best chippy in town, serving mostly takeout, but with a few stools. It's not fast, because they cook the fish fresh to order. They serve generous portions—consider splitting—and are also good for burgers (daily 13:00-22:00, near SuperValu grocery store on Holyground, tel. 066/915-1713).

$ The Wren's Nest is a mellow coffeehouse, reflecting musician-owner John Ryan's philosophical demeanor. This lunch-only refuge, with an ultra-appealing back garden, serves wholesome omelets, sandwiches, cakes, and tea. A small corner stage hosts occasional open-mic acoustic music gigs; you can also check out the schedule of *bodhrán* and music lessons (daily 11:00-17:00, Dykegate Street, mobile 086-177-3119).

$ An Café Liteartha, a simple refuge hidden behind a wonderfully cluttered bookstore, serves soup and sandwiches to a good-natured crowd of Irish speakers (daily 10:00-18:00, Oct-April until 17:00 and closed Sun, Dykegate Street, tel. 066/915-2204).

$ Bean in Dingle is an inviting and hip coffee shop run by Justin and Luke Burgess. They serve baked goodies and fresh sandwiches along with good coffee drinks (daily 8:30-18:00, Green Street).

Ice Cream: For two decades Murphy's ice cream has been a Dingle favorite. Their famously adventurous flavors include lavender, candied chili pepper, rosewater, clove, and even gin (daily 11:00-22:00, shorter hours off-season, two locations on Strand Street).

ON SLEA HEAD DRIVE

$$ The Stone House is an appealing lunch or dinner option about seven miles (12 km) west of Dingle on Slea Head Drive. Serving local specialties, from scones to fresh seafood and steak dishes, David and Michelle Foran nurture a cozy atmosphere. Their front porch outdoor tables are popular seaview perches on warm summer evenings, and the fresh Dingle Bay crab salad is a favorite (daily 10:00-18:00, June-Aug until 20:00, reservations smart, tel. 066/915-9970, www.stonehouseventry.com).

DINGLE PENINSULA

All Roads Lead to Daingean Ui Chuis

The western half of the Dingle Peninsula is part of the Gaeltacht, where locals speak the Irish Gaelic language. In an effort to ward off English-language encroachment, all place names on road signs were controversially changed to Irish-only in the past decade, though some are now back in English (see "Dingle, An Daingean, or Daingean Ui Chuis?" sidebar on page 261). As you travel along Slea Head Drive (known as Ceann Sléibhe in Irish), refer to this cheat sheet of the most useful destination names. A complete translation of all Irish place names is included in the Gazetteer section at the back of the *Complete Road Atlas of Ireland* by Ordnance Survey.

English Name	Irish Gaelic Name
Dingle	*Daingean Ui Chuis* (DANG-un e koosh)
Ventry	*Ceann Trá* (k'yown—rhymes with "crown" traw)
Slea Head	*Ceann Sléibhe* (k'yown SHLAY-veh)
Dunquin	*Dún Chaoin* (doon qween)
Blasket Islands	*Na Blascaodaí* (nuh BLAS-kud-ee)
Great Blasket Island	*An Blascoad Mór* (on BLAS-kade moor)
Ballyferriter	*Baile an Fheirtearaigh* (BALL-yuh on ERR-ter-ee)
Reasc Monastery	*Mainistir Riaisc* (MON-ish-ter REE-isk)
Gallarus	*Gallaras* (GAHL-russ)
Kilmalkedar	*Cill Mhaoil-cheadair* (kill moyle-KAY-dir)
Annascaul	*Abhainn an Scáil* (ow'en on skahl)
Lispole	*Lios Póil* (leesh pohl)
Tralee	*Trá Lí* (tra-LEE)

Dingle Connections

Tralee (Trá Lí), 30 miles from Dingle, is the region's transportation hub (with the nearest train station to Dingle). Most bus trips make connections in Tralee.

From Dingle by Bus to: Galway (5/day, 6 hours), **Dublin** (4/day, 8 hours, transfer in Tralee and Limerick), **Rosslare** (3/day, 9 hours), **Tralee** (5/day, fewer off-season and Sun, 1.5 hours). Most bus trips out of Dingle require at least one or two (easy) transfers.

Remember, buses stop on the waterfront behind the SuperValu (bus info toll tel. 1850-836-611, www.buseireann.ie, or Tralee station at 066/712-3566; Tralee train info tel. 066/712-3522). For more information, see "Tralee Connections" at the end of this chapter.

Dingle Peninsula Loop Trip

The gloriously green Dingle Peninsula is 10 miles wide and runs 40 miles from Tralee to Slea Head. The top of its mountainous spine is Mount Brandon—at 3,130 feet, it's the second-tallest mountain in Ireland. While only a few tiny villages lie west of Dingle town, the peninsula is home to 50,000 sheep. A loop trip around the peninsula (known locally as Slea Head Loop), worth ▲▲▲, is about 30 miles (45 km) long and must be driven or biked in a clockwise direction. It's easy by car, or a demanding five hours by bike.

While you can take a great guided tour of the peninsula (see "Tours in Dingle" on page 255), the self-guided tour that follows allows you to do it on your own. To help locate points of interest, I've given distances (in kilometers so you can follow along with your car odometer).

The route is littered with similar minor sights. I've suggested my favorites so you don't burn out or waste time with redundancy. Ideally, pull safely off the road at or near each stop and read the next section (which can generally be enjoyed from that viewpoint). Then as you drive, you'll get more fascination and less stress out of the drive.

Along the way, you'll see lots of grass-fed Friesian (or Holstein) cows and the belted Galloway breed from Scotland (looking like they have a white blanket tossed over them). The only wild animal you'll encounter is a rabbit. In spring or summer, you'll likely enjoy a festival of flowers all along the way as you follow the blue signs with white squiggles—a stylized "WAW"—reminding you that this is "The Wild Atlantic Way" (part of a marketing campaign by the Irish Tourist Board).

To get the most out of your trip, read through this entire section before departing.

Tips for Drivers: Set your odometer to zero (if possible) at Oceanworld, as you leave Dingle. Even if you get off track, the kilometers listed let you judge the distance from one sight to the next. Then go step-by-step (staying on R-559 the entire way and follow-

Dingle Peninsula Loop Trip

Three Sisters

To Tiduff

Smerwick Harbor

KILMALKEDAR CHURCH

GALLARUS ORATORY
(See detail map)

Sybil Head

Ballyferriter
(Baile an Fheirtearaigh)

Clogher Head

R-559

REASC MONASTERY

To Tralee via Conor Pass

Dingle
(Daingean Ui Chuis)

R-559

SCHOOL-HOUSE

LONG'S HORSERIDING CENTRE

GREAT BLASKET CENTRE
(Ionad An Blascaod Mór)

Mt. Eagle

Ventry
(Ceann Trá)

Dingle Harbor

To Killarney

PUB

FOLLY

Dunquin
(Dún Chaoin)

BEEHIVE HUTS

STONE HOUSE

Ventry Bay

LORD VENTRY'S MANOR

EASK TOWER

BULL'S LIGHT-HOUSE

ABANDONED VILLAGE

R-559

DUNBEG FORT

Slea Head
(Ceann Sléibhe)

Great Blasket Island
(An Blascaod Mór)

Dingle Bay

N

2 Kilometers
2 Miles

Note: Driving route width exaggerated for clarity

- - - - Recommended Driving Loop

ing the brown *Slea Head Drive* signs most of the way—through kilometer 37). The road is narrow and can be congested mid-July to late August.

Warning for Cyclists: Bikers often find this route dangerous and stressful (the road is narrow with high hedges and cliffs crowding the traffic). If biking, try to leave early (consider renting your bike the night before), as the road can be jammed with buses and cars on busy summer days.

Dingle Driving/Biking Tour

For this self-guided tour, leave Dingle town west along the waterfront (0.0 km at Oceanworld). Driving out of town, on the left you'll see a row of humble "two up and two down" cottages from a 1908 affordable-housing government initiative.

0.5 km: Dingle Harbor has an eight-foot tide. The seaweed was used to make formerly worthless land arable. (Seaweed is a natural source of potash—organic farming, before it was trendy.) Across the River Milltown estuary, the white **Milltown House** was Robert Mitchum's home during the 1969 filming of *Ryan's Daughter*. (Behind that is Dingle's pitch-and-putt golf course.) Look for the narrow mouth of this blind harbor (behind you, in the distance at the opposite end of the harbor, where Fungie the dolphin frolics) and the Ring of Kerry beyond that. Dingle Harbor is so hidden that ships needed the Eask Tower to find its mouth. If a group of small boats are gathered at the mouth of the harbor, Fungie has come out to play.

0.7 km: At the roundabout, turn left over the bridge. On the far side, the blue building on the right was the site of a corn-grinding mill in the 18th century (with a ghostly black waterwheel hiding behind it). Today it's a modern warehouse that shelters the **Dingle Distillery** (tours daily—see page 266). Just beyond that on the right, you'll pass the junction where you'll complete this loop trip 30 miles from now. The gas station on your left is the western-most on the peninsula (you won't see another on this drive).

1.3 km: The Milestone B&B is named for the stone **pillar** (*gallaun* in Irish) in its front yard. This pillar may have been a pre-historic grave or a boundary marker between two tribes. Half of the stone's length is buried underground. This peninsula, literally an open-air archaeological museum, is dotted with more than 2,000 such monuments dating from the Neolithic Age (roughly 3000 B.C.) through early Christian times. Another stone pillar stands in the field across the street (100 yards away, on the left). The pillar's function today: cow scratcher.

The land ahead on the left holds the estate and mansion of Lord Ventry, whose family came to Dingle as post-Cromwellian War landlords in 1666. Today his mansion (built in 1750, out of view and closed to the public) houses an all-Irish-language girls boarding school.

As you drive past the **Ventry estate** (at 2.8 km, on the right, is Ventry's slate-roofed blacksmith shop), you'll pass palms, mag-nolias, and exotic flora, which were introduced to Dingle by Lord Ventry. The Gulf Stream is the source of the mild climate, which supports subtropical plants (it rarely snows here). Fuchsias—im-ported from Chile and spreading like weeds—line the roads all over the peninsula and redden the countryside from June through September. More than 100 inches of rain a year gives this area its "40 shades of green."

4.6 km: Stay off the "soft margin" as you enjoy views of Ven-try Harbor, its long beach (to your right as you face the water), and distant Skellig Michael, which you'll see all along this part of the route. **Skellig Michael**—the pyramid-shaped island in the dis-tance—holds the rocky remains of a sixth-century monastic settle-ment (described in previous chapter). It's trendy these days because the last scene of *Star Wars: The Force Awakens* (2015) was filmed on its dramatic crags.

In 1866, the first transatlantic cable was laid from nearby Val-entia Island to Canada's Newfoundland (see sidebar on page 245).

Mount Eagle (1,660 feet), rising across the bay, marks the end of Ireland—and that's where you're heading.

6.6 km: In the town of **Ventry**—a.k.a. Ceann Trá (translated roughly as "beach head")—Irish is the first language. Ventry is little more than a bungalow holiday village today. Urban Irish families love to come here in the summer to immerse their kids in the traditional culture and wild nature. A large hall at the edge of the village is used as a classroom where big-city students come to learn the Irish language.

Just past town, a lane leads left to a fine beach and mobile-home vacation community. An information board explains the history, geology, and bird life of the harbor. The humble trailer park has no running water or electricity. Locals like it for its economy and proximity to the beach. From here, a lane leads inland to **Long's Horseriding Centre** (described earlier, under "Sights in Dingle").

At the start of World War II (1939), a German U-boat churned into this bay and put 28 Greek sailors ashore (depositing them on neutral Irish soil). The Greeks were survivors from a merchant ship that the sub had sunk...not the kind of humanitarian gesture that German U-boat captains were known for making.

7.3 km: The bamboo-like **rushes** on either side of the road are the kind used to make the local thatched roofs. Thatching, which nearly died out because of fire danger, is more popular now that anti-flame treatments are available. It's expensive, as few qualified thatchers remain in Ireland. Black-and-white magpies fly overhead.

8.5 km: This intersection has the "Three Gs"—God (a church), groceries, and Guinness. The pub just past the church is **Paddy O'Shea's.** The Irish football star Páidí Ó Sé (Paddy O'Shea) was a household name in Ireland. He won eight all-Ireland football titles for Kerry as a player from 1970 to 1988. He then trained the Kerry team for many years before further endearing himself to his fans by running this pub. A heroic **statue** remembers Paddy, who died in 2012.

10.7 km: *Taisteal go Mall* means "go slowly"; the building on the right, surrounded by a tall net to keep the balls in, is the **village schoolhouse.** In summer it's used for Irish Gaelic courses for kids from the big cities. On the left is the small Celtic and Prehistoric Museum, a quirky private collection of prehistoric artifacts, including arrowheads and ancient jewelry, collected by a retired busker (musician) named Harris (€5, daily 10:00-17:00).

11.1 km: The circular mound (which looks like a big round hedge) on the right is a late-Stone

Age **ring fort.** It was a petty Celtic chieftain's headquarters—a stone-and-earth stockade filled with little thatched dwellings. Such mysterious sites survived untouched through the centuries because of superstitious beliefs that they were "fairy forts." While this site is unexcavated, archaeologists have found evidence that people have lived on this peninsula since about 4000 B.C. (There must be a dozen such minor sights along this route. I'll recommend my favorites.)

11.7 km: Look ahead up Mount Eagle at the patchwork of stone-fenced fields. In the distance on the left is another view of Skellig Michael.

12.5 km: Dunbeg Fort (50 yards downhill on the left) is made up of a series of defensive ramparts and ditches around a central *clochan* (€3, May-Sept 9:00-18:00, July-Aug until 19:00). A third of the fort fell into the sea during a violent storm in 2014. Forts like this are the most important relics left from Ireland's Iron Age (500 B.C.-A.D. 500).

The modern stone-roofed dwelling across the street was built to blend in with the landscape and the region's ancient rock-slab architecture (A.D. 2000). It's the welcoming and recommended **Stone House Restaurant,** with an adjacent visitors center, where you can check out a 10-minute video that gives a bigger picture of the prehistory of the peninsula (included with Dunberg Fort ticket). A traditional *currach* boat is permanently dry-docked in the parking lot.

Roughly 50 yards up the road and 100 yards off the road to the right is a thatched **cottage** abandoned by a family named Kavanaugh during the Famine (around 1848). With a few rusty and chipped old artifacts and good descriptions, it offers an evocative peek into the simple lifestyles of the area in the 19th century (€3, daily 10:00-18:00, closed Nov-April). The owner, Gabriel, also runs working sheep dog demonstrations (in Irish for the dogs, English for tourists; €5/person, must book ahead by phone, mobile 087-762-2617, www.dinglesheepdogs.com).

13.2 km: A group of **beehive huts** *(clochans)* is a short walk uphill (€3, daily 9:00-19:00, WC). While reconstructed, these mysterious stone igloos, which cluster together within a circular wall, are a better sight than the similar group of beehive huts down the road.

Farther on (at 14.0 km), you'll ford a stream. There's never been a bridge here; this bit of road—nicknamed the "upside-down bridge"—was designed as a ford.

14.7 km: Pull off to the left at this second group of beehive huts. (Aedan runs this family enterprise where you can see more *clochans,* hold a baby lamb, and use the WC for €3.) Look downhill at the rocky field. In the movie *Far and Away,* that's where Lord Ventry evicted (read: torched) peasants from their cottages. Even without Hollywood, this is a bleak and godforsaken land. Look across the bay at the Ring of Kerry in the distance and ahead at the Blasket Islands.

16.0 km: At **Slea Head** (Ceann Sléibhe)—marked by a crucifix, a pullout, and great views of the Blasket Islands (described later)—you turn the corner on this tour. On stormy days, the waves are "racing in like white horses."

16.7 km: Pull into the little parking lot (at *Dún Chaoin* sign) for views of **Great Blasket Island** and **Dunmore Head** (the west-

ernmost point in Europe) and to review the roadside map (which traces your route) posted in the parking lot.

Great Blasket Island is an icon of traditional Irish culture. Because the islanders subsisted off the sea, rather than on potatoes, they survived the Famine. The most traditional of Irish communities, about 100 people lived there until 1953, when the government evacuated the island. While the island is uninhabited today, small tour boats shuttle visitors from Dingle and from Dunquin Harbor (just ahead). To read more about this fascinating island, see page 293. And to learn more, visit the Blasket Island Centre (a few miles farther down the road).

As you drive on, notice the ruined stone houses (and the sheep oblivious to the amazing views). The scattered village just down the road was abandoned during the Famine. Some homes are now fixed up, as this is a popular place these days for summer vacationers. You can see more good examples of land reclamation, patch by patch, climbing up the hillside. Mount Eagle was the first bit of land that Charles Lindbergh saw after crossing the Atlantic on his way to Paris in 1927. Villagers here were as excited as he was—they had never seen anything so big in the air.

Look above, at the patches of land slowly made into farmland by the inhabitants of this westernmost piece of Europe. Rocks were cleared and piled into fences. Sand and seaweed were laid on the clay, and in time it was good for grass. The created land, if at all tillable, was generally used for growing potatoes; otherwise, it was only good for grazing. Much of this farmland has now fallen out of use.

About a kilometer down a road on the left, a plaque celebrates the 30th anniversary of the filming of *Ryan's Daughter*. From here, a trail leads down to a wild beach.

19.0 km: The Blasket Islands' residents had no church or cemetery on the island. On the left stretches their **cemetery.** The famous Blascaod storyteller Peig Sayers (1873-1958) is buried at its center. Just off this coast is the 1588 shipwreck of the *Santa María de la Rosa* of the Spanish Armada. And ahead is the often-tempestuous Dunquin Harbor. Blasket Island farmers—who on a calm day could row across in 30 minutes—would dock here and hike over the saddle and 12 miles into Dingle to sell their produce.

Hey! There's a dead man floating out at sea. Oh, it's just an island. (While its official name is The Sleeping Giant, that island has always been known to Blasket Islanders as "The Dead Man.")

21.3 km: From here a lane leads a kilometer to the **Great Blasket Centre,** described on page 294. This excellent modern cultural museum offers the best look at the island culture.

23.1 km: Grab the scenic **Clogher Head pullout.** The view from here is spectacular. Ahead is Mount Brandon, Ireland's second highest peak (at 3,123 feet). Working to the left you'll see Butter Harbor (the name believed to originate from times when Vikings stopped here to grease up their hulls). Then spot the three swoopy peaks—the Three Sisters. Left of that is Sybil Head (where scenes from *Star Wars: The Force Awakens* were shot). On the summit of Sybil Head, the tiny black square is a watchtower from the days when Britain feared an invasion from Napoleon. The entire coast was lined with these, all within sight of each other to relay a warning signal if under attack by the bloody French. And under the Three Sisters is the popular Dingle Links golf course.

Ahead, on the right, study the top fields, untouched since the planting of 1845, when the potatoes didn't grow, but rotted in the ground. The faint vertical ridges of the potato beds can still be seen—a reminder of the Famine. Before the Famine, 40,000 people inhabited this peninsula. After the Famine, the population was so small that there was never again a need to farm so high up. Today, only 10,000 people live on the peninsula.

From this pullout, a breezy 15-minute walk leads out to **Clogher Head.** The dirt road stretches off to the left and peters out after 200 yards. But it's all open ground and easy to navigate. Just step carefully over bog puddles and head uphill through the rocky heather to the lumpy summit. There you'll be rewarded with postcard-worthy panoramic views.

DINGLE PENINSULA

Building a Rock Fence

The Emerald Isle is as rocky as it is green. When the English took the best land, they told the Irish to "go to hell or go to Connaught" (the rugged western part of Ireland where the soil was particularly poor and rocky). Every spring, farmers "harvest" rocks driven up by the winter frost in order to plant more edible fare. Over generations, Irish farmers stacked these rocks into fences, which still divide so much of the land.

The fences generally have no visible gates. But upon closer look, you'll see a "V" built into the wall by larger rocks, which are then filled in with smaller rocks. When a farmer needs to move some cattle, he slowly unstacks the smaller rocks, moves the cattle through, and then restacks them. Flying low over western Ireland, the fields—alligatored by these rock fences—seem to stretch forever. And nearly all have these labor-intensive V-shaped gates built in.

28.0 km: The town of **Ballyferriter**, established by a Norman family in the 12th century, is the largest on this side of Dingle Peninsula. The pubs serve grub, the fine old church dates to the 1860s, and the old schoolhouse (on the left) is a museum with modest exhibits that provide the best coverage of this very historic peninsula (€3, generally daily 10:00-17:00, closed Oct-May, tel. 066/915-6333, www.westkerrymuseum.com). The early Christian slab cross in front of the schoolhouse looks real. Tap it...it's fiberglass—a prop from the *Ryan's Daughter* bus-stop scenes. Across the street, next to the church, is the handy Your Stop market.

Keep on Slea Head Drive (R-559), following signs to *Dingle*.

30.0 km: The road bends over a tiny yellow bridge, past a pub and microbrewery (on the right); 50 yards after that watch for a tiny unmarked paved road going uphill on the right. Detour right up this lane, where you'll find the scant remains of **Reasc Monastery** about 300 yards up (no sign).

This is the stony footprint of a monastic settlement dating from the 6th to 12th centuries (free, always open). The inner wall divided the community into sections for prayer and business (cottage industries helped support the monastery). In 1975, only the stone pillar was visible, as the entire site was buried. The layer of black tar paper (near the base of the walls) marks where the original rocks stop and the excavators' reconstruction begins. The stone pillar is Celtic (c. 500 B.C.).

When Christians arrived in the fifth century, they didn't throw out the Celtic society. Instead, they carved a Maltese-type cross over the Celtic scrollwork. The square building was an oratory (church, which is facing east—you'll see an intact oratory at the next stop). The round buildings would have been *clochans*—those stone igloo-type dwellings.

One of the cottage industries operated by the monastery was a double-duty kiln. Just outside the wall (opposite the oratory, past the duplex *clochan*, at the bottom end), find a stone hole with a passage facing the southwest wind. This was the kiln—fanned by the wind, it was used for cooking and drying grain. Locals would bring their grain to be dried and ground, and the monks would keep a tithe (their 10 percent cut). With the arrival of the Normans in the 12th century, these small religious communities were pushed aside by a militaristic feudal system.

Return to the main road and continue on.

32.0 km: Go left at big Dingle Peninsula Hotel, following *Gallarus* signs and staying on Slea Head Drive.

33.0 km: Turn right up the narrow lane. The "free" car park is a private enterprise on private land (with a short video, WC, and shop), where you'll be charged €3 to see the site. To park for free, go farther up the lane (at 33.4 km) to a tiny five-car pullout on the left, where a path leads through a gate 200 yards to the amazing **Gallarus Oratory** (free, always open).

Built about 1,300 years ago, the Gallarus Oratory is one of Ireland's best-preserved early Christian churches. Shaped like an

upturned boat, its finely fitted drystone walls are still waterproof. As you step in, notice how thick the walls are. A simple, small arched window offers scant daylight over where the altar would have stood. Picture the interior lit by candles during medieval monastic services.

It would have been tough to fit more than about a dozen monks inside. Notice the holes once used to secure covering at the door, and the fine alternating stonework on the corners.

From the oratory, return to the main road and continue, following the brown *Slea Head Drive* signs. (To skip the Kilmalkedar Church—last stop on this tour—and go directly back to Dingle,

DINGLE PENINSULA

continue up the narrow lane and turn right when you hit the bigger road.)

35.5 km: At the junction in the center of the next village, leave Slea Head Drive by taking a right on R-559 (signed with *Dingle, 10 km*). For an optional stop (your own private mini Gallarus Oratory), pull off at 37.1 km at the cemetery, cross the road, and hike 200 yards to St. Brandon's Oratory, which dates to the sixth century (even older than Gallarus).

37.3 km: The **ruined church of Kilmalkedar** (Cill Mhaoilcheadair, on the left at the yellow hiker sign) was the Norman cen-

ter of worship for this end of the peninsula. It was built when England replaced the old monastic settlements in an attempt to centralize their rule. The 12th-century Irish church has a classic Romanesque arch and a well-worn cross atop its roof. It's surrounded by a densely populated graveyard (which has risen noticeably above the surrounding fields over the centuries). In front of the church, you'll find the oldest (late medieval) tombs, a stately early Christian cross (substantially buried by the rising graveyard and therefore oddly proportioned), and a much older ogham stone. This stone, which had already stood here 900 years when the church was built, is notched with the mysterious Morse code-type ogham script used from the third to seventh centuries. It may have marked a grave or a clan border, indicating this was an important pre-Christian gathering place. The hole was drilled through the top of the stone centuries ago as a place where people would come to seal a deal by touching thumbs through this stone. The church fell into ruin during the Reformation.

38.0 km: Continue uphill, overlooking the water. You'll pass another ancient **"fairy fort"** on the right. The bay stretched out below you is Smerwick Harbor. In 1580 a force of 600 Italian and Spanish troops (sent by the pope to aid a rebellion against the Protestant English) surrendered at this bay to the English. All 600 were beheaded by the English forces, which included Sir Walter Raleigh.

41.7 km: At the crest of the hill you may see the belted Galloway beef cattle with their white blankets. The spruce forest on the right was planted with government supplements (to meet EU forest standards for minimizing Ireland's carbon footprint). From here, enjoy a long coast back into Dingle town (sighting, as oldtime mariners did, the Eask Tower).

44.0 km: Take a left past the Dingle Distillery, go over the bridge, and head back into Dingle. At 45 km, you're back at the Oceanarium where you started. Well done!

Blasket Islands

This rugged group of six islands off the tip of Dingle Peninsula seems particularly close to the soul of Ireland. The population of Great Blasket Island, once home to as many as 160 people, dwindled until the government moved the last handful of residents to the mainland in 1953. Life here was hard, but the sea provided for all, and no one went hungry. Each family had a cow, a few sheep, and a plot of potatoes. They cut their peat from the high ridge and harvested fish from the sea. To these folk, World War I provided a bonus, as occasional valuable cargo washed ashore from merchant ships sunk by U-boats. There was no priest, pub, or doctor. Because they were not entirely dependent upon the potato, island inhabitants survived the Famine relatively unscathed. These people formed the most traditional Irish community of the 20th century—the symbol of ancient Gaelic culture.

A special closeness to an island—combined with a knack for vivid storytelling—is inspirational. From this simple but proud fishing/farming community came three writers of international repute whose Gaelic works—basically tales of life on Great Blasket Island—have been translated into many languages. You'll find *Peig* (by Peig Sayers) and *The Islandman* (Thomas O'Crohan) in shops everywhere. But the most readable and upbeat is *Twenty Years A-Growing* (Maurice O'Sullivan), a somewhat-true, Huck Finn-esque account of the author's childhood and adolescence and of island life as it was a hundred years ago.

The island's café closed down some time ago, but the simple hostel reopened several years ago on a seasonal basis (see page 278). Today Great Blasket is little more than a ghost town overrun with rabbits on a peaceful, grassy, three-mile-long poem. There are often free guided walks on the island in season (for details ask at the Great Blasket Centre).

Getting There: In summer, various boats run between **Dingle town** and the Blasket Islands, with a 3.5-hour stop to explore the Great Blasket Island. The ride (which may include a quick look at Fungie the dolphin) traces the spectacular coastline all the way to Slea Head. Competing boats offer similar services from Dingle town and operate when there's enough demand. The tricky landing at Great Blasket Island's primitive and slippery little boat ramp makes getting off a challenge and landing virtually impossible in wet weather. Boats generally depart from the marina pier in Dingle at 11:00 and return from Great Blasket at 17:30. For details, see the boat tour listings on page 257. These boats also do three-hour eco-tours for those interested in puffins, dolphins, and seals.

Boats also go from **Dunquin Harbor** to the Blasket Islands (book ahead; see Blasket Island Ferry listing on page 257).

▲▲Great Blasket Centre

Note that this sight isn't on the Blasket Islands, but on the mainland facing the islands. It's an essential stop before visiting the islands—or a good place to learn about them without making the crossing (fits neatly with my recommended "Dingle Peninsula Loop Trip," earlier).

This state-of-the-art Blascaod and Gaelic heritage center gives visitors the best look possible at the language, literature, and way of life of Blasket Islanders. The building's award-winning design mixes interpretation and the surrounding countryside. Its spine, a sloping village lane, leads to an almost sacred view of the actual island. Don't miss the exceptional 20-minute video, a virtual visit to the island back when it was inhabited (shows on the half-hour), then hear the sounds, read the poems, browse through old photos, and gaze out the big windows at those rugged islands...and imagine. Even if you never got past limericks, the poetry of these people—so pure and close to each other and nature—will have you dipping your pen into the cry of the birds.

Cost and Hours: €5, daily 10:00-18:00, closed Nov-Easter, fine cafeteria run by friendly Christy, well-signposted on the Slea Head Drive near Dunquin/Dún Chaoin, tel. 066/915-6444, www.blasket.ie.

Tralee

While Killarney is the tour-bus capital of County Kerry, Tralee (Trá Lí in Irish, both pronounced Tra-LEE) is its workaday market and transit hub. For drivers zipping between Dingle and Galway, this amiable town near the base of the Dingle Peninsula is worth an hour's stop.

The town comes alive for the famous Rose of Tralee International Festival, usually held in mid-August. It's a celebration of arts and music, culminating in the election of the Rose of Tralee—the most beautiful woman at the festival (no matter which country she was born in, as long as she has Irish heritage).

Sights in Tralee

▲Kerry County Museum

Easily the best place to learn about life in Kerry, this museum (located in Ashe Memorial Hall in the center of town) has three parts: Kerry slide show, museum, and medieval-town walk.

Cost and Hours: €5; daily 9:30-17:30, Oct-May until 17:00 and closed Sun-Mon; tel. 066/712-7777, www.kerrymuseum.ie.

Visiting the Museum: Get in the mood by relaxing for 10 minutes through the Enya-style continuous slide show of Kerry's spectacular scenery. Then wander through 7,000 years of Kerry history in the museum (well-described, no need for free headphones). The Irish joke that when a particularly stupid guy moved from Cork to Kerry, he raised the average IQ in both counties—but this museum is pretty well done. It starts with good background info on the archaeological sites of Dingle, progresses through Viking artifacts found in the area, and goes right up to a video showing highlights of the Kerry football team (a fun look at Irish football, which is more like rugby than soccer). Good coverage is given to adventurous Kerryman Tom Crean, who survived three Antarctic expeditions with Scott and Shackleton (see sidebar on page 270). The lame finale is a stroll back in time on a re-creation of Tralee's circa-1450 Main Street. Before leaving, horticulture enthusiasts will want to ramble through the rose garden in the adjacent park.

Blennerville Windmill

On the western edge of Tralee, just off the N-86 Dingle road, spins a restored mill originally built in 1780. Its eight-minute video tells the story of the windmill, which ground grain to feed Britain as that country steamed into the Industrial Age. In the 19th century, Blennerville was a major port for America-bound emigrants. It was also the home port where the *Jeanie Johnston* was built. This modern-day replica of a 19th-century ship occasionally tours Atlantic ports, explaining the Irish emigrant experience. Most of the time, it's docked and available to tour in Dublin, on the north shore of the River Liffey (see page 78).

DINGLE PENINSULA

Cost and Hours: €5 gets you a one-room emigration exhibit, the video, and a peek at the spartan interior of the working windmill; daily 9:00-18:00, April-May and Sept-Oct 9:30-17:30, closed Nov-March, last entry 45 minutes before closing, tel. 066/712-1064.

Tralee Connections

Travelers headed for Dingle using public transportation will likely find themselves passing through Tralee.

From Tralee by Train to: Dublin (every 2 hours, 6/day on Sun, 1 direct in morning, otherwise change in mellow Mallow, 4 hours, arrives at Heuston Station), **Killarney** (8/day, 35 minutes). Train info: Tel. 066/712-3522, www.irishrail.ie.

By Bus to: Dingle (5/day, fewer off-season and on Sun, 1.5 hours), **Galway** (8/day, 4 hours), **Limerick** (7/day, 2 hours), **Doolin/Cliffs of Moher** (2/day, 5 hours), **Ennis** (6/day, 3.5 hours, change in Limerick), **Rosslare** (2/day, 7 hours), **Shannon** (7/day, 3 hours), **Dublin** (7/day, 6 hours). Tralee's bus station is across the parking lot from the train station. Bus info: Tel. 066/716-4700, www.buseireann.ie.

By Plane: Kerry Airport is a 20-minute drive from Tralee and a one-hour drive from Dingle (airport code: KIR, tel. 066/976-4644,

www.kerryairport.ie). It's just off the main N-22 road, halfway between Killarney and Tralee. It has a half-dozen handy rental-car outlets and an ATM. Dingle Shuttle Bus is your best connection to Dingle town, but you must reserve in advance (€25/person one-way, minimum 3 passengers, mobile 087-250-4767, www.dingleshuttlebus.com). You can also connect to the airport via taxi (€30 from Tralee, €80 from Dingle) or bus (3/day to Dingle via Tralee). The Kerry Airport offers two flights per day to **Dublin**. International destinations served from this tiny airport include London's Stanstead and Luton airports as well as Frankfurt Hahn airport (about 75 miles from Frankfurt).

Route Tips for Drivers: If you're **driving to Dingle,** you have two choices as you enter the neck of the Dingle Peninsula: the narrow, but very exciting, Conor Pass road; or the faster, easier, N-86 through Lougher and Annascaul (Abhainn an Scáil). On a clear day, Conor Pass comes with incredible views over Tralee Bay and Brandon Bay. On the north slope approaching the pass, pull out at the waterfall. From here, there's a fun five-minute scramble to a dramatic little glacier-created lake. Pause also at the summit viewpoint to look down on Dingle town and harbor.

If you're **driving from Dingle,** heading north straight to Galway, the inland Limerick route is fastest and cheapest (roughly €2 in tolls). But if you're going to the Cliffs of Moher and the Burren, the 20-minute Killimer-Tarbert ferry connection allows you to avoid the 80-mile detour around the River Shannon and is more scenic (€19/carload, departs hourly, June-Sept every 30 minutes; generally departs at :30 past the hour going north and on the hour going south—check timetables online; no need to reserve, tel. 065/905-3124, www.shannonferries.com).

COUNTY CLARE & THE BURREN

Ennis • Cliffs of Moher • Doolin • Lisdoonvarna • Irish Workhouse Centre

Those connecting Dingle in the south with Galway up the coast to the north can entertain themselves along the way by joyriding through the fascinating landscape and tidy villages of County Clare. Ennis, the county's major city, is a workaday Irish place with a medieval history, a great traditional Irish music scene, and a market bustle—ideal for anyone tired of the tourist crowds. Overlooking the Atlantic, the dramatic Cliffs of Moher offer tenderfeet a thrilling hike. The Burren is a unique, windblown limestone moonscape that hides an abundance of flora, fauna, caves, and history. The sobering Irish Workhouse Centre in Portumna offers an opportunity to contemplate the country's harsh Victorian-era options for the destitute. And at the other end of the spectrum, for your evening entertainment, join a tour-bus group for a medieval banquet in a castle in Kinvarra or meet up with trad music enthusiasts from around Europe for tin-whistling in Doolin.

PLANNING YOUR TIME

By Car: A car is the best way to experience County Clare and the Burren. The region can be an enjoyable daylong drive-through or a destination itself. None of the sights take much time. But do get out and walk a bit.

If you're driving from Dingle to Galway, I'd recommend the following day plan: Rather than taking the main N-21 road via Limerick, drive north from Tralee on N-69 via Listowel to catch the Tarbert-Killimer car ferry (avoiding Limerick's rush-hour traffic). Even though the ferry is slower and more expensive, it's more direct to the Burren (see the end of the previous chapter). From Killimer, drive north on N-67 via Kilkee and Milltown Malbay.

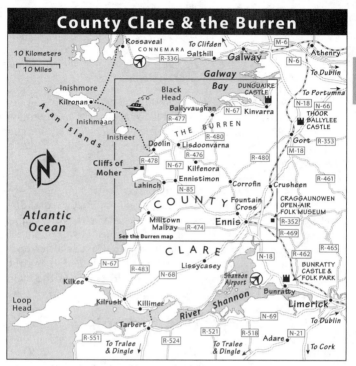

The little surfer-and-golfer village of Lahinch makes a good lunch stop. Then drive the coastal route to the Cliffs of Moher for an hour-long break. (You could wait to eat at the cafeteria at the cliffs, but big-bus tour groups can clog it at midday in summer.) The scenic drive from the cliffs through the Burren, with a couple of stops, takes about two hours. Consider partaking in the 17:30 medieval banquet at Dunguaire Castle, near Kinvarra (one hour south of Galway).

By Train or Bus: Using public transportation, your gateways to this region are Ennis from the south and Galway from the north; Limerick (via Ennis) and Galway are connected by rail—a big plus for those staying in Ennis without a car. Linking the smaller sights within County Clare and the Burren by bus is difficult: Book a tour instead (see page 314).

Tips: Visit an **ATM** in Ennis, Galway, or Lahinch before you enter this region (there are no ATMs in Doolin, Lisdoonvarna, Kilfenora, or Ballyvaughan). Skip the crowded **Bunratty Castle and Folk Park**—I'd leave this to the jet-lagged, big-bus American tour groups (it's located just a potty stop from the Shannon Airport, past Limerick on the road to Ennis).

County Clare

Ennis

This bustling market town (pop. 25,000), the main town of County Clare, provides those relying on public transit with a handy transportation hub (good rail connections to Limerick, Dublin, and Galway). Ennis is 15 miles from Shannon Airport and makes a good first- or last-night base in Ireland for travelers not locked into Dublin flights. It also offers a chance to wander around an Irish town that is not reliant upon the tourist dollar (though not shunning it either). Muhammad Ali visited the town in 2008 after discovering that one of his great-grandfathers had been born in Ennis. Locals credit his success to his fightin' Irish side.

The center of Ennis is a tangle of contorted streets (often one-way). Use the steeple of Saints Peter and Paul Cathedral and the Daniel O'Connell monument column (at either end of the main shopping drag, O'Connell Street) as landmarks.

Orientation to Ennis

TOURIST INFORMATION

The TI is just off O'Connell Street Square (Mon-Sat 9:30-17:30, closed Sun year-round and Mon Oct-May; some lunchtime closures, tel. 065/682-8366).

ARRIVAL IN ENNIS

By Car: If you're not spending the night (i.e., stowing your car at your B&B), parking is best in one of several pay-and-display lots (€1.30/hour, enforced Mon-Sat 9:30-17:30, free on Sun, usually 3-hour maximum). The centrally located multistory lot on Market Place Square charges €5 per day (Mon-Sat 7:30-19:30, closed Sun).

By Train or Bus: The train and bus station is located southeast of town, a 15-minute walk from the town center. To reach town, exit the station parking lot and turn left on Station Road, passing through a roundabout and past the recommended Grey Gables B&B. Turn right after the recommended Old Ground Hotel onto O'Connell Street.

By Plane: Shannon Airport is about 15 miles south of Ennis. For information on this airport, see page 307.

HELPFUL HINTS

Festival: Crowds flock to the **Fleadh Nua** (*fleadh*, pronounced "flah") to celebrate Irish culture at the end of May, making it a challenge to find accommodations (www.fleadhnua.com).

Bookstore: The **Ennis Bookshop** has a good selection (Mon-Fri 9:30-18:30, Sat until 18:00, closed Sun, 13 Abbey Street, tel. 065/682-9000).

Laundry: Fergus launderette is opposite the Parnell Street parking lot (Mon-Sat 8:30-18:00, closed Sun, tel. 065/682-3122).

Supermarket: Dunnes Stores has a location in the shopping center on O'Connell Street (Mon-Sat 8:00-22:00, Sun until 21:00).

Taxi: A good local bet is **Burren Taxis** (tel. 065/682-3456).

Walking Tours: Jane O'Brien leads 1.5-hour walking tours of Ennis departing from the TI (€10, mid-May-mid-Sept Mon-Tue and Thu-Sat at 11:00; no regularly scheduled tours Wed, Sun, or off-season; available for private tours, mobile 087-648-3714, www.enniswalkingtours.com).

Bus Tours: Barratt Tours runs bus tours of the Cliffs of Moher and the Burren (€27, April-Oct daily, none Nov-March, departs from the TI at 10:30 and returns by 17:30, call to confirm schedule, tel. 061/333-100, mobile 087-237-5986, www.barrattstours.ie).

Sights in Ennis

Clare Museum

This small but worthwhile museum, housed in the large TI building, has eclectic displays about ancient ax heads, submarine development, and local boys who made good—from 10th-century High King Brian Ború to 20th-century statesman Éamon de Valera. Coverage includes the Battle of Dysert O'Dea in 1318. One of the few Irish victories over the invading Normans, it delayed English domination of most of County Clare for another 200 years.

Cost and Hours: Free, Mon-Sat 9:30-12:30 & 14:00-17:00, closed Sun year-round and Mon Oct-May, tel. 065/682-3382, www.clarelibrary.ie.

Ennis Friary

The Franciscan monks arrived here in the 13th century, and the town grew up around their friary (which is like a monastery). Today, it's still worth a look for its 15th-century limestone carvings (now protected by a modern roof to keep their details from further deterioration).

Cost and Hours: €5, sometimes includes tour—depends on staffing, daily 10:00-18:00, closed Nov-March, tel. 065/682-9100.

Visiting the Friary: If more than one guide is on duty, ask for a brief introduction to the five carvings taken from the McMahon

NEW ROAD

River Fergus

CUSACK PARK STADIUM

FRANCIS STREET

ENNIS SHOPPING CENTRE

CLON ROAD

GLÓR IRISH MUSIC CENTRE

PARKING GARAGE

FRIARS WALK

PARK AVE.

CLON ROAD

To Galway

⟶ One-way streets

100 Meters

100 Yards

N

CLON ROAD MOR

TRAIN & BUS STATION

R-469

To Craggaunowen Open-Air Folk Museum

To Limerick

Ennis

Accommodations
1. Old Ground Hotel & Poet's Corner Pub
2. Temple Gate Hotel
3. Grey Gables B&B
4. Rowan Tree Hostel

Eateries & Other
5. The Cloisters Rest. & Pub
6. Knox's Pub & Bistro
7. Numero Uno Pizzeria
8. Cruise's Pub
9. Quinn's Pub
10. Brogan's Pub
11. To Cois na hAbhna Show
12. Ennis Bookshop
13. Launderette
14. Dunnes Stores

family tomb. The last one, of Christ rising on the third day, has a banner with a tiny swastika. But look closely: it's rotating as the rising sun would. Despite the swastika's detestable WWII association, it's actually a centuries-old symbol of good luck (the word "swastika" comes from Sanskrit and means "well-being"). Postwar visitors, unaware of the symbol's older meaning, misunderstood it and tried to rub it out of the carving, thus its very faint presence today.

The guides can also fully explain the crucifixion symbolism in the 15th-century *Ecce Homo* carving on a nearby pillar. Every item surrounding Christ on the cross has its own purposeful meaning (nothing on this carving is done just for the sake of decoration). It's a fascinating glimpse into how illiterate worshippers 600 years ago could understand icons even though they couldn't read.

NEAR ENNIS
▲Craggaunowen

This open-air folk museum nestles in a pretty forest, an easy 20-minute drive east of Ennis. All the structures are replicas, except for the small 16th-century castle (tower house), which the park was built around. A friendly weaver, spinning her wool on the castle's ground floor, is glad to tell you the tricks of her trade. A highlight is the Crannog, a fortified Iron Age thatch-roofed dwelling built on a small man-made island, which gives you a grubby idea of how clans lived 2,000 years ago. A modern surprise hides in a corner of the park under a large glass teepee: the *Brendan,* the original humble boat that scholar Tim Severin sailed from Ireland to North America in 1976 (via frosty stepping stones like Iceland and Greenland). He built this boat out of tanned hides, sewn together using primitive methods, to prove that Ireland's St. Brendan may indeed have been the first to discover America on his legendary voyage, 900 years before Columbus and 500 years before the Vikings.

Cost and Hours: €10, daily 10:00-17:00, shorter hours off-season, last entry one hour before closing, tel. 061/360-788, www.shannonheritage.com.

Getting There: The park is well-signposted nine miles (15 km) east of Ennis off R-469, which leads out of town past the train station.

Nightlife in Ennis

Glór Irish Music Centre

The town's modern theater center (*glór* is Irish for "sound") connects you with Irish culture. It's worth considering for traditional music, dance, or storytelling performances (€10-25, year-round

The Voyage of St. Brendan

It has long been part of Irish lore that St. Brendan the Navigator (A.D. 484-577) and 12 followers sailed from the southwest of Ireland to the "Land of Promise" (what is now North America) in a *currach*—a wood-frame boat covered with ox hide and tar. According to a 10th-century monk who poetically wrote of the journey, St. Brendan and his crew encountered a paradise of birds, were attacked by a whale, and suffered the smoke of a smelly island in the north before finally reaching their Land of Promise.

The legend and its precisely described locations still fascinate modern readers. Parts of the tale hold up: The smelly island could well be the sulfuric volcanoes of Iceland. Other parts seem like devoted delirium: The holy monks claimed to have come upon Judas, chained to a rock in the middle of the ocean for all eternity.

A British scholar of navigation, Tim Severin, re-created the entire journey in 1976-1977. He and his crew set out from Brendan Creek in County Kerry in a *currach*. The prevailing winds blew them to the Hebrides, the Faroe Islands, Iceland, and finally to Newfoundland. While this didn't successfully prove that St. Brendan sailed to North America, it did prove that he could have. (You can visit Tim Severin's boat at the Craggaunowen open-air folk museum.)

According to his 10th-century biographer, "St. Brendan sailed from the Land of Promise home to Ireland. And from that time on, Brendan acted as if he did not belong to this world at all. His mind and his joy were in the delight of heaven."

usually at 20:00, 5-minute walk behind TI on Friar's Walk, ticket office open Mon-Sat 10:00-17:00, closed Sun, tel. 065/684-3103, www.glor.ie).

Cois na hAbhna

This original stage show, housed in the local Cois na hAbhna Hall, is a fine way to spend an evening. Sponsored by Comhaltas, a non-profit focused on Irish traditional music, it's a celebration of Irish performing arts presented in two parts. The first features great Irish music, song, and dance. After the break, you're invited to kick up your heels and take the floor as the dancers teach some famous Irish set dances. Phone ahead to see if a *ceilidh* is scheduled on off nights (€10-15, sporadically May-Sept Wed and Fri at 20:30, call ahead to confirm, at edge of town on N-18 Galway road, tel. 065/682-4276, www.coisnahabhna.ie).

Traditional Music

Live music begins in the pubs at about 21:30. The best is **Cruise's** on Abbey Street, with music nightly year-round and good food (bar is cheaper than restaurant, tel. 065/682-8963). Other pubs offering weekly traditional music nights (generally on weekends, but schedules vary) are **Quinn's** on Lower Market Street (tel. 065/682-8148) and **Brogan's** on O'Connell Street (tel. 065/682-9480). The **Old Ground Hotel** hosts live music year-round in its pub (Tue-Sun, open to anyone); although tour groups stay at the hotel, the pub is low-key and feels real, not staged.

Sleeping in Ennis

My first two listings are fancy hotels that you'll share with tour groups.

$$$$ Old Ground Hotel is a stately, ivy-covered 18th-century manse (minister's residence) with 105 rooms and a family feel. Pan Am clipper pilots stayed here during the early days of transatlantic seaplane flights (four blocks from station at intersection of Station Road and O'Connell Street, tel. 065/682-8127, www.flynnhotels.com, reservations@oldgroundhotel.ie).

$$$ Temple Gate Hotel's 70 rooms are more modern and less personal (breakfast extra, just off O'Connell Street, in courtyard with TI, tel. 065/682-3300, www.templegatehotel.com, info@templegatehotel.com).

$ Grey Gables B&B has 12 tastefully decorated rooms (cash only, wheelchair access, family rooms, parking, on Station Road 5 minutes from train station toward town center, tel. 065/682-4487, www.greygables.ie, info@greygables.ie, Mary Keane).

¢ Rowan Tree Hostel is a well-run budget option, centrally located beside the gurgling River Fergus. It incorporates a grand old gentleman's club into its modern additions with better-than-expected private rooms and tidy dorm rooms. A pleasant café/bar rounds out the complex (on Harmony Row next to the bridge, tel. 065/686-8687, www.rowantreehostel.ie, info@rowantreehostel.ie).

Eating in Ennis

The Cloisters, next door to Ennis Friary, inhabits equally historic 800-year-old walls. Its steak, lamb, and fish dishes are the best in town and are served in a tasteful atmosphere, either in the upstairs **$$$$ restaurant** (Tue-Sun 17:30-21:00) or the downstairs **$$$ pub** (Tue-Sun 12:00-17:30, both sections closed Mon, Abbey Street, tel. 065/686-8198).

The Old Ground Hotel serves up hearty meals in its **$$$ Poet's Corner pub** (Mon-Sat 12:00-21:00, Sun 16:00-21:00).

For better than average pub grub, I like **$ Knox's Pub** on Abbey Street (daily 12:00-21:00, tel. 065/682-287). Or try one of the places mentioned under "Nightlife in Ennis," earlier.

The simple **$ Numero Uno Pizzeria** is good for an easy pub-free dinner (Mon-Sat 12:00-23:00, Sun from 15:00, on Old Barrack Street off Market Place, tel. 065/684-1740).

Ennis Connections

From Ennis by Train to: Galway (5/day, 1.5 hours), **Limerick** (9/day, 40 minutes), **Dublin** (9/day, 3-4 hours, change in Limerick, Limerick Junction, or Athenry). Train info: Tel. 065/684-0444, www.irishrail.ie.

By Bus to: Galway (hourly, 1.5 hours), **Dublin** (almost hourly, 4-5.5 hours), **Rosslare** (4/day, 6.5 hours), **Limerick** (hourly, 1 hour), **Lisdoonvarna** (5/day, 2 hours), **Ballyvaughan** (1/day, 2.5 hours), **Tralee** (6/day, 3.5 hours, change in Limerick), **Doolin** (5/day, 2 hours). Bus info: Tel. 065/682-4177, www.buseireann.ie.

SHANNON AIRPORT

The major airport in western Ireland comes with far less stress than Dublin's overcrowded airport (airport code: SNN, airport tel. 061/712-000, www.shannonairport.ie). It has a TI (daily 6:30-19:30, Oct-May until 17:30, tel. 061/471-664), ATMs, Wi-Fi, and a baggage storage desk.

From Shannon Airport by Bus to: Ennis (bus #51 runs between the airport and the Ennis train station hourly, 20 minutes after the hour starting at 8:20, 30 minutes), **Galway** (bus #51, hourly, 1.5 hours), **Limerick** (hourly, 1 hour, can continue to Tralee—2 hours more, and Dingle—4/day, another 2 hours; bus tel. 061/313-333, www.buseireann.ie).

Sleeping near Shannon Airport: Consider **$$ Park Inn by Radisson Shannon Airport** (tel. 061/471-122, www.parkinn.com).

Cliffs of Moher

A visit to the Cliffs of Moher (pronounced "MO-hur")—a ▲▲▲ sight—is one of Ireland's great natural thrills. For five miles, the dramatic cliffs soar as high as 650 feet above the Atlantic.

GETTING THERE
By Car

The Cliffs of Moher are located on R-478, south of Doolin. The parking lot across the road from the visitors center is for the general public; pay the attendant as you drive in. The lot next to the visitors center is for tour buses and visitors with disabilities.

Without a Car

From Galway: Galway Tour Company offers direct shuttle service (not a tour) to and from the Cliffs of Moher (€25, includes cliffs admission; see listing on page 328 for contact details). If the weather cooperates, you can add a Cliffs of Moher cruise (€15). They also offer a tour that includes the Burren (see page 315).

You can also get here by public bus from Galway (8/day in summer, some with change in Ennis, 2 hours, www.buseireann.ie).

From Ennis: Barratt Tours has a bus tour combining the cliffs and the Burren (see page 301).

From Doolin: The Cliffs of Moher are reachable by coastal hike or shuttle bus, or you can take a cruise from Doolin to see (but not visit) the cliffs. For details on these options, see page 311.

ORIENTATION TO THE CLIFFS OF MOHER

Cost: €8, €4 if you book online and visit before 11:00 or after 16:00, includes parking and admission to the visitors center and its exhibit. It costs €2 to climb O'Brien's Tower (not worth it).

Hours: Daily 8:00-19:00, gradually later closing times toward midsummer (as late as 21:00 May-Aug), Nov-Feb 9:00-17:00.

Information: Tel. 065/708-6141, www.cliffsofmoher.ie.

Services: You'll find an information desk and ATM in the visitors center—the Tolkienesque labyrinth tucked under the grassy hillside—flanked by six hobbit garages housing gift shops (across the street from the parking lot). **Cliffs View Café**, upstairs in the visitors center, serves coffee and substantial cafeteria-style hot meals until 16:30. There's also the **Puffin's Nest**, a small sandwich café downstairs.

VISITING THE CLIFFS OF MOHER

The visitors center is designed smartly to orient you to the cliffs experience, spiraling up and finally out onto the cliffs themselves in this order: entry (TI, shop, café); nature exhibit; short film in theater; main restaurant and WC; and outside to the cliffs. (While this is ideal, if the weather seems iffy and you see a sun break, you could do the cliff walk first.)

Visitors Center: The Atlantic Edge exhibit, downstairs, focuses mainly on natural and geological history, native bird and marine life, and virtual interactive exhibits aimed at children. You may even learn why the cliffs are always windy. A small theater shows *The Ledge Experience*, a film following a gannet as he flies along the cliffs and then dives underwater, encountering puffins, seals, and even a humpback whale along the

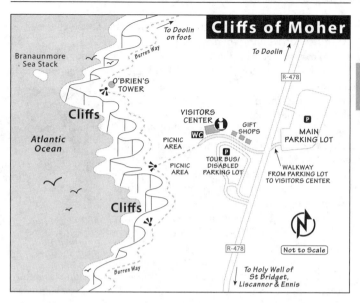

way. (The film is on a five-minute loop with the start-time clock ticking down above the theater door.)

The Cliffs: After leaving the visitors center, walk 200 yards to the **cliff** edge. A protective wall of the local Liscannor slate (notice the squiggles made by worms, eels, and snails long ago when the slate was still mud on the seafloor) keeps visitors safely back from the cliff. You can walk behind the protective wall in either direction. The trail to the right (north, toward the castle-like tower) is the most rewarding.

For years, the Irish didn't believe in safety fences, just natural selection. Anyone could walk right up to the cliffs, until numerous fatal accidents (and suicides) prompted the hiring of "rangers"—ostensibly there to answer questions and lead guided tours, but mainly there to keep you from getting too close to the edge (wind gusts can be sudden, strong, and deadly).

As you gaze down at the waves crashing far, far below you, consider this: Surfing in wet suits is popular in Ireland. Most sane Irish surfers stick to the predictable waves at Lahinch (5 miles south of here). But the monster waves that rear up beneath the Cliffs of Moher on stormy days are coveted by extreme surfers, who work in tandem with tow/rescue helpers skimming the waves on Jet Skis. (You can check it out on YouTube.)

O'Brien's Tower, built in 1835, marks the highest point of the cliffs (but isn't worth the fee to climb...30 feet up doesn't improve the views much). Hike five minutes up to the tower and look to the north (your right). In the distance, on windy days, you can see the Aran Islands wearing their white necklace of surf.

Nearby: Before leaving the area, drivers can take 10 minutes to check out the **Holy Well of St. Bridget,** located beside the tall column about a half-mile (1 km) south of the cliffs on the main road to Liscannor. In the short hall leading into the hillside spring, you'll find a treasure of ex-votos (religious offerings) left behind by devoted visitors seeking cures and blessings. A trickle of water springs from the hillside at the far end. To the right of the simple hall entrance is a stairway heading up into a peaceful graveyard. Be sure to check out the wishing tree (sometimes called a fairy bush or rag tree) halfway up the left side of the stairway. It's usually draped in ribbons tied to branches. These were offerings to saints as

part of a healing ritual. The simple gray column outside was a folly erected over 150 years ago by a local landlord with money and ego to burn.

Doolin

This town was once a strange phenomenon: It had long been a mecca for Irish musicians, who came together here to play before a few lucky aficionados. Many music lovers would come here directly from Paris or Munich, as the town was on the tourist map for its traditional music. But now crowds have overwhelmed the musicians, and I prefer Dingle's richer music scene. Still, as Irish and European fans crowd the pubs, the *bodhrán* beat goes on.

Orientation to Doolin

Doolin has plenty of accommodations and a Greek-island-without-the-sun ambience. The "town" is just a few homes and shops strung out along a valley road from the tiny harbor. Residents generally divide the town into an Upper Village and Lower Village. The Lower Village is the closest thing to a commercial center (it has a couple of pubs and a couple of music shops).

Doolin is without an official and unbiased **TI**. The Upper Village has a privately owned TI at Hotel Doolin that generally exists to book lodging and Aran Islands boat trips (daily 8:30-19:00, closed in off-season tel. 065/707-5642). You'll find a similar boat-booking outfit in the Lower Village.

The Lodge Doolin offers **laundry** service (drop-off only, pick up clothes in 8 hours, daily 8:00-20:00). **Alamo Cabs** is handy for folks without wheels wanting to link a night of fun in Doolin with a bed in Lisdoonvarna (mobile 086-235-3100).

Activities in Doolin

Traditional Music

Doolin is famous for three pubs, all featuring Irish folk music: Nearest the harbor, in the Lower Village, is **Gus O'Connor's Pub** (tel. 065/707-4168). A mile farther up the road, the Upper Village—straddling a bridge—is home to two other destination pubs: **McGann's** (tel. 065/707-4133) and **McDermott's** (tel. 065/707-4328). Music starts between 21:30 and 22:00, finishing at about midnight. Get there before 21:00 if you want a place to sit, or pop in later and plan on standing. The *craic* is fine regardless. Pubs serve decent dinners before the music starts.

Hike, Bus, or Cruise to the Cliffs of Moher

From Doolin, you can hike up the Burren Way along the coast to the Cliffs of Moher. Local guide and farmer Pat Sweeny operates **Doolin Cliff Walk,** leading walking tours that depart daily at 10:00 from O'Connor's Pub. The five-mile walk to the cliffs takes three hours and is not safe for kids under age 10; you catch the 13:30 bus back to Doolin (€10, May-Sept, mobile 086-822-9913, www.doolincliffwalk.com, phone ahead to reserve and check weather/trail conditions).

Alternatively, the **Hop-on, Hop-off Coastal Shuttle Bus** (16 seats) stops throughout Doolin, along the Cliffs of Moher coastal walk, and in the town of Liscannor (€6, departs every 90 minutes starting at 9:00 from Doolin Park & Ride lot—next to R-478, down the hill halfway between N-67 and Doolin Pier, tel. 065/707-5599, mobile 087-775-5098, www.cliffsofmohercoastalwalk.ie). Serious hikers could make a day of it by catching the 9:00 bus southbound, arriving at Liscannor at 10:00, and hiking 7.5 miles (about three hours) back to Doolin. Wear solid footwear for the rugged terrain. Local guide Pat Sweeny can be hired to join you (see above, contact him for cost) or just follow the coastal trail yourself. You can't get lost, unless you take a few too many steps to the left.

To get a different perspective of the cliffs, take a boat cruise along their base. Try for an afternoon cruise, when the sun is coming from the west, illuminating the detail on the dramatic cliffs. Two companies—**Doolin2Aran Ferries** (tel. 065/707-5949, mobile 087-245-3239, www.doolin2aranferries.com) and **O'Brien Line** (tel. 065/707-5618, www.obrienline.com)—offer almost identical cruises. Both make the one-hour voyage past sea stacks and crag-perching birds. Boats depart from the pier in Doolin (same dock as Aran Islands boat, €20, runs daily April-Oct, 3/day, weather and tides permitting, call or go online for sailing schedule and to reserve). They also operate day-trip cruises from Doolin to Inisheer (the closest Aran Island), then along the base of the Cliffs of Moher and back to Doolin (for details, see page 357).

Sleeping in Doolin

$$ Harbour View B&B offers six rooms in a fine modern house overlooking the coast a mile from the Doolin fiddles. Amy Lindner keeps the place immaculate (on main road halfway between Lisdoonvarna and Cliffs of Moher, next to Aran View Market and gas station, tel. 065/707-4154, www.harbourviewdoolin.com, clarebb@eircom.net).

$$ Half Door B&B is the coziest place around, with six woody rooms and a pleasant sun porch. It's just a short walk from the best pubs in the Upper Village (cash only, family rooms, a keg's roll from McDermott's pub, tel. 085/864-2388, www.halfdoordoolin.com, ann@halfdoordoolin.com).

$ The Lodge Doolin is a modern compound of four stone buildings with 21 bright, airy, good-value rooms (located halfway between Upper and Lower Villages, tel. 065/707-4888, www. doolinlodge.com, info@doolinlodge.com). The lodge offers laundry service.

¢ Doolin Inn & Hostel, right in Doolin's Lower Village, caters creatively to the needs of backpackers in town for the music. Friendly Anthony and Dierdre are on top of the local scene. The upper house has the Inn, which offers good-value double rooms and a café. The lower house across the road is the hostel (mobile 087-282-0587, www.doolinhostel.ie, reservationsanthony@ doolinhostel.ie).

Eating in Doolin

The only gourmet option is **$$$ Cullinans,** facing the T-intersection as you come down the hill into the Upper Village (Mon-Tue and Thu-Sat 18:00-21:00, closed Sept-Easter and Wed and Sun year-round, reservations smart in summer, tel. 065/707-4183, www.cullinansdoolin.com, info@cullinansdoolin.com).

The **$$ Ivy Cottage** in the Lower Village, just past the bridge, has a pleasant, leafy tea garden out front. They do a dish of the day as well as simple sandwiches, quiche, or chowder (daily 10:00-18:00, mobile 089-977-1873). You can order fish-and-chips to take away.

$$ The Cliff Coast Café, across the bridge in the Doolin Inn, serves dependable dishes (daily 11:00-21:00, shorter hours off-season, mobile 087-282-0587).

Doolin has earned a reputation for consistently good pub grub.

In the Lower Village, try **$$ Gus O'Connor's Pub,** and in the Upper Village, give **$$ McGann's** a spin. **Mac's Daybreak** is the town market and gas station (daily 7:30-21:00, on R-478 above town next to the Harbour View B&B).

Doolin Connections

From Doolin by Bus to: Galway (5/day, 1.5 hours), **Ennis** (5/day, 2 hours). Buses depart from Doolin's hostel.

By Ferry to the Aran Islands: Doolin2Aran Ferries or O'Brien Line both take you to the closest island, Inisheer (with time to explore), then back along the Cliffs of Moher (they also go to Inishmore, the farthest island; if doing that, it's best to spend the night). For the full rundown on ferries from Doolin, see page 357.

Lisdoonvarna

Treated almost like an inland extension of Doolin, this town of 1,000 (4.3 miles/7 km from Doolin) is a bit bigger, with a few more amenities but no coastal charm. It was known for centuries for its spa, its matchmakers, and its traditional folk music festivals. Today, it's pretty sleepy, except for a few weeks in September, during its Matchmaking Festival (www.matchmakerireland.com), which partially inspired the 1997 film *The Matchmaker.* The nearest ATMs are in Lahinch or Ennistymon. Still, it's more of a town than Doolin and, apart from festival time, less touristy.

Sleeping in Lisdoonvarna: $$ Ballinsheen House is the best value in town. It's perched on a hill with five tastefully decorated rooms and a pleasant, glassed-in breakfast terrace (parking, 5-minute walk north of town on N-67 Galway Road, tel. 065/707-4806, mobile 087-124-1872, www.ballinsheen.com, ballinsheenhouse@ hotmail.com, Mary Gardiner).

Eating in Lisdoonvarna: The **$$ Roadside Tavern** is a favorite local hangout with filling pub grub, great atmosphere, and occasional traditional-music sessions (daily, tel. 065/707-4084, on N-67 in town tucked behind the Royal Spa Hotel in hard-to-miss bright red). **$$$ The Burren Storehouse** is the tavern's modern addition next door, serving chargrilled steaks and seafood, along with pizza and salad options (Mon-Thu 18:00-22:00, Fri-Sat from 14:00, closed Sun, tel. 087-830-0069).

The Burren

Literally the "rocky place," the Burren is just that. This 10-square-mile limestone plateau, a ▲▲ sight, is so barren that a disappointed Cromwellian surveyor of the 1650s described it as "a savage land, yielding neither water enough to drown a man, nor a tree to hang him, nor soil enough to bury him." But he wasn't much of a botanist, because the Burren is in fact a unique ecosystem, with flora that has managed to adapt since the last Ice Age, 10,000 years ago. It's also rich in prehistoric and early Christian sites. This limestone land is
littered with hundreds of historic stone structures, including dozens of Iron Age stone forts. When the first human inhabitants of the Burren came about 6,000 years ago, they cut down its trees with shortsighted slash-and-burn methods, which accelerated erosion of the topsoil (already scoured to a thin layer by glaciers)—making those ancient people partially responsible for the stark landscape we see today.

You can either get a quick overview using my self-guided driving tour, or take your time and really get a feel for the land with one of the walking tours below. Travelers without a car can see the Burren with a bus tour.

Tours in the Burren

Walking Tours

Most travelers zip through the seemingly barren Burren without stopping, grateful for the soft soil they garden back home. But healthy hikers and armchair naturalists may want to slow down and take a closer look. Be sure to wear comfortable shoes for the wet, uneven, rocky bedrock. These guides can bring the harsh landscape to life.

From Ballyvaughan (at the northern entrance to the Burren): **Shane Connolly** leads in-depth, three-hour guided walking tours, explaining the region's history, geology, and diverse flora, and the role humans have played in shaping this landscape. This proud farmer really knows his stuff (€15, daily at 10:00 and 15:00, call to book and confirm meeting place in Ballyvaughan, tel. 065/707-7168, http://homepage.eircom. net/~burrenhillwalks).

From Kilfenora (at the southern entrance to the Burren): **Tony Kirby** leads regularly scheduled two-hour "Heart of Burren Walks" during the summer, and the rest of the year by appointment. His expertise peels back the rocky surface to reveal the surprisingly fascinating natural and human history that has created this unique region (€20, June-Aug Tue-Thu at 10:30, Fri-Sun at 14:15, meet at the Burren Centre in Kilfenora, tel. 065/682-7707, mobile 087-292-5487, www.heartofburrenwalks.com, info@ heartofburrenwalks.com).

Bus Tours

From Galway: Galway Tour Company's standard all-day bus tour of the Burren covers Kinvarra, Aillwee Cave, Poulnabrone Dolmen, and the Cliffs of Moher (€30, discounts if you book online, departs at 10:00, returns about 18:00, confirm schedule ahead). For €15 more, you can add a boat ride out from nearby Doolin to the Aran Island of Inisheer. **Lally Tours** and **Healy Tours** run similar day trips (see page 328 for contact information for all three companies).

From Ennis: Barratt Tours has a bus tour combining the Burren and Cliffs of Moher (see page 301).

Burren Drive

This drive from Kilfenora to Kinvarra offers the best quick swing through the historic Burren (and easily can be done on the way to Galway). Covering about 30 miles from start to finish, it packs a lot of interesting sights and will give you a feel for the unique geology, history, and culture of the region. Music lovers with more time might want to loop back to Kilfenora to join the locals on their set-dancing nights.

⊙ SELF-GUIDED DRIVING TOUR

• *Begin in the town of Kilfenora, 8 kilometers (5 miles) southeast of Lisdoonvarna, at the T-intersection where R-476 meets R-481.*

Kilfenora

This town's hardworking, community-run **Burren Centre** shows an informative 10-minute video explaining the geology and botany of the region, and then ushers you into its enlightening museum exhibits (€6, daily June-Aug 9:30-17:30, mid-March-May and Sept-Oct 10:00-17:00, closed in winter, tel. 065/708-8030, www. theburrencentre.ie). You'll also see copies of a fine eighth-century golden collar and ninth-century silver brooch (originals in Dub-

The Burren

Black Head • Galway Bay • To Galway
DUNGUAIRE CASTLE
Kinvarra

To Kilronan (Inishmore)

Inisheer

R-477 • N-67
Ballyvaughan
AILLWEE CAVE

Lisdoon-varna

THE BURREN

To Irish Workhouse Centre

R-479
Doolin

POULNABRONE DOLMEN
R-480

R-460

Cliffs of Moher
See detail map

R-478

R-476
BURREN CENTRE

CAHERCONNELL RING FORT
LEAMANEH CASTLE

To Gort, Thoor, Ballylee & Portumna

N-67
Kilfenora

Liscannor • Ennistimon
Lahinch

Corrofin

Crusheen

N-18

N-85
R-476

River Fergus

Milltown Malbay

R-460
Inagh

Fountain Cross

Ennis

R-352

CRAGGAUNOWEN FOLK MUSEUM
R-469

To Kilkee, Kilrush & Killimer

5 Kilometers
5 Miles

R-474

N-68

To Shannon Airport, Limerick, Tralee & Dingle

N-18

To Kilrush & Killimer (ferry to Tarbert—road connection to Tralee & Dingle)

lin's National Museum). Brief coverage of the Kilfenora Ceili Band (a national fixture since 1909) primes the set-dancing pumps for what to expect in the town's Barn Pub dance hall (see below). Ceili bands play a form of Irish traditional music embellished with piano and snare drums to create the driving beat popular for set dancing, something County Clare excels in.

The ruined **church** next door has a couple of 12th-century crosses, but there isn't much to see. Mass is still held in the church, which claims the pope as its bishop by papal dictate. As the smallest and poorest diocese in Ireland, Kilfenora was almost unable to function after the Great Potato Famine, so in 1866 Pope Pius IX supported the town as best he could—by personally declaring himself its bishop.

For lunch in Kilfenora, consider the cheap and cheery **Burren Centre Tea Room** (daily 9:30-17:30, located at far back of building) or the more atmospheric **Vaughan's Pub.** If you're spending the night in County Clare, make a real effort to join the locals at the fun set-dancing get-togethers run by the Vaughans in the **Barn Pub,** adjacent to their regular pub. This local dance scene is a memorable treat (€5, Sun at 21:30, also Thu in July-Aug, call ahead to confirm schedule, tel. 065/708-8004).

• *To continue from Kilfenora into the heart of the Burren, head east out of town on R–476. After about 5 kilometers (3 miles), you'll come to the junction with northbound R–480. Take the sharp left turn onto R–480, and slow down to gaze up (on the left) at the ruins of…*

Leamaneh Castle

This ruined shell of a fortified house is closed to everyone except the female ghost that supposedly haunts it. From the outside, you can see how the 15th-century fortified tower house (the right quarter of the remaining ruin) was expanded 150 years later (the left three-quarters of the ruin). The castle evolved from a refuge into a manor, and windows were widened to allow for better views as defense became less of a priority.

• *From the castle, continue north on R–480 (direction: Ballyvaughan). After about 8 kilometers (5 miles), you'll hit the start of the real barren Burren. Keep an eye out for the next stop.*

Caherconnell (Cahercommaun) Ring Fort

Of many ring forts in the area, this one is the most accessible. You can see the low stone profile of Caherconnell to the left on the crest of a hill just off the road. You can park in the gravel lot and walk up to the small visitors center and handy café for an informative 20-minute film followed by a quick wander through the small fort. The fort sometimes features a sheepherding demo with dogs (generally at 12:00 and 15:00—call to confirm).

Cost and Hours: €7, €9.60 with sheepherding demo, daily 10:00-18:00, Easter-June and Sept-Oct 10:30-17:30, closed in winter, tel. 065/708-9999, www.caherconnell.com.

• *The stretch from the ring fort north to Ballyvaughan offers the starkest scenery. Soon you'll see a 10-foot-high stone structure a hundred yards off the road to the right (east, toward an ugly gray metal barn). Pull over for a closer look.*

Poulnabrone Dolmen

While it looks like a stone table, this is a portal tomb. Two hundred years ago, locals called this a "druids' altar." Five thousand years ago, it was a grave chamber in a cairn of stacked stones. Amble over for a look. (It's crowded with tour buses at midday, but it's all yours early or late.)

Wander about for some quiet time with the wildflowers and try to think like a geologist. You're walking across a former seabed, dating from 250 million years ago when Ireland was at the equator (before continental drift nudged it north). Look for white smudges of fossils. Stones embedded in the belly of an advancing glacier ground the scratches you see in the rocks. The rounded boulders came south from Connemara, carried on a giant conveyor belt of ice, then left behind when the melting glaciers retreated north.

• *As you drive away from the dolmen (continuing north), look for the 30-foot-deep sinkhole beside the road on the right (a collapsed cave). From here, R-480 winds slowly downhill for about 6 kilometers (4 miles), eventually leaving the rocky landscape behind and entering a comparatively lush green valley. Eventually, on the right, you'll find the turn up to...*

Aillwee Cave

As this is touted as "Ireland's premier show cave," I couldn't resist a look. While fairly touristy and not worth the time or money if you've seen a lot of caves, it's the easiest way to sample the massive system of caves that underlies the Burren. Your guide walks you 300 yards into the plain but impressive cave, giving a serious 40-minute geology lesson. During the Ice Age, underground rivers carved countless caves such as this one. Brown bears, which became extinct in Ireland a thousand years ago, found them great for hibernating. If you take the tour, you'll need a sweater: The cave is a constant 50°F.

Just below the cave (and on the same property) is the **Burren Birds of Prey Centre,** which houses owls, eagles, hawks, and falcons. During the demo talks, you'll see raptors in action and may be able to briefly hold one as the leather glove is passed around the crowd (bird demonstrations May-Aug at 12:00, 14:00, and 16:00, Sept-April at 12:00 and 15:00—but call for daily schedule).

Adjacent to the cave, the **Hawk Walk** gets visitors face-to-beak with a Harris hawk, "the world's only social raptor." After a brief training session, an instructor leads a small group on a 45-minute hike up a nearby mountain trail. Those paying the stiff €70 fee get to launch and call back the bird to perch on their arm (€18 for a companion—but no participating; limited slots, must reserve).

Cost and Hours: Cave-€12, bird center-€10, €18 combo-ticket includes both sights but not Hawk Walk; open daily at 10:00, last tour at 18:30 July-Aug, otherwise 17:30, Dec-Feb call ahead for limited tours; clearly signposted just south of Ballyvaughan, tel. 065/707-7036, www.aillweecave.ie.

• *Continuing on, our final destination is...*

Botany of the Burren in Brief

The Burren is a story of water, rock, geological force, and time. It supports the greatest diversity of plants in Ireland. Like no-where else, Mediterranean and Arctic wildflowers bloom side by side in the Burren. It's an orgy of cross-pollination that attracts more insects than Doolin does music lovers—even beetles help out. Limestone, created from layers of coral, sea-shells, and mud, is the bedrock of the Burren. (The same formation resurfaces 10 miles or so out to sea to form the Aran Islands.)

Geologic forces in the earth's crust heaved up the land, and the glaciers swept it bare and shattered it like glass under their weight—dropping boulders as they receded. Rain, reacting naturally with the limestone to create a mild but determined acid, slowly drilled potholes into the surface. Rainwater cut through the limestone's weak zones, leaving crevices on the surface and one of Europe's most extensive systems of caves below. Algae grew in the puddles, dried into a powder, and combined with bug parts and rabbit turds (bunnies abound in the Burren) to create a very special soil. Plants and flowers fill the cracks in the limestone. Grasses and shrubs don't do well here, and wild goats eat any trees that try to grow, giving tender little blossoms a chance to enjoy the sun. Different blooms appear throughout the months, sharing space rather than competing. The flowers are best in June and July.

Kinvarra

This tiny town, between Ballyvaughan and Galway, is waiting for something to happen in its minuscule harbor. It faces Dunguaire Castle, a four-story tower house from 1520 that stands a few yards out in the bay.

The touristy but fun **Dunguaire Castle medieval banquet** is Kinvarra's most worthy attraction (€57, cheaper if you book online, most evenings at 17:30 and sometimes at 20:30, mid-April-mid-Oct, reservations required, tel. 061/360-788, castle tel. 091/637-108, www.shannonheritage.com). **Warning:** This company also operates banquets at two other castles in the region, so be sure that you make your reservation for the correct castle.

The evening is as intimate as a gathering of 55 tourists under one time-stained, barrel-vaulted ceiling can be. You get a decent four-course meal with wine (or mead if you ask sweetly), served amid an entertaining evening of Irish tales and folk songs. Remember that in medieval times, it was considered polite to flirt with wenches. It's a small and mul-titalented cast: one harpist and three singer/actors who serve the "lords and ladies" between tunes. The highlight is the 40-minute stage show, which features songs and poems by local writers, and comes with dessert.

You can visit the castle itself by day without taking in an evening banquet (€6, daily 10:00-16:30).

Irish Workhouse Centre

For those who want to see the Victorian "cure" for poverty, the Irish Workhouse Centre in Portumna is a memorable side-trip from Ennis. It's a sad story, of most interest to history buffs or those with Irish heritage, but it sets the stage for Ireland's most cataclysmic tragedy (the Potato Famine).

This is one of the few remaining intact workhouses in Ireland. There were once 163; most were either knocked down or repurposed after Ireland's first step toward independence in 1922. Portumna's workhouse has been restored but not renovated; it stands, grim and foreboding, in much the same condition it was when it was closed.

GETTING THERE
The workhouse is about an hour east of Ennis or Kinvarra, located just over the border in County Galway (and best fits into a jaunt from neighboring County Clare). From Ennis, it's a rural, winding one-hour drive—stay on R-352 the entire way. As you enter Portumna, turn left at Bank of Ireland, continue on, and the Irish Workhouse Centre is on your right.

ORIENTATION TO THE CENTER
Cost and Hours: €7, daily 9:30-17:00, closed Nov-Feb, St. Brigid's Road, Portumna, tel. 090/975-9200, www.irishworkhousecentre.ie.

Tours: Helpful guides give 45-minute tours that add a human angle to the spartan buildings.

VISITING THE CENTER

Workhouses were British institutions, set up by the government in the 1830s (unaware that Ireland's Great Potato Famine was less than a decade away) to provide vagrants with an alternative to starvation and death. However, as the government didn't want the "poorhouse" alternative to be too "tempting," punitive Poor Laws made them a gruesome alternative. To enter the poorhouse, you had to give up any assets you still had, and while you were allowed to enter with your family, you'd likely never see them again once you arrived. Men and women were housed separately; children were also separated by gender. Children over age three were expected to work. There were no common areas for mingling.

Imagine these soul-sapping surroundings during the Great Potato Famine. Since their alternative was starvation, people flooded into these packed quarters—but since workhouses were often not funded properly, the inhabitants were also malnourished. Like cramped emigration "coffin ships," workhouses became transmission points for disease.

Law dictated that workhouses not compete with any local trades or businesses, and therefore they offered the dregs of labor, such as rock-breaking for men and corn-grinding for women. Unraveling old, worn rope and reweaving the salvageable strands into new rope was a task for anyone too weak to do heavy labor.

Life was bleak, food was scarce and of poor quality, and conditions were notoriously inhumane, especially for children. Ironically, it was cheaper for landlords to pay for the boat passage of their paupers to North America than it was to keep them in poorhouses (workhouses were financed by a property tax). Another way to escape was to commit a crime: The food was better in prison, and the regimen was less strict.

GALWAY

Galway offers the most easily accessible slice of Ireland's west coast. Until the recession hit in 2008, it was also the fastest growing city in Ireland. And it's still its most international city, as one out of every four residents was born outside of Ireland. With 76,000 people, this is Galway County's main city, a lively university town and the region's industrial and administrative center. As it's near the traditional regions of Connemara and the Aran Islands, it's also a gateway to these Gaelic cultural preserves.

While Galway has a long and interesting history, precious little from old Galway survives. What does remain has the interesting disadvantage of being built in the local limestone, which, even if medieval, looks like modern stone construction. Galway's reason for being was its ideal position on a large, placid bay, centrally located for trade with all other points on the west coast, as well as beyond to continental Europe.

What Galway lacks in sights it makes up for in ambience. Spend an afternoon just wandering its medieval streets, with their delightful mix of colorful facades, labyrinthine pubs, weather-resistant street musicians, and steamy eateries. Galway also offers tourists plenty of traditional music, easy train connections to Dublin, and a convenient jumping-off point for a visit to the Aran Islands. After dark, blustery Galway heats up, with a fine theater and a pub scene that attracts even Dubliners. Visitors mix with old-timers and students as the traditional music goes round and round.

PLANNING YOUR TIME

Galway merits two nights and a day. The city's sights are little more than pins upon which to hang the old town, and can be seen in just

Galway's History

In 1234, the medieval fishing village of Galway went big time, when the Normans captured the territory from the O'Flaherty family. Making the town a base, the Normans invited in their Anglo friends, built a wall (1270), and kicked out the Irish. Galway's Celtic name (Gaillimh) comes from an old Irish word *gall*, which means "foreigner." Except for a small section in the Eyre Square Shopping Centre and a chunk at the Spanish Arch, that Norman wall is gone.

In the 14th century, 14 merchant families, or "tribes," controlled Galway's commercial traffic, including the lucrative wine trade with Spain and France. These English families constantly clashed with the local Irish. Although the wall was built to "keep out the O's and the Macs," it didn't always work. A common prayer at the time was, "From the fury of the O'Flahertys, good Lord deliver us."

Galway's support of the English king helped it prosper. But with the rise of Oliver Cromwell in the 1640s (see sidebar on page 186), Galway paid for that prosperity. After sieges by Cromwell's troops (in 1651) and those of Protestant King William of Orange (in 1691), Galway declined. It wasn't until the last half of the 20th century that it regained some of its importance and wealth.

GALWAY

a couple of hours. The real joy of Galway is in its street and traditional music scene. On your first night, stroll from Eyre Square through old Galway, seeking out a pub with music. On the next day, visit the Aran Island of Inishmore, or consider day trips to the Burren and Cliffs of Moher, or the Connemara region, which are all doable by car or with a bus tour (all of these destinations are covered in other chapters). At night, return to Galway to enjoy another music-filled evening.

Note for Drivers: Instead of day-tripping, you can visit a number of these sights on the way into or out of Galway. If you're driving north from Dingle to Galway, you can visit the Cliffs of Moher and the Burren en route (see page 298 for route tips). If heading to Northern Ireland from Galway, you can tour Connemara on the way (see page 361 for a plan).

Orientation to Galway

The center of Galway is Eyre (pronounced "air") Square. Within three blocks of the square, you'll find the TI, Aran boat offices, a tour pickup point, accommodations (from the best cheap hostel beds to fancy hotels), and the train station. The train and public bus station butt up against the Hotel Meyrick, a huge gray railroad hotel that overlooks and dominates Eyre Square. The lively old

GALWAY

Galway

To Knock & Sligo via N-17

ST. BRIDGET'S PLACE

NA MBAN

ROSEMARY ST.

PROSPECT HILL

BOTHAR ULEITHIR

CITY HALL

MAGDALENE LAUNDRY MEMORIAL

COLLEGE ROAD

To 🕡, Galway Airport & The Burren

COACH STATION (PRIVATE BUS TOURS)

FRENCHVILLE LANE

BROWNE DOORWAY

GATE

"HOOKER" SCULPTURE

FORSTER STREET

Eyre Square

STATION RD.

PUBLIC BUS STATION

VICTORIA PLACE

EYRE SQUARE SHOPPING CENTRE

TRAIN STATION

Lough Atalia

QUEEN STREET

DOCK ROAD

LOUGH ATALIA ROAD

Bay

100 Meters
100 Yards

Accommodations

1 Park House Hotel
2 Hotel Meyrick
3 Jurys Inn Galway
4 Kinlay Hostel
5 Petra House
6 Balcony House B&B
7 Asgard Guest House

Eateries & Other

8 Ard Bia at Nimmo's
9 To Kai Café/Rest., The Universal & The Crane
10 The Seafood Bar at Kirwan's
11 McDonagh's Fish-and-Chips
12 Rouge Restaurant
13 Murphy's Ice Cream
14 Galway Bakery Co. (GBC)
15 The Lighthouse Vegetarian Café
16 Supermarket
17 To The Huntsman Inn
18 Monroe's Pub
19 Tig Cóilí Pub
20 Taaffe's Pub
21 The Quays Pub
22 Barr An Chaladh
23 Laundry
24 Bike Rental
25 Dubray Books

town lies between Eyre Square and the river. From Eyre Square, Williams Gate leads a pedestrian parade right through the old town (changing street names several times) to Wolfe Tone Bridge. Nearly everything you'll see and do is within a few minutes' walk of this spine.

TOURIST INFORMATION

The well-organized TI, located a block from the bus/train station, has regional as well as local information (Mon-Sat 9:00-17:00, closed Sun, Forster Street, tel. 091/537-700, www.discoverireland. ie). Pick up the TI's free city guide with its simplified town map.

ARRIVAL IN GALWAY

Trains and most buses share the same station, virtually on Eyre Square (which has the nearest ATMs). The train station can store your bag (Mon-Fri 8:00-18:00, closed Sat-Sun). To get from the station to the TI, go left on Station Road as you exit the station (toward Eyre Square), and then turn right on Forster Street.

Don't confuse the public bus station (in same building as the train station) with the coach station (a block away, across the street from the TI), which handles only privately owned coaches. City-link buses from Dublin and Dublin's airport, as well as regional day-tour buses, use the coach station.

Drivers staying overnight at a College Road B&B can park there for free (each has a small lot in front). For daytime parking, the most central and handiest parking garage is under the recommended Jurys Inn Galway in the town center (€2.20/hour, €30/24 hours, Mon-Sat 8:00-1:00 in the morning, Sun 9:00-18:00). Otherwise, you'll have to buy a pay-and-display ticket and put it on your dashboard (€2, 2-hour maximum).

HELPFUL HINTS

Crowd Control: Expect huge crowds—and much higher prices—during the **Galway Arts Festival** (mid to late July, www.galwayartsfestival.com) and **Galway Oyster Festival** (late Sept, www.galwayoysterfest.com). The **Galway Races** are heaven for lovers of horse racing and hell for everyone else (summer races in late July-early Aug, fall races in mid-Sept and late Oct, www.galwayraces.com); prices double for food and lodging, and simple evening strolls feel like punt returns.

Markets: On Saturdays year-round and Sundays in summer, a fun market clusters around St. Nicholas' Church (all day, best 9:00-14:00).

Bookstore: Dubray Books is directly across the pedestrian drag from Lynch's Castle (Mon-Sat 9:00-18:00, Thu-Fri until 21:00, Sun 12:00-18:00, 4 Shop Street, tel. 091/569-070).

Laundry: Galway Dry Cleaners is close to the recommended B&Bs on College Road (drop-off service, Mon-Sat 9:30-17:30, closed Sun, on Bothar Ui Eithir, 2-minute walk uphill from TI, tel. 091/568-393).

Bike Rental: On Yer Bike rents bikes to tool around flat Galway town. Consider a pleasant ride out to the end of Salthill's beachfront promenade and back (€10-15/day, Mon-Sat 9:00-19:00, Sun 12:00-18:00, shorter hours off-season, 42 Prospect Hill, tel. 091/563-393, mobile 087-942-5479, www.onyourbikecycles.com).

Taxi: Give **Big-O-Taxis** a try (tel. 091/585-858).

Tours in Galway

▲Hop-On, Hop-Off City Bus Tours

Guided, one-hour double-decker bus tours compete for your euros. They depart from the northwest end of Eyre Square (opposite end of the square from the huge Hotel Meyrick), have similar schedules and prices, and make the dozen most important stops, including the cathedral, Salthill, and the Spanish Arch. These large coaches can't penetrate some of the winding medieval back streets, but you can get off, explore, and hop back on later. **Galway City** buses are blue (€10, April-Sept daily at 11:00, 12:30, 14:00, and 15:30, tel. 091/770-066, www.galwaybustours.ie). **City Sightseeing** buses are red (€12, April-Sept daily at 10:30, 12:00, 13:30, and 15:00, tel. 091/562-905, www.lallytours.com).

Walking Tours

There are many walking tours in this town full of stories waiting to be told. Most are flexible in their start time and location (call ahead to confirm). **Galway Walking Tours** are led by Fiona Brennan, who takes her guests on leisurely 1.5-hour explorations of the city (€10, mobile 087-290-3499, www.galwaywalkingtours.com, fiona@galwaywalkingtours.com). **Liam Silke** comes from one of Galway's oldest families and portrays Galway's town crier as he leads 1.5-hour tours (€10, departs at 11:30 from TI, tel. 091/588-897, mobile 086-348-0958, www.walkingtoursgalway.com, info@walkingtoursgalway.com). **Galway Walk and Talk Tours** operate with the motto that "a walker has plenty of stories to tell" (€10, departs at 10:30 from TI, mobile 087-690-1452, www.walkandtalk-tour.com).

Food Tours

Sheena Dignam's **Galway Food Tours** take you on 2.5-hour strolls that introduce you to eight "culinary hotspots," including the marketplace. You're encouraged to graze along the way (as a replacement for lunch). Stops run the gamut from sushi to doughnuts, with traditional yet creative options between (€35, Thu-Sun at 11:30, meet in front of McCambridge's food and wine shop, 38 Shop Street, mobile 086-733-2885, www.galwayfoodtours.com).

Excursions from Galway

Good day-trip options from Galway include the Aran Islands, the Burren and Cliffs of Moher, and the Connemara region. Multiple Galway-based companies offer day tours.

Galway Tour Company runs bus tours all over the region, including to the Burren, Cliffs of Moher, and Connemara (office located just a few doors down Forster Street from TI, toward Eyre Square, tours depart from private coach station on Fairgreen Road—across from TI, tel. 091/566-566, www.galwaytourcompany.com, info@galwaytourcompany.com). If Galway Tour Company is booked up, try similar **Lally Tours** (tel. 091/562-905, www.lallytours.com) or **Healy Tours** (tel. 091/770-066, mobile 087-259-0160, www.healytours.ie). All three companies offer discounts if you book two separate tours. Drivers take cash only; to pay with a credit card, book in advance. For details on what these tours cover, see page 315 for the Burren and Cliffs of Moher and page 360 for Connemara.

For details on the ferry to the Aran Island of Inishmore, from Rossaveal (20 miles from Galway), see page 356.

Sights in Galway

EYRE SQUARE AND THE MEDIEVAL "LATIN QUARTER"

Walking from Eyre Square down the pedestrian (and tourist) spine of old Galway to the River Corrib takes you past the essential sights in town. I've connected these sights in an easy downhill stroll.

▲Eyre Square

Galway is dominated by its main, park-like square. On a sunny day, Eyre Square is filled with people just hanging out. In the Middle Ages, it was a field right outside the town wall. The square is named for the mayor who gave the land to the city in 1710. While still called Eyre Square, it now contains John F. Kennedy Park—established in memory of the Irish-American president's visit in 1963 when he filled this space with adoring Irish for one of his speeches, a few months before he was assassinated (a JFK bust near the kids' play area commemorates his visit). Though Kennedy is celebrated as America's first Irish-Catholic president, several US presidents were descended from Protestant Ulster stock (even Barack Obama is part Irish).

Walk to the rust-colored "Hooker" sculpture, built in 1984 to celebrate the 500th anniversary of the incorporation of the city. The sails represent Galway's square-rigged fishing ships ("hookers") and the vessels that made Galway a trading center so long ago. The Browne Doorway, from a 1627 fortified townhouse, is a reminder of the 14 family tribes that once ruled the town (Lynch's Castle, nearby, gives you a feel for an intact townhouse). Each family tribe had a town castle—much like the towers that characterize the towns of Italy, with their feuding noble families. So little survives of medieval Galway that the town makes a huge deal of any remaining window or crest. Each of the 14 colorful flags lining the west end of the square represents a different original Norman founding tribe.

• *From the top of Eyre Square, walk down Williams Gate—a street named for the old main gate of the Norman town wall that once stood here. The spine of medieval Galway, the road changes names several times (to William, Shop, High, and Quay streets) as it leads downhill to the River Corrib. (As you stroll, remember that this is Galway's tourist slalom—with about 80 percent of its tourists and tourist traps.) After about three blocks you'll see a bold limestone "town castle" on your right.*

Lynch's Castle

Now a bank, this limestone tower, Galway's best late-15th-century fortified townhouse, was the home of the Lynch family—the most powerful of the town's 14 tribes—and the only one of their mansions to survive. More than 80 of the mayors who ruled Galway in the 16th and 17th centuries were from the Lynch family.

• *Continuing another block downhill, you'll veer half a block to the right off the main pedestrian flow, to the big church.*

Collegiate Church of St. Nicholas

This church, the finest medieval building in town (1320), is dedicated to St. Nicholas of Myra, the patron saint of sailors. Columbus is said to have worshipped here in 1477, undoubtedly contemplating a scary voyage. Its interior is littered with obscure bits of town history—fine windows, historic tombs, lots of limestone—all described in a handy

GALWAY

23-point flier (€2 suggested donation). Consider attending an evening concert of traditional Irish music in this atmospheric venue (see "Nightlife in Galway," later).

An **open-air market** surrounds the church most Saturdays year-round and also on Sundays in summer.

• *Returning to the pedestrian mall, carry on another block and a half downhill. Look for The Quays pub on your left.*

The Quays

This pub was once owned by "Humanity Dick," an 18th-century Member of Parliament who was the original animal-rights activist. His efforts led to the world's first conviction for cruelty to animals in 1822. It's worth a peek inside for its lively interior.

• *Head down the lane just before the pub, about 50 yards, to the big glass windows on the right...*

Hall of the Red Earl

A big glass wall shows the excavation site of the Hall of the Red Earl. Wall diagrams and storyboards explain that these are the dusty foundations of Galway's oldest building, once the 13th-century hall of the Norman lord Richard de Burgo (free, closed Sun).

Across the lane is the **Druid Theatre**. This 100-seat venue offers top-notch contemporary Irish theater. Although the theater company is away on tour more often than not, it's worth checking their schedule online or dropping by to see if anything's playing tonight (€20-30 tickets, Chapel Lane, tel. 091/568-660, www.druid.ie).

• *Finally, walk to the end of the pedestrian mall, cross the busy street, and follow it to the Wolfe Tone Bridge, where you'll find two gray stone monuments (each about as tall as you are). Above the bridge, a sign says* Welcome to Galway's West End. *You just walked the tourist gauntlet. (Across the river and to the right is a trendy foodie zone.) Stand between the two stone monuments.*

Columbus Monument

The monument (closest to the bridge) was given to Galway by the people of Genoa, Italy, to celebrate the 1477 visit here of Christopher Columbus—Cristoforo Colombo in Italian. (That acknowledgment, from an Italian town so proud and protective of its favorite son, helps to substantiate the famous explorer's legendary visit.) The other memorial is dedicated to sailors lost at sea.

• *Don't cross the bridge. Instead, stroll left downstream to the old fortified arch.*

Spanish Arch

Overlooking the River Corrib, this makes up the best remaining chunk of the old city wall. A reminder of Galway's former importance in trade, the arch (c. 1584) is the place where Spanish ships would unload their cargo (primarily wine).

• *Walk through the arch and take an immediate right. Go past the stone steps to the far corner of the embankment over the river.*

River Corrib Sights

Enjoy this river scene. On either side is a park—a constant party on sunny days. (It's ideal for a picnic of fish-and-chips from the recommended McDonagh's chipper, near the end of the pedestrian mall.) Across the river is the modern housing project that replaced the original Claddagh in the 1930s. **Claddagh** was a picturesque, Irish-speaking fishing village with a strong tradition of independence—and open sewers. This gaggle of thatched cottages functioned as an independent community with its own "king" until the early 1900s, when it was torn down for health reasons.

The old Claddagh village is gone, but the tradition of its popular ring (sold all over town) lives on. **The Claddagh ring** shows two hands holding a heart that wears a crown. The heart represents love, the crown is loyalty, and the hands are friendship. If the ring is worn with the tip of the heart pointing in, it signifies that the wearer is taken. However, if the tip of the heart points out, it means the wearer is available.

Survey the harbor. A few of Galway's famous square-rigged "hooker" fishing ships are often tied up and on display. Called "hookers" for their method of fishing with multiple hooks on a single line, these sturdy yet graceful boats were later used to transport turf from Connemara, until improved roads and electric heat made them obsolete. Beyond that, a huge park of reclaimed land is popular with the local kids for Irish football and hurling. From there, the promenade leads to the resort town of Salthill.

• *Your town intro walk is finished. Just behind the Spanish Arch is a stony riverside warehouse called Nimmo's that contains Ard Bia, one of the best restaurants in town. And just beyond that (see the name towering overhead) is the...*

City Museum

Fragments of old Galway are kept in this modern museum. Check out the intact Galway "hooker" fishing boat hanging from the ceiling. The ground floor houses the archaeological exhibits: prehistoric and ancient Galway-related treasures such as medieval pottery, Iron Age ax heads, and Bronze Age thingamajigs. The first floor sheds light on Galway's role in the Irish struggle for independence in the early 1900s. The top floor is devoted to "sea science" (oceanography).

Cost and Hours: Free, Tue-Sat 10:00-17:00, Sun 12:00-17:00, closed Sun Oct-March and Mon year-round, handy café with cheap lunches, tel. 091/532-460, www.galwaycitymuseum.ie.

Galway Legends and Factoids

Because of the dearth of physical old stuff, the town milks its legends. Here are a few that you'll encounter repeatedly:

- In the 15th century, the mayor, one of the Lynch tribe, condemned his son to death for the murder of a Spaniard. When no one in town could be found to hang the popular boy, the dad—who loved justice more than he loved his son—did it himself.

- Columbus is said to have stopped in Galway in 1477. He may have been inspired by tales of the voyage of St. Brendan, the Irish monk who is thought by some (mostly Irish) to have beaten Columbus to the New World by almost a thousand years.

- On the main drag, you'll find a pub called The King's Head. It was originally given to the man who chopped off the head of King Charles I in 1649. For his safety, he settled in Galway—about as far from London as an Englishman could get back then.

- William Joyce, born in America, spent most of his childhood in Galway and later was seduced by fascist ideology in the 1930s. He moved to Germany and became "Lord Haw-Haw," infamous as the radio voice of Nazi propaganda during World War II. After the war, he was hanged in London for treason. His daughter had him buried in Galway.

MORE SIGHTS IN GALWAY

▲Cathedral of St. Nicholas

Opened by American Cardinal Cushing in 1965, this is one of the last great stone churches built in Europe. The interior is a treat and is worth a peek.

Cost and Hours: Free, open to visitors daily 8:30-18:30 as long as you don't interrupt Mass, church bulletins at doorway list upcoming Masses and concerts, located across Salmon Weir Bridge on outskirts of town, tel. 091/563-577.

Visiting the Cathedral: Inside, you'll see mahogany pews set on green Connemara marble floors under a Canadian cedar ceiling. The acoustically correct cedar enhances the church's fine pipe organ. Two thousand worshippers sit on three sides facing the central altar. A Dublin woman carved the 14 larger-than-life Stations of the Cross. The carving above the chapel (left of entry) is from the old St. Nicholas church. Explore the modern stained glass. Find the Irish Holy Family—with Mary knitting and Jesus offering Joseph a cup of tea. The window depicting the Last Supper is particularly creative—find the 12 apostles.

Next, poke your head into the side chapel with a mosaic of Christ's resurrection (if you're standing in the nave facing the main altar, it's on the left and closest to the front). Take a closer look at the profiled face in a circular frame, below and to the right of Christ—the one looking up while praying with clasped hands. It's JFK, nearly a saint in Irish eyes at the time this cathedral was built.

Salmon Weir Bridge

This bridge was the local "bridge of sighs." It led from the courthouse (opposite the church) to the prison (torn down to build the cathedral). Today, the bridge provides a fun view of the fishing action. Salmon run up this river most of the summer (look for them). Fishermen, who wear waders and carry walking sticks to withstand the strong current, book long in advance to get half-day appointments for a casting spot.

Canals multiplied in this city (once called the "Venice of Ireland") to power more water mills.

OUTER GALWAY
▲Salthill

This small resort town packs pubs, discos, a splashy water park, amusement centers, and a fairground up against a fine, mile-long beach promenade (Ireland's longest). Watch for local power walkers "kicking the wall" when they reach the western end of the promenade to emphasize that they've gone the entire distance.

At the **Atlantaquaria Aquarium,** which features native Irish aquatic life and some Amazonian species, kids can help feed the fish at 13:00 (fresh water), 15:00 (big fish), 16:00 (small fish), and 17:00 (naughty kids fed to piranhas). They can cuddle the crustaceans anytime (€12, Mon-Fri 10:00-17:00, Sat-Sun until 18:00, touch tanks, The Promenade, tel. 091/585-100, www.nationalaquarium. ie).

For beach time, a relaxing sunset stroll, late-night traditional music, or later-night disco action, Salthill hops.

Getting There: To get to Salthill, catch bus #401 from Eyre Square in front of the AIB bank, next to the Meyrick Hotel (3/hour, €2).

Magdalene Laundries Memorial

Documentaries and films such as *The Magdalene Sisters* and *Philomena* have highlighted the 20th-century plight of unmarried, pregnant Irish women who were incarcerated and put to work doing laundry as virtual slaves. Viewing premarital pregnancy as one step short of prostitution, various Catholic orders operated these infamous "Magdalene laundries." (No such stigma applied to the men involved.) Across from the TI (at 47 Forster Street), a modest and easy-to-miss statue stands on the site of one such facility, operated by the Sisters of Mercy, which opened in 1824 with a capacity of 110 young women, and closed in 1984 with 18 inmates remaining. It's estimated that upwards of 10,000 women passed through the Magdalene

laundry system. Magdalene survivors claim that they were held against their will, forced to work without pay, and physically abused...and their children were sold for adoption. The Irish government apologized in 2013 for turning a blind eye to the mistreatment of these "fallen women," who were imprisoned out of sight, often with the consent of their shamed families.

Nightlife in Galway

▲TRADITIONAL IRISH MUSIC

Galway, like Dingle and Doolin, is a mecca for good Irish music (nightly 21:30-23:30). But unlike Dingle and Doolin, this is a university town (enrollment: 12,000), and many pubs are often overrun with noisy students. Still, your chances of landing a seat close to a churning band surrounded by new Irish friends are good any evening of the year.

Pubs

Touristy and student pubs are found and filled along the main drag down from Eyre Square to the Spanish Arch, and across Wolfe Tone Bridge (along William Street West and Dominick Street).

Across the Bridge: A good place to start is at **Monroe's,** with its vast, music-filled interior (check website for trad music schedule, Dominick Street, tel. 091/583-397, www.monroes.ie). Several other pubs within earshot frequently feature traditional music. **The Crane,** near Monroe's, has trad sessions nightly at 21:30 downstairs, a variety of other music upstairs, and Celtic Tales storytelling sessions on Thursdays from May to October (€10 for storytelling at 20:00, other sessions free, 2 Sea Road, tel. 091/587-419, www.thecranebar.com).

On the Main Drag: Pubs known for Irish music include **Tig Cóilí,** featuring Galway's best trad sessions (Mon-Sat at 18:00 and 22:00, Sun at 14:00 and 21:00, intersection of Main Guard Street and High Street, tel. 091/561-294); **Taaffe's** (nightly music sessions at 17:30 and 21:30, Shop Street, across from St. Nicholas Church, tel. 091/564-066); and **The Quays** (trad music most nights at 21:30, sporadic schedule, young scene, Quay Street, tel. 091/568-347). A bit off the main drag, **Barr An Chaladh** is a scruffy little place offering nightly trad or ballad sessions and more locals (3 Daly's Place, tel. 091/895-762).

Performances

Instead of a pub, you can also attend a concert or performance.

Trad on the Prom: This fine, traditional, music-and-dance troupe was started by Galway-born performers, who returned home after years of touring with *Riverdance* and the Chieftains. Their show—so popular that it's lasted for more than a decade—is a great way to enjoy live step dancing and accomplished musicians in a fairly intimate venue (€30, mid-May-Sept only, shows at 20:30 on Tue, Thu, and Sun—call to confirm, and best to reserve ahead online; at Leisureland Theatre beside Salthill Park, 30-minute walk west of town along the Salthill promenade or short ride on bus #401 from Eyre Square; tel. 091/582-860, mobile 087-674-1877, www.tradontheprom.com).

Tunes in the Church: The Collegiate Church of St. Nicholas is a mellow, medieval venue with great acoustics, hosting a rotating lineup of accomplished trad musicians. The 1.5-hour concerts are fun for early birds who don't want to stay up to catch the same great players in a local pub later that night (€15; June-July Mon-Fri at 20:00, daily in Aug; where High Street and Shop Street intersect, mobile 087-962-5425, www.tunesinthechurch.com).

GALWAY

Sleeping in Galway

There are three price tiers for most beds in Galway: off-season, high season (Easter-Oct), and charge-what-you-like festival and race weekends (see "Crowd Control" on page 326).

Note: With easy train access from Dublin, Galway is a popular weekend destination for rambunctious stag and hen parties. If you want a good night's sleep on a Friday or Saturday, steer clear of hotels with bars downstairs or nearby; instead, opt for a smaller B&B or guesthouse (I list several, though these are becoming harder to find as they struggle to compete with bigger hotels).

HOTELS

$$$$ Park House Hotel, a plush, business-class hotel, offers the best value for a fancy place. Ideally located a block from the train station and Eyre Square, it has 84 spacious rooms and all the comforts you'd expect (expensive full Irish breakfast, elevator, pay parking, great restaurant, helpful staff, Forster Street, tel. 091/564-924, www.parkhousehotel.ie, reservations@parkhousehotel.ie).

$$$$ Hotel Meyrick, filled with palatial Old World elegance and 97 rooms, marks the end of the Dublin-Galway train line and the beginning of Galway. Since 1845, it has been Galway's landmark hotel...JFK stayed here in 1963 when it was the Great Southern (at the head of Eyre Square, tel. 091/564-041, www. hotelmeyrick.ie, reshm@hotelmeyrick.ie).

$$$$ Jurys Inn Galway has 130 American-style rooms in a modern hotel, centrally located where the old town hits the river. The big, bright rooms have double beds and huge modern bathrooms (breakfast extra, elevator, lots of tour groups, pay parking, Quay Street, tel. 091/566-444, US tel. 800-423-6953, www. jurysinns.com, jurysinngalway@jurysinns.com).

¢ Kinlay Hostel is a no-nonsense place just 100 yards from the train station, with 224 beds in bare, clean, and simple rooms, including 15 doubles/twins. Easygoing people of any age feel welcome here, but if you want a double, book well ahead—several months in advance for weekends (private rooms available, elevator, baggage storage, on Merchants Road just off Eyre Square, tel. 091/565-244, www.kinlaygalway.ie, info@kinlaygalway.ie).

B&BS

These B&Bs are homey, reasonably priced, and about a 10-minute walk from Eyre Square (from the train or bus stations, walk up Forster Street, which turns into College Road). The following places are lined up like battleships and all have free parking. They're quieter than the rowdy weekend scene at bigger hotels in the city center. Although there are other B&Bs on this road, my favorites are the ones where the owner lives on-site (and whose pride of ownership shows). All B&Bs include a full "Irish fry" breakfast.

$$ Petra House is Galway's best lodging value. Consistently helpful and attentive owners Frank and Joan Maher maintain a peaceful-feeling brick building with nine fresh rooms. It's homey, lovingly maintained, and topped off by breakfasts I look forward to (family rooms, elegant sitting room, 29 College Road, tel. 091/566-580, mobile 087-451-1711, www.petrahousegalway.net, petrahouse@eircom.net).

$$ Balcony House B&B rents eight pleasant, large rooms (family rooms, 27 College Road, tel. 091/563-438, www. balconyhouse.ie, info@balconyhouse.ie). Teresa Coyne is the mellow lady of the house.

$$ Asgard Guesthouse offers eight rooms and an appealing glass-atrium breakfast room (family rooms, 21 College Road, tel. 091/566-855, www.galwaycityguesthouse.com, info@ galwaycityguesthouse.com, Mary O'Flynn).

Eating in Galway

This college town is filled with colorful, inexpensive eateries. People everywhere seem to be enjoying their food. While there are countless scruffy and touristy eateries along the main pedestrian lane, you'll eat better by getting a few blocks away from the tourists.

NEAR THE BOTTOM OF THE OLD TOWN

Each of these places is within a few minutes' walk of Jurys Inn at the river. The first four offer fine dining at a good price. Kai and the Universal are about a five-minute walk into the West End from the Wolfe Tone Bridge.

$$$ Ard Bia at Nimmo's fills an old stone warehouse behind the Spanish Arch. It's rustically elegant, with beautifully presented dishes from a farm-to-table menu. If parsnip crisps, pickled rhubarb, beetroot risotto, and pan-roasted baby squid sound good, you'll enjoy this place (open daily, café lunches 12:00-15:30, finer dinners 18:00-21:30, Long Walk Street, tel. 091/561-114 or 091/539-897, run by Aoibheann—pronounced "aye-von").

$$$ Kai Café and Restaurant is a stylish little place with a candlelit, stone-and-hardwood ambience. A café at lunch and a restaurant at dinner, it serves local foodies quirky, contemporary Irish. This is your kind of place if taste treats like Indian red pepper ratatouille, gooseberry chutney, ox tongue press, and stuffed courgette flowers are your thing. David and Jess Murphy change their menu daily, use organic ingredients, and always serve a good vegetarian dish (daily 12:00-15:00 & 18:30-22:00, reservations required for dinner, 20 Sea Road, tel. 091/526-003, www.kaicaferestaurant. com).

$$$ The Universal gastropub is another hit with Galway foodies. This feels more like a food lover's pub with an open kitchen, stools at the bar, and eight little tables. Choose tapas or full plates of creative, ingredient-driven cuisine, with lots of craft beers on tap (food served Tue-Sat 18:00-22:00, 9 William Street West, tel. 091/728-271).

$$$ The Seafood Bar at Kirwan's is a good place in the touristy center for quality seafood in a romantic setting (Mon-Sat 12:30-14:30 & 18:00-22:00, Sun 17:00-21:00, Kirwan's Lane, tel. 091/568-266, www.kirwanslane.com).

$ McDonagh's Fish-and-Chips is a favorite among residents. It has a fast, cheap, all-day **chipper** on one side and a more expensive sit-and-stay-awhile dinner-only **restaurant** on the other. The restaurant serves the same food, but you'll pay €4 extra to enjoy a nice table setting and a side of mushy peas. Both have a couple of outside tables right in the Quay Street action (chipper open Mon-Sat 12:00-23:00, Sun 14:00-21:00; restaurant open Mon-Sat 17:00-22:00, closed Sun; 22 Quay Street, tel. 091/565-001). If ordering oysters, remember Galway oysters are in season September through April, and Pacific oysters are best May through August.

$$$ Rouge is a French splurge with leather couches and live jazz or mellow music almost nightly. Instead of à la carte, you'll choose between two set menus (daily 18:00-24:00, reservations wise, 38 Lower Dominick Street, tel. 091/530-681, www. rougegalway.com).

Dessert: For ice cream, try **Murphy's**, made from locally sourced, homemade ingredients. While you'll pay a premium for even a small cup (€4.50), it's worth it for flavors like Dingle sea salt (hand-harvested) and caramelized brown bread (daily 12:00-20:00, 12 High Street).

NEAR EYRE SQUARE

$$ Galway Bakery Company (GBC) is a popular, basic place for a quick Irish meal with a self-serve buffet line (daily 8:00-18:00, later in summer, 7 Williams Gate, near Eyre Square, tel. 091/563-087). They have a simple, good-value restaurant upstairs (open later).

$$ The Lighthouse Vegetarian Café is a calm and cozy little vegetarian haven (lunch only) with creative, well-presented plates and fresh-baked goods, just steps behind Lynch's Castle (daily 12:00-17:00, 8 Abbeygate Street Upper, mobile 087-352-0198).

Supermarket: Dunnes is tucked in the Eyre Square Shopping Centre (Mon-Sat 9:00-19:00, Thu-Fri until 21:00, Sun 11:00-19:00, supermarket in basement). Lots of smaller grocery shops are scattered throughout town.

NORTH END OF COLLEGE ROAD

$$ The Huntsman Inn is an easy 10-minute walk north of my College Road B&Bs. It's modern, friendly, and far from the tourist action, with dependable dishes that draw mostly locals (daily 12:00-21:00, 164 College Road, tel. 091/562-849).

OUTSIDE GALWAY

If you have a car, consider a Dunguaire Castle medieval banquet in Kinvarra, a 30-minute drive south of Galway (for details, see page 319). You can fit in the banquet very efficiently when you're driving into Galway (B&Bs can accommodate late arrivals if you call ahead).

Galway Connections

From Galway by Train to: Dublin (8/day, 3 hours), **Limerick** (4/day, 2 hours), **Ennis** (5/day, 1.5 hours). For **Belfast, Tralee,** and **Rosslare,** you'll change in or near Dublin. Train info: Tel. 091/561-444, www.irishrail.ie.

By Bus to: Dublin (hourly, 3.5 hours; also see Citylink, below), **Kilkenny** (3/day, 5 hours), **Cork** (hourly, 4.5 hours), **Ennis** (hourly, 1.5 hours), **Shannon Airport** (hourly, 2 hours), **Cliffs of Moher** (8/day in summer, some with change in Ennis, 2 hours), **Doolin** (5/day, 1.5 hours), **Limerick** (hourly, 2 hours), **Dingle** (5/day, 6 hours), **Tralee** (8/day, 4 hours), **Westport** (6/day, 2-4 hours), **Rosslare** (2/day, 8 hours), **Belfast** (every 2 hours, 6 hours, change in Dublin), **Derry** (6/day, 5.5 hours). Bus info: Tel. 091/562-000, www.buseireann.ie.

Citylink runs cheap and fast bus service from the coach station near the TI to **Dublin** (arriving at Bachelor's Walk, a block from Tara Street DART station; hourly, 2.5 hours), **Dublin Airport** (hourly, 3 hours), and **Cork Airport** (6/day, 4 hours). Bus info: Tel. 091/564-164, www.citylink.ie.

By Car: For ideas on driving from Galway to Derry in Northern Ireland, see the Westport & Connemara chapter for a suggested sightseeing route through Connemara, and the Donegal & the Northwest chapter for some worthwhile stops farther north (near and in Donegal).

ARAN ISLANDS

Inishmore • Inisheer

Strewn like limestone chips hammered off the jagged west coast, the three Aran Islands—Inishmore, Inishmaan, and Inisheer—confront the wild Atlantic with stubborn grit ("Inish" is Irish for "island"). The largest, Inishmore ("big island," 9 miles by 2 miles), is by far the most populated, interesting, and visited. Easily reached from Galway, it's my island of choice (try to spend a night here). Inisheer ("east island") is the smallest at 1.5 miles square. Best reached from Doolin, it's worth considering for travelers with less time. Snoozing between them is Inishmaan ("middle island," 3.5 miles square and not covered in this chapter).

The landscape of all three islands is harsh. Craggy, vertical cliffs fortify the southern flanks of each island (particularly Inishmore). Windswept rocky fields, stitched together by stone walls, blanket the interiors. And the island's precious few sandy beaches hide in coves that dimple the northern shores. During the winter, severe gales sweep through; because of this, most of the settlements on the islands are found on the more sheltered northeastern side.

There's a stark beauty about the Aran Islands and the simple lives their inhabitants eke out of a mean sea and less than six inches of topsoil. Precious little of the land is productive. In the past, people made a precarious living here from fishing and farming. The scoured bedrock offered little in the way of soil, so it was created by the islanders—the result of centuries of layering seaweed with limestone sand and animal dung. Fields are small, divided by several thousand miles of "drystone" wall (made without mortar). Most of these are built in the Aran "gap" style, in which spaces between angled upright stones are filled with smaller stones. This allows a farmer who wants to move livestock to dismantle a short section of wall as a temporary gate, and then rebuild that section afterward. It also allows the harsh winter winds to blow through without knocking down the wall. Nowadays, tourism boosts the islands' economy.

The islands are a Gaeltacht area. While the islanders speak Irish among themselves, they happily speak English for their visitors. Many islanders have direct, personal connections with close relatives in America. I once met an Aran minivan driver who served in the US Navy aboard a destroyer before coming back home to Inishmore. Five of his six children now have American passports.

Today, the 800 people of Inishmore greet as many as 2,000 visitors a day. The vast majority of these are daytrippers. They'll hop on a minivan at the dock for a 2.5-hour visit to Dun Aengus (the must-see Iron Age fort), grab a simple lunch, and then spend an hour or two browsing through the few shops or sitting at a picnic table outside a pub with a pint of Guinness. Inisheer and Inishmaan are smaller, much less populated, and less touristy. While relatively quiet, they do have B&Bs, daily flights, and ferry service. For most, Inishmore is quiet enough—though Inisheer is slowly gaining steam as an alternative to the big island.

Inishmore

The largest of the Aran Islands has a blockbuster sight: the striking Dun Aengus fort, set on a sheer cliff. Everyone arrives at Kilronan, the Aran Islands' biggest town, though it's just a village. Groups of backpackers wash ashore with the docking of each ferry. Minivans, bike shops, and a few men in pony carts sop up the tourists.

PLANNING YOUR TIME

Most travelers visit Inishmore (Inis Mór) as a day trip by boat from Galway. (Boats from distant Doolin are slower and weather-dependent, allowing less time for a same-day round-trip to Inishmore.) Here's a good framework for a day trip: Leave Galway at 9:00 on the shuttle bus to Rossaveal, where you'll catch the 10:30 boat. You'll step off the boat in Kilronan at about 11:15. Arrange minivan transport or rent a bike, visit Dun Aengus, and grab a bite at one of the two simple cafés near the base of the Dun Aengus fort trail (or bring a picnic). Explore the island during low tide, and depart on the boat when high tides return between 16:00 and 18:00. You can squeeze an extra three to four hours out of your day trip by booking an early flight over and a late flight back from Connemara Regional Airport, near Rossaveal. For more details on these options, see "Aran Islands Connections" at the end of this chapter.

Staying Overnight: Travelers spending the night can savor the quiet time before and after the day-trip crowds. Here's how I'd suggest you spend your arrival day: Since most day-trippers make a beeline straight off the boat to Dun Aengus, head in the opposite direction to check out the subtle charms of the less-visited eastern end of the island. Buy a picnic at the Spar supermarket in Kilronan. Then walk to either the ruins of tiny St. Benen's Church (an easy 45-minute hike one way from Kilronan) or the rugged Black Fort ruins (a rocky 1-hour scramble one way from Kilronan). Save Dun Aengus for later in the afternoon, after the midday crowds have subsided. Enjoy an evening in the pubs and take a no-rush midmorning boat trip or flight back to the mainland the next day.

Orientation to Inishmore

Your first stop on Inishmore is the town of Kilronan, huddling around the pier. There are about a dozen shops and B&Bs, about half as many restaurants, and a couple of **bike-rental huts** (regular 21-speed bikes about €10/day plus €10 deposit, electric bikes €25/day plus €20 deposit).

A few blocks inland up the high road, you'll find the best folk-music **pub** (Joe Watty's), a **post office**, and a tiny **bank** across from the roofless Anglican church ruins.

A friendly **café/shop** with free Wi-Fi lurks on the back side of the stony Aran Sweater Market building, across from the high cross (daily 10:00-20:00, shorter hours off-season; also has Irish lessons for tourists, a detailed map for hikers, and the *Man of Aran* film described below). Public **WCs** are 100 yards beyond the TI (see below) on the harbor road.

The huge Spar **supermarket,** two blocks inland from the harbor, seems too big for the tiny community and has the island's only **ATM.** If you don't have plenty of cash on you, get some here—most B&Bs and quite a few other businesses don't accept credit cards.

TOURIST INFORMATION

Kilronan's TI is helpful (daily 10:00-17:00, may close during lunch, shorter hours in winter, faces the harbor, tel. 099/61263). The free map given out by the TI or ferry operator is all the average day-tripper or leisure biker will need to navigate. But serious hikers who plan on scampering out to the island's craggy fringes will want to invest in the detailed black-and-white *Oileáin Árann* map and companion book by Tim Robinson (€16, sold at the Man of Aran Coffee & Craft Shop behind the Aran Sweater Market, and at some bookstores in Galway).

Events: Late June is when Inishmore shakes off its slumber and kicks up its heels. The **Patrún** is a three-day annual celebra-

ARAN ISLANDS

Currach and *Navogue* Boats

These are the traditional fishing boats of the west coast of Ireland—lightweight and easy to haul. In your coastal travels,

you'll see a few actual *currach* or *navogue* boats—generally retired and stacked where visitors can touch them and ponder the simpler age when they were a key part of the economy. The *currach* is native to the Aran Islands, while the *navogue* is native to the Dingle Peninsula. It's primarily a case of semantics and, to us, they look almost the same. But a fisherman would build a boat to suit his needs: a higher bow to deal with more surf, higher sides to lean over when pulling up lobster pots, a flat stern, etc. Few raw materials were needed to make the boats: a wooden frame with canvas (originally cowhide) and paint with tar. But the skill in making them came from generations of fine-tuning by fishermen who knew their environment intimately. The advantage of both boats was maneuverability on the sea and ease in getting them in and out of the water (the seamanship of these skilled sailors is too often underestimated). Their disadvantage was their fragility when hauling anything other than men or fish. When transporting sheep, farmers would lash each sheep's pointy little hooves together and place it carefully upside-down in the *currach*—so it wouldn't puncture the frail little craft's canvas skin.

tion during the last weekend in June (*currach* boat races, Galway "hooker" boat races, fun run). June 23 is **St. John's Eve Bonfire Night,** a Christian/pagan tradition held the night before St. John's Day, close to (but not on) the summer solstice. Each community stokes a raging fire around dusk, and dozens are visible not only on the island, but also on the distant shore of Connemara.

GETTING AROUND INISHMORE

Just about anything on wheels functions as a taxi here. A trip from Kilronan to Dun Aengus to the Seven Churches and back to Kilronan costs €15 per person in a shared minivan. Pony carts cost about €50 for two people (€80 for 4) for a trip to Dun Aengus and back.

Biking is great. Before heading out, check that your bike seat is set at the correct height and stable enough so that you can fully extend both legs as you pedal. (The most frequent bike rental complaint is a seat that won't stay in place and slowly slips down... cramping your legs when you're far down the island.) Take it for a short test spin while you're still near the rental shop.

Novice bikers should be aware that the terrain is hilly and there are occasional headwinds and unpredictable showers (figure 30 minutes to ride from Kilronan to start of trailhead up to Dun Aengus). Cyclists should take the high road over and the low road back—fewer hills, scenic shoreline, and at low tide, a dozen seals basking in the sun.

Keep a sharp lookout along the roads for handy, modern limestone signposts (with distances in kilometers) that point the way to important sights. They're in Irish, but you'll be clued in by the small metal depictions of the sights embedded within them.

Tours on Inishmore

▲▲Island Minivan Tours

Fewer than 100 vehicles roam the island, and most of them seem to be minivans. A line of vans (seating 8-18 passengers) awaits the

arrival of each ferry, offering €15 island tours. They're basically a shared taxi service that will take you to the various sights, drop you off, and return at an agreed time to take you to the next attraction.

Chat with a few drivers to find one who likes to talk. On my tour, I learned that 800 islanders live in 14 villages (actually just crossroads), with three elementary schools and three churches. Most islanders own a small detached field where they keep a couple of cows (sheep are too much trouble). When pressed for more information, my guide explained that there are 400 types of flowers and 19 types of bees on the island. Then he pointed to the 2,000-year-old ring fort on the hilltop and grinned, saying, "It's so popular with visitors that we plan to build another 2,000-year-old ring fort next year."

The tour, a convenient time-saver, zips you to the end of the island for a quick stroll in the desolate fields, gives you 15 minutes to wander through the historic but visually unimpressive Seven Churches, and then drops you off for two hours at Dun Aengus (30 minutes to hike up, 30 minutes at the fort, 20-minute hike back down, 40 minutes in café for lunch or shopping at drop-off point) before running you back to Kilronan. These sights can be linked together in various sequences, but the trailhead crossroads below Dun Aengus—with two cafés—makes the best lunch stop. Ask your driver to take you back along the smaller coastal road (scenic beaches and sunbathing seals at low tide).

Audio Tours

Visitors can rent a mobile phone-size audioguide for a day. Its clear and informative commentary covers the island's major sights, and it comes with a numbered, color-coded map to follow along with. The audioguide offers more scholarly, bite-sized info segments and is no substitute for the fun and colorful ad-libbing by a local minivan driver or pony cart handler. But it's particularly useful for bikers and hikers, who are not being driven around the island by a local (€8/day, rent from recommended Bayview Restaurant facing harbor, tel. 086/792-9925).

Sights and Activities on Inishmore

IN KILRONAN
Man of Aran Film

This Oscar-winning 1934 movie (1.25 hours) is a documentary, partly staged, about traditional island life. It's basically a silent movie, with an all-local cast and the sounds of surf, seagull, and sailor (muttering in barely audible Irish) dubbed in. It's a strangely fascinating glimpse of the past and was groundbreaking in its time. The movie tries to re-create life in the early 1900s—when you couldn't rent bikes—and features *currach*s (canoe-like boats) in a storm, shark fishing with handheld harpoons, kids fishing off cliffs, and farmers creating soil and cultivating the patches from bare rock. But make this film a rainy-day option: Don't waste time indoors when the real thing is right outside at your feet.

Cost and Hours: €5, 3 showings/day—usually on request, plays in café (upstairs) behind Aran Sweater Market—see page 343 for hours.

Irish Lessons: Gearóid (pronounced gair-OH-id), who runs the café, also teaches one-hour Irish lessons to tourists for €5. Learn how to say "please" and "thank you," order a beer, and more in this unusual language (don't worry, he writes everything down phonetically).

Music

Kilronan's pubs offer music sporadically on summer nights. Nothing is dependably scheduled, so ask at your B&B or look for posted notices on the front of the Spar supermarket or post office. **Joe Watty's Bar,** on the high road 100 yards past the post office, is worth the 10-minute walk from the dock. Its appealing front porch goes great with a pint, and Irish folk music warms the interior most nights. The more central **Joe Mac's Pub** (next to the hostel) and **The Bar** (next to the high cross at the base of the high road) are also possibilities.

BEYOND THE TOWN
▲▲▲Dun Aengus (Dún Aonghasa)

This is the island's blockbuster sight. The stone fortress hangs spectacularly and precariously on the edge of a cliff 200 feet above the Atlantic. The crashing waves seem to say, "You've come to the end of the world." Gaze out to sea and consider this: Off this coast, Hy-Brasil—a phantom island cloaked in mist—was said to pop into view once every seven years. This mythical place appeared on maps as late as the mid-1800s.

Little is known about this 2,000-year-old Iron Age fort. Its concentric walls are 13 feet thick and 10 feet high. As an added defense, the fort is ringed with a commotion of spiky stones, sticking up like lances, called *chevaux-de-frise* (literally, "Frisian horses," named for the Frisian soldiers who used pikes to stop charging cavalry). Slowly, as the cliff erodes, hunks of the fort fall into the sea.

Dun Aengus doesn't get crowded until after 11:00. I enjoyed a half-hour completely alone at 10:00 in the height of tourist season; if you can, get there early or late. A small visitors center (housing the ticket office and controlling access to the trail) displays aerial views of the fort and tells the story of its inhabitants. Trail access to the fort is open and free when the visitors center is closed.

Cost and Hours: €5; daily March-Oct 9:30-18:00, off-season until 16:00, closed Mon-Tue in Jan-Feb; last entry one hour before closing, during June-Aug guides at the trailhead answer questions and can sometimes give free tours up at the fort if you call ahead, 5.5 miles from Kilronan, tel. 099/61008.

Warnings: Like the Burren (its nearby mainland limestone cousin), this is rocky, irregular ground with primitive steps of varying heights and some smooth surfaces that can get slippery when wet. The trail is gravel for the first half of the hike and lined with rock walls (you can't get lost). But watch your step on bare rock—some stable-looking rocks can be surprisingly shaky. Rangers advise visitors to wear sturdy walking shoes and watch kids closely; there's no fence between you and a crumbling 200-foot cliff overlooking the sea. Also, be very careful about unexpected gusts of

ARAN ISLANDS

wind and uncertain footing near the edge. The Irish don't believe in litigation, just natural selection.

Seven Churches (Na Seacht Teampaill)

Close to the western tip of the island, this gathering of ruined chapels, monastic houses, and fragments of a high cross dates from the 8th to 11th century. Inishmore is dotted with reminders that Christianity was brought to the islands in the fifth century by St. Enda, who established a monastery here. Many great monks studied under Enda. Among these "Irish apostles" who started Ireland's "Age of Saints and Scholars" (A.D. 500-900) was Columba (Colmcille in Irish), the founder of a monastery on the island of Iona in Scotland—home of the Irish monks who produced the Book of Kells. Check out the ornate gravestones (best detail on sunny days) of the "seven Romans," located in the slightly elevated back corner of the graveyard, farthest from the road. These pilgrims came here from Rome in the ninth century, long after the fall of the Roman Empire.

Kilmurvey

The island's second-largest village nestles below Dun Aengus. More a simple crossroads than a village, it sports two soup-and-sandwich cafés, a gaggle of homes, and a great sheltered swimming beach with a blue flag. Throughout Ireland, "blue flag" beaches proclaim clean water, safe currents, and the color of your toes when you shiver back to your towel. This is the place for peaceful solitude. Located on the narrowest section of the island, it also has the best grazing land, a fact not lost on the local landlord who claimed it for himself.

The Worm Hole (Poll na bPeist)

Off the beaten path and accessible only by hiking, this site (also called the "Serpent's Lair") takes the "logic" out of geo-*logic*. It's a large, perfectly rectangular, 40-by-100-foot seawater-filled pool (60 feet deep) that was cut by nature into the flat coastal bedrock. You'd swear that God used a cake knife to cut out this massive slab—just to mess with us. But limestone often fractures at right angles. So, the Worm Hole was formed when the roof of the hidden cave underneath (cut by tidal action) collapsed just so. To add to the surreal scene, Red Bull has featured this site several times in its annual cliff-diving competition from the 90-foot cliff above it (search YouTube for thrilling video clips).

Boulder-hopping your way across the narrowest section of the island, you'll find the Worm Hole beneath the island's southern cliffs, one mile straight south of Kilmurvey's fine beach. Consult your map and start with the primitive gravel lane leading in the direction of the tiny inland community of Gort na gCapall. From there you'll be using dead reckoning. It's signposted from the Main Road as *Pol na bPeist*, but Tim Robinson's detailed map (see "Tourist Information," earlier) is handy for navigating here.

Aran Artisan Garden

This private residence and garden should be viewed from the road only (please respect their privacy...they're not trying to get famous). It's a "back to basics" family homestead, fronted by a creative garden (spelling out "LOVE" in block letters), and inspired by an appreciation of a holistic lifestyle. It's a refreshing addition to the island landscape that blends in beautifully. To better appreciate it, check out Melissa Gillian's blog (www.thearanartisan.com). The garden is located about halfway between Kilronan and Kilmurvey, downhill on the right side if you are heading west on the High Road.

Ancient Sites near Killeany

The quiet eastern end of Inishmore offers ancient sites in evocative settings for overnight visitors with more time, or for those seeking rocky hikes devoid of crowds. First, get a good hiking map. Then consider assembling a picnic, to fuel up either before or after you spend a couple of hours exploring these sights on foot. Ask the folks in town for directions (almost always a memorable experience in Ireland).

Closest to the road, amid the dunes one mile past the Tigh Fitz B&B and just south of the airport, is the eighth-century **St. Enda's Church** (Teaghlach Einne). Protected from wave erosion by a stubborn breakwater, it sits half-submerged in a sandy graveyard, surrounded by a sea of sawgrass and peppered with tombstones. St. Enda is said to be buried here, along with 125 other saints who flocked to Inishmore in the fifth century to learn from him.

St. Benen's Church (Teampall Bheanáin) perches high on a desolate ridge opposite the Tigh Fitz B&B. Walk up the stone-walled lane, passing a holy well and the stubby remains of a round tower. Then take another visual fix on the church's silhouette on the horizon, and zigzag up the stone terraces to the top. The 30-minute hike up from the B&B pays off with a great view. Dedicated to St. Benen, a young disciple of St. Patrick himself, this tiny (12-by-6-foot) 10th-century oratory is aligned north-south (instead of the usual east-west) to protect the doorway from prevailing winds. It's

thought that this structure was built, not as a place to say Mass, but primarily to house holy relics (a splinter from Christ's cross, a thorn from his crown, etc.), which at the time were highly sought after. Also, its prominent location served something like a beacon to those many pilgrims who had made the arduous journey to this remote holy island on the edge of the then-known world.

About a five-minute walk past the Tigh Fitz B&B (on your left as you head toward the airport), you'll notice an abandoned stone pier and an adjacent, modest medieval ruin. This was **Arkin Fort,** built by Cromwell's soldiers in 1652 using cut stones taken from the round tower and the monastic ruins that once stood below St. Benen's Church. The fort was used as a prison for outlawed priests before they were sent by English authorities to the West Indies to be sold into slavery.

Hidden on a remote, ragged headland an hour's walk from Kilronan to the south side of the island, you'll find the **Black Fort** (Dún Duchathair). After Dun Aengus, this is Inishmore's most dramatic fortification. A good map is essential to navigate here. Built on a promontory with cliffs on three sides, its defenders would have held out behind drystone ramparts, facing the island's interior attackers. Watch your step on the uneven ground, be ready to course-correct as you go, and chances are you'll have this wind-swept ruin all to yourself. Imagine the planning and cooperative effort that went into building these life-saving structures 2,000 years ago, before Gore-Tex and granola bars.

Sleeping on Inishmore

All of the following places are in Kilronan. Remember, this is a rustic island. Many rooms are plain, with simple plumbing. Luxury didn't make the leap from the mainland.

$$ The Aran Islands (Ostan Aran) Hotel is the most modern option on the island. Its 20 rooms (four with large harbor-facing porches) have the comforts you'd expect. Beware of loud weekend stag/hen parties drawn to their downstairs pub (tel. 099/61104, www.aranislandshotel.com, info@aranislandshotel.com, 10-minute walk east of the dock on the coast road heading toward Killeany).

$$ The Pier House stands solidly, 50 yards from the pier, offering 12 decent rooms, a good restaurant downstairs, and sea views from many of its rooms (tel. 099/61417, www.pierhousearan. com, pierhousearan@gmail.com).

$ Clai Ban, the only really cheery place in town, is run by friendly Marion and Bartley Hernon. Their six rooms and warm hospitality are worth the 10-minute uphill walk from the pier. The place is energized by their affectionate adolescent hound, Porter (cash only, family rooms, walk past bank out of town and up the

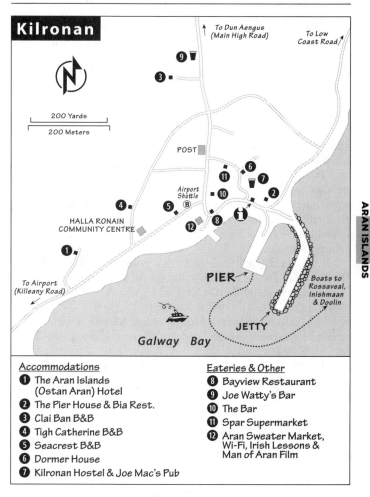

Kilronan

To Dun Aengus (Main High Road)

To Low Coast Road

POST

Airport Shuttle

HALLA RONAIN COMMUNITY CENTRE

To Airport (Killeany Road)

PIER

Boats to Rossaveal, Inishmaan & Doolin

JETTY

Galway Bay

200 Yards
200 Meters

ARAN ISLANDS

Accommodations
1 The Aran Islands (Ostan Aran) Hotel
2 The Pier House & Bia Rest.
3 Clai Ban B&B
4 Tigh Catherine B&B
5 Seacrest B&B
6 Dormer House
7 Kilronan Hostel & Joe Mac's Pub

Eateries & Other
8 Bayview Restaurant
9 Joe Watty's Bar
10 The Bar
11 Spar Supermarket
12 Aran Sweater Market, Wi-Fi, Irish Lessons & Man of Aran Film

50-yard-long lane on left, tel. 099/61111, claibanhouse@gmail.com).

$ Tigh Catherine is a well-kept B&B with four homey rooms overlooking the harbor (cash only, on Church Road up behind the Halla Ronain community center, tel. 099/61464, mobile 087-980-9748, catherineandstiofain@gmail.com, Catherine Mulkerrin).

$ Seacrest B&B offers six uncluttered rooms in a central location behind the Aran Sweater Market (cash only, tel. 099/61292, mobile 087-161-6507, seacrestaran@gmail.com, Geraldine and Tom Faherty).

$ Dormer House is centrally located and not particularly hung up on modern communication technology (no Internet, only phone). But Alice Joyce has run it for 30 years and prices her rooms fairly. They're on par with the neat, no-frills vibe of the rest of the options in town (cash only, next to Spar Market, tel. 099/61125).

¢ **Kilronan Hostel,** overlooking the harbor near the TI, is cheap but noisy above Joe Mac's Pub (tel. 099/61255, www. kilronanhostel.com, kilronanhostel@gmail.com).

Eating on Inishmore

There are few restaurants in Kilronan and none are fancy. Plan on comfort food at reasonable prices.

The island's most central and stylish (a relative term) option is the **Bayview Restaurant**, standing proudly purple beside the high cross. Soup, salads, burgers, and pizza fuel up tired bikers and hikers (daily 12:00-21:00, tel. 086/792-9925). This is also where you can rent audioguides for touring the island (described earlier, under "Tours on Inishmore").

I like the friendly vibe and tasty grub up the hill at **$$ Joe Watty's Bar.** Try the chicken goulash with a pint and stick around for the music (daily April-Oct 12:30-15:30 & 17:00-21:00, tel. 099/20892, pleasant front-porch seating).

The **Aran Islands Hotel** has a modern **$$ pub** serving simple soup-and-sandwich lunches and hot dinners (daily 12:00-21:00, tel. 099/61104).

The Pier House operates the dependable **$$$ Bia Restaurant** on the ground floor of its guesthouse (daily May-Sept 11:00-21:30, tel. 099/61811).

Otherwise, Kilronan's modest cafés dish up hearty soup, soda bread, sandwiches, and tea.

Supermarket: The **Spar** has all the groceries you'll need (Mon-Sat 9:00-18:00, Sun 10:00-17:00).

Inisheer

The roughly circular little island of Inisheer (Inis Oírr) has less than a quarter of the land area and population of Inishmore. But Inisheer's close proximity to the mainland makes it an easy 35-minute boat journey from Doolin and a good option for those with limited time who aren't going north to Galway.

Inisheer offers a vivid glimpse of Aran Island culture and has an engaging smorgas-

Inisheer

To Inishmaan & Inishmore

To Doolin

Galway Bay

PIER

SEAL COLONY

ST. CAVAN'S CHURCH

AIRSTRIP

Lake

O'BRIEN'S CASTLE

Hidden Valley

NAPOLEONIC TOWER

Cliffs

SHIPWRECK

Cliffs

LIGHTHOUSE

1 Kilometer

1 Mile

ARAN ISLANDS

❶ South Aran House

❷ Bru Hostel Radharc na Mara & Tigh Ned Pub

❸ Tigh Rauraí Pub

❹ Ostan Inis Oírr Pub & Grocery

❺ South Aran Restaurant

bord of salty but modest sights. It's also slowly gaining in popularity as an alternative to Inishmore. Inisheer is now being combined with the Cliffs of Moher on some Galway-based bus/boat/bus day tours. Also, boat service from the mainland is becoming more dependable following completion of a second pier at Doolin, allowing Inisheer to siphon off some of the summer crowds from Inishmore.

Planning Your Time: Take an early boat from Doolin to maximize your time on Inisheer. For more details, see "Aran Islands Connections" at the end of this chapter.

Orientation to Inisheer

You'll dock on the north side of the island in its only settlement. Facing inland with your back to the pier, you'll be able to see nearly all of the island's landmarks (except for the *An Plassy* shipwreck and the lighthouse on the southern shore). Although some pony carts and minivan drivers meet you at the pier, I'd rely on them only on a rainy day (€10).

For me, the joy of compact Inisheer is seeing it on a bike ride or a long breezy walk. The bike-rental outfit is right at the base of the pier (€10/2 hours, €12/day, tel. 099/75049, www.rothai-inisoirr. com, no deposit necessary "unless you look suspicious"). Any of the boat operators in Doolin can give you a free map of the island showing Inisheer's primitive road network. That's all you'll need to navigate.

There are three pubs on the island, one small grocery store, and no ATMs. All of the sights, with the exception of the lonely lighthouse on the southern coast, are concentrated on the northern half.

Inisheer lacks the dramatic (and much higher) coastal cliffs of Inishmore, but has its own unique photogenic charms. Fans of the 1990s British sitcom *Father Ted* may recognize parts of the island, which were featured in the show's intro depicting its fictional Craggy Island location.

Sights on Inisheer

The following sights are free, open all the time, and marked on your free boat company map. See them in the order listed, from west to east, across the northern half of the island. If you bike rather than hike, be prepared to walk the bike up (or down) short, steep hills.

O'Brien's Castle (Caislean Ui Bhriain)

The ruins of this castle dominate the hilltop and are visible from almost anywhere on the northern half of the island. It's a steep 20-minute walk from the pier up to the castle ruins. The small castle was built as a tower house refuge around 1400 by the O'Brien clan from nearby County Clare. It sits inside a low wall of a much older Iron Age ring fort. Cromwell's troops destroyed the castle in 1652, leaving the evocative ruins you see today.

If you've huffed your way up to O'Brien's Castle, then go another easy five minutes to the **Napoleonic Tower (An Tur Faire),** which was built in the early 1800s to watch for a feared French invasion that never took place. The views from this highest point on the island are worth it.

• *Consult your map and continue walking (south) on the paved road into the heart of the island. Take your first right turn, roughly 100 yards* *after the Napoleonic Tower, onto a rocky, grassy cow lane that zigzags downhill into a lush **hidden valley**, displaying the prettiest mosaic of ivy-tangled rock walls and small green fields I've seen anywhere on the Aran Islands.*

Once you've wound your way back down to the main north-shore road again, turn right and continue east with the airstrip on your left. On your right, you'll soon see a time-passed graveyard up atop a sandy hill. Hike the 50 yards up into the graveyard to find...

St. Cavan's Church (Teampall Chaomhain)

St. Cavan was the brother of St. Kevin, who founded the monastery at Glendalough in the Wicklow Mountains (see page 139). In the middle of the graveyard is a sunken sandpit holding the rugged, roofless remains of an 11th-century church. The shifting sand dunes almost buried it before sawgrass stabilized the hill. St. Cavan's reputed gravesite is protected by a tiny modern structure worth poking your head into for its candlelit atmosphere. Local folklore held that if you spent a night sleeping on the tomb lid, your particular illness would be cured.

• *Walk back down to the north-shore road and head out on the coast road (to the southeast) 30 minutes to the remote...*

Shipwreck of the *An Plassy*

This freighter was wrecked offshore on Finn's Rock in 1960. But islanders worked with the coastal patrol to help rescue the crew with no loss of life. A couple of weeks later the unmanned ship was washed high up onto the rocky shore, where it still sits today, a rusty but fairly intact ghost ship with a broken back. The fierce winter winds and record-breaking waves of 2013 shifted the wreck, further weakening it, and discussions are under way to remove it as it deteriorates. A local told me, "We may have to go out some night with lanterns to bring in a new shipwreck."

Beware of unstable footing on the rounded cobbles thrown up by the surf near the wreck. It's extremely dangerous to touch the wreck, and those trying to climb it are begging for a rusty puncture wound...or worse.

• *With more time, consult your map and seek out the remaining intimate little church ruins and holy wells that the island has to offer. Or head back to town for a beverage while you await the return ferry.*

ARAN ISLANDS

Sleeping on Inisheer

A scattering of B&Bs dots the northern half of the island. Here are two good options:

$ South Aran House is a quiet, well-run place with five spic-and-span, black-and-white rooms. Humorous Enda and friendly Maria Conneely are generous with local tips and also run the nearby South Aran Restaurant, where you'll have breakfast (easy 10-minute walk west of pier on north-shore road, call ahead with your ferry arrival time so they can meet you with keys, tel. 099/75073, mobile 087-340-5687, www.southaran.com, info@southaran.com). Their small rental cottage sleeps two.

¢ Bru Hostel Radharc na Mara is a simple, economical, 40-bed option just 100 yards west of the pier, next to Tigh Ned Pub. They also offer five basic doubles in their adjacent B&B directly behind (includes continental breakfast, open mid-March-Oct, tel. 099/75024, radharcnamara@hotmail.com).

Eating on Inisheer

Inisheer's three main pubs offer decent pub grub (usually 12:30-20:30). **$$ Tigh Rauraí Pub** (House of Rory) is the epicenter of island social life (from the pier, head east to the edge of the beach and turn right—inland—up a narrow lane for 100 yards). Just below it, closer to the beach, **$$ Ostan Inis Oírr Pub** (Hotel Inisheer) sports a colorful collage of international flags draping the pub's ceiling and stag/hen parties on weekends. **$$$ Tigh Ned Pub** (House of Ned) is right next door to the hostel, near the pier on the north-shore road. Life could be worse than to sit outside at their appealing front tables on a summer evening, enjoying a pint in the salt air.

For a mellow evening meal, try the **$$ South Aran Restaurant,** a five-minute walk west of the pier on the north-shore road (daily 18:00-21:00, tel. 099/75073, mobile 087-340-5687).

Picnic lovers flock to the island's small **grocery,** Siopa XL, behind Ostan Inis Oírr Pub and below Tigh Rauraí Pub (Mon-Sat 9:00-18:00, Sun 10:00-14:00).

Aran Islands Connections

For an overview map of the region, see page 299.

BY FERRY
From Rossaveal (near Galway)

Island Ferries sails to Inishmore from the port of Rossaveal, 20 miles west of Galway. The company runs a shuttle bus from Galway to the Rossaveal dock (3/day April-Oct, 2/day Nov-March, bus ride and ferry crossing each takes 45 minutes; coming from Galway, allow 2 hours total; €25 round-trip boat crossing plus €9 round-trip for shuttle bus, 10 percent discount if you book online, WCs on board). Catch shuttle buses from Galway on Queen Street, a block behind the Kinlay Hostel (check-in 1.5 hours before sailing); shuttles return to Galway immediately after each boat arrives. Ferry schedule for mid-April-Sept: from Rossaveal at 10:30, 13:00, and 18:30; from Inishmore at 8:15 (9:00 on Sun), 12:00, and 17:00 (plus 16:00 in June and 18:30 in July-Aug). Island Ferries has two offices in Galway: on Forster Street across from the TI and at 19 Eyre Square (tel. 091/568-903, after-hours tel. 091/572-273, www.aranislandferries.com).

Note: The boat you take out to the islands may not be the same as the one you come back on. And sometimes you'll board by walking up the gangplank of one boat and walking across its deck to another boat docked beside or behind it. Make sure to ask.

Driving to Rossaveal: Drivers should go straight to the ferry landing in Rossaveal, passing several ticket agencies and pay parking lots. At the boat dock, you'll find a convenient €8/day lot and an office that sells tickets for Island Ferries (with better WCs than on the ferry). Check to see what's going when and for how much.

From Doolin

Boats from Doolin sail to all three Aran Islands. However, service is patchier and less reliable than the bigger boats out of Rossaveal—though recent completion of a second, deeper-water pier at Doolin has improved things, as boats are less at the mercy of the tides that bedeviled crossings from the original port.

While it's possible to travel from Doolin to Inishmore and back in one day, keep in mind that it's a long trip to distant Inishmore (1.25 hours compared with 45 minutes from Rossaveal), leaving less time ashore. Instead, consider an overnight stay on Inishmore, or opt for a day trip to nearby, though less spectacular, Inisheer.

Parking in Doolin: With a car, Doolin is easy to reach; without one, it's better to get to Inishmore from Rossaveal. Parking at the Doolin dock is pay-and-display (€1/2 hours, €5 overnight). Give yourself enough time to deal with parking and the line to pay at the machine.

Buying Tickets: The scene at the Doolin ferry dock is a confusing mosh pit of competition. Two ferry companies operate from three ticket huts with one thing in mind: snaring your business. They have similar schedules and prices.

Doolin2Aran Ferries is run by the Garrihy family (to Inishmore: €25 round-trip, 1.25 hours, generally departs Doolin at

10:00, 11:00, and 13:00, departs Inishmore at 11:30 and 16:00; to Inisheer: €20 same-day round-trip, 30 minutes, departs Doolin at 10:00, 11:00, 13:00, and 17:30, departs Inisheer at 8:30, 12:15, 14:00, and 16:45. They also offer a fun €35 triangular day trip that takes you from Doolin to Inisheer, drops you off on Inisheer for about 3.5 hours, then sails along the base of the Cliffs of Moher before docking back in Doolin (departs at 10:00 and 11:00, has you back in Doolin by 16:45, runs April-Oct, tel. 065/707-5949, mobile 087-245-3239, www.doolin2aranferries.com).

Doolin Ferry/O'Brien Line, run by Bill O'Brien, has been at it the longest, with similar schedules and occasionally cheaper prices. They also offer a cruise along the base of the Cliffs of Moher that includes a stop at Inisheer (tel. 065/707-5618, www.obrienline. com).

No matter which company you choose, it's smart to check on-line for discounts. It's also important to double-check schedules, arrive at least 15 minutes early, be alert, and be patient. Boats can be 30 minutes late...or 10 minutes early. You're on Irish time.

For details on staying in Doolin, see page 312.

BY PLANE

Aer Arann Islands, a friendly and flexible little airline, flies daily from Connemara Regional Airport, serving all three islands (3/

day, up to 11/day in peak season, €25 one-way, €49 round-trip, groups of 4 or more pay €44 each, 10-minute flight, tel. 091/593-034, www. aerarannislands.ie, info@ aerarannislands.ie). These eight-seat planes get booked up—reserve as soon as you are sure of your dates (by email, with a credit card). Note that the baggage weight limit is 40 pounds total, so pack an overnight bag and leave your remaining clothes (but not your valuables) locked in the trunk of your car or stored in your Galway hotel.

You can charter a sightseeing-only Aer Arann flight that leaves from the same airport (by reservation only). Cruising at 500 feet, you'll fly above all three Aran Islands with an extra swoop past the Cliffs of Moher (€960 for seven-passenger air-craft, 35 minutes).

Getting to and from the Airports: Connemara Regional Airport is 20 slow miles west of Galway—allow 45 minutes for the drive, plus 30 minutes to check in before the scheduled departure. A minibus shuttle—€5 one-way—runs from Victoria Hotel off Eyre Square in Galway an hour before each flight. Be sure to reserve a space on the shuttle bus at the same time you book your flight. The Kilronan airport on Inishmore is minuscule. A minibus shuttle (€3 one-way, €5 round-trip) travels the two miles between the airport and Kilronan (stop is behind the Aran Sweater Market).

WESTPORT & CONNEMARA

Cong • Westport • Connemara Loop Drive Sights • East of Connemara

If you have a car, consider spending a day exploring the wild western Irish fringe known as Connemara. The best home base in this area is the prim and charming town of Westport (home to a pub owned by a member of the traditional Irish music group the Chieftains). From here, you can easily reach the highlights of Connemara. Hike the peak of Croagh Patrick, the mountain from which St. Patrick supposedly banished the snakes from Ireland. Pass through the desolate Doo Lough Valley on a road stained with tragic famine history. Bounce on a springy peat bog.

This beautiful area also claims a couple of towns—Cong and Leenane—where classic Irish movies were filmed, as well as the photogenic Kylemore Abbey. At the end of the chapter, I've also described a few interesting stops east of Westport, including a Virgin Mary shrine and the thoughtful Irish National Famine Museum.

PLANNING YOUR TIME

By Car: The Connemara area makes a satisfying day trip by car from Galway. I've listed the region's prime towns and sights in a loop that starts and ends in Galway (driving north, then back south). But drivers who are aiming for Northern Ireland from Galway can easily modify the loop route and still see the main sights. Both routes are described next.

Without a Car: It's most efficient to take a **day tour** from Galway. Three Galway-based organizations—Galway Tour Company, Lally Tours, and Healy Tours—run all-day tours of nearby regions. Most tours of Connemara include the Quiet Man Museum in Cong, Kylemore Abbey, Clifden, and a "famine village" (or some combination of these places). Tours go most days, heading out at 10:00 and returning at 17:30 (call to confirm exact itinerary, see page 328 for contact information).

Public transportation in this region (except to and from Westport) is patchy, and some areas are not served at all. Buses run between Galway and Westport, but by train you must connect through Dublin.

CONNEMARA DRIVING ROUTES

Connemara Loop Drive (from Galway)

With a long and well-organized day, you can loop around from Galway and enjoy the most important sights of Connemara (five hours of driving and 200 miles). You'll be thankful you picked up a good map before departing. For maximum coverage, lace together the sights described in this chapter in a route that goes in this order: Cong, Westport, Murrisk, Louisburgh, through the Doo Lough Valley to Leenane, then on to Clifden (passing Kylemore Abbey and Connemara National Park), along the coast to Roundstone, and finally back to Galway.

Galway to Northern Ireland Drive (via Westport)

If heading from Galway to Northern Ireland (Derry or Portrush), visit the described sights in this order: Cong, then across the Maam Valley to Leenane, up to Louisburgh and Murrisk on the way to Westport (consider spending the night). From there you'll head northeast to Sligo, Donegal, and across the border into Northern Ireland.

One of the most interesting parts of this route is the stretch from Cong through the remote **Maam Valley** to Leenane. The brooding and desolate valley feels like a land of ghosts, as the region, once densely populated with potato-eating peasants, was depopulated in the Famine and remains that way to this day. The old sod cottages are long washed away, but you can still make out the sad corduroy ridges where those last potatoes were planted.

The direct route between Westport and Derry (or Portrush) comes with a series of worthwhile little stops and detours. They are all fast and easy, and don't take much time. For highlights, see page 382 of the Donegal & the Northwest chapter.

Cong

The town of Cong offers a fascinating mix of attractions: a medieval ruined abbey, a modern church with exquisite stained-glass windows, a museum about a John Ford film *(The Quiet Man)*, and a falconry experience on the grounds of the extravagant Ashford

WESTPORT & CONNEMARA

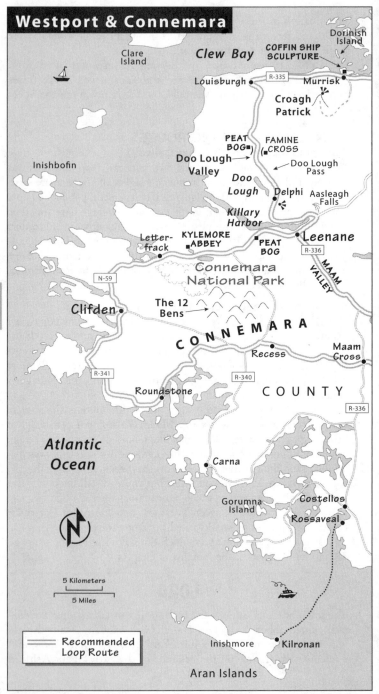

Westport & Connemara

Clare Island

Clew Bay

Dorinish Island

COFFIN SHIP SCULPTURE

Louisburgh • R-335 • Murrisk

Croagh Patrick

PEAT BOG

FAMINE CROSS

Doo Lough Valley

Doo Lough Pass

Inishbofin

Doo Lough

Delphi

Aasleagh Falls

Killary Harbor

Letter-frack

KYLEMORE ABBEY

PEAT BOG

Leenane

R-336

MAAM VALLEY

Connemara National Park

N-59

The 12 Bens

CONNEMARA

Clifden

Recess

Maam Cross

COUNTY

R-341

R-340

R-336

Roundstone

Atlantic Ocean

Carna

Gorumna Island

Costellos

Rossaveal

Inishmore • Kilronan

Aran Islands

5 Kilometers

5 Miles

Recommended Loop Route

To Ballina

Castlebar

N-5

To Strokestown Park, Irish National Famine Museum & Donegal

Westport

N-60

R-330

Knock

N-64

N-17

COUNTY

Partry

Lough Carra

Claremorris

N-60

N-84

R-331

M A Y O

N-17

Lough Mask

Ballinrobe

Cong

Neale

STONE CIRCLE

ASHFORD CASTLE

Cross

N-84

R-345

R-334

Tuam

Lough Corrib

Oughterard

N-17

QUIET MAN STONE BRIDGE

G A L W A Y

N-59

N-84

CONNEMARA LOOP DRIVE BEGINS

Athenry

M-6

Spiddal

Galway

To Dublin

N-18

Galway Bay

Kilcolgan

Black Head

N-67

Bally-vaughan

To Cliffs of Moher

Kinvarra

To Ennis & Limerick

THE BURREN

WESTPORT & CONNEMARA

Castle. Everything is within a short walk of the parking lot in front of the abbey.

The **TI,** where you can pick up a handy map, is across from the entrance to Cong Abbey (Tue-Sat 9:15-17:00, closed Sun-Mon and Nov-Feb, tel. 094/954-6542). There are no banks or **ATMs** in Cong. Public **WCs** are 50 yards down the street from the TI.

On the way in or out of Cong, you may see a dry 19th-century canal as you pass over a scenic bridge. Cong (from *conga,* Irish for "isthmus") lies between two large lakes. Built between 1848 and 1854, this canal was a Great Potato Famine work project that stoked only appetites. The canal, complete with locks, would have linked Lough Mask to the north with Lough Corrib to the south. But the limestone bedrock proved too porous, making the canal an idea that just wouldn't hold water. So, after all that work and expense, it was abandoned. It sits there, dry to this day, as an embarrassment to English engineering.

Sights in Cong

Cong Abbey

The ruins of Cong Abbey (free and always open) are the main attraction in town. The abbey was built starting in the early 1100s in Romanesque style and then into the Gothic age. You'll notice a mix of styles—with both round Romanesque and pointed Gothic arches (especially around the doorway). The famous Cross of Cong, which was believed to have held a splinter of the True Cross (now on display in Dublin's National Museum), was hoisted aloft at the front of processions of Augustinian monks during High Masses in this church. Rory O'Connor, the last Irish high king, died in this abbey in 1198. After O'Connor realized he could never outfight the superior Norman armies, he retreated to Cong and spent his last years here in monastic isolation.

Nearby: Take a walk through the cloister and down the gravel path behind the abbey. The forested grounds are lush, and the stream water is clear. Cong's salmon hatchery contributes to western Ireland's reputation for great fishing. From a little bridge you'll see the **monks' stone house.** It was designed so part of the stream would flow directly under it. The monks simply lowered a net through the floor and attached a bell to the rope; whenever a fish was netted, the bell would ring.

Next to the abbey's cemetery

is the modern, concrete, bunker-like **Church of St. Mary of the Rosary.** Drop in to marvel at its three exquisite windows, made by Irish artist Harry Clarke in 1933. Step behind the altar to get up really close (free, daily 8:00-22:00).

Quiet Man Museum

This cottage-museum is interesting (only) for fans of the 1951 movie. This town (but not this cottage) is where John Wayne and Maureen O'Hara made the famous John Ford film *The Quiet Man*. You'll see modest historical exhibits and film props.

Cost and Hours: €5, daily 10:00-16:00, closed Nov-mid-March, tel. 094/954-6089, www.quietman-cong.com.

Ashford Castle

This massive stone palace (now a hotel) sits on a vast, exclusive estate that's a lush and peaceful 15-minute walk from town. Its river serves as a modern-day moat: To cross the bridge you'll need to pay €10 (unless you're a guest at the hotel or have a falconry appointment—see next listing). While you won't be allowed in the building, the grounds are a gardener's delight, creating a lakeside paradise of greenery. Many scenes from *The Quiet Man* were filmed on these grounds.

▲▲Ireland School of Falconry

If you've never experienced falconry, this is a great chance. Animal lovers, aviation engineers, and wannabe medieval hunters will thrill to the Ireland School of Falconry, hidden on the Ashford Castle grounds. You must have an appointment to visit the school, but if you're walking the castle grounds you may see a group and their guide, strolling around as a hawk flies to and from a tourist's well-padded arm.

Cost and Hours: You must reserve ahead for this hour-long experience. It's €90 for one participant, €70 each for two, €60 each for three, €50 each for 4-10 participants, no charge for spectators who don't launch and land the birds; ask about convenient parking, tel. 094/954-6820, mobile 087-297-6092, www.falconry.ie, info@ falconry.ie.

Getting There: It's about a 10-minute walk from the castle to the school: Cross the bridge onto the castle grounds, circle right through the parking lot, and around the right side toward the back. Then follow "falconry" signs; eventually—deep in the forest— you'll reach a gate with a buzzer and you're there.

Visiting the School: Your falconry experience starts in the courtyard surrounded by pens housing hawks. After a brief Hawks 101 lesson, you're led on a "hawk walk" through the forest with an expert handler, sporting on his forearm a Harris hawk—a breed the school's brochure says is "renowned for its easygoing temperament and unusually sociable nature." The handler teaches you the fascinating intricacies of falconry, and then you have an opportunity to launch and land a bird from your own arm...a unique opportunity you didn't realize you had on your bucket list.

You'll spend a half-hour or so on the castle grounds as your hawk flies away in search of his prey and returns for the tasty reward the trainer has tucked into your protective mitt. You'll do this again and again, all the while shooting lots of amazing photographs and getting into the food-centric mind of your graceful and majestic bird.

Eating in Cong

Fuel up with a light lunch or cakes and coffee at the **$$ Hungry Monk Café** (Mon-Sat 10:00-17:00, closed Sun, shorter hours off-season, on Abbey Street across from public WCs, tel. 094/954-5842).

A solid pub-grub lunch can be had at **$$ The Crowe's Nest** (daily 12:00-21:00, in Ryan's Hotel on Main Street, tel. 094/954-6243).

Westport

Westport, with just 9,000 people, is "the big city" in this part of Ireland. While other villages seem organic and grown out of the Middle Ages, this is a planned town. It was built in the late 1700s with a trendy-back-then Georgian flair by celebrated architect James Wyatt, who designed it to support the adjacent estate of the English Lord Browne. The town thrived in its early days on linen created on local Irish handlooms. But, after the Act of Union with Britain in 1801, Westport was unable to compete with the industrialized British linen makers and fell into decline. With the Famine, things got even worse. The town is still pretty (famously "tidy") and well worth a stop. If in need of an overnight between Galway and Derry or Portrush, this would be my choice.

Orientation to Westport

Westport's main street, Bridge Street, stretches from the clock tower up to the river. A block from the clock tower is the eight-sided main "square" called the Octagon. To get oriented to the town, follow my "Westport Walk" or join the guided walk (both described below).

TOURIST INFORMATION

Westport's TI (called the "Discover Ireland Centre") is on Bridge Street (Mon-Sat 9:00-17:45, closed Sun, tel. 098/25711).

HELPFUL HINTS

Parking: You can park for free on the streets for one hour. Otherwise, there are several handy, inexpensive pay-and-display lots in the center.

Laundry: You can get same-day service if you drop off early at **Gills** (Mon-Sat 9:00-18:30, closed Sun, James Street, tel. 098/25819).

Bookstore: Run by friendly Seamus, **The Bookshop** is a delightful place (Mon-Sat 9:30-18:30, Sun 11:00-18:00, later in summer, Bridge Street).

Local Theater: The **Town Hall Theatre** is worth checking out for music concerts or stage plays (€12-15 tickets, in Town Hall facing the Octagon, tel. 098/28459, www.westporttheatre. com).

Walk with a Local Guide: For a lighthearted and entertaining hour, join Stephen Clarke on his guided walk around town. It's a fun chance to feel like you've made friends with a local and get a sense for the town's pride and personality. Stephen even includes a tea-and-scones stop at the end. Just show up at the Octagon and look for a sprightly man in a yellow jacket (€5, no need to reserve, departs Mon-Fri at 10:00 and 12:00, May-Sept only, mobile 087-410-1363, www.westportwalkingtours. ie).

Westport Walk

This little walk—almost a complete loop—will acquaint you with Westport's charms, beginning at the Octagon and ending at the clock tower on Bridge Street.

Octagon: This is Westport's main square, but as it's eight-sided, it's called the "Octagon." Surrounded by 30 townhouses, it was the centerpiece of the planned town back in the 1760s. The big limestone structure with the clock was the old market house, where trade was organized, and taxes and customs paid.

The monument in the center of the Octagon was built in 1843 (just before the Famine) to honor Lord Browne's banker, George Glendenning. But the statue of the English banker was shot to pieces by Irish patriots in 1922, during the civil war (notice the gunfire-pocked column). Today, St. Patrick perches on top, garbed in Roman clothes (recalling his kidnapping).

As you wander around town, you'll see Westport is a proud little place with a strong community spirit. It's competitive too. In 2012 Westport got "the best Irish town to live in" award. The skinny bronze statue just up the hill from the Octagon celebrates Westport's claim to be the most livable town in Ireland.

James Street: Stroll downhill from the Octagon along James Street. Notice a few things. First, there are no stop signs. That's because traffic is supposed to be so friendly that drivers yield to anyone in a crosswalk without being reminded. Second, there are no chain stores—by popular demand, the town council has allowed no big chains to open up in the town center. Finally, note how locals seem to have almost no expressions on their faces. (I'm told that's because the biggest employer here is Allergan Pharmaceuticals, and about a thousand people in Westport earn their living making Botox.)

Halfway down the street, on the left, you'll see a bike-rental shop (Westport Bikes for Hire), one of several in town. They're all busy because of the Great Western Greenway bike path (see page 370). Photos in the window show the popular 26-mile route, which runs from here to Achill Island over the abandoned right-of-way of a narrow-gauge railway that operated from 1895 to 1937.

Along the River: At the bottom of James Street, stand at the bridge and notice the fancy Anglican church across the river (wealthy English Protestants). Rather than crossing the bridge, head right, to the more humble Catholic church (poor indigenous Catholics, not much inside).

In front of the church, by the water, is a bust of Westport-born **Major John MacBride,** one of the more colorful rebels of the 1916 Easter Rising. MacBride joined a band of insurgents marching into position in Dublin at the start of the rebellion, and was among the 14 men executed at Kilmainham Gaol after its failure.

The river feels like a canal here. Lord Browne, inspired by the embankments he saw in Paris, decided to show off by having this promenade built here, at the western fringe of Western civilization. The flowers along the embankment and on the bridges sure are tidy.

Bridge Street to the Clock Tower: At the next bridge, turn right and go uphill on Westport's main street. McGreevy's general store (on the corner) gets heat from townsfolk for its tacky **giant ice cream cones,** which the owner insists on posting on the sidewalk

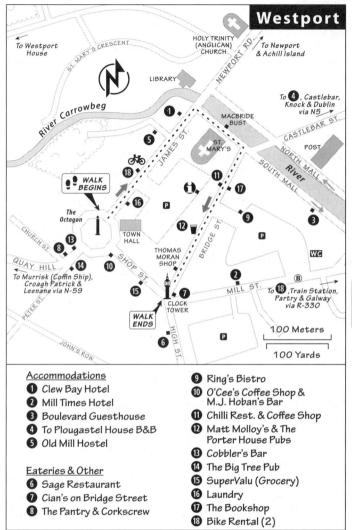

Westport

To Westport House
ST. MARY'S CRESCENT
HOLY TRINITY (ANGLICAN) CHURCH
NEWPORT RD.
To Newport & Achill Island

LIBRARY
River Carrowbeg

❶
MACBRIDE BUST
To ❹ , Castlebar, Knock & Dublin via N5
CASTLEBAR ST.
POST
NORTH MALL
River
SOUTH MALL

❺
ST. MARY'S
JAMES ST.

🚲
❶❽
WALK BEGINS

The Octagon
CHURCH ST.

❶❻
P
P

❶❶
🚻
❶❼
❾
❸

TOWN HALL
❶❷
BRIDGE ST.
P
WC

❶❸
❽
QUAY HILL
❶❹
❿
SHOP ST.
THOMAS MORAN SHOP
❷
MILL ST.
To ❶❽ , Train Station, Partry & Galway via R-330
B

To Murrisk (Coffin Ship), Croagh Patrick & Leenane via N-59
❶❺
PETER ST.
❼
CLOCK TOWER

WALK ENDS
HIGH ST.
P

JOHN'S ROW
❻

100 Meters
100 Yards

WESTPORT & CONNEMARA

Accommodations
❶ Clew Bay Hotel
❷ Mill Times Hotel
❸ Boulevard Guesthouse
❹ To Plougastel House B&B
❺ Old Mill Hostel

Eateries & Other
❻ Sage Restaurant
❼ Cian's on Bridge Street
❽ The Pantry & Corkscrew

❾ Ring's Bistro
❿ O'Cee's Coffee Shop & M.J. Hoban's Bar
⓫ Chilli Rest. & Coffee Shop
⓬ Matt Molloy's & The Porter House Pubs
⓭ Cobbler's Bar
⓮ The Big Tree Pub
⓯ SuperValu (Grocery)
⓰ Laundry
⓱ The Bookshop
⓲ Bike Rental (2)

(not tidy). Bridge Street is, nevertheless, lined by some of the finest old storefronts in Ireland.

Farther up the street, **Matt Molloy's Pub** is the biggest draw in town—famous because its namesake owner is the flutist for the trad group the Chieftains. You can hear music here nightly (see "Entertainment in Westport," later). Explore the pub during the day when it's quiet and empty. The back room is a small theater with photos of celebrated guests on the wall.

At the top of Bridge Street you'll reach the classic storefront of

Thomas Moran—so classic it's on an Irish stamp. Try out a hurling stick.

Tidy flower patches (tended by an army of volunteers) surround the **clock tower,** which dates to 1947. Back when people needed a reliable timekeeper to set their watches to, this tower had a practical function. The tower marks the town's second square—and the end of our walk.

Activities in Westport

▲▲▲Biking the Great Western Greenway

For an easy way to enjoy Ireland's great and scenic natural beauty, consider the popular 26-mile ride along the Great Western Greenway. From 1895 to 1937, a narrow-gauge railway operated from Westport to Achill Island. In 2010, the rails were replaced by a level, paved path, creating an ideal rural route dedicated to bikers and walkers—no vehicles allowed (www.greenway.ie).

Bike rental places will shuttle you by bus to Achill Island (connected to the mainland by bridge); you then bike scenically for three hours (with the wind generally at your back) along the old train bed back to Westport. You'll cross stone bridges, wind through forested and open bog stretches, and usually have the sea in sight as you hug the coastline. About midway, you'll pass Mulranny village (with a pub and its old station renovated into an inviting café). At Newport village you'll bike over an old viaduct.

Westport has several good bike rental places (smart to reserve in advance). **Westport Bikes for Hire** runs daily shuttles at 10:00 and 12:00 to Achill, included with the price of a bike (€30/day for 21-speed bike, €50/day for electric bike, includes yellow vest and helmet, daily 9:00-18:00, James St, tel. 086/088-0882, www.westportbikes4hire.com, Jerry). **Clew Bay Bike Hire** also rents bikes and has shuttle-bus options to Newport, Mulranny, or Achill, plus they offer kayaking trips (€20/day for bikes, €50/day for electric bikes, daily 9:00-18:00, Distillery Road, tel. 098/24818 or 098/37675, www.clewbaybikehire.ie).

Entertainment in Westport

Westport has plenty of live traditional music nightly in its pubs.

On Bridge Street: The most popular place in town is **Matt Molloy's Pub,** whose owner plays with the Chieftains, the group credited with much of the worldwide resurgence of interest in Irish music over the past 50 years. They have traditional music nightly at 21:30 (be there early or stand all night, no food, tel. 098/26655).

The Porter House (next door to Matt Molloy's), an award-winning pub for its traditional music, also has nightly sessions at

21:30. You'll find more room and fewer crowds here. Larry, the head barman, is proud of his craft beers.

On or near the Octagon: Three pubs have live trad music most evenings in summer: **M. J. Hoban's Bar**, **Cobbler's Bar**, and **The Big Tree Pub** (on Lower Peter Street, marked by a big tree a couple of steps up the hill from the Octagon).

Sleeping in Westport

$$$ Clew Bay Hotel has 54 large, modern rooms decked out in cherrywood furniture (free use of adjacent pool and fitness center, James Street, tel. 098/28088, www.clewbayhotel.com, info@clewbayhotel.com).

$$$ Mill Times Hotel has a fresh, woody feel, with 34 comfortable rooms and convenient, free underground parking (Mill Street, tel. 098/29200, www.milltimeshotel.ie, info@milltimeshotel.ie).

$ Boulevard Guesthouse is the best value in town. Located right on the leafy South Mall, it has six large, quiet, tasteful rooms and a cushy lounge with an interesting guest library under the stairs. Sadie and John Moran make you feel welcome (family rooms, cash only, discount with multiple-night stay, light continental breakfast, parking, South Mall, mobile 087-284-4018, www.boulevard-guesthouse.com, boulevardguesthouse@gmail.com).

$ Plougastel House B&B, named after Westport's sister town in Brittany, has six inviting, smartly furnished earth-tone rooms with marble-floored bathrooms (cash only, Distillery Road, tel. 098/25198, www.plougastel-house.com, info@plougastel-house.com, Sandra Corcoran).

¢ Old Mill Hostel is a thick-walled stone structure that could stop a tank. Like many hostels, it's an inexpensive ramshackle bunkhouse for an international mix of youthful vagabonds (James Street, tel. 098/27045, www.oldmillhostel.com, info@oldmillhostell.com).

Eating in Westport

CONTEMPORARY IRISH

Each of these places serves contemporary Irish cuisine in a cozy and inviting space, and generally offers a three-course early-bird special for about €25 if you get your order in before 18:30. They are all popular enough to merit making reservations.

$$$ Sage Restaurant is filled with a happy energy. Shteryo (a talented Bulgarian chef) cooks while his wife Eva serves (daily from 17:30, 10 High Street, tel. 098/56700, www.sagewestport.ie).

$$$ Cian's on Bridge Street, serving beautifully presented dishes and always a good vegetarian plate, is the current choice of foodies, so reservations are a must (Mon-Sat 17:00-22:00, closed Sun, top of Bridge Street at #1, tel. 098/25914).

$$$ The Pantry & Corkscrew is another local favorite, serving modern Irish with a dash of Asian in a woody, welcoming atmosphere (Tue-Sun 17:00-22:00, closed Mon, The Octagon, tel. 098/26977, www.thepantryandcorkscrew.com).

BUDGET EATING

You'll find plenty of options along Bridge Street; for pub grub, consider J. J. O'Malley's.

$ Ring's Bistro, presided over by hard-working Joe and Eithne Ring, is a friendly and filling locals' hangout for breakfast or lunch (Mon-Sat 8:00-17:30, closed Sun, hidden up Market Lane off Bridge Street, tel. 098/29100).

$ O'Cee's Coffee Shop serves good, basic cafeteria-style lunches (Mon-Sat 8:30-18:30, Sun 9:00-16:00, on the Octagon, tel. 098/27000).

$ Chilli Restaurant & Coffee Shop is another reliable local diner (daily 9:30-17:00, also Wed-Sun 18:00-21:00, Bridge Street, tel. 098/27007).

Groceries: The **SuperValu** market has picnic fare; it's just off the Octagon on Shop Street (daily 8:00-22:00).

Westport Connections

By Bus to: Galway (6/day, 2-4 hours), Derry (3/day, 6 hours, change in Sligo), or Dublin (6/day, 4-6 hours). For details, see www.buseireann.ie. You can also reach Dublin by **train** (5/day, 3.25 hours, www.irishrail.ie).

Connemara Loop Drive Sights

The towns and sights below are arranged in the order you will reach them on my "Connemara Loop Drive" as you leave Westport and circle back to Galway (for route details, see "Planning Your Time" on page 360). The first two stops on the drive—Cong and Westport—are covered earlier.

Murrisk, Croagh Patrick, and a Coffin Ship Sculpture

In the tiny town of Murrisk you'll find the trailhead for the long hike up Croagh Patrick and a monument remembering the Famine.

Croagh Patrick: This fabled mountain

pilgrimage destination rises 2,500 feet above the bay from Murrisk. In the fifth century, St. Patrick is said to have fasted on its summit for the 40 days of Lent. It's from here that he supposedly rang his bell, driving all the snakes from Ireland. The snakes never existed, of course, but they represent the pagan beliefs that Patrick's newly arrived Christianity replaced. Every year on the last Sunday of July, "Reek Sunday" (a "reek" is a mountain peak), as many as 30,000 pilgrims hike three hours up the rocky trail to the summit in honor of St. Patrick. The most penitent attempt the hike barefoot (and often come down on a stretcher). On that Sunday, Mass is celebrated throughout the day in a modest cinderblock chapel at the summit.

A few years ago, valuable gold deposits were discovered within Croagh Patrick. Luckily, public sentiment has kept the sacred mountain free of any commercial mining activity.

Hiking Croagh Patrick: From the trailhead at Murrisk (where you'll find a big pay-and-display parking lot and a visitors center), you can see the ruddy trail worn by a thousand years of pilgrims heading up the hill and along the north ridge to the summit. Hikers should allow three hours to reach the top and two hours to get back down (wear solid boots if you have them, and bring plenty of water, sunscreen, and rain gear). There is a primitive WC on the summit. The trail is easy to follow, but the upper half of the mountain is a steep slope of loose, shifting scree that can bang or turn exposed ankles. I'd advise buying (or renting) a walking stick in nearby Westport.

Coffin Ship Sculpture: Across the street from the Croagh Patrick trailhead is a modern bronze ship sculpture. A memorial to the Famine, it depicts a "coffin ship," like those of the late 1840s that carried the sick and starving Famine survivors across the ocean in hope of a new life. But many of the ships contracted to take the desperate emigrants were worn out and barely seaworthy. The poor were weak from starvation and vulnerable to "famine fever," which they spread to others in the putrid, cramped holds of these ships. Many who lived through the six- to eight-week journey died shortly after reaching their new country. Pause a moment to look at the silent skeletons swirling around the ship's masts.

Now contemplate the fact that famine still exists in the world—in virtually every country—even though there's enough food grown worldwide to feed the hungry. The challenge is distribution and buying power. If my cat has more buying power than your child, my cat gets the tuna. That's simply the free market system.

Clew Bay

Stretching west on R-335 from Murrisk is Clew Bay, peppered with more than 300 humpbacked islands of glacial gravel dumped by retreating glaciers at the end of the last Ice Age. A notorious 16th-century local named Grace O'Malley (dubbed the "Pirate Queen") once ruled this bay, even earning the grudging respect of Queen Elizabeth I with her clever exploits.

Doo Lough Valley and a Famine Cross

The Doo Lough Valley, unfolding between Louisburgh and Delphi (on R-335), is some of the most desolate country in Ireland. Signs of human habitation vanish from the bogland, and it seems ghosts might appear beside the road. Stop at the summit (north end of the valley, about 13 kilometers south of Louisburgh) when you see a simple gray stone cross. The lake below is Doo Lough (Irish for "Black Lake"). This is the site of one of the saddest famine tales.

County Mayo's rural folk depended almost exclusively on the potato for food and were the hardest hit when the Great Potato Famine came in 1845. In the winter of 1849, about 600 starving Irish walked 19 kilometers (12 miles) from Louisburgh over this summit and south to Delphi Lodge, hoping to get food from their landlord. But they were turned away. On the walk back, almost 200 of them died along the side of this road. Today, the road still seems to echo with the despair of those hungry souls,

and it inspires an annual walk that commemorates the tragedy. Archbishop Desmond Tutu made the walk in 1991, shortly before South Africa ended its apartheid system.

Killary Harbor and Aasleagh Falls

As you drive toward the town of Leenane, you'll skirt along Killary Harbor, an Irish example of a fjord. This long, narrow body of water was carved by an advancing glacier. The rows of blue floats in the harbor mark mussel farms, with the molluscs growing on hanging nets in the cold seawater.

At the east end of Killary Harbor, stop to enjoy the scenic Aasleagh Falls. In late May, the banks below the falls explode with lush, wild, purple rhododendron blossoms.

Leenane

The "town" of Leenane (actually just a crossroads) is a good place for a break. The 1990 movie *The Field,* starring Limerick-born Richard Harris, was filmed here. Glance at the photos of the making of the movie on the wall of Hamilton's Pub. While you're there, find the old photo of the British dreadnought battleships that filled Killary Harbor when King Edward VII visited a century ago. Drop into the Leenane Sheep and Wool Centre (across the street) to see interesting wool-spinning and weaving demonstrations (€5, daily 9:30-18:00, closed Nov-March; demos run June-Aug at 10:00, 11:30, 14:00, and 15:30; café, tel. 095/42323, www.sheepandwoolcentre.com).

Bog Fun

About eight kilometers west of Leenane, you'll find some areas on the south side of the road that offer a good, close look at a turf cut in a peat bog. Be sure to get out and frolic in the peat fields...with decent footwear and an eagle eye for mushy spots.

Walk a few yards onto the spongy green carpet. (Watch your step on wet days to avoid squishing into a couple of inches of water.) Find a dry spot and jump up and down to get a feel for it. Have your companion jump; you'll feel the vibrations 30 feet away. Rip off a piece of turf and squeeze the water out of it. It's almost all water.

These bogs once covered almost 20 percent of Ireland. As the climate got warmer at the end of the last Ice Age, plants began growing along the sides of the many shallow lakes and ponds. When the plants died in these waterlogged areas, there wasn't enough oxygen for them to fully decompose. Over the centuries, the moss built up, layer after dead layer, helping to slowly fill in the lakes. During World War I, this sphagnum moss was collected to use in bandages to soak up blood (it absorbs many times its weight in fluids).

It's this wet, oxygen-starved ecosystem that has preserved ancient artifacts so well, many of which can be seen in Dublin's National Museum. Even forgotten containers of butter, churned centuries ago and buried to keep cool, have been discovered. But most bizarre are the wrinkled bog mummies that are occasionally unearthed. These human remains (many over 2,000 years old) are so incredibly intact that their eyelashes, hairstyles, and the last meal in their stomachs can be identified. They were likely sacrificial offerings to the pagan gods of Celtic times.

Ireland's Misunderstood Nomads

When you see a small cluster of trailers at the side of an Irish road, you're looking at a dying way of life. These are the Travellers, a nomadic throwback to the days when wandering craftsmen, musicians, and evicted unfortunates crowded rural Ireland. Often mislabeled as gypsies, they have no ethnic ties to those Eastern European nomads, but rather have an Irish heritage going back centuries.

There were once many more Travellers, who lived in tents and used horse-drawn carts as they wandered the countryside in search of work. Before the Famine, when Irish hospitality was a given, Travellers filled a niche in Irish society. They would do odd jobs, such as repairing furniture, sweeping chimneys, and selling horses. Skilled tinsmiths, they mended pots, pans, and stills for *poitín*—Irish moonshine. (Travellers used to be called "tinkers," but this label is now considered derogatory.) Settled-down farm folk, who rarely ventured more than 20 miles from home their entire lives, depended on the roaming Travellers for news and gossip from farther-flung regions. But post-Famine rural depopulation and the gradual urbanization of the countryside forced this nomadic group to adapt to an almost sedentary existence on the fringes of towns.

Today, the 30,000 remaining Travellers are outsiders, usually treated with suspicion by other Irish. Locals often complain that petty thefts go up when Travellers set up camp in a nearby "halting site," and that they leave garbage behind when they depart.

Travellers tend to keep to themselves, marry young, have large families, and speak their own Irish Gaelic-based language (called Shelta, Gammon, or Cant). They are very religious and often camp near the pilgrimage town of Knock. Attempts to settle Travellers in government housing and integrate their children into schools have met with mixed success, as portrayed poignantly in the 1992 movie *Into the West*.

Since these acidic bogs contain few nutrients, unique species of carnivorous plants have adapted to life here by trapping and digesting insects. The tiny pink sundew (less than an inch tall) has delicate spikes glistening with insect-attracting fluid. Find a mossy area and look closely at the variety of tiny plants. In summer, you'll see white tufts of bog cotton growing in marshy areas.

People have been cutting, drying, and burning peat as a fuel source for more than a thousand years. The cutting usually begins in April or May, when drier weather approaches. You'll probably see stacks of "turf" piled up to dry along recent cuts. Pick up a brick and fondle it. Dried peat is surprisingly light and stiff. In central Ireland, there are even industrial peat cuts that were begun after World War II to fuel power stations. But in the past few decades, bogs have been recognized as a rare habitat, and conservation efforts have been encouraged. These days, the sweet, nostalgic smell of burning peat is becoming increasingly rare.

Kylemore Abbey

This Neo-Gothic country house was built by the wealthy English businessman Mitchell Henry in the 1860s, after he and his wife had honeymooned in the area. Now they are both buried on the grounds. After World War I, refugee Benedictine nuns from Ypres, Belgium, took it over and ran it as an exclusive girls' boarding school—which peaked at 200 students—until it closed in 2010. In 2015 the Indiana-based University of Notre Dame signed a 30-year lease to use part of the facility for summer classes and student housing. The nuns still live upstairs, but you can visit the half-dozen open rooms downstairs that display the Henry family's cushy lifestyle.

For me, the best thing about the abbey is the view of it from the lakeshore. But garden enthusiasts will seek out the extensive walled Victorian gardens. From the abbey, the gardens are a one-mile, level walk or quick shuttle bus ride (runs every 15 minutes). Hourly tours of the abbey and gardens are so-so; it's best just to enjoy the setting.

Cost and Hours: Overpriced €13 combo-ticket for abbey and gardens; daily 9:00-18:00, July-Aug until 19:00, shorter hours off-season; WCs in gift shop next to parking lot, the cafeteria can be overwhelmed by multiple big-bus tour groups, tel. 095/52001, www.kylemoreabbeytourism.ie.

Connemara National Park

This park encompasses almost 5,000 acres of wild bog and mountain scenery. The visitors center (just outside Letterfrack) displays worthwhile exhibits of local flora and fauna, which are well-explained in the 15-minute *Man and the Landscape* film that runs every half-hour (free; park open daily year-round; visitors center open daily 9:00-17:30, closed Nov-Feb; tel. 095/41054, www.connemaranationalpark.ie). For a quick visit, take a nature walk along the boardwalk raised above the bog. Nature lovers may want to enjoy a two-hour walking tour with a park naturalist (July-Aug, Wed and Fri at 11:00, departs from visitors center). Call ahead to confirm walking tour schedules, and bring rain gear and hiking shoes.

Coastal Connemara

If you're short on time, you can connect Clifden and Galway with the fast main road (N-59). But the slower coastal loop along R-341 rewards drivers with great scenery. The essence of scenic Connemara—rocky yet seductive—is captured in this neat little 38-kilometer stretch. The 12 Bens (peaks) of Connemara loom deeper inland. In the foreground, broad shelves of bare bedrock are netted with stone walls, which interlock through the landscape. The ocean slaps the hardscrabble shore. Fishermen cast into their favorite little lakes, and ponies trot in windswept fields. Abandoned, roofless stone cottages stand mute. While the loop is pretty desolate, Roundstone is a perfect place to stop for a cup of coffee to fuel your ride back to Galway.

East of Connemara

The following sights are due east of Westport (about 45 minutes to the shrine and 1.5 hours to the museum).

Knock Shrine

In 1879, locals in the little town of Knock claimed to see the Virgin Mary, St. Joseph, and St. John appear against the south gable of their humble church.

Pilgrims started coming. Word of miraculous healings on that spot turned the trickle of pilgrims into a flood and put Knock solidly on the pilgrimage map. And the pilgrims keep coming. Today, you can visit the shrine. At the edge of the site, a small but earnest folk museum shows Knock's knickknacks, photos of a papal visit, and sturdy slices of traditional life.

Cost and Hours: Shrine-free, museum-€4, daily 10:00-18:00, Aug until 19:30, tel. 094/938-8100, www.knockshrine.ie.

Getting There: The shrine is located on N-17, midway between Galway and Sligo (about 45 kilometers east of Westport).

Virgin Mary Shrines

During your time in Ireland, you'll frequently see pretty little roadside shrines and grottoes honoring the Virgin Mary. The older ones were built in 1929 to celebrate 100 years of Catholic emancipation (the Roman Catholic Relief Act of 1829, spearheaded by Daniel O'Connell—see page 243). The majority were constructed in the "Marian Year" (devoted to Mary) of 1954. This was the 100th anniversary of Pope Pius IX's 1854 proclamation of the dogma of the Immaculate Conception (God kept the Virgin Mary "from the stain of original sin" from the moment she was conceived). A record number of devout Catholics flocked to the holy pilgrimage village of Knock to pray during the centenary, and many Irish girls born that year were named Marian.

A more recent, related event happened in 1985 at a shrine devoted to the Virgin Mary on the other side of the country, outside the tiny hamlet of Ballinspittle (4 miles southwest of Kinsale in County Cork). A number of locals claimed they had witnessed the statue of Mary moving spontaneously, and thousands of pilgrims flocked there that summer. Some pilgrims said they also witnessed the statue moving. But the Catholic Church remained neutral on the Ballinspittle event, and interest in it eventually subsided.

WESTPORT & CONNEMARA

▲▲Strokestown Park and Irish National Famine Museum

The Great Potato Famine of 1845-1849 was the bleakest period in Irish history—so traumatic that its effects halved the Irish population over the next 50 years and started a great Irish diaspora—sending desperate, hungry peasants across the globe. It also crystallized Irish nationalist hatred of British rule.

Cost and Hours: You have several options: museum (with a good café), house tour, six-acre Georgian walled gardens, or a combination of the three. One sight costs €9, two cost €12, and a combo-ticket for all three is €13.50. Open daily 10:30-17:30, Nov-mid-March until 16:00; "Big House" tours (45 minutes) go daily in high season at 12:00, 14:30, and 16:00; tel. 071/963-3013, www.strokestownpark.ie.

Getting There: The National Famine Museum fills a mansion on the former estate of the Mahon family in the market town of

Strokestown, 90 kilometers northeast of Galway and 110 kilometers east of Westport (about 1.5 hours from either).

Visiting the Museum: Thoughtful exhibits explain how three million Irish peasants survived on a surprisingly nutritious prefamine diet of buttermilk and potatoes (12 pounds per day per average male laborer...potatoes are 80 percent water). When a fungus destroyed the potato crop, it sparked the Great Potato Famine, and as many as a million Irish people died of starvation.

Major Mahon, the ill-fated landlord here during the Famine, found it cheaper to fill three "coffin ships" bound for America with his evicted, starving tenants than pay the taxes for their upkeep in the local workhouse. When almost half died at sea of "famine fever," he was assassinated.

The tours of the musty Big House provide insights into the gulf that divided the Protestant ascendancy and their Catholic house staff. Afterward, find the servants' tunnel—connecting the kitchen to the stable—built to avoid cluttering the Mahon family's views with unsightly common laborers.

DONEGAL &
THE NORTHWEST

County Donegal, the northernmost part of the island (and west of Derry), is about as far-flung as Ireland gets. It's not on the way to anywhere, and it wears its isolation well. With more native Irish speakers than in any other county, the old ways are better preserved here.

Donegal is connected to the Republic by a slim, five-mile-wide umbilical cord of land on its southern coast. A forgotten economic backwater (part of the Republic but riding piggyback on the North), it lacks blockbuster museums or sights. But it's also Ireland's second-biggest county, with a wide-open "big sky" interior and a shattered-glass, 200-mile, jagged coastline of islands and inlets. A visit here is about the journey, and adventurous drivers—a car is a must—will be rewarded with a time-capsule peek into old Irish ways and starkly beautiful scenery.

For drivers who want to explore the region fully, I've laid out a day-trip loop through the northernmost reaches of County Donegal (starting and ending in the Northern Ireland town of Derry, and best for people home-basing there). Drivers connecting the Republic (Galway or Westport) and Northern Ireland without time for a Donegal deep dive can easily hit several interesting sights en route, including a swing through a swath of County Donegal and the town of the same name (with a worthwhile reconstructed castle).

PLANNING YOUR TIME

To drive in a single day between the Republic (Galway or Westport) and Northern Ireland (Derry or Portrush), get an early start so you have time to stop at your pick of several worthwhile sights lined up along the N-15 road between Sligo and Derry (listed under the "Between Westport and Derry" section). Donegal town makes a good lunch stop. From there, you can continue straight to the border and into Derry, or on to Portrush (both covered in later chapters).

If coming from Galway, consider breaking the drive into two days (sleeping in Westport) so you can follow my suggested route for touring the Connemara area first (see page 361).

To see more of Donegal, consider sleeping two nights in Derry, with one day spent crossing back into the Republic for a scenic driving loop through a remote part of this county (covered at the end of this chapter). For details on Derry, see the Derry chapter later in this book.

Between Westport and Derry

Each of these stops is either on N-15 (the route between Sligo and Derry) or within a few kilometers of it. I've listed these sights in the order you'd reach them if driving north from the Republic to Northern Ireland. (Heading north on N-15, navigation is easy as, after Sligo, Derry is signposted the whole way.) To see more of County Donegal, consider adding in a few sights from my "County Donegal Driving Tour" (see page 385).

Drumcliff Village

For a classic medieval high cross, the nub of a round tower, and the grave of the poet W.B. Yeats, pull off N-15 just north of Sligo at Drumcliff (easy parking). Look for the brown signs for Yeats' grave and the stout stone church spire peeking above the trees just off the road. Walking from the car park you'll see, in this order, the following: church, grave, café/gift shop/WC, high cross, trail to the river, and round tower.

The stately little **church** has a delightful and stony interior (with an interesting video playing in the entryway). To the left of the church (as you face it, about 10 paces) is the simple **grave** of the beloved Irish poet, William Butler Yeats (1865-1939) and his wife, George. The tombstone reads: "Cast a cold eye on life, on death. Horsemen pass by."

Benbulben, the mountain that inspired Yeats, looms behind the graveyard, looking like a sphinx.

Just past the café/gift shop, find the highest cross in the graveyard. This classic **high cross**—along with the stub of a **round tower** (with its defensive door high above ground level) across the busy highway—were part of a monastic settlement a thousand years ago. These symbols of medieval Ireland once dotted and spiked the countryside.

The cross (once colorfully painted) is carved with high reliefs designed to help teach the people Bible lessons. Find Adam and Eve, Cain clubbing Abel, and Christ in Majesty on one side and a camel (trying to get through the eye of a needle) on the other.

This is a historic spot, the site of a monastery founded in A.D. 574 by St. Columba. He and another saint had a quarrel over the rights to a book, which actually led to a battle here in which 3,000 people were killed. Columba was so distraught by the bloodshed that he eventually banished himself from Ireland and sailed to Iona (in Scotland), where he founded another monastery (famous as the original home of the magnificent Book of Kells).

Across from the high cross, a small path leads to a river path with dramatic views of Benbulben, ideal for getting into the spirit of Yeats for a moment (for more on Yeats, see page 509).

Mullaghmore Head Loop

A few kilometers north of Drumcliff, leave N-15 at Cliffoney for a 10-kilometer (6-mile) loop side-trip around Mullaghmore Head. It was just off this scenic bluff that, on August 27, 1979, the IRA detonated a radio-controlled bomb on the vacation yacht of Lord Louis Mountbatten (79-year-old second cousin of Queen Elizabeth II), killing him and members of his family.

As you drive around this scenic loop, you'll see a rugged coastline and desolate beaches with the lonely castle retreat of the royal Mountbatten family crowning the horizon. Drive past beech tree forests (from which Lord Mountbatten constructed his boat) and a rough little stone harbor (from where he and his family sailed that fateful day), and stop at the peninsula's far end (just 12 miles south of the border of Northern Ireland). Check out the views across Donegal Bay to where the bomb went off, just a few hundred yards off the shore. Continue circling the bluff as the road brings you back to N-15.

Belleek Pottery Visitors Centre

If you're interested in pottery, consider a slight detour, about 10 kilometers (6 miles) off N-15, over the Northern Ireland border to the cute town of Belleek. The Belleek Parian China factory welcomes visitors with a small gallery and museum, a 20-minute video, a cheery cafeteria, and 30-minute guided tours of its working factory. Crazed shoppers who forget to fill out a VAT refund form will find their finances looking Belleek.

Cost and Hours: Free, tours-£5; Mon-Fri 9:00-17:30, Sat from 10:00, Sun from 14:00;

longer hours in July-Sept, shorter hours in Oct-Feb and possibly closed weekends; call to confirm tour schedule and reserve a spot (Sat tours June-Sept only, none on Sun), tel. 028/6865-9300, www.belleekpottery.ie, takethetour@belleek.ie.

Donegal Town

The main town (Donegal) in the Republic of Ireland's northern-most county (Donegal) has a striking, reconstructed castle. Do-negal means "Fort of Foreigners"—a reminder that the Vikings invaded here in the 9th century. Detour 5 kilometers (3 miles) off N-15 for a quick visit.

The charming town's main square ("The Diamond") is lined by inviting shops and eateries. Try the comfy café above Magee's tweed shop (Mon-Sat 10:00-18:00, Sun from 14:00). The monu-ment in the center honors four friars who created a record of early Irish history. The small but historic Donegal Castle is half a block beyond that (look for the pointy church spire).

Donegal Castle: This was originally the fortified base of the mighty O'Donnell clan (originally built by Hugh O'Donnell in about 1500). Around 1600, the English defeated the O'Donnells and made the castle closer to what exists today. This castle offers a fine chance to see a reconstructed version of the fortified towers so common in Ireland. Your €5 entry includes an info sheet or a half-hour guided tour (at least hourly with demand, open daily 10:00-18:00, off-season 9:30-16:30).

Wandering through Donegal Castle, you'll notice the original stone floor and 10-foot-thick walls on the ground floor, a spiral "trip staircase" winding clockwise to give the right-handed de-fender the advantage, the banqueting hall with its finely carved fireplace, and a top floor with historical exhibits under 40 tons of Irish oak beams—a 17th-century design with only wooden pegs holding it all together. The extension outside the tower dates from the English lord's manor house (c. 1620).

Remember that most of these fortified towers are post-1601 and were built by the English landlords to assert their control over the Irish. Castles like this remind locals of the devastating Nine Years' War (1594-1603), when the tribal royalty of Ireland fled the island and English rule was firmly and brutally established.

Border Crossing

When you cross the border between the Republic of Ireland and Northern Ireland you'll notice lots of changes. If traveling north along N-15, you'll cross the border in the town of Lifford (in the Republic) into the town of Strabane (in Northern Ireland). As you cross the River Foyle you enter the "United Kingdom of Great Brit-ain and North Ireland" (as of now, you don't need to show a passport, though Brexit could change that). Kilometers become miles, euros become British pounds (actually, Ulster pounds, which are the same as English pound sterling and legal tender in England), the farmland becomes richer and more productive, and Derry is now signposted as "Londonderry"—although, even today, many of the signs will have the "London" spray-painted out. On the south side of the river the sign reads: "Derry, 24 km." On the other side of the bridge, suddenly it reads: "Londonderry, 14 miles." As you drive deeper into Northern Ireland, you'll see lots of Union Jack flags and even towns with their curbs painted red, white, and blue. For more on the differences you'll encounter here, see the Northern Ireland chapter.

County Donegal Driving Tour

Donegal is the most remote (and perhaps the most ruggedly beautiful) county in Ireland. This is the home turf of St. Colmcille (St. Columba in English; means "dove of the church" in Irish), who was born here in 521. In the hierarchy of revered Irish saints, he's second only to St. Patrick. A proud Gaelic culture held out in Donegal to the bitter end, when the O'Donnells and the O'Dohertys, the two most famous local clans, were finally defeated by the English in the early 1600s. After their defeat, the region became known as Dun na nGall ("the fort of the foreigner"), which was eventually anglicized to Donegal.

As the English moved in, four Donegal-dwelling friars (certain that Gaelic ways would be lost forever) painstakingly wrote down Irish history from Noah's Ark to their present. This labor of love became known as the Annals of the Four Masters, and without it, much of our knowledge of early Irish history and myth would have been lost. An obelisk stands in their honor in the main square of Donegal town.

The hardy people of County Donegal have come out on the short end of the modern technology stick. They were famous for their quality tweed weaving, a cottage industry that has gradually given way to modern industrial production in far-off cities. A small but energetic Irish fishing fleet still churns offshore—in the wake of larger EU factory ships scooping traditionally Irish waters (see sidebar on page 393).

But culturally, the county shines. The traditional Irish musicians of Donegal play a driving style of music with a distinctively fast and forceful rhythm. Meanwhile, Enya (local Gweedore gal made good) has crafted languid, ethereal tunes that glide from mood to mood. Capturing the feel of County Donegal on screen, *The Secret of Roan Inish* was filmed here. Today, emigration has taken its toll, and the region relies on a trickle of tourism spilling over from Northern Ireland.

DONEGAL LOOP TRIP FROM DERRY

Here's my choice for a scenic mix of Donegal highlands and coastal views, organized as a self-guided daylong circuit for drivers based across the border in Derry. If you're coming north from Galway or Westport, you could incorporate parts of this drive into your itinerary. Remember, Derry is part of the UK (pounds, miles); Donegal is the Republic (euros, kilometers).

Route Summary: The total drive is about 240 km (150 miles). Drive west out of Derry (direction: Letterkenny) on Buncrana Road, which becomes A-2 (and then N-13 across the border in the Republic). Follow the signs into Letterkenny, and take R-250 out the other (west) end of town. Veer right (north) onto R-251, and stay on it through Church Hill, all the way across the highlands, until you link up with N-56 approaching Bunbeg. After a couple of kilometers on N-56, take R-258 from Gweedore; it's another six kilometers (four miles) into Bunbeg. Depart Bunbeg going north on R-257, around Bloody Foreland, and rejoin N-56 near Gortahork. Take N-56 through Dunfanaghy (possible additional Horn Head miniloop option here) and then south, back into Letterkenny. Retrace your route from Letterkenny via N-13 and A-2 back into Derry.

Driving Tips: An early start is essential, and an Ordnance Survey atlas is helpful. It's cheapest to top off your gas tank in Letterkenny. Consider bringing along a picnic lunch to enjoy from a scenic roadside pullout along the Bloody Foreland R-257 road, or out on the Horn Head loop. Bring your camera and remember—not all who wander are lost.

The sights along this route are well-marked. Don't underestimate the time it takes to get around here, as the narrow roads are full of curves and bumps. Dogs, bred to herd sheep, dart from side lanes to practice their bluffing techniques. If you average 65 kilometers per hour (about 40 mph) over the course of the day, you've got a very good suspension system. Folks wanting to linger at more than a couple of sights will need to slow down and consider an overnight stop in Dunfanaghy.

❍ Self-Guided Drive

• *Leave Derry on A-2, which becomes N-13 near the town of Bridge End. You'll see a sign for the Grianan Aileach Ring Fort posted on N-13, not far from the junction with R-239. Turn up the steep hill at the modern church with the round roof, and follow signs three kilometers (2 miles) to find...*

▲Grianan Aileach Ring Fort

This dramatic, ancient ring fort perches on an 800-foot hill just inside the Republic, a stone's throw from Derry. It's an Iron Age for-

tification, built about the time of Christ, and was once the royal stronghold of the O'Neill clan, which dominated Ulster for centuries. Its stout dry-stone walls (no mortar) are 12 feet thick and 18 feet high, creating an interior sanctuary 80 feet in diameter (entry is free and unattended).

Once inside, you can scramble up the stairs, which are built into the walls, to enjoy panoramic views in all directions. Murtagh O'Brien, King of Desmond (roughly, today's Limerick, Clare, and Tipperary counties), destroyed the fort in 1101...the same power-play year in which he gave the Rock of Cashel to the Church. Legend says he had each of his soldiers carry away one stone, attempting to make it tougher for the O'Neill clan to find the raw materials to rebuild. What you see today is mostly a reconstruction from the 1870s.

Skip the nearby well-signposted Old Church Visitors Center beside the N-13 road. Accessed through a modern hotel, it contains a couple of earnest models, costume props, and an uninterested staff.

• *Return to N–13 and head to and through Letterkenny, continuing out the other (west) end of town on R–250. Eight kilometers (5 miles) west of Letterkenny on this road, you'll reach the...*

Newmills Corn and Flax Mills

Come here for a glimpse of long-gone rural industry (the oldest building in the compact complex is close to 400 years old).

Linen, which comes from flax, was king in this region. The 15-minute film does a nifty job of explaining the process, showing how the common flax plant ends up as cloth. Working in a mill sounds like a mellow job, but conditions were noisy, unhealthy, and exhausting. Veteran mill workers often braved respiratory disease, deafness, lost fingers, and extreme fire danger. For their trouble, they usually got to keep about 10 percent of what they milled.

The corn mill is still in working condition but requires a

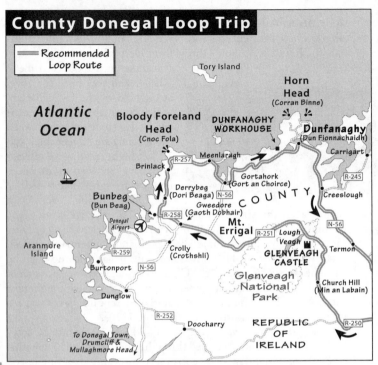

County Donegal Loop Trip

Recommended Loop Route

Tory Island

Horn Head
(Corran Binne)

Atlantic Ocean

Bloody Foreland Head
(Cnoc Fola)

DUNFANAGHY WORKHOUSE

Dunfanaghy
(Dún Fionnachaidh)

Carrigart

Meenlaragh

Brinlack

R-257

Gortahork
(Gort an Choirce)

R-245

Derrybeg
(Doiri Beaga)

N-56

C O U N T Y

Creeslough

Bunbeg
(Bun Beag)

Gweedore
(Gaoth Dobhair)

R-258

Mt. Errigal

R-251

Lough Veagh

N-56

Donegal Airport

Aranmore Island

R-259

Crolly
(Crothshli)

GLENVEAGH CASTLE

Termon

Burtonport

N-56

Glenveagh National Park

Church Hill
(Mín an Labain)

Dunglow

R-252

Doocharry

REPUBLIC OF IRELAND

R-250

To Donegal Town,
Drumcliff &
Mullaghmore Head

skilled miller to operate it. This mill ground oats—"corn" meant oats in Ireland. (What we call corn, they called maize.) The huge waterwheel, powered by the River Swilly, made five revolutions per minute and generated eight horsepower.

The entire operation could be handled by one miller, who knew every cog, lever, and flume in the joint. Call ahead to see when working mill demonstrations are scheduled; otherwise, tours last 45 minutes and are available on request.

Cost and Hours: Free, daily 10:00-18:00, closed mid-Sept-mid-May, last entry 45 minutes before closing, Churchill Road, Letterkenny, tel. 074/912-5115.

• *Continue on R-250, staying right at Driminaught as the road becomes R-251. Watch for Glenveagh Castle and National Park signs, and park in the visitors center lot.*

▲▲Glenveagh Castle and National Park

One of Ireland's six national parks, Glenveagh's jewel is pristine Lough Veagh (Loch Ghleann Bheatha in Irish). The lake is three miles long, occupying a U-shaped valley scoured out of the Derryveagh Mountains by powerful glaciers during the last Ice Age.

In the 1850s, this scenic area attracted the wealthy land speculator John George Adair, who bought the valley in 1857. Right away, Adair clashed with local tenants, whom he accused of stealing his sheep. After his managing agent was found murdered, he evicted all 244 of his bitter tenants to great controversy, and set about creating a hunting estate in grand Victorian style.

His pride and joy was his country mansion, Glenveagh Castle, finished in 1873 on the shore of Lough Veagh. After his death, his widow added to the castle and introduced rhododendrons and rare red deer to the estate. After her death, Harvard art professor Kingsley Porter bought the estate and promptly disappeared on the Donegal coast. (He's thought to have drowned.) The last owner was Philadelphia millionaire Henry McIlhenny, who filled the mansion with fine art and furniture while perfecting the lush surrounding gardens. He donated the castle to the Irish nation in 1981.

Cost and Hours: Park entry-free, guided castle tour-€7, garden tour-€5 (advance reservation required), daily 9:00-18:00, Nov-Feb until 17:00, tel. 076/1002-537, www.glenveaghnationalpark.ie,

DONEGAL & THE NORTHWEST

glenveaghbookings@ahg.gov.ie. Without a car, you can reach Glen-veagh Castle and National Park by bus tour from Derry (see page 408 of the Derry chapter).

Visiting the Castle and National Park: The **Glenveagh National Park Visitors Centre** explains the region's natural history. Hiking trails in the park are scenic and tempting, but beware of the tiny midges that seem to want to nest in your nostrils.

The **castle** is accessible by a 30-minute hike or a 10-minute shuttle-bus ride (€3 round-trip, 4/hour, depart from visitors center, last shuttle 1.25 hours before closing). You can also rent a bike in the parking lot (June-Aug) as a pleasant alternative. Take the 45-minute castle tour, letting your Jane Austen and Agatha Christie fantasies go wild. Antlers abound on walls, in chandeliers, and in paintings by Victorian hunting artists. A table crafted from rare bog oak (from ancient trees hundreds of years old, found buried in the muck) stands at attention in one room, while Venetian glass chandeliers illuminate a bathroom. A round pink bedroom at the top of a tower is decorated in Oriental style, with inlaid mother-of-pearl furnishings. The library, which displays paintings by George Russell, has the castle's best lake views.

Afterward, stroll through the gardens and enjoy the lovely setting. A lakeside swimming pool had boilers underneath it to keep it heated. It's no wonder that Greta Garbo was an occasional guest, coming to visit whenever she "vanted" to be alone.

• *Leave the national park and follow R-251 west, watching for the Mount Errigal trailhead. It's southeast of the mountain, and starts at the small parking lot beside R-251 on the mountain's lower slope (easy to spot, with a low surrounding stone wall in the middle of open bog land).*

Mount Errigal (An Earagail)

The mountain (2,400 feet) dominates the horizon for miles around. Rising from the relatively flat interior bog land, it looks taller from a distance than it is. Beautifully cone-shaped (but not a volcano), it offers a hearty, nontechnical climb with panoramic views (four hours round-trip, covering five miles). Hikers should get a weather report before setting out (frequent mists squat on the summit). Ask the TI in Letterkenny or Donegal town for more detailed hiking directions.

• *Continue on R-251 as it merges into N-56 headed west; at Gweedore, stay west on R-258. After 6 kilometers (4 miles), you'll reach R-257,*

Donegal or Bust

Part of western County Donegal is in the Gaeltacht, where locals speak the Irish Gaelic language. In the spring of 2005, a controversial law was passed that erased all English place names from local road signs in Gaeltacht areas. Signs now have only the Irish-language equivalent, an attempt to protect the region from the further (and inevitable) encroachment of the English language.

Here's a cheat sheet to help you decipher the signs as you drive the Donegal loop (parts of which are in the Gaeltacht). There's also a complete translation of all Irish place names in the recommended *Complete Road Atlas of Ireland* by Ordnance Survey (€10-13), in the Gazetteer section in the back.

Irish	English
Leitir Ceanainn *(LET-ir CAN-ning)*	Letterkenny
Min an Labain *(MEEN on law-BAWN)*	Churchill
Loch Ghleann *(LOCKH thown)*	Lough (Lake)
Bheatha *(eh-VEH-heh)*	Veagh
An Earagail *(on AIR-i-gul)*	Mt. Errigal
Gaoth Dobhair *(GWEE door)*	Gweedore
Crothshli *(CROTH-lee)*	Crolly
Bun Beag *(bun bee-OWG)*	Bunbeg
Dori Beaga *(DOR-uh bee-OWG-uh)*	Derrybeg
Cnoc Fola *(NOK FAW-luh)*	Bloody Foreland
Gort an Choirce *(gurt on HER-kuh)*	Gortahork
Dun Fionnachaidh *(doon on-AH-keh)*	Dunfanaghy
Corran Binne *(COR-on BIN-eh)*	Horn Head

where you'll turn right and pass through the hamlet of Bunbeg (Bun Beag).

The 8 kilometers (5 miles) of road heading north—as Bunbeg blends into Derrybeg (Dori Beaga) and a bit beyond—are some of the most densely populated sections of this loop tour. Modern holiday cottages pepper the landscape in what the Irish have come to call "Bungalow Bliss" (or "Bungalow Blight" to nature lovers). Next you'll come to the...

Bloody Foreland (Cnoc Fola)

Named for the shade of red that heather turns at sunset, this scenic headland is laced with rock walls and forgotten cottage ruins. Pull off at one of the lofty roadside viewpoints and savor a picnic lunch and rugged coastal views.

• *Continue on R-257, meeting N-56 near Gortahork. Stay on N-56 to the Dunfanaghy Workhouse, about a kilometer south of Dunfanaghy town.*

Dunfanaghy Workhouse

Opened in 1845, this structure was part of an extensive workhouse compound (separating families by gender and age)—a dreaded last resort for the utterly destitute of coastal Donegal. There were once many identical compounds built across Ireland (serious history buffs should seek out the most intact and evocative example in Portumna—see page 320). A rigid Victorian solution to the spiraling problem of Ireland's rapidly multiplying poor, authorities at the time thought that poverty stemmed from laziness and should be punished. So, to motivate those lodging at the workhouse to pull themselves up by their bootstraps, conditions were made hard. But the system was unable to cope with the starving, homeless multitudes who were victims of the Famine.

The harsh workhouse experience is told through the true-life narrative of Wee Hannah Herrity, a wandering orphan and former resident of this workhouse. During the Famine, more than 4,000 young orphan workhouse girls from across Ireland were shipped to Australia as indentured servants in an attempt to offset the mostly male former convict population there. But Hannah's fate was different. She survived the Famine by taking meager refuge here, dying at age 90 in 1926. With the audioguide, you'll visit three upstairs rooms where stiff papier-mâché figures relate the powerful episodes in her life.

Cost and Hours: €4.50, includes audioguide; daily 9:30-17:30, Oct-April until 16:30, call to confirm winter hours; good bookstore, coffee shop, and helpful TI desk—pick up map for Horn Head loop here, tel. 074/913-6540, www.dunfanaghyworkhouse. ie.

• *Now continue into the town of...*

Dunfanaghy (Dun Fionnachaidh)

This planned town, founded by the English in the early 1600s for local markets and fairs, has a prim and proper appearance. In Dunfanaghy (dun-FAN-ah-hee), you can grab a pub lunch or some picnic fixings from the town market. Enjoy them from a scenic viewpoint on the nearby Horn Head loop drive (described later).

The modest town square, mostly a parking lot, marks the center of Dunfanaghy. Groceries are sold in the **Centra Market** (daily 7:30-21:00) on the main road opposite the town square.

Sleeping in Dunfanaghy: $$$ The Mill Restaurant and Accommodation is a diamond in the Donegal rough. Susan Alcorn nurtures seven wonderful rooms with classy decor, while her

Irish Fishermen Feel the Squeeze

The biggest fishing port in Ireland is Killybegs, about 30 kilometers (19 miles) west of Donegal town. But today, fishing is a

 sadly withering lifestyle. When Ireland joined the EU in 1973, Irish farmers and infrastructure benefited most from generous subsidies that helped transform the country a generation later into the "Celtic Tiger." But as the country reaped over €35 billion from the EU in its first 25 years of membership, the Irish fishing industry suffered. With the Mediterranean overfished, other EU nations set sail for rich Irish waters that were newly opened to them. Some estimate that 40 percent of the fish caught each year in Europe—valued at €175 billion—come from Irish territorial seas. Huge factory ships from Spain are far more efficient at hauling in a catch than the 1,500 remaining Irish boats (most of which are under 40 feet long). Irish fishermen lament that for every €1 accepted in EU subsidies, €5 have gone out in foreign nets. And the irony is that much of the fish sold in Irish grocery stores and restaurants is now imported from other EU nations...who caught the fish off the Irish coast.

husband Derek is the chef in their fine restaurant downstairs (one mile out of town past the Dunfanaghy Workhouse on the right, parking, tel. 074/913-6985, www.themillrestaurant.com, info@ themillrestaurant.com).

$$$ Arnold's Hotel is a comfortable, old-fashioned place that's been in the Arnold family since 1922. In the center of town, it has 30 cozy rooms that are well-kept by a helpful staff (family rooms, parking, tel. 074/913-6208, www.arnoldshotel.com, enquiries@arnoldshotel.com).

$ The Whins B&B has five inviting rooms with tasteful furnishings, which range from exotic African accents to a sturdy four-poster bed (cash only, parking, 10-minute walk north of town, tel. 074/913-6481, mobile 087-707-3985, www.thewhins.com, barbara@thewhins.com, John & Barbara Scholz).

Eating in Dunfanaghy: Gourmet all the way, **$$$$ The Mill Restaurant and Accommodation** specializes in memorable lamb or lobster dinners. It's worth booking days ahead (July-Aug Tue-Sun 19:00-21:00, closed Mon, Sept-June variable hours and closed days, tel. 074/913-6985, www.themillrestaurant.com). **$ Muck & Muffin** is a simple sandwich café, great for quick, cheap

DONEGAL & THE NORTHWEST

lunches. It's above the pottery shop in the stone warehouse on the town square (daily 9:30-17:00, until 18:00 in summer, tel. 074/913-6780). **$ The Great Wall** is a hole-in-the-wall Chinese takeaway place (daily 16:30-23:00, tel. 074/910-0111, next door to Centra Market). A few doors down, **$$ The Oyster Bar** does pub grub and live music on Friday and Saturday nights. My vote for most atmospheric pub in town is **Patsy Dan's,** with trad tunes Monday and Friday nights (18:00-21:00). Pub grub is served only in summer, when their pizza-porch out back becomes a local fair-weather favorite (daily 17:00-22:00, Main Street, tel. 074/910-0604).

• *From Dunfanaghy, you can head back to Derry via Letterkenny. If you have time, consider a detour to Horn Head.*

Horn Head Loop (Corran Binne)

If you have extra time, take an hour to embark on a lost-world plateau drive. This heaving headland with few trees has memorable coastal views that have made it popular with hikers in recent years.

Consult your map and get off N-56, following the *Horn Head* signs all the way around the eastern lobe of the peninsula. There are fewer than eight kilometers (5 miles) of narrow, single-lane road out here, with very little traffic. But be alert and willing to pull over at wide spots to cooperate with other cars.

This stone-studded peninsula was once an island. Then, shortly after the last Ice Age ended, ocean currents deposited a sandy spit in the calm water behind the island. A hundred years ago, locals harvested its stabilizing dune grass, using it for roof thatching and sending it abroad to Flanders, where soldiers used it to create beds for horses during World War I. With the grass gone, the sandy spit was free to migrate again. It promptly silted up the harbor, created a true peninsula, and ruined Dunfanaghy as a port town.

A short spur road leads to the summit of the headland, where you can park your car and walk another 50 yards up to the abandoned WWII lookout shelter. The views from here are dramatic, looking west toward Tory Island and south to Mount Errigal. Some may choose to hike an additional 30 minutes across the heather, to the ruins of the distant signal tower (not a castle, but instead a lookout for a feared Napoleonic invasion), clearly visible near the cliffs. But from here, it's still easy to bushwhack your way through (in sturdy footwear) to the rewarding cliff views at the base of the old signal tower. Navigate back to your car, using the lookout shelter on the summit as a landmark.

NORTHERN IRELAND

NORTHERN IRELAND

Northern Ireland is a different country from the Republic—both politically (it's part of the United Kingdom) and culturally (a combination of Irish, Scottish, and English influences). Occupying the northern one-sixth of the island of Ireland, it's only about 13 miles from Scotland at the narrowest point of the North Channel, and bordered on the south and west by the Republic.

That border is almost invisible. But when you leave the Republic of Ireland and enter Northern Ireland, you *are* crossing an international border (although you don't have to flash your passport). The 2016 British referendum vote to leave the EU may change the way this border crossing is handled in the future, but for now it's business as usual (see "The Brexit Effect" sidebar, later).

You won't use euros here; Northern Ireland issues its own Ulster pound, which, like the Scottish pound, is interchangeable with the English pound (€1 = about £0.88; £1 = about $1.40). Price differences create a lively daily shopping trade for those living near the border. Some establishments near the border may take euros, but at a lousy exchange rate. Keep any euros for your return to the Republic, and get pounds from an ATM inside Northern Ireland instead. And if you're heading to Britain next, it's best to change your Ulster pounds into English ones (free at any bank in Northern Ireland, England, Wales, or Scotland).

A generation ago, Northern Ireland was a sadly contorted corner of the world. On my first visit, I remember thinking that even the name of this region sounded painful ("Ulster" seemed to me like a combination of "ulcer" and "blister"). But today, Northern Ireland has emerged from the dark shadow of the decades-long political strife and violence known as the Troubles. And while not as popular among tourists as its neighbor to the south, Northern Ireland offers plenty to see and do...and learn.

It's important for visitors to Northern Ireland to understand the ways in which its population is segregated along political, religious, and cultural lines. Roughly speaking, the eastern seaboard is more Unionist, Protestant, and of English-Scottish heritage, while the south and west (bordering the Republic of Ireland) are Nation-

Northern Ireland Almanac

Official Name: Since Northern Ireland (pronounced "Norn Iron" by locals) is not an independent state, there is no official country name. Some call it Ulster (although historically that has included three counties that today lie on the Republic's side of the border), while others label it the Six Counties.

Size: 5,400 square miles (about the size of Connecticut), constituting a sixth of the island. With 1.8 million people, it's the smallest of the four United Kingdom countries (the others are England, Wales, and Scotland).

Geography: Northern Ireland is shaped roughly like a doughnut, with the UK's largest lake in the middle (Lough Neagh, 150 square miles and a prime eel fishery). Gently rolling hills of green grass rise to the 2,800-foot Slieve Donard. The weather is temperate, cloudy, moist, windy, and hard to predict.

Latitude and Longitude: 54°N and 5°W (as far north as parts of the Alaskan panhandle).

Biggest Cities: Belfast, the capital, has 300,000 residents. Half a million people—nearly one in three Northern Irish—inhabit the greater Belfast area. Derry (called Londonderry by Unionists) has 95,000 people.

Economy: Northern Ireland's economy is more closely tied to the UK than to the Republic of Ireland, and is subsidized by the UK and EU. Traditional agriculture (potatoes and grain) is fading fast, though modern techniques and abundant grassland make Northern Ireland a major producer of sheep, cows, and grass seed. Modern software and communications companies are replacing traditional manufacturing. Shipyards are rusty relics, and the linen industry is now threadbare (both victims of cheaper labor in Asia).

Government: Northern Ireland is not a self-governing nation, but is part of the UK, ruled from London by Queen Elizabeth II and Prime Minister Theresa May, and represented by 18 elected Members of Parliament. For 50 years (1922-1972), Northern Ireland was granted a great deal of autonomy and self-governance, known as "Home Rule." The current National Assembly (90-seat Parliament)—after an ineffective decade of political logjams—has recently begun to show signs of rejuvenation.

Flag: The official flag of Northern Ireland is the Union flag of the UK. But you'll also see the green, white, and orange Irish tricolor (waved by Nationalists) and the Northern Irish flag (white with a red cross and a red hand at its center), which is used by Unionists (see "The Red Hand of Ulster" sidebar on page 469).

alist, Catholic, and of indigenous Irish descent. Cities are often clearly divided between neighborhoods of one group or the other. Early in life, locals learn to identify the highly symbolic (and highly charged) colors, jewelry, music, names, accents, and vocabulary that distinguish the cultural groups.

Over the last century, the conflict between these two groups has been not about faith, but about politics: Will Northern Ireland stay part of the United Kingdom (Unionists), or become part of the Republic of Ireland (Nationalists)?

The roots of Protestant and Catholic differences date back to the time when Ireland was a colony of Great Britain. Four hundred years ago, Protestant settlers from England and Scotland were strategically "planted" in Catholic Ireland to help assimilate the island into the British economy. In 1620, the dominant English powerbase in London felt entitled to call both islands—Ireland as well as Britain—the "British Isles" on maps (a geographic label that irritates Irish Nationalists to this day). These Protestant settlers established their own cultural toehold on the island, laying claim to the most fertile land. Might made right, and God was on their side. Meanwhile, the underdog Catholic Irish held strong to their Gaelic culture on their ever-diminishing, boggy, rocky farms.

By the beginning of the 20th century, the sparse Protestant population could no longer control the entire island. When Ireland won its independence in 1921 (after a bloody guerrilla war against British rule), 26 of the island's 32 counties became the Irish Free State, ruled from Dublin with dominion status in the British Commonwealth—similar to Canada's level of sovereignty. In 1949, these 26 counties left the Commonwealth altogether and became the Republic of Ireland, severing all political ties with Britain. Meanwhile, the six remaining northeastern counties—the only ones with a Protestant majority who considered themselves British—chose not to join the Irish Free State and remained part of the UK.

But within these six counties—now joined as the political entity called Northern Ireland—was a large, disaffected Irish (mostly Catholic) minority who felt marginalized by the drawing of the new international border. This sentiment was represented by the Irish Republican Army (IRA), who wanted all 32 of Ireland's counties to be united in one Irish nation—their political goals were "Nationalist." Their political opponents were the "Unionists"—Protestant British eager to defend the union with Britain, who were primarily led by two groups: the long-established Orange Order, and the military muscle of the newly mobilized Ulster Volunteer Force (UVF).

In World War II, the Republic stayed neutral while the North enthusiastically supported the Allied cause—winning a spot close

Northern Ireland

to London's heart. Derry (a.k.a. Londonderry) became an essential Allied convoy port, while Belfast lost more than 800 civilians during four Luftwaffe bombing raids in 1941. After the war, the split between North and South seemed permanent, and Britain invested heavily in Northern Ireland to bring it solidly into the UK fold.

In the Republic of Ireland (the South), where the population was 94 percent Catholic and only 6 percent Protestant, there was a clearly dominant majority. But in the North, at the time it was formed, Catholics were a sizable 35 percent of the population—enough to demand attention when they complained about anti-Catholic discrimination on the part of the Protestant government. It was this discrimination that led to the Troubles, the conflict that filled headlines from the late 1960s to the late 1990s.

Partly inspired by Martin Luther King Jr. and the civil rights movement in America—beamed into Irish living rooms by the new magic of television news—in the 1960s the Catholic minority in Northern Ireland began a nonviolent struggle to end discrimination, advocating for better jobs and housing. Extremists polarized issues, and once-peaceful demonstrations—also broadcast on TV news—became violent.

Unionists were afraid that if the island became one nation, the relatively poor Republic of Ireland would drag down the comparatively affluent North, and feared losing political power to a Catholic majority. As the two sides clashed in 1969, the British Army entered the fray. Their role, initially a peacekeeping one, gradually evolved into acting as muscle for the Unionist government. In 1972, a tragic watershed year, more than 500 people died as combatants moved from petrol bombs to guns, and a new, more violent IRA emerged. In the 30-year (1968-1998) chapter of the struggle for an independent and united Ireland, more than 3,000 people died.

In the 1990s—with the UK (and Ireland's) membership in the EU, the growth of its economy, and the weakening of the Catholic Church's authority—the influence of the Republic of Ireland became less threatening to the Unionists. Optimists hailed the signing of a breakthrough peace plan in 1998, called the "Good Friday Peace Accord" by Nationalists, or the "Belfast Agreement" by Unionists. This led to the release of political prisoners on both sides in 2000—a highly emotional event.

British Army surveillance towers in Northern Ireland cities were dismantled in 2006, and the army formally ended its 38-year-long Operation Banner campaign in 2007. In 2010, the peace process was jolted forward by a surprisingly forthright apology offered by then British Prime Minister David Cameron, who expressed regret for the British Army's offenses on Bloody Sunday (see sidebar on page 415). The apology was prompted by the Saville Report—the results of an investigation conducted by the UK government as part of the Good Friday Peace Accord. It found that the 1972 shootings of Nationalist civil-rights marchers on Bloody Sunday by British soldiers was "unjustified" and the victims innocent (vindication for the victims' families, who had fought since 1972 to clear their loved ones' names).

Major hurdles to a lasting peace persist, but downtown checkpoints and "bomb-damage clearance sales" have been gone for decades. Replacing them are a forest of construction cranes, especially in rejuvenated Belfast. Tourists in Northern Ireland were once considered courageous (or reckless). Today, more tourists than ever are venturing north to Belfast and Derry, and cruise-ship crowds disembark in Belfast to board charter buses that fan out to visit the Giant's Causeway (see page 437) and Old Bushmills Distillery (see page 440).

When locals spot you with a map and a lost look on your face, they're likely to ask, "Wot yer lookin fer?" in their distinctive Northern accent. They're not suspicious of you, but trying to help you find your way. They may even "giggle" (Google) it for you. You're safer in Belfast than in many UK cities—and far safer, statistically, than in most major US cities. You'd have to look for

Northern Ireland Terminology

You may hear Northern Ireland referred to as **Ulster**—the traditional name of Ireland's ancient northernmost province. When the Republic of Ireland became independent in 1922, six of the nine counties of Ulster elected to form Northern Ireland, while three counties joined the Republic.

The mostly Protestant **Unionist** majority—and the more hardline, working-class **Loyalists**—want the North to remain in the UK. The **Ulster Unionist Party** (UUP) is the political party representing moderate Unionist views (Nobel Peace Prize co-winner David Trimble led the UUP from 1995 to 2005). The **Democratic Unionist Party** (DUP) takes a harder stance in defense of Unionism. The **Ulster Volunteer Force** (UVF), the **Ulster Freedom Fighters** (UFF), and the **Ulster Defense Association** (UDA) are Loyalist paramilitary organizations: All three are labeled "proscribed groups" by the UK's 2000 Terrorism Act.

The mostly Catholic **Nationalist** minority—and the more hardline, working-class **Republicans**—want a united and independent Ireland ruled by Dublin. The **Social Democratic Labor Party** (SDLP), founded by Nobel Peace Prize co-winner John Hume, is the moderate political party representing Nationalist views. **Sinn Fein** takes a harder stance in defense of Nationalism. The **Irish Republican Army** (IRA) is the now-disarmed Nationalist paramilitary organization formerly linked with Sinn Fein. The **Alliance Party** wants to bridge the gap between Unionists and Nationalists.

The long-simmering struggle to settle Northern Ireland's national identity precipitated the **Troubles,** the violent, 30-year conflict (1968-1998) between Unionist and Nationalist factions. To gain more insight into the complexity of the Troubles, the 90-minute documentary *Voices from the Grave* provides an excellent overview (easy to find on YouTube). Also check out the University of Ulster's informative and evenhanded Conflict Archive at http://cain.ulst.ac.uk/index.html.

Northern Ireland Politics

NATIONALISTS
(MOSTLY CATHOLICS)
"Feel Irish""

UNIONISTS
(MOSTLY PROTESTANTS)
"Feel British"

SINN FEIN
Mary Lou McDonald

ALLIANCE
Naomi Long

DUP
Arlene Foster

SDLP
Colum Eastwood
*John Hume
(retired)*

UUP
Robin Swann
*David Trimble
(retired)*

MODERATES

REPUBLICANS

LOYALISTS

GREEN

ORANGE

Not to scale &
not all opinions shown

The Brexit Effect

A hundred years ago, the British Isles were ruled from one place: London. Today, three sections of this geographic area (Ireland, Scotland, and England/Wales) drift in separate directions. And Northern Ireland, with strong cultural, geographic, and economic connections to all three, is being stretched uncomfortably.

In 2016, the people of the United Kingdom narrowly approved a referendum to leave the European Union (the "Brexit"). But in Northern Ireland (as in Scotland), a majority of people voted to stay. So where does that leave their relationship with the English and Welsh, who predominately voted to exit?

Among the Unionist community in the North, most of their ancestors came across from Scotland, with cherished cultural ties still evident. But Scotland is flirting with staying in the EU (and separating from the UK). The Republic of Ireland fills 80 percent of the island of Ireland, and a large minority in the North would like to see the island as a single Irish nation. Which direction will the North lean? Special status within the UK? Reunification with the Republic?

When the UK leaves the EU, the current "soft border" between the Republic and Northern Ireland will be reevaluated. It's not yet clear what form the new border will take. Few want the hassle and economic complications of a "hard border" (trade tariffs and border controls between EU and non-EU zones). People over 30 also remember the days when the border between Northern Ireland and the Republic was a closely patrolled line in a war zone. A hard border could rekindle tension between dormant Republican and Loyalist extremists. Borders add fuel to "them and us" perceptions.

Stay tuned to see how the swirling currents of Brexit, the Scottish independence movement, and the Irish reunification dream will affect this unique corner of the world...perched precariously between diverging cultural and economic powers: Ireland, Scotland, and England.

trouble to find it here. Just don't seek out spit-and-sawdust pubs in working-class neighborhoods and spew simplistic opinions about sensitive local topics. Tourists notice lingering tension mainly during the "marching season" (Easter-Aug, peaking in early July). July 12—"the Twelfth"—is traditionally the most confrontational day of the year in the North, when proud Protestant Unionist Orangemen march to celebrate their Britishness (often through staunchly Nationalist Catholic neighborhoods—it's still good advice to lie low if you stumble onto any big Orange parades).

As the less-fractured Northern Ireland enters the 21st century, one of its most valuable assets is its industrious people—and their legendary work ethic. When they emigrated to the US, they became known as the Scots-Irish and played a crucial role in our nation's founding. They were signers of our Declaration of Independence, a dozen of our presidents, and the ancestors of Davy Crockett and Mark Twain.

Northern Irish workers have a proclivity for making things that go. They've produced far-reaching inventions like Dunlop's first inflatable tire. The Shorts aircraft factory (in Belfast) built the Wright Brothers' first six aircraft for commercial sale and the world's first vertical takeoff jet. The *Titanic* was the only flop of Northern Ireland's otherwise successful shipbuilding industry. The once-futuristic DeLorean sports car was made in Belfast.

Notable people from Northern Ireland include musicians Van Morrison and James Galway, and actors Liam Neeson, Roma Downey, Ciarán Hinds, and Kenneth Branagh. The North also produced Christian intellectual and writer C.S. Lewis, Victorian physicist Lord Kelvin, engineer Harry Ferguson (inventor of the modern farm tractor and first four-wheel drive Formula One car), and soccer-star playboy George Best—who once famously remarked, "I spent most of my money on liquor and women...and the rest I wasted."

As in the Republic, sports are big in the North. Northern-born golfers Rory McIlroy, Graeme McDowell, and Darren Clarke have won a fistful of majors over the past decade, filling local hearts with pride. With close ties to Scotland, many Northern Irish fans follow the exploits of Glasgow soccer teams—but which team you root for betrays which side of the tracks you come from. Those who cheer for Glasgow Celtic are Nationalist and Catholic; those waving banners for the Glasgow Rangers are Unionist and Protestant. To maintain peace, some pubs post signs on their doors banning patrons from wearing sports jerseys. Luckily, sports with no sectarian history are now being introduced, such as the Belfast Giants ice hockey team—a hit with both communities.

Northern Ireland seems poised to do great things. As you travel through Northern Ireland today, you'll encounter a fascinating country with a complicated, often tragic history—and a brightening future.

DERRY

No city in Ireland connects the kaleidoscope of historical dots more colorfully than Derry. From a leafy monastic hamlet to a Viking-pillaged port, from a cannonball-battered siege survivor to an Industrial Revolution sweatshop, from an essential WWII naval base to a wrenching flashpoint of sectarian Troubles... Derry has seen it all.

Though Belfast is the capital of Northern Ireland, this pivotal city has a more diverse history and a prettier setting. Derry was a vibrant city back when Belfast was just a mudflat. With roughly a third of Belfast's population (95,000), Derry feels more welcoming and manageable to visitors.

The town is the mecca of Ulster Unionism. When Ireland was being divvied up, the River Foyle was the logical border between the North and the Republic. But, for sentimental and economic reasons, the North kept Derry, which is otherwise on the Republic's side of the river. Consequently, this predominantly Catholic-Nationalist city was much contested throughout the Troubles.

Even its name is disputed. While most of its population and its city council call it "Derry," some maps, road signs, and all UK train schedules use "Londonderry," the name on its 1662 royal charter and the one favored by Unionists. I once asked a Northern Ireland rail employee for a ticket to "Derry"; he replied that there was no such place, but he would sell me one to "Londonderry." I'll call it Derry in this book since that's what the majority of the city's inhabitants do.

The past 15 years have brought some refreshing changes. Manned British Army surveillance towers were taken down in 2006, and most British troops finally departed in mid-2007, after

38 years in Northern Ireland. In June 2011, a new, curvy pedestrian bridge across the River Foyle was completed. Locals dubbed it the Peace Bridge because it links the predominantly Protestant Waterside (east bank) with the predominantly Catholic Cityside (west bank). Today, you can feel comfortable wandering the streets and enjoying this "legend-Derry" city.

PLANNING YOUR TIME

If just passing through (say, on your way to Portrush—see the next chapter), it takes a few hours to see the essential Derry sights: Visit the Tower Museum and catch some views from the town wall.

With more time, spend a night in Derry, so you can see the powerful Bogside murals and take a walking tour around the town walls—you'll appreciate this underrated city. With two nights in Derry, consider crossing back into the Republic for a scenic driving loop through part of remote County Donegal (see page 385).

Orientation to Derry

The River Foyle flows north, slicing Derry into eastern and western chunks. The old town walls and almost all worthwhile sights are on the west side. (The tiny train station and Ebrington Square—at the end of the Peace Bridge—are the main reasons to spend time on the east side.) Waterloo Place and the adjacent Guildhall Square, just outside the north corner of the old city walls, are the pedestrian hubs of city activity. The Strand Road area extending north from Waterloo Place makes a comfortable home base, with the majority of lodging and restaurant suggestions within a block or two. The Diamond (main square) and its War Memorial statue mark the heart of the old city within the walls.

TOURIST INFORMATION

The TI sits on the riverfront and rents bikes (£5/2 hours, £8/4 hours, £12/8 hours), and can book bus and walking tours (Mon-Sat 9:00-18:00, Sun 10:00-17:00, closes earlier in off-season; 44 Foyle Street, tel. 028/7126-7284, www.visitderry.com).

ARRIVAL IN DERRY

By Train: Next to the river on the east side of town, Derry's little end-of-the-line train station (no storage lockers) has service to Portrush, Belfast, and Dublin. Each arriving train is greeted by free shuttle buses to Ulsterbus Station on the west side of town, a couple of minutes' walk south of Guildhall Square on Foyle Street (luggage storage at post office around corner in same building, fee based on bag size, Mon-Fri 9:30-17:30—beware of lunch closure, closed Sat-Sun). Otherwise, it's a £5 taxi ride to Guildhall Square.

Derry

To **13** & County Donegal via A-2

100 Meters
100 Yards

River Foyle

ST. EUGENE'S CATHEDRAL

QUAYSIDE SHOPPING CENTRE

See Bogside Murals map

BLOODY SUNDAY MONUMENT

BOGSIDE

"H" BLOCK MONUMENT

FREE DERRY CORNER

ROYAL BASTION

APPRENTICE BOYS HALL

MAGAZINE GATE

Waterloo Place

POST

GUILD-HALL

Guildhall Square

PEACE BRIDGE

To **9** Waterside & Train Station

TOWER MUSEUM

SHIPQUAY GATE

NERVE CENTRE

CRAFT VILLAGE

Ulsterbus Station

CASTLE GATE

BUTCHER GATE

MILLENNIUM FORUM

CITY WALLS

The Diamond

WAR MEMORIAL

FOYLESIDE SHOPPING CENTRE

ST. AUGUSTINE CHAPEL

SIEGE MUS.

VERBAL ARTS CENTRE

ST. COLUMB'S CATHEDRAL

FERRYQUAY GATE

NEW GATE

LONG TOWER CHURCH

DOUBLE BASTION

BISHOP'S GATE

CITY WALLS

& BIKE RENTAL

JAIL TOWER

FOUNTAIN

PEACE WALL

FORMER SHIRT FACTORY SITE

HANDS ACROSS THE DIVIDE STATUES

To Train Station, Portrush via A-2 & Belfast via A-6

To County Donegal (Republic of Ireland) via A-40

CRAIGAVON BRIDGE

DERRY

Accommodations
1. Bishop's Gate Hotel
2. Maldron Hotel
3. Merchant's House
4. Saddler's House

Eateries & Other
5. Entrada
6. Exchange Rest. & Wine Bar
7. Fitzroy's
8. Browns in Town
9. To Walled City Brewery
10. Mandarin Palace
11. Peadar O'Donnell's Pub
12. Supermarket (2)
13. To Laundry
14. Playhouse Theatre

The same free shuttle service leaves Ulsterbus Station 15 minutes before each departing train. Unfortunately, there's not yet a footpath from the train station to the pedestrian Peace Bridge.

By Bus: All intercity buses stop at the Ulsterbus Station, on Foyle Street close to Guildhall Square.

By Car: Drivers stopping for a few hours can park at the Foyleside parking garage across from the TI (£1/hour, £3/4 hours, Mon-Sat 8:00-19:00 or later, Sun from 12:00, tel. 028/7137-7575). Drivers staying overnight can ask about parking at their B&B, or try the Quayside parking garage behind the Travelodge (£0.80/hour, £3/4 hours, £8 additional for overnight, daily 7:30-21:00, closes earlier on weekends).

HELPFUL HINTS

Money: Danske Bank is on Guildhall Square and the Bank of Ireland is on Strand Road.

Bookstore: Foyle Books is a dusty little pleasure for random browsing (Mon-Sat 11:00-17:00, closed Sun, 12 Magazine Street at entrance to Craft Village, tel. 028/7137-2530).

Laundry: Bubbles has drop-off service—bring it in the morning, pick up later that day (Mon-Fri 9:00-17:00, Sat from 10:00, closed Sun, 141 Strand Road, tel. 028/7136-3366).

Taxi: Try **City Cabs** (tel. 028/7126-4466), **The Taxi Company** (tel. 028/7126-2626), or **Foyle Taxis** (tel. 028/7127-9999).

Car Rental: Enterprise is handy (70 Clooney Road, tel. 028/7186-1699, www.enterprise.co.uk). Another option is **Desmond Motors** (173 Strand Road, tel. 028/7136-7136, www.desmondmotors.co.uk).

Tours in Derry

Walking Tours

McCrossan's City Tours leads insightful hour-long walks, giving a rounded view of the city's history. Tours depart from 11 Carlisle Road, just below Ferryquay Gate (£4; daily at 10:00, 12:00, 14:00, and 16:00; tel. 028/7127-1996, mobile 077-1293-7997, www.derrycitytours.com, derrycitytours@aol.com). They also offer private group tours (£60).

Bogside History Tours offers walks led by Bogside residents who lost loved ones in the tragic events of Bloody Sunday (£6, £9 combo-ticket with Museum of Free Derry; April-Sept daily at 11:00 and 13:00, Mon-Fri also at 15:00; depart from in front of the Guildhall, mobile 077-3145-0088 or 078-0056-7165, www.bogsidehistorytours.com, paul@bogsidehistorytours.com). Tour guides also offer various taxi tours (£25/hour, call or email for options).

Hop-On, Hop-Off Bus Tour

City Sightseeing's double-decker buses are a good option for a general overview of Derry. The one-hour loop covers both sides of the river (seven stops overall), including the Guildhall, the old city walls, political wall murals, cathedrals, and former shirt factories. Your ticket is good for 24 hours (£12.50, pay driver, bus departs April-Sept daily on the hour 10:00-16:00 from in front of TI and Guildhall Square, tel. 028/7137-0067, www.citysightseeingderry.com).

City Sightseeing also offers trips from Derry to the Giant's Causeway, Dunluce Castle, Old Bushmills Distillery, and Carrick-a-Rede Rope Bridge in County Antrim (£25, price does not include Bushmills entry, runs daily May-Sept, depart TI at 10:00, return by 17:00, minimum 10 people). In addition, they offer tours to Glenveagh National Park in County Donegal (depart TI at 9:00, return by 15:00, minimum 10 people). You can book any of their tours online or by phone.

Walks in Derry

Though calm today, Derry is stamped by years of tumultuous conflict. These two self-guided walks (each taking less than an hour) will increase your understanding of the town's history. Walk the Walls, starting on the old city walls and ending at the Anglican Cathedral, focuses on Derry's early days. My Bogside Murals Walk guides you to the city's compelling murals, which document the time of the Troubles. These tours, each worth ▲▲, can be done separately or linked, depending on your time.

WALK THE WALLS

Squatting determinedly in the city center, the old city walls of Derry (built 1613-1618 and still intact, except for wider gates to handle modern vehicles) hold an almost mythic place in Irish history.

It was here in 1688 that a group of brave apprentice boys, some of whom had been shipped to Derry as orphans after the great fire of London in 1666, made their stand. They slammed the city gates shut in the face of the approaching Catholic forces of deposed King James II. With this act, the boys galvanized the city's indecisive Protestant defenders inside the walls.

Months of negotiations and a grinding 105-day siege followed, during which a third of the 20,000 refugees and defenders crammed into the city perished. The siege was finally broken in 1689, when supply ships broke through a boom stretched across the River Foyle. The sacrifice and defiant survival of the city turned the tide in favor of newly crowned Protestant King William of Orange, who arrived in Ireland soon after and defeated James at the pivotal Battle of the Boyne.

To fully appreciate the walls, take a walk on top of them (free and open from dawn to dusk). Almost 20 feet high and at least as thick, the walls form a mile-long oval loop that you can cover in less than an hour. But the most interesting section is the half-circuit facing the Bogside, starting at Magazine Gate (stairs face the Tower Museum Derry inside the walls) and finishing at Bishop's Gate.

• *Enter the walls at Magazine Gate and find the stairs opposite the Tower Museum. Once atop the walls, head left.*

Walk the wall as it heads uphill, snaking along the earth's contours. In the row of buildings on the left (just before crossing over Castle Gate), you'll see an arch entry into the **Craft Village,** an alley lined with a cluster of cute shops and cafés that showcase the economic rejuvenation of Derry (Mon-Sat 9:30-17:30, closed Sun).

• *After crossing over Butcher Gate, stop in front of the grand building with the four columns to view the...*

First Derry Presbyterian Church: This impressive-looking building is the second church to occupy this site. The first was built by Queen Mary in the 1690s to thank the Presbyterian community for standing by their Anglican brethren during the dark days of the famous siege. That church was later torn down to make room for today's stately Neoclassical, red-sandstone church finished in 1780. Over the next 200 years, time took its toll on the structure, which was eventually closed due to dry rot and Republican firebombings. But in 2011, the renovated church reopened to a chorus of cross-community approval (yet one more sign of the slow reconciliation taking place in Derry). The **Blue Coat School** exhibit behind the church highlights the important role of Presbyterians in local history (free but donation encouraged, closed Sat-Tue in summer and all of Oct-April, tel. 028/7126-1550).

• *Just up the block is the...*

Apprentice Boys Memorial Hall: Built in 1873, this houses the private lodge and meeting rooms of an all-male Protestant organization. The group is dedicated to the memory of the original 13 apprentice boys who saved the day during the 1688 siege. Each year, on the Saturday closest to the August 12 anniversary date, the modern-day Apprentice Boys Society celebrates the end of the siege with a controversial march atop the walls. These walls are considered sacred ground for devout Unionists, who claim that many who died during the famous siege were buried within

Derry's History

Once an island in the River Foyle, Derry (from *doire,* Irish for "oak grove") was chosen by St. Colmcille (St. Columba in English) circa A.D. 546 for a monastic settlement. He later banished himself to the island of Iona in Scotland out of remorse for sparking a bloody battle over the rights to a holy manuscript that he had secretly copied.

A thousand years later, the English defeated the last Ulster-based Gaelic chieftains in the Battle of Kinsale (1601). With victory at hand, the English took advantage of the power vacuum. They began the "plantation" of Ulster with loyal Protestant subjects imported from Scotland and England. The native Irish were displaced to less desirable rocky or boggy lands, sowing the seeds of resentment that eventually fueled the Troubles.

A dozen wealthy London guilds (grocers, haberdashers, tailors, and others) took on Derry as an investment and changed its name to "Londonderry." They built the last great walled city in Ireland to protect their investment from the surrounding—and hostile—Irish locals. The walls proved their worth in 1688-1689, when the town's Protestant defenders, loyal to King William of Orange, withstood a prolonged siege by the forces of Catholic King James II. "No surrender" is still a passionate rallying cry among Ulster Unionists determined to remain part of the United Kingdom.

The town became a major port of emigration to the New World in the early 1800s. Then, when the Industrial Revolution provided a steam-powered sewing factory, the city developed a thriving shirt-making industry. The factories here employed mostly Catholic women who had honed their skills in rural County Donegal. Although Belfast grew larger and wealthier, Unionists tightened their grip on "Londonderry" and the walls that they regarded with almost holy reverence. In 1921, they insisted that the city be included in Northern Ireland when the province was partitioned from the new Irish Free State (later to become the Republic of Ireland). A bit of gerrymandering (with three lightly populated Unionist districts outvoting two densely populated

the battered walls because of lack of space. The **Siege Museum** stands behind the hall, giving a narrow-focus Unionist view of the siege (£3, Mon-Sat 10:00-16:30, closed Sun, 18 Society Street, tel. 028/7126-1219).

Next, you'll pass a large, square pedestal on the right atop Royal Bastion. It once supported a column in honor of Governor

Nationalist districts) ensured that the Protestant minority maintained control of the city, despite its Catholic majority.

Derry was a key escort base for US convoys headed for Britain during World War II, and 60 surviving German U-boats were instructed to surrender here at the end of the war. After the war, poor Catholics—unable to find housing—took over the abandoned military barracks, with multiple families living in each dwelling. Only homeowners were allowed to vote, and the Unionist minority, which controlled city government, was not eager to build more housing that would tip the voting balance away from them. Over the years, sectarian pressures gradually built—until they reached the boiling point. The ugly events of Bloody Sunday on January 30, 1972, brought worldwide attention to the Troubles (for more details, see "Bloody Sunday" sidebar on page 415).

Today, life has stabilized in Derry, and the population has increased by 25 percent in the last 30 years. The Foyleside Shopping Centre, bankrolled by investors from Boston, opened in 1995. The 1998 Good Friday Peace Accord provided significant progress toward peace, and the British Army withdrew 90 percent of its troops in mid-2007. With a population that is over 70 percent Catholic, the city has agreed to alternate Nationalist and Unionist mayors. There is a feeling of cautious optimism as Derry—the epicenter of bombs and bloody conflicts in the 1960s and 1970s—now boasts a history museum that airs all viewpoints.

The city continues to work on building a happier image. The wall—with all its troubled imagery and once nicknamed "the noose"—is now called "the necklace." With its complicated history, you're damned-if-you-do and damned-if-you-don't when it comes to calling it Derry (pro-Catholic, Nationalist) or Londonderry (pro-Protestant, Unionist). Some call it Derry/Londonderry or Londonderry/Derry. Others just say "Slashtown." And the tourist board calls it "legend-Derry."

DERRY

George Walker, the commander of the defenders during the famous siege. In 1972, the IRA blew up the column, which had 105 steps to the top (one for each day of the siege). An adjacent plaque shows a photo of the column before it was destroyed.

• *Opposite the empty pedestal is the small Anglican...*

St. Augustine Chapel: Set in a pretty graveyard, this Anglican chapel is where some believe the original sixth-century monastery of St. Columba stood. The quaint grounds are open to visitors (Mon-Sat 10:30-16:30, closed Sun except for worship). In Victorian times, this stretch of the walls was a fashionable promenade walk.

As you walk, you'll pass a long wall (on the left)—all that's left of a former **British Army base,** which stood here until 2006. Two 50-foot towers used to loom out of it, bristling with cameras and listening devices. Soldiers built them here for a bird's-eye view of the once-turbulent Catholic Bogside district below. The towers' dismantlement—as well as the removal of most of the British Army from Northern Ireland—is another positive sign in cautiously optimistic Derry. The walls of this former army base now contain a parking lot.

Stop at the **Double Bastion** fortified platform that occupies this corner of the city walls. The old cannon is nicknamed "Roaring Meg" for the fury of its firing during the siege.

From here, you can see across the Bogside to the not-so-far-away hills of County Donegal in the Republic. Derry was once an island, but as the River Foyle gradually changed its course, the area you see below the wall began to drain. Over time, and especially after the Great Potato Famine (1845-1849), Catholic peasants from rural Donegal began to move into Derry to find work during the Industrial Revolution. They settled on this least desirable land...on the soggy bog side of the city. From this vantage point, survey the Bogside with its political murals and Palestinian flags.

Directly below and to the right are Free Derry Corner and Rossville Street, where the tragic events of Bloody Sunday took place in 1972 (see page 415). Down on the left is the 18th-century Long Tower Catholic church, named after the monk-built round tower that once stood in the area (see page 423).

• *Head to the grand brick building behind you. This is the...*

Verbal Arts Centre: A former Presbyterian school, this center promotes the development of local literary arts in the form of poetry, drama, writing, and storytelling. You can drop in and see what performances might be on during your visit (Mon-Fri 9:00-17:00, Sat 12:00-14:00, closed Sun, tel. 028/7126-6946, www. verbalartscentre.co.uk).

• *Go left another 50 yards around the corner to reach...*

Bishop's Gate: From here, look up Bishop Street Within (inside the walls). This was the site of another British Army surveillance tower. Placed just inside the town walls, it overlooked the neighborhood until 2006. Now look in the other direction to see Bishop Street Without (outside the walls). You'll spot a modern wall topped by a high mesh fence, running along the left side of Bishop Street Without.

This is a so-called **"peace wall,"** built to ensure the security of the Protestant enclave living behind it in Derry's Fountain neighborhood. When the Troubles reignited almost 50 years ago, 20,000 Protestants lived on this side of the river. This small housing development of 1,000 people is all that remains of that proud community today. The rest have chosen to move across the river to the mostly Protestant Waterside district. The stone tower halfway down the "peace wall" is all that remains of the old jail that briefly held doomed rebels after a 1798 revolt against the British.

• *From Bishop's Gate, those short on time can descend from the walls and walk 15 minutes directly back through the heart of the old city, along Bishop Street Within and Shipquay Street to Guildhall Square. With more time, consider visiting St. Columb's Cathedral, the Long Tower Church, and the murals of the Bogside.*

BOGSIDE MURALS WALK

The Catholic Bogside area was the tinderbox of the modern Troubles in Northern Ireland. Bloody Sunday, a terrible confrontation during a march that occurred nearly 50 years ago, sparked a sectarian inferno, and the ashes have not yet fully cooled. Today, the murals of the Bogside give visitors an accessible glimpse of this community's passionate perception of those events.

Getting There: The events are memorialized in 12 murals painted on the ends of residential flats along a 300-yard stretch of Rossville Street and Lecky Road, where the march took place. For the purposes of this walk, you can reach them from Waterloo Place via William Street. They are also accessible from the old city walls at Butcher Gate via the long set of stairs extending below Fahan Street on the grassy hillside, or by the stairs leading down from the Long Tower Church. These days, this neighborhood is gritty but quiet and safe.

The Artists: Two brothers, Tom and William Kelly, and their childhood friend Kevin Hasson are known as the Bogside Artists. They grew up in the Bogside and witnessed the tragic events that took place there, which led them to begin painting the murals in 1994. One of the brothers, Tom, gained a reputation as a "heritage mural" painter, specializing in scenes of life in the old days. In a surprising and hopeful development, Tom was later invited into Derry's Protestant Fountain neighborhood to work with a youth club there on three proud heritage murals that were painted over paramilitary graffiti. For more about this unique trio, visit their website, BogsideArtists.com.

DERRY

Bogside Murals Walk

1. Peace
2. The Hunger Strikers
3. John Hume
4. The Saturday Matinee
5. Civil Rights
6. The Runners
7. Operation Motorman
8. Bloody Sunday
9. Bernadette
10. Petrol Bomber
11. The Death of Innocence
12. Bloody Sunday Commemoration

50 Meters
50 Yards

WILLIAM ST.

WALK BEGINS

To Waterloo Place

BOGSIDE

MUSEUM OF FREE DERRY

"H" BLOCK MONUMENT

BLOODY SUNDAY MONUMENT

BUTCHER GATE

FIRST DERRY PRESBYTERIAN CHURCH

FREE DERRY CORNER

CITY WALLS

APPRENTICE BOYS HALL

SIEGE MUSEUM

WALK ENDS

BOGSIDE INN PUB

ROYAL BASTION

ST. AUGUSTINE CHAPEL

WALLED CITY

LISFANNON PK.
ABBEY ST.
CHAMBERLAIN
FAHAN ST.
ROSSVILLE ST.
WESTLAND ST.
LECKY RD.
FAHAN ST.
SOCIETY ST.
PALACE ST.

DERRY

The Murals: Start out at the corner of Rossville and William streets.

The Bogside murals face different directions (and some are partially hidden by buildings), so they're not all visible from a single viewpoint. Plan on walking three long blocks along Rossville Street (which becomes Lecky Road) to see them all. Residents are used to visitors and don't mind if you photograph the murals. Local motorists are uncommonly courteous with allowing visitors to cross the busy street.

From William Street, walk south along the right side of Ross-

Bloody Sunday

Inspired by civil rights marches in America in the mid-1960s, and the Prague Spring uprising and Paris student strikes of 1968, civil rights groups began to protest in Northern Ireland around this time. Initially, their goals were to gain better housing, secure fair voting rights, and end employment discrimination for Catholics in the North. Tensions mounted, and clashes with the predominantly Protestant Royal Ulster Constabulary police force became frequent. Eventually, the British Army was called in to keep the peace.

On January 30, 1972, about 10,000 people protesting internment without trial held an illegal march sponsored by the Northern Ireland Civil Rights Association. British Army barricades kept them from the center of Derry, so they marched through the Bogside neighborhood.

That afternoon, some youths rioted on the fringe of the march. An elite parachute regiment had orders to move in and make arrests in the Rossville Street area. Shooting broke out, and after 25 minutes, 13 marchers were dead and 13 were wounded (one of the wounded later died). The soldiers claimed they came under attack from gunfire and nail-bombs. The marchers said the army shot indiscriminately at unarmed civilians.

The clash, called "Bloody Sunday," uncorked pent-up frustration as moderate Nationalists morphed into staunch Republicans overnight and released a flood of fresh IRA volunteers. An investigation at the time exonerated the soldiers, but the relatives of the victims called it a whitewash and insisted on their innocence.

In 1998, then-British Prime Minister Tony Blair promised a new inquiry, which became the longest and most expensive in British legal history. In 2010, a 12-year investigation—the Saville Report—determined that the Bloody Sunday civil rights protesters were innocent and called the deaths of 14 protesters unjustified.

In a dramatic 2010 speech in the House of Commons, then-British Prime Minister David Cameron apologized to the people of Derry. "What happened on Bloody Sunday was both unjustified and unjustifiable. It was wrong," he declared. Cheers rang out in Derry's Guildhall Square, where thousands had gathered to watch the televised speech. After 38 years, Northern Ireland's bloodiest wound started healing.

DERRY

ville Street toward Free Derry Corner. The murals will all be on your right.

The first mural you'll walk past is the colorful ❶ *Peace,* showing the silhouette of a dove in flight (left side of mural) and an oak leaf (right side of mural), both created from a single ribbon. A peace campaign asked Derry city schoolchildren to write suggestions for positive peacetime images; their words inspired this artwork. The dove is a traditional symbol of peace, and the oak leaf is a traditional symbol of Derry—recognized by both communities. The dove flies from the sad blue of the past toward the warm yellow of the future.

❷ *The Hunger Strikers,* repainted during the summer of 2015, features two Derry-born participants of the 1981 Maze Prison hunger strike, as well as their mothers, who sacrificed and supported them in their fatal decision (10 strikers died). The prison was closed after the release of all prisoners (both Unionist and Nationalist) in 2000.

Smaller and easy to miss (above a ramp with banisters) is ❸ *John Hume.* It's actually a collection of four faces (clockwise from upper left): Nationalist leader John Hume, Martin Luther King Jr., Nelson Mandela, and Mother Teresa. The Brooklyn Bridge in the middle symbolizes the long-term bridges of understanding that the work of these four Nobel Peace Prize-winning activists created. Born in the Bogside, Hume still maintains a home here.

Now look for ❹ *The Saturday Matinee,* which depicts an outgunned but undaunted local youth behind a screen shield. He holds

a stone, ready to throw, while a British armored vehicle approaches (echoing the famous Tiananmen Square photo of the lone Chinese man facing the tank). Why *Saturday Matinee?* It's because the weekend was the best time for locals to engage in a little "recreational rioting" and "have a go at" the army; people were off work and youths were out of school.

Nearby is ❺ *Civil Rights,* showing a marching Derry crowd carrying an antisectarian banner. It dates from the days when Martin Luther King Jr.'s successful nonviolent marches were being seen worldwide on TV, creating a dramatic, global ripple effect. Civil rights marches, inspired by King and using the same methods to combat a similar set of grievances, gave this long-suffering community a powerful new voice.

All along this walk you'll notice lots of flags, including the red, black, white, and green Palestinian flag. Palestinians and Catholic residents of Northern Ireland have a special empathy for each other—both are indigenous people dealing with the persistent realities of sharing what they consider their rightful homeland with more powerful settlers planted there for political reasons.

In the building behind this mural, you'll find the intense **Museum of Free Derry** (£6, £9 combo-ticket with Bogside History Tours, open Mon-Fri 9:30-16:30 year-round, also open April-Sept Sat-Sun 13:00-16:00, 55 Glenfada Park, tel. 028/7136-0880, www.museumoffreederry.org). Photos, shirts with bullet holes, and video documentary convey the experiences of the people of the Bogside during the worst of the Troubles. At the far end of the museum's outdoor wall (high up on the second floor of an adjacent residential building) is a copy of a famous painting by Francisco Goya depicting another massacre—this one in Spain—called the *Third of May 1808*. This reproduction draws a stark parallel to the local events that occurred here. Below and to the left of the painting (next to a gated alley) are two large bullet holes in the wall, inflicted on Bloody Sunday and preserved behind glass.

Cross over to the other side of Rossville Street to see the **Bloody Sunday Monument.** This small, fenced-off stone obelisk lists the names of those who died that day, most within 50 yards of this spot. Take a look at the map pedestal by the monument, which shows how a rubble barricade was erected to block the street. A 10-story housing project called Rossville Flats stood here in those days. After peaceful protests failed (with Bloody Sunday being the watershed event), Nationalist youths became more aggressive. British troops were wary of being hit by Molotov cocktails thrown from the rooftop of the housing project.

Cross back again, this time over to the grassy median strip that runs down the middle of Rossville Street. At this end stands a granite letter *H* inscribed with the names of the 10 IRA hunger strikers who died (and how many days they starved) in the H-block of Maze Prison in 1981 (see *"The Hunger Strikers,"* earlier in the walk).

From here, as you look across at the corner of Fahan Street, you get a good view of two murals. In ❻ *The Runners* (right), three rioting youths flee tear gas from canisters used by the British Army to disperse hostile crowds. More than 1,000 canisters were used during the Battle of the Bogside; "nonlethal" rubber bullets killed 17 people over the course of the Troubles. Meanwhile, in ❼ *Operation Motorman* (left), a soldier wields a sledgehammer to break through a house door, depicting the massive push by the British

Army to open up the Bogside's barricaded "no-go" areas that the IRA had controlled for three years (1969-1972).

Walk down to the other end of the median strip where the white wall of **Free Derry Corner** announces "You are now enter-

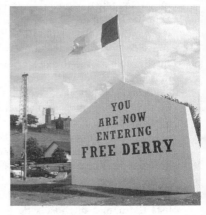

ing Free Derry" (imitating a similarly defiant slogan of the time in once-isolated West Berlin). This was the gabled end of a string of houses that stood here more than 40 years ago. During the Troubles, it became a traditional meeting place for speakers to address crowds. A portion of this mural changes from time to time, calling attention to injustice suffered by kindred spirits around the world (the plight of Palestinians and Basques are common themes).

Cross back to the right side of the street (now Lecky Road) to see ❽ *Bloody Sunday,* in which a small group of men carry a body from that ill-fated march. It's based on a famous photo of Father Edward Daly that was taken that day. Hunched over, he waves a white handkerchief to request safe passage in order to evacuate a mortally wounded protester. The bloodstained civil rights banner was inserted under the soldier's feet for extra emphasis. After Bloody Sunday, the previously marginal IRA suddenly found itself swamped with bitterly determined young recruits.

Near it is a mural called ❾ *Bernadette.* The woman with the megaphone is Bernadette Devlin McAliskey, an outspoken civil rights leader, who at age 21 became the youngest elected member of British Parliament. Behind her kneels a female supporter, banging a trash-can lid against the street in a traditional expression of protest in Nationalist neighborhoods. Trash-can lids were also used to warn neighbors of the approach of British patrols.

❿ *Petrol Bomber,* showing a teen wearing an army-surplus gas mask, captures the Battle of the Bogside, when locals barricaded their community, effectively shutting out British rule. Though the main figure's face is obscured by the mask, his body clearly communicates the resolve of an oppressed people. In the background, the long-gone Rossville Flats housing project still looms, with an Irish tricolor flag flying from its top.

In ⓫ *The Death of Innocence,* a young girl stands in front of bomb wreckage. She is Annette McGavigan, a 14-year-old who was killed on this corner by crossfire in 1971. She was the 100th fatality of the Troubles, which eventually took more than 3,000

DERRY

Political Murals

The dramatic and emotional murals you'll encounter in Northern Ireland will likely be one of your trip's most enduring travel memories.

During the 19th century, Protestant neighborhoods hung flags and streamers each July to commemorate the victory of King William of Orange at the Battle of the Boyne in 1690. Modern murals evolved from these colorful annual displays. With the advent of industrial paints, temporary seasonal displays became permanent territorial statements.

Unionist murals were created during the extended Home Rule political debate that eventually led to the partitioning of the island in 1921 and the creation of Northern Ireland. Murals that expressed opposing views in Nationalist Catholic neighborhoods were outlawed. The ban remained until the eruption of the modern Troubles, when staunchly Nationalist Catholic communities isolated themselves behind barricades, eluding state control and gaining freedom to express their pent-up passions. In Derry, this form of symbolic, cultural, and ideological resistance first appeared in 1969 with the simple "You are now entering Free Derry" message that you'll still see painted on the surviving gable wall at Free Derry Corner.

Found mostly in working-class neighborhoods of Belfast and Derry, today's political murals have become a dynamic form of popular culture. They blur the line between art and propaganda, giving visitors a striking glimpse of each community's history, identity, and values.

lives (and she was also a cousin of one of the artists). The broken gun beside her points to the ground, signifying that it's no longer being wielded. The large butterfly above her shoulder symbolizes the hope for peace. For years, the artists left the butterfly an empty silhouette until they felt confident that the peace process had succeeded. They finally filled in the butterfly with optimistic colors in the summer of 2006.

Finally, around the corner, you'll see a circle of male faces. This mural, painted in 1997 to observe the 25th anniversary of the tragedy, is called ⑫ *Bloody Sunday Commemoration* and shows the 14 victims. They are surrounded by a ring of 14 oak leaves—the symbol of Derry. When relatives of the dead learned that the three

Bogside Artists were beginning to paint this mural, many came forward to loan the artists precious photos of their loved ones, so they could be more accurately depicted.

Across the street, drop into the **Bogside Inn** for a beverage and check out the black-and-white photos of events in the area during the Troubles. This pub has been here through it all, and lives on to tell the tale.

While these murals preserve the struggles of the late 20th century, today sectarian violence has given way to negotiations and a settlement that seems to be working in fits and starts. The British apology for the Bloody Sunday shootings was a huge step forward. Former Nationalist leader John Hume (who shared the 1998 Nobel Peace Prize with then-Unionist leader David Trimble) once borrowed a quote from Gandhi to explain his nonviolent approach to the peace process: "An eye for an eye leaves everyone blind."

Sights in Derry

▲▲Tower Museum Derry

Occupying a modern reconstruction of a fortified medieval tower house that belonged to the local O'Doherty clan, this well-organized museum provides an excellent introduction to the city. Combining modern audiovisual displays with historical artifacts, the exhibits tell the story of the city from a skillfully unbiased viewpoint, sorting out some of the tangled historical roots of Northern Ireland's Troubles.

Cost and Hours: £4, includes audioguide for Armada exhibits, daily 10:00-17:30, last entry 16:00, Union Hall Place, tel. 028/7137-2411, www.derrystrabane.com/towermuseum.

Visiting the Museum: The museum is divided into two sections: the Story of Derry (on the ground floor) and the Spanish Armada (on the four floors of the tower).

Start with the **Story of Derry,** which explains the city's monastic origins 1,500 years ago. The exhibit moves through pivotal events, such as the 1688-1689 siege, as well as unexpected blips, like Amelia Earhart's emergency landing. Don't miss the thought-provoking 15-minute film in the small theater—it offers an even-handed local perspective on the tragic events of the modern sectarian conflict, giving you a better handle on what makes this unique city tick. Scan the displays of paramilitary paraphernalia in the hallway lined with colored curbstones—red, white, and blue Union Jack colors for Unionists; and the green, white, and orange Irish tricolor for Nationalists.

The tower section holds the **Spanish Armada** exhibits, filled with items taken from the wreck of *La Trinidad Valencera*. The ship sank off the coast of Donegal in 1588 in fierce storms nicknamed the "Protestant Winds." A third of the Armada's ships were lost in storms off the coasts of Ireland and Scotland. Survivors who made it ashore were hunted and killed by English soldiers. But a small number made it to Dunluce Castle (see page 442), where the sympathetic lord, who was no friend of the English, smuggled them to Scotland and eventual freedom in France.

Guildhall

This Neo-Gothic building, complete with clock tower, is the ceremonial seat of city government. It first opened in 1890 on reclaimed lands that were once the mudflats of the River Foyle. Destroyed by fire and rebuilt in 1913, it was massively damaged by IRA bombs in 1972. In an ironic twist, Gerry Doherty, one of those convicted of the bombings, was elected as a member of the Derry City Council a dozen years later. (When I first visited Derry with tour groups back in the 1990s, a bus of curious Americans was such a rarity that the mayor actually invited our entire group into his office here for tea and a friendly Q&A session.)

Cost and Hours: Free, daily 10:00-17:30, free and clean WCs on ground floor, tel. 028/7137-6510, www.derrystrabane.com/guildhall.

Visiting the Hall: Inside the hall are the Council Chamber, party offices, and an assembly hall featuring stained-glass windows showing scenes from Derry history. Take an informational pamphlet from the front window and explore, if civic and cultural events are not taking place inside. Rotating exhibits fill a ground-floor hall just to the right of the front reception desk. The Ulster Plantation exhibition is worth a visit. A mighty pipe organ fills much of a wall in the grand hall. It's lonely and loves to be played (if you play the piano and would like to give it a go, just ask a guard).

On the back terrace, facing the river, you'll find locals lunching at the pleasant Guild Café (daily 9:30-17:00). And across the

DERRY

street is the modest but heartfelt Peace Park, with hopeful, nonsectarian children's quotes on tiles that line the path.

Peace Bridge Stroll

A stroll across the architecturally fetching Peace Bridge rewards you with great views as you look back west over the river toward the city center. The €14 million pedestrian Peace Bridge opened in 2011, linking neighborhoods long divided by the river (Catholic Nationalists on the west bank and Protestant Unionists on the east bank). On the far side from the old city walls, the former Ebrington Barracks British Army base (1841-2003) sits on prime real estate and surrounds a huge square that was once the military parade ground. This area features a fun gastropub, and serves as an outdoor concert venue and gathering place for the community. Plans are in progress to develop this area further with a hotel and museum complex.

Hands Across the Divide

Designed by local teacher Maurice Harron, this powerful metal sculpture of two figures extending their hands to each other was

inspired by the growing hope for peace and reconciliation in Northern Ireland (located in a roundabout at the west end of Craigavon Bridge).

The Tillie and Henderson's shirt factory (opened in 1857 and burned down in 2003) once stood on the banks of the river beside the bridge, looming over the figures. In its heyday, Derry's shirt industry employed more than 15,000 workers (90 percent of whom were women) in sweathouses typical of the human toll of the Industrial Revolution. Karl Marx mentioned this factory in *Das Kapital* as an example of women's transition from domestic to industrial work lives.

St. Columb's Cathedral

Marked by the tall spire inside the walls, this Anglican cathedral was built from 1628 to 1633 in a style called "Planter's Gothic." Its construction was financed by the same London companies that backed the Protestant plantation of Londonderry. The first Protestant cathedral built in Britain after the Reformation, St. Columb's played an important part in the defense of the city during the siege. During that time, cannons were mounted on its roof, and the original spire was scavenged for lead to melt into cannon shot.

Cost and Hours: £2 donation, Mon-Sat 9:00-17:00, closed Sun, tel. 028/7126-7313, www.stcolumbscathedral.org.

Visiting the Cathedral: Before you enter, walk over to the "Heroes' Mound" at the end of the churchyard closest to the town wall. Underneath this grassy dome is a mass grave of some of those who died during the 1689 siege.

In the cathedral entryway, you'll find a hollow cannonball that was lobbed into the city—it contained the besiegers' surrender terms. Inside, along the nave, hangs a musty collection of battle flags and Union Jacks that once inspired troops during the siege, the Crimean War, and World War II. The American flag hangs among them, from the time when the first GIs to enter the European theater in World War II were based in Northern Ireland. Check out the small chapter-house museum in the back of the church to see the huge original locks of the gates of Derry and more relics of the siege.

Long Tower Church

Built below the walls on the hillside above the Bogside, this modest-looking church is worth a visit for its stunning high altar. The name comes from a stone monastic round tower that stood here for centuries but was dismantled and used for building materials in the 1600s.

Cost and Hours: Free, generally open Mon-Sat 8:30-20:30, Sun 7:30-18:00—depending on available staff and church functions, tel. 028/7126-2301, www.longtowerchurch.org.

Visiting the Church: Long Tower Church, the oldest Catholic church in Derry, was finished in 1786, during a time of enlightened relations between the city's two religious communities. Protestant Bishop Hervey gave a generous-for-the-time £200 donation and had the four Corinthian columns shipped in from Naples to frame the Neo-Renaissance altar.

Outside, walk behind the church and face the Bogside to find a simple shrine hidden beneath a hawthorn tree. It marks the spot where outlawed Masses were secretly held before this church was built, during the infamous Penal Law period of the early 1700s. Through the Penal Laws, the English attempted to weaken Catholicism's influence by banishing priests and forbidding Catholics from buying land, attending school, voting, and holding office.

Nearby: The adjacent **St. Columba Heritage Centre** fleshes out the life of Derry's patron saint and founding father (free, Mon-Fri 9:30-16:30, Sat-Sun 13:00-16:00, closed Mon Oct-April, tel. 028/7136-8491, www.stcolumbaheritage.org).

DERRY

Nightlife in Derry

The **Millennium Forum** is a modern venue that reflects the city's revived investment in local culture, concerts, and plays (box office open Mon-Sat 9:30-17:00, inside city walls on Newmarket Street near Ferryquay Gate, tel. 028/7126-4455, www.millenniumforum. co.uk, boxoffice@millenniumforum.co.uk).

The **Nerve Centre** shows a wide variety of art-house films and live concerts (inside city walls at 7 Magazine Street, near Butcher Gate, tel. 028/7126-0562, www.nervecentre.org).

The **Playhouse Theatre** is an intimate venue for plays (£9-20 tickets, inside the walls on Artillery Street, between New Gate and Ferryquay Gate, tel. 028/7126-8027, www.derryplayhouse.co.uk).

To get away from tourists and mingle with Derry residents, try **Peadar O'Donnell's** pub on Waterloo Street for Derry's best nightly traditional music sessions (often start late, at 23:00; 53 Waterloo Street, tel. 028/7137-2318).

Sleeping in Derry

The first two options are located inside the city's walls and feature all the modern comforts. The others are in historic buildings with creaky charm and friendly hosts.

$$$$ Bishop's Gate Hotel is Derry's top lodging option and priced that way. A former gentlemen's club once frequented by Winston Churchill, it has 30 rooms that ooze with cushy refinement (fine bar, 24 Bishop Street, tel. 028/7114-0300, www. bishopsgatehotelderry.com, sales@bishopsgatehotelderry.com).

$$ Maldron Hotel features 93 modern and large rooms, a bistro restaurant, and 20 private basement parking spaces (Butcher Street, tel. 028/7137-1000, www.maldronhotelderry.com, info. derry@maldronhotels.com).

$ Merchant's House, on a quiet street a 10-minute stroll from Waterloo Place, is a fine Georgian townhouse with a grand, colorful drawing room and nine rooms sporting marble fireplaces and ornate plasterwork (family rooms, 16 Queen Street, tel. 028/7126-9691, www.thesaddlershouse.com, saddlershouse@btinternet. com). Joan and Peter Pyne also run the Saddler's House (see below), and offer appealing self-catering townhouse rentals inside the walls (great for families or anyone needing extra space, 3-night minimum).

$ Saddler's House, run by the owners of Merchant's House, is a charming Victorian townhouse with seven rooms located a couple of blocks closer to the old town walls. Their dog Bruno (a boxer) provides loveable comic relief (36 Great James Street,

tel. 028/7126-9691, www.thesaddlershouse.com, saddlershouse@
btinternet.com).

Eating in Derry

$$$ Entrada is a crisp, modern restaurant with a faintly Spanish
theme, serving great meals and fine wines in a posh, calm space. It
faces the river a block from the Guildhall (Wed-Sat 12:00-21:30,
Sun until 20:00, closed Mon-Tue, Queens Quay, tel. 028/7137-
3366).

The hip, trendy **$$$ Exchange Restaurant and Wine Bar** of-
fers lunches and quality dinners with flair, in a central location near
the river behind Waterloo Place (Mon-Sat 12:00-14:30 & 17:30-
22:00, Sun 16:00-21:00, Queen's Quay, tel. 028/7127-3990).

$$$ Fitzroy's, tucked below Ferryquay Gate and stacked with
locals, serves good lunches and dinners (Mon-Sat 12:00-22:00,
Sun 13:00-20:00, 2 Bridge Street, tel. 028/7126-6211).

$$ Browns in Town is a casual, friendly lunch or dinner option
near most of my recommended lodgings (Mon-Sat 12:00-15:00 &
17:30-21:00, Sun 17:00-20:30, 21 Strand Road, tel. 028/7136-2889).

$$ Walled City Brewery, across the Peace Bridge, is a fun
change of pace. The brewpub ambience and dependable comfort
food can be washed down with a local fave: Derry chocolate milk
stout (Wed-Thu 17:00-23:30, Fri-Sun from 14:00, closed Mon-
Tue, 70 Ebrington Square, tel. 028/7134-3336).

$ Mandarin Palace is crowded with loyal locals eating filling
Chinese fare; easy takeout is available (Mon-Sat 16:00-23:00, Sun
from 13:00, Queens Quay, tel. 028/7137-3656).

Supermarkets: You'll find everything you need for picnics and
road munchies at **Tesco** (Mon-Sat 8:00-21:00, Sun 13:00-18:00,
corner of Strand Road and Clarendon Street) or **SuperValu** (Mon-
Sat 8:30-19:00, Sun 12:30-17:30, Waterloo Place).

Derry Connections

From Derry, it's an hour's drive to Portrush. If you're using public
transportation, consider spending £17.50 for a Zone 4 iLink smart-
card (£16.50 top-up for each additional day), good for all-day train
and bus use in Northern Ireland (see page 453). Translink has
updated schedules and prices for both trains and buses in Northern
Ireland (tel. 028/9066-6630, www.translink.co.uk). Keep in mind
that some bus and train schedules, road signs, and maps may say
"Londonderry" or "L'Derry" instead of "Derry."

From Derry by Train to: Portrush (8/day, 1.5 hours, change in Coleraine), **Belfast** (10/day, 2.5 hours), **Dublin** (6/day, 5.5 hours, change in Belfast).

By Bus to: Galway (6/day, 5.5 hours), **Westport** (3/day, 6 hours, change in Sligo), **Portrush** (5/day, 1.5 hours, change in Coleraine), **Belfast** (hourly, 2 hours), **Dublin** (12/day, 4 hours).

Near Derry

▲Ulster American Folk Park

This combination museum and folk park (in a wonderfully scenic and walkable rural forest) commemorates the many Irish who left their homeland during the hard times of the 18th century. Your visit progresses through four sections. You'll start by walking through the excellent museum, then head outdoors to visit the remaining three sections in chronological order: life in Ulster before emigration, passage on the boat, and the adjustment to life in unfamiliar America. You'll gain insight into the origins of the tough Scots-Irish stock—think Davy Crockett (his people were from Derry) and Andrew Jackson (Carrickfergus roots)—who later shaped America's westward migration. You'll also find good coverage of the *Titanic* tragedy, and its effect on the Ulster folk who built the ship and the loved ones it left behind.

Cost and Hours: £9; March-Sept Tue-Sun 10:00-17:00; Oct-Feb Tue-Fri 10:00-16:00, Sat-Sun 11:00-16:00; closed Mon year-round; cafeteria, 2 Mellon Road, tel. 028/8224-3292, www.nmni.com.

Getting There: The folk park is 48 kilometers (30 miles) south of Derry on A-5—about a 40-minute drive.

Nearby: The adjacent **Mellon Centre for Migration Studies** is handy for genealogy searches (Tue-Fri 10:00-16:00, Sat from 11:00, closed Sun-Mon, tel. 028/8225-6315, www.qub.ac.uk/cms).

DERRY

PORTRUSH & THE ANTRIM COAST

The Antrim Coast—the north of Northern Ireland—is one of the most interesting and scenic coastlines in Ireland. Portrush, at the end of the train line, is an ideal base for exploring the highlights of the Antrim Coast. Within a few miles of the train terminal, you can visit evocative castle ruins, tour the world's oldest whiskey distillery, catch a thrill on a bouncy rope bridge, and hike along the famous Giant's Causeway.

PLANNING YOUR TIME

You need a full day to explore the Antrim Coast, so allow two nights in Portrush. With a car, you can visit the Giant's Causeway, Old Bushmills Distillery, Carrick-a-Rede Rope Bridge, and Dunluce Castle in one busy day.

On this day, get an early start. My ideal day would start with the Giant's Causeway, arriving by 9:00, when crowds are lightest; choose between a one-hour quickie visit or the scenic three-hour, five-mile "Clifftop Experience" guided hike (from Dunseverick Castle to the causeway). Early birds will find that the trails are always open.

Follow this with a tour of Old Bushmills Distillery (call ahead to reserve). For lunch, you can bring a picnic, or eat cheaply in either the visitors center at the causeway or the Old Bushmills hospitality room.

After lunch, drive to Carrick-a-Rede (about 20 minutes from the distillery). Note, though, that crossing the rope bridge now requires timed-entry tickets, which can sell out in peak season (only available same-day and assigned starting at 9:30). If tickets are sold out, you can still enjoy the scenic cliff-top trail hike all the way to the bridge, as well as the nearby viewpoint for dramatic views of the bridge. But if crossing the actual bridge is your priority, consider going to Carrick-a-Rede first thing in the morning to ensure tickets.

From here, hop in your car and double back west all the way to dramatically cliff-perched Dunluce Castle for a late-afternoon tour. The castle is only a five-minute drive from Portrush. In summer months, the long days this far north extend your sightseeing time (and most golf courses stay open until dusk).

If driving on to Belfast from Portrush, consider the slower-but-scenic coastal route via the Glens of Antrim.

GETTING AROUND THE ANTRIM COAST

By Car: A car is the best way to explore the charms of the Antrim Coast. Distances are short and parking is easy.

By Bus: In peak season, an all-day bus pass helps you get around the region economically. The **Causeway Rambler** links Portrush to Old Bushmills Distillery, the Giant's Causeway, and the Carrick-a-Rede Rope Bridge (stopping at the nearby town of Ballintoy). The bus journey from Portrush to Carrick-a-Rede takes 45 minutes (£6.50/day, runs roughly 10:00-18:00, hourly May-Sept, every two hours March-April, fewer off-season). Pick up a Rambler bus schedule at the TI, and buy the ticket from the driver (in Portrush, the Rambler stops at Dunluce Avenue, next to public WC, a 2-minute walk from TI; operated by Translink, tel. 028/9066-6630, www.translink.co.uk).

By Bus Tour: If you're based in Belfast, you can visit most of the sights on the Antrim Coast with a **McComb's** tour (see page 456). Those based in Derry can get to the Giant's Causeway and Carrick-a-Rede Rope Bridge with City Sightseeing (see page 408).

By Taxi: Groups (up to four) can reasonably visit most sights by taxi (except the more distant Carrick-a-Rede and Rathlin Island sailings from Ballycastle). Approximate one-way prices from Portrush: £6 (Dunluce Castle), £8 (Old Bushmills Distillery), £11 (Giant's Causeway). Try **Andy Brown's Taxi** (tel. 028/7082-2223), **Hugh's Taxi** (mobile 077-0298-6110), or **North West Taxi** (tel. 028/7082-4446).

Portrush

Homey Portrush used to be known as "the Brighton of the North." It first became a resort in the late 1800s, as railroads expanded to offer the new middle class a weekend by the shore. Victorian society believed that swimming in salt water would cure many common ailments.

This is County Antrim, the Bible Belt of Northern Ireland. When a large supermarket chain decided to stay open on Sundays, a local reverend called for a boycott of the store for not honoring the Sabbath. And in 2012, when the Giant's Causeway Visitor Centre opened, local Creationists demanded that, alongside modern geologic explanations about the age of the unique rock formations, an exhibit be added explaining their viewpoint (that, according to the Bible, the earth here was only 6,000 years old—not 60 million—carbon dating be damned).

While it's seen its best days, Portrush retains the atmosphere and architecture of a genteel seaside resort. Its peninsula is filled with lowbrow, family-oriented amusements, fun eateries and B&Bs. Summertime fun seekers promenade along the tiny harbor and tumble down to the sandy beaches, which extend in sweeping white crescents on either side.

Superficially, Portrush has the appearance of any small British seaside resort (and Union Jacks fly with a little extra gusto around here), but its history and large population of young people (students from nearby University of Ulster at Coleraine) give the town a little more personality. Along with the usual arcade amusements, there are nightclubs, restaurants, summer theater productions (July-Aug) in the town hall, and convivial pubs that attract customers all the way from Belfast.

Orientation to Portrush

Portrush's pleasant and easily walkable town center features sea views in every direction. On one side are the harbor and most of the restaurants, and on the other are Victorian townhouses and vast, salty vistas. The tip of the peninsula is filled with tennis courts, lawn-bowling greens, putting greens, and a park.

The town is busy with students during the school year. July and August are beach-resort boom time. June and September are laid-back and lazy. There's a brief but intense spike in visitors in mid-May for a huge annual motorcycle race (see "Helpful Hints," below). Families pack Portrush on Saturdays, and revelers from Belfast crowd its hotels on Saturday nights.

Tourist Information: The TI is located underneath the very central, red-brick Town Hall (July-Aug Mon-Sat 9:00-18:00, Sun from 11:00; shorter hours off-season and closed Oct-March; Kerr Street, tel. 028/7082-3333). Consider the Collins Northern Ireland Visitors Map (£5), the free *Visitor Attractions* brochure, and, if needed, a free Belfast map.

Arrival in Portrush: The train tracks stop at the base of the tiny peninsula that Portrush fills (no baggage storage at station). Most of my listed B&Bs are within a 10-minute walk of the train station. The bus stop is two blocks from the train station.

Helpful Hints: Over a four-day weekend in mid-May, thousands of die-hard motorcycle fans converge on Portrush, Port Stewart, and Coleraine to watch the Northwest 200 Race. Fearless racers scorch the roads at 200 miles per hour on the longest straightaway in motorsports. Accommodations fill up a year ahead, and traffic is the pits (dates and details at www.northwest200.org). **Causeway Laundry** offers full service (Mon-Tue and Thu-Fri 9:00-16:30, Wed and Sat until 13:00, closed Sun, 68 Causeway Street, tel. 028/7082-2060).

Sights in Portrush

Barry's Old Time Amusement Arcade

This fun arcade is bigger than it looks and offers a chance to see Northern Ireland at play. Older locals visit for the nostalgia as many of the rides and amusements go back 50 years. Prices for the various rides are listed at the door. Everything runs with tokens (£0.50 each, buy a pile from coin-op machines). Located just below the train station on the harbor, Barry's is filled with "candy floss" (cotton candy) and crazy "scoop treats" (July-Aug daily 12:30-22:00, weekends only Easter-May, closed Sept-Easter, www.barrysamusements.com).

Royal Portrush Golf Club

Irish courses, like those in Scotland, are highly sought after for their lush greens in glorious settings. Serious golfers can get a tee time at the Royal Portrush, which hosted the British Open in 1951 and is set to host it again in 2019 (green fees generally £205, less most days in off-season). Those on a budget can play the adjacent, slightly shorter Valley Course (green fees £25-£55, 10-minute walk from station, tel. 028/7082-2311, www.royalportrushgolfclub.com).

Portrush

Eateries & Other

7 Ground Espresso Bar
8 Babushka Kitchen Café
9 Café 55 Bistro & 55 North Restaurant
10 Mr. Chips Diner & Mr. Chips
11 Spar Market
12 Harbour Road Eateries & Waterworld
13 Ocho Tapas Bistro
14 Neptune & Prawn Rest. & Cocktail Bar
15 Spring Hill Pub
16 Laundry

Accommodations

1 To Shola Coach House B&B
2 Adelphi Portrush Hotel
3 Anvershiel B&B
4 Beulah Guest House
5 Harbour Heights B&B
6 Portrush Holiday Hostel

Atlantic Ocean

200 Meters
200 Yards

RECREATION GROUNDS

LANDOWNE AVE
RAMORE AVE
LOWER LANDOWNE RD
BATH TERR.
MARK ST
MAIN ST
KERR ST
WC
Harbor
CAUSEWAY ST
East Strand
BARRY'S ARCADE
TRAIN STATION
POST
West Strand
EGLINTON ST
SANDHILL DR
DUNLUCE AVE
CROCKNAMAC
To Royal Portrush Golf Club & Giant's Causeway
BALLYWILLAN RD
To
To Coleraine, Derry & Belfast

Portrush Recreation Grounds

For some easygoing exercise right in town, this well-organized park offers lawn-bowling greens (£5/hour with gear), putting greens, tennis courts, and a great kids' play park. You can rent tennis shoes, balls, and rackets, all for £10/hour (Mon-Sat 10:00-dusk, Sun from 12:00, closed mid-Sept-May, tel. 028/7082-4441).

Waterworld

For more fun, consider Waterworld, with pools, waterslides, and bowling (£5, Mon-Sat 10:30-18:00, Sun from 12:00, closed Sept-May; wedged between Harbour Bistro and Ramore Wine Bar, tel. 028/7082-2001).

Sleeping in Portrush

Portrush has a range of hotels, from depressing to ritzy. Some B&Bs can be well-worn. August and Saturday nights can be tight (and loud) with young party groups. Otherwise, it's a "you take half a loaf when you can get it" town. Rates vary with the view and season—probe for softness. Many listings face the sea, though sea views are worth paying for only if you get a bay window. Ask for a big room (some doubles can be very small; twins are bigger). Lounges are invariably grand and have bay-window views. Most places listed have lots of stairs. All but Shola Coach House are perfectly central and within a few minutes' walk of the train station. Parking is easy.

$$$ Shola Coach House is a memorable treat that exceeds other B&B experiences in Northern Ireland. About 1.5 miles south of town, it's easiest for drivers (otherwise it's a 30-minute uphill walk or £5 taxi ride). The secluded, 170-year-old, renovated stone structure once housed the coaches and horses for a local landlord. The decor of the four rooms is tasteful, the garden patio is delightful, and Sharon and David Schindler keep it spotless (parking, no kids under 18, 2-night minimum, 110A Gateside Road at top of Ballywillan Road, tel. 028/7082-5925, mobile 075-6542-7738, www.sholabandb.com, sholabandb@gmail.com).

$$$ Adelphi Portrush is a breath of fresh air, with 28 tastefully furnished modern rooms, an ideal location, friendly staff, and a hearty bistro downstairs (family rooms, 67 Main Street, tel. 028/7082-5544, www.adelphiportrush.com, stay@adelphiportrush.com).

$ Anvershiel B&B, with seven nicely refurbished rooms, is a great value (RS%, family rooms, parking, 10-minute walk south of train station, 16 Coleraine Road, tel. 028/7082-3861, www.anvershiel.com, enquiries@anvershiel.com, Alan and Janice Thompson).

$ Beulah Guest House is a traditional, old-fashioned place. It's centrally located and run by cheerful Helen and Charlene McLaughlin, with 11 prim rooms (parking at rear, 16 Causeway Street, tel. 028/7082-2413, www.beulahguesthouse.com, stay@beulahguesthouse.com).

$ Harbour Heights B&B rents nine retro-homey rooms, each named after a different town in County Antrim. It has an inviting guest lounge, supervised by two tabby cats, overlooking the harbor. Friendly South African hosts Sam and Tim Swart—a photographer—manage the place with a light hand (family rooms, 17 Kerr Street, tel. 028/7082-2765, mobile 078-9586-6534, www.harbourheightsportrush.com, info@harbourheightsportrush.com).

¢ Portrush Holiday Hostel offers clean, well-organized, economical lodging for bottom-feeding vagabonds (private rooms available, tel. 028/7082-1288, mobile 078-5037-7367, 24 Princess Street, www.portrushholidayhostel.com, info@portrushholidayhostel.com).

Eating in Portrush

As a family getaway from Belfast and a beach escape for students from the nearby university in Coleraine, Portrush has more than enough fish-and-chips joints. And in recent years, the refined tastes of affluent golfers and urban professionals out for a weekend has prompted the town to up its culinary game.

LUNCH SPOTS

$ Ground Espresso Bar makes fresh sandwiches and *panini,* soup, and great coffee (daily July-Aug 9:00-22:00, Sept-June until 17:00, 52 Main Street, tel. 028/7082-5979).

$ Babushka Kitchen Café serves fresh sandwiches and creative desserts with an unbeatable view—actually out on the pier (daily 9:15-17:00, West Strand Promenade, tel. 077-8750-2012).

$$ Café 55 Bistro serves basic sandwiches with a great patio view (daily 9:00-17:00, longer hours in summer, shorter hours off-season, 1 Causeway Street, beneath fancier 55 North restaurant, tel. 028/7082-2811).

$ Mr. Chips Diner and **Mr. Chips** are the local favorites for cheap, quality fish-and-chips (daily 12:00-22:00, 12 and 20 Main Street). Both are mostly takeout while the diner also has tables. The smaller Mr. Chips cooks with lard (less healthy, more traditional). The bigger Mr. Chips cooks with vegetable oil (healthier) and hangs the stars and bars of the Confederate flag on the wall (when it comes to the Catholic/Protestant issue, this is a conservative town with some redneck tendencies).

Groceries: For picnic ingredients, try **Spar Market** (daily

7:00-20:00, June-Aug until 23:00, across from Barry's Arcade on Main Street, tel. 028/7082-5447).

HARBOUR ROAD EATERIES

A creative, diverse, and lively quintet of restaurants clusters together overlooking the harbor. With the same owner, they all have a creative and fun energy, are often jammed with diners, and are basically open nightly from 17:00 to 22:00 (exceptions noted below). All are described at RamoreRestaurant.com (only the Mermaid Kitchen & Bar takes reservations).

$$ Ramore Wine Bar is a salty, modern place, with an inviting menu ranging from steaks to vegetarian food. It's very casual but with serious cuisine. Order at the bar and take a table (also open for lunch, tel. 028/7082-4313).

$$ Coast Pizzeria is a hit for its pizza, pasta, and burgers. It's noisy and youthful with tight seating (tel. 028/7082-3311).

$$$ Harbour Bistro is dark, noisy, and sprawling with a sloppy crowd enjoying chargrilled meat and fish (tel. 028/7082-2430).

$$ Mermaid Kitchen & Bar is all about fresh fish dishes with a Spanish twist and great harbor views. Those at the bar get a bird's-eye view of the fun banter and precision teamwork of the kitchen staff (closed Mon-Tue, tel. 028/7082-6969).

$$$ Neptune & Prawn (just across the inlet from the others) is the most yacht-clubby of the bunch. Serving Asian and other international food, with a fancy presentation and many plates designed to be shared, this place is noisy and high-energy, with rock music playing (tel. 028/7082-2448).

OTHER DINING OPTIONS OFF THE HARBOR

$$$ 55 North (named for the local latitude) has the best sea views in town, with windows on three sides. The filling pasta-and-fish dishes, along with some Asian plates, are a joy. Their lunch and early-bird special (order by 18:45) is three courses at the cost of the entrée (daily 12:30-14:00 & 17:00-21:00, 1 Causeway Street, tel. 028/7082-2811).

$$ Ocho Tapas Bistro brings sunny Spanish cuisine to the chilly north, featuring a great early-bird menu—choose any three tapas from a varied list (Tue-Fri 17:00-21:30, Sat-Sun 12:30-14:30 and 17:00-22:00, closed Mon, 92 Main Street, tel. 028/7082-4110).

PUBS

Harbour Bar is an old-fashioned pub next to the Harbour Bistro (see listing above). **Harbour Gin Bar** (above Harbour Bar) is romantic and classy—a rustic, spacious, and inviting place with live acoustic folk music from 20:30 (almost nightly) and a fun selection of 45 gins.

Neptune & Prawn Cocktail Bar (above the restaurant by the same name; see earlier listing) has great views over the harbor and is the most classy-yet-inviting place in town for a drink.

Spring Hill Pub is also a good bet for its friendly vibe and occasional live music (17 Causeway Street, tel. 028/7082-3361).

Portrush Connections

Consider a £17.50 Zone 4 iLink smartcard, good for all-day Translink train and bus use in Northern Ireland (£16.50 top-up for each additional day; for more on iLink cards, see page 453). Translink's website has updated schedules and prices for both trains and buses in Northern Ireland (tel. 028/9066-6630, www.translink.co.uk).

From Portrush by Train to: Coleraine (hourly, 12 minutes), **Belfast** (15/day, 2 hours, transfer in Coleraine), **Dublin** (7/day, 5 hours, transfer in Coleraine or Belfast). Note that on Sundays, service is greatly reduced.

By Bus to: Belfast (12/day, 2 hours; scenic coastal route, 2.5 hours), **Dublin** (4/day, 5.5 hours).

Antrim Coast

The craggy 20-mile stretch of the Antrim Coast extending eastward from Portrush to Ballycastle rates second only to the tip of the Dingle Peninsula as the prettiest chunk of coastal Ireland. From your base in Portrush, you have a varied grab bag of sightseeing choices: Giant's Causeway, Old Bushmills Distillery, Dunluce Castle, Carrick-a-Rede Rope Bridge, and Rathlin Island.

It's easy to weave these sights together by car, but connections are patchy by public transportation. Bus service is viable only in summer, and taxi fares are reasonable only for the sights closest to Portrush (Dunluce Castle, Old Bushmills Distillery, and the Giant's Causeway). For details on how to plan your day on the Antrim Coast, and for more on your transportation options, see "Planning Your Time" and "Getting Around the Antrim Coast," at the beginning of this chapter.

The Scottish Connection

The Romans called the Irish the "Scoti" (meaning pirates). When the Scoti crossed the narrow Irish Sea and invaded the land of the Picts 1,500 years ago, that region became known as Scoti-land. Ireland and Scotland were never conquered by the Romans, and they retained similar clannish Celtic traits. Both share the same Gaelic branch of the linguistic tree.

On clear summer days from Carrick-a-Rede, the island of Mull in Scotland—only 17 miles away—is visible. Much closer on the horizon is the boomerang-shaped Rathlin Island, part of Northern Ireland. Rathlin is where Scottish leader Robert the Bruce (a compatriot of William "Braveheart" Wallace) retreated in 1307 after defeat at the hands of the English. Legend has it that he hid in a cave on the island, where he observed a spider patiently rebuilding its web each time a breeze knocked it down. Inspired by the spider's perseverance, Robert gathered his Scottish forces once more and finally defeated the English at the decisive Battle of Bannockburn.

Flush with confidence from his victory, Robert the Bruce decided to open a second front against the English...in Ireland. In 1315, he sent his brother Edward over to enlist their Celtic Irish cousins in an effort to thwart the English. After securing Ireland, Edward hoped to move on and enlist the Welsh, thus cornering England with their pan-Celtic nation. But Edward's timing was bad—Ireland was in the midst of famine. His Scottish troops had to live off the land and began to take food and supplies from the starving Irish. He might also have been trying to destroy Ireland's crops to keep them from being used as a colonial "breadbasket" to feed English troops. The Scots quickly wore out their welcome, and Edward the Bruce was eventually killed in battle near Dundalk in 1318.

This was the first time in history that Ireland was used as a pawn by England's enemies. Spain and France saw Ireland as the English Achilles' heel, and both countries later attempted invasions of the island. The English Tudor and Stuart royalty countered these threats in the 16th and 17th centuries by starting the "plantation" of loyal subjects in Ireland. The only successful long-term settlement by the English was here in Northern Ireland, which remains part of the United Kingdom today.

It's interesting to imagine how things might be different today if Ireland and Scotland had been permanently welded together as a nation 700 years ago. You'll notice the strong Scottish influence in this part of Ireland when you ask a local a question and he answers, "Aye, a wee bit." The Irish joke that the Scots are just Irish people who couldn't swim home.

Sights on the Antrim Coast

▲▲Giant's Causeway

This five-mile-long stretch of coastline is famous for its bizarre basalt columns. The shore is covered with largely hexagonal pillars that stick up at various heights. It's as if the earth were offering God a choice of 37,000 six-sided cigarettes.

Geologists claim the Giant's Causeway was formed by volcanic eruptions more than 60 million years ago. As the surface of the lava flow quickly cooled, it contracted and crystallized into columns (resembling the caked mud at the bottom of a dried-up lakebed, but with far deeper cracks). As the rock later settled and eroded, the columns broke off into the many stair-like steps that now honeycomb the Antrim Coast.

Of course, in actuality, the Giant's Causeway was made by a giant Ulster warrior named Finn MacCool who knew of a rival giant living across the water in Scotland. Finn built a stone bridge over to Scotland to spy on his rival, and found out that the Scottish giant was much bigger. Finn retreated back to Ireland and had his wife dress him as a sleeping infant, just in time for the rival giant to come across the causeway to spy on Finn. The rival, shocked at the infant's size, fled back to Scotland in terror of whomever had sired this giant baby. Breathing a sigh of relief, Finn tore off the baby clothes and prudently knocked down the bridge. Today, proof of this encounter exists in the geologic formation that still extends undersea and surfaces in Scotland (at the island of Staffa).

Cost and Hours: The Giant's Causeway is free and open all the time. But in practice, anyone parking there needs to pay £11.50, which includes an audioguide (or guided walk) and entrance to the visitors center (daily 9:00-18:00, June-Sept until 19:00, Nov-March until 17:00, tel. 028/2073-1855, www.nationaltrust.org.uk/giantscauseway). A gift shop and café are in the visitors center.

Visiting the Causeway: For cute variations on the Finn story, as well as details on the ridiculous theories of modern geologists, start in the **Giant's Causeway Visitor Centre.** It's filled with kid-friendly interactive exhibits giving a worthwhile history of the Giant's Causeway, with a regional overview. On the far wall opposite the entrance, check out the interesting three-minute video showing the evolution of the causeway from molten lava to the geometric, geologic wonderland of today. The large 3-D model of the causeway offers a bird's-eye view of the region. There's also an exhibit about the history of tourism here from the 18th century.

The **causeway** itself is the highlight of the entire coast. The audioguide (included with the visitors center ticket) highlights 15 stops along the causeway, each with a photo of the formation being described; all stops are shown on the map you'll receive with your ticket. (Your admission also includes a one-hour guided walk—leaving regularly with demand—covering the same information as the audioguide.)

From the visitors center, you have several options for visiting the causeway:

Short and Easy: A **shuttle bus** (4/hour from 9:00, £1 each way) zips tired tourists a half-mile from the visitors center down a paved road to the causeway. This standard route (the blue dashed line on your map) offers the easiest access and follows the stops on your audioguide. Many choose to walk down and then take the shuttle back up.

RATHLIN ISLAND SEABIRD CENTER

Rathlin Island

Bull Point

Church Bay

C O A S T

CARRICK-A-REDE ROPE BRIDGE

Ballintoy

A-2

B-147

B-67

A-44

Rue Point

3 Kilometers

3 Miles

Ballycastle

Ballyvoy

A-2

"DARK HEDGES"

Armoy

To Belfast

To Glens of Antrim, Glenariff Forest Park, The Gobbins Cliff Path & Carrickfergus Castle

Cushendun

Mid-Level Hike: For a longer hike and a more varied dose of causeway views, consider the cliff-top trail (red dashed line on your map). Take the easy-to-follow trail uphill from the visitors center 10 minutes to Weir's Snout, the great fence-protected precipice viewpoint. Then hike 15 minutes farther (level) to reach the Shepherd's Steps. Then grab the banister on the steep (and slippery-when-wet) stairs that zigzag down the switchbacks toward the water. At the T-junction, go 100 yards right, to the towering rock pipes of "the Organ." (You can detour another 500 yards east around the headland, but the trail dead-ends there.) Now retrace your steps west on the trail (don't go up the steps again), continuing down to the tidal zone, where the "Giant's Boot" (6-foot boulder, on the right) provides some photo fun. Another 100 yards farther is the dramatic point where the causeway meets the sea. Just beyond that, at the asphalt turnaround, is the shuttle bus stop.

Just below the bus stop is a fine place to explore the uneven, wave-splashed rock terraces, watching your every easy-to-trip step. Look for "wishing coins"—rusted and bent—that have been jammed into the cracks of rock just behind the turnaround (where the trail passes through a notch in the 20-foot-high rock wall).

Return to the visitors center by hiking up the paved lane (listening to the audioguide at stops along the way). Or, from the turnaround, you can catch the shuttle bus back to the visitors center (just line up and pay the driver).

Longer Hike: Hardy hikers and avid photographers can join the guided three-hour **Clifftop Experience** trek exploring the trail that runs along a five-mile section of the Causeway Coast, starting at the meager ruins of Dunseverick Castle (yellow dashed line on your map). Operated by the National Trust, the hike is led by a naturalist, who ventures beyond the usual big-bus tourist crowds to explore the rugged rim of this most-scenic section of the Antrim Coast. Expect undulating grass and gravel paths with no WC options and no shelter whatsoever from bad weather (£35, daily March-Oct at 12:15, must prebook, no kids under 12, includes bus from visitors center to Dunseverick trailhead, tel. 028/2073-3419, www.giantscausewaytickets.com, northcoastbookings@nationaltrust.org.uk).

This same hike could also be done on your own. Occasional rock falls and slides can close this trail (ask first at Portrush TI, or call ahead to visitors center). If going independently, a good plan is to take the Causeway Rambler bus (see "Getting Around the Antrim Coast," earlier) or a taxi from Portrush to Dunseverick Castle (east of Giant's Causeway on B-146). Get off there and hike west, following the cliff-hugging contours of Benbane Head back to the visitors center. You'll have a fence on your left and the cliff on the right, so there's no doubt about the route. When you're finished, travel back to Portrush by taxi or Rambler bus (check bus schedules ahead of time at Portrush TI or at www.translink.co.uk). For more info on hiking the route without a naturalist, see www.visitcausewaycoastandglens.com and search for "North Antrim Cliff Path."

▲▲Old Bushmills Distillery

Bushmills claims to be the world's oldest distillery. Though King James I (of Bible translation fame) only granted Bushmills its license to distill "Aqua Vitae" in 1608, whiskey has been made here since the 13th century. Distillery tours waft you through the process, making it clear that Irish whiskey is triple distilled—and therefore smoother than Scotch whisky (distilled merely twice and minus the "e").

Cost and Hours: £8 for 45-minute tour followed by a tasting; tours go on the half-hour Mon-Sat 9:30-16:00 (last tour), Sun from 12:00; Nov-March tours run Mon-Sat 10:00-15:30 (last tour), Sun from 12:00; tours are limited to 30 people and book

For *Game of Thrones* Fans

Even if you don't give a bloody Stark about the *Game of Thrones* TV saga, you'll notice references to it as you travel around Northern Ireland. Much of the series is filmed here, both on location and in the Titanic Quarter studio in Belfast. Other scenes are shot in Croatia, Spain, Morocco, and Iceland, but the cast is subjected most often to Irish weather. An average visit to the Antrim Coast is a traipse through the set: Dragonstone, the Stormlands, and the Iron Islands were brought to life along the same route that travelers use to see Dunluce Castle and Carrick-a-Rede Rope Bridge. For those who are truly interested in the approach of a very long winter, there are several options: both McComb's (www.mccombscoaches.com; see page 456) and Game of Thrones Tours (www.gameofthronestours.com) run £40 day tours from Belfast to various spots in the seven kingdoms.

With a car, use the map at www.discovernorthernireland.com/GameofThrones to find filming locations. Without leaving County Antrim, you can visit Ballintoy Harbour (Stormlands), Larrybane (Iron Islands), Murlough Bay (Storm's End), and the Dark Hedges (King's Road) with no more than an hour's driving time. Just avoid any re-enactments, as the nearest major hospital that treats dragon burns is in Belfast.

up—reserve ahead in summer; note that in July, you can still tour, but the distillery machinery is shut down for annual maintenance; tel. 028/2073-3218, www.bushmills.com.

Visiting the Distillery: Tours start with the mash pit, which is filled with a porridge that eventually becomes whiskey. (The leftovers of that porridge are fed to the county's particularly happy cows.) Bushmills is made of only three ingredients: malted barley, water, and yeast. You'll see a huge room full of whiskey aging in oak casks—casks already used to make bourbon, sherry, and port. Whiskey picks up its color and personality from this wood (which breathes and has an effective life of 30 years). Bushmills shapes the flavor of its whiskey by carefully finessing the aging process—often in a mix of these casks.

To see the distillery at its lively best, visit when the 100 workers are staffing the machinery—Monday morning through Friday noon. (The still is still on weekends and in July.) The finale, of course, is the opportunity for a sip in the 1608 Bar—the former malt barn. Visitors get a single glass of their choice. Hot-drink enthusiasts might enjoy a cinnamon-and-cloves hot toddy. Teetotalers can just order tea. After the tour, you can get a decent lunch in the hospitality room.

Warning to Shoppers: Customs allowance is one liter per person, which the distillery cannot ship home. To bring some home, you must pack it in your checked bag (pad it well and put it in a plastic bag in case it leaks; airlines will not accept liability for bottles breaking).

Nearby: The distillery is just outside of **Bushmills town,** which is a loyalist festival of red, white, and blue flags and bunting. Banners posted throughout the town celebrate illustrious Ulster men and women and people far and wide with Ulster heritage (like Mark Twain and Dolly Parton).

▲▲Carrick-a-Rede Rope Bridge

For 200 years, fishermen hung a narrow, 90-foot-high bridge (planks strung between wires) across a 65-foot-wide chasm be-

tween the mainland and a tiny island. Today, the bridge (while not the original version) gives access to the sea stack where salmon nets were set (until 2002) during summer months to catch the fish turning and hugging the coast's corner. (The complicated system is described at the gateway.) A pleasant, 30-minute, one-mile walk from the parking lot takes you down to the rope bridge. Cross over to the island for fine views and great seabird-watching, especially during nesting season. A coffee shop and WCs are near the parking lot.

Cost and Hours: £8 trail and bridge fee; daily 9:30-18:00, June-Aug until 20:00, Nov-Feb until 15:30; last entry 45 minutes before closing, tel. 028/2076-9839, www.nationaltrust.org.uk.

Timed-Entry Tickets: Due to an increase in visitors, timed tickets are now required to cross the bridge. Arrive as early as possible; they sell only 240 tickets (same-day only) for each hour-long entry window. If you arrive on a busy day, you may have to wait an hour or even find that all the day's tickets are sold. Cruise groups and big buses arrive after 11:00. (If you're frustrated at the ticket booth, you're welcome to hike down to the bridge for free but won't be able to venture onto it.)

Nearby Viewpoint: If you have a car and a picnic lunch, don't miss the terrific coastal scenic rest area one mile steeply uphill and east of Carrick-a-Rede (on B-15 to Ballycastle). This grassy area offers one of the best picnic views in Northern Ireland (tables but no WCs). Feast on bird's-eye views of the rope bridge, nearby Rathlin Island, and the not-so-distant Island of Mull in Scotland.

▲Dunluce Castle

These romantic ruins, perched dramatically on the edge of a rocky headland, are a testimony to this region's turbulent past. During the Middle Ages, the castle was a prized fortification. But on a stormy night in 1639, dinner was interrupted as half of the kitchen fell into the sea, taking the servants with it. That was the last straw for the lady of the castle. The countess of Antrim packed up and moved inland, and the castle "began its slow submission to the forces of nature."

Cost and Hours: £5, daily 10:00-17:00, winter until 16:00, tel. 028/2073-1938.

Visiting the Castle: While it's one of the largest castles in Northern Ireland and is beautifully situated, there's precious little left to see among Dunluce's broken walls.

Before entering, catch the eight-minute video about the history of the castle (across from the ticket desk). The ruins themselves are dotted with plaques that show interesting artists' renditions of how the place would have looked 400 years ago.

The 16th-century expansion of the castle was financed by treasure salvaged from a shipwreck. In 1588, the Spanish Armada's *Girona*—overloaded with sailors and the valuables of three abandoned sister ships—sank on her way home after the aborted mission against England. More than 1,300 drowned, and only five survivors washed ashore. The shipwreck was more fully excavated in 1967, and a bounty of golden odds and silver ends wound up in Belfast's Ulster Museum.

Rathlin Island

The only inhabited island off the coast of Northern Ireland, Rathlin is a quiet haven for hikers, birdwatchers, and seal spotters. Less

than seven miles from end to end, this "L"-shaped island is reachable by ferry from the town of Ballycastle.

Getting There: The Rathlin Island passenger-only ferry departs from Ballycastle, just east of Carrick-a-Rede (10 trips per day in summer). Six are fast 25-minute trips, and four are slower 45-minute trips (£12 round-trip per passenger, smart to prebook, as the ferry can sell out on summer days; tel. 028/2076-9299, www.rathlinballycastleferry.com).

Travelers with rental cars park in Ballycastle (only special-permit holders can take a car onto the ferry). A taxi from Portrush to Ballycastle runs £25 one-way. Bus service from Portrush to Bal-

PORTRUSH & ANTRIM COAST

lycastle is spotty (check with the TI in Portrush, or contact Translink—tel. 028/9066-6630, www.translink.co.uk).

Visiting Rathlin Island: Rathlin's population of 110 islanders clusters around the ferry dock at Church Bay. Here you'll find the **Rathlin Boathouse Visitor Centre,** which operates as the island's TI (daily 10:00-12:30 & 13:00-17:00, closed in winter, on the bay 100 yards east of the ferry dock, mobile 077-0886-9605).

In summer, a shuttle bus (£5 round-trip) meets arriving ferries and drives visitors to the **Rathlin Island Seabird Centre** at the west end of the island. Entry to the Seabird Centre (£5) includes a tour of its unique lighthouse, extending down the cliff with its beacon at the bottom. It's upside-down because the coast guard wants the light visible only from a certain distance out to sea. The bird observation terrace at the center (next to the lighthouse) overlooks one of the most dramatic coastal views in Ireland—a sheer drop of more than 300 feet to craggy sea stacks just offshore that are draped in thousands of seabirds. Bring your most powerful zoom lens for photos.

Rathlin has seen its fair share of history. Flint ax heads were quarried here in Neolithic times. The island was one of the first in Ireland to be raided by Vikings, in 795. Robert the Bruce hid out from English pursuers on Rathlin in the early 1300s (see "The Scottish Connection" sidebar, earlier). In the late 1500s, local warlord Sorely Boy MacDonnell stashed his extended family on Rathlin and waited on the mainland at Dunluce Castle to face his English enemies...only to watch in horror as they headed for the island instead to massacre his loved ones. And in 1917, a WWI U-boat sank the British cruiser HMS *Drake* in Church Bay. The wreck is now a popular scuba-dive destination, 60 feet below the surface.

▲Antrim Mountains and Glens

Not particularly high (never more than 1,500 feet), the Antrim Mountains are cut by a series of large glens running northeast to the sea. Glenariff, with its waterfalls—especially the Mare's Tail— is the most beautiful of the nine glens (described next). Travelers going by car can take a pleasant drive from Portrush to Belfast, sticking to the (more scenic but less direct) A-2 road that stays near the coast and takes in parts of all the Glens of Antrim.

▲Glenariff Forest Park

Glenariff Forest Park offers scenic picnic spots and hiking trails as well as a cozy tea shop. The parking lot alone has a lovely view down the glen to the sea. You'll find more spectacular scenery on the two-mile waterfall trail along the river gorge, while an easy-going half-mile stroll on the viewpoint trail via the ornamental gardens also provides lovely views (£5 parking fee, daily 10:00-

dusk, trail map available at café onsite, tel. 028/7034-0870, www. nidirect.gov.uk).

Getting There: The entry is off A-43 (via A-26; eight miles south of Cushendall, follow signs).

Nearby: Continue along the A-2 scenic coastal route and take a short jog up to Cushendall, where there's a nice beach for a picnic, or just head south on A-2 toward the Gobbins Cliff Path and the castle at Carrickfergus (see listings in the Belfast chapter).

BELFAST

Seventeenth-century Belfast was just a village. With the influx, or "plantation," of English and (more often) Scottish settlers, the character of the place changed. After the Scots and English were brought in—and the native Irish were subjugated—Belfast blossomed, spurred by the success of the local linen, rope-making, and especially shipbuilding industries. The Industrial Revolution took root here with a vengeance. While the rest of Ireland remained rural and agricultural, Belfast earned its nickname ("Old Smoke") during the time when many of the brick buildings that you'll see today were built. The year 1888 marked the birth of modern Belfast. After Queen Victoria granted city status to this boomtown of 300,000, its citizens built Belfast's centerpiece, City Hall.

Belfast is the birthplace of the *Titanic* (and many other ships that didn't sink). In 2012, to mark the 100th anniversary of the *Titanic* disaster, a modern new attraction was launched in Belfast's shipyard, telling the ill-fated ship's fascinating and tragic story. Nearby, two huge, mustard-colored cranes (built in the 1970s, and once the biggest in the world, nicknamed Samson and Goliath) rise like skyscrapers. They stand idle now, but serve as a reminder of this town's former shipbuilding might...strategic enough to be the target of four Luftwaffe bombing raids in World War II.

At the beginning of the 21st century, the peace process (substantially defusing the sectarian Troubles) began to take root, and investments from south of the border—the Republic of Ireland—injected quiet optimism into the dejected shipyards where the *Titanic* was built. Like everywhere else in Ireland, the 2008 economic crash gave investors a sobering lesson. But Belfast officials have

BELFAST

Greater Belfast

To Portrush & the Antrim Coast — A-43

To Antrim Coast via Glens of Antrim

To Cairnryan, Scotland — A-2

Larne

THE GOBBINS CLIFF PATH

Irish Sea

Ballymena

A-8

5 Kilometers

5 Miles

A-26

To Derry

M-22

A-57

A-6

Antrim

A-8

M-2

CARRICK-FERGUS CASTLE

To Cairnryan, Scotland & Liverpool (port of Birkenhead), England

Bangor

A-5   B-39

Cultra

A-2

A-21

Belfast International Airport

A-52

ULSTER FOLK & TRANSPORT MUSEUM

SOMME HERITAGE CENTRE

Crumlin

Belfast

George Best City Airport

Newtownards

Lough Neagh

See Belfast map

Stormont

MOUNT STEWART HOUSE

A-20

Lisburn   B-76   A-24

To Newcastle   To Downpatrick

Strangford Lough

To Dublin

resumed hope that the historic Titanic Quarter will continue to attract development...and lots of tourists.

It feels like a new morning in Belfast. A forest of cranes stand sentinel over numerous building sites. The skyline is changing rapidly, especially along the once depressing Lagan riverfront. It's hard to believe that the bright and bustling pedestrian center was once a subdued, traffic-free security zone. There's no longer any hint of security checks, once a tiresome daily routine. These days, both Catholics and Protestants root for the Belfast Giants ice hockey team. And aggressive sectarian murals are slowly being repainted with scenes celebrating heritage pride...less carnage, more culture.

Still, it's a fragile peace. Hateful bonfires, built a month before they're actually set ablaze, still scorch the pavement each July. Pubs with security gates are reminders that the island is still split—and 900,000 Protestant Unionists in the North prefer it that way.

PLANNING YOUR TIME

Big Belfast is thin on sights. For most, one day of sightseeing is plenty. But I've also included advice for longer stays.

Day Trip from Dublin

Using the handy, two-hour Dublin-Belfast train (about €40 for "day return" tickets), you could make Belfast a day trip:

7:35	Catch the train from Dublin's Connolly Station (arriving in Belfast's Central Station at 9:45; confirm train times)
11:00	Take the City Hall tour (12:00 on Sat-Sun), browse the pedestrian zone, have lunch, and ride a shared black taxi up Falls Road
15:00	Visit Titanic Belfast (after midday crowds subside) or side-trip to the Ulster Folk Park and Transport Museum in nearby Cultra (closed Mon)
Evening	Return to Dublin (last train departs Belfast Mon-Sat at 20:05 and arrives in Dublin at 22:15)

Note about Sundays: Trains depart later and return earlier on this day, compressing your already limited sightseeing time (first train departs Dublin at 10:00 and arrives in Belfast at 12:08; last train departs Belfast at 19:05 and pulls into Dublin at 22:15).

Staying Overnight

Belfast makes a pleasant overnight stop, with plenty of cheap hostels, reasonable B&Bs, weekend hotel deals, and a relaxed neighborhood full of B&Bs 30 minutes away in Bangor.

Two Days in Belfast: On the first day, follow my day-trip itinerary described earlier. For your second day, take the City Sightseeing bus tour in the morning, then visit Carrickfergus Castle in the afternoon.

Two Days in Small-Town Northern Ireland: From Dublin (via Belfast), take the train to Portrush; allow two nights and a day to tour the Causeway Coast (castle, whiskey distilleries, Giant's Causeway, resort fun), then follow the Belfast-in-a-day plan described earlier. With a third day, add Derry.

Coming from Scotland or England: With cheap flights from Edinburgh or Glasgow, as well as slow ferry connections (from Cairnryan in Scotland or Liverpool in England; see "Belfast Connections," later), it's easy to begin your exploration of the Emerald Isle in Belfast, and then head south to Dublin and the Republic.

Orientation to Belfast

Belfast is flat and spread out, with the following zones of interest: **Titanic Quarter** (northeast of city center; docklands with Odyssey entertainment complex and Titanic Belfast), **western Belfast** (working-class sectarian neighborhoods west of A-12 freeway), **city center** (Donegall Square, City Hall, pedestrian shopping, TI), **Cathedral Quarter** (north of City Hall; Ulster-Scots Centre, Northern Ireland War Memorial, lively nightlife), and **southern Belfast** (Botanic Gardens, Queen's University, Ulster Museum).

The eastern part of Belfast is more affluent and residential, with little of interest to the average sightseer, except for Stormont (the seat of government in Northern Ireland).

The modern bookends of sightseeing interest are the Titanic Belfast attraction (in the Titanic Quarter to the north) and the Lyric Theatre (near the university district to the south). Their contemporary angularities are hard to miss, as they contrast sharply with the red-brick uniformity of old Belfast. But the core of your city navigating will hinge on four more central landmarks (listed from north to south): St. Anne's Cathedral, City Hall, Shaftesbury Square, and Queen's University. Find them on your map, and use them to navigate as you stroll the town.

Belfast's "Golden Mile" commercial drag—stretching from Hotel Europa to the university district—connects the central and southern zones with some of the best dinner and entertainment spots.

TOURIST INFORMATION

The modern TI (look for *Visit Belfast* sign) has a courteous staff and baggage storage (£3.50/bag for 4 hours, £5/bag for 8 hours; Mon-Sat 9:00-17:30, June-Sept until 19:00, Sun 11:00-16:00 year-round; a couple of doors down from the Linen Hall Library, just across Chichester Street, north of City Hall at 9 Donegall Square North, tel. 028/9024-6609, http://visitbelfast.com). City walking tours depart from the TI (see "Tours in Belfast," later). Pick up a free copy of *Visit Belfast*, which lists all the sightseeing and evening entertainment options.

ARRIVAL IN BELFAST

By Train: Arriving by train, you'll go directly to Belfast's Central Station (with an ATM in the lobby). From the station, a free Centrelink bus loops to Donegall Square, with stops near Shaftesbury Square (recommended hostel), the bus station (some recommended hotels), and the TI (free with any train or bus ticket, 4/hour, none on Sun; during morning rush hour, bus runs only between station and Donegall Square). Allow about £5 for a taxi from Central Station to Donegall Square, or £8 to my accommodation listings south of the university.

Slower trains arc through the city, stopping at several downtown stations, including Central Station, Great Victoria Station (most central, near Donegall Square and most hotels), and Botanic Station (close to the university, Botanic Gardens, and some recommended lodgings). It's easy and cheap to connect stations by train (£1.50).

BELFAST

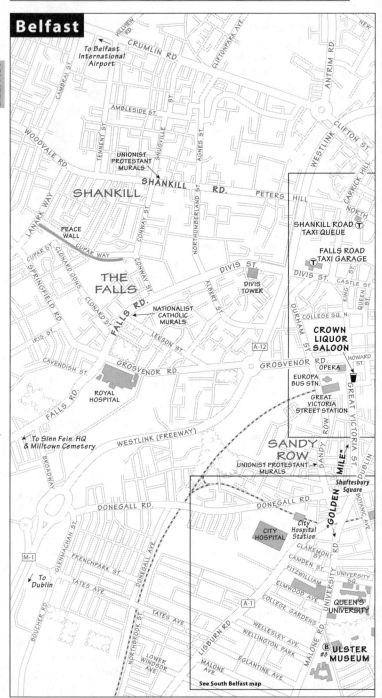

Belfast

To Belfast International Airport

HILLVIEW RD.
CRUMLIN RD.
CLIFTONPARK AVE.
CAMBRAI ST.
WOODVALE RD.
AMBLESIDE ST.
TENNENT ST.
SNUGVILLE ST.
AGNES ST.
CONWAY ST.

UNIONIST PROTESTANT MURALS

SHANKILL
SHANKILL RD.
PETERS HILL

LANARK WAY
PEACE WALL
CUPAR WAY
CUPAR ST.
CLONARD GDNS.
CLONARD ST.
SPRINGFIELD RD.

THE FALLS
FALLS RD.

NATIONALIST CATHOLIC MURALS

NORTHUMBERLAND ST.
DIVIS ST.
DIVIS TOWER
ALBERT ST.
LEESON ST.
A-12

IRIS ST.
CAVENDISH ST.
GROSVENOR RD.
GROSVENOR RD.
DURHAM ST.
COLLEGE SQ. N

ROYAL HOSPITAL
FALLS RD.

To Sinn Fein HQ & Milltown Cemetery

WESTLINK (FREEWAY)

BROADWAY
M-1
To Dublin
GLENMACHAN ST.
FRENCHPARK ST.
DONEGALL RD.
DONEGALL AVE.
TATES AVE.
TATES AVE.
BOUCHER RD.
NORTHBROOK ST.
LOWER WINDSOR AVE.

WESTLINK
CLIFTON ST.
ANTRIM RD.
NEW
CARRICK HILL
NORTH

SHANKILL ROAD TAXI QUEUE (T)
FALLS ROAD TAXI GARAGE (T)

DIVIS ST.
CASTLE ST.
KING ST.
QUEEN ST.

CROWN LIQUOR SALOON

HOWARD ST.
OPERA
EUROPA BUS STN.
GREAT VICTORIA STREET STATION
GREAT VICTORIA ST.

SANDY ROW
UNIONIST PROTESTANT MURALS
SANDY ROW
"GOLDEN MILE"
DUBLIN RD.
BOTANIC AVE.
Shaftesbury Square

DONEGALL RD.
CITY HOSPITAL
City Hospital Station
CLAREMONT ST.
CAMDEN ST.
FITZWILLIAM
ELMWOOD AVE.
UNIVERSITY RD.
UNIVERSITY SQ.
QUEEN'S UNIVERSITY

LISBURN RD.
COLLEGE GARDENS
WELLESLEY AVE.
WELLINGTON PARK
EGLANTINE AVE.
MALONE AVE.
MALONE RD.
A-1
(B) #5
ULSTER MUSEUM

See South Belfast map

BELFAST

By Car: Driving in Belfast, although not as bad as in Dublin, is still a pain. Avoid it if possible. Street parking in the city center is geared for short stops (use pay-and-display machines, £0.30/15 minutes, one-hour maximum, Mon-Sat 8:00-18:00, free in evenings and on Sun).

HELPFUL HINTS

Belfast Visitor Pass: This pass combines iLink smartcards for free bus and rail travel, with sightseeing discounts, for one day or two or three consecutive days within the Belfast Visitor Pass Zone (all of downtown Belfast as far out as the Ulster Folk and Transport Museum in Cultra, but not as far as Carrickfergus or Bangor). The handy one-day pass saves money for anyone visiting Titanic Belfast (£3 discount) and the Ulster Folk and Transport Museum (30 percent discount) while connecting them by train or bus (free with pass). Buy it at the TI, any train station, either airport, Europa Bus station, or online (£6.50 for 1-day pass, £11 for 2 days, £14.50 for 3 days, tel. 028/9066-6630, www.translink.co.uk).

Market: On Friday, Saturday, and Sunday, the Victorian confines of **St. George's Market** is a commotion of commerce and a people-watching delight. Friday is a variety market (6:00-14:00), Saturday blooms with food and garden items (9:00-15:00), and Sunday creaks with crafts and antiques (10:00-16:00). It's located at the corner of Oxford and East Bridge streets (5 blocks east of Donegall Square, tel. 028/9043-5704, www.belfastcity.gov.uk/markets).

Shopping Mall: Victoria Square is a glitzy American-style mall. Its huge glass dome reflects Belfast's economic rejuvenation. For fine city views, ride the free elevator to the observation platform high up inside the dome (Mon-Sat 9:30-18:00, Wed-Fri until 21:00, Sun 13:00-18:00; 3 blocks east of City Hall—bordered by Chichester, Victoria, Ann, and Montgomery streets; www.victoriasquare.com).

Phone Tips: For details on making calls between the Republic of Ireland and Northern Ireland, see page 556.

Post Office: The main post office, with lots of fun postcards, is at the intersection of High and Bridge streets (Mon-Fri 9:00-17:30, Sat until 12:30, closed Sun, 3 long blocks north of Donegall Square).

Services: Located directly across University Road from the red-brick university building, **Queen's University Student Union** is just as handy for tourists as it is for college students. Inside you'll find an ATM, WCs, a minimarket, and Wi-Fi. Grab a quick and cheap sandwich and coffee at **Clement's Coffee Shop** (long hours Mon-Sat, closed Sun).

Laundry: Globe Launderers has both self-serve and drop-off service (Mon-Fri 8:00-21:00, Sat until 18:00, Sun 12:00-18:00, 37 Botanic Avenue, tel. 028/9024-3956). For the hotel neighborhood south of the university, the closest is **Whistle Cleaners** (drop-off service, Mon-Fri 8:30-18:00, Sat 9:00-17:30, closed Sun, 160 Lisburn Road, at intersection with Eglantine Avenue, tel. 028/9038-1297). For locations, see the map on page 473.

Bike Rental: Belfast Bike Tours rents bikes only if reserved in advance (£15/day, daily but no set hours, off Wellington Park behind Wellington Park Hotel, mobile 078-1211-4235, www. belfastbiketours.com).

GETTING AROUND BELFAST

If you line up your sightseeing logically, you can do most of this flat town on foot. On wheels, you have several options. For most visitors, the Belfast Visitor Pass will save time and money. It combines iLink smartcards for local bus and train trips with sightseeing discounts (see "Helpful Hints," earlier).

By Train or Bus: Ask about iLink smartcards, which give individuals one day of unlimited train and bus travel. The Zone 1 card (£5) covers the city center, Cultra (Ulster Folk Park and Transport Museum), and George Best Belfast City Airport. The handy Zone 2 card (£10) includes Bangor and Carrickfergus Castle. The Zone 3 card (£13.50) is really only useful for reaching Belfast's distant international airport. Zone 4 (£16) gets you anywhere in Northern Ireland, including Portrush and Derry (£16.50 top-up for each additional day). For those lingering in the North, one-week cards offer even better deals. Buy your iLink card at any train station in the city.

If you're traveling from Belfast to only one destination—Carrickfergus Castle, Cultra, or Bangor—a "day return" ticket is cheaper than two one-way tickets.

Pink-and-white city buses go from Donegall Square East to Malone Road and my recommended accommodations (any #8 bus, 3/hour, £2, all-day pass costs £4 Mon-Sat before 9:30—after 9:30 and on Sun it's £3.70). Sunday service is much less frequent.

For more information on iLink smartcards, trains, and buses in Belfast, contact Translink (tel. 028/9066-6630, www.translink. co.uk).

By Taxi: Taxis are reasonable and a good option. For general transport, as opposed to the taxi tours described later, try **Valu Cabs** (tel. 028/9080-9080). Cabs charge a flat £3 rate for any ride (£3.40 from 22:00 to 6:00) and £2 per mile after that. If you're going up Falls Road, ride a shared cab (explained later, under "Sights in Belfast").

BELFAST

Tours in Belfast

ON FOOT

▲General Walking Tours

Belfast Compass Tours introduces you to the city's 300-year history on a balanced two-hour stroll. Highlights include City Hall, St. George's Market, Albert Clock, and the opulent Merchant Hotel (£7, must book in advance, mobile 079-4425-6560 or 079-3440-7751, www.belfastcompasstours.com).

Belfast Hidden Tours focuses on the culture of North Belfast, going heavier on trade and industry with a sprinkling of rebel sedition and Luftwaffe destruction, while leading visitors to less obvious "hidden" corners of the city (£10, March-Oct daily at 10:00, 12:00, and 14:00, no 10:00 tour on Sun, meet at Visit Belfast TI, tel. 079-7189-5746, www.belfasthiddentours.com).

Belfast Trad Trail Tours hosts this musical pub crawl. It's led by two local musicians, who walk you between three fun drinking establishments, and play and explain traditional Irish music at each pub. It's a great intro to Irish music and the pulsing evening scene of the Cathedral Quarter. It starts at 16:00 and lasts about 2.5 hours, allowing you time afterward to dine and explore the neighborhood (£15, mid-May-Aug daily at 16:00, meet at Dirty Onion Pub, 3 Hill Street, tel. 028/9028-8818, www.tradtrail.com).

Local Guides

Susie Millar is a sharp former BBC TV reporter who thrives on showing visitors around her native Belfast. With family connections to the *Titanic* tragedy, she knows that sad, yet inspiring chapter inside and out. She can also take you farther afield by car (yours or hers) when she is not busy guiding Rick Steves tours (£25/person for half-day tour, book in advance, mobile 078-5271-6655, www.titanictours-belfast.co.uk, info@titanictours-belfast.co.uk).

Lynn Corken is a friendly, knowledgeable, and flexible Jill-of-all-trades, with a passion for her hometown. She's willing to customize her guiding to your interests (on foot or with her car) when she's not on the road leading Rick Steves tours (£100/half-day, £200/day, book in advance, mobile 077-7910-2448, lynncorken@hotmail.co.uk).

Sectarian Neighborhoods Walking Tours

Two walking tours offer opposite viewpoints on the Troubles and local culture. Listen and learn. Or, as an Irish friend once told me, "Never give unsolicited advice...wise men don't need it and fools won't heed it."

Coiste Irish Political Tours offers the Nationalist/Republican perspective on extended, two-hour walks along Falls Road. Led by former IRA prisoners, you'll visit murals, gardens of remembrance, peace walls, and community centers in this slowly re-juvenating section of gritty Belfast. Tours meet beside the Divis Tower (the 20-story apartment house at the east end of the Divis Road near the A-12 Westlink motorway overpass) and end at the Milltown Cemetery (£10; Tue, Thu, and Sat at 11:00, Sun at 14:00; best to book in advance, tel. 028/9020-0770, www.coiste.ie).

Sandy Row Walking Tours provides the Unionist/Loyalist point of view during its 1.5-hour walks centering on Sandy Row, Belfast's oldest residential neighborhood. Tours cover the city's industrial heritage, the Orange Order, both World Wars, and historic local churches. They depart from the King William Mural at the intersection of Sandy Row and Linfield Road (£7.50; daily at 10:00, 14:00, and 17:00; best to book in advance, mobile 079-0925-4849, www.historicsandyrow.co.uk).

ON WHEELS
▲Hop-On, Hop-Off Bus Tours
City Sightseeing offers the best quick introduction to the city's political and social history. Their open-top, double-decker buses link major sights and landmarks, including the Catholic and Protestant working-class neighborhoods, the Stormont Parliament building, Titanic Belfast, and City Hall, with commentary on political murals and places of interest. The route also has convenient stops near several lodging options listed later: Fisherwick Place (Jurys Inn), Shaftsbury Square (Benedicts Hotel and Belfast International City Hostel), and Malone Road (Malone Lodge and Wellington Park Hotel). Pay cash on bus or book online in advance (£12.50 for 48 hours, 2/hour, fewer in winter, daily 10:00-16:00, 20 stops, 1.5-hour loop; departs from Castle Place on High Street, 2 blocks west of Albert Clock Tower; tel. 028/9032-1321, http://belfastcitysightseeing.com).

City Tours offers a route with more than 20 stops. It starts on High Street (near Albert Clock), then veers westward to take in Falls and Shankill roads (£10 for 48 hours, runs 2/hour 9:45-16:45, pay cash on bus or book in advance, tel. 028/9032-1912, www.citytoursbelfast.com).

Sectarian Taxi Tours
This is the easiest way to view the evolving murals of the Catholic and Protestant communities with a local who has lived through the events that inspired them. In recent years, these taxi tours have begun venturing onto each other's turf to give a more balanced, yet still opinionated personal perspective. Their unscripted commentary is as varied as their individual personalities. See "Sectarian Neighborhoods in West Belfast," later, for details on Falls and Shankill roads.

Avoid squeezing more than four passengers into a cab because the views from the middle seats are restricted. However, drivers are willing to stop (where traffic allows) to let you out for photos.

Taxi Trax Black Taxi Tours—from a Nationalist Catholic area—gives 90-minute **Falls Road**-based tours (£35/1-3 people, £12/additional person, cheap for small groups, at the intersection of Castle and King streets in Castle Junction Car Park, tel. 028/9031-5777 or mobile 078-9271-6660, www.taxitrax.com).

NI Black Taxi Tours—from a Unionist Protestant area—takes you on 90-minute tours around **Shankill Road** (£30/1-3 people, £10/additional person, cheap for small groups, book in advance, mobile 077-2968-3104, www.niblacktaxitours.com).

Bike Tours

Belfast Bike Tours offers 2.5-hour rides in the countryside south of town. Departing from the front gate of Queen's University, you'll pedal along an old canal towpath to the Giant's Ring (ancient dolmen) and back on generally flat terrain (£15; April-Aug Mon, Wed, Fri-Sat at 10:30 and 14:00; Sept-March Sat 10:30 and 14:00; bikes, helmets, and bottle of water provided; must reserve ahead by phone or email, mobile 078-1211-4235, www.belfastbiketours.com, info@belfastbiketours.com).

Minibus Tours

McComb's Giant's Causeway Tour visits Carrickfergus Castle, the Giant's Causeway, Dunluce Castle (photo stop only), Carrick-a-Rede Rope Bridge, and Old Bushmills Distillery (£25, doesn't include distillery admission, daily depending on demand, book through and depart from the recommended Belfast International City Hostel, pickup around 9:00, back to Belfast by 19:00). Their *Game of Thrones* tour (see sidebar on page 441) visits many of the sites where the hit fantasy TV series was filmed (£35, starts around 8:30, back to Belfast by 19:00). They also have private guides (book in advance, tel. 028/9031-5333, www.mccombscoaches.com).

BY BOAT

Titanic Tours

The **Lagan Boat Company** shows you shipyards on this one-hour cruise, narrated by a member of the Belfast Titanic Society. The tour shows off the fruits of the city's £800 million investment in its harbor, including a weir built to control the tides and stabilize the depth of the harbor (it doubles as a free

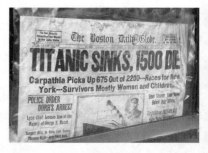

pedestrian bridge over the River Lagan). The heart of the tour is a lazy harbor cruise past rusty dry-dock gates, brought alive by the guide's proud commentary and passed-around historical photos (£10; April-Oct daily sailings at 12:30, 14:00, and 15:30; fewer off-season, tel. 028/9024-0124, www.laganboatcompany.com). Tours depart from the Lagan Pedestrian Bridge and Weir on Donegall Quay. The quay is located just past the leaning Albert Clock Tower, a 10-minute walk from the TI.

Sights in Belfast

TITANIC QUARTER

Up until the mid-1990s, this district was a barren wasteland of cement slabs and rusting industrial relics. But during the Celtic Tiger boom years (which spilled over into the North), shrewd investors saw the real-estate potential and began building posh, high-rise condos.

The first landmark project to be completed was the Odyssey entertainment complex (in 2000). To draw more visitors and commemorate the proud shipbuilding industry of the Victorian and Edwardian Ages, another flagship attraction was needed. The 100th anniversary of the *Titanic* disaster in 2012 provided the perfect opportunity, and the result is the Titanic Belfast.

The Odyssey

This huge millennium-project complex offers a food pavilion, bowling alley, and W5 science center with interactive, educational exhibits for youngsters. Where else can a kid play a harp with laser-light strings? The "W5" stands for "who, what, when, where, and why" (£9.80, kids-£6.50, Mon-Fri 10:00-17:00, Sat until 18:00, Sun 12:00-18:00, last entry one hour before closing, 2 Queen's Quay, 10-minute walk north of Belfast's Central Station, tel. 028/9046-7790, www.w5online.co.uk).

There's also a 12-screen cinema and the 11,000-seat SSE Odyssey Arena, where the Belfast Giants professional hockey team skates from September to March on Friday or Saturday nights (£16 game tickets, tel. 028/9073-9074, www.belfastgiants.com).

▲▲▲Titanic Belfast

This £97 million attraction stands right next to the original slipways where the *Titanic* was built. Creative displays tell the tale of the famous ocean liner, proudly heralded as the largest man-made moving object of its time. The sight has no actual artifacts from the underwater wreck (out of respect for the fact that it's a mass grave). The artifacts on display are from local shipbuilding offices and personal collections.

Cost and Hours: £18:50; daily 9:00-18:00, June-Aug until

Belfast at a Glance

▲▲▲**Titanic Belfast** Excellent but crowded high-tech exhibit covering the famously infamous ship and local shipbuilding, housed in a stunning structure on the site where the *Titanic* was built. **Hours:** Daily 9:00-18:00, June-Aug until 19:00; Oct-March 10:00-17:00. See page 457.

▲▲ **Sectarian Neighborhoods Taxi Tours** Local cabbies drive visitors through West Belfast's Falls Road and Shankill Road neighborhoods, offering personal perspectives on the slowly fading Troubles. See page 455.

▲▲**City Hall** Central Belfast's polished and majestic celebration of Victorian-era pride built with industrial wealth. **Hours:** Daily 8:30-17:00. See page 463.

▲**Ulster Museum** Mixed bag of local artifacts, natural history, and coverage of political events; a good rainy-day option near Queen's University. **Hours:** Tue-Sun 10:00-17:00, closed Mon. See page 467.

▲**Botanic Gardens** Belfast's best green space, featuring the Palm House loaded with delicate tropical vegetation. **Hours:** Daily 8:00 until dusk; Palm House open daily 10:00-17:00, Oct-March until 16:00. See page 468.

Near Belfast

▲▲**Ulster Folk Park and Transport Museum** A glimpse into Northern Ireland's hard-working heritage, split between a charming re-creation of past rural life and halls of innovative vehicular advances (8 miles east of Belfast). **Hours:** March-Sept Tue-Sun 10:00-17:00; Oct-Feb Tue-Fri 10:00-16:00, Sat-Sun 11:00-16:00; closed Mon year-round. See page 468.

▲**Carrickfergus Castle** Northern Ireland's first and most important fortified refuge for invading 12th-century Normans (14 miles northeast of Belfast). **Hours:** Daily 10:00-17:00, Oct-March until 16:00. See page 470.

▲**The Gobbins** Rugged, unique, wave-splashed hiking trail cut into coastal rock, accessible by guided tour (34 miles northeast of Belfast). **Hours:** Visitor center daily 9:30-17:30, guided hikes about every hour in good weather. See page 470.

Near Bangor

▲**Mount Stewart House** Fine 18th-century manor house displaying ruling-class affluence, surrounded by lush and calming gardens (18 miles east of Belfast). **Hours:** Daily 10:00-16:30, closed Nov-Feb. See page 480.

19:00; Oct-March 10:00-17:00; last admission about 90 minutes before closing (though the Late Saver Ticket is sold one hour before closing for £10); audioguide-£3, but you get plenty of info without it; located on Queen's Island, tel. 028/9076-6399, www. titanicbelfast.com.

Crowd-Beating Tips: Go early or late as big bus-tour or cruise-ship crowds can clog the exhibits from 10:00 to 14:00. Book ahead online to get the entry time you want.

Getting There: From Donegall Square, take bus #26 or #26B (both stop behind Belfast Metropolitan College, infrequent buses on Sun), or go by taxi (£6 ride). The Titanic Quarter train station is a 15-minute walk to the south of the Titanic Belfast.

Tours: The **Discovery Tour** explains the striking architecture of the Titanic Belfast building and the adjacent slipways where the ship was built (£9, 1 hour, call ahead for tour times).

Eating: The ground floor includes a **$ Galley Express** (sandwich café) as well as **$$ Bistro 401** (a carvery-style restaurant). Or, walk one block east (away from the tourist crowds), through the arch in the Drawing Offices building and across Queens Road to the battleship-gray **$$ Cast & Crew** for a sandwich, soup, or salad (daily 12:00-18:00).

Visiting the Sight: The spacey architecture of the Titanic Belfast building is a landmark on the city's skyline. Six stories tall, it's clad in more than 3,000 sun-reflecting aluminum panels. Its four corners represent the bows of the many ships (most of which didn't sink) that were built in these yards during the industrial Golden Age of Belfast.

The exhibit's nine galleries are numbered differently than the floors, but it doesn't matter as you'll be routed on a one-way path through six floors. If you have any questions, there are helpful "crew" everywhere you look.

The "shipyard ride" near the beginning is a fun (if cheesy) five-minute experience. Six people share a gondola as you glide through a series of vignettes that attempt to capture what it was like to be a worker building the ship. (There can be a 20-minute wait—if strapped for time, I'd skip it and use that time more productively in the fascinating displays that follow.)

Continuing on, you'll find a big window overlooking the actual construction site (which you'll visit after leaving the building). Next, you'll see exhibits on the construction, historic photographs, proud displays of the opulence on board, the disaster (with Morse code transmissions sent after the ship hit the iceberg) and, in the

200-seat Discovery Theatre, the seven-minute *Titanic Beneath* video, with eerie footage of the actual wreckage sprouting countless "rusticles" 12,000 feet down on the ocean floor. Don't miss the see-through floor panels at the foot of the movie screen where the wreck passes slowly under your feet.

The last escalator leaves you on the ground floor facing the back door of the center. Step outside. Just beyond the door, in the pavement, is a big, stylized map showing the route of the *Titanic*'s one and only voyage. The brown benches are long and short—set up in dots and dashes to represent the Morse code distress transmissions sent on that fateful day. Just beyond two dashes, a few steps to the left, find the symbolic steel tip of the ship in the pavement and stand there looking out. This was where the bow was; the lampposts (stretching 300 yards before you) mark the size of the ship built here. Fifty yards ahead is a memorial with the names of all who perished.

Nearby: The SS *Nomadic* tender ship, which once ferried passengers between the dock and the *Titanic,* is docked 50 yards south of Titanic Belfast and easily visible (included with Titanic Belfast ticket, same hours as Titanic Belfast).

Thompson Dry Dock and Pump-House

Those with an unsinkable interest in the *Titanic* may want to walk down into the massive footprint where it last rested on dry land, to get a feel for how colossal the vessel was. The pump house filled the dry dock with water—and emptied it—in record time. Slipways rolled hulls down a slope into the water, where they were then towed to a dry dock. It's here that the final outfitting was completed, adding extra weight before the final watertight launch. Standing on the floor of this humongous concrete bathtub is humbling, especially when looking at the well-placed historic photos that show how snugly the ship fit here.

Cost and Hours: £3, daily 10:30-16:00, www.titanicsdock. com.

Getting There: From the Titanic Belfast, it's a 15-minute walk north to the Dry Dock and Pump-House. En route, you'll pass the huge **Titanic Studios** building, where interiors of *Game of Thrones* and *City of Ember* were filmed.

SECTARIAN NEIGHBORHOODS IN WEST BELFAST

It will be a happy day when the sectarian neighborhoods of Belfast have nothing to be sectarian about. For a look at three of the original home bases of the Troubles, explore the working-class neighborhoods of Catholic Falls Road and Protestant Shankill Road (west of the Westlink motorway), or Protestant Sandy Row (south of the Westlink motorway).

Murals (found in working-class, sectarian areas) are a memorable part of any visit to Belfast. But with more peaceful times, the character of these murals is slowly changing. The Re-Imaging Communities Program has spent £3 million in government money to replace aggressive murals with positive ones. Paramilitary themes are gradually being covered over with images of pride in each neighborhood's culture. The *Titanic* was built primarily by proud Protestant Ulster stock and is often seen in their neighborhood murals—reflecting their industrious work ethic. Over in the Catholic neighborhoods, you'll see more murals depicting mythological heroes from the days before the English came.

Hop-on, hop-off bus tours regularly drive these roads. But taxi tours of Falls Road or Shankill Road are more interactive (quiz the cabbie, who grew up here) and allow you to pull over to take photos.

▲▲Falls Road (Catholic)

At the intersection of Castle and King streets, you'll find the Castle Junction Car Park. On the ground floor of this nine-story parking garage, a passenger terminal (entrance on King Street) connects travelers with old black cabs—and the only Irish-language signs in downtown Belfast. These shared black cabs efficiently shuttle residents from outlying neighborhoods up and down Falls Road and to the city center. This service originated almost 50 years ago at the beginning of the Troubles, when locals would hijack city buses and use them as barricades in the street fighting. When bus service was discontinued, local sectarian groups established the shared taxi service. Although the buses are now running again, these cab rides are still a great value for their drivers' commentaries.

Any cab goes up Falls Road, past Sinn Fein headquarters and lots of murals, to the Milltown Cemetery (£6, sit in front and talk

to the cabbie). Hop in and out. Easy-to-flag-down cabs run every minute or so in each direction on Falls Road. Or, take a one-hour tour from a trained black-taxi cabbie (see page 455).

Visiting Falls Road: The Sinn Fein office and bookstore are near the bottom of Falls Road. The **bookstore** is worth a look. Page through books featuring color photos of the political murals that decorated these buildings. Money raised here supports the families of deceased IRA members.

A sad, corrugated structure called the **peace wall** runs a block or so north of Falls Road (along Cupar Way), separating the Catholics from the Protestants in the Shankill Road area. The first cement wall was 20 feet high—it was later extended another 10 feet by a solid metal addition, and then another 15 feet with a metal screen. Seemingly high enough now to deter a projectile being lobbed over, this is one of many such walls erected in Belfast during the Troubles. Meant to be temporary, these barriers stay up because of old fears among the communities on both sides. In 2013, the Northern Ireland Assembly announced its ambitious goal to remove all of these walls by 2023, but a lack of resources and weak community unity have resulted in little progress.

At the **Milltown Cemetery,** walk past all the Gaelic crosses down to the far right-hand corner (closest to the highway), where

little green railings set apart the IRA Roll of Honor from the thousands of other graves. These martyrs are treated like fallen soldiers. Notice the memorial to Bobby Sands and nine other hunger strikers. They starved themselves to death in the nearby Maze Prison in 1981, protesting for political prisoner status as opposed to terrorist criminal treatment. Maze Prison closed in the fall of 2000.

Shankill Road and Sandy Row (Protestant)

A shared black cab brings you though the Shankill Road area (see page 456), but an easier and cheaper way to get a dose of the Unionist side is to walk **Sandy Row.** From Hotel Europa, walk a block

down Glengall Street, then turn left for a 10-minute walk along a working-class Protestant street. A stop in a Unionist memorabilia shop, a pub, or one of the many cheap eateries here may give you an opportunity to talk to a local. You'll see murals filled with Unionist symbolism. The mural of William of Orange's victory over the Catholic King James II (Battle of the Boyne, 1690) thrills Unionist hearts. You'll find it at the northern end of Sandy Row at the corner with Linfield Road.

CENTRAL BELFAST
▲▲City Hall

This grand structure's 173-foot-tall copper dome dominates the town center. Built between 1898 and 1906, with its statue of Queen Victoria scowling down Belfast's main drag and the Neoclassical dome looming behind her, the City Hall is a stirring sight. Take a close look at the Queen Victoria monument and how it celebrates the industrial might of Belfast: shipping, linen (the woman with the bobbin), and education (the student). Facing the building, if you go around to the left, you'll find the Titanic Memorial Garden.

Cost and Hours: Free, daily 8:30-17:00; handy Bobbin coffee shop on ground floor, tel. 028/9032-0202, www.belfastcity.gov.uk/cityhall.

Tours: Free 45-minute tours of City Hall run Mon-Fri at 10:00, 11:00, 14:00, 15:00, and 16:00; Sat-Sun at 12:00, 14:00, 15:00, and 16:00 (fewer off-season); call or check online to confirm schedule.

Visiting City Hall: If you can't manage a tour, at least step into the main lobby to admire the marble-swirl staircase and the view up into the dome. In 1912, at the center of the marble floor design beneath the dome, Sir Edward Carson signed the Ulster Covenant—to be followed by 470,000 other Unionists at dozens of desks surrounding City Hall that day. Some signed with their own blood. The Covenant stated Unionists would use "all means necessary" (including the might of the 100,000-strong UVF militia) to resist the Home Rule bill that had just passed in Parliament. The bill would have given the entire island of Ireland limited autonomy from Britain. These Protestant Unionists did not want this new level of political distance from Britain and feared that "Home Rule is Rome Rule." They would have become the minority in a more independent Catholic Ireland. World War I interrupted the implementation of Home Rule, and the partition of Ireland followed shortly after the war's end.

Belfast History and Culture Exhibit: A worthwhile, 16-room exhibit fills the ground floor of City Hall. It covers the history of the city, culture, industry, the WWII bombings, and the Troubles (free, open same hours as the building).

Linen Hall Library

Across the street from City Hall, the 200-year-old Linen Hall Library welcomes guests (notice the red hand above the front door

Central Belfast

1. Hotel Europa & Piano Lounge
2. Jurys Inn
3. The Morning Star Pub & Restaurant
4. Robinson & Cleaver
5. Coco Restaurant
6. Crown Liquor Saloon & Dining Room
7. Kelly's Cellars
8. Bobbin Café
9. Linen Hall Library Café
10. Merchant Hotel & The Cloth Ear Pub
11. 2 Taps Wine Bar
12. The Dirty Onion & Yardbird
13. Wagamama & Bittles Bar
14. Marks & Spencer
15. Tesco Supermarket
16. Falls Road Taxi Garage
17. Shankill Road Taxi Queue
18. Madden's Pub (Belfast Story)
19. Discover Ulster-Scots Centre
20. Northern Ireland War Memorial

facing Donegall Square North; for more on its meaning, see the sidebar on page 469). Described as "Ulster's attic," the library takes pride in being a neutral space where anyone trying to make sense of the sectarian conflict can view the Troubled Images, a historical collection of engrossing political posters. It has a fine hardbound ambience, a coffee shop (nice light lunches), and a royal newspaper reading room. Climb to the top floor and then go down the back staircase, where the walls are lined with fascinating original posters from those tough times.

Cost and Hours: Free; Mon-Fri 9:30-17:30, Sat until 16:00, closed Sun; 45-minute tours for £5—daily at 11:30, 17 Donegall Square North, tel. 028/9032-1707, www.linenhall.com.

Golden Mile

This is the overstated nickname of Belfast's liveliest dining and entertainment district, which stretches from the Opera House (Great Victoria Street) to the university (University Road).

The **Grand Opera House,** originally built in 1895, bombed and rebuilt in 1991, and bombed and rebuilt again in 1993, is extravagantly Victorian and *the* place to take in a concert, play, or opera (ticket office open Mon-Sat 10:00-17:30, closed Sun; ticket office to right of main front door on Great Victoria Street, tel. 028/9024-1919, www.goh.co.uk). The recommended **Hotel Europa,** next door, while considered to be the most-bombed hotel in the world (33 times during the Troubles), actually feels pretty casual (but is expensive).

Across the street is the museum-like **Crown Liquor Saloon.** Built in 1849, it's now a part of the National Trust. A wander through its mahogany, glass, and marble interior is a trip back into the days of Queen Victoria, although the privacy provided by the snugs—booths—allows for un-Victorian behavior (consider a lunch stop—see "Eating in Belfast," later). Upstairs, the Crown Dining Room serves pub grub and is decorated with historic photos.

CATHEDRAL QUARTER

This rejuvenating district is about a 15-minute walk north of City Hall, in the oldest part of the city. You'll find an unexpected cluster of culture that will make you rethink your preconceptions about Belfast. Besides being home to the following sights, it's a memorable maze for a wander, where mind-bending murals put the "fun" in "funky" and show the artistic alternative to the sectarian murals found elsewhere. For the best scene, head for the intersection of Hill Street and Commercial Court and peek into nearby breezeways. It's also a good place for a lively dinner (see listings on page 475).

Discover Ulster-Scots Centre

This bright and inviting gallery is designed to promote the Ulster-Scots heritage. Ulster and Scotland are 13 miles apart, and this exhibit feels almost like propaganda, trying to make it clear that the first Scots were from northeastern Ireland and the cultures are rightfully intertwined. If your heritage is Scots-Irish (as they be-

1916

This pivotal year means vastly different things to Northern Ireland's two communities. When you say "1776" to most Ameri-

Republican Socialist Movement
IRSP - INLA - RSYM

National
1916
Easter Rising
Commemoration

Assemble: 11am, Easter Sunday
Dunville Park, Falls Road, Belfast

Honour Ireland's Dead - Wear an Easter Lily

cans, it means revolution and independence from tyranny (unless, perhaps, you're a Native American). But when you say "1916" to someone in Northern Ireland, the response depends on who's talking.

To Nationalists (who are usually Catholic), "1916" brings to mind the Easter Rising—which took place in Dublin in April of that year and was the beginning of the end of 750 years of British rule for most of Ireland (see sidebar on page 66). Some Nationalist murals still use images of Dublin's rebel headquarters or martyred leaders like Patrick Pearse and James Connolly. To this community, 1916 emphasizes their proud Gaelic identity, their willingness to fight to preserve it, and their stubborn anti-British attitude.

To Unionists (who are usually Protestant), "1916" means the brutal WWI Battle of the Somme in France, which began that July. (For more on the Somme, visit the Somme Heritage Centre in Bangor, described on page 481.) Although both Catholic and Protestant soldiers died in this long and bloody battle, the first wave of young men who went over the top were the sons of proud Ulster Unionists. The Unionists hoped this sacrifice would prove their loyalty to the Crown—and assurance that the British would never let them be gobbled up by an Irish Nationalist state (a possible scenario just before the Great War's outbreak). You'll see Tommies heroically

climbing out of their trenches in some of Belfast's Unionist murals. For the Unionists, 1916 is synonymous with devout, almost righteously divine, Britishness.

came known in America) this is the place to begin your genealogy research.

Cost and Hours: Free, Mon-Fri 10:00-16:00, closed Sat-Sun, one block from clock tower at 1 Victoria Street, tel. 028/9043-6710, http://discoverulsterscots.com.

BELFAST

Northern Ireland War Memorial

This one-room sanctuary is dedicated to the lives lived and lost in this corner of the U.K. during World War II. Coverage includes the American troops based here during the war and the damage done by multiple German bombing raids during the Blitz.

Cost and Hours: Free, Mon-Fri 10:00-16:30, closed Sat-Sun, 21 Talbot Street, tel. 028/9032-0392, www.niwarmemorial.org.

St. Anne's Cathedral

Also known as Belfast Cathedral, this Anglican church was built in the early 1900s, at the peak of Belfast's industrial power. The novel spire is a spike like the one so famous in Dublin. Goofy nicknames are a passion throughout Ireland: This one's dubbed "the Rod to God."

Cost and Hours: £5, Mon-Sat 9:00-17:00, evensong on Sun at 15:30, Donegall Street, tel. 028/9032-8332.

SOUTH BELFAST
▲Ulster Museum

This is Belfast's most venerable museum. It offers an earnest and occasionally thought-provoking look at the region's history, with a cross-section of local artifacts.

Cost and Hours: £3 suggested donation; Tue-Sun 10:00-17:00, closed Mon; in Botanic Gardens on Stranmillis Road, south of downtown, tel. 028/9044-0000, www.nmni.com.

Visiting the Museum: The five-floor museum is pretty painless. Ride the elevator to the top floor and follow the spiraling exhibits downhill through various zones. The top two floors are dedicated to rotating art exhibits, the next floor down covers local nature, and the two below that focus on history. The ground floor covers the Troubles, and has a coffee shop and gift shop.

The Art Zone displays beautifully crafted fine crystal and china. In the Nature Zone, audiovisuals trace how the Ice Age affected the local landscape. Dinosaur skeletons lurk, stuffed wildlife plays possum, and geology rocks. Kids will enjoy the interactive Discover History room.

The delicately worded History Zone has an interesting British slant (such as the implication that most deaths in the Great Potato Famine of 1845-1849 were caused by typhus and fever epidemics—with little mention of the starvation that made peasants susceptible to these diseases in the first place). But the coverage of the modern-day Troubles is balanced and thought-provoking.

After a peek at a pretty good mummy, top things off with the *Girona* treasure. Soggy bits of gold, silver, leather, and wood were salvaged from the Spanish Armada's shipwrecked *Girona*, lost off the Antrim Coast north of Belfast in 1588.

BELFAST

▲Botanic Gardens

This is the backyard of Queen's University, and on a sunny day, you couldn't imagine a more relaxing park setting. On a cold day, step into the Tropical Ravine for a jungle of heat and humidity. Take a quick walk through the Palm House, reminiscent of the one in London's Kew Gardens, but smaller. The Ulster Museum is on the garden's grounds.

Cost and Hours: Free, gardens open daily 8:00 until dusk; Palm House open daily 10:00-17:00, Oct-March until 16:00; tel. 028/9031-4762, www.belfastcity.gov.uk/parks.

Nearby: Just south of the gardens is the **Lyric Theatre**, an architecturally innovative building rebuilt in 2011 (no tours, but there are performances; see "Entertainment in Belfast," later).

NEAR BELFAST
▲▲Ulster Folk Park and Transport Museum

This sprawling 180-acre, two-museum complex straddles the road and rail line at Cultra, midway between Bangor and Belfast (8 miles east of town).

Cost and Hours: £9 for each museum, £11 combo-ticket for both, £29 for families; March-Sept Tue-Sun 10:00-17:00; Oct-Feb Tue-Fri 10:00-16:00, Sat-Sun 11:00-16:00; closed Mon year-round; check the schedule for the day's special events, tel. 028/9042-8428, www.nmni.com.

Getting There: From Belfast, you can reach Cultra by taxi (£15), bus #502 (2/hour, 30 minutes, from Laganside Bus Centre), or train (2/hour, 15 minutes, from any Belfast train station or from Bangor). Buses stop right in the park, but schedules are skimpy on Saturday and Sunday. Train service is more dependable (and more frequent on the weekend): Get off at the Cultra stop, which puts off between the two parks, a bit closer to the Transport Museum than to the Folk Park.

Planning Your Time: Allow three hours for your visit, and expect lots of walking. Most people will spend an hour in the Transport Museum and a couple of hours at the Folk Park. You'll arrive (by rail or car) between the two museums a bit closer to the Transport Museum. From here, you have a choice of going downhill to the Transport Museum or 200 panting yards uphill into the Folk Park. Assess your energy level and plan accordingly. Those with a car can drive between the museum and the folk park. Note that the Transport Museum is all indoors. The Folk Park involves more walking between buildings spread across the upper hillside.

Visiting the Museums: The **Transport Museum** consists of three buildings. Start at the bottom and trace the evolution of transportation from 7,500 years ago—when people first decided to load an ox—to the first vertical takeoff jet. In 1909, the Belfast-

The Red Hand of Ulster

All over Belfast, you'll notice a curious symbol: a red hand facing you as if swearing a pledge or telling you to halt. You'll spot it, faded, above the Linen Hall Library door, in the wrought-iron fences of the Merchant Hotel, on old-fashioned clothes wringers (in the Ulster Folk Park and Transport Museum at Cultra), above the front door of a bank in Bangor, in the shape of a flowerbed at Mount Stewart House, in Loyalist paramilitary murals, on shield emblems in the gates of Republican memorials, and even on the flag of Northern Ireland (the white flag with the red cross of St. George). It's known as the Red Hand of Ulster—and it is one of the few emblems used by both communities in Northern Ireland.

Nationalists display a red-hand-on-a-yellow-shield as a symbol of the ancient province of Ulster. It was the official crest of the once-dominant O'Neill clan (who fought tooth and nail against English rule) and today signifies resistance to British rule in these communities.

But you'll more often see the red hand in Unionist areas. They see it as a potent symbol of the political entity of Northern Ireland. The Ulster Volunteer Force chose it for their symbol in 1913 and embedded it in the center of the Northern Irish flag upon partition of the island in 1921. You may see the red hand clenched as a fist in Loyalist murals. One Loyalist paramilitary group even named itself the Red Hand Commandos.

The origin of the red hand comes from a mythological tale of two rival clans that raced by boat to claim a far shore. The first clan leader to touch the shore would win it for his people. Everyone aboard both vessels strained mightily at their oars, near exhaustion as they approached the shore. Finally, in desperation, the chieftain leader of the slower boat whipped out his sword and lopped off his right hand...which he then flung onto the shore, thus winning the coveted land. Moral of the story? The fearless folk of Ulster will do *whatever it takes* to get the job done.

based Shorts Aviation Company partnered with the Wright brothers to manufacture the first commercially available aircraft. The middle building holds an intriguing section on the sinking of the Belfast-made *Titanic*. The top building covers the history of bikes, cars, and trains. The car section rumbles from the first car in Ireland (an 1898 Benz), through the "Cortina Culture" of the 1960s, to the local adventures of controversial auto-mobile designer John DeLorean and a 1981 model of his sleek sports car.

The **Folk Park,** an open-air collection of 34 reconstructed buildings from all over the nine counties of Ulster, showcases the region's traditional lifestyles. After wandering through the old-town site (church, print shop, school-house, humble Belfast row house, silent movie theater, and so on), you'll head off into the country to nip into cottages, farmhouses, and mills. Some houses are warmed by a wonderful peat fire and a friendly attendant. Your visit can be dull or vibrant, depending upon whether attendants are available to chat. Drop a peat brick on the fire.

▲Carrickfergus Castle

Built during the Norman invasion of the late 1100s, this historic castle stands sentry on the shore of Belfast Lough. William of

Orange landed here in 1690, when he began his Irish campaign against deposed King James II. In 1778, the American priva-teer ship *Ranger* (the first ever to fly the Stars-and-Stripes), under the com-mand of John Paul Jones, defeated the HMS *Drake* just up the coast. These days the castle feels a bit sanitized and geared for kids, but it's an easy excursion if you're seeking a castle experience near the city.

Cost and Hours: £5; daily 10:00-17:00, Oct-March until 16:00; tel. 028/9335-1273.

Getting There: It's a 20-minute train ride from Belfast (on the line to Larne). Turn left as you exit the train station and walk straight downhill for five minutes—all the way to the waterfront—passing under the arch of the old town wall en route. You'll find the castle on your right.

▲The Gobbins Cliff Path

Newly reopened in 2016, the Gobbins Cliff Path is an Edward-ian adventure with birds, beautiful scenery, and occasional rogue waves. Located 20 miles northeast of Belfast via Carrickfergus, this complex path—a mix of tunnel bridges, railings, and steps carved, hammered, or fastened to the cliff—was first opened in 1902, designed to boost tourism. Once popular, it fell into disrepair during World War II and was closed for decades. The newly reinforced path (which, to spoil all the turn-of-the-century fun, now requires helmets and guides) takes two to three hours to hike, and is awkward and steep in places, but not terribly strenuous. You'll spot puffins, cormorants, and kittiwakes in nesting areas along the way.

Cost and Hours: £10, visitor center open daily 9:30-17:30, required guided hikes generally hourly (weather permitting), book in advance as tours can fill up, tel. 028/9337-2318, 68 Middle Road, Islandmagee, www.thegobbinscliffpath.com.

Getting There: By car, take the A-2 from Belfast to Larne, turn right on B-90, and follow the signs to *Islandmagee* and *The Gobbins*. Without a car, take a train to Ballycarry (on the Larne line) and walk a mile to the center, or take a taxi (Ballycarry Cabs, tel. 028/9303-8131).

Entertainment in Belfast

Consider the following, as well as the musical pub crawl offered by Belfast Trad Trail Tours (described earlier, under "Tours in Belfast").

Theater
Located beside the River Lagan (near Queen's University), the **Lyric Theatre** is a Belfast institution. Rebuilt in 2011, it represents the cultural rejuvenation of the city—the building was partially funded by donations from actors such as Liam Neeson, Kenneth Branagh, and Meryl Streep. While there are no public tours, it's a good place to see quality local productions (tickets £15-25; box office open daily 10:00-17:00; 55 Ridgeway Street, tel. 028/9038-1081, www.lyrictheatre.co.uk).

Traditional Music and Dance
Belfast Story features former *Riverdance* musicians and dancers for an energetic hour celebrating the people, poetry, and music of Belfast. It's set in a characteristic pub—with the local crowd on the ground floor and the tourists packed into a tiny performance room upstairs (£25; May-Oct Wed and Fri-Sat at 20:00, upstairs in Madden's Pub at 74 Berry Street, tel. 079-7189-5746, www.belfasthiddentours.com).

Sleeping in Belfast

Belfast is more of a business town than a tourist town, so business-class room rates are lower or soft on weekends. For cozy B&Bs, check out the Queen's University area or the nearby seaside town of Bangor.

IN CENTRAL BELFAST

To locate these hotels, see the map on page 464.

$$$$ Hotel Europa is Belfast's landmark hotel—fancy, comfortable, and central—with four stars and lower weekend rates. Modern yet elegant, this place is the choice of visiting diplomats (breakfast extra, Great Victoria Street, tel. 028/9027-1066, www. hastingshotels.com, res@eur.hastingshotels.com).

$$$ Jurys Inn, an American-style hotel that rents 190 identical modern rooms, is perfectly located two blocks from City Hall (breakfast extra, Fisherwick Place, tel. 028/9053-3500, www. jurysinns.com, jurysinnbelfast@jurysinns.com).

SOUTH OF QUEEN'S UNIVERSITY

Many of Belfast's best budget beds cluster in a comfortable, leafy neighborhood just south of Queen's University (near the Ulster Museum). The Botanic, Adelaide, and City Hospital train stations are nearby (I find Botanic the most convenient), and buses zip down Malone Road every 20 minutes. Any bus on Malone Road goes to Donegall Square East. Taxis take you downtown for about £6 (your host can call one).

$$$ Malone Lodge Hotel, by far the classiest listing in this neighborhood, provides slick, business-class comfort in 119 spacious rooms on a quiet street (elevator, restaurant, parking, 60 Eglantine Avenue, tel. 028/9038-8000, www.malonelodgehotel.com, info@malonelodgehotel.com).

$$ Gregory Guesthouse, with its stately red brick, ages gracefully behind a green lawn with 15 large, fresh rooms. It's a good value with subtle charm on a quiet street (family room, parking, 32 Eglantine Ave, tel. 028/9066-3454, www.thegregorybelfast.com, info@thegregorybelfast.com).

$$ Wellington Park Hotel is a dependable, if unimaginative, chain-style hotel with 75 rooms. It's predictable but in a good location (parking extra, 21 Malone Road, tel. 028/9038-1111, www. wellingtonparkhotel.com, info@wellingtonparkhotel.com).

$ Elms Village, a huge Queen's University dorm complex, rents 100 basic, institutional rooms (all singles) to travelers during summer break (July and Aug only, coin-op laundry, self-serve kitchen; reception building is 50 yards down entry street, marked *Elms Village* on low brick wall, 78 Malone Road; tel. 028/9097-4525, www.stayatqueens.com, accommodation@qub.ac.uk).

BETWEEN QUEEN'S UNIVERSITY AND SHAFTESBURY SQUARE

$$ Benedicts Hotel has 32 rooms in a good location at the northern fringe of the Queen's University district. Its popular bar is a maze of polished wood and can be loud on weekend nights (eleva-

South Belfast

To Central Belfast →

BLYTHE ST.

UNIONIST
PROTESTANT
MURALS

← To Dublin
via M-1

Shaftesbury
Square

DONEGALL RD.

DONEGALL PASS

ORMEAU RD.

SANDY ROW

GREAT VICTORIA

DUBLIN ROAD

MARYVILLE ST.

VIRGINIA WAY

POST

❼

❺

❶❶

Botanic
Station

VERNON ST.

City
Hospital
Station

CITY HOSPITAL

GOLDEN MILE

BOTANIC AVE.

❶⓪

CROMWELL RD.

CLAREMONT

CAMDEN ST.

FITZWILLIAM ST.

ELMWOOD AVE.

❾

RD.

UNIVERSITY SQ.

UNIVERSITY

WESTMINSTER ST.

UNIVERSITY ST.

❻

RUGBY RD.

UNIVERSITY AVE.

❶⓶

COLLEGE GARDENS

POST

QUEEN'S
UNIVERSITY

RUGBY RD.

AGINCOURT AVE.

A-1

LISBURN RD.

WELLESLEY AVE.

WELLINGTON PARK

❶❶

❷

EGLANTINE AVE.

❶

MALONE RD.

STRANMILLIS RD.

PALM
HOUSE

ULSTER
MUSEUM

Botanic
Gardens

River Lagan

MALONE AVE.

❸

❽

100 Meters
100 Yards

← To Adelaide Station

To Lyric
Theatre

↙ To ❹

Accommodations
❶ Malone Lodge Hotel
❷ Gregory Guesthouse
❸ Wellington Park Hotel
❹ To Elms Village
❺ Benedicts Hotel
❻ Ibis Belfast Queens Quarter
❼ Belfast International City Hostel

Eateries & Other
❽ The Barking Dog
❾ Villa Italia
❶⓪ Maggie May's
❶❶ Laundry (2)
❶⓶ Queen's University
Student Union

tor, 7 Bradbury Place, tel. 028/9059-1999, www.benedictshotel.
co.uk, info@benedictshotel.co.uk).

$$ Ibis Belfast Queens Quarter, part of a major European
hotel chain, has 56 practical rooms in a convenient location. It's a
great deal if you're not looking for cozy character (breakfast extra,
elevator, a block north of Queen's University at 75 University Street,
tel. 028/9033-3366, www.ibisbelfast.com, h7288-fo@accor.com).

¢ Belfast International City Hostel, big and creatively run,
provides the best value among Belfast's hostels. It is located near
Botanic Station, in the heart of the lively university district, and
has 24-hour reception. Paul, the manager, is a veritable TI, with
a passion for his work (private rooms available, 22 Donegall Road,
tel. 028/9031-5435, www.hini.org.uk, info@hini.org.uk).

Eating in Belfast

DOWNTOWN

For locations, see the map on page 464.

The Morning Star is woody and elegant, with a **$$$ restaurant** upstairs (daily 12:00-22:00) and a **$ afternoon buffet** (Mon-Sat 12:00-16:00; down alley just off High Street at 17 Pottinger's Entry, alley entry is roughly opposite the post office, tel. 028/9023-5986).

$$ Robinson & Cleaver has a great central location, perfect for light lunches or tasty dinners. In good weather, their balcony has terrific views of City Hall (Mon-Sat 12:00-15:00, Wed-Sat also 17:00-21:30, closed Sun; Donegall Square North, a few doors east of the TI, tel. 028/9031-2666).

$$$ Coco Restaurant is a spacious, high-end place with a quirky sense of style serving reliably tasty modern Irish and Continental dishes. Their early-bird special makes it a budget find if you order before 19:00 (open nightly from 17:30, a couple of blocks behind City Hall at 7 Linen Hall Street, tel. 028/9031-1150).

$$ Crown Liquor Saloon, a recommended stop along the Golden Mile, is small and antique. Its mesmerizing mishmash of mosaics and shareable snugs (booths—best to reserve) is topped with a smoky tin ceiling (food served Sun-Thu 11:30-19:00, Fri-Sat until 17:00, 46 Great Victoria Street, across from Hotel Europa, tel. 028/9024-3187, www.nicholsonspubs.co.uk). The **$$$ Crown Dining Room** upstairs offers dependable meals (daily 11:30-20:00, tel. 028/9024-3187, use entry on Amelia Street when the Crown Liquor Saloon is closed).

$$$ Europa Piano Lounge rests serenely above the lobby of the Europa Hotel, with refined service and possibly the best club sandwich in town. It's a great hideaway for quietly recharging your sightseeing batteries (daily 10:00-22:00, tel. 028/9027-1066).

$$ Kelly's Cellars, once a rebel hangout (see plaque above door), still has a very gritty Irish feel. It's 300 years old and hard to find, but worth it. The pub grub is basic, but the atmosphere is delicious (Mon-Sat 11:30-24:30, Sun 13:00-23:30; live traditional music Tue-Fri and Sun at 21:30, Sat at 16:30; 32 Bank Street, 100 yards behind Tesco supermarket, access via alley on left side when facing Tesco, tel. 028/9024-6058).

Lunch Spots: The **$ Bobbin Café** at City Hall is a good, cheap, and cheery little cafeteria serving soups, sandwiches, and hot dishes (open daily, same hours as City Hall). Across the street, the **$ Linen Hall Library Café** is more elegant (it's like eating with professors in a library) but with a more limited lunch menu (daily 9:30-16:00).

Supermarkets: Consider a picnic on the City Hall lawn with food from one of the following. **Marks & Spencer** has a coffee shop and a supermarket in its basement (daily until 18:00, WCs on second floor, Donegall Place, a block north of Donegall Square). **Tesco** is a block north of Marks & Spencer and two blocks north of Donegall Square (open slightly later than Marks & Spencer, Royal Avenue and Bank Street).

CATHEDRAL QUARTER

For restaurant locations, see the map on page 464.

$$$$ Check out the lobby of **Merchant Hotel** (a grand former bank) for a glimpse of crushed-velvet Victorian splendor under an opulent dome, and consider indulging in Belfast's best afternoon tea splurge. Don't show up in shorts and sneakers (£25 for Mon-Fri 12:00-16:30, £29.50 for Sat-Sun, reserve ahead for seating at 12:30 or 15:00, 35 Waring Street, tel. 028/9023-4888, www.themerchanthotel.com).

$$$ 2 Taps Wine Bar is a whiff of Mediterranean warmth in this cold brick city. Try a cheerful tapas or paella meal washed down with sangria (Tue-Sun 12:00-21:00, closed Mon, 42 Waring Street, tel. 028/9031-1414).

$$ The Cloth Ear is a friendly, modern, often-crowded bar serving better-than-average pub grub from the kitchen of the posh Merchant Hotel next door (daily 12:00-20:30, 33 Waring Street, tel. 028/9026-2719).

$$ The Dirty Onion and **Yardbird** are a hip combo filling a dimly lit and woody warehouse with enthusiastic young-at-heart locals. The Yardbird (upstairs) serves the grub, specializing in rotisserie chicken that's "clucking good." The Dirty Onion (downstairs) is a popular pub that spills suds and live music into its packed outer courtyard on summer nights (daily 12:00-23:30, 3 Hill Street, tel. 028/9024-3712).

VICTORIA SQUARE AREA

Although Victoria Square is a big, glitzy mall, a couple of fun options are worth considering—one inside the mall (for food) and one next door (for drinks). For locations, see the map on page 464.

$$ Wagamama, part of a British chain, is a Japanese noodle bar located on the first floor of the mall. Hearty portions of chicken ramen, *yakisoba,* and cumin beef salad are menu highlights (Sun-Wed 12:00-21:00, Thu-Sat until 22:00, Victoria Square, tel. 028/9023-6098).

Bittles Bar is a good place to stop for a pint. It's a tiny, wedge-shaped throwback to Victorian days, hidden in the shadows on the east side of the mall next to the ornate, yellow Victorian fountain. The minuscule, terraced interior is decorated with caricatures of literary and political figures (daily generally 12:00 until late, no food, 70 Upper Church Lane just off Victoria Street, mobile 077-9396-2329).

NEAR QUEEN'S UNIVERSITY

For locations, see the map on page 473.

$$$ The Barking Dog is closest to my cluster of accommodations south of the university. It's a trendy grill serving tasty burgers, duck, scallops, and other filling fare. If the weather's fine, the outdoor tree-shaded front tables are ideal for people-watching (Mon-Sat 12:00-15:00 & 17:00-22:00, Sun 12:00-21:00, near corner of Eglantine Avenue at 33 Malone Road, tel. 028/9066-1885).

$$$ Villa Italia packs in crowds hungry for linguini and *bistecca*. With its checkered tablecloths and a wood-beamed ceiling draped with grape leaves, it's a little bit of Italy in Belfast (Mon-Sat 17:00-23:00, Sun 12:30-21:30, 3 long blocks south of Shaftesbury Square, at intersection with University Street, 39 University Road, tel. 028/9032-8356).

$$ Maggie May's serves hearty, simple, affordable meals (Sun-Thu 8:00-22:00, Fri-Sat until 23:00, one block south of Botanic Station at 50 Botanic Avenue, tel. 028/9032-2662).

Belfast Connections

BY TRAIN OR BUS

For updated schedules and prices for both trains and buses in Northern Ireland, check with Translink (tel. 028/9066-6630, www.translink.co.uk). Consider a Belfast Visitor Pass (see page 452) if you're visiting just Belfast. Those going beyond Belfast can make use of the Zone 4 iLink smartcard, good for all-day train and bus use in Northern Ireland (see page 453). Service is less frequent on Sundays.

From Belfast by Train to: Dublin (8/day, 2 hours), **Derry** (10/day, 2.5 hours), **Larne** (hourly, 1 hour), **Portrush** (15/day, 2 hours, transfer in Coleraine), **Bangor** (2/hour, 30 minutes). Expect less-frequent service on Sundays.

By Bus to: Portrush (12/day, 2 hours; scenic-coast route, 2.5 hours), **Derry** (hourly, 2 hours), **Dublin** (hourly, most via Dublin Airport, 3 hours), **Galway** (every 2 hours, 6 hours, change in Dublin), **Glasgow** (3/day, 6 hours), **Edinburgh** (3/day, 7 hours). The Europa Bus Centre is behind Hotel Europa (Ulsterbus tel. 028/9033-7003 for destinations in Scotland and England).

BY PLANE

Belfast has two airports. **George Best Belfast City Airport** (airport code: BHD, tel. 028/9093-9093, www.belfastcityairport.com) is a five-minute taxi ride from town (near the docks) or a £2.50 ride on the Airport Express bus #600 (hourly from Europa Bus Centre). Meanwhile, **Belfast International Airport** (airport code: BFS, tel. 028/9448-4848, www.belfastairport.com) is 18 miles west of town—a £7.50 ride on the Airport Express bus #300 (hourly from Europa Bus Centre).

If you're headed for Edinburgh or Glasgow, flying is generally better than taking the ferry (slow and not that scenic), as it's a fairly cheap, short trip.

BY FERRY

To Scotland: You can sail between Belfast and **Cairnryan** on the Stena Line ferry. A Rail Link coach connects the Cairnryan port to Ayr, where you'll catch a train to Glasgow Central station (7/day, 2.5 hours by ferry plus 2.5 hours by bus and train, tel. 028/9074-7747, www.stenaline.co.uk). The P&O Ferry (toll tel. 087-1664-2121, www.poferries.com) goes from **Larne,** 20 miles north of Belfast, to **Cairnryan** (7/day, 2 hours), with bus or rail connections from there to Glasgow and Edinburgh. There are hourly trains between Belfast and Larne (1-hour trip, Larne TI tel. 028/2826-2495).

To England: You can sail from Belfast to **Liverpool** (generally 2/day, 8 hours, arrives in port of Birkenhead—10 minutes from Liverpool, tel. 028/9074-7747, www.stenaline.co.uk).

Bangor

To stay in a laid-back seaside hometown—with more comfort per pound—sleep 12 miles east of Belfast in Bangor (BANG-grr).

With elegant old homes facing its spruced-up harbor and not even a hint of big-city Belfast, the city has appeal, and it's a handy alternative for travelers who find Belfast booked up by occasional conventions and conferences.

Formerly a Victorian resort and seaside escape from the big city nearby, Bangor now has a sleepy residential feeling. To visit two worthwhile sights near Bangor—the Somme Heritage Centre and Mount Stewart House—consider renting a car for the day (bus service to these sights is sporadic) at nearby George Best Belfast City Airport, a 15-minute train trip from Bangor. The harbor is a 10-minute walk from the train station.

GETTING THERE

Catch the train to Bangor from either Belfast's Central or Great Victoria Street stations; both are on the same line and cost the same (2/hour, 30 minutes, go to the end of the line—don't get off at Bangor West). Consider stopping en route at Cultra (Ulster Folk Park and Transport Museum; see page 468). The journey gives you a good, close-up look at the giant Belfast harbor cranes.

If day-tripping into Belfast from Bangor, get off at Central Station (free shuttle bus to town center, 4/hour, none on Sun; some trains may also stop at the more convenient Great Victoria Street Station), or stay on until Botanic Station for the Ulster Museum, the Golden Mile, and Sandy Row. Trains cost the same from Bangor to all three Belfast stations (Central Station, Great Victoria Station, and Botanic Station).

Orientation to Bangor

Tourist Information: Bangor's TI is in a stone tower house (from 1637) on the harborfront (Mon-Fri 9:15-17:00, Sat from 10:00, Sun 13:00-17:00 except closed Sun Sept-April, 34 Quay Street, tel. 028/9127-0069, www.visitardsandnorthdown.com).

Helpful Hints: You'll find **Speediwash Launderette** at 96 Abbey Street, a couple of blocks south of the train station (Mon-Sat 9:00-18:00, closed Sun, tel. 028/9127-0074). **Kare Cabs** provides local taxi service (tel. 028/9145-6777 or 028/9181-8001).

Sights in Bangor

Walks

For sightseeing, your time is better spent in Belfast. But if you have time to burn in Bangor, enjoy a walk next to the water on the **Coastal Path,** which leads west out of town from the marina. A pleasant three-mile walk along the water leads you to Crawfordsburn Country Park in the suburb of Helen's Bay. Hidden in the trees above Helen's Bay beach is Grey Point Fort, with its two WWI artillery bunkers guarding the shore (generally Sat-Sun 12:00-16:00, tel. 028/9185-3621). Allow 1.5 hours each way as you share the easy-to-follow and mostly paved trail with local joggers, dog walkers, and bikers.

For a shorter walk with views of the marina, head to the end of the **North Pier,** where you'll find a mosaic honoring the D-Day

Bangor

- ❶ Shelleven House
- ❷ Hargreaves House
- ❸ Bramble Lodge
- ❹ Bangla Indian Rest.
- ❺ Rabbit Rooms Rest.
- ❻ Little Wing Pizza
- ❼ Café Brazilia
- ❽ Jamaica Inn
- ❾ Launderette

fleet that rendezvoused offshore in 1944, far from Nazi reconnaissance aircraft. Keep an eye out in the marina for Rose the seal. Little kids may enjoy the **Pickie Fun Park** next to the marina, with paddleboat swan rides and miniature golf. The **Bangor Castle** grounds are good for picnics, and include a peaceful walled garden (free, open Mon-Thu 10:00-17:00, Fri-Sun until 18:00).

North Down Museum

This museum covers local history, from monastic days to Viking raids to Victorian splendor. It's hidden on the grassy grounds behind the City Hall, uphill and opposite from the train station.

Cost and Hours: Free, July-Aug daily 10:00-16:30; Sept-June Tue-Sat 10:00-16:30, Sun from 12:00, closed Mon, tel. 028/9127-1200.

NEAR BANGOR

The eastern fringe of Northern Ireland is populated mostly by people who consider themselves true-blue British citizens with a history of loyalty to the Crown that goes back more than 400 years. Two sights within reach by car from Bangor highlight this area's firm roots in British culture: the Somme Heritage Centre and Mount Stewart House. Call ahead to confirm sight opening hours.

Getting There: Bus service from Bangor is patchy (bus #6; check schedule with Bangor TI). I'd rent a car instead at nearby George Best Belfast City Airport (described on page 477), which is only 15 minutes by train from Bangor or 10 minutes from Belfast's Central Station. Because the airport is east of Belfast, your drive to these rural sights skips the headache of urban Belfast.

▲Mount Stewart House

No manor house in Ireland better illuminates the affluent lifestyle of the Protestant ascendancy than this lush estate. After the defeat of James II (the last Catholic king of England) at the Battle of the Boyne in 1690, the Protestant monarchy was in control—and the privileged status of landowners of the same faith was assured. In the 1700s, Ireland's many Catholic rebellions seemed finally to be squashed, so Anglican landlords felt safe flaunting their wealth in manor houses surrounded by utterly perfect gardens. The Mount Stewart House in particular was designed to dazzle.

Cost and Hours: £9.50 for house and gardens; daily 10:00-16:30, closed Nov-Feb; 8 miles south of Bangor, just off A-20 beside Strangford Lough, tel. 028/4278-8387, www.nationaltrust. org.uk, enquiries@nationaltrust.org.uk.

Visiting the House: Hourly tours give you a glimpse of the cushy life led by the Marquess of Londonderry and his heirs over the past three centuries. The main entry hall is a stunner, with a black-and-white checkerboard tile floor, marble columns, classical statues, and pink walls supporting a balcony with a domed ceiling and a fine chandelier. In the dining room, you'll see the original seats occupied by the rears of European heads of state, brought back from the Congress of Vienna after Napoleon's 1815 defeat. A huge painting of Hambletonian, a prize-winning racehorse, hangs above the grand staircase, dwarfing a portrait of the Duke of Wellington in a hall nearby. The heroic duke (worried that his Irish birth would be seen as lower class by British blue bloods) once quipped in Parliament, "Just because one is born in a stable does not make him a horse." Irish emancipator Daniel O'Connell retorted, "Yes, but it could make you an ass."

Afterward, wander the expansive manicured **gardens.** The fantasy life of parasol-toting, upper-crust Victorian society seems to ooze from every viewpoint. Fanciful sculptures of extinct dodo birds and monkeys holding vases on their heads set off predictably classic Italian and Spanish sections. An Irish harp has been trimmed out of a hedge a few feet from a flowerbed shaped like the Red Hand of Ulster. Swans glide serenely among the lily pads on a small lake.

Somme Heritage Centre

World War I's trench warfare was a meat grinder. More British soldiers died in the last year of that war than in all of World War II. Northern Ireland's men were not spared—especially during the bloody Battle of the Somme in France, starting in July 1916 (see the "1916" sidebar on page 466). Among the Allied forces was the British Army's 36th Ulster Division, which drew heavily from this loyal heartland of Northern Ireland. The 36th Ulster Division suffered brutal losses at the Battle of the Somme—of the 760 men recruited from the Shankill Road area in Belfast, only 10 percent survived.

Exhibits portray the battle experience through a mix of military artifacts, photos, historical newsreels, and life-size figures posed in trench warfare re-creations. To access the majority of the exhibits, it's essential to take the one-hour guided tour (leaving hourly, on the hour). Visiting this place is a moving experience, but it can only hint at the horrific conditions endured by these soldiers.

Cost and Hours: £6.50; July-Aug Mon-Fri 10:00-16:00, Sat from 11:00, closed Fri Sept-June and Sun year-round; hourly tours, 3 miles south of Bangor just off A-21 at 233 Bangor Road, tel. 028/9182-3202, www.irishsoldier.org. A coffee shop is located at the center.

Sleeping in Bangor

Visitors arriving in Bangor (by train) come down Main Street to reach the harbor marina. You'll find Hargreaves House to the right, along the waterfront east of the marina on Seacliff Road. The other two listings are to the left, just uphill and west of the marina.

$$$ Shelleven House is an old-fashioned, well-kept, stately place with 13 prim rooms on the quiet corner of Princetown Road and Tennyson Avenue (RS%, parking, 61 Princetown Road, tel. 028/9127-1777, www.shellevenhouse.com, info@shellevenhouse.com, Sue and Paul Toner).

$$ **Hargreaves House,** a homey Victorian waterfront refuge with three cozy rooms, is Bangor's best value (RS%—use code HHRS18, 15-minute walk from train station but worth it, 78 Seacliff Road, tel. 028/9146-4071, mobile 079-8058-5047, www.hargreaveshouse.com, info@hargreaveshouse.com, Pauline Mendez).

$$ **Bramble Lodge** is closest to the train station (10-minute walk), offering three inviting and spotless rooms (1 Bryansburn Road, tel. 028/9145-7924, mobile 077-9262-8001, jacquihanna_bramblelodge@yahoo.co.uk, Jacquiline Hanna).

Eating in Bangor

Be aware that most restaurants in town stop seating at about 20:30.

$$$ **Bangla** serves fine Indian cuisine with attentive service and a good-value early-bird option before 19:00 (daily 12:00-14:30, also Thu-Sun 16:30-23:00, 115 Main Street, tel. 028/9127-1272).

$$ The **Rabbit Rooms** serves hearty Irish food to local crowds (daily 12:00-21:00, near the harbor at 33 Quay Street, tel. 028/9146-7699).

$ **Little Wing Pizza** is a friendly joint serving tasty pizza, pasta, and salads. Grab your food to go and munch by the marina. It's also one of the few places in town that serves food later at night (daily 11:00-22:00, 37 Main Street, tel. 028/9147-2777).

$ **Café Brazilia,** a popular locals' lunch hangout with a simple menu, is across from the stubby clock tower (Mon-Sat 8:00-16:30, Sun from 10:00, 13 Bridge Street, tel. 028/9127-2763).

The $$ **Jamaica Inn** offers pleasant pub grub and a breezy waterfront porch (food served about 12:00-21:00, 10-minute walk east of the TI, 188 Seacliff Road, tel. 028/9147-1610).

IRELAND: PAST & PRESENT

Ireland is rich with history, culture, and language. The country continues to transform and grow today, learning from its experience with the Celtic Tiger economy, making progress toward peace, and reexamining some of its long-held social customs.

Irish History

PREHISTORY

Ireland became an island when rising seas covered the last land bridge (7000 B.C.), a separation from Britain that the Irish would fight to maintain for the next 9,000 years. Snakes were too slow to migrate before the seas cut Ireland off, despite later legends about St. Patrick banishing them. By 6000 B.C., Stone Age hunter-fishers had settled on the east coast, followed by Neolithic farmers (from the island of Britain). These early inhabitants left behind impressive but mysterious funeral mounds (passage graves) and large Stonehenge-type stone circles.

THE CELTS (500 B.C.-A.D. 450)

Perhaps more an invasion of ideas than of armies, the Celtic culture from Central Europe (particularly that of the most influential tribe, called the **Gaels**) settled in Ireland, where it would dominate for a thousand years. A warrior people with more than a hundred petty kings, they feuded constantly with rival clans and gathered in ring forts for protection. There were more than 300 *tuatha* (kingdoms) in Ireland, each with its own *rí* (king), who would've happily chopped the legs off anyone who called him "petty." The island was nominally ruled by a single *Ard Rí* (high king) at the **Hill of Tara** (north of Dublin), though there was no centralized nation.

Druid priests conducted pagan, solar-calendar rituals among

What's a Celt?

The Irish are a Celtic people. The Celts, who came from Central Europe, began migrating west in about 1500 B.C. Over time, many settled in the British Isles and in western France. When the Angles and Saxons came later, grabbing the best land in the British Isles (which became Angle-land...or England), the Celts survived in Brittany, Cornwall, Wales, Scotland, and Ireland. Today, this "Celtic Crescent" still nearly encircles England. The word "Celtic" (pronounced with a hard C) comes from the Greek "Keltoi," meaning barbarian.

From about 700 B.C. on, various Celtic tribes mixed, mingled, and fought in Ireland. The last and most powerful of the Celtic tribes to enter the fray were the Gaels, who probably came to Ireland from Scotland. The Irish and Scottish language, Gaelic, is named for them.

Celtic society revolved around warrior kings, who gathered groups of families into regional kingdoms. These small kingdoms combined to make the five large provincial kingdoms of ancient Ireland (whose names survive on maps today): Leinster, Munster, Connacht, Ulster, and the Middle Kingdom (now County Meath).

For defensive purposes, these early Irish peoples lived in small thatched huts built on man-made islands or on high ground surrounded by ditches and a stone or earthen wall. A strictly observed hierarchy governed Celtic societies: the king on top, followed by poets, druids (priests), legal men, skilled craftsmen, freemen, and slaves. Only once did a high king rule the entire island (Brian Ború: 941-1014). Loyalty to one's clan came first, and alliances between clans were often temporary, lasting only until a more advantageous alliance could be struck with a rival clan. This fluid system of alliances ebbing and flowing meant that the warrior Celts would never unite as a single nation. It also meant that an invading army could not destroy one main capital or kill one king to bring the entire island to its knees. Celtic culture was a multiheaded monster... tough to slay.

Unlike the Celtic tribes living in Western Europe and England, the Celts in Ireland were never conquered by the Romans. This gives Ireland a cultural continuity and uniqueness rare in Europe. Their culture—which evolved apart from Europe—remained strong and independent for centuries. Then, in the 12th century, English dominance led to suppression of the Gaelic language and Celtic traditions. But with Irish independence—won only in the 20th century—Irish ways are no longer threatened. The most traditional areas (generally along the west coast, such as the Dingle Peninsula) are protected as a Gaeltacht. The Gaeltacht (literally, places where the Irish Gaelic language is spoken) is a kind of national park for the traditional culture. If much of Ireland's charm can be credited to its Celtic roots, that charm is most vivid in the Gaeltacht.

the megalithic stones erected by earlier inhabitants. The Celtic people peppered the countryside with thousands of Iron Age monuments. While most of the sights are little more than rock piles that take a vigorous imagination to reconstruct (ring forts, wedge tombs, standing stones, and so on), just standing next to a megalith that predates the pharaohs is stirring.

The Celtic world lives on today in the Gaelic language and in legends of Celtic warriors such as **Finn MacCool,** who led a merry band of heroes in battle and in play. Tourists marvel at large ritual stones decorated with ogham (rhymes with "poem") script, the peculiar Celtic-Latin alphabet that used lines as letters. The **Tara Brooch** and elaborately inscribed, jewel-encrusted daggers in Dublin's National Museum attest to the sophistication of this warrior society.

In 55 B.C., the Romans conquered the Celts in England, but Ireland and Scotland remained independent, their history forever skewed in a different direction—Gaelic, not Latin. The Romans called Ireland **Hibernia,** meaning Land of Winter; it was apparently too cold and bleak to merit colonization. The biggest non-event in Irish history is that the Romans never invaded. While the mix of Celtic and Roman is part of what makes the French French and the English English, the Irish are purely Celtic. Hurling, the wild Irish national pastime, goes back more than 2,000 years to Celtic days, when it was played almost as a substitute for warfare. Perhaps best described as something like airborne hockey with no injury time-outs, hurling is as central to the Irish culture as cricket is to the English, or *boules* to the French.

THE AGE OF SAINTS AND SCHOLARS (A.D. 450-800)

When Ancient Rome fell and took the Continent—and many of the achievements of Roman culture—with it, Gaelic Ireland was

unaffected. There was no Dark Age here, and the island was a beacon of culture for the rest of Europe. Ireland (population c. 750,000) was still a land of many feuding kings, but the culture was stable.

Christianity and Latin culture arrived first as a trickle from trading contacts with Christian Gaul (France), then more emphatically in A.D. 432 with **St. Patrick,** who persuasively converted the sun-and-nature-worshipping Celts. (Perhaps St. Patrick had an easy time converting the locals because they had so little sun to worship.) Patrick (c. 389-461), a Latin-speaking Christian from Roman Britain, was kidnapped as a teenager and carried off into slavery for six years in Ireland. He escaped back to Britain, then traveled to Gaul to study for a life in the clergy. Inspired by a dream, he eventually returned to Ireland, determined to convert the pagan, often hostile, Celtic inhabitants. Legends say he drove Ireland's snakes (symbolic of pagan beliefs) into the sea and explained the Holy Trinity with a shamrock—three leaves on one stem.

Later monks (such as **St. Columba,** 521-597) continued Christianizing the island, and foreign monks flocked to isolated Ireland. They withdrew to scattered, isolated monasteries, living in stone beehive-shaped huts, translating and illustrating (illuminating) manuscripts. Perhaps the greatest works of art from all of Dark Age Europe are these manuscripts, particularly the ninth-century **Book of Kells,** which you'll see at Dublin's Trinity College Library. Irish monks—heads shaved crosswise across the top of the skull from ear to ear, like the druids before them—were known throughout Europe as ascetic scholars.

St. Columbanus (c. 600; different from St. Columba) was one of several traveling missionary monks who helped to bring Christianity back to Western Europe, which had reverted to paganism and barbarism after the fall of the Roman Empire. The monks established monastic centers of learning that produced great Christian teachers and community builders. One of the monks, **St. Brendan,** may even have sailed to America.

By 800, **Charlemagne** was importing educated and literate Irish monks to help organize and run his Frankish kingdom. Meanwhile, Ireland remained a relatively cohesive society based on monastic settlements rather than cities. Impressive round towers from those settlements still dot the Irish landscape—silent reminders of this scholarly age.

VIKING INVASION AND DEFEAT (800-1100)

In 795, Viking pirates from Norway invaded, first testing isolated island monasteries, then boldly sailing up Irish rivers into the interior. The many raids immediately wreaked havoc on the monasteries and continued to shake Irish civilization for two chaotic centuries. The Vikings raped, pillaged, and burned Christian churches, making off with prized monastic booty such as gold chalices, silver candlestick holders, and the jeweled book covers of sacred illuminated manuscripts. Monks stood guard from their round towers to spy approaching marauders, ring the warning bells, and protect the citizens. In 841, a conquering Viking band decided to winter in

Ireland. The idea caught on as subsequent raiders eventually built the island's first permanent walled cities, Dublin and Waterford. Viking raiders slowly evolved into Viking traders. They were the first to introduce urban life and commerce to Ireland.

In response, **High King Brian Ború** led a Gaelic revival, briefly controlling the entire island in the late 900s. His rule ended at the Battle of Clontarf (1014), near Dublin. Though he defeated a mercenary Viking army, which had allied with rebellious clans, Ború and most of his sons died in the battle, and his unified kingdom quickly fell apart. Over the centuries, Viking settlers married Gaelic natives and slowly blended in.

ANGLO-NORMAN ARRIVAL (1100-1500)

The Normans were Ireland's next aggressive guests. In 1169, a small army of well-armed and fearless soldiers of fortune invaded Ire-

land under the pretense of helping a deposed Irish king regain his lands. With the blessing of the only English pope in history (Adrian IV and his papal bull), a Welsh conquistador named **Strongbow** (c. 1130-1176) took Dublin and Waterford, married the local king's daughter, then succeeded his father-in-law as king of Leinster. This was the spearhead of a century-long invasion by the so-called Anglo-Normans—the French-speaking rulers of England, descended from William the Conqueror and his troops, who had invaded and conquered England a hundred years earlier at the Battle of Hastings (1066).

King Henry II of England soon followed (1171) to remind Strongbow who was boss, proclaiming the entire island under English (Anglo-Norman) rule. By 1250, the Anglo-Normans occupied two-thirds of the island, controlling the best land while clustered in walled cities surrounded by hostile Gaels. These invaders, who were big-time administrators, ushered in a new age in which society (government, cities, and religious organizations) was organized on a grander scale. They imposed feudalism and scoffed at the old Gaelic clan system. Riding on the coattails of the Normans, monastic orders (Franciscans, Augustinians, Benedictines, and Cistercians) came over from the Continent and eclipsed Ireland's individual monastic settlements, once the foundation of Irish society.

Normans lived in tightly packed settlements surrounded by their superior fortifications. But when the **Black Death** came in 1348, it spread more rapidly and fatally in these tight Norman quarters than it did in rural, far-flung Gaelic clan settlements. The plague, along with Normans intermarrying with Gaels, eventually diluted Norman identity and shrank English control.

Stone Circles: The Riddle of the Rocks

Ireland is home to more than 200 evocative stone circles. These jaggedly sparse boulder rings are rudimentary in comparison to Britain's more famous Stonehenge. But their misty, mossy settings provide curious travelers with an intimate and accessible glimpse of the mysterious people who lived in Ireland before the arrival of the Celts.

Bronze Age Ireland (2000-600 B.C.) was populated by farming folk who had mastered the craft of smelting heated tin and copper together to produce bronze, which was used to produce more durable tools and weapons. Late in the Bronze Age, many of these primitive, clannish communities also put considerable time and effort into gathering huge rocks and arranging them into ceremonial circles for use in rituals with

long-forgotten meanings. Scholars believe that these circles may have been used as solar observatories, to calculate solstices and equinoxes as they planned life-sustaining seasonal crop-planting cycles. Archaeologists have discovered a few ancient remains in the center of some circles, but their primary use seems to have been ceremonial rather than as burial sites. And without any written records, we can only make educated guesses as to their exact purpose.

In the Middle Ages, superstitious people believed that the stones had been arranged by an earlier race of giants. Later, some thought that at least one circle was made up of petrified partiers

England, preoccupied with the Hundred Years' War with France and its own internal Wars of the Roses, "ruled" Ireland through deputized locals such as the earls of Kildare. Many Irish landowners actually resided in England, a pattern of absentee-landlordism that would persist for centuries. England's laws were fully enforced only in a 50-mile foothold around Dublin (**the Pale**—from the Norman-French word for a defensive ditch). A couple of centuries after invading, the Anglo-Normans saw their area of control shrink to only the Pale (perhaps 20 percent of the island)—with the rest of the island "beyond the Pale."

Even as their power eroded, the English kings considered Ireland theirs. To keep their small islands of English culture undiluted by Irish heathen ways, they passed the **Statutes of Kilkenny** (1366). These laws prohibited the settlers from going native and being seduced by Gaelic ways...or people. Intermarriage between Irish locals and English settlers, adoption of Irish dress, and the who had dared to dance on the Sabbath. A nearby standing stone was supposed to be the frozen figure of the piper who had been playing the dance tunes.

Irish stone circles are concentrated in two main regional clusters consisting of more than a hundred circles each: central Ulster, in the North (radiocarbon-dated 1500-700 B.C.); and County Cork and County Kerry, in the south (radiocarbon-dated 1000-700 B.C.). The remaining dozen circles are scattered across central Ireland. Some circles have only recently been rediscovered, having been buried over the centuries by rapidly accumulating bog growth.

Dedicated travelers seeking stone circles will find them marked in the Ordnance Survey atlas and signposted along rural Irish roads. Ask a local farmer for directions—and savor the experience (wear shoes impervious to grass dew and sheep doo).

Here are my five favorite Irish stone circles, all within a druid's dance of other destinations mentioned in this book:

Kenmare is in County Kerry, on the western fringe of Kenmare town. It's the most easily accessible of the circles listed here.

Drombeg is in County Cork, 35 miles (56 km) southwest of Kinsale, up a narrow winding lane just south of the R-597 coastal road.

Glebe is in County Mayo, two miles (3 km) east of Cong and 100 yards south of the R-345 road to Neale (across a minefield of sheep droppings).

Beltany is in County Donegal, 10 miles (16 km) southeast of Letterkenny, straight south of Raphoe.

Beaghmore is in County Tyrone, 20 miles (32 km) east of Omagh, north off A-505 (Cookstown Road).

speaking of the Irish Gaelic language were all outlawed. In practice, the statutes were rarely enforced.

THE END OF GAELIC RULE (1500s)

As European powers raced west to establish profitable colonies in North and South America, Ireland's location on the western edge of Europe took on more strategic importance. England's naval power grew to threaten Spain's monopoly on New World riches. Meanwhile, Spain viewed Ireland as England's vulnerable back door—the best place to attack. (Think of how the USSR used Cuba to threaten the US in the early 1960s.) Martin Luther's **Reformation** split the Christian churches into Catholic and Protestant, making Catholic Ireland an even hotter potato for newly Protestant England to handle. Catholic Spain and, later, France would use their shared Catholicism with Ireland as divine justification for alliances against heretical England.

PAST & PRESENT

Typical Castle Architecture

Castles were fortified residences for medieval nobles. In Ireland, they were introduced by Norman (evolving into English) warlords in the late 1100s. Castles come in all shapes and sizes, but knowing a few general terms will help you understand them.

Barbican: A fortified gatehouse, sometimes a stand-alone building located outside the main walls.

Crenellation: A gap-toothed pattern of stones atop the parapet.

Drawbridge: A bridge that could be raised or lowered, using counterweights or a chain-and-winch.

Great Hall: The largest room in the castle, serving as throne room, conference center, and dining hall.

Hoardings (or Gallery or Brattice): Wooden huts built onto the upper parts of the stone walls. They served as watchtowers, living quarters, and fighting platforms.

Keep (or Donjon): A high, strong stone tower in the center of the complex; the lord's home and refuge of last resort.

Loopholes (or Embrasures): Narrow wall slits through which soldiers could shoot arrows.

Machicolation: A stone ledge jutting out from the wall, with holes through which soldiers could drop rocks or boiling liquid onto wall-scaling enemies below.

Moat: A ditch encircling the wall, sometimes filled with water.

Parapet: Outer railing of the wall walk.

Portcullis: An iron grille that could be lowered across the entrance.

Postern Gate: A small, unfortified side or rear entrance. In wartime, it became a "sally-port" used to launch surprise attacks, or as an escape route.

Towers: Square or round structures with crenellated tops or conical roofs serving as lookouts, chapels, living quarters, or the dungeon.

Turret: A small lookout tower rising from the top of the wall.

Wall Walk (or Allure): A pathway atop the wall where guards could patrol and where soldiers stood to fire at the enemy.

Yard (or Bailey): An open courtyard inside the castle walls.

Typical Church Architecture

The oldest stone churches that survive in Ireland were designed and built by religious orders (Cistercians, Benedictines, Franciscans, and Dominicans) that came to Ireland from the Continent in the mid-1100s, and were supported by the Norman invaders who soon followed. Even if you wouldn't know your apse from a hole in the ground, learning a few simple terms will enrich your experience.

Aisles: The long, generally low-ceilinged arcades that flank the nave.

Altar: The raised area with a ceremonial table (often adorned with candles or a crucifix), where the priest prepares and serves the bread and wine for Communion.

Apse: The space beyond the altar, often bordered with small chapels.

Barrel Vault: A continuous round-arched ceiling that resembles an extended upside-down U.

Choir: A cozy area, often screened off, located within the church nave and near the high altar where services are sung in a more intimate setting.

Cloister: Covered hallways bordering a square or rectangular open-air courtyard, traditionally where monks and nuns got fresh air.

Facade: The front exterior of the church's main (west) entrance, generally highly decorated.

Groin Vault: An arched ceiling formed where two equal barrel vaults meet at right angles. Less common usage: term for a medieval jock strap.

Narthex: The area (portico or foyer) between the main entry and the nave.

Nave: The long, central section of the church (running west to east, from the entrance to the altar) where the congregation sits or stands through the service.

Transept: In a traditional cross-shaped floor plan, the transept is one of the two parts forming the "arms" of the cross. The transepts run north-south, perpendicularly crossing the east-west nave.

West Portal: The main entry to the church (on the west end, opposite the main altar).

In 1534, angered by **Henry VIII** and his break with Catholicism (and taking advantage of England's Reformation chaos), the **Earls of Kildare** (father, then son) led a rebellion. Henry crushed the revolt, executed the earls, and confiscated their land. Henry's daughter, **Queen Elizabeth I,** gave the land to colonists ("planters"), mainly English Protestants. The next four centuries would see a series of rebellions by Catholic, Gaelic-speaking Irish farmers fighting to free themselves from rule by Protestant, English-speaking landowners.

Hugh O'Neill (1540-1616), a Gaelic chieftain educated in Queen Elizabeth's court, was angered by planters and English abuses. He soon led a Gaelic revolt, in 1595. The rebels were supported by the Spanish, who were fellow Catholics and England's archrival on the high seas. At the Battle of Yellow Ford (1598), guerrilla tactics brought about an initial Irish victory.

But the **Battle of Kinsale** (1601) ended the revolt. The exhausted Irish, who had marched the length of Ireland in winter, arrived to help Spanish troops, who were pinned down inside the town. Though the Irish were skilled at guerrilla warfare on their own turf, they were no match for the English cavalry on open and unfamiliar ground, and were crushed before they could join the Spanish. The Spanish soon surrendered, and O'Neill knelt before the conquering general, ceding half a million acres to England. Then he and other proud, Gaelic, Ulster-based nobles unexpectedly abandoned their remaining land and sailed to the Continent (the Flight of the Earls, 1607). They searched for further support on the Continent, but died before they could enlist additional armies to bring back to Ireland. Their flight signaled the end of Gaelic Irish rule.

ENGLISH COLONIZATION AND IRISH REBELLIONS (1600s)

King James I took advantage of the Gaelic power vacuum and sent 25,000 Protestant English and Scottish planters into the confiscated land (1610-1641), making Ulster (in the northeast) the most English area of the island. The Irish responded with two major rebellions.

In 1642, with England embroiled in a civil war between a divine-right monarch (who answered only to God) and a power-hungry Parliament, Irish rebels capitalized on the instability. Tensions were already high, as tenant farmers had recently taken up pitchforks against their English landlords, slaughtering 4,000 in the **Massacre of the Planters** (1641). The landless, Irish-speaking rebels hadn't attacked the middle tier of Irish society—the English-speaking, but still Irish, landed gentry (descendants of the first Anglo-Norman invaders, they were called, rather confusingly, "Old English"). Like the peasant rebels, the "Old English" were Catholic, and they wanted more autonomy for Ireland. Both groups feared the rise of Protestant power in England, and together they formed a pro-Royalist confederation in opposition to the new Protestant Parliament of **Oliver Cromwell.** (This meant, oddly enough, that the Irish now found themselves on the side of the English monarchy.)

Once Cromwell had pulled off his coup d'état and executed King Charles I, he invaded Ireland with 12,000 men (1649-1650). Out to obliterate the last Royalist forces and to exact retaliation for the Massacre of the Planters, and armed with puritanical, anti-Catholic religious zeal, he conquered the country—brutally. Thousands were slaughtered, priests were tortured, villages were pillaged, and rebels were sold into slavery. Cromwell confiscated 11 million acres of land from Catholic Irish landowners to give to English Protestants. Cromwell's scorched-earth invasion was so harsh that it became known as the "curse of Cromwell"—and it still raises hackles in Ireland (for more on Cromwell, see the sidebar on page 186). After Cromwell died in 1658, the English were fed up with austerity and asked Charles II to come back to Ireland and retake the monarchy that his father had lost.

In 1688-1689, rebels again took advantage of England's political chaos. They rallied around Catholic **King James II,** who had been deposed by the English Parliament in the "Glorious Revolution" of 1688 and then had fled to France. He wound up in Ireland, where he formed an army to retake the crown. In the **Siege of Londonderry,** James' Catholic army surrounded the city, the last loyal Protestant power base. But some local apprentice boys locked them out, and after months of negotiations and a 105-day siege, James went away empty-handed.

The showdown came at the massive **Battle of the Boyne** (1690), north of Dublin. Catholic James II and his 25,000 men were defeated by the 36,000 troops of Protestant **King William III** of Orange. From this point on, the color orange became a symbol in Ireland for pro-English, pro-Protestant Irish forces.

As the 17th century came to a close, Protestant England had successfully put down every rebellion. To counter Irish feistiness, the ruling English out-and-out attacked the indigenous Gaelic culture through legislation called the **Penal Laws.** Catholics couldn't vote, hold office, buy land, join the army, play the harp, or even own a horse worth more than £5. Catholic education was banned and priests were outlawed. But the Penal Laws were difficult to enforce, and many Catholics were taught at hidden outdoor "hedge schools," and worshipped in private or at secluded "Mass rocks" in the countryside.

PROTESTANT RULE (1700s)

During the 18th century, urban Ireland thrived economically, and even culturally, under the English. Dublin in the 1700s (pop. 50,000) was Britain's second city, one of Europe's wealthiest and most sophisticated. It's still decorated in Georgian (Neoclassical) style, named for the English kings of the time (consecutive kings George I, II, III, and IV, who ruled for more than a century).

But beyond the Pale surrounding Dublin, rebellion continued to brew. Over time, greed on the top and dissent on the bottom led to more repressive colonial policies. The Enlightenment provided ideas of freedom, and the Revolutionary Age emboldened the Irish masses. Irish nationalists were inspired by budding democratic revolutions in America (1776) and France (1789). The Irish say, "The Tree of Liberty sprouted in America, blossomed in France, and dropped seeds in Ireland." Increasingly, the issue of Irish independence was less a religious question than a political one, as poor, disenfranchised colonists demanded a political voice.

In Dublin, **Jonathan Swift** (1667-1745), the dean of St. Patrick's Cathedral, published his satirical *Gulliver's Travels* with veiled references to English colonialism. He anonymously wrote pamphlets advising, "Burn all that's British, except its coal."

The **Irish Parliament** was an exclusive club, and only Protestant male landowners could be elected to a seat (1 percent of the population qualified). In 1782, led by **Henry Grattan** (1746-1820), the Parliament negotiated limited autonomy from England (while remaining loyal to the king) and fairer treatment of the Catholics. England, chastened by the American Revolution (and soon preoccupied with the French Revolution), tolerated a more-or-less independent Irish Parliament for two decades.

Then, in 1798, came the bloodiest Irish Rebellion. Inspired by the American and French revolutionary successes and buoyed by an "if they can do it, so can we" attitude, a band of Irish idealists rose up. The **United Irishmen** (whose goals included introducing the term "Irishman" for all Irish, rather than labeling people as either Protestant or Catholic) revolted against Britain, led by **Wolfe Tone** (1763-1798), a Protestant Dublin lawyer. Tone, trained in the French Revolution, had gained French aid for the Irish cause (though a French naval invasion in 1796 already had failed after a freakish "Protestant wind" blew the ships away from Ireland's shores). The Rebellion was marked by bitter fighting—30,000 died over six weeks—before British troops crushed the revolt.

England tried to solve the Irish problem politically by forcing Ireland into a "Union" with England as part of a "United Kingdom" (**Act of Union, 1801**). The 500-year-old Irish Parliament was dissolved, with its members becoming part of England's Parliament in London—but Catholics were not allowed. When the movers and shakers of the Anglo-Irish aristocracy followed members of Parliament in moving to London, Dublin slowly began to decay. From then on, "Unionists" have been those who oppose Irish independence, wanting to preserve the country's union with England.

PAST & PRESENT

VOTES, VIOLENCE, AND THE FAMINE (1800s)

Irish politicians lobbied in the British Parliament for Catholic rights, reform of absentee-landlordism, and for **Home Rule**—i.e., the return of an Irish Parliament and more self-government. Meanwhile, secret societies of revolutionaries pursued justice through violence.

Daniel O'Connell (1775-1847), known as The Liberator, campaigned for Catholic equality and for the repeal of the Act of Union (to gain autonomy). Having personally witnessed the violence of the French Revolution in 1789 and the 1798 United Irishman Rebellion, O'Connell chose peaceful, legal means to achieve his ends. He was a charismatic speaker, drawing half a million people to one of his "monster meeting" demonstrations at the Hill of Tara (1843). But any hope of an Irish revival was soon snuffed out by the biggest catastrophe in Irish history: the Great Potato Famine.

The **Great Potato Famine** (1845-1849) was caused by a fungus *(Phytophthora infestans)* that destroyed Ireland's main food crop. Legions of people starved to death or died of related diseases (estimates range between 500,000 and 1.1 million). Another one to two million emigrated—most to America and others to Canada and Australia.

The poorest were hardest hit. They depended on potatoes because other crops—grown by tenant farmers on their landlords' land—went to pay the rent and were destined for export.

Britain—then the richest nation on earth, with an empire stretching around the globe—could seemingly do nothing to help its starving citizens. A toxic combination of laissez-faire economic policies, racial bigotry, and religious self-righteousness conspired to blind the English to the plight of the Irish. While the British tend to blame the Famine on overpopulation among the undisciplined and backward Irish (Ireland's population had doubled in the 45 years leading up to this period), some Irish believe it was a calculated attempt to take advantage of a natural disaster to starve down the local population through lack of effective relief. While the potato crop failed, there was more than enough food, in the form of other crops and cattle, to feed the starving, but it was exported off the island instead. For this reason, many do not refer to this period as "the Famine" (implying a lack of food) but rather as "An Gorta Mór" (The Great Hunger...imposed by British colonial policies). Over the course of five long years, Ireland was ruined. To this day, Irish weather reports include mention of potential potato-blight conditions.

The island's population was suddenly cut by almost a third (from 8.4 million to 6 million). Many of their best and brightest had fled, and the island's economy—and spirit—took generations to recover. The Irish language, spoken by the majority of the population before the Famine, became a badge of ignorance and was considered useless to those hoping to emigrate.

By 1900, emigration had further cut the island's population to just over 4 million (half of what it had been just before the Famine). Before the Famine, land was subdivided—each son got a piece of the family estate (so individual plots shrunk with each generation). Afterwards, the oldest son got the estate, and the younger siblings—with fewer options for making a living in Ireland (primarily joining the priesthood)—emigrated to Britain, Australia, Canada, or the US. Meanwhile, women could make more money than men abroad by working as domestic servants, thus more quickly saving up enough to bring their siblings over. As a result, women often beat men to new homes in foreign lands.

The tradition of an "American Wake" was a sad farewell by family and friends who gathered the night before an emigrant boarded the ship (likely never to be seen by them again, but at least heard from by letter). Because of the huge emigration to the US (today there are 45 million Irish Americans), US influence increased. (During the negotiations between Northern Ireland and the Irish Republic, US involvement in the talks was welcomed and considered essential by nearly all parties.)

Occasional violence demonstrated the fury of Irish nationalism, with the tragedy of the Famine inflaming the movement. In 1848, the **Young Irelander** armed uprising was easily squelched. In 1858, the **Irish Republican Brotherhood** was formed (the forerunner of the IRA). Also called the **Fenians,** they launched a campaign for independence by planting terrorist bombs. Irish Americans sent money to help finance these revolutionaries. Uprising after uprising made it clear that Ireland was ready to close this 800-year chapter of invasions and colonialism.

Home Rule Party leader **Charles Stuart Parnell** (1846-1891), an Irishman educated in England, made "the Irish problem" the focus of London's Parliament. Parnell lobbied for independence and for the rights of poor tenant farmers living under absentee landlords, pioneering the first boycott tactics. Then, in 1890, at the peak of his power and about to achieve Home Rule for Ireland, he was drummed out of politics by a scandal involving his mistress, scuttling the Home Rule issue for another 20 years (for more on Parnell, see page 54).

Culturally, the old Gaelic, rural Ireland was being crushed under the Industrial Revolution and the political control wielded by Protestant England. The **Gaelic Athletic Association** was founded in 1884 to resurrect pride in ancient Irish sports such as hurling (see sidebar on page 91). Soon after, in 1893, writers and educators formed the **Gaelic League** to preserve the traditional language, music, and poetry. Building on the tradition of old Celtic bards, Ireland turned out a series of influential writers: **W. B. Yeats, Oscar Wilde, George Bernard Shaw,** and **James Joyce** (see "Irish Literature," later).

EASTER RISING, WAR OF INDEPENDENCE, PARTITION, AND CIVIL WAR (1900-1950)

As the century turned, Ireland prepared for the inevitable showdown with Britain.

The **Sinn Fein** party (meaning "Ourselves") lobbied politically for independence. The **Irish Volunteers** were more Catholic and more militant. Also on the scene was the **Irish Citizens Army,** with a socialist agenda to protect labor unions and clean up Dublin's hideous tenements, where 15 percent of children died before the age of one.

Of course, many Irish were Protestant and pro-British. The **Ulster Volunteers** (Unionists, and mostly Orangemen) feared that Home Rule would result in a Catholic-dominated state that would oppress the Protestant minority.

Meanwhile, Britain was preoccupied with World War I, where it was "fighting to protect the rights of small nations" (except Ireland's), and so it delayed granting Irish independence. The increasingly militant Irish rebels, believing that England's misfortune was Ireland's opportunity, decided to rise up and take independence while the time was ripe.

On Easter Monday, April 24, 1916, 1,500 Irish Volunteers,

PAST & PRESENT

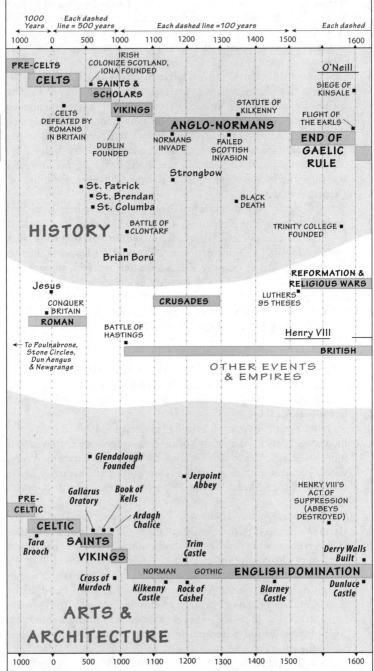

1000 Years	Each dashed line = 500 years		Each dashed line =100 years					Each dashed
1000	0	500	1000	1100	1200	1300	1400	1500	1600

PRE-CELTS

CELTS

IRISH COLONIZE SCOTLAND, IONA FOUNDED

■ **SAINTS & SCHOLARS**

O'Neill

SIEGE OF KINSALE ■

CELTS DEFEATED BY ROMANS IN BRITAIN

VIKINGS

STATUTE OF KILKENNY ■

ANGLO-NORMANS

FLIGHT OF THE EARLS ↗

DUBLIN FOUNDED

NORMANS INVADE

FAILED SCOTTISH INVASION

END OF GAELIC RULE

Strongbow

■ St. Patrick
■ St. Brendan
■ St. Columba

■ BLACK DEATH

HISTORY

BATTLE OF ■ CLONTARF

TRINITY COLLEGE ■ FOUNDED

Brian Ború

REFORMATION & RELIGIOUS WARS

Jesus

■

LUTHERS 95 THESES ■

CONQUER BRITAIN

CRUSADES

ROMAN

BATTLE OF HASTINGS

Henry VIII

← To Poulnabrone, Stone Circles, Dun Aengus & Newgrange

BRITISH

OTHER EVENTS & EMPIRES

■ Glendalough Founded

■ Jerpoint Abbey

HENRY VIII'S ACT OF SUPPRESSION (ABBEYS DESTROYED) ■

Gallarus Oratory

Book of Kells

PRE-CELTIC

Ardagh Chalice

CELTIC

Tara Brooch ■

SAINTS

Trim Castle

Derry Walls Built ■

VIKINGS

NORMAN   GOTHIC   **ENGLISH DOMINATION**

Cross of Murdoch ■

Kilkenny Castle

Rock of Cashel

Blarney Castle

Dunluce Castle

ARTS & ARCHITECTURE

| 1000 | 0 | 500 | 1000 | 1100 | 1200 | 1300 | 1400 | 1500 | 1600 |

Irish History & Art Timeline

line = 50 years   Each dashed line = 25 years

1700   1800   1900   1950   2000

WORKHOUSES ■ ■ POTATO FAMINE
BUILT
Meagher   De Valera
Adams
MASSACRE   Wolfe   Pearse   BORDER   MOUNTBATTEN
OF THE   Tone   Collins   CAMPAIGN   ■ KILLED
PLANTERS   O'Connell   IRA
BATTLE OF   HUNGER ■   ■ PEACE
THE BOYNE   Parnell   WWI   WWII   STRIKE
■ 1690   1798   YOUNG   FENIAN   JOINS   EU &
ENGLISH   REBELLION   IRELANDER   REBELLION   EC   EURO
PENAL   PROT. RULE   UPRISING   EASTER   IRISH   GLOBAL
LAWS   VOTES &   UPRISING   CIVIL WAR   RECESSION
ENGLISH &   VIOLENCE   UPRISING   CELTIC TIGER
SCOTTISH   ACT OF   IRISH   IRISH   BOOM
SETTLERS   UNION   FREE STATE   REPUBLIC   POST-WAR
JAMESON   GUINNESS   GAA   FOUNDED   PEACE
FOUNDED ■   FOUNDED ■   FOUNDED
KNOCK   GOOD FRIDAY
BUSHMILLS   APPARITION ■   PEACE ACCORDS
FOUNDED ■   TITANIC BUILT   PARTITION ■   "BLOODY   TROUBLES
WATERLOO ■   BELFAST   SUNDAY" ■
Napoleon   LUSITANIA   NORTHERN IRELAND
FRENCH REV. ■   SINKS ■   Paisley
Churchill
Cromwell   George III   Victoria   Elizabeth II
EMPIRE
AMERICAN   USA
REVOLUTION   MILLIONS ■   ■ CIVIL WAR   JFK PRESIDENCY
EMIGRATE   The
INDUSTRIAL REV.   Quiet Man   Steves
W.B. Yeats
Joyce   Van Morrison
Swift   Wilde   U-2
Shaw
IRISH LITERATURE
GAELIC LEAGUE ■
FOUNDED   Synge   Heaney
Beckett
O'Casey   Keane
Meeting on the
Turret Stairs ■
J.B. Yeats
Merrion   City Hall   Keating
Square   Dublin   Muckross   Henry
■ ■   House
GEORGIAN   VICTORIAN
Charles   Powers-   Four   Kylemore   GAELIC
Fort   court   Courts   Abbey   REVIVAL   POST-WAR
CONTEMP.
NEO-CLASSICAL   Belfast   Titanic
Custom House ■   City Hall ■   Museum

1700   1800   1900   1950   2000

united with members of the Irish Citizens Army, marched on Dublin, occupied the General Post Office (and six other key buildings across town), and raised a green, white, and orange flag. The teacher and poet **Patrick Pearse** stood in front of the post office and proclaimed Ireland an independent republic.

British troops struck back—in a week of street fighting and intense shelling, some 300 died. By Saturday, the greatly outnumbered rebels had been killed or arrested. The small-scale rebellion—which failed to go national and was never popular even in Dublin—was apparently over.

The British government, however, overreacted by swiftly executing the 16 ringleaders, including Pearse. Ireland was outraged, no longer seeing the rebels as troublemakers but as martyrs. From this point on, Ireland was resolved to win its independence at all costs. A poem by W. B. Yeats, "Easter, 1916," captured the struggle with his words: "All changed, changed utterly: A terrible beauty is born."

In the 1918 elections, the Sinn Fein party won big, but the new members of Parliament refused to go to London, instead forming their own independent Irish Parliament in Dublin. Then Irish rebels began ambushing policemen—seen as the eyes and ears of British control—sparking two years of confrontations called the **War of Independence.** The fledgling Irish Republican Army faced 40,000 British troops, including the notorious Black and Tans (named for the color of their clothes: black for police and tan for army-surplus uniforms). More than 1,000 people died in this war of street fighting, sniper fire, jailhouse beatings, terrorist bombs, and reprisals (for a more detailed timeline of the war and events leading up to it, see the sidebar on page 66).

Finally, Britain, tired of extended war after the slaughterhouse of World War I, agreed to negotiate Irish independence. But Ireland itself was a divided nation—the southern three-quarters of the island was mostly Catholic, Gaelic, rural, and for Home Rule; the northern quarter was 65 percent Protestant, English, industrial, and Unionist. The solution? In 1920, in the **Government of Ireland Act,** the British Parliament partitioned the island into two independent, self-governing countries within the British Commonwealth: **Northern Ireland** and the **Irish Free State.** While the northern six counties (the only ones without a Catholic majority) chose to stay with Britain as Northern Ireland, the remaining counties became the Irish Free State. (For a review of the issues between the North and the Republic, see the Northern Ireland chapter.)

Ireland's various political factions wrestled with this compromise solution, and the island plunged into a yearlong **Civil War**

(1922-1923). The hard-line IRA opposed the partition, unwilling to accept a divided island, an oath of loyalty to the Crown, or the remaining British navy bases on Irish soil. They waged a street war on the armies of the Irish Free State, whose leaders supported the political settlement as a stepping-stone toward future independence. Dublin and the southeast were ravaged in a year of bitter fighting before the Irish Free State, led by the charismatic young Nationalist **Michael Collins,** emerged victorious. The IRA went underground, moving its fight north and trying for the rest of the century to topple the government of Northern Ireland.

Out of the ashes of the Civil War came the two parties that still dominate Ireland's politics today. **Fine Gael** spawned from those who approved the treaty and the creation of the Irish Free State. **Fianna Fáil** was founded by **Eamon de Valera,** the figurehead of the antitreaty side. Interestingly, Fianna Fáil, which developed from the losing side of the Civil War, has been in power 70 percent of the time since its inception.

In 1937, the Irish Free State severed more ties with the British Commonwealth, writing up a new national constitution and taking an old name—**Éire** (pronounced AIR-uh). This new constitution reflected De Valera's conservative views, giving the Catholic Church "special status" and decreeing that a woman's place was in the home. Ireland called World War II "The Emergency" and remained neutral. In 1949, the separation from Britain was completed, as the Irish Free State left the Commonwealth and officially became the **Republic of Ireland.**

CELTIC TIGER IN THE SOUTH, TROUBLES IN THE NORTH (1950-2000)

In the 1950s, Ireland hemorrhaged its best and brightest as emigration soared. But beginning in the 1960s, the Republic of Ireland—formerly a poor, rural region—began its transformation into a modern, economic nation. The dropping of trade-strangling tariffs lured foreign investors. In 1973, membership in the European Union opened new Continental markets to Irish trade. No longer would Britain be the dominant trade partner. At the same time, reforms to Ireland's antiquated education system created a new generation of young people prepared for more than life on the farm.

The big social changes in the Republic were reflected in the 1990 election of Mary Robinson (a feminist lawyer who was outspoken on issues of divorce, contraception, and abortion) as the first female president of a once ultraconservative Ireland. Her much-respected seven-year tenure was followed by the equally graceful presidency of Mary McAleese (1997-2011). Born in the North, McAleese is another example of the shrinking divide between the two political states that occupy the island.

Through the late 1990s, the Republic's booming, globalized economy grew a whopping 40 percent, and Dublin's property values tripled (between 1995 and 2007), earning the Republic's economy the nickname "The Celtic Tiger." (Like elsewhere, the global recession hit hard here in 2008—the property bubble burst, sending home values plummeting and driving up unemployment.)

Meanwhile, as the Republic moved toward prosperity, Northern Ireland—with a slight Protestant majority and a large, disaffected Catholic minority—was plagued by the **Troubles.** In 1967, the Northern Ireland Civil Rights Movement, inspired by the African American rights movement in the US, organized marches and demonstrations demanding equal treatment for Catholics (better housing, job opportunities, and voting rights). But they didn't have a moral authority like Martin Luther King Jr. or a Desmond Tutu to advocate for them. Protestant **Unionist Orangemen** countered by continuing their marches through Catholic neighborhoods, flaunting their politically dominant position (disguised as tradition), and provoking riots. In 1969, Britain sent troops to help Northern Ireland keep the peace and met resistance from the IRA, which saw them as an occupying army supporting the Protestant pro-British majority.

From the 1970s to the 1990s, the North was a low-level battlefield, with the IRA using terrorist tactics to advance their political

agenda. The Troubles, which claimed some 3,000 lives, continued with bombings, marches, hunger strikes, rock-throwing, and riots (notably Derry's **Bloody Sunday** in 1972—see sidebar on page 415). These were interrupted by periods of cease-fires, broken cease-fires, and a string of failed peace agreements.

Then came the watershed 1998 settlement known as the **Good Friday Peace Accord** (to pro-Irish Nationalists) or the **Belfast Agreement** (to pro-British Unionists).

NORTHERN IRELAND IN THE 21ST CENTURY

The 1998 **Good Friday Peace Accord** gave Northern Ireland the freedom to leave the UK—if a majority of the population ever approves a referendum to do so. At the same time, the Republic of Ireland withdrew its constitutional claim to the entire island of Ireland. Northern Ireland now has limited autonomy from London, with its own democratically elected, power-sharing government. It will be up to this body to untie this stubborn Gordian knot.

After years of negotiation, in 2005 the IRA formally announced an end to its armed campaign, promising to pursue peaceful, democratic means to achieve its goals. In response, after almost 40 years, in 2007 the British Army withdrew 90 percent of its forces from Northern Ireland. In 2010, the long-awaited Saville Report—the result of a 12-year investigation by the British government—found that the Bloody Sunday shootings were unjustified, and the victims legally innocent.

Great Britain is also trying to mend its relationship with the Republic. In 2011, Queen Elizabeth II became the first British monarch to visit the Republic of Ireland since it broke away in 1921 (she has been to the North numerous times). The Queen took the gutsy step of visiting Dublin's Croke Park stadium, where British Black and Tan troops massacred 14 people at a 1921 Gaelic football match (see sidebar on page 91). She also visited Dublin's Garden of Remembrance, a quiet urban plot devoted to the 1916 Easter Rising. In 2012, she went a step further by shaking hands with ex-IRA leader and then-Deputy First Minister of Northern Ireland, the late Martin McGuinness. These acts of reconciliation, though controversial and dramatic, were an important step toward building an amicable relationship between the two countries.

In 2016, the unexpected British referendum vote to leave the European Union (the so-called **Brexit**) reshuffled the political cards in the region. Northern Ireland had voted to remain in the EU, as did Scotland. With Scotland debating its own independence from the UK, the Unionist community in Northern Ireland (which holds both their Britishness and Scottish ancestry dear) is split on whether to remain part of the UK or instead prioritize membership in the EU. One thing is certain: Only extremists want a hard border to replace the soft and cooperative one that exists today between Northern Ireland and the Republic.

GLOBAL NATIONS (2000 AND BEYOND)

In the Republic of Ireland, the challenges of **immigration** (new arrivals into Ireland) eventually replaced problems associated with the generations of emigration (young people leaving Ireland). Ireland once had the most liberal citizenship laws in the European Union, granting Irish citizenship to anyone born on Irish soil (even if neither parent had an Irish passport). This led to a flood of pregnant immigrant women arriving from Eastern Europe and Africa to give birth in Ireland so their children would gain EU citizenship. A 2004 Irish referendum closed that legal loophole.

During its **Celtic Tiger economic boom**, the Irish imported labor and temporarily surpassed the English in per-capita income—both for the first time ever. Starting in 1980, when Apple set up its European headquarters here, streams of multinational and US corporations opened offices in Ireland. Ireland has one of the youngest populations in Europe. And those young Irish, beneficiaries of one of Europe's best education systems, provide these corporations with a highly skilled workforce. Ireland's big pharmaceutical and software industries (although usually foreign-owned) are well-established—this little country is second only to the US in the exportation of software. The island's close business ties to its American partners mean its economy is highly reactive to US market fluctuations. The Irish say, "When America sneezes, we get pneumonia."

By 2003, the rising economic tide had lifted Ireland to float beside Finland as one of the two most expensive countries in the European Union. But in 2008, the irrationally exuberant Irish housing bubble burst, wiping out retirement nest eggs. By 2011 that tide had receded: The global recession was a cold shower on Ireland's long period of economic good times, and the Irish economy fell further, by percentage, than any other EU country during that period.

The final stage of this humbling financial buzzkill came in the fall of 2010, when the EU bailed out Ireland's teetering banks (an event wedged painfully between similar bailouts in Greece and Portugal). To Ireland's credit, it fulfilled its banking obligations and bounced back from the bailout faster than the other troubled European economies. Now the Irish economy is growing again. Help-wanted signs and expanded road construction are visible evidence of a resurgence.

As 2016 marked the **hundredth anniversary of the Easter Rising**, the Irish could look back in amazement at the highs and lows of its turbulent first hundred years of modern nationhood. No longer an agricultural backwater in the shadow of British colonial domination, the country has forged a unique identity and proved it can compete successfully in the ever-accelerating 21st century. In the past decade, the Irish enjoyed views from their lofty Celtic Tiger peak (with the hottest economy in the EU) and then suffered the helpless free fall of the merciless global recession. But now the roller coaster has bottomed out and tentative "green shoots" have given way to blossoming optimism once again.

While the Irish are embracing the new economies and indus-

Irish Brogue with a Polish Accent

Walking down the street in an Irish city these days, you might overhear an unfamiliar language. It's Polish, and it is to Ireland what Spanish is to the US: the language needed to communicate with a huge immigrant population. Polish food sections are popping up in grocery stores, and English-Polish menus appearing in some restaurants. Ask that chambermaid or waiter with the unusual accent where they're from; the likely response is Warsaw or Kraków.

When 10 mostly Eastern European nations joined the EU in 2004, Ireland's booming economy at that time needed a cheap labor force to fill the growing number of minimum-wage jobs. Hardworking, ambitious young Poles headed west to the land of opportunity. Ireland was their first choice because of its Catholicism, stronger economy, and opportunity to learn English (the international language of business). From 2006 to 2011, the number of Polish residents in the Republic of Ireland increased by 93.7 percent, beating out UK nationals as the largest group of non-Irish nationals living in Ireland. And Polish has replaced Irish Gaelic as Ireland's second most-spoken language.

tries of the 21st century, some still see their island as an oasis of morality and **traditional values** when it comes to sex and marriage. A seismic shift began when homosexuality was decriminalized in 1993. In 2015, the doors were blown off the closet when the Republic of Ireland became the first country to legalize same-sex marriage by a referendum (62 percent were in favor). In 2017, 38-year-old Leo Varadkar became the new Taoiseach (prime minister) of Ireland... as the openly gay son of an Indian immigrant. And in 2018, Ireland voted to repeal a decades-old ban on abortion.

The Catholic Church, once the main moral force in Irish society, is becoming less influential. The popular demands of the youngest population in Europe will likely continue to push the Irish government to make changes on birth control (which is employed here at rates lower than in any other EU nation) and divorce (which requires that strict conditions be met).

Irish Art

Megalithic tombs, ancient gold- and metalwork, illuminated manuscripts, high crosses carved in stone, paintings of rural Ireland, and provocative political murals—Ireland comes with some fascinating art. To best appreciate this art in your travels, kick off your tour in Ireland's two top museums, both in Dublin: the **National Museum of Ireland** and the **National Gallery.** Each provides a good context to help you enjoy Irish art and architecture—from ancient to modern and both rural and urban. Here's a quick survey.

Megalithic Period: During the Stone Age, 5,000 years ago, farmers living in the **Boyne Valley,** north of Dublin, built a "cemetery" of approximately 40 **burial mounds.** The most famous of these mound tombs is the passage tomb at Newgrange (part of Brú na Bóinne). About 250 feet across, 40 feet high, and composed of 200,000 tons of loose stone, Newgrange was constructed so that the light from the winter solstice sunrise (Dec 21) would pass through the eastern entrance to the tomb, travel down a 60-foot passage, and illuminate the inner burial chamber (not bad engineering for Stone Age architects). The effect is now re-created daily, so visitors can experience this ancient ritual of renewal and rebirth any time of year (see the Near Dublin chapter).

Some of Europe's best examples of megalithic (big rock) art are also at Newgrange. Carved on the tomb's stones are zigzags, chevrons, parallel arcs, and concentric spirals. Scholars think these designs symbolize a belief in the eternal cycle of life and the continuation of the life force, or that they pay homage to the elements in nature on which these ancient peoples depended for their existence.

Exploring these burial mounds (only Newgrange and Knowth are open to the public), you begin to understand the reverence that these ancient people had for nature, and the need they felt to bury their dead in these great mound tombs, returning their kin to the womb of Mother Earth.

Bronze Age: As ancient Irish cultures developed from 2000 B.C., so did their metalworking skills. Gold and bronze were used to create **tools, jewelry,** and **re-ligious objects.** (The National Museum: Archaeology in Dublin houses the most dazzling of these works.) Gold neck rings worn by both men and women, cufflink-like dress fasteners, bracelets, and lock rings (to hold hair in place) are just a few of the personal adornments fashioned by the ancient Irish.

Most of these objects were deliberately buried, often in bogs, as votive offerings to their gods or to prevent warring tribes from stealing them. Like the earlier megaliths, they're decorated with geometric and organic motifs.

Iron Age: The Celts, a warrior society from Central Europe, arrived in Ireland perhaps as early as the seventh century B.C. With their metalworking skills and superior iron weaponry, they soon overwhelmed the native population. And, though the Celts may have been fierce warriors, they wreaked havoc with a flair for the aesthetic. **Shields, swords,** and **scabbards** were embellished with delicate patterns, often enhanced with vivid colors. The dynamic energy of these decorations must have reflected the ferocious power of the Celts.

The Age of Saints and Scholars: Christianity grew in Ireland from St. Patrick's first efforts in the fifth century A.D. In the sixth and seventh centuries, its many great saints (such as St. Columba) established monastic settlements throughout Ireland, Britain, and the Continent, where learning, literature, and the arts flourished. During this Golden Age of Irish civilization, monks, along with metalworkers and stonemasons, created imaginative designs and distinctive stylistic motifs for **manuscripts, metal objects,** and **crosses.**

Monks wrote out and richly decorated manuscripts of the Gospels. These manuscripts—which preserved the written word in Latin, Greek, and Irish—eventually had more power than the oral tales of the ancient pagan heroes.

The most beautiful and imaginative of these illuminated man-uscripts is the **Book of Kells** (c. A.D. 800), on display in the Old Library at Trinity College in Dublin. Crafted by Irish monks at a monastery on the Scottish island of Iona, the book was brought to Ireland for safekeeping from rampaging Vikings. The skins of 150 calves were used to make the vellum, which is painted with rich pigments from plants and minerals. The entire manuscript is colorfully decorated with flat, stylized human or angelic forms and intricate, interlacing animal and knot patterns. Full-page illustra-tions depict the life of Christ, and many pages are given over to highly complex yet symmetrical designs that resemble an Eastern carpet. Many consider this book the finest piece of art from Eu-rope's Dark Ages.

The most renowned metalwork of this period is the **Ardagh Chalice,** made sometime in the eighth century. Now on display at the National Museum: Archaeology in Dublin, the silver and bronze gilt chalice is as impressive as the Book of Kells. Ribbons of gold wrap around the chalice stem, while intricate knot patterns ring the cup. A magnificent gold ring and a large glass stone on the chalice bottom reflect the desire to please God. (He would see this side of the chalice when the priest drank during the Mass.)

The monks used Irish high crosses to celebrate the triumph of Christianity and to provide a means of educating the illiterate masses through simple stone carvings. The **Cross of Murdock** (Muiredach's Cross, A.D. 923) is 18 feet tall, towering over the remains of the monastic settlement at Monasterboice. It is but one of many monumental crosses that you'll come across throughout Ireland. Typically, stone carvers depicted Bible stories and surrounded these with the same intricate patterns seen in the Book of Kells and the Ardagh Chalice.

Early Irish art focused on organic, geometric, and linear designs. Unlike Mediterranean art, Irish art of this early period was not preoccupied with a naturalistic representation of people, animals, or the landscape. Instead, it reflects Irish society's rituals and the elements and rhythms of nature.

Suppression and Revival of Native Irish Art: After invading Ireland in 1169, the English suppressed Celtic Irish culture. English traditions in architecture, painting, and literature replaced native styles until the late 19th century, when revivals in Irish language, folklore, music, and art began to surface.

Painters in the late 19th and early 20th centuries went to the west of Ireland, which was less affected by English dominance and influence, in search of traditional Irish subject matter. **Jack B. Yeats** (1871-1957, brother of the poet W. B. Yeats), Belfast-born painter **Paul Henry** (1876-1958), and **Sean Keating** (1889-1977) were among those who looked to the west for inspiration. The National Gallery in Dublin holds many of these artists' greatest works, with an entire gallery dedicated to Jack Yeats. Many of his early paintings illustrate scenes of his beloved Sligo. His later paintings are more expressionistic in style and patriotic in subject matter.

Henry's paintings depict the rugged beauty of the Connemara region and its people, with scenes of rustic cottages, mountains, and boglands. Keating, the most political of the three painters, featured stirring scenes from Ireland's struggle against the English for independence.

Contemporary Irish art is often linked to the social, political, and environmental issues that face Ireland today. Themes include the position of the Church in the daily lives of the modern Irish, the effects of development on the countryside, the changing roles of women in Ireland, and the Troubles. Look for this provocative art at the Irish Museum of Modern Art in Dublin (on Military Road, www.imma.ie) and at city galleries.

Today's Irish respect the artistic process,

so much so that a provision in the tax system in the Republic of Ireland allows income from art sales to go untaxed. This is one reason many artists immigrate to Ireland.

In Northern Ireland, murals in sectarian neighborhoods (such as the Shankill and Falls roads in Belfast and the Bogside in Derry) are stirring public testaments to the martyrs and heroes of the Troubles.

To learn more about Irish history, consider *Europe 101: History and Art for the Traveler,* written by Rick Steves and Gene Openshaw (available at www.ricksteves.com).

Irish Literature

Since the Book of Kells, Ireland's greatest contributions to the world of art have been through words. As there was no Irish Gaelic written language, the inhabitants of Ireland were illiterate until Christianity came in the fourth century. Far from ignorant, Celtic society maintained a complex set of laws and historical records and legends...verbally. The druid priests and bards who passed down this rich oral tradition from generation to generation were the most respected members of the clan, next to the king. After Christianity transformed Ireland into a refuge of literacy (while the rest of Europe crumbled into the Dark Ages), Charlemagne's imported Irish monks invented "minuscule," which became the basis of the lower-case letters we use in our alphabet today. The cultural importance placed on the word (spoken, and for the past 1,500 years, written) is today reflected in the rich output of modern Irish writers.

Three hundred years ago, Dublin native **Jonathan Swift** created his masterpiece, *Gulliver's Travels,* as an acidic satire of British colonialism. It pokes fun at religious hard-liners and the pompous bureaucrats in London who shaped England's misguided Irish policies, and ironically has survived as a children's classic.

William Butler Yeats, also born and raised in Dublin, dedicated his early writings in the 1880s to the "Celtic Twilight" rebirth of pride in mythic Irish heroes and heroines. His early poems and plays are filled with fairies and idyllic rural innocence, while his later poems reflect Ireland's painful transition to independence. Yeats' Nobel Prize for literature (1923) was eventually matched by three later, Nobel-winning Irish au-

DUBLIN TOURISM
SENATOR
WILLIAM
BUTLER YEATS
1865 – 1939

POET & PLAYWRIGHT

LIVED HERE 1922 – 1928

thors: **George Bernard Shaw** (1925), **Samuel Beckett** (1969), and **Seamus Heaney** (1995).

Oscar Wilde, born in Dublin and a graduate of Trinity College, wowed London with his quick wit, outrageous clothes, and flamboyant personality. Wilde wrote the darkly fascinating novel *The Picture of Dorian Gray* (1890) and skewered upper-class Victorian society in witty comedic plays (such as *The Importance of Being Earnest,* 1895), with characters who speak very elegantly about the trivial concerns of the idle rich. He was the toast of London in the 1890s—before the scandal of his homosexuality turned Victorian society against him. Meanwhile, **Bram Stoker** was conjuring up a Gothic thriller called *Dracula* (1897).

Most inventive of all, perhaps, was **James Joyce,** who broke new ground and captured literary lightning in a bottle when he focused on Dublin's seedier side in a modern, stream-of-consciousness style. His famous novel *Ulysses,* set on a single day (June 16, 1904), follows Dubliners on an odyssey through the city's pubs, hospitals, libraries, churches, and brothels.

The **Abbey Theatre** (championed by W. B. Yeats) was the world's first national theater, built to house plays intended to give a voice to Ireland's flowering playwrights. When **J. M. Synge** staged *The Playboy of the Western World* there in 1907, his unflattering comic portrayal of Irish peasant life (and mention of women's underwear) caused riots. Twenty years later, **Sean O'Casey** provoked more riots at the Abbey when his *Plough and the Stars* production depicted the 1916 Rising in a way that was at odds with the audience's cherished views of their heroes.

In recent decades, the bittersweet Irish literary parade has been inhabited by tragically volcanic characters like **Brendan Behan,** who exclaimed, "I'm not a writer with a drinking problem...I'm a drinker with a writing problem." Bleak poverty experienced in childhood was the catalyst for **Frank McCourt**'s memorable *Angela's Ashes.* Among the most celebrated of today's Irish writers is **Roddy Doyle,** whose feel for working-class Dublin resonates in his novels of contemporary life (such as *The Commitments*) as well as in historical slices of life (such as *A Star Called Henry*). **Seamus Heaney,** a poet who has won the Nobel and Pulitzer prizes, published a new translation in 1999 of the Old English epic *Beowulf*—wedding the old with the new.

Irish Language

The Irish have a rich oral tradition that goes back to their ancient fireside storytelling days. Part of the fun of traveling here is getting an ear for the way locals express themselves.

Irish Gaelic is one of four surviving Celtic languages, along with Scottish Gaelic, Welsh, and Breton (spoken in parts of French Brittany). A couple of centuries ago, there were seven surviving Celtic languages. But Cornish (spoken in Cornwall) is on life support, and two others—Manx (from the Isle of Man) and Gallaic (spoken in Northern Spain)—have died out. Some proud Irish choose to call their native tongue "Irish" instead of "Gaelic" to ensure that there is no confusion with what is spoken in parts of Scotland.

I ᵹcuiṁne aᵹus in onóir na nᵹael, sa ċeanᴛair seo, a ᵹlaċ páirᴛ san éirí amaċ 1'98 ar san saoirse na h-éireann. ar óeis láṁ óé ᵹo raiḃ siaó.

PAST & PRESENT

Only 165 years ago, the majority of the Irish population spoke Irish Gaelic. But most of the speakers were of the poor laborer class that either died or emigrated during the Famine. After the Famine, Irish Gaelic was seen as a badge of backwardness. Parents and teachers understood that English was the language that would serve children best when they emigrated to better lives in the US, Canada, Australia, or England. Children in schools wore a tally stick around their necks, and a notch was cut by teachers each time a child was caught speaking Irish. At the end of the day, the child received a whack for each notch in the stick. It wasn't until the resurgence of cultural pride, brought on by the Gaelic League in 1884, that an attempt was made to promote use of the language again.

Gaeltacht Regions

N. BELFAST
IRE.

GALWAY

REP.
OF
IRELAND

DINGLE
(AN DAINGEAN)

DUBLIN

CORK

AREAS SHOWN IN GREY
ARE PART OF THE GAELTACHT

These days, less than 5 percent of the Irish population is fluent in their native tongue. However, it's taken seriously enough that all national laws passed must first be written in Irish, then translated into English. Irish Gaelic can be heard most often in the western counties of Kerry, Galway, Mayo, and Donegal. Each of these counties has a slightly different dialect. You'll know you're entering an Irish Gaelic-speaking area when you see a sign saying *Gaeltacht* (GAIL-takt).

Irish Gaelic doesn't use the letters *j, k, q, x,* or *z.* And there's no "th" sound—which you can hear today when an Irish person says something like "turdy-tree" (33, mostly in the Dublin accent). There is also no equivalent of the simple words "yes" or "no." Instead, answers are given in the affirmative or negative rephrasing of the question. For example, a question like "Did you mail the letter today?" would be answered with "I did," rather than a simple "yes." Or "It's a nice day today, isn't it?" would be answered with "It is," or "'Tis."

IRISH PUB AND MUSIC WORDS

The Irish love to socialize. Pubs are like public living rooms, where friends gather in a corner to play tunes and anyone is a welcome guest. Here are some useful pub and music words:

Irish	English
poitín (po-CHEEN)	moonshine, homemade liquor
craic (crack)	fun atmosphere, good conversation
bodhrán (BO-run)	traditional drum
uilleann (ILL-in)	elbow (*uilleann* pipes are elbow bagpipes)
trad (trad)	traditional Irish music
ceilidh (KAY-lee)	Irish dance gathering
fleadh (flah)	music festival
Slainte! (SLAWN-chuh)	Cheers! (To your health!)
Táim súgach! (taw im SOO-gakh)	I'm tipsy!
lei thras (LEH-hrass)	Toilets
mná (min-AW)	women's room
fír (fear)	men's room

IRISH POLITICS

Politics is a popular topic of conversation in Ireland. Whether you pick up a local newspaper or turn on your car radio, you're likely to encounter these Irish political terms in the media:

Irish	English
Taoiseach (TEE-shock)	Prime minister of Irish Republic
Seanad (SHAN-ud)	Irish Senate
Dáil (DOY-ill)	Irish House of Representatives
Teachta Dála (TD) (TALK-tah DOLL-ah)	Member of Irish Parliament
Fine Gael (FEE-nuh GWAIL)	Political party "Clan of the Gaels"
Fine Fáil (FEE-nuh FOIL)	Political party "Soldiers of Destiny"
Sinn Féin (shin-FAIN)	Political party "We Ourselves"

IRISH WORDS

Here are a few words that appear in Irish place names. You'll see these on road signs or at tourist sights.

Irish	English
alt (ahlt)	cliff
an lár (ahn lar)	city center
ard (ard)	high, height, hillock
baile (BALL-yah)	town, town land
beag (beg)	little
bearna (bar-na)	gap
boireann (burr-en)	large rock, rocky area
bóthar (boh-er)	road
bun (bun)	end, bottom
caiseal (CASH-el)	circular stone fort
caisleán (cash-LAWN)	castle
cathair (CAHT-her)	circular stone fort, city
cill (kill)	church
cloch (clockh)	stone
doire (dih-ruh)	oak
droichead (DROCKH-ed)	bridge
drumlin (DRUM-lin)	small hill
dún (doon)	fort
fionn (fi-UN)	white, fair-haired person
gaeltacht (GAIL-takt)	Irish language district
gall (gaul)	foreigner
garda (gar-dah)	police officer
gort (gort)	field
inis (in-ish)	island
mileac (MIL-yach)	low marshy ground
mór (mor)	large
muc (muck)	pig
oifig an phoist (UFF-ig un fusht)	post office
poll (poll)	hole, cave
rath (rath)	ancient earthen fort
ros (ross)	wood or headland
sí (shee)	fairy mound, bewitching
slí (slee)	route, way
sliabh (sleeve)	mountain
sráid (shrayd)	street
teach (chockh)	house
trá (traw)	beach, strand

PAST & PRESENT

IRISH PLEASANTRIES

When you reach the more remote western fringe of Ireland, you're likely to hear folks speaking Irish. Although locals in these areas can readily converse with you in English, it's fascinating to hear their ancient Celtic language spoken. Here are some basic Irish phrases:

Irish	English
Fáilte. (FAHLT-chuh or FAHLT-uh)	Welcome.
Conas tá tú? (CONN-us A-ta too)	How are you?
Go raibh maith agat. (guh rov mah UG-ut)	Thank you.
Slán. (slawn)	Bye.
Dia dhuit. (DEA-gwitch)	God be with you.

IRISH NAMES

Here are some of the most common Celtic first names you'll encounter in your travels. Amaze your new Irish friends by pronouncing them correctly, or at least not mangling them.

Irish	English
Aoife (EE-fuh)	Ava
Áine (ON-yuh)	Anna
Eammon (A-mun)	Edmond
Liam (LEE-um)	William
Mairéad (mahr-AID)	Margaret
Michael (ME-hall)	Michael
Niall (NILE)	Neil
Pádraig (POD-rig)	Patrick
Peadar (PAD-er)	Peter
Roisín (ROW-sheen)	Rosaleen
Seamus (SHAME-us)	James
Sean (SHAWN)	John
Sinéad (shin-AID)	Jane
Siobhán (shiv-AWN)	Joan

Irish-Yankee Vocabulary

If some of these words seem more British than Irish, those are ones you're likely to hear more often in Northern Ireland (part of the UK).

advert: advertisement

anticlockwise: counterclockwise

aubergine: eggplant

banger: sausage

bang on: correct

banjaxed: messed up

bank holiday: government holiday
bar: except
beer mat: coaster
bespoke: custom
billion: a thousand of our billions (a trillion)
biro: ballpoint pen
biscuit: cookie
Black Mariah: police van
black pudding: sausage made from pig's blood
black stuff: Guinness
blather: rambling, empty talk
blinkered: narrow-minded
bloody: damn (from medieval blasphemy: "Christ's blood")
blow off: fart
boffin: nerd
bog: slang for toilet
boho: bohemian
bolshy: argumentative
bonnet: car hood
boot: car trunk
braces: suspenders
bridle way: path for walkers, bikers, and horse riders
brilliant: cool
bum: bottom or "backside"
busker: street musician
cacks: trousers, underpants
candy floss: cotton candy
caravan: trailer
car boot sale: temporary flea market, often for charity
car park: parking lot
carry on: nonsense
casualty: emergency room
cat's eyes: road reflectors
ceilidh (pronounced "KAY-lee"): dance, party
champ: mashed potatoes and onions
chemist: pharmacist
chicory: endive
chippy: fish-and-chips shop
chips: French fries
chock-a-block: jam-packed
chuffed: pleased
cider: alcoholic apple cider
clearway: road where you can't stop
coach: long-distance bus
concession: discounted admission
cos: romaine lettuce

cotton buds: cotton swabs
courgette: zucchini
craic (pronounced "crack"): fun, good conversation
crèche (pronounced "creesh"): preschool
crisps: potato chips
Croker: Croke Park (GAA Dublin sports stadium)
crusties: New Age hippies
culchie: hick, country yokel
cuppa: cup of tea
CV: résumé (curriculum vitae)
Da: father
deadly: really good
dear: expensive
digestives: round graham crackers
dinner: lunch or dinner
diversion: detour
dodgy: iffy, risky
dole: welfare
done and dusted: completed
donkey's years: until the cows come home, forever
draughts (pronounced "drafts"): checkers
draw: marijuana
dual carriageway: divided highway (four lanes)
Dubs: people from Dublin
Dutch courage: alcohol-induced bravery
eejit: moron
Emergency, The: World War II
en suite: bathroom attached to room
face flannel: washcloth
fair play (to you): well done, good job
fanny: vagina
fiddler's fart: worthless thing
first floor: second floor (one floor above ground)
fiver: five-euro note
flat: apartment
fluthered: drunk
flutter: a bet
football: Gaelic football
fortnight: two weeks
full monty: the whole shebang, everything
GAA: Gaelic Athletic Association
gallery: balcony
gammon: ham
gangway: aisle
gaol: jail (same pronunciation)
Garda: police

gargle: to have an alcoholic drink
gasman: the life of the party
give way: yield
giving out: chewing out, yelling at
glen: valley
gob: mouth
gobsmacked: astounded
grand: good, well ("How are you?" "I'm grand, thanks")
guards: police *(Garda)*
gurrier: hooligan
half eight: 8:30 (not 7:30)
hen night: bachelorette party
holiday: vacation
homely: likable or cozy
hooley: party or informal shindig
hoover: vacuum cleaner
hurling: Irish field hockey
iced lolly: popsicle
interval: intermission
ironmonger: hardware store
jacket potato: baked potato
jacks: toilet
jars: drinks (alcohol)
jelly: Jell-O
Joe Soap: dim stranger
jumble: sale, rummage sale
jumper: sweater
just a tick: just a second
kipper: smoked herring
knackered: exhausted
knickers: ladies' panties
knocked: torn down (buildings)
knocking shop: brothel
knock up: wake up or visit
ladybird: ladybug
lash: a try ("give it a lash")
left luggage: baggage check
let: rent
lift: elevator
listed: protected historic building
lorry: truck
Ma, Mam, Mammy: mother
mac: mackintosh (trench) coat
mangetout: snow peas
mate: buddy (boy or girl)
mean: stingy

mental: crazy
minced meat: hamburger
minerals: soft drinks
mobile (MOH-bile): cellphone
mod cons: modern conveniences (not convicts in bell-bottoms)
naff: dorky, tacky
nappy: diaper
natter: talk and talk
"Norn Iron": Northern Ireland
nought: zero
noughties: the decade from 2000-2009
noughts & crosses: tic-tac-toe
OAP: old-age pensioner (qualified for senior discounts)
off-license: liquor store
Oirish: exaggerated Irish accent
on offer: for sale
paddywhackery: exaggerated Irish accent
paralytic: passed-out drunk
pasty (PASS-tee): crusted savory (usually meat) pie
pavement: sidewalk
pear-shaped: messed up, gone wrong
petrol: gas
pissed (rude), paralytic, bevvied, wellied, popped up, ratted, pissed as a newt: drunk
pitch: playing field
plaster: Band-Aid
publican: pub manager
pull: to attract romantic attention
punter: partygoer, customer
put a sock in it: shut up
quay (pronounced "key"): waterside street, ship offloading area
queue: line
queue up: line up
quick smart: immediately
quid: pound (money in Northern Ireland, worth about $1.40)
ramps: speed bumps
randy: horny
rat run: shortcut
redundant, made: laid off
return ticket: round-trip
ride: have sex with
ring up: call (telephone)
ROI: Republic of Ireland
roundabout: traffic circle
RTE: Irish Republic's broadcast network
rubber: eraser

runners: tennis shoes
sanitary towel: sanitary pad
sat-nav: satellite navigation technology
sausage roll: sausage wrapped in a flaky pastry (like a pig in a blanket)
scarlet: embarrassed
Scotch egg: hard-boiled egg wrapped in sausage meat
self-catering: apartment with kitchen
sellotape: Scotch tape
serviette: napkin
session: musical evening
shag: have sex with
shag all: hardly any
shebeen: illegal drinking hole
single ticket: one-way ticket
skint: broke, poor
skip: Dumpster
slag: to ridicule, tease
smalls: underwear
snogging: kissing, making out
solicitor: lawyer
sort out: figure out, organize
spanner: wrench
spend a penny: urinate
splash out: splurge
stag night: bachelor party
starkers: buck naked
starters: appetizers
stick: criticism
stone: 14 pounds (weight)
strand: beach
stroppy: bad-tempered
subway: underground pedestrian passageway
sultanas: golden raisins
surgical spirit: rubbing alcohol
swede: rutabaga
take the mickey: tease
tatty: worn out or tacky
taxi rank: taxi stand
tenner: 10-euro note
theatre: live stage
tick: a check mark
tight as a Scotsman (derogatory): cheapskate
tights: panty hose
Tipp: County Tipperary
tipper lorry: dump truck
tin: can

to let: for rent
top up: refill a drink or your mobile-phone credit
torch: flashlight
towpath: path along a river
trad: traditional music
Travellers: itinerants, once known as Tinkers
turf accountant: bookie
twee: corny, too cute
twitcher: bird-watcher
verge: grassy edge of road
victualler: butcher
wain: small child
way out: exit
wee (v.): urinate
wee (n.): tiny (in the North)
Wellingtons, wellies: rubber boots
whacked: exhausted
whinge (rhymes with hinge): whine
witter on: gab and gab
woolies: warm clothes
your man: that guy, this guy
zebra crossing: crosswalk
zed: the letter Z

PRACTICALITIES

This chapter covers the practical skills of European travel: how to get tourist information, pay for things, sightsee efficiently, find good-value accommodations, eat affordably but well, use technology wisely, and get between destinations smoothly. To round out your knowledge, check out "Resources from Rick Steves." For more information on these topics, see www.ricksteves.com/travel-tips.

Tourist Information

Ireland's two government-funded tourist offices (one for the Republic and one for the North) offer a wealth of information. **Before your trip,** scan their websites. For the Republic of Ireland, visit www.discoverireland.ie. For Northern Ireland, use www.discovernorthernireland.com. At either site, you can download brochures, maps, ask questions, and request that information be mailed to you (such as a free vacation-planning packet, regional and city maps, walking routes, and festival schedules).

In Ireland, a good first stop in any town is generally the tourist information office (abbreviated **TI** in this book). Avoid ad agencies masquerading as TIs, especially in Dublin—use the official TI. Fáilte Ireland TIs are information dispensaries with trained staff that don't sell anything or take commissions. I make a point to swing by the local TI to confirm sightseeing plans, pick up a city map, and get information on public transit, walking tours, special events, and nightlife. Prepare a list of questions and a proposed plan to double-check. Many TIs have information on the entire country or at least the region, so try to pick up maps and printed information for destinations you'll be visiting later in your trip. Be aware that TI phone numbers for some towns often simply connect you to a centralized national tourist office, with staff that may not have the "local" knowledge you are seeking.

In Dublin, try to get everything you'll need for all of Ireland in one stop at the TI (see page 38). The general nationwide tourist-information phone number for travelers calling from within Ireland is 1-850-230-330 (office open Mon-Sat 9:00-17:00, closed Sun).

Travel Tips

Emergency and Medical Help: In Ireland, dial 999 for police or a medical emergency. If you get sick, do as the locals do and go to a pharmacist for advice. Or ask at your hotel for help—they'll know the nearest medical and emergency services.

Theft or Loss: To replace a passport, you'll need to go in person to an embassy (see page 579). If your credit and debit cards disappear, cancel and replace them (see "Damage Control for Lost Cards" on page 528). File a police report, either on the spot or within a day or two; you'll need it to submit an insurance claim for lost or stolen rail passes or travel gear, and it can help with replacing your passport or credit and debit cards. For more information, see www.ricksteves.com/help.

Time Zones: Ireland, which is one hour earlier than most of continental Europe, is five/eight hours ahead of the East/West coasts of the US. The exceptions are the beginning and end of Daylight Saving Time: Ireland and Europe "spring forward" the last Sunday in March (two weeks after most of North America) and "fall back" the last Sunday in October (one week before North America). For a handy online time converter, see www.timeanddate.com/worldclock.

Business Hours: In Ireland, most stores are open Monday through Saturday from roughly 10:00 to 17:30, with a late night on Wednesday or Thursday (until 19:00 or 20:00), depending on the neighborhood. Saturdays are virtually weekdays, with earlier closing hours and no rush hour (though transportation connections can be less frequent than on weekdays). Sundays have the same pros and cons as they do for travelers in the US: Sightseeing attractions are generally open (with limited hours), while banks and many shops are closed. You'll notice special events, limited public transportation, no rush hours, and street markets lively with shoppers. Friday and Saturday evenings are rowdy; Sunday evenings are quiet.

Watt's Up? Europe's electrical system is 220 volts, instead of North America's 110 volts. Most newer electronics (such as laptops, battery chargers, and hair dryers) convert automatically, so you won't need a converter, but you will need an adapter plug with three square prongs, sold inexpensively at travel stores in the US. Avoid bringing older appliances that don't automatically convert voltage; instead, buy a cheap replacement in Europe. Low-cost hair dryers and other small appliances are sold at Dunnes and Tesco stores in bigger cities; ask your hotelier for the closest shop.

Discounts: Discounts for sights (called "concessions" in Ireland) are generally not listed in this book. However, many Irish sights offer discounts for youths (up to age 18), students (with proper identification cards, www.isic.org), families, seniors (loosely defined as retirees or those willing to call themselves seniors), and groups of 10 or more. Always ask. Some discounts are available only for citizens of the European Union (EU).

Laundry: If you're not planning to wash your clothes in your hotel sink, it's a good idea to plan ahead for laundry. Basic wash-and-wear clothes have nothing to fear from an Irish launderette (but don't tempt fate with your favorite silk shirt—it might come back leprechaun-size). At most launderettes, you drop off your load first thing in the morning and pick it up late that afternoon (washed, dried, and kind-of folded). This works well for travelers—the savings from doing it yourself are not worth the lost sightseeing time. Note that late-morning drop-off may delay delivery until the next day, and most places are closed on Sunday; a Monday morning pick-up time may cramp your plans. Confirm closing time when you drop off, and set an alarm to remind you to pick up.

Money

Here's my basic strategy for using money in Europe:

- Upon arrival, head for a cash machine (ATM) at the airport and load up on local currency, using a debit card with low international transaction fees.

- Withdraw large amounts at each transaction (to limit fees) and keep your cash safe in a money belt.
- Pay for most items with cash.
- Pay for larger purchases with a credit card with low (or no) international fees.

PLASTIC VERSUS CASH

Although credit cards are widely accepted in Europe, day-to-day spending is generally more cash-based than in the US. I find cash is

the easiest—and sometimes only—way to pay for cheap food, bus fare, taxis, tips, and local guides. Some businesses (especially smaller ones, such as B&Bs and mom-and-pop cafés and shops) may charge you extra for using a credit card—or might not accept credit cards at all. Having cash on hand helps you out of a jam if your card randomly doesn't work.

I use my credit card to book and pay for hotel reservations, to buy advance tickets for events or sights, and to cover major expenses (such as car rentals or plane tickets). It can also be smart to use plastic near the end of your trip, to avoid another visit to the ATM.

WHAT TO BRING

I pack the following and keep it all safe in my money belt.

Debit Card: Use this at ATMs to withdraw local cash.

Credit Card: Use this to pay for larger items (at hotels, larger shops and restaurants, travel agencies, car-rental agencies, and so on).

Backup Card: Some travelers carry a third card (debit or credit; ideally from a different bank), in case one gets lost, demagnetized, eaten by a temperamental machine, or simply doesn't work.

US Dollars: I carry $100-200 US dollars as a backup. While you won't use it for day-to-day purchases, American cash in your money belt comes in handy for emergencies, such as if your ATM card stops working.

What NOT to Bring: Resist the urge to buy euros and pounds before your trip or you'll pay the price in bad stateside exchange rates. Wait until you arrive to withdraw money. I've yet to see a European airport that didn't have plenty of ATMs.

BEFORE YOU GO

Use this pre-trip checklist.

Know your cards. Debit cards from any major US bank will

Exchange Rates

I've priced things throughout this book in the local currencies. The Republic of Ireland uses the euro currency. Northern Ireland, which is part of the United Kingdom, has retained its traditional currency, the British pound sterling. Border towns in the North might take euros, but at a lousy exchange rate. (Check www.oanda.com for the latest exchange rates.)

1 euro (€1) = about $1.20
1 British pound (£1) = about $1.40

Republic of Ireland: To convert prices in euros to dollars, add about 20 percent: €20 = about $24, €50 = about $60. Just like the dollar, one euro (€) is broken down into 100 cents. You'll find coins ranging from €0.01 to €2, and bills ranging from €5 to €200 (bills over €50 are rarely used; €500 bills are being phased out).

Northern Ireland: To convert prices in pounds to dollars, add 40 percent: £20 = about $28, £50 = about $70. The British pound (£), also called a "quid," is broken into 100 pence (p). Pence means "cents." You'll find coins ranging from 1p to £2 and bills from £5 to £50. Fake pound coins are easy to spot (real coins have an inscription on their outside rims; the edges of fakes resemble tree bark).

Northern Ireland issues its own currency, which is worth the same as an English pound. If you're traveling on to Great Britain, note that English and Northern Ireland's Ulster pounds are technically interchangeable in both regions, although Ulster pounds are "undesirable" in Britain. Banks in either region will convert your Ulster pounds into English pounds at no charge. Don't worry about the coins, which are accepted throughout Great Britain and Northern Ireland.

work in any standard European bank's ATM (ideally, use a debit card with a Visa or MasterCard logo). As for credit cards, Visa and MasterCard are universal, American Express is less common, and Discover is unknown in Europe.

Know your PIN. Make sure you know the numeric, four-digit PIN for all of your cards, both debit and credit. Request it if you don't have one and allow time to receive the information by mail.

All credit and debit cards now have chips that authenticate and secure transactions. Europeans insert their chip cards into the payment machine slot, then enter a PIN. American cards should work in most transactions without a PIN—but may not work at self-service machines at train stations, toll booths, gas pumps, or parking lots. I've been inconvenienced a few times by self-service payment machines in Europe that wouldn't accept my card, but it's never caused me serious trouble.

If you're concerned, a few banks offer a chip-and-PIN card that works in almost all payment machines, including those from Andrews Federal Credit Union (www.andrewsfcu.org) and the State Department Federal Credit Union (www.sdfcu.org).

Report your travel dates. Let your bank know that you'll be using your debit and credit cards in Europe, and when and where you're headed.

Adjust your ATM withdrawal limit. Find out how much you can take out daily and ask for a higher daily withdrawal limit if you want to get more cash at once. Note that European ATMs will withdraw funds only from checking accounts; you're unlikely to have access to your savings account.

Ask about fees. For any purchase or withdrawal made with a card, you may be charged a currency conversion fee (1-3 percent), a Visa or MasterCard international transaction fee (1 percent), and—for debit cards—a $2-5 transaction fee each time you use a foreign ATM (some US banks partner with European banks, allowing you to use those ATMs with no fees—ask).

If you're getting a bad deal, consider getting a new debit or credit card. Reputable no-fee cards include those from Capital One, as well as Charles Schwab debit cards. Most credit unions and some airline loyalty cards have low-to-no international transaction fees.

IN EUROPE
Using Cash Machines

European cash machines have English-language instructions and work just like they do at home—except they spit out local currency instead of dollars, calculated at the day's standard bank-to-bank rate.

In most places, ATMs are easy to locate. When possible, withdraw cash from a bank-run ATM located just outside that bank. Ideally use it during the bank's opening hours; if your card is munched by the machine, you can go inside for help.

If your debit card doesn't work, try a lower amount—your request may have exceeded your withdrawal limit or the ATM's limit. If you still have a problem, try a different ATM or come back later—your bank's network may be temporarily down.

Avoid "independent" ATMs, such as Travelex, Euronet, Moneybox, Cardpoint, and Cashzone. These have high fees, can be less secure than a bank ATM, and may try to trick users with "dynamic currency conversion" (see below).

Exchanging Cash

Avoid exchanging money in Europe; it's a big rip-off. In a pinch you can always find exchange desks at major train stations or airports—convenient but with crummy rates. Banks in some countries may not exchange money unless you have an account with them.

Using Credit Cards

US cards no longer require a signature for verification, but don't be surprised if a European card reader generates a receipt for you to sign. Some card readers will accept your card as is; others may prompt you to enter your PIN (so it's important to know the code for each of your cards). If a cashier is present, you should have no problems.

At self-service payment machines (transit-ticket kiosks, parking, etc.), results are mixed, as US cards may not work for unattended transactions. If your card won't work, look for a cashier who can process your card manually—or pay in cash.

Drivers Beware: Be aware of potential problems using a US card to fill up at an unattended gas station, enter a parking garage, or exit a toll road. Carry cash and be prepared to move on to the next gas station if necessary. When approaching a toll plaza, use the "cash" lane.

Dynamic Currency Conversion

Some European merchants and hoteliers cheerfully charge you for converting your purchase price into dollars. If it's offered, refuse this "service" (called dynamic currency conversion, or DCC). You'll pay extra for the expensive convenience of seeing your charge in dollars. Some ATM machines also offer DCC, often in confusing or misleading terms. If an ATM offers to "lock in" or "guarantee" your conversion rate, choose "proceed without conversion." Other prompts might state, "You can be charged in dollars: Press YES for dollars, NO for euros or pounds." Always choose the local currency.

Security Tips

Pickpockets target tourists. To safeguard your cash, wear a money belt—a pouch with a strap that you buckle around your waist like a belt and tuck under your clothes. Keep your cash, credit cards, and passport secure in your money belt, and carry only a day's spending money in your front pocket or wallet.

Before inserting your card into an ATM, inspect the front. If anything looks crooked, loose, or damaged, it could be a sign of a card-skimming device. When entering your PIN, carefully block other people's view of the keypad.

Don't use a debit card for purchases. Because a debit card pulls funds directly from your bank account, potential charges incurred by a thief will stay on your account while the fraudulent use is investigated by your bank.

While traveling, to access your accounts online, be sure to use a secure connection (see page 558).

Damage Control for Lost Cards

If you lose your credit or debit card, report the loss immediately to the respective global customer-assistance centers. Call these 24-hour US numbers collect: Visa (tel. 303/967-1096), MasterCard (tel. 636/722-7111), and American Express (tel. 336/393-1111). In the Republic of Ireland, to make a collect call to the US, dial 1-800-550-000. In Northern Ireland, dial 0-800-89-0011. Press zero or stay on the line for an English-speaking operator. European toll-free numbers (listed by country) can be found at the websites for Visa and MasterCard.

You'll need to provide the primary cardholder's identification-verification details (such as birth date, mother's maiden name, or Social Security number). You can generally receive a temporary card within two or three business days in Europe (see www.ricksteves.com/help for more).

If you report your loss within two days, you typically won't be responsible for unauthorized transactions on your account, although many banks charge a liability fee of $50.

TIPPING

Tipping in Ireland isn't as automatic and generous as it is in the US. For special service, tips are appreciated, but not expected. As in the US, the proper amount depends on your resources, tipping philosophy, and the circumstances, but some general guidelines apply.

Restaurants: At a pub or restaurant with waitstaff, check the menu or your bill to see if the service is included; if not, tip about 10 percent. At pubs where you order food at the counter, a tip is not expected but is appreciated.

Taxis: For a typical ride, round up your fare a bit (for instance, if the fare is €9, give €10). If the cabbie hauls your bags and zips you to the airport to help you catch your flight, you might want to toss in a little more. But if you feel like you're being driven in circles or otherwise ripped off, skip the tip.

Services: In general, if someone in the tourism or service industry does a super job for you, a small tip of a euro or two is appro-

PRACTICALITIES

priate...but not required. If you're not sure whether (or how much) to tip, ask a local for advice.

GETTING A VAT REFUND

Wrapped into the purchase price of your Irish souvenirs is a Value-Added Tax (VAT); it's 23 percent in the Republic and 20 percent in Northern Ireland. You're entitled to get most of that tax back if you purchase more than €30/£30 (about $36/$40) worth of goods at a store that participates in the VAT-refund scheme. Typically, you must ring up the minimum at a single retailer—you can't add up your purchases from various shops to reach the required amount. (If the store ships the goods to your US home, VAT is not assessed on your purchase.)

Getting your refund is straightforward...and worthwhile if you spend a significant amount on souvenirs.

Get the paperwork. Have the merchant completely fill out the necessary refund document, called a "Tax-Free Shopping Cheque." You'll have to present your passport. Get the paperwork done before you leave the store to ensure you'll have everything you need (including your original sales receipt).

Get your stamp at the border or airport. Process your VAT document at your last stop in the European Union (such as at the airport) with the customs agent who deals with VAT refunds. Arrive an additional hour before you need to check in to allow time to find the customs office—and to stand in line. Some customs desks are positioned before airport security; confirm the location before going through security.

It's best to keep your purchases in your carry-on. If they're too large or dangerous to carry on (such as knives), pack them in your checked bags and alert the check-in agent. You'll be sent (with your tagged bag) to a customs desk outside security; someone will examine your bag, stamp your paperwork, and put your bag on the belt. You're not supposed to use your purchased goods before you leave. If you show up at customs wearing your new Irish sweater, officials might look the other way—or deny you a refund.

Collect your refund. Many merchants work with a service, such as Global Blue or Premier Tax Free, that have offices at major airports, ports, or border crossings (either before or after security, probably strategically located near a duty-free shop). These services, which extract a 4 percent fee, can refund your money immediately in cash or credit your card (within two billing cycles). Other refund services may require you to mail the documents from home, or more quickly, from your point of departure (using an envelope you've prepared in advance or one that's been provided by the merchant). You'll then have to wait—it can take months.

PRACTICALITIES

PRACTICALITIES

CUSTOMS FOR AMERICAN SHOPPERS

You can take home $800 worth of items per person duty-free, once every 31 days. Many processed and packaged foods are allowed, including vacuum-packed cheeses, dried herbs, jams, baked goods, candy, chocolate, oil, vinegar, mustard, and honey. Fresh fruits and vegetables and most meats are not allowed, with exceptions for some canned items. As for alcohol, you can bring in one liter duty-free (it can be packed securely in your checked luggage, along with any other liquid-containing items).

To bring alcohol (or liquid-packed foods) in your carry-on bag on your flight home, buy it at a duty-free shop at the airport. You'll increase your odds of getting it onto a connecting flight if it's packaged in a "STEB"—a secure, tamper-evident bag. But stay away from liquids in opaque, ceramic, or metallic containers, which usually cannot be successfully screened (STEB or no STEB).

For details on allowable goods, customs rules, and duty rates, visit http://help.cbp.gov.

Sightseeing

Sightseeing can be hard work. Use these tips to make your visits to Ireland's finest sights meaningful, fun, efficient, and painless.

MAPS AND NAVIGATION TOOLS

A good map is essential for efficient navigation while sightseeing. The maps in this book are concise and simple, designed to help you locate recommended destinations, sights, and local TIs, where you can pick up more in-depth maps. Maps with even more detail are sold at newsstands and bookstores.

Train travelers do fine with a simple rail map (available as part of the free Intercity Timetable found at Irish train stations) and city maps from the TI offices. (You can get free maps of Dublin and Ireland from the national tourist-office websites before you go; see "Tourist Information" at the beginning of this chapter.)

You can also use a mapping app on your mobile device. Be aware that pulling up maps or looking up turn-by-turn walking directions on the fly requires an Internet connection: To use this feature, it's smart to get an international data plan (see page 554). With Google Maps or City Maps 2Go, it's possible to download a map while online, then go offline and navigate without incurring data-roaming charges, though you can't search for an address or get real-time walking directions. A handful of other apps—including Apple Maps, OffMaps, Maps.me, and Navfree—also allow you to use maps offline.

PLAN AHEAD

Set up an itinerary that allows you to fit in all your must-see sights. For a one-stop look at opening hours, see the "At a Glance" sidebars for Dublin, Dingle, and Belfast. Most sights keep stable hours, but you can easily confirm the latest by checking with the TI or visiting museum websites.

Don't put off visiting a must-see sight—you never know when a place will close unexpectedly for a holiday, strike, or restoration. Many museums are closed or have reduced hours at least a few days a year, especially on holidays such as Christmas, New Year's, and Labor Day (first Monday in May). A list of holidays is on page 580; check online for possible museum closures during your trip. In summer, some sights may stay open late; in the off-season, hours may be shorter.

Going at the right time helps avoid crowds. This book offers tips on the best times to see specific sights. Try visiting popular sights very early or very late. Make that first sight of the day the one that is the most physically or mentally demanding, while you've still got wind in your sails. Evening visits are usually peaceful, with fewer crowds.

If you plan to hire a local guide, reserve ahead by email. Popular guides can get booked up.

Study up. To get the most out of the self-guided walks and sight descriptions in this book, read them before you visit.

AT SIGHTS

Here's what you can typically expect:

Entering: Be warned that you may not be allowed to enter if you arrive less than 30 to 60 minutes before closing time. And guards start ushering people out well before the actual closing time, so don't save the best for last.

Many sights have a security check, where you must open your bag or send it through a metal detector. Allow extra time for these lines in your planning. Some sights require you to check daypacks and coats. (If you'd rather not check your daypack, try carrying it tucked under your arm like a purse as you enter.)

Photography: If the museum's photo policy isn't clearly posted, ask a guard. Generally, taking photos without a flash or tripod is allowed. Some sights ban photos altogether; others ban selfie sticks.

Temporary Exhibits: Museums may show special exhibits in addition to their permanent collection. Some exhibits are included in the entry price, while others come at an extra cost (which you may have to pay even if you don't want to see the exhibit).

Expect Changes: Artwork can be on tour, on loan, out sick, or shifted at the whim of the curator. Pick up a floor plan as you enter, and ask museum staff if you can't find a particular item.

Audioguides and Apps: Many sights rent audioguides, which generally offer dry-but-useful recorded descriptions (sometimes included with admission). If you bring your own earbuds, you can enjoy better sound and avoid holding the device to your ear. To save money, bring a Y-jack and share one audioguide with your travel partner. Museums and sights often offer free apps that you can download to your mobile device (check their websites).

Services: Important sights may have a reasonably priced on-site café or cafeteria (handy places to rejuvenate during a long visit). The WCs at sights are free and generally clean.

Before Leaving: At the gift shop, scan the postcard rack or thumb through a guidebook to be sure that you haven't overlooked something that you'd like to see.

Every sight or museum offers more than what is covered in this book. Use the information in this book as an introduction—not the final word.

SIGHTSEEING PASSES

Ireland offers two passes (each covering a different set of sights) that can save you money. Both are smart, although the second packs more punch for two people traveling together (2-for-1 entries for couples as compared to 10-25 percent off for individuals).

Heritage Card: This pass gets you into 98 historical monuments, gardens, and parks maintained by the OPW (Office of Public Works) in the Republic of Ireland. It will pay off if you visit eight or more included sights over the course of your trip (€40; seniors age 60 and older-€30, students-€10, families-€90, covers entry to all Heritage sights for one year, comes with handy map and list of sights' hours and prices, purchase at first Heritage

sight you visit, cash only, tel. 01/647-6592, www.heritageireland.ie, heritagecard@opw.ie). People traveling by car are most likely to get their money's worth out of the card.

An energetic sightseer with three weeks in Ireland will probably pay to see nearly all 20 of the following sights (covered in this book). Without the Heritage Card, your costs will add up fast, and you'll waste time buying tickets. (Be aware that advance reservations are recommended for both Kilmainham Gaol and Brú na Bóinne.)

• Dublin Castle-€10
• Kilmainham Gaol-€8 (Dublin)

- Brú na Bóinne (Knowth and Newgrange tombs and Visitors Centre-€13—Boyne Valley)
- Battle of the Boyne-€5
- Hill of Tara-€5 (Boyne Valley)
- Old Mellifont Abbey-€5 (Boyne Valley)
- Trim Castle-€5 (Boyne Valley)
- Glendalough Visitors Centre-€5 (Wicklow Mountains)
- Kilkenny Castle-€8
- Rock of Cashel-€8
- Reginald's Tower-€5 (Waterford)
- Charles Fort-€5 (Kinsale)
- Desmond Castle-€5 (Kinsale)
- Muckross House-€9 (near Killarney)
- Derrynane House-€5 (Ring of Kerry)
- Garnish Island Gardens-€5 (near Kenmare)
- Great Blasket Centre-€5 (near Dingle)
- Ennis Friary-€5 (Ennis)
- Dun Aengus-€5 (Inishmore, Aran Islands)
- Glenveagh Castle and National Park-€7 (Donegal)

Together these sights total €128; a pass saves you €88 per person over paying individual entrance fees. Note that scheduled tours given by OPW guides at any of these sites are included in the price of admission—regardless of whether you have the Heritage Card. The card covers no sights in Northern Ireland.

Heritage Island Visitor Attraction Map: Ambitious travelers covering more ground can grab this free map adorned with discount coupons (get it at any TI or participating site; skip the €8.45 accompanying 56-page booklet sold online). The map doesn't overlap with the above Heritage Card sights and provides a variety of discounts (usually 2-for-1 entries, but occasionally 10-25 percent off) at 88 sights in both the Republic of Ireland and Northern Ireland. This is a great no-brainer addition, especially for two people traveling together. At some sites that already have free admission, you may get 10 percent off purchases at their shop or café. Study the full list of sights first (tel. 01/775-3870, www.heritageisland. com).

Discounted sights on this map include:
- Trinity College Library (Book of Kells, Dublin)
- St. Patrick's Cathedral (Dublin)
- Dublin City Hall
- Dublinia
- Guinness Storehouse (Dublin)
- *Jeanie Johnston* Tall Ship and Famine Museum (Dublin)
- Irish National Stud (Kildare)
- Powerscourt Gardens (Enniskerry)
- Avondale House (Wicklow Mountains)

- *Dunbrody* Famine Ship (New Ross)
- Waterford Crystal Visitor Centre
- Blarney Castle (County Cork)
- Burren Centre (Kilfenora)
- Aillwee Cave (Burren)
- Atlantic Edge exhibit (Cliffs of Moher)
- Clare Museum (Ennis)
- Kylemore Abbey (Letterfrack)
- Strokestown Park National Famine Museum (Strokestown)
- Mount Stewart House (near Bangor)
- Titanic Belfast (Belfast)
- Ulster Museum (Belfast)
- Ulster Folk Park and Transport Museum (Cultra)
- Belleek Pottery Visitors Centre (Belleek)
- Ulster American Folk Park (Omagh)

Sleeping

I favor hotels and restaurants that are handy to your sightseeing activities. Rather than list hotels scattered throughout a city, I choose hotels in my favorite neighborhoods. My recommendations run the gamut, from dorm beds to fancy rooms with all the comforts. Outside of Dublin you can expect to find good doubles for $100-150, including tax and a cooked breakfast.

Extensive and opinionated listings of good-value rooms are a major feature of this book's Sleeping sections. I like places that are clean, central, relatively quiet at night, reasonably priced, friendly, small enough to have a hands-on owner or manager and stable staff, and run with a respect for Irish traditions. I'm more impressed by a convenient location and a fun-loving philosophy than flat-screen TVs and a fancy gym. Most places I recommend fall short of perfection. But if I can find a place with most of these features, it's a keeper.

Book your accommodations as soon as your itinerary is set, especially to stay at one of my top listings or if you'll be traveling during busy times. Also reserve in advance for Dublin for any weekend, for Galway during its many peak-season events, and for Dingle throughout July and August. See page 580 for a list of major holidays and festivals throughout Ireland; for tips on making reservations, see page 538.

Some people make reservations as they travel, calling hotels and B&Bs a few days to a week before their arrival. If this is you, understand that beggars can't be choosers and many options might be booked up. If you anticipate crowds (worst weekdays at business destinations and weekends at tourist locales), on the day you want to check in, call hotels at about 9:00 or 10:00, when the receptionist knows who'll be checking out and which rooms will be available. Some apps—such as HotelTonight.com—specialize in last-minute rooms, often at business-class hotels in big cities.

The Republic of Ireland and Northern Ireland have banned smoking in the workplace (pubs, offices, taxicabs, etc.), but some hotels still have a floor or two of rooms where guests are allowed to smoke. If you don't want a room that a smoker might have occupied before you, let the hotelier know when you make your reservation. All of my recommended B&Bs prohibit smoking. Even in places that allow smoking in the sleeping rooms, breakfast rooms are nearly always smoke-free.

Loud and rowdy Irish stag/hen (bachelor/bachelorette) parties are plentiful on weekends. This enthusiastic, alcohol-assisted merriment can interfere with a much-needed night's sleep. If you're a light sleeper, bring earplugs and think twice before booking a weekend room in a hotel with a pub on the ground floor. Steer clear of establishments that trumpet "stags and hens welcome" on their websites.

RATES AND DEALS

I've categorized my recommended accommodations based on price, indicated with a dollar-sign rating (see sidebar). The price ranges suggest an estimated cost for a one-night stay in a double room with a private toilet and shower in high season, include a hearty breakfast, and assume you're booking directly with the hotel (not through a booking site, which extracts a commission). Room prices can fluctuate significantly with demand and amenities (size, views, room class, and so on), but these relative price categories remain constant.

Room rates are especially volatile at larger hotels that use "dynamic pricing" to set rates. Prices can skyrocket during festivals and conventions, while business hotels can have deep discounts on weekends when demand plummets. Of the many hotels I recommend, it's difficult to say which will be the best value on a given day—until you do your homework.

Once your dates are set, check the specific price for your preferred stay at several hotels. You can do this either by comparing prices on a site such as Hotels.com or Booking.com, or by checking the hotels' own websites. To get the best deal, contact my family-run hotels directly by phone or email. When you go direct, the owner avoids the 20 percent commission, giving them wiggle room to offer you a discount, a nicer room, or free breakfast if it's not already included (see the "Making Hotel Reservations" sidebar, later). If you prefer to book online or are considering a hotel chain, it's to your advantage to use the hotel's website.

Some hotels offer a discount to those who pay cash or stay lon-

PRACTICALITIES

PRACTICALITIES

Sleep Code

Hotels are classified based on the average price of a typical en suite double room with breakfast in high season.

$$$$	**Splurge:**	Most rooms over €170/£140
$$$	**Pricier:**	€130-170/£110-140
$$	**Moderate:**	€90-130/£80-110
$	**Budget:**	€50-90/£50-80
¢	**Backpacker:**	Under €50/£50
RS%	**Rick Steves discount**	

Unless otherwise noted, credit cards are accepted and free Wi-Fi is available. Comparison-shop by checking prices at several hotels (on each hotel's own website, on a booking site, or by email). For the best deal, *book directly with the hotel*. Ask for a discount if paying in cash; if the listing includes **RS%**, request a Rick Steves discount.

ger than three nights. To cut costs further, try asking for a cheaper room (for example, with a shared bathroom or no window) or offer to skip breakfast (if included).

Additionally, some accommodations offer a special discount for Rick Steves readers, indicated in this guidebook by the abbreviation "**RS%.**" Discounts vary: Ask for details when you reserve. Generally, to qualify you must book direct (that is, not through a booking site), mention this book when you reserve, show this book upon arrival, and sometimes pay cash or stay a certain number of nights. In some cases, you may need to enter a discount code (which I've provided in the listing) in the booking form on the hotel's website. Rick Steves discounts apply to readers with ebooks as well as printed books. Understandably, discounts do not apply to promotional rates.

When establishing prices, confirm if the charge is per person or per room (if a price is too good to be true, it's probably per person). Because many places in Ireland charge per person, small groups often pay the same for a single and a double as they would for a triple. In this book, I've categorized hotels based on the per-room price, not per person.

LODGING VOUCHERS

Many US travel agents sell vouchers for lodging in Ireland. In essence, you're paying ahead of time for your lodging, with the assurance that you'll be staying in B&Bs and guesthouses that live up to certain standards. I don't recommend buying these, since your choices will be limited to only the places in Ireland that accept vouchers. Sure, there are hundreds in the program to choose from. But in this guidebook, I list any place that offers a good value—a useful location, nice hosts, and a comfortable and clean room—regardless of what club they do or don't belong to. Lots of great B&Bs choose not to participate in the voucher program because they have to pay to be part of it, slicing into their already thin profit. And many Irish B&B owners lament the long wait between the date a traveler stays with them and the date the voucher company reimburses them. In short, skip it. The voucher program is just an expensive middleman between you and the innkeeper.

TYPES OF ACCOMMODATIONS

Ireland has a rating system for hotels and B&Bs. These stars and shamrocks are supposed to imply quality, but I find that they mean only that the place sporting symbols is paying dues to the tourist board. These rating systems often have little to do with value: One of my favorite Irish B&Bs (also loved by readers) will never be tourist-board approved because it has no dedicated breakfast room (a strict requirement in the eyes of the board). Instead, guests sit around a large kitchen table and enjoy a lively chat with the friendly hosts as they cook breakfast 10 feet away.

Hotels

Know the terminology: "Twin" means two single beds, "double" means one double bed. If you'll take either one, let them know, or you might be needlessly turned away. An "en suite" room has a bathroom (toilet and shower/tub) inside the room; a room with a "private bathroom" can mean that the bathroom is all yours, but it's across the hall; and a "standard" room has access to a bathroom down the hall that's shared with other rooms. Figuring there's little difference between "en suite" and "private" rooms, some places charge the same for both. If you want your own bathroom inside the room, request "en suite." If money's tight, ask for a standard room. You'll almost always have a sink in your room, and as more rooms go "en suite," the hallway bathroom is shared with fewer standard rooms.

Some hotels can add an extra bed (for a small charge) to turn a double into a triple; some offer larger rooms for four or more people (I call these "family rooms" in the listings). If there's space for an extra cot, they'll cram it in for you. In general, a triple room is cheaper than the cost of a double and a single. Three or four people can economize by requesting one big room.

Most hotels offer family deals, which means that parents with young children can easily get a room with an extra child's bed or a discount for a larger room. Call to negotiate the price. Teenagers are generally charged as adults. Kids under five sleep almost free.

Note that to be called a "hotel," a place technically must have

Making Hotel Reservations

Reserve your rooms as soon as you've pinned down your travel dates. For busy national holidays, it's wise to reserve far in advance (see page 580).

Requesting a Reservation: For family-run hotels, it's generally cheaper to book your room direct via email or a phone call. For business-class hotels, or if you'd rather book online, reserve directly through the hotel's official website (not a booking agency's site). For complicated requests, send an email.

Here's what the hotelier wants to know:

- type(s) of rooms you need and size of your party
- number of nights you'll stay
- your arrival and departure dates, written European-style—day/month/year (for example, 18/06/20 or 18 June 2020); include the total number of nights
- special requests (such as en suite bathroom vs. down the hall, cheapest room, twin beds vs. double bed, quiet room)
- applicable discounts (such as a Rick Steves reader discount, cash discount, or promotional rate).

Confirming a Reservation: Most places will request a credit-card number to hold your room. If you're using an online reservation form, look for the *https* or a lock icon at the top of your browser. If you book direct, you can email, call, or fax this information.

Canceling a Reservation: If you must cancel, it's courteous—and smart—to do so with as much notice as possible, especially for smaller family-run places. Cancellation policies can be strict;

certain amenities, including a 24-hour reception (though this rule is loosely applied). TVs are standard in rooms.

Arrival and Check-In: Hotel elevators are becoming more common, though some older buildings still lack them. You may have to climb a flight of stairs to reach the elevator (if so, you can ask the front desk for help carrying your bags up). Elevators are typically very small—pack light, or you may need to send your bags up without you.

When you check in, the receptionist will normally ask for your passport and keep it for anywhere from a couple of minutes to a couple of hours. The EU requires that hotels collect your name, nationality, and ID number. Relax. Americans are notorious for making this chore more difficult than it needs to be.

If you're arriving in the morning, your room probably won't be ready. Drop your bag safely at the hotel and dive right into sightseeing.

In Your Room: More pillows and blankets are usually in the

From: rick@ricksteves.com
Sent: Today
To: info@hotelcentral.com
Subject: Reservation request for 19-22 July

Dear Hotel Central,

I would like to stay at your hotel. Please let me know if you have a room available and the price for:
• 2 people
• Double bed and en suite bathroom in a quiet room
• Arriving 19 July, departing 22 July (3 nights)

Thank you!
Rick Steves

read the fine print or ask about these before you book. Many discount deals require prepayment, with no cancellation refunds.

Reconfirming a Reservation: Always call or email to reconfirm your room reservation a few days in advance. For B&Bs or very small hotels, I call again on my day of arrival to tell my host what time to expect me (especially important if arriving late—after 17:00).

Phoning: For tips on calling hotels overseas, see page 556.

closet or available on request. Towels and linens aren't always replaced every day. Hang your towel up to dry.

Most hotel rooms have a TV, telephone, and free Wi-Fi (although in old buildings with thick walls, the Wi-Fi signal doesn't always make it to the rooms; sometimes it's only available in the lobby). There's often a guest computer with Internet access in the lobby. Simpler places rarely have a room phone, but often have free Wi-Fi.

Breakfast and Meals: Small hotels and B&Bs serve a hearty "Irish fry" breakfast (more about B&B breakfasts later). Because B&Bs owners are often also the cook, there's usually a limited time span when breakfast is served (typically about an hour, starting at about 8:00). Modern hotels usually have an attached restaurant.

Hotelier Help: Hoteliers can be a good source of advice. Most know their city well, and can assist you with everything from public transit and airport connections to finding a good restaurant, the nearest launderette, or a late-night pharmacy.

To guard against theft in your room, keep valuables out of

sight. Some rooms come with a safe, and other hotels have safes at the front desk. I've never bothered using one and in a lifetime of travel, I've never had anything stolen from my room.

Checking Out: While it's customary to pay for your room upon departure, it can be a good idea to settle your bill the day before, when you're not in a hurry and while the manager's in. That way you'll have time to discuss and address any points of contention.

Hotel Hassles: Even at the best places, mechanical breakdowns occur: Sinks leak, hot water turns cold, toilets may gurgle or smell, the Wi-Fi goes out, or the air-conditioning dies when you need it most. Report your concerns clearly and calmly at the front desk. For more complicated problems, don't expect instant results. Above all, keep a positive attitude. Remember, you're on vacation. If your hotel or B&B is a disappointment, spend more time out enjoying the place you came to see.

If you suspect night noise will be a problem (if, for instance, your room is over a rowdy pub), ask for a quieter room in the back or on an upper floor. Pubs are plentiful and packed with revelers on weekend nights. (James Joyce once said it would be a good puzzle to try to walk across Dublin without passing a pub.)

Small Hotels and B&Bs

Compared to hotels, bed-and-breakfast places give you double the cultural intimacy for half the price. While you may lose some of the conveniences of a hotel—such as lounges, in-room phones, frequent bedsheet changes, and being able to pay with a credit card—I happily make the trade-off for the lower rates and personal touches. If you have a reasonable but limited budget, skip hotels and go the B&B way. In 2019, you'll generally pay €45-70 (about $55-80) per person for a double room in a B&B in Ireland. Prices include a big cooked breakfast. The amount of coziness, doilies, tea, and biscuits tossed in varies tremendously.

You'll likely need to pay cash for your room. Think ahead so you have enough cash to pay up when you check out. Paying in cash helps keep prices down: Some of my favorite B&Bs tell me the fee for a small business to accept credit cards can exceed €750 a year (money they likely would not make back by offering the service).

B&Bs range from large guesthouses with 10-15 rooms to small

homes renting out a couple of spare bedrooms, but typically have six rooms or fewer. A "townhouse" or "house" is like a big B&B or a small family-run hotel—with fewer amenities but more character than a hotel. The philosophy of the management determines the character of a place more than its size and facilities offered. Avoid places run as a business by absentee owners (their hired hands often don't provide the level of service that pride of ownership brings). My top listings are run by people who enjoy welcoming the world to their breakfast table.

Book direct. If you buy the lodging vouchers sold by many US travel agents, you'll only be taking money from the innkeeper and putting it in the pocket of a middleman. If you have a local TI book a room for you or use a website like Booking.com, the B&B will pay a 15 percent commission. But if you book direct, the B&B gets it all, and you'll have a better chance of getting a discount. I have negotiated special discounts with this book (often for payment in cash, and always for booking direct).

Small hotels and B&Bs come with their own etiquette and quirks. Keep in mind that B&B owners are subject to the whims

of their guests—if you're getting up early, so are they; and if you check in late, they'll wait up for you. It's polite to call ahead to confirm your reservation the day before and give them a rough estimate of your arrival time. This allows your hosts to plan their day and run errands before or after you arrive...and also allows them to give you specific directions for driving or walking to their place. If you are arriving past the agreed time, please call and let them know.

A few tips: B&B proprietors are selective as to whom they invite in for the night. At some B&Bs, children are not welcome. Risky-looking people (two or more single men are often assumed to be troublemakers) find many places suddenly full. If you'll be staying for more than one night, you are a "desirable." In popular weekend-getaway spots, you're unlikely to find a place to take you for Saturday night only. If my listings are full, ask for guidance. (Mentioning this book can help.) Owners usually work together and can call up an ally to land you a bed.

B&Bs serve a hearty "Irish fry" breakfast (for more about Irish breakfast, see "Eating," later in this chapter). You'll quickly figure out which parts of the "fry" you do and don't like. B&B owners prefer to know this up front, rather than serving you the whole she-bang and throwing out uneaten food. Because your B&B owner is also the cook, there's usually a quite limited time span when break-fast is served (typically about an hour, starting at about 8:00—make sure you know the exact time before you turn in for the night). It's an unwritten rule that guests shouldn't show up at the very end of

Hotels vs. Booking Websites vs. Consumers

In the last decade it's become almost impossible for independent-minded, family-run hotels to survive without playing the game as dictated by the big players in the online booking world. Priceline's Booking.com and Expedia's Hotels.com take roughly 80 percent of this business. Hoteliers note that without this online presence, "We become almost invisible." Online booking services demand about a 20 percent commission. And in order to be listed, a hotel must promise that its website does not undercut the price on the third-party's website. Without that restriction, hoteliers could say, "Sure, sell our rooms for whatever markup you like, and we'll continue to offer a fair rate to travelers who come to us directly"—but that's not allowed.

Here's the work-around: For independent and family-run hotels, book direct by email or phone, in which case hotel owners are free to give you whatever price they like. Research the price online, and then ask them to split the difference—the hotel charges you 10 percent less but pockets 10 percent more. Or you can ask for a free breakfast (if not included) or free upgrade.

If you do book online, be sure to use the hotel's website (you'll likely pay the same price as via a booking site, but your money goes to the hotel, not agency commissions).

As consumers, remember: Whenever you book with an online booking service, you're adding a needless middleman who takes roughly 20 percent. If you'd like to support small, family-run hotels whose world is more difficult than ever, book direct.

the breakfast period and expect a full cooked breakfast. If you do arrive at the last minute (or if you need to leave before breakfast is served), most B&B hosts are happy to let you help yourself to cereal, fruit or juice, and coffee; ask politely if it's possible.

Some B&Bs stock rooms with an electric kettle, along with cups, tea bags, and coffee packets (if you prefer decaf, buy a jar at a grocery, and dump the contents into a baggie for easy packing).

B&Bs are not hotels. Think of your host as a friendly acquaintance who's invited you to stay in her home, rather than someone you're paying to wait on you. Americans often assume they'll get new towels each day. The Irish don't. Hang them up to dry and reuse. And pack a washcloth (many Irish B&Bs don't provide them).

Electrical outlets sometimes have switches that turn the current on or off; if your electrical appliance isn't working, flip the switch at the outlet. When you unplug your appliance, don't forget your adapter—most B&Bs have boxes of various adapters and converters that guests have left behind (which is handy if you left yours at the last place).

Most B&Bs come with thin walls and doors. This can make for a noisy night, especially with people walking down the hall to use the bathroom. If you're a light sleeper, bring earplugs. And please be quiet in the halls and in your rooms (gently shut your door, talk softly, and keep the TV volume low)...those of us getting up early will thank you for it.

Virtually all rooms have sinks. You'll likely encounter unusual bathroom fixtures. The "pump toilet" has a flushing handle that doesn't kick in unless you push it just right: too hard or too soft, and it won't go. (Be decisive but not ruthless.) There's also the "dial-a-shower," an electronic box under the showerhead where you'll turn a dial to select the heat of the water, and (sometimes with a separate dial or button) turn on or shut off the flow of water. If you can't find the switch to turn on the shower, it may be just outside the bathroom.

Your B&B bedroom might not include a phone. Some B&B owners will allow you to use their phone, but understandably they don't want to pay for long-distance charges. If you must use their phone, keep the call short (5-10 minutes max). If you plan to stay in B&Bs and make frequent calls, consider bringing a mobile phone or buying one in Ireland (see page 555). At a B&B, some rooms might have better Wi-Fi reception than others; usually the ground-floor lobby or breakfast room is your best bet.

A few B&B owners are also pet owners. And, while pets are rarely allowed into guest rooms, and B&B proprietors are typically very tidy, those with pet allergies might be bothered. I've tried to list which B&Bs have pets, but if you're allergic, ask about pets when you reserve.

Big, Cheap, Modern Hotels

Hotel chains—popular with budget tour groups—offer predictably comfortable, no-frills accommodations at reasonable prices. These hotels are popping up in big cities in Ireland. They can be located near the train station, in the city center, on major arterials, and outside the city center. What you lose in charm, you gain in savings.

I can't stress this enough: Check online for the cheapest deals. But be sure to go through the hotel's website rather than an online middleman.

Chain hotels are ideal for families, offering simple, clean, and modern rooms for up to four people (two adults/two children) for €110-165, depending on the location. Note that couples often pay the same price for a room as do families (up to four). Most rooms have a double bed, single bed, five-foot trundle bed, private shower, WC, TV, and Wi-Fi. Hotels usually have an attached restaurant,

PRACTICALITIES

good security, an elevator, and a 24-hour staffed reception desk. Of course, they're as cozy as a Motel 6, but many travelers love them. You can book online (be sure to check their websites for deals) or over the phone with a credit card, then pay when you check in. When you check out, just drop off the key, Lee.

The biggies are **Jurys Inn** (call their hotels directly or book online at www.jurysinns.com), **Comfort/Quality Inns** (Republic of Ireland tel. 1-800-500-600, Northern Ireland tel. 0800-444-444, US tel. 877-424-6423, www.choicehotels.com), and **Travelodge** (also has freeway locations for tired drivers, reservation center in Britain tel. 08700-850-950, www.travelodge.co.uk).

Short-Term Rentals

A short-term rental—whether an apartment, house, or room in a local's home—is an increasingly popular alternative, especially if you plan to settle in one location for several nights. For stays longer than a few days, you can usually find a rental that's comparable to—and cheaper than—a hotel room with similar amenities. Plus, you'll get a behind-the-scenes peek into how locals live.

Many places require a minimum night stay, and compared to hotels, rentals usually have less-flexible cancellation policies. And you're generally on your own: There's no hotel reception desk, breakfast, or daily cleaning service.

Finding Accommodations: Aggregator websites such as Airbnb, FlipKey, Booking.com, and the HomeAway family of sites (HomeAway, VRBO, and VacationRentals) let you browse properties and correspond directly with European property owners or managers. If you prefer to work from a curated list of accommodations, consider using a rental agency such as InterhomeUSA.com or RentaVilla.com. Agency-represented apartments typically cost more, but this method often offers more help and safeguards than booking direct. Both of Ireland's tourism websites (www.discoverireland.ie and www.discovernorthernireland.com) are reliable sources.

Before you commit, be clear on the details, location, and amenities. I like to virtually "explore" the neighborhood using the Street View feature on Google Maps. Also consider the proximity to public transportation, and how well-connected the property is with the rest of the city. Ask about amenities (elevator, air-conditioning, laundry, Wi-Fi, parking, etc.). Reviews from previous guests can help identify trouble spots.

Think about the kind of experience you want: Just a key and an affordable bed...or a chance to get to know a local? There are typically two kinds of hosts: those who want minimal interaction with their guests, and hosts who are friendly and may want to interact with you. Read the promotional text and online reviews to help shape your decision.

Apartments and Rental Houses: If you're staying somewhere for four nights or longer, it's worth considering an apartment—sometimes called a "flat" in Ireland—or rental house (shorter stays aren't worth the hassle of arranging key pickup, buying groceries, etc.). Apartment or house rentals can be especially cost-effective for groups and families. European apartments, like hotel rooms, tend to be small by US standards. But they often come with laundry machines and small, equipped kitchens, making it easier and cheaper to dine in. If you make good use of the kitchen (and Europe's great produce markets), you'll save on your meal budget.

Rooms in Private Homes: Renting a room in someone's home is a good option for those traveling alone, as you're more likely to find true single rooms—with just one single bed, and a price to match. Beds range from air-mattress-in-living-room basic to plush-B&B-suite posh. Some places allow you to book for a single night; if staying for several nights, you can buy groceries just as you would in a rental house. While you can't expect your host to also be your tour guide—or even to provide you with much info—some may be interested in getting to know the travelers who come through their home.

Other Options: Swapping homes with a local works for people with an appealing place to offer, and who can live with the idea of having strangers in their home (don't assume where you live is not interesting to Europeans). A good place to start is HomeExchange. To sleep for free, Couchsurfing.com is a vagabond's alternative to Airbnb. It lists millions of outgoing members, who host fellow "surfers" in their homes.

Confirming and Paying: Many places require you to pay the entire balance before your trip. It's easiest and safest to pay through the site where you found the listing. Be wary of owners who want to take your transaction offline to avoid fees; this gives you no recourse if things go awry. Never agree to wire money (a key indicator of a fraudulent transaction).

Hostels

Ireland has hundreds of hostels of all shapes and sizes. Choose yours selectively; hostels can be historic castles or depressing tenements, serene and comfy or overrun by noisy school groups.

A hostel provides cheap beds in dorms where you sleep alongside strangers for about €25 per night. Travelers of any age are welcome if they don't mind dorm-style accommodations and meeting other travelers. Most hostels offer kitchen facilities, guest computers, Wi-Fi, and a self-service laundry. Hostels almost always pro-

Irish Castle Lodging

The stone castles that dot the Irish landscape are some of the most famous and evocative in the world. Built in the 11th to the 15th centuries, they were the fortified homes of Anglo-Norman settlers and Irish chieftains, designed for defense. Modern-day visitors can get an intimate feel for medieval Irish life by spending the night in one of these fortresses of yore.

These are not the modern, boxy hotels with cheesy crenellated rooflines that call themselves "castles," but the real thing (or in some instances a heavily modified version). The true-to-history castle lodgings are rustic, isolated tower houses, while the modified ones amount to fancy mansion splurges. Be honest about how much cushiness you need and don't be swept away with frilly Camelot film-set expectations.

Rustic

For an authentic experience, search out a real tower-house castle built by native Gaelic lords in the 1400s. Usually four to six stories high, these age-old fortifications sleep 8 to 12 and are rented to small groups (3 night minimum stay). A visiting cook may prepare meals, but all have self-catering kitchens so you can whip up some medieval fare of your own.

Authenticity comes with surprises, such as the occasional spider, drafty windowsill, or flake of medieval dust sprinkling down from original wicker-imprinted ceilings. Canopy beds protect you as you sleep...just like the lord and lady 600 years ago. You'll carry your bags up tight stone stairways and may have to share a bathroom. Wi-Fi can't handle the three-foot-thick walls, so unplug for a few days. However, floor heating and electrical lighting take the edge off "roughing it."

These remote castles don't come with fancy landscaping—your windows will likely overlook bogs or grazing land. Get clear directions and be sure to arrive in daylight. Prices vary wildly depending on number of nights and time of year. Figure €1,000 for two nights and up to €3,000 for a week (give or take a crown jewel). Split that cost by 10 friends and you've got the recipe for a unique, good-value evening à la the 15th century. Turn off the lights, light the candles, stoke up the fireplace, and uncork the

vide bedding, but the towel's up to you (though you can usually rent one for a small fee). Family and private rooms are often available.

Independent hostels tend to be easygoing, colorful, and informal (no membership required, www.hostelworld.com). You may pay slightly less by booking direct with the hostel. Ireland's Independent Holiday Hostels (www.hostels-ireland.com) is a network wine—a convivial night in a castle can be truly magical.

Three well worth considering can be found on www.historiccastlesofireland.com.

Ballyportry Castle (10 miles north of Ennis in County Clare) was built by a branch of the O'Brien family in the 15th century.

Turin Castle (9 miles east of Cong in County Mayo) was built by the locally powerful De Burgo family in the 13th century.

Ballybur Castle (5 miles south of Kilkenny town in County Kilkenny) was built in the 16th century as the seat of the Comerford clan.

Fancy

Despite their castle-like exteriors, these fancy versions are now castles in name only. In reality, they are plush, pampered estates with spas and adjacent golf courses. They have all the comforts you could ever expect, and then some. The current structure may indeed include a smaller fortified castle that once stood alone hundreds of years ago. But then wealthy Romantic-age Anglo-Irish aristocrats built luxurious additions and surrounded them with lush gardens and gurgling fountains. Real fortified castles would never have had the ground-floor bay windows you see on these palaces today.

These dolled-up dream-houses are not really a good value for your money unless you're looking for a fanciful indulgence to celebrate an anniversary or honeymoon. In summer months, don't expect basic room prices below €400 per night. The upside? A chance to live like a privileged character in a Victorian novel for a day or two.

A couple to consider:

Dromoland Castle (8 miles south of Ennis or 9 miles north of Shannon Airport, www.dromoland.ie) once secretly hosted Beatles John and George as they attempted to hide out during the height of "Beatlemania."

Ashford Castle (28 miles north of Galway near the town of Cong, www.ashfordcastle.com) has hosted Ron and Nancy Reagan, John Wayne, Maureen O'Hara, and the weddings of both former 007 Pierce Brosnan and champion golfer Rory McIlroy.

PRACTICALITIES

of independent hostels, requiring no membership and welcoming all ages. All IHH hostels are approved by Fáilte Ireland.

Official hostels are part of Hostelling International (HI) and share an online booking site (www.hihostels.com). HI hostels typically require that you be a member or pay extra per night.

The Good and Bad of Online Reviews

User-generated review sites and apps such as Yelp, Booking.com, and TripAdvisor can give you a consensus of opinions about everything from hotels and restaurants to sights and nightlife. If you scan reviews of a hotel and see several complaints about noise or a rotten location, it tells you something important that you'd never learn from the hotel's own website.

But as a guidebook writer, my sense is that there is a big difference between the uncurated information on a review site and a guidebook. A user-generated review is based on the experience of one person, who likely stayed at one hotel in a given city and ate at a few restaurants there (and who doesn't have much of a basis for comparison). A guidebook is the work of a trained researcher who, year after year, visits many alternatives to assess their relative value. I recently checked out some top-rated user-reviewed hotel and restaurant listings in various towns; when stacked up against their competitors, some were gems, while just as many were duds.

Both types of information have their place, and in many ways, they're complementary. If something is well-reviewed in a guidebook, and also gets good ratings on one of these sites, it's likely a winner.

Eating

Denis Leary once quipped, "Irish food isn't cuisine...it's penance." For years, Irish food was something you ate to survive rather than to savor. In this country, long considered the "land of potatoes," the diet reflected the economic circumstances. But times have changed. You'll find modern Irish cuisine delicious and varied. Expatriate chefs have come home with newly refined tastes, and immigrants have added a world of interesting flavors.

Modern Irish cuisine is skillfully prepared with fresh, local ingredients. Irish beef, lamb, and dairy products are among the EU's best. And there are streams full of trout and salmon and a rich ocean of fish and shellfish right offshore. While potatoes remain staples, they're often replaced with rice or pasta in many dishes. Try the local specialties wherever you happen to be eating.

The traditional breakfast, the "Irish Fry" (known in the North as the "Ulster Fry"), is a hearty way to start the day—with juice, tea or coffee, cereal, eggs, bacon, sausage, a grilled tomato, sautéed mushrooms, and optional black pudding (made from pigs' blood). Toast is served with butter and marmalade. Home-baked Irish soda bread can be an ambrosial eye-opener for those of us raised on Wonder Bread. This meal tides many travelers over until dinner. But there's nothing un-Irish about skipping the "fry"—few locals actually start their day with this heavy traditional breakfast. You can simply skip the heavier fare and enjoy the cereal, juice, toast, and tea (surprisingly, the Irish drink more tea per capita than the British).

I look for restaurants that are convenient to your hotel and sightseeing. When restaurant-hunting, choose a spot filled with locals, not tourists. Venturing even a block or two off the main drag leads to higher-quality food for less than half the price of the tourist-oriented places. Locals eat better at lower-rent locales.

Picnicking saves time and money. Try boxes of orange juice (pure, by the liter), fresh bread (especially Irish soda bread), tasty Cashel blue cheese, meat, a tube of mustard, local-eatin' apples, bananas, small tomatoes, a small tub of yogurt (it's drinkable), rice crackers, trail mix or nuts, plain digestive biscuits (the chocolate-covered ones melt), and any local specialties. At open-air markets and supermarkets, you can get produce in small quantities. Supermarkets often have good deli sections, packaged sandwiches, and sometimes salad bars. Hang on to the half-liter mineral-water bottles (sold everywhere for about €1.50). Buy juice in cheap liter boxes, then drink some and store the extra in your water bottle. I often munch a relaxed "meal on wheels" in a car, train, or bus to save 30 precious minutes for sightseeing.

If you're driving, pull over and grab a healthy snack at a roadside stand (Ireland's climate is ideal for strawberries...County Wexford claims the best spring/summer crop).

Tipping: At a sit-down place with table service, tip about 10 percent—unless the service charge is already listed on the bill. If you order at a counter, there's no need to tip.

RESTAURANT PRICING

I've categorized my recommended eateries based on price, indicated with a dollar-sign rating (see sidebar). The price ranges suggest the average price of a typical main course—but not necessarily a complete meal. Obviously, expensive items (like steak and seafood), fine wine, appetizers, and dessert can significantly increase your final bill.

The categories also indicate a place's personality: **Budget** eateries include street food, takeaway, order-at-the-counter shops, basic cafeterias, bakeries selling sandwiches, and so on. **Moderate** eateries are nice (but not fancy) sit-down restaurants, ideal for a

PRACTICALITIES

Restaurant Code

I've assigned each eatery a price category, based on the average cost of a typical main course. Drinks, desserts, and splurge items (steak and seafood) can raise the price considerably.

$$$$ **Splurge:** Most main courses over €25/£20
$$$ **Pricier:** €20-25/£15-20
$$ **Moderate:** €15-20/£10-15
$ **Budget:** Under €15/£10

In the Republic of Ireland, carryout fish-and-chips and other takeout food is **$**, a basic pub or sit-down eatery is **$$**, a gastropub or casual but more upscale restaurant is **$$$**, and a swanky splurge is **$$$$**.

straightforward, fill-the-tank meal. Most of my listings fall in this category—great for a good taste of local cuisine on a budget.

Pricier eateries are a notch up, with more attention paid to the setting, presentation, and cuisine. These are ideal for a memorable meal that doesn't break the bank. This category often includes affordable "destination" or "foodie" restaurants. And **splurge** eateries are dress-up-for-a-special-occasion-swanky—typically with an elegant setting, polished service, pricey and intricate cuisine, and an expansive (and expensive) wine list.

I haven't categorized places where you might assemble a picnic, snack, or graze: supermarkets, delis, ice cream-stands, cafés or bars specializing in drinks, chocolate shops, and so on. At classier restaurants, look for "early-bird specials," which allow you to eat well and affordably, but early (about 17:30-19:00).

PUB GRUB AND BEER

If beer is not your cup of tea, don't wine about it. Pubs are a basic part of the Irish social scene, and whether you're a teetotaler or a beer-guzzler, they should be a part of your travel here. Whether in rural villages or busy Dublin, a pub (short for "public house") is an extended living room where, if you don't mind the stickiness, you can feel the pulse of Ireland.

Smart travelers use pubs to eat, drink, get out of the rain, watch the latest sporting event, and make new friends. Unfortunately, many city pubs have been afflicted with an excess of brass, ferns, and video games. Today the most traditional atmospheric pubs are in Ireland's countryside and smaller towns.

Pub grub gets better every year—it's Ireland's best eating value. But don't expect high cuisine; this is, after all, comfort food. For about $20, you'll get a basic hot lunch or dinner in friendly surroundings. Pubs that are attached to restaurants, advertise their food, and are crowded with locals are more likely to have fresh food and a chef than sell lousy microwaved snacks.

Pub menus consist of a hearty assortment of traditional dishes, such as Irish stew (mutton with mashed potatoes, onions, carrots, and herbs), soups and chowders, coddle (bacon, pork sausages, potatoes, and onions stewed in layers), fish-and-chips, collar and cabbage (boiled bacon coated in bread crumbs and brown sugar, then baked and served with cabbage), boxty (potato pancake filled with fish, meat, or vegetables), and champ (potato mashed with milk and onions). Irish soda bread nicely rounds out a meal. In coastal areas, seafood is available, such as mackerel, mussels, and Atlantic salmon. There's seldom table service in Irish pubs. Order drinks and meals at the bar. Pay as you order, and only tip (by rounding up to avoid excess coinage) if you like the service. Don't expect every pub to offer grub. Some only have peanuts and potato chips.

I recommend certain pubs to eat in, and your B&B host is usually up-to-date on the best neighborhood pub grub. Ask for advice (but adjust for nepotism and cronyism, which run rampant).

When you say "a beer, please" in an Irish pub, you'll get a pint of Guinness (the tall blonde in a black dress). If you want a small beer, ask for a glass, which is a half-pint. Never rush your bartender when he's pouring a Guinness. It's an almost-sacred two-step process that requires time for the beer to settle.

The Irish take great pride in their beer. At pubs, long hand pulls are used to draw the traditional, rich-flavored "real ales" up from the cellar. These are the connoisseur's favorites: They're fermented naturally, vary from sweet to bitter, and often have a hoppy or nutty flavor. Experiment with obscure local microbrews (a small but growing presence on the Irish beer scene). Short hand pulls at the bar mean colder, fizzier, mass-produced, and less interesting keg beers. Stout is dark and more bitter, like Guinness. If you think you don't like Guinness, try it in Ireland. It doesn't travel well and is better in its homeland. Murphy's is a very good Guinness-like stout, but a bit smoother and milder. For a cold, refreshing, basic, American-style beer, ask for a lager, such as Harp. Ale drinkers swear by Smithwick's (I know I do). Caffrey's is a satisfying cross between stout and ale. Try the draft cider (sweet or dry)...carefully. The most common spirit is triple-distilled Irish whiskey. Teetotalers can order a soft drink.

Pubs are generally open daily from 11:00 to 23:30 and Sunday from noon to 22:30. Children are served food and soft drinks in pubs (sometimes in a courtyard or the

PRACTICALITIES

PRACTICALITIES

"My Goodness, My Guinness!"

Every year on March 17, bars around the US serve pint after pint of green beer. But if you go to Ireland on Saint Patrick's Day, the beer is never green. It's black—or actually "dark ruby," according to the Guinness Brewery.

In 1759, Arthur Guinness signed an astounding 9,000-year lease on a dilapidated Dublin brewery. The rent: £45 a year. Competition was fierce among Dublin brewers, and friends of the 34-year-old entrepreneur thought his idea was ridiculous. He began pumping out two varieties of beer—an ale, and a darker "stout porter," so named because it was popular among porters in London. Against big odds, his dark beer thrived. By 1868, Guinness had the largest brewery in the world.

Today, Guinness remains one of the world's largest beer producers, with breweries in 50 countries. Around the world, 10 million pints of Guinness stout are consumed each day (with a few extra on St. Patrick's Day).

Over the years, a clever ad campaign has helped fuel the beer's success. In the 1930s, the brewery was known for its animal cartoons that featured simple but catchy slogans such as, "Guinness is good for you," "My goodness, my Guinness!" and "Have a Guinness when you're tired." Whether or not it's a good idea to drink alcohol when you're fighting fatigue, the slogan certainly helped sell beer.

Guinness stout is known for its dark color and creamy white head. The color and slightly burnt flavor come from roasting the barley before the beer is brewed. The beer is carbonated with nitrous oxide in addition to the usual carbon dioxide, producing the thick white foam on top. Traditionally, Guinness is served at a slightly warmer temperature than most ales and lagers.

Because of the high carbonation, pouring a Guinness takes skill, and ordering one takes patience. To tap a perfect pint, Guinness instructs bartenders to use a "two-part pour." The glass should be tilted at a 45-degree angle and filled to three-quarters capacity. Then you must wait for the surge of bubbles beneath the foam to settle before the glass is filled to the brim. The overall process takes about two minutes.

Several years ago, a Dublin company worked on developing a process to cut down the pouring-and-settling time without disrupting the beer's quality...but Guinness aficionados weren't impressed. A bartender at one of Dublin's oldest pubs told CNN, "Our customers will certainly not go for that. Guinness is a traditional drink and I don't think people will sacrifice that for a little extra speed and efficiency."

restaurant section). You'll often see signs behind the bar asking that children vacate the premises by 20:00. You must be 18 to order a beer, and the Gardí (police) are cracking down on pubs that don't enforce this law.

You're a guest on your first night; after that, you're a regular. A wise Irishman once said, "It never rains in a pub." The relaxed, informal atmosphere feels like a refuge from daily cares. Women traveling alone need not worry—you'll become part of the pub family in no time.

Craic (pronounced "crack"), Irish for "fun" or "a good laugh," is the sport that accompanies drinking in a pub. People are there to talk. To encourage conversation, stand or sit at the bar, not at a table.

In 2004, the Irish government passed a law making all pubs in the Republic smoke-free. Smokers now take their pints outside, turning alleys into covered smoking patios. An incredulous Irishman responded to the law by saying, "What will they do next? Ban drinking in pubs? We'll never get to heaven if we don't die."

It's a tradition to buy your table a round, and then for each person to reciprocate. If an Irishman buys you a drink, thank him by saying, "*Go raibh maith agat*" (guh rov mah UG-ut). Offer him a toast in Irish—"*Slainte*" (SLAWN-chuh), the equivalent of "cheers." A good excuse for a conversation is to ask to be taught a few words of Irish Gaelic.

Staying Connected

One of the most common questions I hear from travelers is, "How can I stay connected in Europe?" The short answer is: more easily and cheaply than you might think.

The simplest solution is to bring your own device—mobile phone, tablet, or laptop—and use it just as you would at home (following the tips here, such as connecting to free Wi-Fi whenever possible). Another option is to buy a European SIM card for your mobile phone—either your US phone or one you buy in Europe. Or you can use European landlines and computers to connect. Each of these options is described next, and more details are at www.ricksteves.com/phoning. For a very practical one-hour talk covering tech issues for travelers, see www.ricksteves.com/mobile-travel-skills.

Because dialing instructions vary between the Republic and Northern Ireland, carefully read "How to Dial," on page 556.

Because dialing instructions vary between the Republic and Northern Ireland, carefully read "How to Dial," on page 556.

PRACTICALITIES

USING A MOBILE DEVICE IN EUROPE

Here are some budget tips and options.

Sign up for an international plan. Using your cellular network in Europe on a pay-as-you-go basis can add up (about $1.70/minute for voice calls, 50 cents to send text messages, 5 cents to receive them, and $10 to download one megabyte of data). To stay connected at a lower cost, sign up for an international service plan through your carrier. Most providers offer a simple bundle that includes calling, messaging, and data. Your normal plan may already include international coverage (T-Mobile's does).

Before your trip, call your provider or check online to confirm that your phone will work in Europe, and research your provider's international rates. Activate the plan a day or two before you leave, then remember to cancel it when your trip's over.

Use free Wi-Fi whenever possible. Unless you have an unlimited-data plan, you're best off saving most of your online tasks for Wi-Fi. You can access the Internet, send texts, and even make voice calls over Wi-Fi.

Most accommodations in Europe offer free Wi-Fi, but some—especially expensive hotels—charge a fee. Many cafés (including Starbucks and McDonald's) have free hotspots for customers; look for signs offering it and ask for the Wi-Fi password when you buy something. You'll also often find Wi-Fi at TIs, city squares, major museums, public-transit hubs, and airports, and aboard trains and buses.

Minimize the use of your cellular network. Even with an international data plan, wait until you're on Wi-Fi to Skype, download apps, stream videos, or do other megabyte-greedy tasks. Using a navigation app such as Google Maps over a cellular network can take lots of data, so do this sparingly or use it offline.

Limit automatic updates. By default, your device constantly checks for a data connection and updates apps. It's smart to disable these features so your apps will only update when you're on Wi-Fi, and to change your device's email settings from "auto-retrieve" to "manual" (or from "push" to "fetch").

When you need to get online but can't find Wi-Fi, simply turn on your cellular network just long enough for the task at hand. When you're done, avoid further charges by manually turning off data roaming or cellular data (either works) in your device's Settings menu. Another way to make sure you're not accidentally using data roaming is to put your device in "airplane" mode (which also disables phone calls and texts), and then turn your Wi-Fi back on as needed.

It's also a good idea to keep track of your data usage. On your device's menu, look for "cellular data usage" or "mobile data" and reset the counter at the start of your trip.

Use Wi-Fi calling and messaging apps. Skype, Viber, Face-Time, and Google+ Hangouts are great for making free or low-cost voice and video calls over Wi-Fi. With an app installed on your phone, tablet, or laptop, you can log on to a Wi-Fi network and contact friends or family members who use the same service. If you buy credit in advance, with some of these services you can call any mobile phone or landline worldwide for just pennies per minute.

Many of these apps also allow you to send messages over Wi-Fi to any other person using that app. Be aware that some apps, such as Apple's iMessage, will use the cellular network if Wi-Fi isn't available: To avoid this possibility, turn off the "Send as SMS" feature.

USING A EUROPEAN SIM CARD

With a European SIM card, you get a European mobile number and access to cheaper rates than you'll get through your US carrier. This option works well for those who want to make a lot of voice calls or need faster connection speeds than their US carrier provides. Fit the SIM card into a cheap phone you buy in Europe (about $40 from phone shops anywhere), or swap out the SIM card in an "unlocked" US phone (check with your carrier about unlocking it).

SIM cards are sold at mobile-phone shops, department-store electronics counters, some newsstands, and vending machines. Costing about $5-10, they usually include prepaid calling/messaging credit, with no contract and no commitment. Expect to pay $20-40 more for a SIM card with a gigabyte of data. If you travel with this card to other countries in the European Union, there should be no extra roaming fees.

I like to buy SIM cards at a phone shop where there's a clerk to help explain the options. Certain brands—including Lebara and Lycamobile, both of which are available in multiple European countries—are reliable and especially economical. Ask the clerk to help you insert your SIM card, set it up, and show you how to use it. In some countries, you'll be required to register the SIM card with your passport as an antiterrorism measure (which may mean you can't use the phone for the first hour or two).

Find out how to check your credit balance. When you run out of credit, you can top it up at newsstands, tobacco shops, mobile-phone stores, or many other businesses (look for your SIM card's logo in the window), or online.

How to Dial

International Calls
Whether phoning from a US landline or mobile phone, or from a number in another European country, here's how to make an international call. I've used recommended hotels in Dublin (tel. 01/679-6500) and in Belfast (tel. 028/9027-1066) as examples.

Initial Zero: Drop the initial zero from international phone numbers—except when calling Italy.

Mobile Tip: If using a mobile phone, the "+" sign can replace the international access code (for a "+" sign, press and hold "0").

US/Canada to Europe
Dial 011 (US/Canada international access code), country code (353 for the Republic of Ireland, 44 for Northern Ireland), and phone number.
▶ To call the Dublin hotel from home, dial 011-353-1-679-6500.
▶ To call the Belfast hotel, dial 011-44-28-9027-1066.

Country to Country Within Europe
Dial 00 (Europe international access code), country code, and phone number.
▶ To call the Dublin hotel, whether from Northern Ireland or elsewhere in Europe, dial 00-353-1-679-6500.
▶ To call the Belfast hotel from the Republic of Ireland or elsewhere in Europe, dial 00-44-28-9027-1066.

Europe to the US/Canada
Dial 00, country code (1 for US/Canada), and phone number.
▶ To call from Europe to my office in Edmonds, Washington, dial 00-1-425-771-8303.

Domestic Calls
To call within the Republic of Ireland or within Northern Ireland (from one Irish landline or mobile phone to another), simply dial the phone number, including the initial 0 if there is one.
▶ To call the Dublin hotel from Wexford, dial 01/679-6500.
▶ To call the Belfast hotel from Derry, dial 028/9027-1066.

More Dialing Tips
Republic of Ireland to Northern Ireland: To avoid international rates when calling from any Republic of Ireland phone number to a landline in Northern Ireland (prefix 028), you can dial 048, then the local number (skipping the access code, country code, and Northern Ireland's area code).
▶ To call the Belfast hotel from a Dublin landline, dial 048-9027-1066.

Dialing from Northern Ireland to Republic of Ireland
From a Northern Ireland phone number, dial 00-353, then the area code without its initial 0, and then the local number.

▶ To call the Dublin hotel from a Belfast number, dial 00-353-1-679-6500.

Irish Phone Numbers: Phone numbers in both the Republic and Northern Ireland can vary in length. I keep things simple by always dialing the full number (including the area code or prefix). Mobile phone numbers in the Republic start with 083, 085, 086, 087, and 089. Mobile phone numbers in Northern Ireland (and the rest of the UK) start with 07. Note that calls to a European mobile phone are more expensive than calls to a landline.

Toll and Toll-Free Calls: In the Republic, numbers starting with 1-800 are toll-free, but numbers starting with 15, 1850, or 0818 are toll numbers. In Northern Ireland, numbers starting with 080 are toll-free, but those beginning with 084, 087, or 03 are inexpensive toll numbers. Numbers beginning with 09 are pricey toll lines. International rates apply to US toll-free numbers dialed from Ireland—they're not free.

More Phoning Help: See www.howtocallabroad.com.

European Country Codes		Ireland & N. Ireland	353 / 44
Austria	43	Italy	39
Belgium	32	Latvia	371
Bosnia-Herzegovina	387	Montenegro	382
Croatia	385	Morocco	212
Czech Republic	420	Netherlands	31
Denmark	45	Norway	47
Estonia	372	Poland	48
Finland	358	Portugal	351
France	33	Russia	7
Germany	49	Slovakia	421
Gibraltar	350	Slovenia	386
Great Britain	44	Spain	34
Greece	30	Sweden	46
Hungary	36	Switzerland	41
Iceland	354	Turkey	90

PRACTICALITIES

Tips on Internet Security

Make sure that your device is running the latest versions of its operating system, security software, and apps. Next, ensure that your device and key programs (like email) are password- or passcode-protected. On the road, use only secure, password-protected Wi-Fi hotspots. Ask the hotel or café staff for the specific name of their Wi-Fi network, and make sure you log on to that exact one.

If you must access your financial info online, use a banking app rather than accessing your account via a browser. A cellular connection is more secure than Wi-Fi. Avoid logging onto personal finance sites on a public computer.

Never share your credit-card number (or any other sensitive information) online unless you know that the site is secure. A secure site displays a little padlock icon, and the URL begins with *https* (instead of the usual *http*).

PUBLIC PHONES AND COMPUTERS

It's possible to travel in Europe without a mobile device. You can make calls from your hotel (or the increasingly rare public phone), and check email or browse websites using public computers.

Most **hotels** charge a fee for placing calls—ask for rates before you dial. Phones are rare in **B&Bs;** if there's no phone in your room, and you have an important, brief call to make, politely ask your hosts if you can use their personal phone.

Public pay phones are hard to find in Northern Ireland, and they're expensive. To use one, you'll pay with a major credit card (which you insert into the phone—minimum charge for a credit-card call is £1.20) or coins (have a bunch handy; minimum fee is £0.60). Only unused coins are returned, so put in biggies with caution.

Most hotels have **public computers** in their lobbies for guests to use; otherwise you may find them at Internet cafés and public libraries (ask your hotelier or the TI for the nearest location). Think ahead, especially if you need to print boarding passes for a flight (Ryanair requires it).

On a European keyboard, use the "Alt Gr" key to the right of the space bar to insert the extra symbol that appears on some keys. If you can't locate a special character (such as @), simply copy it from a Web page and paste it into your email message.

MAIL

You can mail one package per day to yourself worth up to $200 duty-free from Europe to the US (mark it "personal purchases"). If you're sending a gift to someone, mark it "unsolicited gift." For details, visit www.cbp.gov, select "Travel," and search for "Know Before You Go."

The Irish postal service works fine, but for quick transatlantic delivery (in either direction), consider services such as DHL (www.dhl.com). Get stamps at the neighborhood post office, newsstands within fancy hotels, and some minimarts and card shops. Don't use stamps from the Republic of Ireland on postcards mailed in Northern Ireland (part of the UK), and vice versa.

Transportation

To see all of Ireland, especially the sights with far-flung rural charm, I prefer the freedom of a rental car. Connemara, the Ring of Kerry, the Antrim Coast, County Donegal, County Wexford, and the Boyne Valley are really only worth it if you have wheels.

Cars are best for three or more traveling together (especially families with small kids), those packing heavy, and those scouring the countryside. Trains and buses are best for solo travelers, blitz tourists, city-to-city travelers, and those who don't want to drive in Ireland.

Ireland has a good train-and-bus system, though departures are not as frequent as the European norm. Most rail lines spoke outward from Dublin, so you'll need to mix in bus transportation to bridge the gaps. Buses pick you up when the trains let you down.

Given the choice of either a bus or a train between the same two towns, I prefer trains, which are sometimes faster and are not subject to the vehicle traffic that can delay buses (although bus travel can be more direct). Also, unlike bus travel, on a train you can get up and walk around.

The best overall source of schedules for public transportation in the Republic of Ireland as well as Northern Ireland—including rail, cross-country and city buses, and Dublin's LUAS transit—is the Republic of Ireland's domestic website: www.discoverireland.ie (select "Getting Around" near the bottom of the home page).

I've included a sample itinerary for drivers (with tips and tweaks for those using public transportation) to help you explore Ireland smoothly; you'll find it on page 20.

Trains

To research Irish rail connections online, you need to access two sites. For the Republic of Ireland, use www.irishrail.ie. For Northern Ireland, use www.translink.co.uk. For train schedules on the rest of the European continent, check www.bahn.com (Germany's excellent Europe-wide timetable).

It really pays to buy your train tickets online ahead of time. Advance-purchase discounts of up to 50 percent are not unheard

PRACTICALITIES

PRACTICALITIES

Rail Passes and Train Travel in Ireland

A Eurail **Ireland Pass** lets you travel by train in Ireland for three to eight days (north or south, consecutively or not) within a one-month period. Discounted rates are offered for two people traveling together. In addition, Irish Rail sells rail passes good for four or five days of train travel in the Republic of Ireland within a 15-day period.

Ireland can also be included in a Eurail **Select Pass**, which allows travel in two "neighboring" countries (but not Britain) over two months, and it's covered (along with most of Europe) by the classic Eurail **Global Pass**.

Eurail passes are best purchased outside Europe (through travel agents or Rick Steves' Europe); Irish Rail passes can be purchased at rail ticket offices in Ireland. For more on the ins and outs of rail passes, including prices, download my **free guide to Eurail Passes** (http://www.ricksteves.com/rail-guide) or go to www.ricksteves.com/rail.

If you're taking just a couple of train rides, individual **point-to-point train tickets** may save you money over a pass. Use this map to add up approximate pay-as-you-go fares for your itinerary, and compare that to the price of a rail pass. Keep in mind that significant discounts on point-to-point tickets may be available with advance purchase.

Map shows approximate costs, in US$, for one-way, second-class tickets. Dashed lines show bus connections not covered by rail passes.

of, but online fares fluctuate widely and unpredictably. Online and off, fares are often higher for peak travel on Fridays and Sundays. Remember that the quoted price will be in euros or British pounds. Booking ahead online can also help you avoid long ticket lines in Dublin and elsewhere at busy times.

Be aware that very few Irish train stations have storage lockers.

Rail Passes: For most travelers in Ireland, a rail pass is not very useful. Trains fan out from Dublin to major cities but neglect much of the countryside. But if a pass works for your itinerary, keep in mind that Eurail passes cover all trains in both the Republic and Northern Ireland, and give a 30 percent discount on standard foot-passenger fares for some international ferries. Irish Rail also offers passes covering four consecutive days or five days of travel within a 15-day period in the Republic only (purchase at any major rail station in Ireland, www.irishrail.ie). For more detailed advice on train travel options, visit www.ricksteves.com/rail.

Buses

If you opt for public transportation, you'll probably spend more time on Irish buses than Irish trains. But be aware: Public transportation (especially cross-country Irish buses) will likely put your travels into slow motion.

For example, driving across County Kerry from Kenmare to Dingle takes two hours. If you go by bus, the same trip takes almost four hours. The trip by bus usually requires two transfers (in Killarney and Tralee, each involving a wait for the next bus), and the buses often take a rural milk-run route, making multiple stops along the way. But not every Irish coach trip will involve this kind of delay. They're sometimes more direct than trains; for example, the bus from Dublin to Derry takes four hours with few stops, while the train takes six and requires a change. But in general buses tend to be slower than trains (by about a third), so if you opt to go by coach, be realistic about your itinerary and study the schedules ahead of time. The Bus Éireann Expressway Bus Timetable comes in handy (free, available at some bus stations or online at www.buseireann.ie, bus info toll tel. 1850-836-611).

Buses are much cheaper than trains. Round-trip bus tickets usually cost less than two one-way fares. For example, Tralee to Dingle is €14 one-way and €19 round-trip, and Kinsale to Cork is €9 one-way and €13 round-trip when purchased the day before. The Irish distinguish between "buses" (for in-city travel with lots of stops) and "coaches" (long-distance cross-country runs).

You may need to do some trips partly by train. For instance, if you're going from Dublin to Dingle without a car, you'll need to take a train to Tralee and catch a bus from there. Similarly, to go from Dublin to Kinsale without a car, take a train to Cork and then a bus; and from Dublin to Doolin, take a train to Galway or Ennis and then a bus.

If you're traveling up and down Ireland's west coast, buses are best (or a combination of buses and trains); relying on rail only here is too time-consuming. Note that some rural coach stops are by "request only." This means the coach will drive right on by unless you flag it down by extending your arm straight out, with your palm open.

PRACTICALITIES

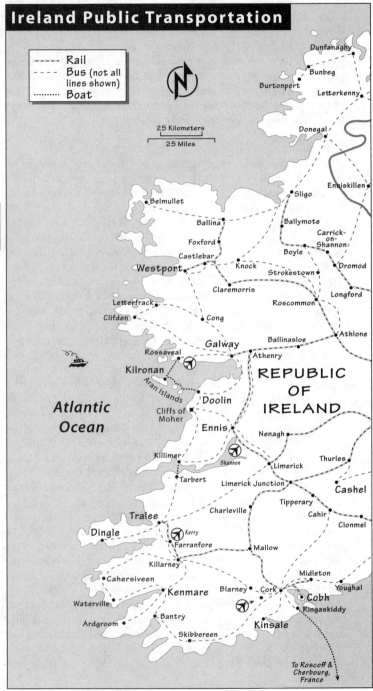

Ireland Public Transportation

Rail
Bus (not all lines shown)
Boat

25 Kilometers
25 Miles

Atlantic Ocean

REPUBLIC OF IRELAND

Dunfanaghy
Bunbeg
Burtonport
Letterkenny
Donegal
Enniskillen
Belmullet
Sligo
Ballina
Ballymote
Carrick-on-Shannon
Foxford
Boyle
Dromod
Castlebar
Knock
Strokestown
Longford
Westport
Claremorris
Roscommon
Letterfrack
Cong
Athlone
Clifden
Ballinasloe
Galway
Athenry
Rossaveal
Kilronan
Aran Islands
Doolin
Cliffs of Moher
Ennis
Nenagh
Thurles
Killimer
Shannon
Limerick
Cashel
Tarbert
Limerick Junction
Charleville
Tipperary
Tralee
Cahir
Dingle
Kerry
Farranfore
Clonmel
Mallow
Killarney
Midleton
Cahersiveen
Blarney
Cork
Youghal
Waterville
Cobh
Bantry
Ringaskiddy
Ardgroom
Kinsale
Skibbereen

Kenmare

To Roscoff & Cherbourg, France

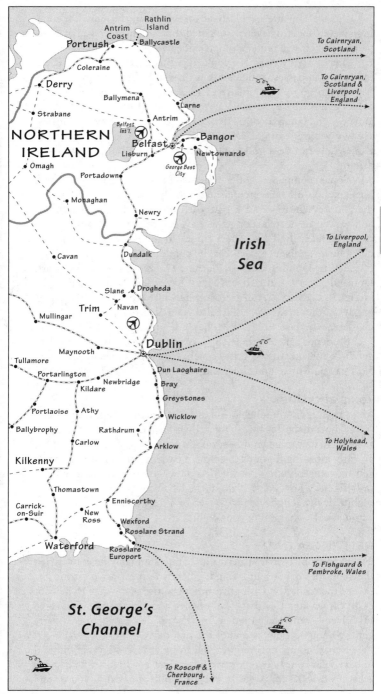

Rathlin Island

Antrim Coast

Portrush

Ballycastle

Coleraine

Derry

Ballymena

Strabane

Larne

Antrim

NORTHERN IRELAND

Belfast Int'l.

Belfast

Bangor

Lisburn

Newtownards

George Best City

Omagh

Portadown

Monaghan

Newry

Cavan

Dundalk

Irish Sea

Slane

Drogheda

Trim

Navan

Mullingar

Dublin

Tullamore

Maynooth

Dun Laoghaire

Portarlington

Newbridge

Bray

Kildare

Greystones

Portlaoise

Athy

Wicklow

Ballybrophy

Rathdrum

Carlow

Arklow

Kilkenny

Thomastown

Enniscorthy

Carrick-on-Suir

New Ross

Wexford

Rosslare Strand

Waterford

Rosslare Europort

St. George's Channel

To Cairnryan, Scotland

To Cairnryan, Scotland & Liverpool, England

To Liverpool, England

To Holyhead, Wales

To Fishguard & Pembroke, Wales

To Roscoff & Cherbourg, France

Bus stations are normally at or near train stations. On some Irish buses, sporting events are piped throughout the bus; have earplugs handy if you prefer a quieter ride.

Busy bus travelers can look into Bus Éireann's **Open Road** tourist travel passes, which start at three days of travel in a six-day period and go up to as many as 15 days in a 30-day period. The passes can be pricey so make sure you add up your point-to-point journeys and compare to the pass prices once you know your itinerary (www.buseireann.ie, select "Tickets" and then "Tourist Travel Passes"). It can be a good option for those who are phobic about driving.

Some companies offer **backpacker's bus circuits.** These hop-on, hop-off bus circuits take mostly youth hostelers around the country cheaply and easily, with the assumption that they'll be sleeping in hostels along the way. For example, Paddy Wagon cuts Ireland in half and offers three- to nine-day "tours" of each half (north and south) that can be combined into one whole tour connecting Dublin, Cork, Killarney, Dingle, Galway, Westport, Donegal, Derry, and Belfast (May-Oct, 5 Beresford Palace, Dublin, tel. 01/823-0822, toll-free from UK tel. 0800-783-4191, www.paddywagontours.com). They also offer day tours to the Giant's Causeway, Belfast, Cliffs of Moher, Glendalough, or Kilkenny.

Students can use their ISIC (student card, www.isic.org) to get discounts on cross-country coaches (up to 50 percent). Children 5-15 pay half-price on trains, and wee ones under age 5 go free.

Taxis and Uber

Most Irish taxis are reliable and cheap. In many cities, couples can travel short distances by cab for little more than two bus or subway tickets. Taxis can be your best option for getting to the airport for an early morning flight or to connect two far-flung destinations. If you like ride-booking services like Uber, these apps usually work in Irish cities just like they do in the US: You request a car on your mobile device (connected to Wi-Fi or a data plan), and the fare is automatically charged to your credit card.

RENTING A CAR

Travelers from North America are understandably hesitant when they consider driving in Ireland, where you must drive on the left side of the road. The Irish government statistics say that 10 percent of all car accidents on Irish soil involve a foreign tourist. But careful drivers—with the patient support of an alert navigator—usually get the hang of it by the end of the first day.

Rental companies require you to be at least 21 years old and to have held your license for two years. Drivers under 25 may incur a young-driver surcharge. In the Republic of Ireland, you gener-

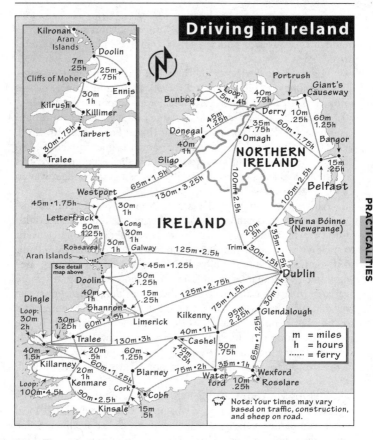

Driving in Ireland

Kilronan • Aran Islands
Doolin
7m .25h
25m .75h
Cliffs of Moher
30m 1h
Ennis
Kilrush
Killimer
30m .75h
Tarbert
Tralee

Bunbeg
Loop 75m • 4h
Portrush
40m .75h
Giant's Causeway
Derry 10m .25h
60m 1.25h
45m 1.25h
35m .75h
60m • 1.75h
Bangor
Donegal
Omagh
NORTHERN IRELAND
40m 1h
Sligo
100m 2.5h
15m .25h
Belfast
65m • 1.5h
130m • 3.25h
105m 2.5h
Westport
30m 1h
IRELAND
20m .5h
Brú na Bóinne (Newgrange)
45m • 1.75h
Letterfrack
50m 1.25h
Cong
30m 1h
35m .75h
Trim
30m .5h
Rossaveal
30m 1h
Galway
125m • 2.5h
Aran Islands
45m • 1.25h
See detail map above
Doolin
50m 1.25h
15m .25h
125m • 2.75h
Dublin
Dingle
40m 1h
Shannon
75m • 1.5h
30m • 1h
Loop: 30m 2h
30m 1.25h
60m • .5h
Limerick
Kilkenny
95m 2.25h
Glendalough
Tralee
130m • 3h
40m • 1h
Cashel
30m .75h
65m • 1.25h
40m 1.5h
20m .5h
60m • 1.25h
45m 1.25h
35m • 1h
Killarney
60m • 1.25h
Blarney
75m • 2h
Water-ford
Wexford
10m .25h
Rosslare
Loop: 100m 4.5h
Kenmare
30m • 2.5h
Cork
Cobh
15m .5h
Kinsale

m = miles
h = hours
...... = ferry

🐑 Note: Your times may vary based on traffic, construction, and sheep on road.

ally can't rent a car if you're 75 or older (unless you have a note from your doctor), and you'll usually pay extra if you're 70-74. Some companies in Northern Ireland won't rent to anyone over 69. (Note that you can't lease a car in Ireland; you can only rent.)

Research car rentals before you go. It's cheaper to arrange most car rentals from the US. Consider several companies to compare rates.

Most of the major US rental agencies (including Avis, Budget, Enterprise, Hertz, and Thrifty) have offices throughout Ireland. Also consider the two major Europe-based agencies, Europcar and Sixt. It can be cheaper to use a consolidator, such as Auto Europe/Kemwel (www.autoeurope.com—or the often cheaper www. autoeurope.eu), which compares rates at several companies to get you the best deal—but because you're working with a middleman, it's especially important to ask in advance about add-on fees and restrictions.

Always read the fine print or query the agent carefully for add-on charges—such as one-way drop-off fees, airport surcharges, or mandatory insurance policies—that aren't included in the "total price."

For the best deal, rent by the week with unlimited mileage. To save money on fuel, request a diesel car. In midsummer expect to pay at least $300 per week (more for an automatic, as much as 50 percent cheaper off-season), not including fuel and minimum insurance, for a basic compact-size car (like a Ford Focus 1.4-liter). With full insurance, the price of the same car goes up about $180 per week (even more for an automatic). Smaller economy-size cars cost about $50 less per week. Minibuses are a good, budget way to go for larger groups (five to nine people).

Although an upgrade to a larger car might be offered, remember that Irish roads can be narrow and winding, and parking tight. Unless you're taller or you need the space for luggage, you may want to stick with a smaller car. Almost all rentals are manual by default, so if you need an automatic, you must request one in advance. Beware that an automatic transmission costs more and is usually more available in larger models. Weigh these considerations against the fact that in Ireland you'll be sitting on the right side of the car and shifting with your left hand...while driving on the left side of the road and tuning out the right side of your brain. The floor pedals are in the same locations as in the US, and the gears are still found in the same basic "H" pattern as at home (i.e., first gear, second, etc.).

Picking Up Your Car: Big companies have offices in most cities; ask whether they can pick you up at your hotel. Small local rental companies can be cheaper but aren't as flexible. Some companies, such as Auto Europe (www.autoeurope.com) or Dan Dooley (www.dan-dooley.ie), will do longer-term rentals at a slight discount.

Compare pickup costs (downtown can be less expensive than the airport—but isn't recommended in congested urban Dublin), and explore drop-off options. Always check the hours of the location you choose: Many rental offices close from midday Saturday until Monday morning and, in smaller towns, at lunchtime.

When selecting a location, don't trust the agency's description of "downtown" or "city center." In some cases, a "downtown" branch can be on the outskirts of the city—a long, costly taxi ride from the center. Before choosing, plug the addresses into a mapping website. You may find that the "train station" location is handier. Returning a car at a big-city train station or downtown agency can be tricky; get precise details on the car drop-off location and hours and allow ample time to find it.

When you pick up the rental car, check it thoroughly and make sure any damage is noted on your rental agreement. Rental agen-

The Wild Atlantic Way

This Irish tourism marketing initiative offers drivers "the world's longest defined touring route." Stretching 1,550 miles (2,500 km) from Kinsale in the south to Derry in the North, the Wild Atlantic Way snakes along the inlets and outcrops of Ireland's west coast, passing through nine counties and bagging some of the best coastal views along the way. This is the scenic, long-way-around route for travelers not in a hurry. You'll frequently see signs with a large blue "WW" meant to symbolize waves, which tells you that you're driving on a section of the route (www.wildatlanticway.com).

cies in Europe tend to charge for even minor damage, so be sure to mark everything. Before driving off, find out how your car's gearshift, lights, turn signals, wipers, radio, and fuel cap function, and know what kind of fuel the car takes (diesel vs. unleaded). When you return the car, make sure the agent verifies its condition with you. Some drivers take pictures of the returned vehicle as proof of its condition.

If your trip covers both Ireland and Great Britain (Scotland, England, and Wales), you're better off with two separate car rentals, rather than paying for your car to ride the ferry between the two islands. On an all-Ireland trip, you can drive your rental car from the Republic of Ireland into Northern Ireland, but be aware of drop-off charges (as much as $150-200) if you return it in the North. You'll pay a smaller drop-off charge (as much as $50-100) for picking up the car at one place and dropping it off at another within the same country (even picking up in downtown Dublin and dropping off at Dublin Airport). If you pick up the car in a smaller city, you'll more likely survive your first day on the Irish roads. If you drop the car off early or keep it longer, you'll be credited or charged at a fair, prorated price.

Car Insurance Options

When you rent a car, you're liable for a very high deductible, sometimes equal to the entire value of the car. Limit your financial risk with one of these two options: Buy Collision Damage Waiver **(CDW)** coverage with a low or zero deductible from the car-rental company, or get coverage through your credit card (more complicated, and few credit cards now offer free coverage in Ireland).

Basic CDW includes a very high deductible (typically $1,000-1,500). Though each rental company has its own variation, basic

PRACTICALITIES

How to Navigate a Roundabout

CORK
M-8

DUBLIN ← → DINGLE
M-7   R-561

NOTE:

- TRAFFIC IN ROUNDABOUTS FLOWS IN A CLOCKWISE DIRECTION.
- WHITE CARS ARE ENTERING THE ROUNDABOUT, GRAY CARS ARE EXITING.
- VEHICLES ENTERING A ROUNDABOUT MUST YIELD TO VEHICLES IN THE ROUNDABOUT.
- LOOK TO YOUR RIGHT AS YOU MERGE! ☺

CDW costs $10-30 a day (figure roughly 30 percent extra) and reduces your liability, but does not eliminate it. When you reserve or pick up the car, you'll be offered the chance to "buy down" the basic deductible to zero (for an additional $10-30/day; this is sometimes called "super CDW" or "zero-deductible coverage").

If you opt for **credit-card coverage** (and your credit card is one of the few accepted for this type of coverage in Ireland), there's a catch. You'll technically have to decline all coverage offered by the car-rental company, which means they can place a hold on your card (which can be up to the full value of the car). In case of damage, it can be time-consuming to resolve the charges with your credit-card company. Before you decide on this option, quiz your credit-card company about how it works.

For more on car-rental insurance, see www.ricksteves.com/cdw.

Navigation Options

If you'll be navigating using your phone or a GPS unit from home, remember to bring a car charger and device mount.

Your Mobile Device: The mapping app on your mobile phone works fine for navigation in Europe, but for real-time turn-by-turn directions and traffic updates, you'll generally need Internet access. And driving all day while online can be very expensive. Helpful exceptions are Google Maps, Here WeGo, and Navmii, which provide turn-by-turn voice directions and recalibrate even when they're offline.

Download your map before you head out—it's smart to select a large region. Then turn off your cellular connection so you're not charged for data roaming. Call up the map, enter your destination, and you're on your way. View maps in standard view (not satellite view) to limit data demands.

GPS Devices: If you prefer the convenience of a dedicated GPS unit, consider renting one with your car ($10-30/day). These units offer real-time turn-by-turn directions and traffic without the data requirements of an app. Note that the unit may only come loaded with maps for its home country; if you need additional maps, ask. Also make sure your device's language is set to English before you drive off.

A less-expensive option is to bring a GPS device from home. Be aware that you'll need to buy and download European maps before your trip.

Maps and Atlases: Even when navigating primarily with a mobile app or GPS, I always make it a point to have a paper map. It's invaluable for getting the big picture, understanding alternate routes, and filling in when my phone runs out of juice. The free maps you get from your car-rental company usually don't have enough detail. It's smart to get a road atlas that covers all of Ireland. Ordnance Survey atlases are best (€11 in gas stations and bookstores). Drivers, hikers, and cyclists may want more detailed maps for Dingle, Connemara, Donegal, Wexford, the Antrim Coast, the Ring of Kerry, and the Boyne Valley (easy to buy locally at bookstores or gas stations).

DRIVING

Ireland's new motorways have vastly improved the cross-country driving experience and now link most major cities (Dublin, Belfast,

PRACTICALITIES

Tips on Driving

Driving gives you access to the most rural sights and is my favorite mode of transportation in Ireland. Here's what I've learned in the school of hard brakes and adrenaline rushes:

- *The Complete Road Atlas of Ireland* by Ordnance Survey (€11, handy ring-binder style, 1:210,000 scale) is the best Irish road map, and includes translations of Irish place names on the last pages. It covers every road your car can wedge onto. Flipping to the next page of an atlas is easier to manage in a cramped front seat than wrestling with a large, ungainly folding map. Buy the atlas at the first bookstore or gas station you come to.
- Study your map before taking off. Get a sense of the areas you'll be visiting, as road numbers are inconsistent.
- Road signs can be confusing, too little, and too late. Driving in Ireland is easier as a team; the person in the passenger seat needs to be engaged and alert when the driver asks for a navigational clarification from a map or device.
- Figure out your lights, wipers, and radio before you're on the road. Nervous Nellie navigators will thank you.
- Adjust your side-view mirrors and get in the habit of using them. Narrow roads with lush vegetation are an Irish fact of life. Get comfortable with the sound of vegetation whisking the side of your car.
- Drive with your lights on to make your vehicle more visible.
- Get used to shifting with your left hand. Find reverse...before you need it. (I love the smell of burnt clutch in the morning.)
- The most common mistake is getting a late start, which causes you to rush, which makes you miss turns, which causes you stress, which decreases your enjoyment, which makes your trip feel less like a vacation.
- Car travel in Ireland isn't fast (although more motorways are being built). Plan your itinerary estimating an average speed of 40 mph (1 km per minute). Give your itinerary a reality check by finding distances and driving times between towns on the driving map (see the chart in this chapter) or online (www.google.com/maps or www.viamichelin.com).
- The shortest distance between any two points is usually the motorway (highway). But miss a motorway exit and you can lose 20 minutes.
- Avoid driving in big cities if possible; use ring roads to skirt the congestion. Dublin is clogged with traffic—you'll find

sightseeing easier on foot, by bus (particularly the hop-on, hop-off tours), or by taxi. Spare yourself the traffic stress and parking expense of trying to drive in Dublin. Real-time traffic conditions are updated on www.aa.ie.

- When it comes to narrow rural roads, adjust your perceptions of personal space. It's not "my side of the road" or "your side of the road." It's just "the road"—and it's shared as a cooperative adventure. Locals are usually courteous, pulling over against a hedgerow and blinking their headlights for you to pass while they wait. Return the favor when you are closer to a wide spot in the road than they are. Pull over frequently—to let faster drivers pass and to check the map.

- Watch the road ahead and expect a slow tractor, a flock of sheep, a one-lane bridge, and a baby stroller to lurk around the next turn. Honk when approaching blind corners to alert approaching drivers.

- On narrow rural roads, buses always have the right of way, so you'll need to back up to give way.

- Tune in to RTE Radio 1, the national radio station (89 FM), for long drives. Its interviews and music are an education in Irish culture (for more on RTE, see page 34). The same goes for BBC Ulster (94.5 FM) in Northern Ireland.

- Make your road trip fun. Establish a cardboard-box pantry of munchies. Keep a rack of liter boxes of juice in the trunk. Buy some window-cleaner and a roll of paper towels for cleaner sightseeing. A bottle of sparkling mineral water makes a dandy windshield cleaner in a pinch.

- Don't drink and drive. The Gardí (police) set up random checkpoints. If you've had more than one pint, you're legally drunk in Ireland.

- If you're driving between the Republic and Northern Ireland, keep these basic differences in mind: In the Republic, the speed limit is in kilometers per hour, unleaded costs about €1.40 per liter ($5.75 per gallon), and the roads can be bumpy, narrow, and winding. In Northern Ireland, the speed limit is in miles per hour, unleaded costs about £1.20 per liter ($5.00 per gallon), and roads are better maintained.

- Diesel fuel pumps (which are usually green in the US) are black in Ireland. Mixing them up while fueling is a sure way to ruin your day. Insurance doesn't cover this mistake.

- Travelers who want to use designated disabled parking spaces in Ireland can bring their Disabled Persons Parking Card from the US (even though the Irish have a different card that they set on their dashboard). For more information, call the Irish Wheelchair Association at tel. 045/893-094 (from the US, dial 011-353-45-893-094).

PRACTICALITIES

Cork, Waterford, Limerick, and Galway). But the best intimate sites still require you to drive on narrow country lanes.

Note that your US credit and debit cards are unlikely to work at self-service gas pumps and automated parking garages, which use chip-and-PIN technology. Even a US card with a chip may not work, since most are chip-and-signature cards, but if you know your PIN, try it anyway. Luckily, the vast majority of Irish gas stations have a live attendant who can process your gas purchase (as long as it's not too late at night). The easiest solution is carrying sufficient cash in euros (pounds in the North).

An Irish Automobile Association membership comes with most rentals (www.theaa.ie). Understand its towing and emergency road-service benefits.

Road Rules: Driving in Ireland is basically wonderful—once you remember to stay on the left and after you've mastered the roundabouts. Don't let a roundabout spook you. After all, you routinely merge into much faster traffic with cars slipping into your blind spot on American highways back home. The traffic in a roundabout has the right-of-way; entering traffic yields (look to your right as you merge). It helps to remember that the driver is always in the center of the road. And pay attention to the instructions painted on the pavement as you approach bigger roundabouts; they tell you which lane to be in for a destination well before you get to the actual roundabout.

Spend a little time using Google's Street View option (www.google.com/maps) to actually see 360-degree views of the roads you'll be driving and how to access lodging or sightseeing you're considering. An advance peek online can settle the nerves of twitchy drivers and give you a heads-up on navigational issues you hadn't thought of yet.

Be warned: Every year I get a few emails from traveling readers advising me that, for them, trying to drive in Ireland was a nerve-wracking and regrettable mistake. If you want to get a little slack on the roads, try to time your car rental to begin on a Sunday morning when you can acclimate to driving on less congested roads at a mellower pace.

Be aware of typical European road rules; for example, many countries require headlights to be turned on at all times, and nearly all forbid talking on a mobile phone without a hands-free headset. In Ireland, you're not allowed to turn left on a red light unless a sign or signal specifically authorizes it, and on motorways it's illegal to pass drivers on the left. Seat belts are mandatory for all, and kids under 12 or under 1.5 meters tall (about 4 feet, 9 inches) must ride in a child-safety seat.

Ask your car-rental company about these rules, read the Department for Transport's *Highway Code* (www.gov.uk/highway-code), or check the US State Department website (www.travel.state.gov, search for your country in the "Learn about your destination" box, then click "Travel and Transportation").

Speed Limits: Speed limits are 50 kilometers per hour (roughly 30 miles per hour) in towns, 80 kph (approximately 50 mph) on rural roads (such as R-257, R-600, etc.), 100 kph (about 60 mph) on national roads (N-8, N-30, etc.), and 120 kph (roughly 75 mph) on motorways (M-1, M-50, etc.). Note that road-surveillance cameras strictly enforce speed limits. Any driver (including foreigners renting cars) photographed speeding will get a nasty bill in the mail. (Cameras—you'll see the foreboding gray boxes—flash on your rear license plate in order not to invade the privacy of anyone sharing the front seat with someone they shouldn't be with.)

Tolls: The M-50 ring road surrounding Dublin carries a €3.10 toll, paid electronically with an eFlow pass. Get details from your rental-car company at Dublin Airport (see page 109; more details at www.eflow.ie). Many rental car companies will charge you automatically, so if you pay the toll, you're paying twice. Be sure to ask. Be aware there is a €10 fee for the Port Tunnel in Dublin at peak hours Mon-Fri; if you avoid driving inside the M-50 ring road as I suggest, however, you won't pass through the tunnel. Other Irish motorways, linking smaller cities farther from Dublin, may carry tolls ranging from €1.30 to €2.90 which must be paid as you pass through (easiest with cash).

Toll motorways are usually blue on maps and are shown with the letter "M" followed by the route number (toll info and map: www.tii.ie/roads-tolling).

Parking: Parking is confusing. One yellow line marked on the pavement means no parking Monday through Saturday during business hours. Double yellow lines mean no parking at any time. Broken yellow lines mean short stops are OK, but you should always look for explicit signs or ask a passerby.

Even in small towns, rather than fight it, I just pull into the most central parking lot I can find. As for street parking, signs along

Ferry Information

INTERNATIONAL FERRY CONNECTIONS

Ireland has good ferry connections with Britain and France. Check the websites listed per route below for specifics on price, frequency, and length of journey.

Republic of Ireland

Irish Port	To...	Web Site
Dublin	Liverpool (England)	www.poirishsea.com and www.poferries.com
Dublin	Holyhead (Wales)	www.irishferries.com and www.stenaline.com
Rosslare	Fishguard (Wales)	www.stenaline.com
Rosslare	Pembroke (Wales)	www.irishferries.com
Rosslare	Cherbourg (France)	www.irishferries.com and www.stenaline.com
Rosslare	Roscoff (France)	www.irishferries.com
Ringaskiddy (near Cork)	Roscoff (France)	www.brittanyferries.ie

Northern Ireland

Belfast	Liverpool (England)	www.stenaline.com
Belfast	Cairnryan (Scotland)	www.stenaline.com
Larne (near Belfast)	Troon (Scotland)	www.poirishsea.com
Larne	Cairnryan (Scotland)	www.poirishsea.com

the street will state whether pay-and-display or parking disk laws are in effect for that area. The modern pay-and-display machines are solar-powered and placed regularly along the street (about six feet tall, look for blue circle with white letter *P*). I keep some extra coins in the console for these machines (no change given for large coins). The use of parking disks is less common these days, but if you need disks, they're sold at nearby shops. You buy one disk for each hour you want to stay. Scratch off the time you arrived on the disk and put it on your dashboard.

FLIGHTS

The best comparison search engine for both international and intra-European flights is Kayak.com. An alternative is Google Flights, which has an easy-to-use system to track prices. For inexpensive flights within Europe, try Skyscanner.com.

Flying to Europe: Start looking for international flights about four to six months before your trip, especially for peak-season travel. Depending on your itinerary, it can be efficient to fly into one city and out of another. If your flight requires a connection in Europe, see our hints on navigating Europe's top hub airports at www.ricksteves.com/hub-airports.

Flying Within Europe: If you're considering a train ride that's more than five hours long, a flight may save you both time and money. When comparing your options, factor in the time it takes to get to the airport and how early you'll need to arrive to check in.

Well-known cheapo airlines include Easyjet, Aer Lingus, Flybe, and Ryanair. For flights within Ireland, try Aer Arann, a regional subsidiary of Aer Lingus.

But be aware of the potential drawbacks of flying with a discount airline: nonrefundable and nonchangeable tickets, minimal or nonexistent customer service, pricey and time-consuming treks to secondary airports, and stingy baggage allowances with steep overage fees. If you're traveling with lots of luggage, a cheap flight can quickly become a bad deal. To avoid unpleasant surprises, read the small print before you book. These days you can also fly within Europe on major airlines affordably—and without all the aggressive restrictions—for around $100 a flight.

Flying to the US and Canada: Because security is extra tight for flights to the US, be sure to give yourself plenty of time at the airport. It's also important to charge your electronic devices before you board because security checks may require you to turn them on (see www.tsa.gov for the latest rules).

Ireland's Airports: There are four major airports planted in the four corners of the island of Ireland: Dublin (east), Cork (south), Shannon (west), and Belfast (north). If you only have a few days and are focused mainly on one region, investigate flying into that airport to save valuable time (rather than assuming Dublin is best because it's biggest, then wasting half a day driving).

All direct flights from the US land in either Dublin, Shannon, or Belfast. Cork has become a handy arrival point as well (via connecting flights from London). If you're offered a choice and have no interest in sightseeing in busy, congested Dublin, you'll find Shannon Airport to be a far less stressful entry or exit point into or out of Ireland. Drivers will especially appreciate getting used to the "other side of the road" around rural Shannon, as compared to urban Dublin. Be aware that smaller regional airports may have fewer car-rental offices.

Resources from Rick Steves

Begin Your Trip at RickSteves.com

My mobile-friendly **website** is *the* place to explore Europe in preparation for your trip. You'll find thousands of fun articles, videos, and radio interviews; a wealth of money-saving tips for planning your dream trip; travel news dispatches; a video library of my travel talks; my travel blog; my latest guidebook updates (www.ricksteves.com/update); and my free Rick Steves Audio Europe app. You can also follow me on Facebook and Twitter.

Our **Travel Forum** is a well-groomed collection of message boards where our travel-savvy community answers questions and shares their personal travel experiences—and our well-traveled staff chimes in when they can be helpful (www.ricksteves.com/forums).

Our **online Travel Store** offers bags and accessories that I've designed to help you travel smarter and lighter. These include my popular carry-on bags (which I live out of four months a year), money belts, totes, toiletries kits, adapters, guidebooks, and planning maps (www.ricksteves.com/shop).

Our website can also help you find the perfect **rail pass** for your itinerary and your budget, with easy, one-stop shopping for rail passes, seat reservations, and point-to-point tickets (www.ricksteves.com/rail).

Rick Steves' Tours, Guidebooks, TV Shows, and More

Small Group Tours: Want to travel with greater efficiency and less stress? We offer more than 40 itineraries reaching the best destinations in this book...and beyond. Each year about 25,000 travelers join us on about 1,000 Rick Steves bus tours. You'll enjoy great guides and a fun bunch of travel partners (with small groups of 24 to 28 travelers). You'll find European adventures to fit every vacation length. For all the details, and to get our tour catalog, visit www.ricksteves.com/tours or call us at 425/608-4217.

Books: *Rick Steves Ireland 2019* is just one of many books in my series on European travel, which includes country and city guidebooks, Snapshots (excerpted chapters from bigger guides), Pocket guides (full-color little books on big cities), "Best Of" guidebooks (condensed, full-color country guides), and my budget-travel skills handbook, *Rick Steves Europe Through the Back Door*. A more complete list of my titles—including phrase

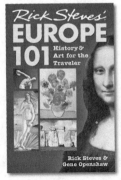

books, cruising guides, and more—appears near the end of this book.

TV Shows and Travel Talks: My public television series, *Rick Steves' Europe*, covers Europe from top to bottom with over 100 half-hour episodes—and we're working on new shows every year (watch full episodes at my website for free). Or, to raise your travel I.Q., check out the video versions of our popular classes (covering most European countries as well as travel skills, packing smart, cruising, tech for travelers, European art, and travel as a political act—www.ricksteves.com/travel-talks).

Radio: My weekly public radio show, *Travel with Rick Steves*, features interviews with travel experts from around the world. It airs on 400 public radio stations across the US, or you can hear it as a podcast. A complete archive of programs is available at www.ricksteves.com/radio.

Audio Tours on My Free App: I've produced dozens of free, self-guided audio tours of the top sights in Europe. For those tours and other audio content, get my free **Rick Steves Audio Europe app,** an extensive online library organized by destination.

PRACTICALITIES

APPENDIX

Useful Contacts

Emergency Needs
Police, Fire, and Ambulance: 112 (Europe-wide in English)
In the Republic of Ireland and Northern Ireland: 999

US Embassies and Consulates
In the Republic of Ireland: 42 Elgin Road, Dublin, Mon-Fri 8:30-17:00, closed Sat-Sun, tel. 01/668-8777, https://ie.usembassy.gov/
In Northern Ireland: Danesfort House, 223 Stranmillis Road, Belfast, Mon-Fri 8:30-17:00, closed Sat-Sun, tel. 028/9038-6100, after-hours emergency mobile 012-5350-1106, http://belfast.usconsulate.gov

Canadian Embassies
In the Republic of Ireland: 7 Wilton Terrace, Dublin, Mon-Fri 9:00-13:00 & 14:00-16:30; consular and passport services Mon-Fri 9:00-12:00, closed Sat-Sun; tel. 01/234-4000, www.canada.ie
In Northern Ireland: Honorary Consul in Belfast, tel. 028/9754-2405. This office does not offer passport services; instead contact the Canadian High Commission in London (www.unitedkingdom.gc.ca).

Holidays and Festivals

This list includes selected festivals in major cities, plus national holidays observed throughout Ireland in 2019. Many sights and banks close on national holidays—keep this in mind when planning your itinerary. Before planning a trip around a festival, verify the dates with the festival website, TI sites (www.discoverireland.ie and www.discovernorthernireland.com), or my "Upcoming Holidays and Festivals in Ireland" web page (www.ricksteves.com/europe/ireland/festivals).

Jan 1	New Year's Day (banks closed)
Jan 23-27	Temple Bar Trad, Dublin (Irish music and culture festival, http://templebartrad.com)
March 15-18	St. Patrick's Day celebration throughout Ireland (parades, drunkenness, 4-day festival in Dublin, www.stpatricksday.ie)
April 19	Good Friday (banks closed)
April 21-22	Easter Sunday and Monday
Mid-April	International Pan Celtic Festival
May 6	Labor Day; Early May Bank Holiday, Ireland and UK (banks closed)
Late May	Fleadh Nua, Ennis (traditional music and dance festival, www.fleadhnua.com)
May 27	Spring Bank Holiday, UK (banks closed)
June 3	June Holiday, Ireland (banks closed)
Mid-June	Bloomsday, Dublin (James Joyce festival, www.jamesjoyce.ie)
Late June	Patrún Festival, Kilronan (*currach* boat races)
Late June	St. John's Eve Bonfire Night (Kilronan)
July 12	Battle of the Boyne anniversary, Northern Ireland (Protestant marches, protests)
Mid- to Late July	Galway Arts Festival
Late July/Early Aug	Galway Races (horse races, www.galwayraces.com)
Aug 5	August Bank Holiday, Ireland (banks closed)
Early Aug	Dingle Races (horse races, www.dingleraces.ie)
Early-Mid-Aug	Dingle Regatta (boat races)
Early-Mid-Aug	Puck Fair, Killorglin, Kerry ("Ireland's Oldest Fair" and drink-fest, www.puckfair.ie)

Early-Mid-Aug	Féile an Phobail, West Belfast (Irish cultural festival, www.feilebelfast.com)
Mid-Aug	Fleadh Cheoil, Drogheda (traditional music festival, www.fleadhcheoil.ie)
Aug 26	Late Summer Bank Holiday, UK only (banks closed)
Late Aug	Rose of Tralee International Festival, Tralee (http://roseoftralee.ie)
Late Aug/Early Sept	Blessing of the Boats, Dingle (maritime festival)
Mid-Sept/Late Oct	Galway Races (www.galwayraces.com)
Late Sept	Galway Oyster Festival (4 days, www.galwayoysterfest.com)
Late Sept/ Early Oct	Dingle Food Festival (www.dinglefood.com)
Oct 28	October Bank Holiday, Ireland (banks closed)
Dec 25	Christmas holiday, Ireland and UK
Dec 26	St. Stephen's Day, Ireland (religious festival); Boxing Day, UK
Dec 31	New Year's Eve

APPENDIX

Books and Films

To learn more about Ireland past and present, check out a few of these books or films:

Nonfiction

Angela's Ashes (Frank McCourt, 1996). This evocative memoir documents an Irish family's struggles during the Great Depression.

Are You Somebody? The Accidental Memoir of a Dublin Woman (Nuala O'Faolain, 1996). A woman steps out of the traditional shoes she was always told to fill.

The Back of Beyond: A Search for the Soul of Ireland (James Charles Roy, 2002). Roy, an authority on Irish history, leads a group of Americans on an unconventional tour through the byways of Ireland.

How the Irish Saved Civilization (Thomas Cahill, 1995). Cahill explains how the "island of saints and scholars" changed the course of world history.

The Immortal Irishman (Timothy Egan, 2016). This well-written biography spans three continents to describe the incredible, passionate, and short life of Thomas Francis Meagher.

Ireland: A Concise History (Máire and Conor Cruise O'Brien, 1972). This is a riveting account of Irish history from pre-Christian Ireland to the Northern Irish civil rights movement.

O Come Ye Back to Ireland (Niall Williams and Christine Breen, 1987). Two New Yorkers adjust to life in a tiny Irish village after leaving their careers for a simpler life.

Round Ireland with a Fridge (Tony Hawks, 1997). For a humorous jaunt through the countryside, read Hawks' account of his attempt to hitchhike around Ireland with a fridge.

A Short History of Ireland (Richard Killeen, 1994). Killeen's well-illustrated book is among the most accessible introductions to Irish history.

To School Through the Fields (Alice Taylor, 1988). In one of the best-selling Irish memoirs of all time, Taylor fondly remembers growing up in a rural Irish town.

Fiction

The Barrytown Trilogy (Roddy Doyle, 1992). This trilogy includes Doyle's first three novels—*The Commitments, The Snapper,* and *The Van*—each capturing the day-to-day lives of working-class Dubliners.

The Bódhran Makers (John B. Keane, 1986). Keane documents the struggles of hard-living farmers in 1950s Ireland.

Circle of Friends (Maeve Binchy, 1990). One of Binchy's many soapy novels, *Circle of Friends* tells the story of a group of friends starting college in Dublin.

Dublin Saga (Edward Rutherfurd, 2004). Rutherfurd's historical saga traces the lives of rich and poor families through key events in Irish history, from A.D. 430 to the fight for independence.

Dubliners (James Joyce, 1914). Joyce's classic short-story collection describes Irish life in the 1900s, told through the experiences of 15 ordinary Dubliners.

Finbar's Hotel and *Ladies' Night at Finbar's Hotel* (Dermot Bolger, 1997/1999). These novels, about a collection of guests at a Dublin hotel, were collaboratively written, with each chapter penned by a different modern Irish author.

Ireland (Frank Delaney, 2004). Delaney's historical epic follows Ronan O'Mara on his journey to find a beloved Irish storyteller.

The Last Prince of Ireland (Morgan Llywelyn, 1992). An Irishman and his clan are determined to hold on to their homeland following the 1601 Battle of Kinsale, in which the Gaelic nobility were defeated by English invaders.

Long Lankin (John Banville, 1970). This collection of short stories by the Man Booker Prize-winning Irish author explores themes of alienation, jealousy, and love lost.

A Star Called Henry (Roddy Doyle, 1999). Doyle's political thriller, set in Ireland during the 1916 Easter Rising, is narrated by the young Henry Smart, a soldier in the Irish Citizen Army.

Trinity (Leon Uris, 1976). Uris dramatizes the sectarian struggles in the decades just prior to modern Irish independence.

Film and TV

Cal (1984). This complicated love story centers on a widow who must cope when her lover is hunted by the Irish Republican Army.

The Commitments (1991). Working-class Dubliners form a soul band in this adaption of Roddy Doyle's popular novel. Other film adaptions of Doyle's books include *The Snapper* (1993) and *The Van* (1996).

Dancing at Lughnasa (1998). This drama following five unmarried sisters in 1930s rural Ireland is based on a play that first opened in Dublin and then on Broadway.

Evelyn (2002). Single dad Pierce Brosnan must fight the Irish courts to keep his kids after being abandoned by his wife.

Far and Away (1992). Tom Cruise and Nicole Kidman star as penniless Irish immigrants seeking their fortune in late 19th century America.

The Field (1990). A farmer fights to keep his land in 1930s Ireland.

Fifty Dead Men Walking (2008). Director Kari Skogland's crime thriller features an IRA informer navigating a brutal world during the Troubles.

In the Name of the Father (1993). Daniel Day-Lewis plays wrongly accused IRA bomber Gerry Conlon in this biopic.

Into the West (1992). Two boys hide their beloved horse in urban Dublin before fleeing cross-country with it in this film written by Jim Sheridan, director of *My Left Foot*.

Leap Year (2009). In this movie set in Dingle (but filmed on the island of Inishmore), Amy Adams plays a woman who travels to Dublin to propose to her boyfriend.

The Magdalene Sisters (2003). Director Peter Mullan tells the story of three unwed Irish mothers struggling to survive an abusive 1960s nunnery.

Man of Aran (1934). Directed by Robert J. Flaherty, this haunting, near-silent documentary about life on the Aran Islands in the early 20th century is a classic.

Michael Collins (1996). Director Neil Jordan's biopic stars Liam Neeson as the famous Irish patriot and revolutionary who was killed in the Irish Civil War.

My Left Foot (1989). Daniel Day-Lewis plays an Irishman with cerebral palsy who learns to write and paint with his left foot.

Odd Man Out (1947). This British film noir, about the early IRA, is set in Northern Ireland with a great scene filmed in Belfast's Crown Bar.

Omagh (2004). "Best Drama" winner of the 2005 British Academy of Film and Television awards, *Omagh* recounts the deadly 1998 IRA bombing that killed 29 people in Northern Ireland.

Once (2006). An Irish street musician joins a Czech classical musician to compose heartfelt melodies in a sensitive tale set in gritty modern Dublin.

Philomena (2013). This poignant but clear-eyed story centers on an Irish woman's search for the son she had to give up.

The Quiet Man (1952). John Wayne plays a disgraced boxer who returns to the Irish village where he was born.

Ryan's Daughter (1970). David Lean's epic WWI love story documents an affair between a married Irish woman and a British officer.

The Secret of Roan Inish (1995). This whimsical and sensitive film explores the Irish and Orcadian folklores of selkies—seals that can shed their skins to become human.

71 (2015). In this true story, a solitary British Army soldier flees on foot through hostile IRA-controlled territory at the height of the Troubles in 1971.

Some Mother's Son (1996). Helen Mirren stars in this movie about families of IRA hunger strikers.

Titanic Town (1998). A brave mother tries to protect her family while living on the bleak front lines of sectarian Belfast during the Troubles.

Veronica Guerin (2003). Cate Blanchett stars as Veronica, an Irish journalist who exposes Dublin's drug lords—and pays the price.

Waking Ned Devine (1998). A deceased villager wins the lottery in this funnier-than-it-sounds comedy that showcases beautiful island landscapes and the wit of the Irish people.

The Wind That Shakes the Barley (2006). Two brothers fight in the Irish Republican Army during the country's struggle for independence from Britain.

Conversions and Climate

NUMBERS AND STUMBLERS

- In Europe, dates appear as day/month/year, so Christmas 2019 is 25/12/19.
- What Americans call the second floor of a building is the first floor in Europe.
- On escalators and moving sidewalks, Europeans keep the left "lane" open for passing. Keep to the right.

METRIC CONVERSIONS

Both the Republic of Ireland and Northern Ireland use the metric system (except for driving signage in Northern Ireland). Weight and volume are typically calculated in metric: A kilogram is 2.2 pounds, and a liter is about a quart. The weight of a person is measured by "stone" (one stone equals 14 pounds). Temperatures are generally given in both Celsius and Fahrenheit.

On the road, signs in the Republic of Ireland show distances and speed limits in kilometers and kilometers per hour, while Northern Ireland uses miles and miles per hour.

APPENDIX

1 foot = 0.3 meter	1 square yard = 0.8 square meter
1 yard = 0.9 meter	1 square mile = 2.6 square kilometers
1 mile = 1.6 kilometers	1 ounce = 28 grams
1 centimeter = 0.4 inch	1 quart = 0.95 liter
1 meter = 39.4 inches	1 kilogram = 2.2 pounds
1 kilometer = 0.62 mile	32°F = 0°C

CLOTHING SIZES

When shopping for clothing, use these US-to-Ireland comparisons as general guidelines (but note that no conversion is perfect).

Women: For pants and dresses, add 4 (US 10 = UK size 14). For blouses and sweaters, add 2. For shoes, subtract 2.5 (US size 8 = UK size 5.5)

Men: For clothing, US and UK sizes are the same. For shoes, subtract about 0.5 (US size 9 = UK size 8.5)

Ireland's Climate

First line, average daily high; second line, average daily low; third line, average days without rain. For more detailed weather statistics for destinations in this book (as well as the rest of the world), check www.wunderground.com.

J	F	M	A	M	J	J	A	S	O	N	D

Dublin

J	F	M	A	M	J	J	A	S	O	N	D
46°	47°	51°	55°	60°	65°	67°	67°	63°	57°	51°	47°
34°	35°	37°	39°	43°	48°	52°	51°	48°	43°	39°	37°
18	18	21	19	21	19	18	19	18	20	18	17

Fahrenheit and Celsius Conversion

Europe takes its temperature using the Celsius scale, while we opt for Fahrenheit. For a rough conversion from Celsius to Fahrenheit, double the number and add 30. For weather, remember that 28°C is 82°F—perfect. For health, 37°C is just right. At a launderette, 30°C is cold, 40°C is warm (usually the default setting), 60°C is hot, and 95°C is boiling. Your air-conditioner should be set at about 20°C.

Packing Checklist

Whether you're traveling for five days or five weeks, you won't need more than this. Pack light to enjoy the sweet freedom of true mobility.

Clothing

- ❑ 5 shirts: long- & short-sleeve
- ❑ 2 pairs pants (or skirts/capris)
- ❑ 1 pair shorts
- ❑ 5 pairs underwear & socks
- ❑ 1 pair walking shoes
- ❑ Sweater or warm layer
- ❑ Rainproof jacket with hood
- ❑ Tie, scarf, belt, and/or hat
- ❑ Swimsuit
- ❑ Sleepwear/loungewear

Money

- ❑ Debit card(s)
- ❑ Credit card(s)
- ❑ Hard cash (US $100-200)
- ❑ Money belt

Documents

- ❑ Passport
- ❑ Tickets & confirmations: flights, hotels, trains, rail pass, car rental, sight entries
- ❑ Driver's license
- ❑ Student ID, hostel card, etc.
- ❑ Photocopies of important documents
- ❑ Insurance details
- ❑ Guidebooks & maps

Toiletries Kit

- ❑ Basics: soap, shampoo, toothbrush, toothpaste, floss, deodorant, sunscreen, brush/comb, etc.
- ❑ Medicines & vitamins
- ❑ First-aid kit
- ❑ Glasses/contacts/sunglasses
- ❑ Sewing kit
- ❑ Packet of tissues (for WC)
- ❑ Earplugs

Electronics

- ❑ Mobile phone
- ❑ Camera & related gear
- ❑ Tablet/ebook reader/laptop
- ❑ Headphones/earbuds
- ❑ Chargers & batteries
- ❑ Phone car charger & mount (or GPS device)
- ❑ Plug adapters

Miscellaneous

- ❑ Daypack
- ❑ Sealable plastic baggies
- ❑ Laundry supplies: soap, laundry bag, clothesline, spot remover
- ❑ Small umbrella
- ❑ Travel alarm/watch
- ❑ Notepad & pen
- ❑ Journal

Optional Extras

- ❑ Second pair of shoes (flip-flops, sandals, tennis shoes, boots)
- ❑ Travel hairdryer
- ❑ Picnic supplies
- ❑ Water bottle
- ❑ Fold-up tote bag
- ❑ Small flashlight
- ❑ Mini binoculars
- ❑ Small towel or washcloth
- ❑ Inflatable pillow/neck rest
- ❑ Tiny lock
- ❑ Address list (to mail postcards)
- ❑ Extra passport photos

APPENDIX

INDEX

INDEX

INDEX

MAP INDEX

MAP INDEX

Explore Europe

At ricksteves.com you can browse through thousands of articles, videos, photos and radio interviews, plus find a wealth of money-saving travel tips for planning your dream trip. And with our mobile-friendly website, you can easily access all this great travel information anywhere you go.

TV Shows

Preview the places you'll visit by watching entire half-hour episodes of Rick Steves' Europe (choose from all 100 shows) on-demand, for free.

ricksteves.com

your travel dreams into affordable reality

Radio Interviews

Enjoy ready access to Rick's vast library of radio interviews covering travel

tips and cultural insights that relate specifically to your Europe travel plans.

Travel Forums

Learn, ask, share! Our online community of savvy travelers is a great resource for first-time travelers to Europe, as well as seasoned pros. You'll find forums on each country, plus travel tips and restaurant/hotel reviews. You can even ask one of our well-traveled staff to chime in with an opinion.

Travel News

Subscribe to our free Travel News e-newsletter, and get monthly updates from Rick on what's happening in Europe.

Audio Europe™

Rick's Free Travel App

Get your FREE **Rick Steves Audio Europe**™ app to enjoy...

- Dozens of self-guided tours of Europe's top museums, sights and historic walks

- Hundreds of tracks filled with cultural insights and sightseeing tips from Rick's radio interviews

- All organized into handy geographic playlists

- For Apple and Android

With Rick whispering in your ear, Europe gets even better.

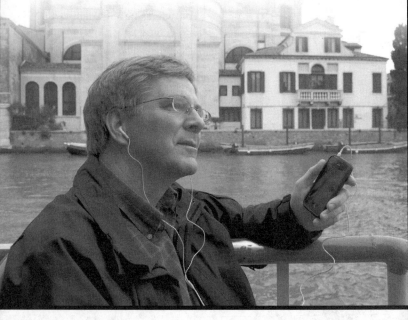

Find out more at ricksteves.com

Save time and energy

This guidebook is your independent-travel toolkit. But for all it delivers, it's still up to you to devote the time and energy it takes to manage the preparation and logistics that are essential for a happy trip. If that's a hassle, there's a solution.

Rick Steves Tours

A Rick Steves tour takes you to Europe's most interesting places with great

great tours, too!

with minimum stress

guides and small groups of 28 or less. We follow Rick's favorite itineraries, ride in comfy buses, stay in family-run hotels, and bring you intimately close to the Europe you've traveled so far to see. Most importantly, we take away the logistical headaches so you can focus on the fun.

travelers—nearly half of them repeat customers—along with us on four dozen different itineraries, from Ireland to Italy to Athens. Is a Rick Steves tour the right fit for your travel dreams? Find out at ricksteves.com, where you can also request Rick's latest tour catalog. Europe is best experienced with happy travel partners. We hope you can join us.

Join the fun

This year we'll take thousands of free-spirited

A Guide for Every Trip

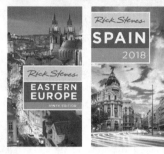

BEST OF GUIDES

Full color easy-to-scan format, focusing on Europe's most popular destinations and sights.

Best of England
Best of Europe
Best of France
Best of Germany
Best of Ireland
Best of Italy
Best of Spain

COMPREHENSIVE GUIDES

City, country, and regional guides with detailed coverage for a multi-week trip exploring the most iconic sights and venturing off the beaten track.

Amsterdam & the Netherlands
Barcelona
Belgium: Bruges, Brussels,
  Antwerp & Ghent
Berlin
Budapest
Croatia & Slovenia
Eastern Europe
England
Florence & Tuscany
France
Germany
Great Britain
Greece: Athens & the Peloponnese
Iceland
Ireland
Istanbul
Italy
London
Paris
Portugal
Prague & the Czech Republic
Provence & the French Riviera
Rome
Scandinavia
Scotland
Spain
Switzerland
Venice
Vienna, Salzburg & Tirol

THE BEST OF ROME

ome, Italy's capital, is studded with
man remnants and floodlit-fountain
ares. From the Vatican to the Colos-
m, with crazy traffic in between, Rome
onderful, huge, and exhausting. The
ds, the heat, and the weighty history

of the Eternal City where Caesars walked
can make tourists wilt. Recharge by taking siestas, gelato breaks, and after-dark
walks, strolling from one atmospheric
square to another in the refreshing evening air.

ired **Pantheon**—which
gest dome until the
rly 2,000 years old
day over 1,500).

l of Athens in the **Vat-**
odies the humanistic
ance.

, gladiators fought
another, entertaining
0.

his Rome *ristorante*.
rds at **St. Peter's**
rk seriously.

Rick Steves guidebooks are published by Avalon Travel,
an imprint of Perseus Books, a Hachette Book Group company.

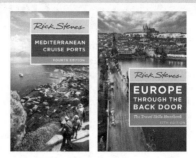

POCKET GUIDES

Compact, full color city guides with the essentials for shorter trips.

Amsterdam	Paris
Athens	Prague
Barcelona	Rome
Florence	Venice
Italy's Cinque Terre	Vienna
London	
Munich & Salzburg	

SNAPSHOT GUIDES

Focused single-destination coverage.

Basque Country: Spain & France
Copenhagen & the Best of Denmark
Dublin
Dubrovnik
Edinburgh
Hill Towns of Central Italy
Krakow, Warsaw & Gdansk
Lisbon
Loire Valley
Madrid & Toledo
Milan & the Italian Lakes District
Naples & the Amalfi Coast
Normandy
Northern Ireland
Norway
Reykjavík
Sevilla, Granada & Southern Spain
St. Petersburg, Helsinki & Tallinn
Stockholm

CRUISE PORTS GUIDES

Reference for cruise ports of call.

Mediterranean Cruise Ports
Scandinavian & Northern European Cruise Ports

Complete your library with...

TRAVEL SKILLS & CULTURE

Study up on travel skills and gain insight on history and culture.

Europe 101
Europe Through the Back Door
European Christmas
European Easter
European Festivals
Postcards from Europe
Travel as a Political Act

PHRASE BOOKS & DICTIONARIES

French
French, Italian & German
German
Italian
Portuguese
Spanish

PLANNING MAPS

Britain, Ireland & London
Europe
France & Paris
Germany, Austria & Switzerland
Ireland
Italy
Spain & Portugal

Credits

CONTRIBUTOR
Gene Openshaw

Gene has co-authored a dozen Rick Steves books, specializing in writing walks and tours of Europe's cities, museums, and cultural sights. He also contributes to Rick's public television series, produces tours for Rick Steves Audio Europe, and is a regular guest on Rick's public radio show. Outside of the travel world, Gene has co-authored *The Seattle Joke Book*. As a composer, Gene has written a full-length opera called *Matter*, a violin sonata, and dozens of songs. He lives near Seattle with his daughter, enjoys giving presentations on art and history, and roots for the Mariners in good times and bad.

ACKNOWLEDGMENTS
Thanks to Rozanne Stringer for her writing on the Celts, the Celtic Tiger, St. Brendan, and Irish art. Thanks also to Dave Fox of Globejotting.com for his writing on Guinness beer.

Avalon Travel
Hachette Book Group
1700 Fourth Street
Berkeley, CA 94710

Printed in Canada by Friesens.
First printing November 2018.

ISBN 978-1-63121-831-6

For the latest on Rick's talks, guidebooks, tours, public television series, and public radio show, contact Rick Steves' Europe, 130 Fourth Avenue North, Edmonds, WA 98020, tel. 425/771-8303, www.ricksteves.com, rick@ricksteves.com.

Rick Steves' Europe
Managing Editor: Jennifer Madison Davis
Assistant Managing Editor: Cathy Lu
Special Publications Manager: Risa Laib
Editors: Glenn Eriksen, Tom Griffin, Suzanne Kotz, Rosie Leutzinger, Jessica Shaw, Carrie Shepherd
Editorial & Production Assistant: Megan Simms
Editorial Intern: Madeline Smith
Contributor: Gene Openshaw
Graphic Content Director: Sandra Hundacker
Maps & Graphics: David C. Hoerlein, Lauren Mills, Mary Rostad
Digital Asset Coordinator: Orin Dubrow

Avalon Travel
Senior Editor and Series Manager: Madhu Prasher
Editors: Jamie Andrade, Sierra Machado
Copy Editor: Denise Silva
Proofreaders: Patrick Collins, Suzie Nasol
Indexer: Stephen Callahan
Production & Typesetting: Krista Anderson, Lisi Baldwin, Rue Flaherty
Cover Design: Kimberly Glyder Design
Maps & Graphics: Kat Bennett

Photo Credits
Front Cover: Carrick-a-Rede rope bridge in Northern Ireland © Chris Hill/Getty Images
Back Cover (left to right): © Albertoloyo/Dreamstime.com; © Wavebreakmediamicro/Dreamstime.com; © Ciprian82/Dreamstime.com
Title Page: Irish musician © Dominic Arizona Bonuccelli
Additional Photography: Dominic Arizona Bonuccelli, Rich Earl, Trish Feaster, David C. Hoerlein, Pat O'Connor, Rick Steves, Wikimedia Commons (PD-Art/PD-US). Photos are used by permission and are the property of the original copyright owners.

COLOR MAPS

LEGEND

- **A-4** Motorway
- Major Roads
- Major Rail Line
- ✈ Airport
- ♠ National Park or Natural Wonder
- Gaeltacht (Irish-speaking Regions)
- ■ Ruin, Museum, Other Point of Interest
- ▪ Castle/Monument/Palace

50 Kilometers

50 Miles

Bloo
Forelar

Bunbeg

Dungloe

Glencolumbkille

Cliffs of
Bunglass

Doneg

Ballyshannon

DRUMCLIFF
(YEATS' GRAVE)■   Bell

Erris
Head

Belmullet

Ballina

Sligo

Lough
Gill

Achill
Island

MAYO

Lough
Conn

N-59

SLIGO

N-1

Clare Island

Clew
Bay

Westport

Castlebar

Knock

Carrick-
on-Shannon

N-5

Louisburgh

CROAGH
PATRICK

N-17

Strokestown

Longfo

KYLEMORE ABBEY■ N-59

Leenane

Ballinrobe

Neale

N-17

Clifden

ASHFORD

Cong

Tuam

Roscommon

Lou
Re

Recess

Lough
Corrib

Ross

Roundstone

N-59

N-84

R E P

Rossaveal

Galway

Athenry

M-6

Athl

Salthill

DUN AENGUS ■   Kilrónan

Galway Bay

DUNGUAIRE

CLONMACNOISE

Aran
Islands

Ballyvaughan

Kinvarra

Doolin Lisdoonvarna

Portumna

I R E

Cliffs of Moher ♠

T H E
B U R R E N

Gort

Lough
Derg

Lahinch

Corrofin

Birr

C L A R E

Ennis

M-18

BUNRATTY
CASTLE
& FOLK PARK

Roscrea

Kilkee

N-67

N-68

*Atlantic
Ocean*

Loop
Head

Killimer

✈ Shannon

Shannon

M-7

T I P P E R A R

Tarbert

Limerick

Killmer

Adare

D I N G L E
P E N I N S U L A

GALLARUS
ORATORY

Tralee

N-69

Limerick
Junction

N-24

M-8

ROCK OF
CASHEL

Slea
Head

Dingle

MINARD
CASTLE

N-86

K E R R Y

✈ Kerry

N-21

N-20

Tipperary

Cashel

Caher

Clonme

Blasket
Islands

*Inch
Strand*

N-72

Killarney

Mallow

Valentia
Island

N-70

Lough
Eane

N-72

W A T E

Port-
magee

R I N G
o f
K E R R Y

MUCKROSS
HOUSE

Dungarvan

Skellig
Michael

DERRYNANE
HOUSE

Sneem

Kenmare

BLARNEY
CASTLE ▪

Macroom

M-8

Midleton

Youghal

B E A R A

Adrigole

Glengarriff

Lee

Blarney

Cork

N-25

Ardmore

Bantry

Bantry Bay

CORK

Cork

✈

Cobh

Kinsale

Skull

N-71

R-600

Mizen
Head

Skibbereen

DROMBEG
STONE CIRCLE

CHARLES
FORT

*To Roscoff,
France*

SIGHTS

1. Abbey Theatre
2. Book of Kells & Trinity Old Library
3. Chester Beatty Library
4. Christ Church Cathedral
5. Dublin Castle
6. Dublin City Hall
7. Dublin Writers Museum
8. Dublinia
9. Duke Pub (Literary Pub Crawl)
10. Epic: The Irish Emigration Museum
11. Garden of Remembrance
12. GPO Witness History Exhibit
13. Gogarty's Pub (Musical Pub Crawl)
14. To Guinness Storehouse & Kilmainham Gaol
15. Ha' Penny Bridge
16. Hugh Lane Gallery
17. James Joyce Centre
18. Jeanie Johnston Tall Ship & Famine Museum
19. Little Museum of Dublin
20. Merrion Square
21. National Gallery
22. National Leprechaun Museum
23. National Library
24. National Museum: Archaeology
25. To National Museum: Decorative Arts & History
26. National Museum: Natural History
27. Number 29 Georgian House
28. Old Jameson Distillery & Smithfield Village
29. St. Patrick's Cathedral
30. St. Stephen's Green

Transportation

31. To Airport & M-1 to Belfast
32. Busáras Central Bus Station
33. Connolly Station
34. To Heuston Station

LEGEND

- Pedestrian-Friendly Area
- Popular Shopping Area
- DART Commuter Rail Line
- Red Line LUAS Tram with stops
- Green Line LUAS Tram with stops
- Landmark or Point of Interest
- Tourist Information

250 Meters

250 Yards

Dublin

To Croke Park Stadium
& GAA Museum

N. GREAT GEORGE'S ST.
W. RUTLAND
SUMMERHILL

JAMES JOYCE
CENTRE
17

OUR LADY
OF LOURDES

To
Howth

GATE
THEATRE

Parnell

BUCKINGHAM

N

SEAN MACDERMOTT LOWER

RAILWAY ST.

FOLEY ST.

CATHAL BRUGHA ST.

PARNELL
STATUE

O'Connell
Upper

GRESHAM
HOTEL

FATHER
MATTHEW
STATUE

UPPER O'CONNELL ST.

MOORE LN.

ST. MARY'S
PRO-CATHEDRAL

MARLBOROUGH ST.

GARDINER ST. LOWER

CORPORATION ST.

MABBOT LN.

Connolly

33

CONNOLLY
STATION

LOWER
SHERIFF ST.

THE
SPIRE

TALBOT ST.

STORE ST.

TALBOT PL.

AMIENS ST.

INNER
DOCK

To
The Point

GPO
WITNESS
HISTORY
EXHIBIT
12

EARL ST.

LOWER O'CONNELL STREET

Marlborough

ABBEY ST. LOWER

MEMORIAL RD.

BUSÁRAS
CENTRAL BUS
STATION
32

ST.
GEORGE'S
DOCK

MAYOR ST.

George's
Dock

EPIC
EMIGRATION
MUSEUM

To
3 Arena
& Car Ferry
Terminal

O'Connell/
GPO

LARKIN
STATUE

Abbey
Street

LIBERTY
HALL

ABBEY
THEATRE

Busáras

IFSC

CUSTOM HOUSE
QUAY

10

O'Connell

PRINCE'S ST. N.

ST. MIDDLE
T.

ACHELORS WALK

CUSTOM
HOUSE

Liffey

N. WALL QUAY

FAMINE
STATUES

O'CASEY
BRIDGE

18

JEANIE
JOHNSTON
SHIP

EDEN QUAY

ROSIE
HACKETT
BRIDGE

GEORGE'S QUAY

CITY QUAY

O'CONNELL
STATUE

O'CONNELL
BRIDGE

BURGH QUAY

POOLBEG

TARA ST.

IMMACULATE
HEART

MOSS ST.

ASTON QUAY

Westmoreland

HAWKINS

TARA STREET
STATION

GLOUCESTER ST.

PRINCE'S ST.

LOMBARD ST. EAST

13

FLEET ST.

ANGLESEA

COLLEGE

DOLIER ST.

WESTMORE.

Trinity

PEARSE ST.

TOWNSEND ST.

MARKS LN.

LWR. SANDWITH ST.

BAR

BANK OF
IRELAND

MAIN
ENTRANCE

CAMPANILE

2

BOOK OF
KELLS

TRINITY
COLLEGE

PEARSE
STREET
STATION

SOUTH CUMBERLAND ST.

BOYNE ST.

UPPER SANDWITH ST.

To Dun
Laoghaire

MOLLY
MALONE
STATUE

COLLEGE
GREEN

OST

SUFFOLK

ANDREW'S

POWERSCOURT
CENTER

NASSAU

ENTRANCE
ST.

ST
ANDREW'S

LEINSTER ST. S.

LINCOLN PL.

FENIAN ST.

DENZILLE LN.

9

Dawson

DUKE ST.

GRAFTON ST.

CLARENDON ST.

ANNE ST. S.

DAWSON ST.

SOUTH FREDERICK ST.

MOLESWORTH ST.

SETANTA

KILDARE ST.

NATIONAL
LIBRARY

23

CLARE ST.

NATIONAL
GALLERY

OSCAR
WILDE
STATUE

MERRION ST.

To
Ballsbridge
& US
Embassy

ST.
ANN'S

NATIONAL
MUSEUM:
ARCHAEOLOGY

24

21

26

MERRION SQUARE NORTH

WEST

Merrion
Square

20

FUSILIERS'
ARCH

19

St.
Stephen's
Green

SHELBOURNE
HOTEL

ST. STEPHEN'S GREEN N.

GOV'T.
BLDGS.

MERRION ST.

MERRION SQUARE SOUTH

MERRION SQUARE EAST

FITZWILLIAM LN.

27

#29
GEORGIAN
HOUSE

WEST

YEATS
STATUE

30

St.
Stephen's
Green

EAST

FAMINE
VICTIMS'
MEMORIAL

To National
Concert Hall

LOWER BAGGOT ST.

FITZWILLIAM ST.

FITZWILLIAM

To
Dun Laoghaire &
Wicklow Mountains

LEGEND

5 Kilometers
5 Miles

— Roads
═══ Recommended Scenic Drives
— Major Rail Line
✈ Airport
■ Ruin, Museum, Other Point of Interest
▲ Mountain Peak
🏰 Castle/Monument/Palace

The Seven Hogs

Rough Point

Brandon Head

Brandon Bay

Castlegregory

Brandon Mountain ▲

Tiduff

Cloghane

Ballyduff

Conor Pass

KILMALKEDAR CHURCH

DINGLE PENINSULA (AN DAINGEAN)

Three Sisters

Sybil Head

Ballyferriter (Baile an Fheirtearaigh)

GALLARUS ORATORY

REASC MONASTERY

Dingle (Daingean Uí Chúis)

Lispole (Lios Póil)

Annascaul

SOUTH POLE INN

N-86

GREAT BLASKET CENTRE

Dunquin (Dún Chaoin)

Ventry (Ceann Trá)

PUICIN WEDGE TOMB

MINARD CASTLE

Inish-tooskert

BEEHIVE HUTS

LORD VENTRY'S MANOR

EASK TOWER

BULL'S LIGHTHOUSE

DUNBEG FORT

Slea Head (Ceann Sléibhe)

Great Blasket Island (An Blascaod Mór)

Dingle Bay

LEACANABUAILE & CAHERGAL RING FORTS

N-70

RING

Kells

IVERAGH "RING

Doulus Head

Cahersiveen

LISSATINNING BRIDGE

Valentia Island

Knightstown

Inny

Derriana Lough

SKELLIG EXPERIENCE CENTRE

Clynacartan

R-565

N-70

River Inny

Bray Head

Portmagee

SKELLIG

R-567

INNY BRIDGE

RING

Lough Currane

STAIGUE FORT

Little Skellig

SKELLIG

RING

Waterville

Ballybrack

St. Finian's Bay

Ballinskelligs

Ballinskelligs Bay

Castle Cove

Skellig Michael

Bolus Head

Hog's Head

Coomakesta Pass

DERRYNANE HOUSE

Caherdaniel

Carroll's Cove

Scariff Island

Deenish Island

Lamb's Head